Guide to
BRITISH DRAMA EXPLICATION

Volume 1

Beginnings to 1640

A
Reference
Publication
in
Literature

Nancy C. Martinez
Editor

Guide to
BRITISH DRAMA EXPLICATION

Volume 1

Beginnings to 1640

KRYSTAN V. DOUGLAS

G. K. HALL & CO.
An Imprint of Simon & Schuster Macmillan
New York

Prenctice Hall International
London   Mexico City   New Delhi   Singapore   Sydney   Toronto

G. K. Hall & Co.
An Imprint of Simon & Schuster Macmillan
1633 Broadway
New York, New York 10019

Library of Congress Catalog Card Number: 95-51781

Printed in the United States of America

Printing Number:

1 2 3 4 5 6 7 8 9 10

Library of Congress Cataloging-in-Publication Data

Douglas, Krystan V.
 Guide to British drama explication / Krystan V. Douglas.
  p. cm.—(A reference publication in literature)
 Includes bibliographical references.
 Contents: v. 1. Beginnings to 1640
 ISBN 0-8161-7372-9 (alk. paper)
  1. English drama—History and criticism—Bibliography. I. Title
II. Series.
 Z2014.D7D68 1996
 [PR625]
 016.822009—dc20   95-51781
                           CIP

This paper meets the requirements of ANSI/NISO A39.48.1992 (Permanence of Paper).

Contents

The Author

Krystan V. Douglas holds a master's degree in English with a specialty in medieval and Renaissance drama, and a doctorate in American studies with a specialty in American theatre history. She teaches at the University of New Mexico and the Albuquerque TVI Community College; at both institutions she has taught courses in all periods of dramatic literature and theatre history. She is the author of several papers and articles on American drama and theatre history.

Preface

This volume continues the explication series that began with *Poetry Explication*, edited by Joseph M. Kuntz; it is a part of the major publishing project by G. K. Hall & Co. Publishers under the general editorship of Nancy Martinez.

This is the first of two volumes focusing on English language explication of British drama. This first volume deals primarily with drama written in the British Isles up to the closing of the theatres in 1640; the second volume will be concerned with drama of the British Isles from the Restoration to the present.

There are two exceptions to the 1640 date. The first of these is that the plays of John Milton are included in this volume, even though they were written after the closing of the theatres; the second exception is that the plays of Sir William Davenant will be included in the second volume, even though many were written prior to 1640. In each instance the determination has been made on the basis of how the plays fit with the tone, themes, and spirit of the other plays of the period and the age itself. Milton's works are more closely allied to the earlier period than to the Restoration, while the works of the Royalist Davenant echo the spirit of the Cavaliers and the Restoration.

The critical works included in this bibliography have been selected according to the general guidelines laid down in the original *Poetry Explication*, although the term "explication" is broadly interpreted. The basic rule for inclusion is that a work must involve a close reading of the drama. New Criticism, by its nature, involves close reading and clearly belongs in this volume. Other critical approaches are not, however, as dependent on close reading to fulfill their purposes. Thus, the decision whether to include a specific work (e.g., psychoanalytic, semiotic, new historical, or postmodernist criticism) depends on the extent to which the criticism focuses on the text or specific passages from the text. In the case of structural approaches, for example, the concern is the degree to which a work deals with the language of specific passages in determining meaning, interpretation, or characterization. In keeping with this practice, criticism that focuses on production and performance, theatre history, or attribution of authorship has been largely excluded from this bibliography unless it contains a strong element of close reading. Also, in the interests of space, extremely short explications, of less than a page, do not appear in this volume.

This said, it must be noted that the critical works that do appear here range from the New Criticism to the New Historicism, from Archetypical Criticism to Semiotics. Certainly some critical schools command greater representation. For example, the New Critical approach to drama has been the backbone of drama criticism for many years; longevity, if nothing else, would account for its greater representation. Semiotics, on the other hand, is a much newer field, and, as a critical approach, it has more often been applied to production and performance than to dramatic texts. Therefore, fewer semiotic entries than New Critical entries appear in this bibliography.

The organization of this *Guide* follows that of the others in this series:

1. Dramatists are listed alphabetically by last names.

2. Plays are listed alphabetically by title (excluding initial articles).

3. Criticism is listed aphabetically by the author's name following each play. Full publication data are included with the citation for all articles and most books. Reprints are cited following the major entry.

4. Books in which multiple entries appear are cited in shortened form within the checklist, and full publication information given in the Main Souces section. Included in this list of works consulted are the journals and periodicals that publish criticism of medieval and Renaissance English drama.

5. Names of journals and periodicals are abbreviated according to the standard MLA abbreviations and are listed immediately after this Preface.

Many Renaissance plays were the products of collaboration, and disagreement exists as to the nature and degree of contributions by various playwrights. To facilitate searches for specific plays, when there are multiple authors the plays will be listed under the name of each collaborator.

No work of this scope can be undertaken without the support of many people. While I have not the space to acknowledge all those who have provided emotional and practical support during this project, there are some who must be recognized: Nancy C. Martinez, General Editor of this series, for thinking of me; Catherine E. Carter, Editor of G. K. Hall, for understanding an impossible situation; Lynn Beene for coffee, commiseration, and handholding; Julie Cunico for support and friendship; the staff of the Interlibrary Loan Department of the University of New Mexico, for not running in terror when they see me; and other bibliographers who pointed the direction. Finally, I wish to thank my mother, Shelley G. Douglas, who has endured more than she should have to.

K. V. D.

Periodicals, Journals, and Abbreviations

ABR   American Benedictine Review

Accent

ACM   Aligarh Critical Miscellany

AI   American Imago

AJES   Aligarh Journal of English Studies

AJP   American Journal of Psychoanalysis

AJS   American Journal of Semiotics

ALLCB   Bulletin for the Association for Literary & Linguistic
               Computing

Allegorica   Allegorica (University of Texas, Arlington)

AN   Acta Neophilologica

PERIODICALS, JOURNALS, AND ABBREVIATIONS

Analysis	Analysis: Quaderni di Angelistica
Anglia	Anglia: Zeitschrift für Englische Philologie
Anglica	Anglica (Kansai University, Osaka)
AnM	Annuale Mediaevale
APSR	American Political Science Review
AR	Antioch Review
Archiv	Archiv für das Studium der Neuren Sprachen und Literaturen
ArielE	Ariel: A Review of International English Literature
ArQ	Arizona Quarterly
Aryan Path	
Asch	American Scholar
ASLBA	Annual Shakespeare Lecture of the British Academy
Assaph	Assaph: Studies in the Arts
Assays	Assays: Critical Approaches to Medieval and Renaissance Texts
Atlantis	Atlantis: A Women's Studies Journal/Journal d'Etudes sur la Femme
AUMLA	Journal of the Australian Language and Literature Association
AUS-PEAS	Acta Universitatis Szegediensis de Attila Jozef Nominatae: Papers in English and American Studies
BJA	British Journal of Aesthetics
BJMP	British Journal of Medical Psychology
BJRL	Bulletin of the John Rylands University Library of Manchester

BNYPL   Bulletin of the New York Public Library

Boundary   Boundary 2: A Journal of Postmodern Literature and Culture

BPLQ   Boston Public Library Quarterly

BRH   Bulletin of Research in the Humanities

BRMMLA   Bulletin of the Rocky Mountain Modern Language Association

BSEAA   Bulletin de la Société d'Etudes Anglo-Américaines des XVII et
            XVIII Siècles

BSUF   Ball State University Forum

Bucknell University Studies

BuR   Bucknell Review

BUSE   Boston University Studies in English

BWVACET   Bulletin of the West Virginia Association of College English
            Teachers

BYUS   Brigham Young University Studies

C&L   Christianity and Literature

C&M   Classica et Mediaevalia

CahiersE   Cahiers Elisabethains

CairoSE   Cairo Studies in English

Caliban

Cambridge Journal

Caribbean Quarterly

Catholic World

PERIODICALS, JOURNALS, AND ABBREVIATIONS

CaudaP   Cauda Pavonis

CCP   City College Papers

CCR   The Claflin College Review

CCTEP   Conference of College Teachers of English Studies

CdIL   Cahiers de l'Institute de Linguistique de Louvain

CE   College English

CEA   CEA Critic: An Official . . .

CEJ   California English Journal

Celestinesca

CentR   Centennial Review

Central States Speech Journal

ChauR   Chaucer Review

ChiR   Chicago Review

CHR   Catholic Historical Review

ChS   Christian Scholar

Chum   Computers and the Humanities

CIEFLB   Central Institute of English and Foreign Languages Bulletin

Cithera   Cithera: Essays in Judeo-Christian Tradition

CL   Comparative Literature (Oregon)

CLAJ   College Language Association Journal Classical Bulletin

CLIO   CLIO: A Journal of Literature, History, and the Philosophy of History

CLQ   Colby Literary Quarterly

CLS   Comparative Literature Studies

CML   Classic and Modern Literature

CollL   College Literature

ColQ   Colorado Quarterly

Columbia University Forum

Comitatus   Comitatus: A Journal of Medieval and Renaissance Studies

CompD   Comparative Drama

Connotations   Connotations: A Journal for Critical Debate

Coranto   Coranto: Journal of the Friends of the Libraries (U. S. C.)

CP   Concerning Poetry

CQ   Cambridge Quarterly

CR   Critical Review

CritI   Critical Inquiry

Criticism & Research

CRCL   Canadian Review of Comparative Literature/Revue Canadienne de Litterature Compative

Criterion

Criticism   Criticism: A Quarterly Review of Literature

CritQ   The Critical Quarterly

CrSurv   Critical Survey

CRUX   CRUX: A Journal on the Teaching of English

CUSECL	Columbia University Studies in English and Comparative Literature
Cycnos	
Daedalus	Daedalus: Journal of the American Academy of Arts and Sciences
Diacritics	Diacritics: A Review of Contemporary Criticism
Diogenes	
Discourse	Discourse: Journal for Theoretical Studies in Media and Culture
Dock Leaves	
DQR	Dutch Quarterly Review of Anglo-American Letters
DR	Dalhousie Review
Drama Critique	
DramaS	Drama Survey
DSGW	Deutsch Shakespeare-Gesellschaft West: Jahrbuch
Dublin Magazine	
DUJ	Durham University Journal
DUS	Dacca University Studies
E&S	Essays and Studies by Members of the English Association
EA	Etudes Anglaises: Grande Bretagne, Etats Unis
EAA	Estudos Anglo-Americanos
EAS	Essays in Arts and Sciences
Edda	Edda: Nordisk Tidsskrift for Litteraturforskning/Scandanavian Journal of Literary Research

EFLL   Essays in Foreign Languages and Literature

EIC   Essays in Criticism

EIRC   Explorations in Renaissance Culture

EiT   Essays in Theatre

EJ   The English Journal (Urbana, IL)

ELH   Journal of English Literary History

ELLS   English Literature and Language

ELN   English Language Notes

ELR   English Literary Renaissance

ELWIU   Essays in Literature

EM   English Miscellany

Emblematica   Emblematica: An Interdisciplinary Journal of Emblem Studies

enclitic

Encyclia   Encyclia: The Journal of the Utah Academy of Sciences, Arts, and Letters

English   English: Journal of the English Association

English Institute Essays

EngR   English Record

ES   English Studies

ESA   English Studies in Africa

ESC   English Studies in Canada

ESRS   Emporia State Research Studies

Essays by Divers Hands

Etc.	ETC: A Review of General Semantics
Eth	Elizabethan Theatre
ETJ	Educational Theatre Journal
EUQ	Emory University Quarterly
Exemplaria	Exemplaria: A Journal of Theory in Medieval and Renaissance Studies
Expl	The Explicator
F&R	Faith & Reason
FCS	Fifteenth-Century Studies
Flor	Florilegium . . .
FMLS	Forum for Modern Language Studies
Folklore	Folklore (London, Eng.)
ForumH	Forum (Houston)
FurmS	Furman Studies
GaR	Georgia Review
Genre	
GettR	The Gettysburg Review
GorR	The Gordon Review
Greyfriar	Greyfriar: Siena Studies in Literature
GyS	Gypsy Scholar: A Graduate Forum for Literary Criticism
HAB	The Humanities Association Bulletin
Helios	Helios (Lubbock, TX)

Hermathena   Hermathena: A Trinity Dublin Review

HIS   Humanities in Society

Hispanica

HLQ   Huntington Library Quarterly

Hogarth Lecture Series

Hopkins Review

Horizontes   Horizontes: Revista de la Universidad Catolica de Puerto Rico

HSL   University of Hartford Studies in Lit: A Journal of
Interdisciplinary Criticism. . .

Hst   Hamlet Studies

HudR   The Hudson Review

HUSL   Hebrew University Studies in Literature and the Arts

IJES   Indian Journal of English Studies

IJPP   Interpretation: A Journal of Political Philosophy

International Journal of Psychoanalysis

IJWS   International Journal of Women's Studies

Interpretations: Studies in Language and Literature

IQ   Italian Quarterly

IR   The Illif Review

Irish Monthly

ISJR   Iowa State Journal of Research

ISLL   Illinois Studies in Language and Literature

JAAR   Journal of the American Academy of Religion

PERIODICALS, JOURNALS, AND ABBREVIATIONS

JAF	Journal of American Folklore
JCL	Journal of Commonwealth Literature
JDECU	Journal of the Department of English (Calcutta)
JDJ	John Donne Journal
JDSG	Jahrbuch der Deutschen Schillergesellshaft
JEGP	Journal of English and German Philology
JEI	Journal of the English Institute
JELL	Journal of English Language and Literature
Jen	Journal of English
JengS	Journal of English Studies
JEP	Journal of Evolutionary Psychology

Jewish Quarterly

JGE	Journal of General Education
JHI	Journal of the History of Ideas
JKSUA	Journal of King Saud University Arts
JMRS	Journal of Medieval and Renaissance Studies

Journal of African Civilizations

Journal of the University of Saugar

JPC	Journal of Popular Culture
JRMMRA	Journal of the Rocky Mountain Medieval and Renissance Association
JWCI	Journal of Warburg and Courtland Institutes

KN	Kwartalnik Neofilologiczny
Komos	
KPAB	Kentucky Philological Association Bulletin
KR	Kenyon Review
Krev	Kentucky Review
KSJ	Keats-Shelley Journal
L&B	Literature and Belief
L&H	Literature and History
L&LC	Literary and Linguistic Computing
L&M	Literature and Medicine
L&P	Literature and Psychology
L&T	Literature and Theology
Landfall	
Lang&C	Language and Culture
Lang&L	Language and Literature
Lang&S	Language & Style
LangQ	Language Quarterly
Lapis	
LCrit	The Literary Criterion
LdD	Letras de Deusto
LeedsSE	Leeds Studies in English
Legacy	

PERIODICALS, JOURNALS, AND ABBREVIATIONS

LHR   Lock Haven Review

Life and Letters Today

Litera

The Literary Half-Yearly

Lore&L Lore & Language

LOS   Literary Onomastics Studies

Lper   Literature in Performance

LWU   Literatur in Wissenschaft und Unterricht

M&H   Medievalia et Humanistica

M&L   Music and Letters

Madison Quarterly

Mainstream

Maledicta Maledicta: The International Journal of Verbal Aggression

Makerere Journal

Mandrake

McNR   McNeese Review

MCRel   Mythes, Croyances et Religions dans le Monde Anglo-Saxon

MD   Modern Drama

MedAe   Medium Aevum

Mediaevalia Mediaevalia: A Journal of Medieval Studies

MEJ   Maryland English Journal

Menninger Quarterly

MET	Middle English Texts
METh	Medieval English Theatre
MichA	Michigan Academy of Science, Arts, and Letters
Mid-Hudson Lang. St.	Mid-Hudson Language Studies
MiltonQ	Milton Quarterly
MiltonS	Milton Studies
MissFR	Mississippi Folklore Register
Missouri English Bulletin	
MissQ	Mississippi Quarterly
MLN	Modern Language Notes
MLQ	Modern Language Quarterly
MLR	Modern Language Review
MLS	Modern Language Studies
Moreana	Moreana Bulletin Thomas More
Mosaic	Mosaic: A Journal for the Comparative Study of Literature and Ideas
Motif	Motif: International Newsletter in Research in Folklore and Literature
MP	Modern Philology
MQ	Midwest Quarterly
MR	Massachusetts Review
MRDE	Medieval and Renaissance Drama in England
MS	Medieval Studies

PERIODICALS, JOURNALS, AND ABBREVIATIONS

MSE   Massachusettes Studies in English

Mspr   Moderna Sprak

N&Q   Notes and Queries

Names   Names: Journal of the American Names Society

NcarF   North Carolina Folklore Journal

NDEJ   Notre Dame English Journal

NDQ   North Dakota Quarterly

Neophil   Neophilologus

NETJ   New England Theatre Journal

New English Review

New Hungarian Quarterly

NewComp   New Comparison

Nimbus

NYLF   New York Literary Forum

NLH   New Literary History (University of VA)

NM   Neuphilologische Mitteilungen

NOR   New Orleans Review

The Norseman

Northern Miscellany of Literary Criticism

NS   Die Neuren Sprachen

OJES   Osmania Journal of English Studies

OL   Orbis Litterarum

Orion

Orpheus

P&L	Philosophy and Literature
PAPA	Publications of the Arkansas Philological Association
PAPS	Proceedings of the American Philosophical Association
Parergon	Parergon: Bulletin of the Australian Association of Medieval and Renaissance Studies
Paunch	
PBA	Proceedings of the British Academy
PBSA	Papers of the Bibliographic Society of America
PCP	Pacific Coast Philology
PE	Pennsylvania English
PE&W	Philosophy East and West: A Quarterly of Asian and Comparative Thought
Person	The Personalist
Perspective	
The Phoenix	
PL	Pamitnik Literacki: Czasopismo Kwartalne Poswiecone Historii i Krytyce Literatury Polskiej
PLL	Papers on Language and Literature
PLPLS	Proceedings of the Leeds Philosophical and Literary Society
PMLA	Publication of the Modern Language Association
PMPA	Publications of the Missouri Philological Association

PERIODICALS, JOURNALS, AND ABBREVIATIONS

Poet Lore

Poetics   Poetics: International Review for Theory

Poetry Magazine

PostS   Post Script: Essays in Film and Humanities

PoT   Poetics Today: Theory and Analysis of Literature and Communication

PP   Philologica Pragensia

PPMRC   Proceedings of the PMR Conference

PQ   Philological Quarterly

Psychoanalytic Quarterly

Psychoanalytic Review

PsyR   Psychology Review

QFG   Quaderni Quaderni di Filologia Germanica della Facoltà di Lettere e Filosofia dell'Università di Bologna

QJS   Quarterly Journal of Speech

QQ   Queens Quarterly

R&L   Religion and Literature

RBPH   Revue Belge de Philologie et d'Histoire

RCEI   Revista Canaria de Estudios Ingleses

ReAL   RE: Artes Liberalis

REALB   REAL: Tearbook for Research in English and American Literature

RecL   Recovering Literature: A Journal of Contextualist Criticism

REEDN	Records of Early English Drama Newsletter
REL	Review of English Literature (Leeds)
Ren&R	Renaissance and Reformation
RenB	The Renaissance Bulletin
RenD	Renaissance Drama
RenP	Renaissance Papers
RenQ	Renaissance Quarterly
RenSt	Renaissance Studies
RES	Review of English Studies
RMLC	Revista di Litterature Modern e Comparate (Firenze)
Rice Institute Pamphlets	
RLC	Revue de Literature Comparee
RMRLL	Rocky Mountain Review of Language and Literature
RMS	Renaissance & Modern Studies
RN	Renaissance News
RoR	Romanian Review
RORD	Research Opportunities in Renaissance Drama
RPLit	Res Publica Litterarum: Essays in the Classical Tradition
RRL	Revue Roumaine de Linguistique
RRWL	Renaissance and Renascenses in Western Literature: A Quarterly Newsletter of Classical Influences
RS	Research Studies (Washington State)

ShAB	Shakespeare Association Bulletin
ShakB	Shakespeare Bulletin
ShakS	Shakespeare Studies (New York)
Shenandoah	
ShJE	Shakespeare Jahrbuch
ShN	Shakespeare Newsletter
SHR	Southern Humanities Review
ShS	Shakespeare Survey
ShSA	Shakespeare in Southern Africa
ShStud	Shakespeare Studies (Tokyo)
ShY	Shakespeare Yearbook
Sicon	Studies in Iconography
Signs	Signs: Journal of Women in Culture and Society
SJS	San Jose Studies
SJW	Shakespeare-Jahrbuch (Weimar, E. Germany)
SlitI	Studies in the Literary Imagination
SMC	Studies in Medieval Culture
Smy	Studia Mystica
SN	Studia Neophilologica
Snew	Sidney Newsletter
SoAR	South Atlantic Review
Social Research	

PERIODICALS, JOURNALS, AND ABBREVIATIONS

SoRA	Southern Review (Australia)
SoQ	Southern Quarterly
Southern Speech Journal	
Southwest Review	
SP	Studies in Philology
Speech Monographs	
SPWVSRA	Selected Papers fron the West Virginia Shakespeare and Renaissance Association
SQ	Shakespeare Quarterly
SR	Sewanee Review
Sren	Studies in the Renaissance
SSEng	Sydney Studies in English
SSL	Studies in Scottish Literature
StHum	Studies in the Humanities
Struct. Rev.	Structuralist Review
SUS	Susquehanna University Studies
T&P	Text & Presentation
TA	Theatre Annual
TAIUS	Texas A&I University Studies
TCEL	Thought Currents in English Literature
TDR	The Drama Review (formerly Tulane Drama Review)
TexP	Textual Practice

TFSB	Tennessee Folklore Society Bulletin
Theology	
ThR	Theatre Research International
ThS	Theatre Survey
TJ	Theatre Journal
TLS	Times Literary Supplement (London)
TN	Theatre Notebook
TPB	Tennessee Philological Bulletin: . . .
TriQ	Tri-Quarterly (Evanston, IL)
TSE	Tulane Studies in English
TSL	Tennessee Studies in Literature
TSLL	Texas Studies in Literature and Language
TSWL	Tulsa Studies in Women's Literature
Ucrow	The Upstart Crow
UCSLL	University of Colorado Studies in English
UDQ	University of Denver Quarterly
UDR	University of Dayton Review
UES	Unisa English Studies
UMPEAL	University of Miami Publications in English and American Literature
UMSE	University of Mississippi Studies in English

PERIODICALS, JOURNALS, AND ABBREVIATIONS

UMSS	University of Michigan Studies in Shakespeare
Universitas	
UR	University of Kansas City Review
USSE	University of Saga Studies in English
UTQ	University of Toronto Quarterly
UWR	University of Windsor Review
Viator	Viator: Medieval and Renaissance Studies
Virginia Eng. Bull.	Virginia English Bulletin
Virginia Hum. Bull.	Virginia Humanities Bulletin
VQR	Virginia Quarterly Review
VSH	Vanderbilt Studies in Humanities
W&D	Works and Days: ...
W&I	Word and Image
WascanaR	Wascana Review
WSCS	Washington State College Research Studies
WHR	Western Humanities Review
WLWE	World Literature Written in English
WS	Women's Studies
WVUBPL	University of West Virginia Philological Bulletin
WVUPP	West Virginia University Philological Papers
XUS	Xavier University Studies

YCC Yearbook of Comparative Criticism

YES Yearbook in English Studies

YIS Yearbook of Italian Studies

YR The Yale Review

ZAA Zeitschrift fur Anglistik und Amerikanstik

Guide to
BRITISH DRAMA EXPLICATION

Volume 1

Beginnings to 1640

Checklist of Interpretation

ANONYMOUS

Abraham and Isaac

Peter Braeger, "Typology as Contrast in the Middle English Abraham and Isaac Plays," in Johnston and Riley, *Proceedings of the Illinois Medieval Association*, 131–53.

Ellis-Fermor, *The Frontiers of Drama*, 21–24.

Thomas Rendall, "Visual Typology in the Abraham and Isaac Plays," *MP* 81 (February 1984): 221–32.

Williams, *Drama in Performance*, 41–45.

Abraham's Sacrifice

Blackburn, *Biblical Drama*, 145–48.

ANONYMOUS, *Adam*

Peter Braeger, "Typology as Contrast in the Middle English Abraham and Isaac Plays," in Johnston and Riley, *Proceedings of the Illinois Medieval Association*, 131–53.

Adam

Erich Aurebach, *Mimesis* (Princeton: Princeton University Press, 1953), 143–51, 156–62.

G. B. Shand, "The Actorly Craft of the Adam Playwright: His Fall of Man," *MRDE* 5 (Spring 1991): 1–10.

Alarum For London

Loftis, *Renaissance Drama in England and Spain*, 218–19.

Appius and Virginia

Cope, *Dramaturgy of the Daemonic*, 41–44.

Inga-Stina Ekiblad, "Storm Imagery in *Appius and Virginia*," *N&Q* 3 (March 1956): 5–7.

Richard Leighton Greene, "Carols in Tudor Drama," in Rowland, *Chaucer and Middle English Studies*, 357–65.

P. Happé, "Tragic Themes in Three Tudor Moralities," *SEL* 5 (Spring 1965): 207–27.

Rosemary Woolf, "The Influence of the Mystery Plays upon the Popular Tragedies of the 1560's," *RenD* 6 (1973): 89–105.

Arden of Feversham

Adams, *English Domestic or Homiletic Tragedies*, 100–08.

Max Bluestone, "The Imagery of Tragic Melodrama in *Arden of Feversham*," *DramS* 5 (August 1966): 171–81.

Cunningham, *Woe or Wonder*, 60–61.

J. Hanratty, "*Arden of Feversham*," *The Use of English* 11 (Spring 1960): 176–80.

Alexander Leggatt, "*Arden of Feversham*," *ShS* 36 (1983): 121–33.

Leanore Lieblein, "The Context of Murder in English Domestic Plays, 1590–1610," *SEL* 23 (Spring 1983): 181–96.

Michael T. Marsden, "The Otherworld of *Arden of Feversham*," *SFQ* 36 (January 1972): 36–42.

Ian Ousby, & Heather D. Ousby, "Art and Language in *Arden of Feversham*," *DUJ* 36 (December 1975): 47–54.

Sybil Truchet, "Alice Arden and the Religion of Love," *Caliban* 17 (1980): 39–44.

Eugene P. Walz, "*Arden of Faversham* as Tragic Satire," *MSE*, 4 no. 2 (1974): 23–41.

Wiggins, *Journeymen in Murder*, 121–27.

Sarah Youngblood, "Theme and Imagery in *Arden of Faversham*," *SEL* 3 (Spring 1963): 207–18

The Arrival of Edward IV

Richard Firth Green, "The Short Version of *The Arrival of Edward IV*," *Speculum* 56 (April 1981): 324–36.

Beauvais Daniel

Jerome Taylor, "Prophetic 'Play' and Symbolist 'Plot' in the Beauvais *Daniel*," *CompD* 11 (Summer 1977): 191–208.

The Birth of Merlin

Traister, *Heavenly Necromancers*, 55–56.

Brome Abraham and Isaac

David Mills, "The Doctor's Epilogue to the Brome *Abraham and Isaac*: A Possible Analogue," *LeedsSE* 11 (Spring 1980): 105–10.

Rei R. Noguchi, "Conversational Interaction, Verbal Strategies, and Literary Response," *Lang&S* 18 (Spring 1985): 192–204.

Janette Richardson, "Affective Artistry of the Medieval Stage," *QJS* 70 (May 1984): 12–22.

ANONYMOUS, *Caesar's Revenge*

Caesar's Revenge

McDonnell, *The Aspiring Mind*, 161–64.

Jacqueline Pearson, "Shakespeare and *Caesar's Revenge*," *SQ* 32 (Spring 1981): 101–04.

Clifford J. Ronan, "*Caesar's Revenge* and the Roman Thoughts in *Antony and Cleopatra*," *ShakS* 19 (1991): 171–82.

Captain Thomas Stukeley

D'Amico, *The Moor in English Renaissance Drama*, 83–84.

Cardenio

Muir, *Shakespeare as Collaborator*, 148–60.

The Castle of Perseverance

Bevington, *From "Mankind" to Marlowe*, 115–23.

David M. Bevington, " 'Man Thinke on Thine Endinge Day': Stage Pictures of Just Judgment in *The Castle of Perseverance*," in *Homo, Memento Finis: The Iconography of Just Judgement in Medieval Art and Drama* (Kalamazoo: Western Michigan University, 1985), 147–77.

G. C. Britton, "Language and Character in Some Late Medieval Plays," *E&S* 33 (1980): 1–15.

Samuel C. Chews, *The Virtues Reconciled* (Toronto: University of Toronto Press, 1947), 44–45.

Merle Fifield, "The Assault on the *Castle of Perseverance*: The Tradition and the Figure," *BSUF* 16 (Autumn 1975): 16–26.

Arvil K. Henry, "*The Castle of Perseverance*: The Stage Direction at Line 1767," *N&Q* 12 (December 1965): 448.

Frances Erdey Hildahl, "Penitence and Parody in *The Castle of Perseverance*," in Tricomi, *Early Drama to 1600*, 129–41.

S. E. Holbrook, "Covetousness, Contrition, and the Town in the *Castle of Perseverance*," *FCS* 13 (1988): 275–89.

Michael Robert Kelley, "Fifteenth-Century Flamboyant Style and *The Castle of Perseverance*," *CompD* 6 (Spring 1972): 14–27.

J. W. McCutchan, "Covetousness in *The Castle of Perseverance*," in *English Studies in Honor of James Southall Wilson*, 175–91.

Robert Potter, "Divine and Human Justice," in Neuss, *Aspects of Early English Drama*, 129–41.

Richard Proudfoot, "The Virtue of Perseverance," in Neuss, *Aspects of Early English Drama*, 92–109.

Michael E. Ralston, "The Four Daughters of God in *The Castle of Perseverance*," *Comitatus* 15 (Spring 1984): 35–44

Thomas Rendall, "The Times of Mercy and Judgment in *Mankind, Everyman*, and the *Castle of Perseverance*," *ESC* 7 (Fall 1981): 255–69.

Milla B. Riggio, "The Allegory of Feudal Acquisition in *The Castle of Perseverance*," in *Allegory, Myth, and Symbol*, ed. Morton W. Bloomfield (Cambridge, MA: Harvard University Press, 1981), 187–208.

Edgar T. Schell, "On the Imitation of Life's Pilgrimage in *The Castle of Perseverance*," *JEGP* 67 (July 1968): 235–48. Reprinted in Taylor and Nelson, *Medieval English Drama*, 279–91.

Edgar T. Schell, *Strangers and Pilgrims*, 27–51.

Natalie Crohn Schmitt, "The Idea of a Person in Medieval Morality Plays," in Davidson, Gianakaris, and Stroupe, *The Drama in the Middle Ages*, 304–15.

F. Towne, "Roister Doister's Assault on the *Castle of Perseverance*," *WSCS* 18 (December 1950): 175–80.

P. J. Umphrey, "*The Castle of Perseverance*, Line 695," *PQ* 59 (Winter 1980): 105–07.

John W. Velz, "From Jerusalem to Damascus: Biblical Dramaturgy in Medieval and Shakspearean Conversion Plays," *CompD* 15 (Winter 1981–82): 311–26.

Chester Cycle
Chester Abraham and Isaac

Peter Braeger, "Typology as Contrast in the Middle English Abraham and Isaac Plays," in Johnston and Riley, *Proceedings of the Illinois Medieval Association*, 131–53.

Joseph Candido, "Language and Gesture in the Chester *Sacrifice of Isaac*," *Comitatus* 3 (Spring 1972): 11–18.

Bert Cardullo, "*The Chester Sacrifice of Isaac*," *Expl* 43 (Spring 1985): 3–4.

ANONYMOUS, *Chester Adoration of the Shepherds*

Phillip McCaffrey, "The Didactic Structure of the Chester 'Sacrifice of Isaac,'" *Comitatus* 2 (Spring 1971): 16–26.

Thomas Rendall, "Visual Typology in the Abraham and Isaac Plays," *MP* 81 (February 1984): 221–32.

Travis, *Dramatic Design in the Chester Cycle*, 78–84, 86–89.

Chester Adoration of the Shepherds

Robert Adams, "The Egregious Feasts of the Chester and Towneley Shepherds," *ChauR* 21 (Fall 1986): 96–107.

Kathleen M. Ashley, "An Anthropological Approach to the Cycle Drama: The Shepherds as Sacred Clowns," *FCS* 13 (1988): 123–36.

Hans-Jürgen Diller, "The Composition of the *Chester Adoration of the Shepards*," *Anglia* 89, no. 2 (1971): 178–98.

Joseph E. Grennen, "Tudd, Tibbys Sonne, and Trowle the Trewe: Dramatic Complexities in the Chester Shepherds' Pageant," *SN* 57 (Summer 1985): 165–73.

Kevin J. Harty, " 'And Sheep will I keepe no more': Birth and Rebirth in the *Chester Adoration of the Shepherds*," *ABR* 29 (December 1978): 348–57.

William F. Munson, "Audience and Meaning in Two Medieval Dramatic Realisms," *CompD* 9 (Spring 1975): 44–67. Reprinted in Davidson, Gianakaris, and Stroupe, *The Drama in the Middle Ages*, 183–206.

Lorraine Kochanske Stock, "Comedy in the English Mystery Cycles: Three Scenes in the Chester *Shepherds' Play*," in *Versions of Medieval Comedy*, ed. Paul D. Ruggiers (Norman: University of Oklahoma Press, 1977), 211–26.

Chester Annunciation and Nativity Play

G. C. Britton, "Language and Character in Some Late Medieval Plays," *E&S* 33 (1980): 1–15.

Kevin J. Harty, " 'Unbeleeffe Is a Fowle Sinne': *The Chester Nativity Play*," *SUS* 11 (1979): 35–41.

Ruth M. Keane, "Kingship in the *Chester Nativity Play*," *LeedsSE* 13 (Spring 1982): 74–84.

Travis, *Dramatic Design in the Chester Cycle*, 108–18.

ANONYMOUS, *Chester Deluge; Noah*

Chester Ascension

Travis, *Dramatic Design in the Chester Cycle*, 197–98.

Chester Christ at Simon's; The Money Lenders; Judas' Plot

Travis, *Dramatic Design in the Chester Cycle*, 163–68, 170–71.

Chester Christ's Ministry; Lazarus

Kathleen M. Ashley, "The Resurrection of Lazarus in the Late Medieval English and French Cycle Drama," *PLL* 22 (Summer 1986): 227–44.

Travis, *Dramatic Design in the Chester Cycle*, 156–62.

Chester Coming of Antichrist

Leslie Howard Martin, "Comic Eschatology in the *Chester Coming of the Antichrist*," *CompD* 5 (Fall 1971): 163–76.

Travis, *Dramatic Design in the Chester Cycle*, 225–27, 230–36, 238–41.

Chester Creation of the World; Adam and Eve; Cain and Abel

Blair W. Boone, "The Skill of Cain in the English Mystery Cycles," *CompD* 16 (Summer 1982): 112–29.

Kevin J. Harty, "Adam's Dream and the First Three Chester Plays," *CahiersE* 21 (April 1982): 1–11.

Travis, *Dramatic Design in the Chester Cycle*, 89–98.

Chester Crucifixion

David Mills, " 'In This Storye Consistethe Oure Chefe Faithe': The Problems of Chester's Play(s) of the Passion," *LeedsSE* 16 (Winter 1985): 326–36.

Chester Deluge; Noah

Richard Jacob Daniels, "*Uxor* Noah: A Raven or a Dove?" *ChauR* 14 (Summer 1979): 23–32.

ANONYMOUS, *Chester Emmaus; Doubting Thomas*

Kevin J. Harty, "Adam's Dream and the First Three Chester Plays," *CahiersE* 21 (April 1982): 1–11.

Sarah Sutherland, " 'Not or I See More Neede': The Wife of Noah in the Chester, York, and Towneley Cycles," in Elton and Long, *Shakespeare and Dramatic Tradition*, 181–93.

Phillip Zarilli, "From Destruction to Conservation in the Chester *Noah* Play," *TJ* 31 (May 1979): 198–209.

Chester Emmaus; Doubting Thomas

Travis, *Dramatic Design in the Chester Cycle*, 237–38.

Chester Fall of Lucifer

Kevin J. Harty, "Adam's Dream and the First Three Chester Plays," *CahiersE* 21 (April 1982): 1–11

Kevin J. Harty, "The Chester *Fall of Lucifer*," *McNR* 22 (1975–1976): 70–79.

Norma Kroll, "Cosmic Characters and Human Form: Dramatic Interaction and Conflict in the Chester Cycle *Fall of Lucifer*," *MRDE* 2 (Spring 1985): 33–50.

Jean Q. Seaton, "Source of Order or Sovereign Lord: God and the Pattern of Relationships in Two Middle English 'Fall of Lucifer' Plays," *CompD* 18 (Fall 1984): 203–21.

Karl Tamburr, "The Dethroning of Satan in the Chester Cycle," *NM* 85 (June 1984): 316–28.

Travis, *Dramatic Design in the Chester Cycle*, 70–75, 92–95.

Chester Fall of Man

Kevin J. Harty, "The Norwich Grocers' Play and Its Three Cyclic Counterparts: Four English Mystery Plays on the Fall of Man," *SN* 53 (Spring 1981): 77–89.

Chester Harrowing of Hell

Thomas N. Grove, "Light in Darkness: The Comedy of the York *Harrowing of Hell* as Seen Against the Backdrop of the Chester *Harrowing of Hell*," *NM* 75 (March 1974): 115–25.

Karl Tamburr, "The Dethroning of Satan in the Chester Cycle," *NM* 85 (June 1984): 316–28.

Travis, *Dramatic Design in the Chester Cycle*, 192–97.

Chester Last Judgement

George Ovitt, Jr., "Christian Eschatology and the *Chester* 'Judgement,'" *ELWIU* 10 (Spring 1983): 3–16.

Travis, *Dramatic Design in the Chester Cycle*, 241–53.

Chester Last Supper and Betrayal

Travis, *Dramatic Design in the Chester Cycle*, 175–77.

Chester Magi

Travis, *Dramatic Design in the Chester Cycle*, 108–12, 130–32.

Chester Moses and the Law; Balaak and Balaam

David Mills, "The Two Versions of Chester Play v: *Balaam and Baluak*," in Rowland, *Chaucer and Middle English Studies*, 366–71.

Travis, *Dramatic Design in the Chester Cycle*, 84–89.

Chester Offering of the Three Kings

Travis, *Dramatic Design in the Chester Cycle*, 108–12, 130–34.

Chester Pentecost

Travis, *Dramatic Design in the Chester Cycle*, 204–06.

Chester Pinacle, with the Woman of Canan

Judith Ferster, "Writing on the Ground: Interpretation in *Chester Play XII*," in *Sign, Sentence, Discourse: Language in Medieval Thought and Literature*, ed. Julian N. Wasserman and Lois Roney (Syracuse, NY: Syracuse University Press, 1989), 179–93.

ANONYMOUS, *Chester Prophets of Antichrist*

Alan H. Nelson, "The Temptation of Christ; or the Temptation of Satan," in Taylor and Nelson, *Medieval English Drama*, 218–29.

Travis, *Dramatic Design in the Chester Cycle*, 152–56.

Chester Prophets of Antichrist

Travis, *Dramatic Design in the Chester Cycle*, 228–30.

Chester Passion

Lorrayne Y. Baird, " 'Cockes face' and the Problem of *poydrace* in the Chester *Passion*," *CompD* 16 (Fall 1982): 227–37.

David Mills, " 'In This Storye Consistethe Oure Chefe Faithe': The Problem of the Chester Play(s) of the Passion," *LeedsSE* 16 (Winter 1985): 326–36.

Travis, *Dramatic Design in the Chester Cycle*, 177–79, 185–91.

Peter W. Travis, "The Dramatic Strategies of Chesyer's Passion Pagina," *CompD* 8 (Fall 1974): 275–89.

Chester Purification; Christ and the Doctors

John J. McGavin, "Sign and Transition: *The Purification* Play in Chester," *LeedsSE* 11 (Spring 1980): 90–104.

Travis, *Dramatic Design in the Chester Cycle*, 138–40.

Chester Ressurection

Travis, *Dramatic Design in the Chester Cycle*, 203–04, 212–15, 218–21.

Chester Shepherds

Robert Adams, "The Egregious Feasts of the Chester and Towneley Shepherds," *ChauR* 21 (Fall 1986): 96–107.

Travis, *Dramatic Design in the Chester Cycle*, 108–12, 118–30.

Chester Slaughter of the Innocents

Travis, *Dramatic Design in the Chester Cycle*, 134–38.

Chester Trial and Flagellation

David Mills, " 'In This Storye Consistethe Oure Chefe Faithe': The Problems of Chester's Play(s) of the Passion," *LeedsSE* 16 (Winter 1985): 326–36.

Travis, *Dramatic Design in the Chester Cycle*, 179–85, 204–06.

The Contention Between Liberality and Prodigality

John Scattergood, "*The Contention between Liberality and Prodigality*—A Late Morality Play," in Tricomi, *Early Drama to 1600*, 153–167.

The Contention—Betwixt the Houses of York and Lancaster

James McManaway, "*The Contention* and *2 Henry VI*," in *Studies in English Presented to Karl Brunner*, ed. Siegfried Korninger (Stuttgart: University of Stuttgart 1957), 143–45.

Coventry Cycle. See *N-Towne Cycle*

The Creation of the World [*Gwryans an Bys*]

Robert M. Longsworth, "Two Medieval Cornish Versions of the Creation of the World," *CompD* 21 (Fall 1987): 249–58.

Croxton Play of the Sacrament

Cecilia Cutts, "The Croxton Play: An Anti-Lollard Piece?" *MLQ* 5 (March 1944): 45–60.

Richard L. Homan, "Devotional Themes in the Violence and Humor of the *Play of the Sacrament*," *CompD* 20 (Winter 1986–87): 327–40.

Richard L. Homan, "Two Exempla: Analogues to the *Play of the Sacrament* and *Dux Moraud*," *CompD* 18 (Fall 1984): 241–251. Reprinted in Clifford and Stroupe, *Drama in the Middle Ages*, Second Series, 199–209.

Sister Nicholas Maltman, "Meaning and Art in the Croxton *Play of the Sacrament*," *ELH* 41 (Spring 1974): 149–64.

Ann Eljenholm Nichols, "The Croxton *Play of the Sacrament*: A Re-Reading," *CompD* 22 (Summer 1988): 117–37.

Ann Eljenholm Nichols, "Lollard Language in the Croxton *Play of the Sacrament*," *N&Q* 36 (March 1989): 23–25.

ANONYMOUS, *Dame Sirith*

Victor I. Sherbe, "The Earthly and Divine Physicians: Christus Medicus in the Croxton *Play of the Sacrament*," in *The Body and the Text: Comparative Essays in Literature and Medicine*, ed. Bruce Clarke and Wendell Aycock (Lubbock: Texas Tech University Press, 1990) 161–71.

Victor I. Sherbe, "Violence and the Social Body in the Croxton *Play of the Sacrament*," in *Violence in Drama*, ed. James Redmond (Cambridge: Cambridge University Press, 1991), 69–78.

Dame Sirith

Bruce More, "The Narrator within the Performance: Problems with Two Medieval 'Plays,'" *CompD* 22 (Spring 1988): 21–36.

Digby Plays

Digby Conversion of St. Paul

John W. Velz, "From Jersulam to Damascus: Biblical Dramaturgy in Medieval and Shakspearean Conversion Plays," *CompD* 15 (Winter 1981–82): 311–26.

Digby Mary Magdalene

Jacob Bennett, "The *Mary Magdalene* of Bishop's Lynn," *SP* 75 (Winter 1978): 1–9.

Robert H. Bowers, "The Tavern Scene in the Middle English Digby Play of Mary Magdalen," in Bryan, et al., *All These to Teach*, 15–32.

Theresa Coletti, "The Design of the Digby Play of *Mary Magdalene*," *SP* 76 (October 1979): 313–33.

Clifford Davidson, "The Digby *Mary Magdalene* and the Magdalene Cult of the Middle Ages," *AnM* 13 (1972): 70–87.

David L. Jeffrey, "English Saints' Plays," in Denny, *Medieval Drama*, 68–89.

Sister Nicholas Maltman, O.P., "Light in and on the Digby *Mary Magdalene*," in vol. 1 of *Saints, Scholars and Heroes: Studies in Medieval Culture in Honour of Charles W. Jones*, ed. Margot H. King and Wesley M. Stevens (Collegeville, MN: Saint John's Abbey and University, 1979), 257–80.

John W. Velz, "From Jerusalem to Damascus: Biblical Dramaturgy in Medieval and Shakspearean Conversion Plays," *CompD* 15 (Winter 1981-82): 311–26.

John W. Velz, "Sovereignty in the Digby *Mary Magdalen*," *CompD* 2 (Spring 1968): 32–43.

Dux Moraud

Constance B. Hieatt, "A Case for *Duk Moraud* as a Play of the Miracles of the Virgin," *MS* 32 (1970): 345–51.

Richard L. Homan, "Two Exempla: Analogues to the Play of the Sacrament and *Dux Moraud*," *CompD* 18 (Fall 1984): 241–51. Reprinted in Davidson and Stroupe, *Drama in the Middle Age*, Second Series, 199–209.

Edmund Ironsides

Ribner, *English History Play*, 243–44.

M. W. A. Smith, "*Edmund Ironsides* and Principles of Authorship Attribution," *ShN* 38 (Fall–Winter 1988): 50.

Edward III

Inna Koskenniemi, "Themes and Imagery in *Edward III*," *NM* 65 (September 1964): 446–81.

John S. Lewis, "The Rash Oath in *Edward III*," *Allegorica* 1 (Summer 1976): 269–77.

Muir, *Shakespeare as Collaborator*, 10–55.

Ribner, *English History Play*, 146–54.

Talbert, *Elizabethan Drama*, 90–92, 110–12.

The Entertainment at Chirk Castle

Cedric C. Brown, "The Chirk Castle Entertainment of 1634," *MiltonQ* 11 (March 1977): 76–86.

Everyman

Mary D. Anderson, *Drama and Imagery in English Medieval Churches* (Cambridge: Cambridge University Press, 1963), 72–84.

Brooks and Heilman, *Understanding Drama*, 100–11.

ANONYMOUS, *Everyman*

Joyce Cary, *Art and Reality* (New York: Cambridge University Press, 1958), 154–59.

John Conley, "Aural Error in *Everyman*?" *N&Q* 22 ((June 1975): 244–45.

John Conley, " 'Cruelly' in *Everyman* 73," *N&Q* 34 (March 1987): 10–11.

John Conley, "The Doctrine of Friendship in *Everyman*," *Speculum* 44 (April 1969): 374–82.

John Conley, "*Everyman* 29: 'Lawe' or 'Love'?" *N&Q* 27 (August 1980): 298–99.

John Conley, "*Everyman* 504: Ase, Behold, or 'Ah, See'?" *N&Q* 29 (October 1982): 399–400.

John Conley, "The Identity of Discretion in *Everyman*," *N&Q* 30 (October 1983): 394–96.

John Conley, "The Phrase 'The oyl of forgyuenes' in *Everyman*: A Reference to Extreme Unction?" *N&Q* 22 (March 1975): 105–06.

John Conley, "A Reference to Judas Maccabeus in *Everyman*," *N&Q* 14 (March 1967): 50–51.

Jim W. Corder, "*Everyman*: The Way to Life," in *Studies in Medieval, Renaissance, American Literature: A Festschrift Honoring Troy C. Crenshaw, Lorraine Sherley, and Ruth Speer Angell*, ed. Betsy F. Colquitt (Fort Worth: Texas Christian University Press, 1971), 53–56.

Douglas Cowling, "The Angels' Song in *Everyman*," *N&Q* 35 (September 1988): 301–03.

Julia Dietrich, "*Everyman*, Lines 364-47," *Expl* 40 (Spring 1982): 5.

Donald F. Duclow, "*Everyman* and the *Ars Moriendi*: Fifteenth-Century Ceremonies of Dying," *FCS* 6 (1983): 93–13.

Garner, *The Absent Voice*, 61–71.

Allen D. Goldhamer, "*Everyman*: A Dramatization of Death," *C&M* 30 (1969): 595–616. Reprinted in *QJS* 59 (February 1973): 87–98.

Randolf Goodman, *Drama on Stage* (NY: Holt, Rinehart, 1961), 61–95.

Richard Hillman, "*Everyman* and the Energies of Stasis," *Flor* 7 (June 1985): 206–26.

Thomas J. Jambeck, "*Everyman* and the Implications of Bernardine Humanism in the Character 'Knowledge,'" *M&H* 8 (March 1977): 103–23.

David Kaula, "Time in *Everyman* and *Dr. Faustus*," *CE* 21 (October 1960): 9–14.

V. A. Kolve, "*Everyman* and the Parable of the Talents," in *The Medieval Drama: Papers of the Third Annual Conference of the Center for Medieval and Early Renaissance Studies, State University of New York at Binghampton, 3–4 May 1969*, ed. Sandro Sticca (Albany: State University of New York Press, 1972), 69–98. Reprinted in Taylor and Nelson, *Medieval English Drama*, 316–40.

H. Kossman, "Felawship His Fer: A Note on Everyman's False Friend," *ES* 45 Supplement (1964): 157–60.

Murdo William McRae, "Everyman's Last Rites and the Digression on Priesthood," *CL* 13 (Fall 1966): 305–09.

Dennis V. Moran, "The Life of *Everyman*," *Neophil* 56 (July 1972): 324–30.

William Munson, "Knowing and Doing in *Everyman*," *ChauR* 19 (Fall 1985): 252–71.

George S. Peek, "Sermon Themes and Sermon Structure in *Everyman*," *SCB* 40 (Winter 1980): 159–60.

Robert Potter, "Divine and Human Justice," in Neuss, *Aspects of Early English Drama*, 129–41.

Thomas Rendall, "The Times of Mercy and Judgment in *Mankind*, *Everyman*, and the *Castle of Perseverance*," *ESC* 7 (Fall 1981): 255–69.

Lawrence V. Ryan, "Doctrine and Dramatic Structure in *Everyman*," *Speculum* 32 (January 1957): 722–35.

Natalie Crohn Schmitt, "The Idea of a Person in Medieval Morality Plays," in Davidson, Gianakaris, and Stroupe, *The Drama in the Middle Ages*, 304–15.

Phoebe S. Spinrad, "The Last Temptation of *Everyman*," *PQ* 64 (Spring 1985): 185–94.

Sinichi Takaku, "Dissappearance of Death in *Everyman*," *SELL* 23 (April 1974): 232–34.

Ron Tanner, "Humor in *Everyman* and the Middle English Morality Play," *PQ* 70 (Spring 1991): 149–61.

Geoffrey Thomas, *The Theatre Alive* (London: Christopher Johnson, 1948), 222–26.

Helen S. Thomas, "The Meaning of the Character Knowledge in *Everyman*," *MissQ* 14 (Spring 1963): 3–13.

Zacharias P. Thundy, "Good Deeds Rediviva: Everyman and the Doctrine of Reviviscence," *FCS* 17 (1990): 421–37.

Carolynn Van Dyke, "The Intangible and Its Image: Allegorical Discourse and the Cast of *Everyman*," in *Acts of Interpretation: The Text in Its Contexts, 700–1600: Essays on Medieval and Renaissance Texts in Honor of E. Talbot Donaldson*, ed. Mary J. Carruthers and Elizabeth D. Kirks (Norman, OK: Pilgrim, 1982), 311–24.

Thomas F. Van Lann, "*Everyman*: A Structural Analysis," *PMLA* 78 (December 1963): 1465–75.

John W. Velz, "Episodic Structure in Four Tudor Plays: A Virtue of Necessity," *CompD* 6 (Summer 1972): 87–102.

Michael J. Warren, "*Everyman*: Knowledge Once More," *DR* 54 (Spring 1974): 136–46.

John M. Webster, "The Allegory of Contradiction in *Everyman* and *The Faerie Queen*," in *Spenser and the Middle Ages*, ed. David A. Richardson (Cleveland, OH: Cleveland State University Press, 1976), 357–86.

Williams, *Drama in Performance*, 46–53.

Wimsatt, *Allegory and Mirror*, 46–49.

The Famous Victories of Henry V

Larry S. Champion, " 'What prerogatiues meanes': Perspective and Political Ideology in *The Famous Victories of Henry V*," *SAB* 53 (November 1988): 1–19.

Clemen, *English Tragedy Before Shakespeare*, 194–97.

Ribner, *English History Play*, 73–74.

The First Part of Hieronimo

Wiggins, *Journeymen in Murder*, 153–56.

The Fortress of Perfect Beauty

Norman Council, "*O Dea Certe*: The Allegory of *The Fortress of Perfect Beauty*," *HLQ* 39 (October 1976): 328–42.

Louis Adrian Montrose, "Celebration and Insinuation: Sir Philip Sidney and the Motives of Elizabethan Courtship," *RenD* 8 (1977): 3–35.

The Four Cardinal Virtues

Frederick S. Boas, "*The Four Cardinal Virtues*," *QQ* 58 (Spring 1951): 85–91.

Godly Queen Hester

Blackburn, *Biblical Drama*, 70–76.

Hegge Play of Joseph's Return. See *N-Town*

Hickscorner

Bevington, *From "Mankind" to Marlowe*, 50–51, 138–39.

Edgar T. Schell, *"Youth* and *Hickscorner*, Which Came First?" *PQ* 45 (April 1966): 468–74.

How a Man May Choose a Good Wife from a Bad

Sherbo, *English Sentimental Drama*, 75–81.

Impatient Poverty

Yukihiro Takemoto, "A Study of the Prodigal Son Plays, II: The Revitalization of the Godly Traditions," *Lang&C* 10 (1989): 1–18.

Interlude of the Clerk and the Girl

Bruce Moore, "The Narrator within the Preformance: Problems with Two Medieval 'Plays,'" *CompD* 22 (Spring 1988): 21–36.

Jacob and Esau

Blackburn, *Biblical Drama*, 148–51.

Richard Leighton Greene, "Carols in Tudor Drama," in Rowland, *Chaucer and Middle English Studies*, 357–65.

Paul Whitfield White, "Predestinarian Theology in the Mid-Tudor Play *Jacob and Esau*," *Ren&R* 24 (Fall 1988): 291–302.

John of Bordeux

Waldo F. McNeir, "Reconstructing the Conclusion to *John of Bordeux*," *PMLA* 66 (June 1951): 540–43.

ANONYMOUS, *King Darius*

Waldo F. McNeir "Robert Green and *John of Bordeux*," *PMLA* 64 (September 1949): 781–801.

King Darius

Bevington, *From "Mankind" to Marlowe*, 175–78.

Blackburn, *Biblical Drama*, 125–28.

King Leir

Mark J. Blechner, "*King Lear, King Leir*, and Incest Wishes," *AI* 45 (Fall 1988): 309–25.

Clemen, *English Tragedy Before Shakespeare*, 205–07, 285–86.

Claudette Hoover, "Goneril and Regan: 'So Horrid as in Woman,'" *SJS* 10 (Fall 1984): 49–65.

Robert A. Law, "*King John* and *King Leir*," *TSLL* 1 (Winter 1960): 472–76.

Stephen J. Lynch, "Sin, Suffering, and Redemption in *Leir* and *Lear*," *ShakS* 18 (1986): 161–74.

Wiggins, *Journeymen in Murder*, 67–70, 111–17.

A Knack to Know an Honest Man

Sherbo, *English Sentimental Drama*, 123–27.

The Life and Death of Jack Straw

Mary Grace Muse Adkins, "A Theory about *The Life and Death of Jack Straw*," *Studies in English* 28 (1949): 57–82.

The Life and Death of Thomas Lord Cromwell

Larry S. Champion, "Dramatic Strategy and Political Ideology in *The Life and Death of Thomas, Lord Cromwell*," *SEL* 29 (Spring 1989): 219–36.

Francis E. Zapatka, and T. R. Murphy, "Two Thomases: An Historical and Literary Comparison of *Thomas Lord Cromwell* and *Sir Thomas More*," *PPMRC* 12–13 (1987–1988): 263–79.

Locrine

Clemen, *English Tragedy Before Shakespeare*, 92–99, 258–62.

Ribner, *English History Play*, 238–41.

Love Feigned and Unfeigned

Leah Lindsay Scragg, "*Love Feigned and Unfeigned*: A Note on the Use of Allegory on the Tudor Stage," *ELN* 3 (December 1966): 248–52.

Ludus Coventriae. See *N-Town Cycle*

Mankind

Adams, *English Domestic or Homiletic Tragedies*, 56–58.

Kathleen M. Ashley, "Titivillus and the Battle of Words in *Mankind*," *AnM* 16 (1975): 128–50.

LynnDianne Beene, "Language Patterns in *Mankind*," *LangQ* 21 (Spring–Summer 1983): 25–29

Sandra Billington, " 'Suffer Fools Gladly': The Fool in Medieval England and the Play *Mankind*," in Williams, *The Fool and the Trickster*, 125–33.

G. C. Britton, "Language and Character in Some Late Medieval Plays," *E&S* 33 (1980): 1–15.

Arthur Brown, "Folklore Elements in Medieval Drama," *Folklore* 63, no. 1 (1952): 65–78.

Lawrence M. Clopper, "*Mankind* and Its Audience," *CompD* 8 (Autumn 1974): 347–55.

W. A. Davenport, "Peter Idley and the Devil in *Mankind*," *ES* 64 (April 1983): 106–12.

Alan J. Fletcher, "The Meaning of 'Gostly to Owr Purpos' in *Mankind*," *N&Q* 31 (September 1984): 301–02.

Garner, *The Absent Voice*, 71–79.

Staunton B. Garner, Jr. "Theatricality in *Mankind* and *Everyman*," *SP* 84 (Summer 1987): 272–85.

Anthony Gash, "Carnival against Lent: The Ambivalence of Medieval Drama," in *Medieval Literature: Criticism, Ideology, and History*, ed. David Aers (New York: St. Martin's, 1986), 74–98.

Paula Neuss, "Active and Idle Language: Dramatic Images in *Mankind*," in Denny, *Medieval Drama*, 40–67.

Robert Potter, "Divine and Human Justice," in Neuss, *Aspects of Early English Drama*, 129–41.

Thomas Rendall, "The Times of Mercy and Judgment in *Mankind*, *Everyman*, and the *Castle of Perseverance*," *ESC* 7 (Fall 1981): 255–269.

Schell, *Strangers and Pilgrims*, 53–54.

Lorraine K. Stock, "The Thematic and Structural Unity of *Mankind*," *SP* 72 (October 1975): 386–407.

The Marriage of Wit and Science

Werner Habicht, "The Wit Interludes and the Form of Pre-Shakespearean 'Romantic Comedy,'" *RenD* 8 (1965): 73–88.

R. S. Varna, "Philosophical and Moral Ideas in *The Marriage of Wit and Science*," *PQ* 44 (January 1965): 120–22.

Merry Devil of Edmonton

Rudolph Fiehler, "I Serve the Good Duke of Norfolk," *MLQ* 10 (December 1949): 364–66.

Traister, *Heavenly Necromancers*, 51–53.

Mucedorus and Amadine

Paul G. Kreuzer, "*Mucedorus*: A Comedy of Transformation," *Thoth* 16, no. 3 (1976): 33–42.

Richard Marientras, *New Perspectives on Shakespeare's World*, trans. J. Lloyd (Cambridge: Cambridge University Press, 1985), 11–15.

George Reynolds, "*Mucedorus*, Most Popular Elizabethan Play," in Bennett, Cargill, and Hall, *Studies in English Renaissance Drama*, 248–68.

Mundus et Infans

G. C. Britton, "Language and Character in Some Late Medieval Plays," *E&S* 33 (1980): 1–15.

Natalie Crohn Schmitt, "The Idea of a Person in Medieval Morality Plays," in Davidson, Gianakaris, and Stroupe, *The Drama in the Middle Ages*, 304–15.

The Nature of the Four Elements

Bevington, *From "Mankind" to Marlowe*, 45–47.

New Custom

Leslie M. Cliver, "John Foxe and the Drama *New Custom*," *HLQ* 10 (January 1947): 407–10.

Newcastle Noah's Ark

Richard Jacob Daniels, "*Uxor* Noah: A Raven or a Dove?" *ChauR* 14 (Summer 1979): 23–32.

Nice Wanton

Adams, *English Domestic or Homiletic Tragedies*, 69–71.

Norwich Grocers' Play

Kevin J. Harty, "The *Norwich Grocers' Play* and Its Three Cyclic Counterparts: Four English Mystery Plays on the Fall of Man," *SN* 53 (Spring 1981): 77–89

N-Towne Cycle
N-Town Agony in the Garden

Travis, *Dramatic Design in the Chester Cycle*, 146–47.

N-Town Annunciation

David Mills, "The House That Joseph Built: The N-Town *Annunciation* and Return," in *KM* 80, 103–04.

Theresa Coletti, "Devotional Iconography in the N-Town Marian Plays," in Davidson, Gianakaris, and Stroupe, *The Drama in the Middle Ages*, 249–71.

Alan J. Fletcher, "Layers of Revision in the N-Town Marian Cycle," *Neophil* 66 (July 1982): 469–78.

N-Town Assumption

Theresa Coletti, "Devotional Iconography in the N-Town Marian Plays," in Davidson, Gianakaris, and Stroupe, *The Drama in the Middle Ages*, 249–71.

Alan J. Fletcher, "Layers of Revision in the N-Town Marian Cycle," *Neophil* 66 (July 1982): 469–78.

Ann Eljenholm Nichols, "The Hierosphthitic Topos, or the Fate of Fergus: Notes on the N-Town *Assumption*," *CompD* 25 (Spring 1991): 29–41.

N-Town Fall of Man

Kevin J. Harty, "The *Norwich Grocers' Play* and Its Three Cyclic Counterparts: Four English Mystery Plays on the Fall of Man," *SN* 53 (Spring 1981): 77–89.

N-Town Joseph's Return

Joseph L. Baird, and Lorrayne Y. Baird, "Fabliau Form and the Hegge Joseph's Return," *CHR* 8 (Fall 1973): 159–69.

Gail McMurray Gibson, " 'Porta haec clausa erit': Comedy, Conception, and Ezekiel's Closed Door in the *Ludus Coventriae* Play of 'Joseph's Return,'" *JMRS* 8 (Spring 1978): 137–56.

David Mills, "The House That Joseph Built: The N-Town *Annunciation* and *Return*," in *KM* 80, 103–04.

N-Town Lamech

C. M. Guilfoyle, "Cain, Lamech, and the 'Quarell Hede,'" *ELN* 25 (December 1987): 13–18

N-Town Play of Mary's Conception

Theresa Coletti, "Devotional Iconography in the N-Town Marian Plays," in Davidson, Gianakaris, and Stroupe, *The Drama in the Middle Ages*, 249–71.

Alan J. Fletcher, "The Design of the N-Town *Play of Mary's Conception*," *MP* 79 (November 1981): 166–73.

N-Town Noah

Daniel P., Poteet, II, "Symbolic Character and Form in the *Ludus Coventriae* 'Play of Noah,'" *ABR* 26 (March 1975): 75–88.

N-Town Pagent of the Weavers

Mikiko Ishii, "Joseph's Proverbs in the Coventry Plays," *Folklore* 93 (Spring 1982): 47–60.

N-Town Passion

Theresa Coletti, "Sacrament and Sacrifice in the N-Town Passion," *Mediaevalia* 7 (October 1981): 239–64

Paula Lozar, "Time in the Corpus Christi Cycles: 'Aesthetic' and 'Realistic' Models," *PLL* 14 (Fall 1978): 385–93.

John F. Plummer, "The Logomachy of the *N-Town Passion Play I*," *JEGP* 88 (July 1989): 311–31.

Daniel P. Poteet, II, "Time, Eternity, and Dramatic Form in Ludus Coventriae 'Passion Play I,'" *CompD* 8 (Fall 1974): 369–85. Reprinted in Davidson, Gianakaris, and Stroupe, *The Drama in the Middle Ages*, 232–48.

Michael J. Wright, "Ludus Coventriae *Passion Play I*: Action and Interpretation," *NM* 86 (March 1985): 70–77.

N-Town Parliament of Heaven; Salutation and Conception

Alan J. Fletcher, "The 'Contemplacio' Prologue to the N-Town Play of the *Parliament of Heaven*," *N&Q* 27 (April 1980): 111–12.

Alan J. Fletcher, "Layers of Revision in the N-Town Marian Cycle," *Neophil* 66 (July 1982): 469–78.

David Mills, "Concerning a Stage Direction in the *Ludus Coventriae*," *ELN* 11 (March 1974): 162–64.

N-Town Shearmen and Taylors Pagent

Mikiko Ishii, "Joseph's Proverbs in the Coventry Plays," *Folklore* 93 (Spring 1982): 47–60.

ANONYMOUS, *N-Town Temptation of Christ*

Pamela M. King, "Faith, Reason and the Prophets' Dialogue in the Coventry *Pageant of the Shearmen and Taylors*," in *Drama and Philosophy*, ed. James Redmond (Cambridge: Cambridge University Press; 1990), 37–46.

N-Town Temptation of Christ

Alan H. Nelson, "The Temptation of Christ; or the Temptation of Satan," in Taylor and Nelson, *Medieval English Drama*, 218–29.

N-Town Woman Taken in Adultery

Elizabeth J. El Itreby, "The N-Town Play of 'The Woman Taken in Adultery': Central to a Recapitulative 'Redemption Trilogy,'" *BSUF* 26 (Summer 1985): 3–13.

Peter Meredith, " 'Nolo Mortem' and the Ludus Coventriae Play of the *Woman Taken in Adultery*," *MedAe* 38, no. 1 (1969): 38–54.

Daniel P. Poteet, II. "Condition, Contrast, and Division in the Ludus Coventriae 'Woman Taken in Adultery,'" *Mediaevalia* 1 (Spring 1975): 78–92.

Travis, *Dramatic Design in the Chester Cycle*, 154–55.

Ordinalia

Sally Joyce Cross, "Torturers as Tricksters in the Cornish *Ordinalia*," *Neophil* 84 (December 1983): 448–55.

Origo Mundi

Robert M. Longsworth, "Two Medieval Cornish Versions of the Creation of the World," *CompD* 21 (Fall 1987): 249–58.

Parnassus Plays

Mann, *The Elizabethan Player*, 128–47.

The Partial Law

T. M. Parrot, "Two Late Dramatic Versions of the Slandered Bride Theme," in McManaway, *Joseph Quincy Adams Memorial Studies*, 542–48.

The Pride of Life

Irmlind Hengstebeck, "*The Pride of Life*, Vers 444," *NM* 72 (December 1971): 739–41.

The Prodigal Son

Blackburn, *Biblical Drama*, 188–90.

Yukihiro Takemoto, "A Study of the Prodigal Son Plays, II: The Revitalization of the Godly Traditions," *Lang&C* 10 (1989): 1–18.

The Puritan

Leinwand, *The City Staged*, 119–21.

Queen Hester and Proud Haman

Blackburn, *Biblical Drama*, 182–88.

Quem Quaeritis

James M. Gibson, "*Quem Quaeritis in Presepe*: Christmas Drama or Christmas Liturgy?" in Davidson and Stroupe, *Drama in the Middle Ages*, 106–28.

The Rare Triumphs of Love and Fortune

Kiefer, *Fortune and Elizabethan Tragedy*, 169–72.

Traister, *Heavenly Necromancers*, 37–39.

The Reign of Edward III

Larry S. Champion, "'Answere to this perillous time': Ideological Ambivalence in *The Raigne of King Edward III* and the English Chronicle Plays," *ES* 69 (April 1988): 117–29.

Lee Ligon-Jones, "Be Absolute: Death and Sex in *Measure for Measure* and *Edward III*," *CCTEP* 55 (September 1990): 7–15

Inna Koskenniemi, "Themes and Imagery in *Edward III*," *NM* 65 (September 1964): 446–81.

ANONYMOUS, *The Revesby Sword Play*

The Revesby Sword Play

Michael Heaney, "New Light on the *Revesby Sword Play*," *N&Q* 35 (June 1988): 191–93.

The Sacrifice of Isaac

Peter Braeger, "Typology as Contrast in the Middle English Abraham and Isaac Plays," in Johnston and Riley, *Proceedings of the Illinois Medieval Association*, 131–53.

Thomas Rendall, "Visual Typology in the Abraham and Isaac Plays," *MP* 81 (February 1984): 221–32.

Sapentia Solomonis

Blackburn, *Biblical Drama*, 142–45.

The Second Maiden's Tragedy

David M. Bergeron, "Art Within *The Second Maiden's Tragedy*," *MRDE* 1 (Summer 1984): 173–86.

Frank Howden, "Horror and the Macabre in Four Elizabethan Tragedies: *The Revenger's Tragedy*, *The Duchess of Malfi*, *The Second Maiden's Tragedy*, *The Atheist's Tragedy*," *CahiersE* 10 (April 1968).

Kistner and Kistner, *Middleton's Tragic Themes*, 43–56.

Levin, *The Multiple Plot in English Renaissance Drama*, 25–34.

Swetnam the Woman-Hater Arraigned by Women

Woodbridge, *Women and the English Renaissance*, 300–22.

The Taming of a Shrew

T. M. Parrot, "*The Taming of a Shrew*: A New Study of an Old Play," *UCSLL* 2 (Summer 1945): 155–65.

John W. Schroeder, "*The Taming of a Shrew* and *The Taming of the Shrew*: A Case Reopened," *JEGP* 57 (October 1958): 424–43.

The Telltale

Kenneth L. Wheelen, "A Critical View of *The Telltale*, an Anonymous Play," *ESRS* 15 (Fall 1966): 34–48.

Temperence and Humility

T. W. Craik, "The Political Interpretation of Two Tudor Interludes: *Temperance and Humility* and *Wealth and Health*," *RES* 4 (1953): 98–108.

Thomas of Woodstock

Clemen, *English Tragedy Before Shakespeare*, 207–10.

Ribner, *English History Play*, 136–45.

A. P. Rossiter, "Prolegomenon to the Anonymous *Woodstock* (alias *1 Richard II*)," *DUJ* 7 (March 1945): 42–51.

Schell, *Strangers and Pilgrims*, 79–112.

The Three Marys

Williams, *Drama in Performance*, 36–40.

Tom Tyler and His Wife

Richard Leighton Greene, "Carols in Tudor Drama," in Rowland, *Chaucer and Middle English Studies*, 357–65.

Towneley Cycle. See *Wakefield Cycle*

The Trial of Treasure

Bevington, *From "Mankind" to Marlowe*, 153–55.

Leslie Oliver, "William Wager and *The Trial of Treasure*," *HLQ* 9 (January 1946): 419–29.

The Troublesome Reign of King John

Clemen, *English Tragedy Before Shakespeare*, 153–55.

John Elson, "Studies in the King John Plays," in McManaway *Joseph Quincy Adams Memorial Studies*, 183–97.

Robert A. Law, "*King John* and *King Leir*," *TSLL* 1 (Winter 1960): 472–76.

Loftis, *Renaissance Drama in England and Spain*, 77–78.

Nicole Rowan, "Some Aspects of the Relationship between *King John* and *The Troublesome Reign*," *SGG* 21 (1980–1981): 233–46.

Wiggens, *Journeymen in Murder*, 90–93.

The True Tragedy of Richard III

Barry, *The King in Tudor Drama*, 123–30.

Clemen, *English Tragedy Before Shakespeare*, 202–04.

Talbert, *Elizabethan Drama and Shakespeare's Early Drama*, 66–67.

The Two Merry Milkmaids

Traister, *Heavenly Necromancers*, 53–55.

Two Noble Ladies and the Converted Conjuror

Traister, *Heavenly Necromancers*, 62–64, 136–37.

Wakefield Cycle
Wakefield Abraham

Robert B. Bennett, "Homiletic Design in the Towneley *Abraham*," *MLS* 7 (Spring, 1977): 5–15.

Lawrence L. Besserman, "The Wakefield *Noah*, Lines 55–56," *PLL* 15 (Spring 1979): 82–84.

Peter Braeger, "Typology as Contrast in the Middle English Abraham and Isaac Plays," in Johnston and Riley, *Proceedings of the Illinois Medieval Association*, 131–53.

G. C. Britton, "Language and Character in Some Late Medieval Plays," *E&S* 33 (1980): 1–15.

John Gardner, "Idea and Emotion in the Townley *Abraham*," *PLL* 7 (Summer 1971): 227–41.

Edgar Schell, The Distinctions of the Towneley *Abraham*," *MLQ* 41 (December 1980): 315–27.

Donna Smith Vinter, "Didactic Characterization: The Towneley *Abraham*," *CompD* 14 (Summer 1980): 117–36. Reprinted in Happé, *Medieval English Drama*, 71–89.

Wakefield Annunciation

Raimo Anttila, "Loanwords and Statistical Measures of Style in the Towneley Plays," *Statistical Methods in Linguistics* 2 (January 1963): 73–93.

Kathleen M. Ashley, "The Specter of Bernard's Noonday Demon in Medieval Drama," *ABR* 30 (June 1979): 205–21.

Joseph L. Baird, and Amy Cassidy. "Humility and the Towneley *Annunciation*," *PQ* 52 (Spring 1973): 301–06.

Janet Cowen, " 'Heven and erthe in lytyl space,'" in Neuss, *Aspects of Early English Drama*, 62–77.

Martin Stevens, "The Dramatic Setting of the Wakefield *Annunciation*," *PMLA* 81 (January 1966): 193–98.

Wakefield Caesar Augustus

Raimo Anttila, "Loanwords and Statistical Measures of Style in the Towneley Plays," *Statistical Methods in Linguistics* (Stockholm) 2 (January 1963): 73–93.

Wakefield Creation

Maris G. Fiondella, "Framing and Ideology in the Towneley Creation Play," *Exemplaria* 1 (Fall 1989): 401–27.

Edith Hartnett, "Cain in the Medieval *Towneley* Play," *AnM* 12 (1971): 21–29.

Wakefield Crucifixion

Maris G. Fiondella, "Medieval Textuality: A Psycholinguistic Function for the Towneley Passion Plays," in *Semiotics* 1987, ed. John Deely (Lanham, MD: University Press of America, 1988), 201–10.

ANONYMOUS, *Wakefield First Shepherds' Play*

Thomas J. Jambeck, "The Dramatic Implications of Anselmian Affective Piety in the Towneley *Play of the Crucifixion*," *AnM* 16 (1975): 110–27.

Wakefield First Shepherds' Play

Robert Adams, "The Egregious Feasts of the Chester and Towneley Shepherds," *ChauR* 21 (Fall 1986): 96–107.

Kathleen M. Ashley, "An Anthropological Approach to the Cycle Drama: The Shepherds as Sacred Clowns," *FCS* 13 (1988): 123–36.

Robert J. Blanch, "The Gifts of the Shepherds in *Prima Pastorum*: A Symbolic Interpretation," *Cithara* 13 (May 1974): 69–75.

Josie P. Campbell, "Farce and Function in the Wakefield Shepherds' Plays," *ChauR* 14 (Spring 1980): 336–43.

Helen Cooper, "A Note on the Wakefield 'Prima Pastorum,'" *N&Q* 20 (September 1973): 326.

Thomas J. Jambeck, "The 'Ayll of Hely' Allusion in the *Prima Pastorum*," *ELN* 17 (September 1979): 1–7.

David Lyle Jeffrey, "Pastoral Care in the Wakefield Shepherd Plays," *ABR* 22 (June 1971): 208–21.

Lauren Ethyl Lepow, " 'What God Has Cleansed': The Shepherds' Feast in the *Prima Pastorum*," *MP* 80 (February 1983): 280–83.

William F. Munson, "Audience and Meaning in Two Medieval Dramatic Realisms," *CompD* 9 (Spring 1975): 44–67. Reprinted in Davidson, Gianakaris, and Stroupe, *The Drama in the Middle Ages*, 183–206.

Alicia K. Nitecki, "The Sacred Elements of the Secular Feast in *Prima Pastorum*," *Mediaevalia* 3 (Summer 1977): 229–37.

Lois Roney, "The Wakefield First and Second Shepherds Plays as Complements in Psychology and Parody," *Speculum* 58 (July 1983): 696–723.

Suzanne Spyser, "Dramatic Illusion and Sacred Reality in the Townley *Prima Pastorum*," *SP* 78 (Winter 1981): 1–19.

Rose A. Zimbardo, "A Generic Approach to the First and Second Shepherds' Plays of the Wakefield Mystery Cycle," *FCS* 13 (1988): 79–89.

Wakefield Harrowing of Hell

Clifford Davidson, "From *Tristia* to *Gaudium*: Iconography and the York-Towneley *Harrowing of Hell*," *ABR* 28 (September 1977): 260–75.

Diana Wyatt, "Two Yorkshire Fragments: Perhaps Dramatic?" *REEDN* 3 (January 1978): 17–21.

Wakefield Herod the Great

Wendy Clein, "The Towneley *Magnus Herodes* and the Comedy of Redemption," *Renascence* 38 (Autumn 1985): 54–63.

Shearle Furnish, "Technique versus Feeling in the Wakefield Master's *Magnus Herodes*," *KPAB* (January 1984): 36–43.

Clarence Steinberg, "Kemp Towne in the Townley [sic] *Herod* Play: A Local Wakefield Allusion?" *NM* 71 (June 1970): 253–60.

Wakefield Isaac

Peter Braeger, "Typology as Contrast in the Middle English Abraham and Isaac Plays," in Johnston and Riley, *Proceedings of the Illinois Medieval Association*, 131–53.

Thomas Rendall, "Visual Typology in the Abraham and Isaac Plays," *MP* 81 (February 1984): 221–32.

Wakefield Judgement

Lister M. Matheson, "Linguistics and Hierarchy: The Demons in the Towneley Judgment Play with a Note on Line 539," *NM* 91, no. 2 (1991): 209–13.

Wakefield Killing of Abel

Blair W. Boone, "The Skill of Cain in the English Mystery Cycles," *CompD* 16 (Summer 1982): 112–29.

Bennett A. Brockman, "Comic and Tragic Counterpoint in the Medieval Drama: The Wakefield *Mactacio Abel*," *MS* 39 (1977): 331–49.

Bennett A. Brockman, "The Law of Man and the Peace of God: Judicial Process as Satiric Theme in the Wakefield *Mactacio Abel*," *Speculum* 49 (October 1974): 699–707.

C. M. Guilfoyle, "Cain, Lamech, and the 'Quarell Hede,'" *ELN* 25 (December 1987): 13–18.

Dorrel T. Hanks, Jr., "The *Mactacio Abel* and the Wakefield Cycle: A Study in Context," *SoQ* 16 (October 1977): 47–57.

David Lyle Jeffrey, Stewardship in the Wakfield *Mactacio Abel* and *Noe* Plays," *ABR* 22 (March 1971): 64–76.

Edmund Reiss, "The Symbolic Plow and Plowman and the Wakefield *Mactacio Abel*," *SIcon* 5 (1975): 3–30.

D. W. Robertson, Jr., "The Question of 'Typology' and the Wakefield *Mactacio Abel*," *ABR* 25 (March 1974): 157–73. Reprinted in *Essays on Medieval Culture*, ed. D. W. Robertson, Jr. (Princeton: Princeton University Press, 1980), 218–32, 317–72.

Wakefield Lazarus

Seth Daniel Riemer, "The Dramatic Significance of Christ's Tears in a French and an English Version of the Lazarus Play," in Tricomi, *Early Drama to 1600*, 37–47.

George A. West, "An Analysis of the Towneley Play of *Lazarus*," *PQ* 56 (Spring 1976): 320–29.

Wakefield Noah

Lawrence L. Besserman, "The Wakefield *Noah*, Lines 55–56," *PLL* 15 (Winter 1979): 82–84.

Josie P. Campbell, "The Idea of Order in the *Wakefield Noah*," *ChauR* 10 (Summer 1975): 76–86.

Richard Jacob Daniels, "*Uxor* Noah: A Raven or a Dove?" *ChauR* 14 (Summer 1979): 23–32.

Mary P. Freier, "Woman as Termagant in the Towneley Cycle," in Johnston and Riley, *Proceedings of the Illinois Medieval Association*, 154–167.

John Gardner, "Imagery and Allusion in the Wakefield Noah Play," *PLL* 4 (Spring 1968): 3–12.

Jeffrey Allen Hirshberg, "Noah's Wife on the Medieval English Stage: Iconographic and Dramatic Values of Her Distaff and Choice of the Raven," *SIcon* 2 (1972): 25–40.

David Lyle Jeffrey, "Stewardship in the Wakfield *Mactacio Abel* and *Noe* Plays," *ABR* 22 (March 1971): 64–76.

Roston, *Biblical Drama*, 45–48.

Edgar Schell, "The Limits of Typology and the Wakefield Master's *Processus Noe*," *CompD* 25 (Summer 1991): 168–87.

Thomas Ramey Watson, "The Wakefield *Noah*," *Expl* 40 (Spring 1982): 5–7.

Wakefield Pharaoh

G. C. Britton, "Language and Character in Some Late Medieval Plays," *E&S* 33 (1980): 1–15.

Wakefield Play of the Talents

Theresa Margaret Coletti, "Theology and Politics in the Towneley *Play of the Talents*," *M&H* 9 (March 1979): 111–26.

Peter Meredith, "The York Millers' Pageant and the Towneley *Processus Talentorum*," *MET* 4 (December 1982): 104–14.

Michael Olmert, "Towneley *Processus Talentorum*: Dicing toward Jerusalem," *Flor* 5 (March 1983): 157–77.

Wakefield Procession of the Prophets

Raimo Anttila, "Loanwords and Statistical Measures of Style in the Towneley Plays," *Statistical Methods in Linguistics* 2 (January 1963): 73–93.

Wakefield Salutation of Elizabeth

Raimo Anttila, "Loanwords and Statistical Measures of Style in the Towneley Plays," *Statistical Methods in Linguistics* 2 (January 1963): 73–93.

G. C. Britton, "Language and Character in Some Late Medieval Plays," *E&S* 33 (1980): 1–15.

Wakefield Second Shepherds' Play

George R. Adams, "Comedy and Theology in the *Second Shepherds' Play*," in Selz, *Medieval Drama*, 63–68.

Kathleen M. Ashley, "An Anthropological Approach to the Cycle Drama: The Shepherds as Sacred Clowns," *FCS* 13 (1988): 123–36.

Kathleen M. Ashley, "The Guiler Beguiled: Christ and Satan as Theological Tricksters in Medieval Religious Literature," *Criticism* 24 (Spring 1982): 126–37.

Robert J. Blanch, "The Symbolic Gifts of the Shepherds in the *Secunda Pastorum*," *TSL* 17 (Spring 1972): 25–36.

Robert A. Brawer, "St. Augustine's Two Cities as Medieval Dramatic Exempla," *Mediaevalia* 4 (Summer 1978): 225–44.

Josie P. Campbell, "Farce and Function in the Wakefield Shepherd's Plays," *ChauR* 14 (Spring 1980): 336–43.

Thomas P. Campbell, "Why Do the Shepherds Prophesy?" *CompD* 12 (1978): 200–13.

Eugene B. Cantelupe, and Richard Griffith, "The Gifts of the Shepherds in the Wakefield *Secunda Pastorum*: An Iconographical Interpretation," *MS* 28 (1966): 328–35.

Nan Cooke Carpenter, "Music in the *Secunda Pastorum*," *Speculum* 26 (October 1951): 696–700. Reprinted in Taylor and Nelson, *Medieval English Drama*, 212–17.

John H. Cleland, "*Second Shepherd's* [sic] and *Homecoming*: Two Dramatic Imitations of Life," *F&R* 3, no. 2 (1977): 46–64.

John P. Cutts, "The Shepherd's Gifts in the *Second Shepherds' Play* and Bosch's 'Adoration of the Magi,'" *CompD* 4 (Summer 1970): 120–24.

Regula Meyer Evitt, "Musical Structure in the *Second Shepherd's* [sic] *Play*," *CompD* 22 (Winter 1988): 304–22.

Mary P. Freier, "Woman as Termagant in the Towneley Cycle," in Johnston and Riley, *Proceedings of the Illinois Medieval Association*, 154–67.

John Gardner, "Structure and Tone in the *Second Shepherds' Play*," *ETJ* 19 (March 1967): 1–8.

Cherrell Guilfoyle, " 'The Riddle Song' and the Shepherds' Gifts in *Secunda Pastorum* with a Note on the 'Tre callyd Persidis,'" *YES* 8 (1978): 208–19.

Jeffrey Helterman, "Satan as Everyshepherd: Comic Metamorphosis in *The Second Shepherds' Play*," *TSLL* 12 (Winter 1971): 515–30.

Thomas J. Jambeck, "The Canvas-Tossing Allusion in *Secunda Pastorum*," *MP* 76 (August 1978): 49–54.

David Lyle Jeffrey, "Pastoral Care in the Wakefield Shepherd Plays," *ABR* 22 (June 1971): 208–21.

Kenneth E. Johnson, "The Rhetoric of Apocalypse in van Eyck's 'Last Judgement' and the Wakefield *Secunda Pastorum*," in vol. 4 of *Legacy of Thespis: Drama Past and Present*, ed. Karelissa V. Hartigan (Lanham, MD, New York, and London: University Press of America, 1984), 31–41.

Robert E. Jungman, "Mak and the Seven Names of God," *Lore&L* 3 (January 1982): 24–28.

Erik Kooper, "Political Theory and Pastoral Care in the Second Shepherds' Play" in *This Noble Craft . . .: Proceedings of the Xth Research Symp. of Dutch & Belgian Univ. Teachers of Old and Middle English & Hist. Ling., Utrecht, 19–20 Jan, 1989*, ed. Erik Kooper (Amsterdam: Rodopi, 1991), 142–51.

David Lampe, "The Magi and Modes of Meaning: The Second Shepherd's Play as an Index of the Criticism of Medieval Drama," in Tricomi, *Early Drama to 1600*, 107–20.

Lauren Lepow, "Daw's Tennis Ball: A Topical Allusion in the *Secunda Pastorum*," *ELN* 22 (December 1984): 5–8.

Maynard Mack, Jr. "*The Second Shepherds' Play*: A Reconsideration," *PMLA* 93 (January 1978): 78–85.

F. P. Manion, S.J., "A Reinterpretation of *The Second Shepherds' Play*," *ABR* 30 (March 1979): 44–68.

Linda E. Marshall, " 'Sacral Parody' in the *Secunda Pastorum*," *Speculum* 47 (October 1972): 720–36.

Lynn Remley, "*Deus Caritas*: The Christian Message of the '*Secunda Pastorum*,'" *NM* 72 (December 1971): 742–48.

J. W. Robinson, "Form in the *Second Shepherds' Play*," *PPMRC* 8 (1983): 71–78.

Lois Roney, "The Wakefield First and Second Shepherds' Plays as Complements in Psychology and Parody," *Speculum* 58 (July 1983): 696–723.

Lawrence J. Ross, "Symbol and Structure in the *Secunda Pastorum*," *CompD* 1 (Summer 1966): 122–49. Reprinted in Taylor and Nelson, *Medieval English Drama*, 177–211.

Roston, *Biblical Drama*, 40–44.

Jennifer Strauss, "Grace Enacted: The *Secunda Pastorum*," *Parergon* 14 (January 1976): 63–68.

Edmund M. Taft, "Surprised by Love: The Dramatic Structure and Popular Appeal of the *Wakefield Second Shepherds' Pageant*," *JPC* 14 (Summer 1980): 131–40.

M. F. Vaughan, "Mak and the Proportions of *The Second Shepherds' Play*," *PLL* 18 (Winter 1982): 355–67.

M. F. Vaughan, "The Three Advents in the *Secunda Pastorum*," *Speculum* 55 (July 1980): 484–504.

Hiroshi Yamamoto, "Religion and Entertainment in the Towneley *Secunda Pastorum*; Essays in Honour of Professor Toyohiko Tatsumi's Seventieth Birthday," in Milward, *Poetry and Faith in the English Renaissance*, 27–36.

Rose A. Zimbardo, "Comic Mockery of the Sacred: *The Frogs* and *The Second Shepherds' Play*," ETJ 30 (October 1978): 398–406.

Wakefield Thomas of India

Robert A. Brawer, "St. Augustine's Two Cities as Medieval Dramatic Exempla," *Mediaevalia* 4 (Summer 1978): 225–44.

A Warning for Faire Women

Adams, *English Domestic or Homiletic Tragedies*, 114–25.

Leanore Lieblein, "The Context of Murder in English Domestic Plays, 1590–1610," *SEL* 23 (Spring 1983): 181–96.

Arthur D. Lewis, "*A Warning for Faire Women*, Line 143," *N&Q* 199 (January 1954): 18–19.

Joseph H. Marshburn, "'A Cruell Murder Done in Kent' and Its Literary Manifestations," *SP* 46 (April 1949): 134–36.

The Wars of Cyrus King of Persia

Barry, *The King in Tudor Drama*, 208–16.

Michael Shapiro, *Children of the Revels: The Boy Companies of Shakespeare's Time and Their Plays* (New York: Columbia University Press, 1977), 158–65.

Traister, *Heavenly Necromancers*, 56–57.

Wealth and Health

T. W. Craik, "The Political Interpretation of Two Tudor Interludes: *Temperance and Humility* and *Wealth and Health*," *RES* 4 (1953): 98–108.

Rainer Pineas, "The Revision of *Wealth and Health*," *PQ* 44 (July 1965): 560–62.

Wily Beguiled

Matthew McDiarmid, "The Stage Quarrel in *Wily Beguiled*," *N&Q* 201 (September 1956): 380–83.

The Wisdom of Doctor Dodypoll

Traister, *Heavenly Necromancers*, 61–62.

Wisdom Who Is Christ, or Mind, Will, and Understanding

Donald C. Baker, "Is Wisdom a 'Professional' Play?" in Riggio, *The Wisdom Symposium*, 67–86.

David Bevington, " 'Blake and Wyght, Fowll and Fayer': Stage Picture in *Wisdom Who Is Christ*," *CompD* 19 (Summer 1985): 136–150. Reprinted in Riggio, *The Wisdom Symposium*, 18–38.

David Bevington, "Political Satire in the Morality *Wisdom Who Is Christ*," *RenP* 1960 (1961): 41–51.

Merle Fifield, "The Use of Doubling and 'Extras' in *Wisdom Who Is Christ*," *BSUF* 6 (Fall 1965): 65–68.

Milton McC. Gatch, "Mysticism and Satire in the Morality of *Wisdom*," *PQ* 53 (Spring 1974): 342–62.

Eugene D. Hill, "The Trinitarian Allegory of the Moral Play of *Wisdom*," *MP* 73 (November 1975): 121–35.

Robert Potter, "Divine and Human Justice," in Neuss, *Aspects of Early English Drama*, 129–41.

Wolfgang Riehle, "English Mysticism and the Morality Play *Wisdom Who Is Christ*," in *The Medieval Mystical Tradition in England: Papers Read at the Exeter Symposium, July 1980*, ed. Marion Glasscoe (Exeter: University of Exeter, 1980), 202–15.

Meg Twycross, " 'Apparell comlye,' " in Neuss, *Aspects of Early English Drama*, 30–49.

York Cycle
York Abraham and Isaac

Richard Beadle, "The Origins of Abraham's Preamble in the York Play of *Abraham and Isaac*," *YES* 11 (1981): 178–87.

ANONYMOUS, *York Christ Led up to Calvary*

Peter Braeger, "Typology as Contrast in the Middle English Abraham and Isaac Plays," in Johnston and Riley, *Proceedings of the Illinois Medieval Association*, 131–53.

A. K. Reed, " 'A Thing Like a Love Affair': A Study of the Passion of Obedience in the York Play of *Abraham and Isaac*," *C&L* 29 (Winter 1980): 34–45.

Thomas Rendall, "Visual Typology in the Abraham and Isaac Plays," *MP* 81 (February 1984): 221–32.

York Christ Led up to Calvary

Paula Lozar, "Time in the Corpus Christi Cycles: 'Aesthetic' and 'Realistic' Models," *PLL* 14 (Fall 1978): 385–93.

York Crucifixion

Clifford Davidson, "Civic Concern and Iconography in the York Passion," *AnM* 15 (1974): 125–49.

Clifford Davidson, "The Realism of the York Realist and the York Passion," *Speculum* 50 (April 1975): 270–83. Reprinted in Happé, *Medieval English Drama*, 101–17.

Paula Lozar, "Time in the Corpus Christi Cycles: 'Aesthetic' and 'Realistic' Models," *PLL* 14 (Fall 1978): 385–93.

David Mills, " 'Look at Me When I'm Speaking to You': The 'Behold and See' Conventions in Medieval Drama," *MET* 7 (July 1985): 4–12.

R. H. Nicholson, "The Trial of Christ the Sorcerer in the York Cycle," *JMRS* 16 (Fall 1986): 125–69.

Alicia Korzeniowska Nitecki, "The Dramatic Impact of the Didactic Voice in the York Cycle of Mystery Plays," *AnM* 21 (1981): 61–76.

Paul Willis, "The Weight of Sin in the York *Crucifixio*," *LeedsSE* 15 (Spring 1984): 109–16.

York Dream of Pilate's Wife: Jesus Before Pilate

Lee Jobling, "The Pilate of the York Mystery Plays," in Barnes, et al., *Words and Wordsmiths*, 49–62.

Sally Mussetter, "The York Pilate and the Seven Deadly Sins," *NM* 81 (March 1980): 57–64.

York Fall of the Angels

Jean Q. Seaton, "Source of Order or Sovereign Lord: God and the Pattern of Relationships in Two Middle English 'Fall of Lucifer' Plays," *CompD* 18 (Fall 1984): 203–21.

York Fall of Man

Blair W. Boone, "The Skill of Cain in the English Mystery Cycles," *CompD* 16 (Summer 1982): 112–29.

Kevin J. Harty, "The Norwich Grocers' Play and Its Three Cyclic Counterparts: Four English Mystery Plays on the Fall of Man," SN 53 (Spring 1981): 77–89.

York Harrowing of Hell

Clifford Davidson, "From *Tristia* to *Gaudium*: Iconography and the York-Towneley *Harrowing of Hell*," *ABR* 28 (September 1977): 260–75.

Thomas N. Grove, "Light in Darkness: The Comedy of the York *Harrowing of Hell* as Seen Against the Backdrop of the Chester *Harrowing of Hell*," *NM* 75 (March 1974): 115–25.

York Moses and Pharaoh

Richard Beadle, "The York Hosiers' Play of *Moses and Pharaoh*: A Middle English Dramatist at Work," *Poetica* 19 (February 1984): 3–26.

York Noah

Richard Jacob Daniels, "*Uxor* Noah: A Raven or a Dove?" *ChauR* 14 (Summer 1979): 23–32.

Roston, *Biblical Drama*, 45–48.

York Second Accusation Before Pilate: Remorse of Judas: Purchase of the Field of Blood

Lee Jobling, "The Pilate of the York Mystery Plays," in Barnes, et al., *Words and Wordsmiths*, 49–62.

ANONYMOUS, *York Second Trial Continued: Judgement on Jesus*

Sally Mussetter, "The York Pilate and the Seven Deadly Sins," *NM* 81 (March 1980): 57–64.

R. H. Nicholson, "The Trial of Christ the Sorcerer in the York Cycle," *JMRS* 16 (Fall 1986): 125–69.

York Second Trial Continued: Judgement on Jesus

Lee Jobling, "The Pilate of the York Mystery Plays," in Barnes, et al., *Words and Wordsmiths*, 49–62.

Sally Mussetter, "The York Pilate and the Seven Deadly Sins," *NM* 81 (March 1980): 57–64.

R. H. Nicholson, "The Trial of Christ the Sorcerer in the York Cycle," *JMRS* 16 (Fall 1986): 125–69.

York Temptation of Christ

Alan H. Nelson, "The Temptation of Christ; or the Temptation of Satan," in Taylor and Nelson, *Medieval English Drama*, 218–29.

The Yorkshire Tragedy

Adams, *English Domestic or Homiletic Tragedies*, 126–32.

Glenn H. Blaynewy, "Dramatic Pointing in *The Yorkshire Tragedy*," *N&Q* 202 (May 1957): 191–92.

A. C. Cawley, "*A Yorkshire Tragedy* Considered in Relation to Biblical and Moral Plays," in *Everyman and Company: Essays on the Theme and Structure of the European Moral Play*, ed. Donald Gilman, David M. Bevington, and Robert Potter (New York: AMS, 1989), 155–68.

Leanore Lieblein, "The Context of Murder in English Domestic Plays, 1590–1610," *SEL* 23 (Spring 1983): 181–96.

Stephen L. Trainor, " 'Guilty Creatures at Play': Rhetoric and Repentance in Renaissance Domestic Tragedy," *BSUF* 24 (Fall 1983): 40–46.

Youth

Edgar T. Schell, "*Youth* and *Hickscorner*, Which Came First?" *PQ* 45 (April 1966): 468–74.

BALE, JOHN

King John

Barry B. Adams, "Doubling in Bale's *King Johan*," *SP* 62 (April 1965): 111–20.

Sarah Carpenter, "John Bale's *Kynge Johan*: The Dramatization of Allegorical and Non-Allegorical Figures," in *Le Théâtre au Moyen Age: Actes du deuxième colloque de le Société International pour l'étude du Théâtre Médiéval, Alençon, 11–14 juillet 1977*, ed. Gari R. Muller (Paris, Brussels, and Quebec: L'Aurore/Univers; Montreal: Les Editions Universe, 1981), 263–69.

John Elson, "Studies in the King John Plays," in McManaway, *Joseph Quincy Adams Memorial Studies*, 191–97.

Hiroshi Ebihara, "The English Political Morality from *Magnyfycence* to *Wealth and Health*, with Special Attention to Bale's Treatment in *King Johan* of the Doctrine of Absolutism," *SEL* 12 (Spring 1972): 141–64.

Peter Happé, "Sedition in *King Johan*: Bale's Development of a 'Vice,'" *MET* 3 (July 1981): 3–6.

S. F. Johnson, "The Tragic Hero in Early Elizabethan Drama," in Bennett, Cargill, and Hall, *Studies in English Renaissance Drama*, 157–64, 169–71.

Carole Levin, "A Good Prince: King John and Early Tudor Propaganda," *SCJ* 11 (Winter 1980): 23–32.

Edwin S. Miller, "The Roman Rite in Bale's *King John*," *PMLA* 64 (September 1949): 802–22.

J. H. P. Pafford, "Two Notes on Bale's *King John*," *MLR* 56 (October 1961): 553–55.

Ribner, *English History Play*, 37–41, 49–50, 52–54.

Yoshiko Uéno, "An Essay on the King John Plays: From History to Romance," *ShStud* 12 (1973-74): 1–30.

Three Laws, of Nature, Moses, and Christ, Corrupted by Sodomites, Pharisees, and Papists

Bevington, *From "Mankind" to Marlowe*, 128–32.

BALE, JOHN, *The Life and Repentaunce of Mary Magdalene*

The Life and Repentaunce of Mary Magdalene

Peter Happé, "The Protestant Adaptation of the Saint Play," in *The Saint Play in Medieval Europe*, ed. Clifford Davidson (Kalamazoo: Western Michigan University Press, 1986), 205–240.

BARNES, BARNABE

The Devil's Charter

Jacqueline E. M. Latham, "Machiavelli, Policy, and *The Devil's Charter*," *MRDE* 1 (Spring 1984): 97–108.

Traister, *Heavenly Necromancers*, 58–60.

BARRY, LORD DAVID

Ram Alley

Leinwand, *The City Staged*, 180–83, 191–92.

BEAUMONT, FRANCIS

The Knight of the Burning Pestle

Lee Bliss, " 'Plot Mee No Plots': The Life of Drama and the Drama of Life in *The Knight of the Burning Pestle*," *MLQ* 45 (March 1984): 3–21.

Cope, *Dramaturgy of the Daemonic*, 59–61.

Cope, *Theatre and the Dream*, 196–210.

D'Amico, *The Moor in English Renaissance Drama*, 61–71.

John Doebler, "Beaumont's *Knight of the Burning Pestle* and the Prodigal Son Plays," *SEL* 5 (Spring 1965): 333–44.

John Doebler, "The Tone of the Jaspar and Luce Scenes in Beaumont's *The Knight of the Burning Pestle*," *ES* 56 (April 1975): 108–13.

Leinwand, *The City Staged*, 64–67.

Ronald F. Miller, "Dramatic Form and Dramatic Imagination in Beaumont's *The Knight of the Burning Pestle*," *ELR* 8 (Spring 1978): 67–84.

W. J. Olive, " 'Twenty Good Nights'—*The Knight of the Burning Pestle*, *The Family of Love*, and *Romeo and Juliet*," *SP* 47 (April 1950): 182–89.

David A. Samuelson, "The Order in Beaumont's *Knight of the Burning Pestle*," *ELR* 9 (Autumn 1979): 302–18.

Wells, *Elizabethan and Jacobean Playwrights*, 233–35.

BEAUMONT, FRANCIS, AND JOHN FLETCHER

The Captain

Ornstein, *Moral Vision of Jacobean Tragedy*, 167–68.

The Coxcomb

Suzanne Gossett, "The Term 'Masque' in Shakespeare and Fletcher, and *The Coxcomb*," *SEL* 14 (Spring 1974): 285–95.

Shaw, *Plays and Players*, 307–11.

A King and No King

Knights, *Drama and Society in the Age of Jonson*, 292–95.

Michael Neill, "The Defence of Contraries: Skeptical Paradox in *A King and No King*," *SEL* 21 (Spring 1981): 319–32.

Robert K. Turner, Jr., "The Morality of *A King and No King*," *RenP* 1959 (1960): 93–103.

Waith, *The Pattern of Tragicomedy in Beaumont and Fletcher*, 27–42.

Wells, *Elizabethan and Jacobean Playwrights*, 15–17.

William C. Woodson, "The Casuistry of Innocence in *A King and No King* and Its Implications for Tragicomedy," *ELR* 8 (Autumn 1978): 312–28.

Love's Pilgrimage

Wells, *Elizabethan and Jacobean Playwrights*, 154–56.

The Maid's Tragedy

Berry, *Poet's Grammar*, 93–96.

Eugene R. Cunnar, "The Wedding Masque's Moral Vision in *The Maid's Tragedy*," *SPWVSRA* 7 (Spring 1982): 37–45.

Danby, *Poets on Fortune's Hill*, 152–210.

A. B. Feldman, "The Yellow Malady: Short Studies of Five Tragedies of Jealousy," *L&P* 5 (May 1956):46–49, 51–52.

Anne M. Hasselkorn, "Sin and the Politics of Penitence: Three Jacobean Adultresses," in Hasselkorn and Travitsky, *The Renaissance Englishwoman in Print*, 119–36.

Ronald Heubert, " 'An Artificial Way to Grieve': The Forsaken Woman in Beaumont and Fletcher, Massinger and Ford," *ELH* 44 (December 1977): 601–21.

Leech, *Shakespeare's Tragedies*, 87–89, 94–-5, 107–08.

Michael Neill, " `The Simetry, Which Gives a Poem Grace': Masque, Imagery, and the Fancy of *The Maid's Tragedy*," *RenD* 3 (1970): 111–15.

Nicoll, *English Drama*, 79–-1.

Ornstein, *Moral Vision of Jacobean Tragedy*, 173–79.

Prior, *Language of Tragedy*, 101–-4.

Ribner, *Jacobean Tragedy*, 15–17.

William Shullenberger, " 'This For the Most Wrong'd of Women': A Reappraisal of *The Maid's Tragedy*," *RenD* 13 (1982): 131–56.

Wells, *Elizabethan and Jacobean Playwrights*, 124–27.

Philaster; or, Love Lies A-Bleeding

Mary G. Adkins, "The Citizens of *Philaster*: Their Function and Significance," *SP* 43 (April 1946): 203–12

Danby, *Poets on Fortune's Hill*, 162–83.

Peter Davidson, "The Serious Concerns of *Philaster*," *ELH* 30 (March 1963): 1–15.

Ornstein, *Moral Vision of Jacobean Tragedy*, 178–79.

Nicholas F. Radel, "'Then Thus I Turn My Language to You': TheTransformation of Theatrical Language in *Philaster*," *MRDE* 3 (Spring 1986): 129–47.

James E. Savage, "Beaumont and Fletcher's *Philaster* and Sidney's *Arcadia*," *ELH* 14 (June 1947): 194–206.

James E. Savage, "The 'Gaping Wounds' in the Text of *Philaster*," *PQ* 48 (October 1949): 443–47.

Wells, *Elizabethan and Jacobean Playwrights*, 122–24.

Jerry D. White, "Irony and the Three Temptations in *Philaster*," *Thoth* 15, no. 2 (1978): 3–8.

The Woman Hater

Philip Finkelpearl, "Beaumont, Fletcher, and 'Beaumont and Fletcher': Some Distinctions," *ELR* 1 (Summer 1971): 144–64.

Levin, *The Multiple Plot in English Renaissance Drama*, 151–54.

The Woman's Prize; or, The Tamer Tamed

M. C. Bradbrook, "Dramatic Role as Social Image: A Study of *The Taming of the Shrew*," *ShJE* 94 (1958): 146–48.

BERKLEY, SIR WILLIAM

The Lost Lady

Hassel, *Renaissance Drama*, 148–50.

B[OWER], R[ICHARD]

Appius and Virginia

Richard Leighton Greene, "Carols in Tudor Drama," in Rowland, *Chaucer and Middle English Studies*, 357–65.

BRETON, NICHOLAS

The Entertainment at Elvetham

Harry H. Boyle, "Elizabeth's Entertainment at Elvetham: War Policy in Pagentry," *SP* 68 (April 1971): 146–66.

BROME, RICHARD

The Antipodes

Butler, *Theatre and Crisis*, 214–20.

Cope, *Theatre and the Dream*, 143–59.

Joe Lee Davis, "Richard Brome's Neglected Contribution to Comic Theory," *SP* 40 (October 1943): 520–28.

Donaldson, *The World Upside-Down*, 78–98.

Charlotte Spivack, "Alienation and Illusion: The Play-within-a-Play on the Caroline Stage," *MRDE* 4 (Summer 1989): 195–10.

Mann, *The Elizabethan Player*, 65–67.

The Court Beggar

Butler, *Theatre and Crisis*, 220–33.

R. J. Kaufman, "Suckling and Davenant Satirised by Brome," *MLR* 55 (July 1960): 332–44.

The Damoiselle

Butler, *Theatre and Crisis*, 210–14.

Kaufmann, *Richard Brome, Caroline Playwright*, 131–50.

The English Moor; or, The Mock Marriage

Catherine M. Shaw, *Richard Brome* (Boston: Twayne, 1980), 48–55.

Tokson, *The Popular Image of the Blackman in English Drama*, 52–53.

A Jovial Crew; or, The Merry Beggars

Butler, *Theatre and Crisis*, 269–79.

Cope, *Theatre and the Dream*, 159–69.

Farley-Hills, *The Comic in Renaissance Comedy*, 147–59.

McPeek, *The Black Book of Knaves*, 165–70.

The Late Lancashire Witches
(with Heywood)

Adams, *English Domestic or Homiletic Tragedy*, 204–05.

The Queen and the Concubine

Butler, *Theatre and Crisis*, 35–42.

Cope, *Theatre and the Dream*, 282–84.

Kaufman, *Richard Brome, Caroline Playwright*, 88–108.

The Queen's Exchange

Cope, *Theatre and the Dream*, 134–40.

The Sparagus Garden

LeRoy L. Panek, "Asparagus and Brome's *The Sparagus Garden*," *MP* 68 (May 1971): 362–63.

The Weeding of Covent Garden; or, The Middlesex Justice of the Peace

Butler, *Theatre and Crisis*, 151–58.

Kaufmann, *Richard Brome, Caroline Playwright*, 67–87.

CAMPION, THOMAS

The Caversham Entertainment

Lindley, *Thomas Campion*, 210–16.

CAMPION, THOMAS, *The Masque at Lord Hay's Marriage*

The Masque at Lord Hay's Marriage

Kogan, *The Hieroglyphic King*, 70–86.

Lindley, *Thomas Campion*, 176–90.

The Masque at Lord Somerset's Marriage

Lindley, *Thomas Campion*, 216–34.

The Lord's Mask

Brooks-Davies, *The Mercurian Monarch*, 96–98.

A. Leigh DeNeef, "Structure and Theme in Campion's *Lord's Masque*," *SEL* 17 (Spring 1977): 95–103.

Lindley, *Thomas Campion*, 190–210.

John Peacock, "Inigo Jones and the Florentine Court Theater," *JDJ* 5, no. 1–2 (1986): 200–34.

CAREW, THOMAS

Coelum Britannicum

Brooks-Davies, *The Mercurian Monarch*, 102–07.

Jennifer Chibnall, " 'To That Secure Fix'd State': The Function of the Caroline Masque Form," in Lindley, *The Court Masque*, 78–93.

Hassel, *Renaissance Drama*, 130–35.

Kogan, *The Hieroglyphic King*, 183–205.

CARLELL, LODOWICK

Arviragus and Philicia

Hassel, *Renaissance Drama*, 144–48.

The Ordinary

Wilson F. Engel, "Cartwright's *The Ordinary*," *Expl* 38 (Spring 1980): 42–43.

CARY, ELIZABETH

Edward II

Tina Krontiris, "Style and Gender in Elizabeth Cary's *Edward II*," in Haselkorn and Travitsky, *The Renaissance Englishwoman in Print*, 137–53.

The Tragedy of Mariam, The Fair Queen of Jewery

Elaine Beilin, "Elizabeth Cary and *The Tragedy of Mariam*," *PLL* 16 (Spring 1979): 45–64.

Margaret W. Ferguson, "The Spectre of Resistance: The Tragedy of *Mariam* (1613)" in Kastan and Stallybrass, *Staging the Renaissance*, 235–50.

Margaret W. Ferguson, "Running On with Almost Public Voice: The Case of 'E. C.,'" in *Tradition and the Talents of Women*, ed. Florence Howe (Urbana: University of Illinois Press, 1991), 37–67.

Sandra K. Fischer, "Elizabeth Cary and Tyranny, Domestic and Religious" in *Silent but for the Word: Tudor Women as Patrons, Translators, and Writers of Religious Works*, ed. Margaret Patterson Hannay (Kent, OH: Kent State University Press, 1985), 225–37.

Nancy A. Gutierrez, "Valuing Mariam: Genre Study and Feminist Analysis," *TSWL* 10 (Fall 1991): 233–51.

Betty S. Travitsky, "The Feme Covert in Elizabeth Cary's *Mariam*," in *Ambiguous Realities: Women in the Middle Ages and Renaissance*, ed. Carole Jeanie Levin and Jeanie Watson (Detroit: Wayne State University Press, 1987), 184–96.

Betty S. Travitsky, "Husband-Murder and Petty Treason in English Renaissance Tragedy" *RenD* 21 (1990): 171–98.

CHAPMAN, GEORGE

All Fools

R. P. Corballis, "George Chapman and Machiavelli," *Parergon* 14 (January 1976): 39–46.

Leonard Goldstein, "Some Aspects of Marriage and Inheritance in Shakespeare's *The Merry Wives of Windsor* and Chapman's *All Fools*," *ZAA* 12, no. 4 (1964): 375–86.

Grant, *Comedies of George Chapman*, 84–102.

CHAPMAN, GEORGE, *The Blind Beggar of Alexandria*

The Blind Beggar of Alexandria

Grant, *Comedies of George Chapman*, 29–43.

Helen A. Kaufman, "*The Blind Beggar of Alexandria*: A Reappraisal," *PQ* 38 (January 1959): 101–106.

Ennis Rees, "Chapman's *Blind Beggar* and the Marlovian Hero," *JEGP* 57 (April 1958): 60–63.

Bussy D'Ambois

Altman, *The Tudor Play of Mind*, 302–20.

C. L. Barber, "The Ambivalence of *Bussy D'Ambois*," *REL* 2 (October 1961): 38–44.

Barber, *Theme of Honour's Tongue*, 104–10.

Bement, *George Chapman*, 104–43.

Peter Bement, "The Imagery of Dark and Lightness in Chapman's *Bussy D'Ambois*," *SP* 64 (July 1967): 187–98.

Albert J. Braunmuller, "The Natural Course of Light Inverted: Chapman's *Bussy D'Ambois*," *JWCI* 34 (September 1971): 356–60.

Roger T. Burbridge, "Speech and Action in Chapman's *Bussy D'Ambois*," *TSL* 17 (Spring 1972): 59–65.

R. P. Carballis, "The Apotheosis of *Bussy D'Ambois*," *N&Q* 26 (March 1979): 145–46.

Clay, *The Role of Anxiety*, 183–209.

Paul Dean, and Jacqueline Johnson, "Structure in the 'Bussy' Plays of Chapman," *ES* 61 (April 1980): 119–26.

Florby, *The Painful Passage to Virtue*, 97–149.

Leonard Goldstein, "George Chapman and the Decadence in Early Seventeenth Century Drama," *S&S* 27 (Winter 1963): 33–37.

Michael Higgins, "The Developement of the 'Senecal Man': Chapman's *Bussy D'Ambois* and Some Precursors," *RES* 23 (January 1947): 30–33.

Clifford Leech, "*The Atheist's Tragedy* as a Dramatic Commentary on Chapman's Bussy Plays," *JEGP* 52 (October 1953): 525–30

Jane Melbourne, "The Inverted World of *Bussy D'Ambois*," *SEL* 25 (Spring 1985): 381–95.

William G. McCollom, "The Tragic Hero and Chapman's *Bussy D'Ambois*," *UTQ* 18 (April 1949): 227–33.

Deborah Montuori, "The Confusion of Self and Role in Chapman's *Bussy D'Ambois*," *SEL* 28 (Spring 1988): 287–99.

Edwin Muir, " 'Royal Man': Notes on the Tragedies of George Chapman," *Orion* 2, no. 1 (1945): 92–100.

Richard H. Perkinson, "Nature and the Tragic Hero in Chapman's Bussy Plays," *MLQ* 3 (September 1942): 263–85.

Ornstein, *Moral Vision of Jacobean Tragedy*, 50–60.

Prior, *Language of Tragedy*, 104–11.

Ribner, *Jacobean Tragedy*, 19–35.

Irving Ribner, "Character and Theme in Chapman's *Bussy D'Ambois*," *ELH* 26 (1959): 482–96.

Robert Roth, "Another World of Shakespeare," *MP* 49 (August 1951): 47–49.

Simpson, *Studies in Elizabethan Drama*, 154–58.

Traister, *Heavenly Necromancers*, 109–22.

Peter Ure, "Chapman's Tragedies," *Stratford-Upon-Avon Studies* 1 (1960): 227–37.

Peter Ure, "Chapman's Tragedy of *Bussy D'Ambois*: Problems of the Revised Quarto," *MLR* 48 (July 1953): 257–69.

Raymond B. Waddington, *The Mind's Empire: Myth and Form in George Chapman's Narrative Poems* (Baltimore: Johns Hopkins University Press, 1974), 19–44.

Raymond B. Waddington, "Prometheus and Hercules: The Dialectic of *Bussy D'Ambois*," *ELH* 34 (March 1967): 21–48.

Waith, *The Herculean Hero*, 88–111.

The Conspiracy and Tragedy of Charles, Duke of Byron, Marshal of France

Bement, *George Chapman*, 144–81.

K. M. Burton, "The Political Tragedies of Chapman and Jonson," *EIC* 2 (October 1952): 406–07.

Patricia Demers, "*The Conspiracy and Tragedy of Charles, Duke of Byron*: The Evaporation of Honour," *Ren&R* 11 (February 1975): 85–96.

Sidney R. Homan, "Chapman and Marlowe: The Paradoxical Hero and the Divided Response," *JEGP* 68 (January 1969): 396–406.

G. K. Hunter, "*Henry IV* and the Elizabethan Two-Part Play," *RES* 5 (July 1954): 238–39.

Ide, *Possessed with Greatness*, 132–42.

Knight, *Golden Labyrinth*, 93–95.

Loftis, *Renaissance Drama in England and Spain*, 71–72, 93–103.

MacLure, *George Chapman*, 132–44.

Ornstein, *Moral Vision of Jacobean Tragedy*, 60–70.

Johnstone Parr, "The Duke of Byron's Malignant *Caput Algoe*," *SP* 43 (April 1946): 194–202.

Elias Schwartz, "Chapman's Renaissance Man: Byron Reconsidered," *JEGP* 58 (October 1959): 613–26.

Louis Charles Stagg, "Characterization Through Nature Imagery in the Tragedies of George Chapman," *BSUF* 9, no. 1 (1968): 39–43.

Traister, *Heavenly Necromancers*, 120–21.

Peter Ure, "Chapman's Tragedies," *Stratford-Upon-Avon Studies* 1 (1960): 237–41, 244–47.

Peter Ure, "The Main Outline of Chapman's *Byron*," *SP* 47 (October 1950): 568–88. Reprinted in Maxwell, *Elizabethan and Jacobean Drama*, 123–44.

Eastward Ho
(with Jonson and Marston)

Barton, *Ben Jonson, Dramatist*, 242–48.

Bradbrook, *Growth and Structure of Elizabethan Comedy*, 149–51.

Ralph Alan Cohen, "The Function of Setting in *Eastward Ho*," *RenP* 1972 (1973): 85–96.

Jackson I. Cope, "Volpone and the Authorship of *Eastward Hoe*," *MLN* 72 (April 1957): 253–56.

Richard Horwich, "*Hamlet* and *Eastward Ho*," *SEL* 11 (Spring 1971): 223–33.

Alexander Leggatt, *Citizen Comedy in the Age of Shakespeare* (Toronto: University of Toronto Press, 1973), 47–53.

Leinwand, *The City Staged*, 113–15, 166–67, 172–74, 190–91.

CHAPMAN, GEORGE, *The Memorable Masque of the Middle Temple*

Levin, *Multiple Plot in English Renaissance Drama*, 88–89.

Nicholl, *The Chemical Theatre*, 107–11.

The Fount of New Fashions

G. A. Wilkes, "Chapman's 'Lost' Play, *The Fount of New Fashions*," *JEGP* 62 (January 1963): 77–81.

The Gentleman Usher

Cope, *Theatre and the Dream*, 33–52.

Grant, *Comedies of George Chapman*, 125–49.

Lacy, *Jacobean Problem Play*, 114–35

MacLure, *George Chapman*, 95–98.

Henry M. Weidner, "The Dramatic Uses of Homeric Idealism: The Significance of Theme and Design in Chapman's *The Gentleman Usher*," *ELH* 28 (March 1961): 121–36.

An Humorous Day's Mirth

Grant, *Comedies of George Chapman*, 44–58.

May Day

William Dean, "Chapman's *May Day*: A Comedy of Social Reformation," *Parergon* 16 (January 1974): 47–55.

Grant, *Comedies of George Chapman*, 103–24.

The Memorable Masque of the Middle Temple and Lincoln's Inn

D. J. Gordon, "Chapman's *Memorable Masque*," in Orgel, *The Renaissance Imagination*, 194–206.

Kogan, *The Hieroglyphic King*, 87–96.

Jack E. Reese, "Unity in Chapman's *Masque of the Middle Temple and Lincoln's Inn*," *SEL* 4 (Spring 1964): 291–306.

CHAPMAN, GEORGE, *Monsieur D'Olive*

Monsieur D'Olive

Grant, *Comedies of George Chapman*, 160–85.

A. P. Hogan, "Thematic Unity in Chapman's *Monsieur D'Olive*," *SEL* 11 (Spring 1971): 295–306.

The Revenge of Bussy D'Ambois

Geoffrey Aggeler, "The Unity of Chapman's *The Revenge of Bussy D'Ambois*," *PCP* 4 (January 1969): 5–18.

Bement, *George Chapman*, 182–231.

Allen Bergson, "The Wordly Stoicism of George Chapman's *The Revenge of Bussy D'Ambois* and *The Tragedy of Chabot, Admiral of France*," *PQ* 55 (Winter 1976): 43–64.

B. J. Cohon, "A Catullian Echo in George Chapman's *The Revenge of Bussy D'Ambois*," *MLN* 60 (January 1945): 29–33.

Paul Dean, and Jacqueline Johnson, "Structure in the 'Bussy' Plays of Chapman," *ES* 61 (April 1980): 119–26.

Patricia Demers, "Chapman's *The Revenge of Bussy D'Ambois*: Fixity and the Absolute Man," *Ren&R* 12 (February 1976): 12–20.

Fred M. Fetrow, "Chapman's Stoic Hero in *The Revenge of Bussy D'Ambois*," *SEL* 19 (Spring 1979): 229–37.

Florby, *The Painful Passage to Virtue*, 181–259.

Leonard Goldstein, "George Chapman and the Decadence in Seventeenth Century Drama," *S&S* 27 (Winter 1963): 37–41.

Michael H. Higgins, "Chapman's Senecal Man: A Study in Elizabethan Psychology," *RES* 47 (July 1945): 186–91.

Richard S. Ide, "Exploiting the Tradition: The Elizabethan Revenger as Chapman's 'Complete Man,'" *MRDE* 1 (Summer 1984): 159–72.

Suzanne F. Kistler, " 'Strange and Far-Removed Shores': A Reconsideration of *The Revenge of Bussy D'Ambois*," *SP* 77 (Spring 1980): 128–44.

Knight, *Golden Labyrinth*, 95–97.

Leech, *Shakespeare's Tragedies*, 23–28, 195–96.

Ornstein, *Moral Vision of Jacobean Tragedy*, 70–76.

Richard H. Perkinson, "Nature and the Tragic Hero in Chapman's Bussy Plays," *MLQ* 3 (September 1942): 263-85.

Wells, *Elizabethan and Jacobean Playwrights*, 91–93.

E. E. Wilson, "The Genesis of Chapman's *The Revenge of Bussy D'Ambois*," *MLN* 71 (December 1956): 567–69.

Sir Giles Goosecap, Knight

Grant, *Comedies of George Chapman*, 58–75.

The Tragedy of Chabot, Admiral of France

Bement, *George Chapman*, 262–73.

Allen Bergson, "The Wordly Stoicism of George Chapman's *The Revenge of Bussy D'Ambois* and *The Tragedy of Chabot, Admiral of France*," *PQ* 55 (Winter 1976): 43–64.

A. R. Braunmuller, " 'A Greater Wound': Corruption and Human Frailty in Chapman's *Chabot, Admiral of France*," *MLR* 70 (July 1975): 241–59.

K. M. Burton, "The Political Tragedies of Chapman and Jonson," *EIC* 2 (October 1952): 400–01.

Lilian Haddakin, "A Note on Chapman and Two Medieval English Jurists," *MLR* 47 (October 1952): 550–53.

Ornstein, *Moral Vision of Jacobean Tragedy*, 76–79.

Ribner, *Jacobean Tragedy*, 35–49.

Irving Ribner, "The Meaning of Chapman's *Tragedy of Chabot*," *MLR* 55 (July 1960): 321–31.

Takashi Sasayama, "*Chabot, Admiral of France*," *ShakS* 1 (1972): 15–32.

Louis Charles Stagg, "Characterization Through Nature Imagery in the Tragedies of George Chapman," *BSUF* 9, no. 1 (1968): 39–43.

The Wars of Caesar and Pompey

Bement, *George Chapman*, 235–46, 250 59.

Allen Bergson, "Stoicism Achieved: Cato in Chapman's *Tragedy of Caesar and Pompey*," *SEL* 17 (Spring 1977): 295–302.

K. M. Burton, "The Political Tragedies of Chapman and Jonson," *EIC* 2 (October 1952): 405–06.

Derek Crawley, "Decision and Character in Chapman's *The Tragedy of Caesar and Pompey*," *SEL* 7 (Spring 1967): 277–97.

Leonard Goldstein, "George Chapman and Decadence in Early Seventeenth Century Drama," *S&S* 27 (Winter 1963): 41–48.

Richard S. Ide, "Chapman's *Caesar and Pompey* and the Uses of History," *MP* 82 (February 1985): 255–68.

J. E. Ingledew, "Chapman's Use of Lucan in *Caesar and Pompey*," *RES* 13 (August 1962): 283–88.

Suzanne F. Kistler, "The Significance of the Missing Hero in Chapman's *Caesar and Pompey*," *MLQ* 40 (September 1979): 339–57.

James F. O'Callaghan, "Chapman's Caesar," *SEL* 16 (Spring 1966): 319–31.

Ornstein, *Moral Vision of Jacobean Tragedy*, 79–83.

Elias Schwartz, "A Neglected Play by Chapman," *SP* 58 (April 1961): 140–59.

Peter Ure, Chapman's Use of North's Plutarch in *Caesar and Pompey*," *RES* 9 (August 1958): 281–84.

The Widow's Tears

Lee Bliss, "The Boys from Ephesus: Farce, Freedom, and Limit in *The Widow's Tears*," *RenD* 10 (1979): 161–83.

Cope, *Theatre and the Dream*, 55–75.

Richard Corballis, "*The Widow's Tears*: Two Plots or Two Parts?" *Parergon* 20 (January 1978): 34–39.

Grant, *Comedies of George Chapman*, 185–213.

Thelma Herring, "Chapman and an Aspect of Modern Criticism," *RenD* 8 (1965): 153–79.

Renu Juneja, "Widowhood and Sexuality in Chapman's *The Widow's Tears*," *PQ* 67 (Spring 1988): 157–75.

J. C. Maxwell, "*The Widow's Tears*, V.iv.39–40," *N&Q* 21 (September 1974): 290.

Arnold W. Preussner, "Chapman's Anti-Festive Comedy: Generic Subversion and Classical Allusion in *The Widow's Tears*," *ISJR* 59 (February 1985): 263–72.

Samuel Schoenbaum, "*The Widow's Tears* and the Other Chapman," *HLQ* 23 (October 1960): 321–38. Reprinted in Stoll, *Shakespeare and Other Masters*, 218–32.

Albert H. Tricomi, "The Social Disorder of Chapman's *The Widow's Tears*," *JEGP* 72 (1973): 350–59.

Peter Ure, "The Widow Ephesus: Some Reflections on an International Comic Theme," *DUJ* 18 (December 1956): 1–9. Reprinted in Maxwell, *Elizabethan and Jacobean Drama*, 221–36.

Henry M. Weidner, "Homer and the Fallen World: Focus of Satire in George Chapman's *The Widow's Tears*," *JEGP* 62 (1963): 518–32.

CHETTLE, HENRY

The Blind Beggar of Bethnel Green
(with Day)

Samuel Schoenbaum, "John Day and Elizabethan Drama," *BPLQ* 5 (July 1953): 148–49.

The Death of Robert, Earl of Huntingdon
(with Munday)

J. M. R. Margeson, "Dramatic Form: The Huntingdon Plays," *SEL* 14 (Spring 1974): 223–38.

Downfall of Robert, Earl of Huntingdon
(with Munday)

J. M. R. Margeson, "Dramatic Form: The Huntingdon Plays," *SEL* 14 (Spring 1974): 223–38.

Hoffman; or, A Revenge for a Father

Simpson, *Studies in Elizabethan Drama*, 165–68.

CHETTLE, HENRY, *Patient Grissel*

Patient Grissel
(with Dekker and Haughton)

Judith Bronfman, "Griselda, Renaissance Woman," in Haselkorn and Travitsky, *The Renaissance Englishwoman in Print*, 211–23.

David Mason Greene, "The Welsh Characters in *Patient Grissel*," *BUSE* 4 (Autumn 1960): 171–80

Harry Keyishian, "Griselda on the Elizabethan Stage: *The Patient Grissil* of Chettle, Dekker, and Haughton," *SEL* 16 (Spring 1976): 253–61.

Levin, *The Multiple Plot in English Renaissance Drama*, 49–51.

William G. Smith, "Thomas Dekker's Welshman," *Dock Leaves* 4 (Summer, 1953): 47–52.

CHRISTOPHERSON, JOHN

Jephthe

Blackburn, *Biblical Drama*, 102–06.

DANIEL, SAMUEL

Hymen's Triumph

Johanna Procter, "*The Queenes Arcadia* (1606) and *Hymen's Triumph* (1615): Samuel Daniel's Court Pastoral Plays," in Salmons and Moretti, *The Renaissance in Ferrara*, 83–109.

Philotas

G. A. Wilkes, "Daniel's *Philotas* and the Essex Case: A Reconsideration," *MLQ* 23 (June 1962): 233–42.

The Queen's Arcadia

Johanna Procter, "*The Queenes Arcadia* (1606) and *Hymen's Triumph* (1615): Samuel Daniel's Court Pastoral Plays," in Salmons and Moretti, *The Renaissance in Ferrara*, 83–109.

Tethys' Festival, or the Queen's Wake

John Pitcher, " 'In Those Figures Which They Seeme': Samuel Daniel's *Tethys' Festival*," in Lindley, *The Court Masque*, 33–46.

The Tragedy of Cleopatra

Altman, *The Tudor Play of Mind*, 288–92.

Arthur M. Z. Norman, "Daniel's *The Tragedie of Cleopatra* and *Antony and Cleopatra*," *SQ* 9 (Winter 1958): 11–18. Reprinted in *MLR* 54 (January 1959): 1–9.

Joan Rees, "Samuel Daniel's *Cleopatra* and Two French Plays," *MLR* 47 (January 1952): 1–10.

Ernest Schanzer, "Daniel's Revision of His *Cleopatra*," *RES* 8 (November 1957): 375–81.

Cecil C. Seronsy, "The Doctrine of Cyclical Recurrence and Some Related Ideas in the Works of Samuel Daniel," *SP* 54 (July 1957): 392–97.

Michael Steppat, "Shakespeare's Response to Dramatic Tradition in *Anthony and Cleopatra*," in Fabian and von Rosador, *Shakespeare: Text, Language, Criticism*, 254–79.

Williamson, *Infinite Variety*, 134–49.

The Vision of the Twelve Goddesses

Brooks-Davies, *The Mercurian Monarch*, 85–87.

Geoffrey Creigh, "Samuel Daniel's Masque *The Vision of the Twelve Goddesses*," *E&S* 24 (1971): 22–35.

Kogan, *The Hieroglyphic King*, 51–69.

DAVENPORT, ROBERT

The City-Night-Cap

W. J. Olive, "Davenport's Debt to Shakespeare in *The City-Night-Cap*," *JEGP* 49 (July 1950): 333–44.

DAVENPORT, ROBERT, *King John and Matilda*

King John and Matilda

Ribner, *English History Play*, 295–99.

A New Trick to Cheat the Devil

W. J. Olive, "Shakespeare Parody in Davenport's *A New Tricke to Cheat the Devil*," *MLN* 66 (November 1951): 478–80.

DAVIDSON, FRANCIS

The Masque of Proteus and the Rock Adamantine

Orgel, *Jonsonian Masque*, 8–18.

DAY, JOHN

The Blind Beggar of Bethnal Green
(with Chettle)

Samuel Schoenbaum, "John Day and Elizabethan Drama," *BPLQ* 5 (July 1953): 148–49.

The Isle of Gulls

Samuel Schoenbaum, "John Day and Elizabethan Drama," *BPLQ* 5 (July 1953): 145–46.

R. Ann Thompson, "The 'Two Buckets' Image in *Richard II* and *The Isle of Gulls*," *Archiv* 213 (1976): 108.

Law Tricks; or, Who Would Have Thought It

Samuel Schoenbaum, "John Day and Elizabethan Drama," *BPLQ* 5 (July 1953): 146–48.

The Parliament of Bees

Samuel Schoenbaum, "John Day and Elizabethan Drama," *BPLQ* 5 (July 1953): 149–51.

The Travels of the Three English Brothers, Sir Thomas, Sir
Anthony, Mr. Robert Shirley
(with Rowley and Wilkins)

H. Neville Davies, "*Pericles* and the Sherley Brothers," in Honigmann, *Shakespeare and His Contemporaries*, 94–113.

Mann, *The Elizabethan Player*, 68–73.

Samuel Schoenbaum, "John Day and Elizabethan Drama," *BPLQ* 5 (July 1953): 142–45.

DEKKER, THOMAS

The Belman of London

McPeek, *The Black Book of Knaves*, 40–42, 142–47.

Cupid and Psyche

W. L. Hatstead, "Dekker's *Cupid and Psyche* and Thomas Heywood," *ELH* 11 (June 1944): 182–91.

The Honest Whore, I and II
(with Middleton)

Blow, *Rhetoric in the Plays of Thomas Dekker*, 18–21, 31–32, 36–39, 46–48, 51–52, 57–58, 60–62, 98–100, 119–20.

Normand Berlin, "Thomas Dekker: A Reappraisal," *SEL* 6 (Spring 1966): 263–77.

Arthur Brown, "Citizen Comedy and Domestic Drama," *Stratford-Upon-Avon-Studies* 1 (1960): 69–73.

Larry S. Champion, "From Melodrama to Comedy: A Study of Dramatic Perspective in Dekker's *The Honest Whore*, Parts I and II," *SP* 69 (Summer 1972): 192–209.

Viviana Comensoli, "Gender and Eloquence in Dekker's *The Honest Whore, Part II*," *ESC* 15 (Fall 1989): 249–62.

Haselkorn, *Prostitution in Elizabethan and Jacobean Drama*, 116–36.

DEKKER, THOMAS, *If This Be Not a Good Play the Devil Is in It*

R. L. Horn, "Thematic Structure of *The Honest Whore*, Part I," *DUJ* 46 (December 1984): 7–10.

A. L. Kistner, and M. K. Kistner, "*I Honest Whore*: A Comedy of Blood," *HAB* 23, no. 4 (1972): 23–27.

Kistner, and Kistner, *Middleton's Tragic Themes*, 103–11.

Lacy, *Jacobean Problem Play*, 60–84.

Leinwand, *The City Staged*, 70–73, 131–33, 175–78.

McPeek, *The Black Book of Knaves*, 82–89.

Michael Manheim, "The Thematic Structure of Dekker's *2 Honest Whore*," *SEL* 5 (Spring 1965): 356–81.

Anne Parten, "Masculine Adultery and Feminine Rejoinders in Shakespeare, Dekker and Sharpham," *Mosaic* 17 (Winter 1984): 9–18.

Neill Rhodes, *Elizabethan Grotesque*, 77–80.

Charlotte Spivack, "Bedlam and Bridewell: Ironic Design in *The Honest Whore*," *Komos* 3, no. 1 (1973): 10–16.

Peter Ure, "Patient Madman and Honest Whore: The Middleton-Dekker Oxymoron," *E&S* 19 (1966): 18–40. Reprinted in Maxwell, *Elizabethan and Jacobean Drama*.

If This Be Not a Good Play the Devil Is in It

J. W. Ashton, "Dekker's Use of Folklore in *Old Fortunatus*, *If This Be Not A Good Play*, and *The Witch of Edmonton*," *PQ* 41 (January 1962): 240–41, 243–45.

Blow, *Rhetoric in the Plays of Thomas Dekker*, 22–23, 78–79, 83–87, 91–92.

Champion, *Thomas Dekker and the Traditions of English Drama*, 91–97.

Julia Gaspar, "A Surplus Coronation in Dekker's *If This Be Not a Good Play*," *N&Q* 35 (December 1988): 490–91.

Leah S. Marcus, *The Politics of Mirth: Johnson, Herrick, Milton, Marvell, and the Defense of Old Holiday Pastimes* (Chicago: University of Chicago Press, 1986), 94–100.

King James, His Royal and Magnificent Entertainment
(with Jonson)

Erskin-Hill, *The Augustan Idea in English Literature*, 123–33.

Goldberg, *James I and the Politics of Literature*, 50–54.

Graham, *The Golden Age Restor'd*, 1–21.

Lust's Dominion; or, The Lacivious Queen

D'Amico, *The Moor in English Renaissance Drama*, 106–19.

Jones, *Othello's Countrymen*, 60–68.

Tokson, *The Popular Image of the Blackman in English Drama*, 2–3, 40–43.

Match Me in London

Blow, *Rhetoric in the Plays of Thomas Dekker*, 24–26, 63–64.

Wiggins, *Journeymen in Murder*, 143–45.

Noble Soldier, The; or, A Contract Broken, Justly Revenged

William Perry, "*The Noble Soldier* and *The Parliament of Bees*," *SP* 48 (April 1951): 219–33.

Northward Ho
(with Webster)

Champion, *Thomas Dekker and the Tradition of English Drama*, 59–63.

Forker, *The Skull Beneath the Skin*, 81–103.

Leinwand, *The City Staged*, 97–99, 154–56.

Old Fortunatus

Adams, *English Domestic or Homiletic Tragedies*, 80–82.

J. W. Ashton, "Dekker's Use of Folklore in *Old Fortunatus*, *If This Be Not A Good Play*, and *The Witch of Edmonton*," *PQ* 41 (January 1962): 240–43.

Blow, *Rhetoric in the Plays of Thomas Dekker*, 40–43, 92–96, 100–02, 114–19.

Fredson Bowers, "Essex's Rebellion and Dekker's *Old Fortunatus*," *RES* 3 (October 1952): 365–66.

James H. Conover, *Thomas Dekker: An Analysis of Dramatic Structure* (The Hague: Mouton, 1969), 51–81.

DEKKER, THOMAS, *Patient Grissel*

Hassel, *Renaissance Drama*, 33–37.

Sidney R. Homan, Jr., "*Doctor Faustus*, Dekker's *Old Fortunatus*, and the Morality Plays," *MLQ* 26 (December 1965): 497–505.

Kiefer, *Fortune and Elizabethan Tragedy*, 107–14.

Lacy, *Jacobean Problem Play*, 48–60.

Patient Grissel
(with Chettle and Haughton)

David Mason Greene, "The Welsh Characters in *Patient Grissel*," *BUSE* 4 (Autumn 1960): 171–80

Harry Keyishian, "Griselda on the Elizabethan Stage: The *Patient Grissil* of Chettle, Dekker, and Haughton," *SEL* 16 (Spring 1976): 253–61.

Levin, *The Multiple Plot in English Renaissance Drama*, 49–51.

William G. Smith, "Thomas Dekker's Welshman," *Dock Leaves* 4 (Summer 1953): 47–52.

Roaring Girl, The; or, Moll Cut-Purse
(with Middleton)

Bradbrook, *Growth and Structure of Elizabethan Comedy*, 172–74.

Champion, *Thomas Dekker and the Traditions of English Drama*, 81–89.

Patrick Cheney, "Moll Cutpurse as Hermaphrodite in Dekker and Middleton's *The Roaring Girl*," *Ren&R* 17 (February 1983): 120–34.

Viviana Comensoli, "Play-Making, Domestic Conduct, and the Multiple Plot in *The Roaring Girl*," *SEL* 27 (Spring 1987): 249–66.

Marjorie Garber, "The Logic of the Transvestite: *The Roaring Girl* (1608)," in Kastan and Stallybrass, *Staging the Renaissance*, 221–34.

Leinwand, *The City Staged*, 73–76, 156–60.

McPeek, *The Black Book of Knaves*, 135–40.

Jo E. Miller, "Women and the Market in *The Roaring Girl*," *Ren&R* 26 (Winter 1990): 11–23.

Mary Beth Rose, "Women in Men's Clothing: Apparel and Social Stability in *The Roaring Girl*," *ELR* 14 (Autumn 1984): 367–91.

Shepherd, *Amazons and Warrior Women*, 74–83.

DEKKER, THOMAS, *The Shoemaker's Holiday; or, The Gentle Craft*

Satiromastix; or, The Untrussing of the Humorous Poet

Blow, *Rhetoric in the Plays of Thomas Dekker*, 14–16, 62–63, 96–97, 126–27.

Robert C. Evans, "Jonson, *Satiromastix*, and the Poetomachia: A Patronage Perspective," *ISJR* 60 (February 1986): 369–83.

Harrison, *Elizabethan Plays and Players*, 272–77.

Mann, *The Elizabethan Player*, 101–11, 210–11.

The Shoemaker's Holiday; or, The Gentle Craft

Normand Berlin, "Thomas Dekker: A Partial Reappraisal," *SEL* 6 (Spring 1966): 263–77.

Blow, *Rhetoric in the Plays of Thomas Dekker*, 49–51, 77–78, 112–13.

Boas, *Introduction to Stuart Drama*, 147–65.

Bradbrook, *Growth and Structure of Elizabethan Comedy*, 119–32.

Arthur Brown, "Citizen Comedy and Domestic Drama," *Stratford-Upon-Avon Studies* 1 (1960): 63–69.

Frederick M. Burelbach, Jr., "War and Peace in *The Shoemaker's Holiday*," *TSL* 13 (Spring 1968): 99–107.

Dee Dee Dominguez, " 'A Woman's Place': The Discrimination against Women in *The Shoemaker's Holiday*," *CCTEP* 56 (September 1991): 35–38.

Farley-Hills, *The Comic in Renaissance Comedy*, 108–17.

Julia Gaspar, "Dekker's Word Play in *The Shoemaker's Holiday*," *N&Q* 32 (March 1985): 58–59.

George K. Hunter, "Bourgeois Comedy: Shakespeare and Dekker," in Honigmann, *Shakespeare and His Contemporaries*, 1–15.

Norman Hidden, "*The Shoemaker's Holiday*," *The Use of English* 13 (Summer 1962): 249–52.

George K. Hunter, "Bourgeois Comedy: Shakespeare and Dekker," in Honigman, *Shakespeare and His Contemporaries*, 1–15.

Joel H. Kaplan, "Virtue's Holiday: Thomas Dekker and Simon Eyre," *RenD* 2 (1969): 103–22.

Arthur F. Kinney, "Thomas Dekker's *Twelfth Night*," *UTQ* 41 (March 1971): 63–73.

Knights, *Drama and Society in the Age of Jonson*, 236–40.

L. M. Manheim, "The King in *The Shoemaker's Holiday*," *N&Q* 202 (October 1957): 432–33.

Michael Manheim, "The Construction of *The Shoemaker's Holiday*," *SEL* 10 (Spring 1970): 315–23.

Peter Mortenson, "The Economics of Joy in *The Shoemaker's Holiday*," *SEL* 16 (Spring 1966): 241–52.

Norman Nathan, "*Julius Caesar* and *The Shoemaker's Holiday*," *MLR* 48 (April 1953): 178–79.

David Novarr, "Dekker's Gentle Craft and the Lord Mayor of London," *MP* 57 (May 1960): 233–39.

Patricia Thomson, "The Old Way and the New Way in Dekker and Massinger," *MLR* 51 (April 1956): 168–78.

Harold E. Toliver, "*The Shoemaker's Holiday*: Theme and Image," *BUSE* 5 (Winter 1961): 209–18.

Wells, *Elizabethan and Jacobean Playwrights*, 219–21.

Gillian West, "Some Word-Play in Dekker's *Shoemaker's Holiday*," *N&Q* 29 (April 1982): 135–36.

Sir Thomas Wyatt
(with Heywood and Webster)

Champion, *Thomas Dekker and the Tradition of English Drama*, 68–75.

Forker, *The Skull Beneath the Skin*, 66–72.

Phillip Shaw, "*Sir Thomas Wyatt* and the Scenario and Lady Jane," *MLQ* 13 (September 1952): 227–38

The Sun's Darling; A Moral Masque
(with Ford)

Stavig, *John Ford and the Traditional Moral Order*, 49–54.

Troia-Nova Triumphans, London Triumphing

Bergeron, *English Civic Pagentry*, 163–70.

Gordon Kipling, "Triumphal Drama: Form in *English Civic Pagentry*," *RenD* 8 (1977): 37–56.

Theodore B. Leinwand, "London Triumphing: The Jacobean Lord Mayor's Show," *CLIOI* 11 (Fall 1982): 137–53.

The Virgin Martyr
(with Massinger)

Larry S. Champion, " 'Disaster with my so many joys': Structure and Perspective in Massinger and Dekker's *The Virgin Martyr*," *MRDE* 1 (Summer 1984): 199–209.

Larry S. Champion, *Thomas Dekker and the Traditions of English Drama*, 105–15.

Peter F. Mullany, "Religion in Massinger and Dekker's *The Virgin Martyr*," *Komos* 2, no. 1 (1970): 89–97.

Westward Ho
(with Webster)

Larry S. Champion, "Westward-Northward: Structural Development of Dekker's *Ho* Plays," *CompD* 16 (Fall 1982): 251–66.

Forker, *The Skull Beneath the Skin*, 81–103.

Leinwand, *The City Staged*, 45–50, 94–96, 149–54.

The Whore of Babylon

Frank R. Ardolino, " 'In Saint Iagoes Parke': Iago as Catholic Machiavel in Dekker's *The Whore of Babylon*," *Names* 30 (March 1982): 1–4.

Blow, *Rhetoric in the Plays of Thomas Dekker*, 45–46, 109–12.

Rainer Pineas, "Dekker's *The Whore of Babylon* and Milton's *Paradise Lost*," *ELN* 2 (June 1965): 257–60.

Ribner, *The English History Play*, 284–88.

Wiggins, *Journeymen in Murder*, 156–57, 160–62.

DEKKER, THOMAS, *The Witch of Edmonton*

The Witch of Edmonton
(with Rowley and Ford)

J. W. Ashton, "Dekker's Use of Folklore in *Old Fortunatus*, *If This Be Not A Good Play*, and *The Witch of Edmonton*," *PQ* 41 (January 1962): 240–43.

David Atkinson, "Moral Knowledge and the Double Action of *The Witch of Edmonton*," *SEL* 25 (Spring 1985): 419–37.

David Atkinson, "The Two Plots of *The Witch of Edmonton*," *N&Q* 31 (June 1984): 229–30.

Leonora L. Brodwin, "The Domestic Tragedy of Frank Thorney in *The Witch of Edmonton*," *SEL* 7 (Spring 1967): 311–28.

Viviana Comensoli, "Witchcraft and Domestic Tragedy in *The Witch of Edmonton*," in Brink, Coudert, and Horowitz, *The Politics of Gender in Early Modern Europe*, 43–60.

Anthony B. Dawson, "Witchcraft/Bigamy: Cultural Conflict in *The Witch of Edmonton*," *RenD* 20 (1989): 77–98.

Harris, *Night's Black Agents*, 90–108.

Michael Hattaway, "Women and Witchcraft: The Case of *The Witch of Edmonton*," *Trivium* 20 (1985): 49–68.

Edward Sackville West, "The Significance of *The Witch of Edmonton*," *Criterion* 17, no. 1 (1973): 23–32.

DRAYTON, MICHAEL

Sir John Oldcastle

Mary G. Adkins, "Sixteenth-Century Religious and Political Implications in *Sir John Oldcastle*," *TSLL* (Spring 1942): 86–104.

Larry S. Champion, " 'Havoc in the Commonwealth': Perspective, Political Ideology, and Dramatic Strategy in *Sir John Oldcastle* and the English Chronicle Plays," *MRDE* 5 (Summer 1991): 165–79.

EDWARDES, RICHARD

Common Conditions

Bevington, *From "Mankind" to Marlowe*, 191–94.

Jackson I. Cope, " 'The Best For Comedy': Richard Edwardes' Canon," *TSLL* 2 (Winter 1961): 501–19.

Cope, *Dramaturgy of the Daemonic*, 36–39.

Damon and Pithias

Cope, *Dramaturgy of the Daemonic*, 44–49.

Richard Leighton Greene, "Carols in Tudor Drama," in Rowland, *Chaucer and Middle English Studies*, 357–65.

Sir Clyomond and Sir Clamides

Jackson I. Cope, " 'The Best For Comedy': Richard Edwardes' Canon," *TSLL* 2 (Winter 1961): 501–19.

Cope, *Dramaturgy of the Daemonic*, 36–49.

Traister, *Heavenly Necromancers*, 35–37.

FIELD, NATHAN

Amends for Ladies

Leinwand, *The City Staged*, 183–84.

The Fatal Dowery
(with Massinger)

Swapan Chakravorty, "Court, City and Country: Social and Political Themes in Philip Massinger," *JDECU* 18, no. 1 (1982): 59–86.

William M. Clements, and Frances M. Malpezzi, "Rationalization of Folklore in *The Fatal Dowry*," *SCB* 41 (Winter 1981): 97–98.

The Knight of Malta
(with Fletcher and Massinger)

Jones, *Othello's Countrymen*, 80–82.

Mullany, *Religion and Artifice*, 65–74.

Wells, *Elizabethan and Jacobean Playwrights*, 150–52.

FIELD, NATHAN, *A Woman Is a Weather-Cock*

A Woman Is a Weather-Cock

Glenn H. Blayney, "Field's Parody of a Murder Play," *N&Q* 200.

FLETCHER, JOHN

Bonduca

Paul D. Green, "Theme and Structure in Fletcher's *Bonduca*," *SEL* 22 (Spring 1982): 305–16.

Shepherd, *Amazons and Warrior Women*, 144–50.

Wells, *Elizabethan and Jacobean Playwrights*, 136–38.

The Custom of the Country
(with Massinger)

W. D. Howarth, "Cervantes and Fletcher: A Theme with Variations," *MLR* 56 (October 1961): 564–66.

Carolyn Prager, "The Problem of Slavery in *The Custom of the Country*," *SEL* 28 (Spring 1988): 301–17.

Sherbo, *English Sentimental Drama*, 22–24.

Wells, *Elizabethan and Jacobean Playwrights*, 152–54.

The Double Marriage
(with Massinger)

Wells, *Elizabethan and Jacobean Playwrights*, 141–43.

The Faithful Shepardess

Lee Bliss, "Defending Fletcher's Shepherds," *SEL* 23 (Spring 1983): 295–310.

Marco Mincoff, "*The Faithful Shepherdess*: A Fletcherian Experiment," *RenD* 9 (1966): 163–77.

Wells, *Elizabethan and Jacobean Playwrights*, 167–75.

Rose A. Zimbardo, "Dramatic Imitation of Nature in the Restoration's Seventeenth-Century Predecessors," in Markley and Fine, *From Renaissance to Restoration*, 57–86.

FLETCHER, JOHN, *Love's Cure; or, The Martial Maid*

Fair Maid of the Inn
(with Massinger)

Loftis, *Renaissance Drama in England and Spain*, 242–44.

The False One
(with Massinger)

Jones, *Othello's Countrymen*, 85–86.

The Island Princess

Perry Gethner, "Providence by Indirection in Seventeenth-Century Tragicomedy," in *Drama and Religion: Themes in Drama 5* (Cambridge: Cambridge University Press, 1983), 39–51.

Loftis, *Renaissance Drama in England and Spain*, 239–40.

The Knight of Malta
(with Field and Massinger)

Jones, *Othello's Countrymen*, 80–82.

Mullany, *Religion and Artifice*, 65–74.

Wells, *Elizabethan and Jacobean Playwrights*, 150–52.

The Little French Lawyer
(with Massinger)

Barber, *The Theme of Honour's Tongue*, 121–25.

N. J. Rigaud, "Mental Cruelty in Fletcher's *The Little French Lawyer*," *CahiersE* 22 (October 1982): 35–39.

Love's Cure; or, The Martial Maid
(with Massinger)

Jonathan Dollimore, "Subjectivity, Sexuality, and Transgression: The Jacobean Connection," *RenD 17* (1986): 53–81.

Loftis, *Renaissance Drama in England and Spain*, 252–56, 259–60.

FLETCHER, JOHN, *The Loyal Subject; or, The Faithful General*

The Loyal Subject; or, The Faithful General

Loftis, *Renaissance Drama in England and Spain*, 244–46.

Waith, *Pattern of Tragicomedy*, 143–51.

Eugene Waith, "A Tragicomedy of Humors: Fletcher's *The Loyal Subject*," *MLQ* 6 (September 1945): 299–313 .

The Mad Lover

John P. Cutts, "Music and *The Mad Lover*," *SRen 8* (1961): 236–48.

Suzanne Gossett, "Masque Influence on the Dramaturgy of Beaumont and Fletcher," *MP* 69 (May 1972): 199–208.

Eugene M. Waith, "Mad Lovers, Vainglorious Soldiers," *RORD* 27 (1984): 13–19.

The Maid in the Mill
(with Rowley)

Klaus P. Steiger, " 'May a Man be Caught with Faces?': The Convention of 'Heart' and 'Face' in Fletcher and Rowley's *The Maid in the Mill*," *E&S* 20 (1967): 47–63.

The Pilgrim

Mignon, *Crabbed Age and Youth*, 150–152.

Rule a Wife and Have a Wife

Levin, *The Multiple Plot in English Renaissance Drama*, 51–54.

Loftis, *Renaissance Drama in England and Spain*, 240–42.

The Sea Voyage
(with Massinger)

Shepherd, *Amazons and Warrior Women*, 133–36.

Sir John Van Oldenbarnevelt
(with Massinger)

Loftis, *Renaissance Drama in England and Spain*, 134–39, 220–21.

Thierry, King of France, and His Brother Theodoret
(with Massinger)

Wells, *Elizabethan and Jacobean Playwrights*, 139–41.

Two Noble Kinsmen
(with Shakespeare)

Paula S. Bergren, " 'For What We Lack, / We Laugh': Incompletion in *The Two Noble Kinsmen*," *MLS* 14 (Fall 1984): 3–17.

Noel R. Blincoe, " 'Sex individual' as Used in *The Two Noble Kinsmen*," *N&Q* 35 (December 1988): 484–85.

Brownlow, *Two Shakespearean Sequences*, 202–05.

John P. Cutts, "Shakespeare's Song and Masque in *The Two Noble Kinsmen*," *EM* 18 (Spring 1967): 55–85.

Philip Edwards, "On the Design of *The Two Noble Kinsmen*," *REL* 5 (October 1964): 99–105.

Helge Kolkeritz, "The Beast-Eating Clown: *The Two Noble Kinsmen*, 3. 5. 131," *MLN* 61 (December 1946): 532–35.

Muir, *Shakespeare as Collaborator*, 98–147.

Smith, *Homosexual Desire in Shakespeare's England*, 69–72.

Eugene M. Waith, "Shakespeare and Fletcher on Love and Friendship," *ShS* 38 (1986): 235–50.

Glynne Wickham, "*The Two Noble Kinsmen* or *A Midsummer Night's Dream, Part II?*" *ETh* 7, no. 2 (1980): 167–96. Reprinted in Hibbard, *The Elizabethan Theatre VII*, 167–96.

Valentinian

Shepherd, *Amazons and Warrior Women*, 169–78.

Wells, *Elizabethan and Jacobean Playwrights*, 133–36.

FLETCHER, JOHN, *The Very Woman; or, The Prince of Tarent*

The Very Woman; or, The Prince of Tarent
(with Massinger)

Roma Gill, "Collaboration and Revision in Massinger's *A Very Woman*," *RES* 18 (1967): 136–48.

The Wild Goose Chase

Gagen, *The New Woman*, 26–29.

Mignon, *Crabbed Age and Youth*, 165–67.

A Wit at Several Weapons
(with Middleton and Rowley)

James E. Savage, "The Effects of Revision in the Beaumont and Fletcher Play, *Wit at Several Weapons*," *UMSE* 1, no. 1 (1960): 32–50.

Wit Without Money

Charles R. Forker, "*Wit Without Money*: A Fletcherian Antecedent to *Keep the Widow Waking*," *CompD* 8 (Summer 1974): 172–83.

The Woman's Prize

Leinwand, *The City Staged*, 159–62.

FORD, JOHN

The Broken Heart

Ali, *Opposing Absolutes*, 47–58.

Donald K. Anderson, Jr., "The Heart and the Banquet: Imagery in Ford's *'Tis Pity* and *The Broken Heart*," *SEL* 2 (Spring 1962): 209–18.

David Atikinson, " 'Married Wives' in *The Broken Heart*," *N&Q* 31 (June 1984): 238.

Anne Barton, "Oxymoron and the Structure of John Ford's *The Broken Heart*," *E&S* 33 (1980): 70–94.

Glenn H. Blayney, "Convention, Plot, and Structure in *The Broken Heart*," *MP* 56 (August 1958): 1–9.

Frederick M. Burelbach, Jr., " 'The Truth' in John Ford's *The Broken Heart* Revisited," *N&Q* 14 (September 1967): 211–12.

Carol A. Burns, "*The Broken Heart* 'Piec'd Up Again,'" *BSUF* 24 (Autumn 1983): 49–54.

Grovanni M. Carsanga, "The 'Truth' in John Ford's *The Broken Heart*," *CL* 10 (Fall 1958): 344–48.

R. Davril, "Shakespeare and Ford," *ShJE* 94 (1958): 127–131.

R. Davril, "John Ford and La Cerda's *Ines de Castro*," *MLN* 66 (November 1951): 464–66.

William D. Dyer, "Holding/Withholding Environments: A Psychoanalytic Approach to Ford's *The Broken Heart*," *ELR* 21 (Autumn 1991): 401–24.

Eliot, *Essays on Elizabethan Drama*, 143–146.

Farr, *John Ford*, 79–104.

A. Bronson Feldman, "The Yellow Malady: Short Studies of Five Tragedies of Jealousy," *L&P* 5 (May 1956): 49–52.

Thelma N. Greenfield, "The Language of Process in Ford's *The Broken Heart*," *PMLA* 87 (March 1972): 397–405.

Sharon Hamilton, "*The Broken Heart*: Language Suited to a Divided Mind," in Anderson, *"Concord in Discord,"* 171–93.

Heubert, *John Ford: Baroque English Dramatist*, 42–43, 51–54, 97–101, 136–40, 155–56.

Marie L. Kessel, "*The Broken Heart*: An Allegorical Reading," *MRDE* 3 (Summer 1986): 217–30.

R. J. Kaufmann, "Ford's 'Waste Land': *The Broken Heart*," *RenD* 3 (1970): 167–88.

Charles O. McDonald, "The Design of John Ford's *The Broken Heart*: A Study in the Development of Caroline Sensibility," *SP* 59 (April 1962): 141–61.

McDonald, *Rhetoric of Tragedy*, 314–33.

Michael Neill, "Ford's Unbroken Art: The Moral Design of *The Broken Heart*," *MLR* 75 (July 1980): 249–68.

Michael Neill, "New Light on 'The Truth' in *The Broken Heart*," *N&Q* 22 (September 1975): 249–50.

FORD, JOHN, *The Fancies, Chaste and Noble*

Orbison, *The Tragic Vision*, 114–49.

Ornstein, *The Moral Vision of Jacobean Tragedy*, 213–16.

Prior, *The Language of Tragedy*, 145–152.

Ribner, *Jacobean Tragedy*, 156–163.

June Schulter, "Ford's *The Broken Heart* as a Multiple-Plot Play," *Thoth* 15, no. 2 (1975): 21–26.

George F. Sensabaugh, "John Ford Revisited," *SEL* 4 (Spring 1964): 195–203.

Sensabaugh, *The Tragic Muse*, 59–66.

Phoebe S. Spinrad, "Ceremonies of Complement: The Symbolic Marriage in Ford's *The Broken Heart*," *PQ* 65 (Winter 1986): 23–37.

Peter Ure, "Marriage and the Domestic Drama of Heywood and Ford," *ES* 32 (October 1951): 211–16.

Eugene M. Waith, "Struggle for Calm: The Dramatic Structure of *The Broken Heart*," in Henning, Kimbrough, and Knowles, *English Renaissance Drama*, 155–66.

Wells, *Elizabethan and Jacobean Playwrights*, 127–29.

The Fancies, Chaste and Noble

Ali, *Opposing Absolutes*, 69–78.

Heubert, *John Ford: Baroque English Dramatist*, 68–71, 120–24.

Juliet Sutton, "Platonic Love in Ford's *The Fancies, Chaste and Noble*," *SEL* 7 (Spring 1967): 299–309.

The Great Favourite; or The Duke of Lerma

G. F. Sensabaugh, "Another Play by John Ford," *MLQ* 3 (December 1942): 595–602.

The Lady's Trial

Ali, *Opposing Absolutes*, 79–88.

Lois E. Bueler, "Role-Splitting and Regeneration: The Tested Woman Plot in Ford," *SEL* 20 (Spring 1980): 326–44.

Farr, *John Ford*, 134–49.

Heubert, *John Ford: Baroque English Dramatist*, 112–16.

Glenn Hopp, "The Speaking Voice in *The Lady's Trial*," in Anderson, *"Concord in Discord,"* 149–70.

James Howe, "Ford's *The Lady's Trial*: A Play of Metaphysical Wit," *Genre* 7 (Fall 1974): 342–61.

Brian Opie, " 'Being all one': Ford's Analysis of Love and Friendship in *Loues Sacrifice* and *The Ladies Triall*," in Neill, *John Ford*, 233–60.

Ian Robson, *The Moral World of John Ford's Drama* (Salzburg: University of Salzburg, 1983), 238–64.

Love's Sacrifice

Ali, *Opposing Absolutes*, 33–46.

Martin Butler, *"Love's Sacrifice*: Ford's Metatheatrical Tragedy," in Neill, *John Ford*, 201–31.

Heubert, *John Ford: Baroque English Dramatist*, 41–42, 47–51, 74–75, 148–61.

R. T. Kaufmann, "Ford's Tragic Perspective," *TSLL* 1 (Winter 1960): 527–32.

Juliet McMaster, "Love, Lust, and Sham: Structural Pattern in the Plays of John Ford," *RenD* 2 (1969): 157–66.

Brian Opie, " 'Being all one': Ford's Analysis of Love and Friendship in *Loues Sacrifice* and *The Ladies Triall*," in Neill, *John Ford*, 233–60.

Orbison, *The Tragic Vision*, 87–113.

Ornstein, *Moral Vision of Jacobean Tragedy*, 216–21.

Ribner, *Jacobean Tragedy*, 162–63.

George F. Sensabaugh, "John Ford Revisited," *SEL* 4 (Spring 1964): 203–09.

Sensabaugh, *The Tragic Muse*, 56–59, 66–68.

Stavig, *John Ford and the Traditional Moral Order*, 122–43.

Peter Ure, "Cult and Initiates in Ford's *Love's Sacrifice*," *MLQ* 11 (July 1950): 298–306. Reprinted in Maxwell, *Elizabethan and Jacobean Drama*, 93–103.

Wells, *Elizabethan and Jacobean Playwrights*, 67–69.

The Lover's Melancholy

Ali, *Opposing Absolutes*, 9–13.

FORD, JOHN, *Perkin Warbeck: A Strange Truth*

Farr, *John Ford*, 16–35.

Michael Neill, "The Moral Artifice of *The Lover's Melancholy*," *ELR* 8 (Spring 1978): 85–106.

Sensabaugh, *The Tragic Muse*, 47–50, 62–64.

Stavig, *John Ford and the Traditional Moral Order*, 68–81.

Perkin Warbeck: A Strange Truth

Ali, *Opposing Absolutes*, 59–68.

Donald K. Anderson, Jr., "Kingship in *Perkin Warbeck*," *ELH* 27 (September 1960): 177–93.

Donald K. Anderson, Jr., "*Richard II* and *Perkin Warbeck*," *SQ* 13 (Spring 1962): 260–63.

Jonas A. Barish, "*Perkin Warbek* as Anti-History," *EIC* 20 (July 1970): 151–71.

Anne Barton, "He That Plays the King: Ford's *Perkin Warbek* and the Stuart History Play," in Axton and Williams, *English Drama*, 69–93.

Joseph Candido, "The 'Strange Truth' of *Perkin Warbek*," *PQ* 59 (Summer 1980): 300–16.

Cope, *Theatre and the Dream*, 122–33.

Edwards, *Threshold of a Nation*, 176–80.

Eliot, *Essays on Elizabethan Drama*, 146–47.

Farr, *John Ford*, 105–24.

Anat Feinberg, "Strength of Passion: On the Method of Characterisation in Ford's 'Perkin Warbeck,'" *NM* 86 (Summer 1985): 216–24.

Verna Ann Foster, "*Perkin* without the Pretender: Reexamining the Dramatic Center of Ford's Play," *RenD* 16 (1985): 141–58.

Coburn Freer, "'The Fate of Worthy Expectation': Eloquence in *Perkin Warbeck*," in Anderson, *"Concord in Discord,"* 131–48.

Sharon Hamilton, "Huntly as Tragic Chorus in Ford's *Perkin Warbeck*," *PLL* 16 (Summer 1976): 250–59.

Alfred Harbage, "The Mystery of *Perkin Warbeck*," in Bennett, Cargill and Hall, *Studies in the English Renaissance Drama*, 125–41.

Heubert, *John Ford: Baroque English Dramatist*, 43–44, 71–3, 101–06.

Jean Howard, " 'Effeminately dolent': Gender and Legitimacy in Ford's *Perkin Warbeck*," in Neill, *John Ford*, 261–79.

Alexander Leggatt, "A Double Reign: *Richard II* and *Perkin Warbek*," in Honigmann, *Shakespeare and His Contemporaries*, 129–39.

Michael Neill, " 'Anticke Pageantrie': The Mannerist Art of *Perkin Warbeck*," *RenD* 7 (1976): 117–50.

Orbison, *The Tragic Vision*, 150–77.

Ribner, *The English History Play*, 299–305.

Winston Weathers, "*Perkin Warbeck*: A Seventeenth-Century Psychological Play," *SEL* 4 (Spring 1964): 217–26.

Wells, *Elizabethan and Jacobean Playwrights*, 104–06.

The Queen; or, The Excellency of Her Sex

Ali, *Opposing Absolutes*, 14–20.

Heubert, *John Ford: Baroque English Dramatist*, 45–47, 62–63, 116–20.

The Sun's Darling; A Moral Masque
(with Dekker)

Stavig, *John Ford and the Traditional Moral Order*, 49–54.

'Tis Pity She's a Whore

Adams, *English Domestic or Homiletic Tragedies*, 177–83.

Ali, *Opposing Absolutes*, 21–32.

Donald K. Anderson, Jr., "The Heart and the Banquet: Imagery in Ford's *'Tis Pity* and *The Broken Heart*," *SEL* 2 (Spring 1962): 209–13.

Larry S. Champion, "Ford's *'Tis Pity She's a Whore* and the Jacobean Tragic Perspective," *PMLA* 90 (January 1975): 78–87.

Champion, *Tragic Patterns*, 180–95.

Claudine Defaye, "Annabella's Unborn Baby: The Heart in the Womb in *'Tis Pity She's a Whore*," *CahiersE* 15 (April 1976): 35–42.

Eliot, *Essays on Elizabethan Drama*, 139–43.

FORD, JOHN, *'Tis Pity She's a Whore*

Farr, *John Ford*, 36–57.

Laurie A. Finke, "Painting Women: Images of Femininity in Jacobean Tragedy," *TJ* (October 1984): 357–70.

Vera Foster, "*'Tis Pity She's a Whore* as City Tragedy," in Neill, *John Ford*, 181–200.

Gomez, *The Alienated Figure in Drama*, 125–31.

Sharon Hamilton, "Ford's *'Tis Pity She's a Whore*," *Expl* 37 (Summer 1979): 15–16.

Heubert, *John Ford: Baroque English Dramatist*, 35–40, 54–5845, 77–90, 141–50, 156–57.

A. P. Hogan, "*'Tis Pity She's a Whore*: The Overall Design," *SEL* 17 (Spring 1977): 303–16.

Sidney R. Homan, Jr., "Shakespeare and Dekker as Keys to Ford's *'Tis Pity She's a Whore*," *SEL* 7 (Spring 1967): 269–76.

Cyrus Hoy, "'Ignorance in Knowledge': Marlowe's Faustus and Ford's Giovanni," *MP* 57 (February 1960): 145–54.

R. T. Kaufmann, "Ford's Tragic Perspective," *TSLL* 1 (Winter 1960): 522–24, 532–37.

Knight, *Golden Labyrinth*, 111–12.

Gordon Millington, "The Art of John Ford," *Mandrake* 1 (February 1946): 11–14.

Giles D. Monsarrat, "The Unity of John Ford: *'Tis Pity She's a Whore* and *Christ's Bloody Sweat*," *SP* 77 (Spring 1980): 247–70.

Michael Neill, " 'What strange riddle's this?' Deciphering *'Tis Pity She's a Whore*," in Neill, *John Ford*, 153–79.

Orbison, *The Tragic Vision*, 50–86.

Ornstein, *Moral Vision of Jacobean Tragedy*, 203–13.

Irving Ribner, "By Nature's Light: *'Tis Pity She's A Whore*," *TSE* 10 (Spring 1960): 39–50.

Ribner, *Jacobean Tragedy*, 163–74.

Carol C. Rosen, "The Language of Cruelty in Ford's *'Tis Pity She's a Whore*," *CompD* 8 (Winter 1974): 356–68.

Carol C. Rosen, "The Language of Cruelty in Ford's *'Tis Pity She's a Whore*," in Davidson, Gianakaris, and Stroupe, *Drama in the Renaissance*, 315–27.

Scott, *Renaissance Drama*, 89–104.

G. F. Sensabaugh, "John Ford Revisited," *SEL* 4 (Spring 1964): 209–16.

Stavig, *John Ford and the Traditional Moral Order*, 95–121.

Nathaniel Strout, "The Tragedy of Annabella in *'Tis Pity She's a Whore*," in Allen and White, *Traditions and Innovations*, 163–6.

Wells, *Elizabethan and Jacobean Playwrights*, 49–52.

Wiggins, *Journeymen in Murder*, 193–96.

The Witch of Edmonton
(with Rowley and Dekker)

Adams, *English Domestic or Homiletic Tragedies*, 132–42.

J. V. Ashton, "Dekker's Use of Folklore in *Old Fortunatus*, *If This Be Not A Good Play*, and *The Witch of Edmonton*," *PQ* 41 (January 1962): 240–41, 245–51.

David Atkinson, "Moral Knowledge and the Double Action of *The Witch of Edmonton*," *SEL* 25 (Spring 1985): 419–37.

Leonora L. Brodwin, "The Domestic Tragedy of Frank Thorney in *The Witch of Edmonton*," *SEL* 7 (Spring 1967): 311–28.

Viviana Comensoli, "Witchcraft and Domestic Tragedy in *The Witch of Edmonton*," in *The Politics of Gender in Early Modern Europe*, ed. Jean R. Brink, Allison P. Coudert, and Maryanne C. Horowitz (Kirksville, MO: Sixteenth Century Journal Publications, 1989) 43–60.

Anthony B. Dawson, "Witchcraft/Bigamy: Cultural Conflict in *The Witch of Edmonton*," *RenD* 20 (1989): 77–98.

Harris, *Night's Black Agents*, 90–108.

Michael Hattaway, "Women and Witchcraft: The Case of *The Witch of Edmonton*," *Trivium* 20 (1985): 49–68.

Edward Sackville West, "The Significance of *The Witch of Edmonton*," *Criterion* 17, no. 1 (1973): 23–32.

Wells, *Elizabethan and Jacobean Playwrights*, 71–75.

FOXE, JOHN

Christus Triumphans

Blackburn, *Biblical Drama*, 106–17.

Henry VIII

Elizabeth H. Hageman, "John Foxe's Henry VIII as *Justitia*," *SCJ* 10 (Spring 1979): 35–43.

FULWELL, ULPIAN

Like Will to Like

Adams, *English Domestic or Homiletic Tragedies*, 63–66.

Bevington, *From "Mankind" to Marlowe*, 155–58.

Robert C. Jones, "Jonson's *Staple of News* Gossips and Fulwell's *Like Will to Like*: 'The Old Way' in a 'New' Morality Play," *YES* 3 (1973): 74–77.

Paula Neuss, "The Sixteenth-Century English 'Proverb' Play," *CompD* 18 (Spring 1984): 1–18.

GAGER, WILLIAM

Oedipus

R. H. Bowers, "William Gager's *Oedipus*," *SP* 46 (April 1949): 141–53.

GARTER, THOMAS

Virtuous and Godly Susanna

Blackburn, *Biblical Drama*, 136–42.

Peter Happé, "Aspects of Dramatic Technique in Thomas Garter's 'Susanna,'" *METh* 8 (July 1986): 61–65.

Marvin T. Herrick, "Susanna and the Elders in Sixteenth Century Drama," in *Studies in Honor of T. W. Baldwin*, ed. Don Cameron Allen (Urbana: University of Illinois Press, 1958), 125–35.

Olga Horner, "Susanna's Double Life," *METh* 8 (December 1986): 76–102.

Heather Kerr, "Thomas Garter's *Susanna*: 'Pollicie' and 'True Report,'" *AUMLA* 72 (November 1989): 183–202

Roston, *Biblical Drama*, 87–100.

GASCOYGNE, GEORGE

The Glass of Government

Abraham Bronson Feldman, "Dutch Humanism and the Tudor Dramatic Tradition," *N&Q* 197 (December 1952): 357–60.

Linda B. Salamon, "A Face in *The Glasse*: Gascoigne's *Glasse of Government* Re-examined," *SP* 71 (Spring 1974): 47–71.

GOFFE, THOMAS

The Tragedy of Orestes

Hallett and Hallett, *The Revenger's Madness*, 244–64.

GREENE, ROBERT

Alphonsus, King of Aragon

Clemen, *English Tragedy Before Shakespeare*, 179–80.

Crupi, *Robert Greene*, 101–07.

Harrison, *Elizabethan Plays and Players*, 82–86.

McDonnell, *The Aspiring Mind*, 152–53.

Irving Ribner, "Greene's Attack on Marlowe: Some Light on *Alphonsus* and *Selimus*," *SP* 52 (April 1955): 162–71.

Norman Sanders, "The Comedy of Greene and Shakespeare," *Stratford-Upon-Avon Studies* 3 (1961): 37–39.

A Disputation

Virginia L. MacDonald, "The Complex Moral View of Robert Greene's *A Disputation*," *ShJE* 119 (1983): 122–136.

Friar Bacon and Friar Bungay

Frank R. Ardolino, "Simnel Cakes and Royal Progress: The Festive Significance of Rafe Simnell in Greene's *Friar Bacon and Friar Bungay*," *Motif* 4 (October 1982): 3–4.

Frank R. Ardolino, " 'Thus glories England over all the West': Setting as National Encomium in Robert Greene's *Friar Bacon and Friar Bungay*," *JEP* 9 (August 1988): 218–29.

Greg Bentley, "Coppernose: The Nature of Burdene's Disease in Robert Greene's *Friar Bacon and Friar Bungay*," *ELN* 22 (June 1985): 28–32.

Bradbrook, *Growth and Structure of Elizabethan Comedy*, 69–71.

Cecil Williamson Cary, "The Iconography of Food and the Motif of World Order in *Friar Bacon and Friar Bungay*," *CompD* 13 (Summer 1979): 150–63.

Clemen, *English Tragedy Before Shakespeare*, 182–85.

Harrison, *Elizabethan Plays and Players*, 91–93.

Jeffrey P. Hart, "Prospero and Faustus," *BUSE* 2 (Winter 1956): 197–206.

Charles W. Hieatt, "Multiple Plotting in *Friar Bacon and Friar Bungay*," *RenD* 16 (1985): 17–34.

Allan H. Maclaine, "Greene's Borrowings from His Own Prose Fiction in *Bacon and Bungay* and *James the Fourth*," *PQ* 30 (January 1951): 22–26.

Waldo F. McNeir, "Traditional Elements in the Character of Greene's Friar Bacon," *SP* 45 (April 1948): 172–79.

Waldo F. McNeir, "Robert Greene and *John of Bordeaux*," *PMLA* 64 (September 1949): 781–801.

Kenneth Muir, "Robert Greene as Dramatist," in Hosley, *Essays on Shakespeare*, 47–50.

Nicoll, *English Drama*, 43–44.

Thomas Marc Parrott, and Robert H. Ball, *A Short View of Elizabethan Drama*, 71–74.

Hereward T. Price, "Shakespeare and His Young Contemporaries," *PQ* 41 (January 1962): 45–46.

Norman Sanders, "The Comedy of Greene and Shakespeare," *Stratford-Upon-Avon Studies* 3 (1961): 40–50.

Joseph H. Stodder, "Magnus and Maiden: Archetypal Roles in Greene's *Friar Bacon and Friar Bungay*," *JEP* 4 (April 1983): 28–37.

Traister, *Heavenly Necromancers*, 67–87.

Weld, *Meaning in Comedy*, 136–53.

Albert Wertheim, "The Presentation of Sin in *Friar Bacon and Friar Bungay*," *Criticism* 16 (Summer 1974): 273–86.

A Groat's Worth of Wit Bought with a Million of Repentance

W. W. Barker, "Rhetorical Romance: The 'Frivolous Toyes' of Robert Greene," in Logan and Teskey, *Unfolded Tales*, 74–97.

John of Bordeaux

Waldo F. McNeir, "Robert Greene and *John of Bordeaux*," *PMLA* 64 (September 1949): 781–801.

Traister, *Heavenly Necromancers*, 47–51.

A Looking Glass for London and England

Blackburn, *Biblical Drama*, 161–71.

Menaphon

W. W. Barker, "Rhetorical Romance: The 'Frivolous Toyes' of Robert Greene," in Logan and Teskey, *Unfolded Tales*, 74–97.

Never Too Late

W. W. Barker, "Rhetorical Romance: The 'Frivolous Toyes' of Robert Greene," in Logan and Teskey, *Unfolded Tales*, 74–97.

GREENE, ROBERT, *Orlando Furioso, One of the Twelve Peers of France*

Orlando Furioso, One of the Twelve Peers of France

William Babula, "Fortune or Fate: Ambiguity in Robert Greene's *Orlando Furioso*," *MLR* 67 (October 1972): 481–85.

Clemen, *English Tragedy Before Shakespeare*, 180–82.

Crupi, *Robert Greene*, 107–14.

D'Amico, *The Moor in English Renaissance Drama*, 41–44.

Norman Gelber, "Robert Greene's *Orlando Furioso*: A Study of Thematic Ambiguity," *MLR* 64 (July 1969): 264–66.

Tetsumaro Hayashi, "*Orlando Furioso*, Robert Greene's Romantic Comedy," *SAP* 6, no. 1–2 (1975): 157–60.

Raymond A. Houk, "Shakespeare's *Shrew* and Greene's *Orlando*," *PMLA* 62 (September 1947): 657–71.

McDonnell, *The Aspiring Mind*, 153–56.

Waldo F. McNeir, "Greene's Medievalization of Aristo," *RLC* 29 (July–September 1955): 351–60.

Norman Sanders, "The Comedy of Greene and Shakespeare," *Stratford-Upon-Avon Studies* 3 (1961): 39–41.

Rolf Soeltner, "The Madness of Hercules and the Elizabethans," *CL* 10 (Fall 1958): 317–18.

The Scottish History of James IV

A. R. Braunmuller, "The Serious Comedy of Greene's *James IV*," *ELR* 3 (Autumn 1973): 335–50.

Clemen, *English Tragedy Before Shakespeare*, 186–91.

Alexander Leggatt, "Bohan and Oberon: The Internal Debate of Greene's *James IV*," in *The Elizabethan Theatre, XI*, ed. A. L. Magnusson and C. E. McGee (Port Credit, Ont.: P. D. Meany, 1990), 95–116.

Allan H. Maclaine, "Greene's Borrowings from His Own Prose Fiction in *Bacon and Bungay* and *James the Fourth*," *PQ* 30 (January 1951): 22–24, 26–27.

Kenneth Muir, "Robert Greene as Dramatist," in Hosley, *Essays on Shakespeare*, 50–54.

Norman Sanders, "The Comedy of Greene and Shakespeare," *Stratford-Upon-Avon Studies* 3 (1961): 40–44, 51–53.

Talbert, *Elizabethan Drama*, 92–95.

Selimus

Clemen, *English Tragedy Before Shakespeare*, 130–34.

McDonnell, *The Aspiring Mind*, 158–61.

Irving Ribner, "Greene's Attack on Marlowe: Some Light on *Alphonsus* and *Selimus*," *SP* 52 (January 1955): 167–71.

GREVILLE, SIR FULKE

Alaham

Ivor Morris, "The Tragic Vision of Fulke Greville," *ShS* 14 (1961): 66–75.

Peter Ure, "Fulke Greville's Dramatic Characters," *RES* 1 (October 1950): 313–18, 320–23.

Mustapha

Dollimore, *Radical Tragedy*, 120–33.

Ivor Morris, "The Tragic Vision of Fulke Greville," *ShS* 14 (1961): 66–75.

Peter Ure, "Fulke Greville's Dramatic Characters," *RES* 1 (October 1950): 318–23.

GRIMALD, NICHOLAS

Archipropheta

Blackburn, *Biblical Drama*, 94–101.

Howard B. Norland, "Grimald's *Archipropheta*: A Saint's Tragedy," *JMRS* 14 (Spring 1984): 63–76.

Christus Redivivus

Blackburn, *Biblical Drama*, 88–94.

Ruth H. Blackburn, "Nicholas Grimald's *Christus Redivivus*: A Protestant Ressurection Play," *ELN* 5 (March 1968): 247–50.

HAUGHTON, WILLIAM

Englishmen for My Money, or A Woman Will Have Her Will

Elizabeth Schafer, "William Haughton's *Englishmen for My Money*: A Critical Note," *RES* 41 (November 1990): 536–538

Patient Grissil
(with Dekker and Chettle)

David Mason Greene, "The Welsh Characters in *Patient Grissel*," *BUSE* 4 (Autumn 1960): 171–180

Harry Keyishian, "Griselda on the Elizabethan Stage: The *Patient Grissil* of Chettle, Dekker, and Haughton," *SEL* 16 (Spring 1976): 253–61.

Levin, *The Multiple Plot in English Renaissance Drama*, 49–51.

William G. Smith, "Thomas Dekker's Welshman," *Dock Leaves* 4 (Summer 1953): 47–52.

HEYWOOD, JOHN

The Four PP

Richard Finkelstein, "Formation of the Christian Self in *The Four P. P.*" in Tricomi, *Early Drama to 1600*, 143–152.

John John, the Husband, Tyb, His Wife, and Sir John the Priest

Stanley Sultan, "The Audience Participation Episode in *Johan Johan*," *JEGP* 52 (October 1953): 491.

Stanley Sultan, "*Johan Johan* and Its Debt to French Farce," *JEGP* 53 (January 1954): 23–37.

The Pardoner and the Friar

Edwin S. Miller, "Guilt and Penalty in Heywood's Pardoner's Lie," *MLQ* 10 (March 1949): 58–60.

Hiroshi Ozawa, "The Structural Innovations of the More Circle Dramatists," *ShStud* 19 (1980-1981): 1–23.

HEYWOOD, THOMAS, *The Captives; or, The Lost Recovered*

A Play of Love

T. W. Craik, "Experiment and Variety in John Heywood's Plays," *RenD* 7 (1964): 6–11.

R. J. Schoeck, "A Common Tudor Expletive and Legal Parody in Heywood's *Play of Love*," *N&Q* 201 (September 1956): 375–76.

The Play of the Weather

David M. Bevington, "Is John Heywood's *Play of the Weather* Really About the Weather?" *RenD* 7 (1964): 11–19.

T. W. Craik, "Experiment and Variety in John Heywood's Plays," *RenD* 7 (1964): 6–11.

HEYWOOD, THOMAS

Appius and Virginia
(with Webster)

Adams, *English Domestic or Homiletic Tragedy*, 75 78.

Forker, *The Skull Beneath the Skin*, 200–24.

Haworth, *English Hymns and Ballads*, 137–48.

R. G. Howarth, "Webster's *Appius and Virginia*," *PQ* 46 (Winter 1967): 135–37.

Mina Irgat, "Disease Imagery in the Plays of J. Webster," *Litera* 2 (1955): 2–24.

Melvin Seiden, "Two Notes on Webster's *Appius and Virginia*," *PQ* 35 (October 1956): 408–17.

The Brazen Age

Ellen R. Belton, " 'A Plaine and Direct Course': The Unity of Thomas Heywood's *Ages*," *PQ* 56 (Spring 1977): 169–82.

The Captives; or, The Lost Recovered

Carolyn Prager, "Heywood's Adaptation of Plautus' Rudens: The Problem of Slavery in *The Captives*," *CompD* 9 (Summer 1975): 116–24.

HEYWOOD, THOMAS, *A Challenge for Beauty*

Freda L. Townsend, "The Artistry of Thomas Heywood's Double Plots," *PQ* 25 (April 1946): 110–14.

A Challenge for Beauty

Baines, *Thomas Heywood*, 130–38.

Johnson, *Images of Women*, 148–51.

Freda L. Townsend, "The Artistry of Thomas Heywood's Double Plots," *PQ* 25 (April 1946): 104–08.

The English Traveller

Adams, *English Domestic or Homiletic Tragedies*, 169–73.

Baines, *Thomas Heywood*, 120–30.

Eliot, *Essays on Elizabethan Drama*, 110–14.

Michel Grivelet, "The Simplicity of Thomas Heywood," *ShS* 14 (1961): 56–65.

Johnson, *Images of Women*, 93–100.

Norman Rabkin, "Dramatic Deception in Heywood's *The English Traveller*," *SEL* 1 (Spring 1961): 1–16.

Stilling, *Love and Death in Renaissance Tragedy*, 183–96.

Freda L. Townsend, "The Artistry of Thomas Heywood's Double Plots," *PQ* 25 (April 1946): 110–12, 114–16.

The Fair Maid of the West, or, A Girl Worth Gold

Baines, *Thomas Heywood*, 42–53.

D'Amico, *The Moor in English Renaissance Drama*, 84–98.

Johnson, *Images of Women*, 139–48.

Jones, *Othello's Countrymen*, 18–19.

Tokson, *The Popular Image of the Blackman in English Drama*, 60–61, 117–18.

The Four Prentices of London

Bevington, *From "Mankind" to Marlowe*, 38–39.

Martin R. Orkin, " 'He Shows a Fair Pair of Heels' in *I Henry IV* and Elsewhere," *ELN* 23 (September 1985): 19–23.

The Golden Age

Ellen R. Belton, " 'A Plaine and Direct Course': The Unity of Thomas Heywood's *Ages*," *PQ* 56 (April 1977): 169–82.

Allan Holaday, "Heywood's Trioa Brittanica and the *Ages*," *JEGP* 45 (October 1946): 430–39.

How a Man May Choose a Good Wife from A Bad

Baines, *Thomas Heywood*, 54–61.

Johnson, *Images of Women*, 111–17.

If You Know Not Me, You Know Nobody, I & II; or, The Troubles of Queen Elizabeth

O. Rauchbauer, "The 'Armada Scene' in Thomas Heywood's '2 If You Know Not Me You Know Nobody,'" *N&Q* 24 (March 1977): 143–44.

Wiggins, *Journeymen in Murder*, 158–61.

The Iron Age

Ellen R. Belton, " 'A Plaine and Direct Course': The Unity of Thomas Heywood's *Ages*," *PQ* 56 (April 1977): 169–82.

King Edward the Fourth

Baines, *Thomas Heywood*, 9–22.

Johnson, *Images of Women*, 62–70.

The Late Lancashire Witches
(with Brome)

Adams, *English Domestic or Homiletic Tragedy*, 204–05.

HEYWOOD, THOMAS, *Love's Mistress; or, The Queen's Masque*

Love's Mistress; or, The Queen's Masque

Baines, *Thomas Heywood*, 147–55.

Cope, *Theatre and the Dream*, 173–96.

W. L. Halstead, "Dekker's *Cupid and Psyche* and Thomas Heywood," *ELH* 11 (September 1944): 182–91.

Raymond C. Shady, "Thomas Heywood's Masque at Court," in Hibbard, *The Elizabethan Theatre VII*, 147–66.

Miseries of Enforced Marriage, The
(with Wilkins)

Leanore Lieblein, "The Context of Murder in English Domestic Plays, 1590–1610," *SEL* 23 (Spring 1983): 181–96.

Rape of Lucrece

Baines, *Thomas Heywood*, 103–12.

Cunningham, *Woe or Wonder*, 57–58, 116–17.

Alan Holaday, "Thomas Heywood's *The Rape of Lucrece*," *ISLL* 34 (March 1950): 1–44.

Ribner, *Jacobean Tragedy*, 59–71.

The Silver Age

Ellen R. Belton, " 'A Plaine and Direct Course': The Unity of Thomas Heywood's *Ages*," *PQ* 56 (April 1977): 169–82.

Sir Thomas Wyatt
(with Dekker and Webster)

Champion, *Thomas Dekker and the Tradition of English Drama*, 68–75.

Forker, *The Skull Beneath the Skin*, 66–72.

Phillip Shaw, "*Sir Thomas Wyatt* and the Scenario and Lady Jane," *MLQ* 13 (September 1952): 227–38.

HEYWOOD, THOMAS, *A Woman Killed with Kindness*

The Wise Woman of Hogsdon

Jean E. Howard, "Scripts and/versus Playhouse: Ideological Production and the Renaissance Public Stage," *RenD* 20 (1989): 31–49.

Johnson, *Images of Women*, 154–58.

Wells, *Elizabethan and Jacobean Playwrights*, 221–23.

A Woman Killed with Kindness

Adams, *English Domestic or Homiletic Tragedy*, 144–59.

David Atkinson, "An Approach to the Main Plot of Thomas Heywood's *A Woman Killed with Kindness*," *ES* 70 (February 1989): 15–27.

Baines, *Thomas Heywood*, 79–103.

Lloyd E. Berry, "A Note on Heywood's *A Woman Killed With Kindness*," *MLR* 58 (January 1963): 64–65.

Rick Bowers, "*A Woman Killed with Kindness*: Plausibility on a Smaller Scale," *SEL* 24 (Spring 1984): 293–306.

Laura G. Bromley, "Domestic Conduct in *A Woman Killed with Kindness*," *SEL* 26 (Spring 1986): 259–76.

Margaret B. Bryan, "Food Symbolism in *A Woman Killed with Kindness*," *RenP* 1973 (1974): 9–17.

John Canuetson, "The Theme of Forgiveness in the Plot and Subplot of *A Woman Killed with Kindness*," *RenD* 2 (1969): 123–41.

Cecil W. Cary, " 'Go Break This Lute': Music in Heywood's *A Woman Killed with Kindness*," *HLQ* 37 (February 1974): 111–22.

D. J. Cook, "*A Woman Killed With Kindness*: An Unshakespearian Tragedy," *ES* 45 (October 1964): 353–72.

Herbert R. Coursen, "The Subplot of *A Woman Killed with Kindness*," *ELN* 2 (March 1965): 180–85.

Eliot, *Essays on Elizabethan Drama*, 107–10.

Eliot, *Selected Essays*, 149–58.

Harry Garlick, "Anne Frankford's Fall: A Complementary Perspective," *AUMLA* 61 (May 1984): 20–28.

Nancy A. Gutierrez, "The Irresolution of Melodrama: The Meaning of Adultery in *A Woman Killed with Kindness*," *Exemplaria* 1 (Fall 1989): 265–91.

Diana E. Henderson, "Many Mansions: Reconstructing *A Woman Killed with Kindness*," *SEL* 26 (Spring 1986): 277–94.

A. G. Hooper, "Heywood's *A Woman Killed With Kindness*," *ESA* 4 (March 1961): 54–57.

Gilford Hooper, "Heywood's *A Woman Killed with Kindness* Scene xiv: Sir Charles's Plan," *ELN* 11 (March 1974): 181–88.

Johnson, *Images of Women*, 81–88.

Frederick Kiefer, "Heywood as Moralist in *A Woman Killed with Kindness*," *MRDE* 3 (Spring 1986): 83–98.

Levin, *The Multiple Plot in English Renaissance Drama*, 93–97.

Leanore Lieblein, "The Context of Murder in English Domestic Plays, 1590–1610," *SEL* 23 (Spring 1983): 181–96.

Robert Ornstein, "Burgeois Morality and Dramatic Convention in *A Woman Killed with Kindness*," in Henning, Kimbrough, and Knowles, *English Renaissance Drama*, 128–41.

Prior, *The Language of Tragedy*, 94–99,

Otto Rauchbauer, "Visual and Rhetorical Imagery in Th. Heywood's *A Woman Killed with Kindness*," *ES* 57 (July 1976): 200–10.

Ribner, *Jacobean Tragedy*, 8–9, 51–58,

Patricia Meyer Spacks, "Honor and Perception in *A Woman Killed With Kindness*," *MLQ* 20 (December 1959): 321–32.

Freda L. Townsend, "The Artistry of Thomas Heywood's Double Plots," *PQ* 25 (April 1946): 99–102.

Peter Ure, "Marriage and the Domestic Drama of Heywood and Ford," *ES* 32 (October 1951): 203–07.

Michael Wentworth, "Thomas Heywood's *A Woman Killed with Kindness* as Domestic Morality," in Allen and White, *Traditions and Innovations*, 150–62.

HUGHES, THOMAS

The Misfortunes of Arthur

William A. Armstrong, "Elizabethan Themes in *The Misfortunes of Arthur*," *RES* 7 (July 1956): 238–49.

Clemen, *English Tragedy Before Shakespeare*, 85–91.

McDonnel, *The Aspiring Mind*, 86–90.

Gertrude Reese, "Political Import of *The Misfortunes of Arthur*," *RES* 21 (April 1945): 81–91.

Gertrude Reese, "The Succession Question in Elizabethan Drama," *Studies in English* 21 (1942): 68–69 .

Ribner, *The English History Play*, 229–36.

JEFFERE, JOHN

The Bugbears

Francis Guinle, "The Songs in a 16th Century Manuscript Play: *The Bugbears*, by John Jeffere," *CahiersE* 21 (April 1982): 13–26.

JONSON, BEN

The Alchemist

Michael Cameron Andrews, "Jonson's *The Alchemist*," *Expl* 37 (Fall 1978): 24–26.

Judd Arnold, "Lovewit's Triumph and Jonsonian Morality: A Reading of *The Alchemist*," *Criticism* 11 (Spring 1969): 151–66.

Wallace A. Bacon, "The Magnetic Field: The Structure of Jonson's Comedies," *HLQ* 19 (February 1956): 142–45.

William Blissett, "The Venter Tripartite in *The Alchemist*," *SEL* 8 (Spring 1968): 323–34.

Carol A. Carr, "Play's the Thing: A Study of Games in *The Alchemist*," *CLQ* 18 (June 1982): 113–25.

JONSON, BEN, *The Alchemist*

James H. Conover, "Art Criticism as a Tool for Play Analysis: *Epicoene* and *The Alchemist*," *TJ* 28 (April 1976): 78–87.

Gerard H. Cox, "Apocalyptic Projection and the Comic Plot of *The Alchemist*," *ELR* 13 (Winter 1983): 70–87.

Curry, *Deception in Elizabethan Comedy*, 142–43.

R. W. Dent, "*The Alchemist* III.i.4–14," *ELN* 16 (September 1979): 18–20.

Alan Dessen, "*The Alchemist*: Jonson's 'Estates Play,'" *RenD* 7 (1964): 35–54.

Dessen, *Jonson's Moral Comedy*, 105–37.

Ian Donaldson, "Language, Noise, and Nonsense: *The Alchemist*," in *Seventeenth-Century Imagery: Essays on Uses of Figurative Language from Donne to Farquhar*, ed. E. Miner (Berkeley: University of California Press, 1971), 69–82.

Edgar Hill Duncan, "Jonson's *Alchemist* and the Literature of Alchemy," *PMLA* 61 (September 1946): 699–710.

Edgar Hill Duncan, "Jonson's Use of Arnald of Villa Nova's *Rosarium*," *PQ* 21 (October 1942): 435–38.

A. Richard Dutton, "*Volpone* and *The Alchemist*: A Comparison in Satiric Techniques," *RMS* 18 (1974): 36–62.

William Empson, "*The Alchemist*," *HudR* 22 (Winter 1969–70): 595–608.

Farley-Hills, *Comic in Renaissance Comedy*, 51–80.

Michael Flachmann, "Ben Johnson and the Alchemy of Satire," *SEL* 17 (Spring 1977): 259–80.

Donald Gertmenian, "Comic Experience in *Volpone* and *The Alchemist*," *SEL* 17 (Spring 1967): 247–58.

Paul Goodman, *The Structure of Literature*, 80–103.

James V. Halleran, "Character Transmutation in *The Alchemist*," *CLAJ* 11 (December 1967): 221–27.

Haselkorn, *Prostitution in Elizabethan and Jacobean Drama*, 34–38.

Hawkins, *Likeness of Truth in Elizabethan and Restoration Drama*, 8–9.

Jonathan Haynes, "Representing the Underworld: *The Alchemist*," *SP* 86 (Winter 1989): 18–41.

Edgar Duncan Hill, "Jonson's *Alchemist* and the Literature of Alchemy," *PMLA* 61 (December 1945): 699–710.

Cyrus H. Hoy, *The Hyacinth Room*, 119–27.

Cyrus H. Hoy, "The Pretended Piety of Jonson's *Alchemist*," *RenP* 1956 (1957): 15–19.

Maurice Hussey, "Ananias the Deacon: A Study of Religion in Jonson's *The Alchemist*," *English* 9 (Autumn 1953): 207–12.

Myrrddin Jones, "Sir Epicure Mamon: A Study in 'Spiritual Fornication,'" *RenQ* 22 (1969): 223–42.

Renu Juneja, "Rethinking about Alchemy in Jonson's *The Alchemist*," *BSUF* 24 (Autumn 1983): 3–14.

Robert E. Knoll, "How to Read *The Alchemist*," *CE* 21 (May 1960): 456–60 .

Edgar C. Knowlton, Jr., " 'Kiss'd Our Anos' in Ben Jonson's *The Alchemist*," *Maledicta* 8 (Winter 1984–1985): 119–22.

Louis Kronenberger, *The Thread of Laughter*, 19–24.

Leinwand, *The City Staged*, 128–30.

Richard Levin, " 'No Laughing Matter': Some New Readings of *The Alchemist*," *SLitI* 6, no. 1 (1973): 85–99.

Joseph T. McCullen, Jr., "Conference With the Queen of Fairies: A Study of Jonson's Workmanship in *The Alchemist*," *SN* 23 (Spring 1951): 87–95.

F. H. Mares, "Comic Procedures in Shakespeare and Jonson: *Much Ado* and *The Alchemist*," in Donaldson, *Jonson and Shakespeare*, 101–18.

John S. Mebane, "Renaissance Magic and the Return of the Golden Age: Utopianism and Religious Enthusiasm in *The Alchemist*," *RenD* 10 (1979): 117–26.

G. D. Monsarrat, "Editing the Actor: Truth and Deception in *The Alchemist*, V.3–5," *CahiersE* 23 (April 1983): 61–71.

Ruth Evans Netscher, "The Moral Vision of *The Alchemist*: Tricks, Psychotherapy, and Personality Traits," *L&M* 7 (Spring 1988): 177–94.

Nicholl, *The Chemical Theatre*, 97–100, 111–15.

Marianna da Vinci Nichols, "Truewit and Sir Epicure Mammon: Jonson's Creative Accidents," *ArielE* 7 (January 1976): 4–21.

Parfitt, *Ben Jonson*, 100–03.

Johnstone Parr, "Non-Alchemical Pseudosciences in *The Alchemist*," *PQ* 24 (January 1945): 95–99.

JONSON, BEN, *The Alchemist*

Partridge, *The Broken Compass*, 114–60.

Dave Rankin, "Ben Jonson: Semanticist," *Etc* 19 (October 1962): 289–97.

Wayne A. Rebhorn, "Jonson's 'Jovy Boy': Lovewit and the Dupes in *The Alchemist*," *JEGP* 79 (July 1980): 355–75.

Cheryl Lynn Ross, "The Plague of *The Alchemist*," *RenQ* 41 (Autumn 1988): 439–58.

Robert M. Schuler, "Jonson's Alchemists, Epicures, and Puritans," *MRDE* 2 (Summer 1985): 171–208.

M. A. Shaaber, "The 'Unclear Birds' in *The Alchemist*," *MLN* 65 (February 1950): 106–09.

Shapiro, *Rival Playwrights*, 64–67.

C. J. Sission, "A Topical Reference in *The Alchemist*," in McManaway, *Joseph Q. Adams Memorial Studies*, 739–41.

R. L. Smallwood, " 'Here in the Friars': Immediacy and Theatricality in *The Alchemist*," *RES* 32 (1981): 142–60.

Geraldo U. de Sousa, "Boundaries of Genre in Ben Jonson's *Volpone* and *The Alchemist*," *EiT* 4 (May 1986): 134–46.

Stoll, *Shakespeare and Other Masters*, 104–06.

Barry Targan, "The Dramatic Structure of *The Alchemist*," *Discourse* 5 (Autumn 1963): 315–24 .

Thayer, *Ben Jonson*, 84–111.

C. G. Thayer, "Theme and Structure in *The Alchemist*," *ELH* 26 (March 1959): 23–35.

Townsend, *Apologie for Bartholomew Fayre*, 66–70.

Joyce Van Dyke, "The Game of Wits in *The Alchemist*," *SEL* 19 (Spring 1979): 253–69.

John W. Velz, "Scatology and Moral Meaning in Two English Renaissance Plays," *SCRev* 1 (Spring–Summer 1984): 4–21.

Robert Viau, "Jonson's Sir Epicure Mammon: 'The Perpetual Possession of Being Well Deceived,' " *SCN* 36 (Spring 1978): 44–48.

Robert N. Watson, "*The Alchemist* and Jonson's Conversion of Comedy," in Lewalski, *Renaissance Genres*, 332–65.

Watson, *Ben Jonson's Parodic Strategy*, 113–38.

Dennis M. Welch, "A Sucker's Delight: Piscatorial Imagery in *The Alchemist*," *BSUF* 19 (Summer 1978): 20–25.

Wells, *Elizabethan and Jacobean Playwrights*, 200–03.

David Young, "Where the Bee Sucks: A Triangular Study of *Doctor Faustus*, *The Alchemist*, and *The Tempest*," in McGinnis and Jacobs, *Shakespeare's Romances Reconsidered*, 149–66.

Bartholomew Fair

Wallace A. Bacon, "The Magnetic Field: The Structure of Jonson's Comedies," *HLQ* 19 (February 1956): 145–49.

Jonas A. Barish, "*Bartholomew Fair* and its Puppets," *MLQ* 20 (March 1959): 3–17.

Barish, *Ben Jonson and the Language of Prose Comedy*, 187–239.

Barton, *Ben Jonson, Dramatist*, 198–218.

Baum, *The Satiric and Didactic in Ben Jonson's Comedies*, 126–31.

Mary W. Bledsoe, "The Function of Linguistic Enormity in Ben Jonson's *Bartholomew Fair*," *Lang&S* 17 (Spring 1984): 149–60.

Boas, *Introduction to Stuart Drama*, 117–20.

Larry D. Bradfield, "Prose Decorum and the Anatomy of Folly in *Bartholomew Fair*," *ESRS* 32 (Fall 1983): 5–53.

Canfield, *Word as Bond*, 126–35.

Thomas Cartelli, "*Bartholomew Fair* as Urban Arcadia: Jonson Responds to Shakespeare," *RenD* 14 (1983): 151–72.

Ron Childress, "Jonson's *Bartholomew Fair*," *Expl* 47 (Fall 1988): 5–7.

Ralph Alan Cohen, "The Strategy of Misdirection in *A Midsummer Night's Dream* and *Bartholomew Fair*," *RenP* 1981 (1982): 65–75

John Scott Colley, "*Bartholomew Fair*: Ben Jonson's *A Midsummer Night's Dream*," *CompD* 11 (1977): 63–72.

Jackson I. Cope, "*Bartholomew Fair* as Blasphemy," *RenD* 8 (1965): 127–52.

Cope, *Dramaturgy of the Daemonic*, 72–90.

D. H. Craig, "The Idea of the Play in *A Midsummer Night's Dream* and *Bartholomew Fair*," in Donaldson, *Jonson and Shakespeare*, 89–100.

JONSON, BEN, *Bartholomew Fair*

Clifford Davidson, "Judgment, Iconoclasm, and Anti-Theatricalism in Jonson's *Bartholomew Fair*," *PLL* 25 (Fall 1989): 349–63.

Dessen, *Jonson's Moral Comedy*, 138–220.

Donaldson, *World Upside-Down*, 46–77.

Enck, *Jonson and the Comic Truth*, 188–208.

Judith K. Gardiner, "Infantile Sexuality, Adult Critics, and *Bartholomew Fair*," *L&P* 24 (May 1974): 124–32.

Guy Hamel, "Order and Judgement in *Bartholomew Fair*," *UTQ* 43 (January 1974): 48–67.

Haselkorn, *Prostitution in Elizabethan and Jacobean Drama*, 38–41.

H. R. Hays, "Satire and Identification: An Introduction to Ben Jonson," *KR* 19 (Spring 1957): 276–93.

Jonathan Haynes, "Festivity and the Dramatic Economy of Jonson's *Bartholomew Fair*," *ELH* 51 (Winter 1984): 645–68.

Ray L. Heffner, "Unifying Symbols in the Comedy of Ben Jonson," *English Institute Essays* (1954): 89–97. Reprinted in Bluestone and Rabkin, *Shakespeare's Contemporaries*, 196–202.

Irena Janika, "Figurative Language in *Bartholomew Fair*," *DSGW* 111 (1975): 156–67.

Renu Juneja, "Eve's Flesh and Blood in Jonson's *Bartholomew Fair*," *CompD* 12 (Winter 1978): 340–55.

Joel H. Kaplan, "Dramatic and Moral Energy in *Bartholomew Fair*," *RenD* 3 (1970): 137–56.

W. David Kay, "*Bartholomew Fair*: Ben Jonson in Praise of Folly," *ELR* 6 (Autumn 1976): 299–316.

Louis Kronenberger, *The Thread of Laughter*, 30–34.

Jacqueline E. M. Latham, "Form in *Bartholomew Fair*," *English* 21 (Spring 1972): 8–11.

Richard Levin, "The Structure of *Bartholomew Fair*," *PMLA* 80 (January 1965): 172–79. Reprinted in Levin, *The Multiple Plot*, 202–14.

Don Mager, "The Paradox of Tone in *Bartholomew Fayre*," *Thoth* 9, no. 1 (1968): 39–47.

McPeek, *The Black Book of Knaves*, 93–100, 244–48.

David McPherson, "The Origins of Overdo: A Study in Jonsonian Invention," *MLQ* 37 (June 1976): 221–33.

W. J. Olive, "A Chaucer Allusion in Johnson's *Bartholomew Fair*," *MLQ* 13 (March 1952): 21–22.

Parfitt, *Ben Jonson*, 98–103.

R. B. Parker, "The Themes and Staging of *Bartholomew Fair*," *UTQ* 39 (July 1970): 293–309.

Vincent F. Petronella, "Jonson's *Bartholomew Fair*: A Study in Baroque Style," *Discourse* 13, no. 3 (1970): 325–37.

John M. Porter, "Old Comedy in *Bartholomew Fair*," *Criticism* 10 (Autumn 1968): 209–99.

James E. Robinson, "*Bartholomew Fair*: Comedy of Vapors," *SEL* 1 (Spring 1961): 65–80.

Alexander H. Sackton, "The Paradoxical Encomium in Elizabethan Drama," *Studies in English* 28 (1949): 100–01.

Leo Salingar, "Crowd and Public in *Bartholomew Fair*," *RenD* 10 (1979) 141–59.

Shapiro, *Rival Playwrights*, 68–71, 154–56.

Debora K. Shuger, "Hypocrites and Puppets in *Bartholomew Fair*," *MP* 82 (August 1984): 70–73.

Calvin C. Smith "*Bartholomew Fair*: Cold Decorum," in *Essays in the Renaissance: In Honour of Allan H. Gilbert*, ed. Philip Traci and Marilyn Williamson. *SAQ* 71, special issue (1982): 548–56.

Barry Targan, "The Moral Structure of *Bartholomew Fair*," *Discourse* 8, no. 2 (1965): 276–84.

Watson, *Ben Jonson's Parodic Strategy*, 139–71.

Wells, *Elizabethan and Jacobean Dramatists*, 204–06.

The Case Is Altered

Barton, *Ben Jonson, Dramatist*, 29–44.

John J. Enck, "*The Case Is Altered*: Initial Comedy of Humours," *SP* 50 (April 1953): 195–214.

Enck, *Jonson and the Comic Truth*, 21–33.

JONSON, BEN, *Cataline His Conspiracy*

Stephen Hannaford, "Gold Is But Muck: Jonson's *The Case Is Altered*," *StHum* 8 (June 1980): 11–16.

J. M. Nosworhy, "*The Case Is Altered*," *JEGP* 51 (January 1952): 61–70.

Cataline His Conspiracy

Barton, *Ben Jonson, Dramatist*, 154–69.

Joseph A. Bryant, "*Cataline* and the Nature of Jonson's Tragic Fable," *PMLA* 69 (March 1954): 265–77.

K. M. Burton, "The Political Tragedies of Chapman and Jonson," *EIC* 2 (October 1952): 401–04, 411–12.

Champion, *Tragic Patterns*, 76–88.

Ellen M. T. Duffy, "Ben Jonson's Debt to Renaissance Scholarship in *Sejanus* and *Cataline*," *MLR* 42 (January 1947): 24–30.

A. R. Dutton, " 'What Ministers Man Must for Practice Use': Ben Jonson's *Cicero*," *ES* 59 (October 1968): 324–35.

Michael J. C. Echeruo, "The Conscience of Politics and Jonson's *Cataline*," *SEL* 6 (Spring 1966): 341–56.

Eliot, *Essays on Elizabethan Drama*, 68–73.

Enck, *Jonson and the Comic Truth*, 172–82.

Wilson F. Engel, III, "The Dynamics of *Pietas* in Ben Jonson's *Cataline*," *JRMM-RA* 2 (January 1981): 117–28.

Goldberg, *James I and the Politics of Literature*, 193–203.

Geoffrey Hill, "The World's Proportion: Jonson's Dramatic Poetry in *Sejanus* and *Cataline*," *Stratford-Upon-Avon Studies* 1 (1960): 113–12.

Jackson, *Vision and Judgement*, 128–35.

Leo Kirschbaum, "Jonson, Seneca, and *Mortimer*," in Wallace, *Studies in Honor of John Wilcox*, 16–18.

J. S. Lawry, "*Cataline* and 'The Sight of Rome in Us'," in *Rome in the Renaissance: The City and the Myth*, ed. Paul A. Ramsey (Binghamton: Medieval & Renaissance Texts & Studies, 1982), 395–407.

Ralph Nash, "Ben Jonson's Tragic Poems," *SP* 55 (April 1958): 164–86.

Ornstein, *Moral Vision of Jacobean Tragedy*, 97–103.

Clifford J. Ronan, "Snakes in *Cataline*," *MRDE* 3 (Spring 1986): 149–63.

Alexander H. Sackton, "The Rhymed Couplet in Ben Jonson's Plays," *Studies in English* 30 (1951): 101–03.

Raymond V. Utterback, "Oratory and Political Action in Jonson's *Cataline His Conspiracy*," *ISJR* 57 (November 1982): 193–203.

J. I. Villiers, "Ben Jonson's Tragedies," *ES* 45 (December 1964): 440–42.

Womack, *Ben Jonson*, 87–96.

Yumiko Yamada, "Classics That Revolt: Modernizing Factors in *Sejanus*, *Epicoene* and *Cataline*," *ShStud* 24 (1985–1986): 31–51.

Chloridia: Rites to Chloris and Her Nymphs

R. I. C. Graziani, "Ben Jonson's *Chlorida*: Fame and Her Attendants," *RES* 7 (January 1956): 56–58.

Kogan, *The Hieroglyphic King*, 111–22.

Christmas His Masque

Marcus, *The Politics of Mirth*, 76–85.

Cynthia's Revels

Wallace A. Bacon, "The Magnetic Field: The Structure of Jonson's Comedies," *HLQ* 19 (February 1956): 132–33.

Ralph Berringer, "Jonson's *Cynthia's Revels* and the War of the Theatre," *PQ* 22 (January 1943): 1–22.

Boyce, *Theophrastan Character in England to 1642*, 102–07.

Beaurline, *Jonson and Elizabethan Comedy*, 121–32.

Chan, *Music in the Theatre of Ben Jonson*, 46–63.

Edwards, *Threshold of a Nation*, 144–49.

Judith Kegan Gardiner, "'A Wither'd Daffodil': Narcissism and *Cynthia's Revels*," *L&P* 30 (May 1980): 26–43.

Allan H. Gilbert, "The Function of the Masques in *Cynthia's Revels*," *PQ* 22 (July 1943): 211–30.

JONSON, BEN, *The Devil Is an Ass*

Harrison, *Elizabethan Plays and Players*, 233–36.

Martin Kallich, "Unity of Time in *Every Man in His Humor* and *Cynthia's Revels*," *MLN* 57 (June 1942): 445–48.

Kathryn A. McEuen, "Jonson and Juvenal," *RES* 21 (April 1945): 102–04.

McPeek, *The Black Book of Knaves*, 206–10.

James A. S. McPeek, "The Thief 'Deformed' and Much Ado About 'Noting,'" *BUSE* 4 (Summer 1960): 77–84.

Abbie Findlay Potts, "*Cynthia's Revels*, *Poetaster* and *Troilus and Cressida*," *SQ* 5 (Summer 1954): 297–99.

Alexander H. Sackton, "The Paradoxical Encomium in Elizabethan Drama," *Studies in English* 28 (1949): 95–96.

James E. Savage, "Ben Jonson in Ben Jonson's Plays," *UMSE* 3, no. 1 (1962): 8–13, 16–17.

E. M. Thron, "Jonson's *Cynthia's Revels*: Multiplicity and Unity," *SEL* 11 (Spring 1971): 235–47.

Toshihiko Shibata, "On the Palinodial Ending of *Cynthia's Revels*," *ShStud* 10 (1971–72): 1–15.

Ernest W. Talbot, "Classical Mythology and the Structure of *Cynthia's Revels*," *PQ* 22 (July 1943): 193–210.

Robet Wittenburg, *Ben Jonson and Self-Love: The Subtlest Maze of All* (Columbia: University of Missouri Press, 1990), 5–20.

Karl F. Zender, "The Unveiling of the Goddess in *Cynthia's Revels*," *JEGP* 77 (January 1978): 37–52.

The Devil Is an Ass

Mami Adachi, "Song as Device: Ben Jonson's Use of Seduction Songs in *Volpone* and *The Devil Is an Ass*," *ShStud* 25 (1986–1987): 1–24.

Barton, *Ben Jonson, Dramatist*, 219–36.

Champion, *Ben Jonson's "Dotages,"* 22–44.

Dessen, *Jonson's Moral Comedy*, 221–35.

Gagen, *The New Woman*, 102–04.

Nicoll, *The Chemical Theatre*, 118–19.

Thayer, *Ben Jonson*, 156–77.

Watson, *Ben Jonson's Parodic Strategy*, 172–209.

Womack, *Ben Jonson*, 43–47.

Yumiko Yamada, "*Volpone* and *The Devil Is an Ass*: Damnation and Salvation through Metamorphosis," *SEL* 18 (December 1978): 195–211.

Eastward Ho
(with Chapman and Marston)

Bradbrook, *Growth and Structure of Elizabethan Comedy*, 149–51.

Jackson I. Cope, "*Volpone* and the Authorship of *Eastward Hoe*," *MLN* 72 (April 1957): 253–56.

Nicholl, *The Chemical Theatre*, 10–11, 107–12, 182–83.

Epicoene; or, The Silent Woman

Mark A. Anderson, "The Successful Unity of *Epicoene*: A Defense of Ben Jonson," *SEL* 10 (Spring 1970): 349–66.

Michael Cameron Andrews, "Truewit and the Tone of *Epicoene*," in *Jacobean Miscellany* 3 (Salzburg: Institut fur Anglistik & Amerikanistik, Universität Salzburg, 1983), 32–59.

P. K. Ayers, "Dreams of the City: The Urban and the Urbane in Jonson's *Epicoene*," *PQ* 66 (Winter 1987): 73–86.

Wallace A. Bacon, "The Magnetic Field: The Structure of Jonson's Comedies," *HLQ* 19 (February 1956): 132–33.

Barbara J. Baines, and Mary C. Williams, "The Contemporary and Classical Antifeminist Tradition in Jonson's *Epicoene*," *RenP 1976* (1977): 43–58.

Barish, *Ben Jonson and the Language of Prose Comedy*, 147–86.

Jonas A. Barish, "Ovid, Juvenal, and *The Silent Woman*," *PMLA* 71 (March 1956): 213–24.

Boas, *Introduction to Stuart Drama*, 110–13.

Cristy Campbell-Furtick, "Deviations from the Norm: The Epicene in Ben Jonson's *Epicoene, or The Silent Woman*," *CCTEP* 55 (September 1990): 75–81.

Charles A. Carpenter, "*Epicoene* Minus Its Secret: Surprise as Expectation," *XUS* 7, no. 3 (1968): 15–22.

James H. Conover, "Art Criticism as a Tool for Play Analysis: *Epicoene* and *The Alchemist*," *TJ* 28 (April 1976): 78–87.

Joseph A. Dane, "The Ovids of Ben Jonson in *Poetaster* and in *Epicoene*," in Davidson, Giankaris, and Stroup, *Drama in the Renaissance*, 103–15.

Ian Donaldson, " 'A Martyr's Resolution': Jonson's *Epicoene*," *RES* 18 (1967): 1–15.

Donaldson, *World Upside-Down*, 24–45.

Eliot, *Selected Essays*, 127–39.

Enck, *Jonson and the Comic Truth*, 132–50.

John Ferns, "Ovid, Juvenal and *The Silent Woman*: A Reconsideration," *MLR* 65 (April 1970): 248–53.

Michael Flachmann, "*Epicoene*: A Comic Hell for a Comic Sinner," *MRDE* 1 (Summer 1984): 131–42.

Haselkorn, *Prostitution in Elizabethan and Jacobean Drama*, 41–44.

Hawkes, *Shakespeare's Talking Animals*, 158–65.

Ray L. Heffner, "Unifying Symbols in the Comedy of Ben Jonson," *English Institute Essays* (1954): 74–89. Reprinted in E. K. Wimsatt, ed., *English Stage Comedy* (New York: Columbia University Press, 1955), 74–97.

Huston D. Hallahan, "Silence, Eloquence, and Chatter in Jonson's *Epicoene*," *HLQ* 40 (February 1977): 117–27.

Dorothy Jones, " 'Th' Adulteries of Art': A Discussion of *The Silent Woman*," in Brissenden, *Shakespeare and Some Others*, 83–103.

Kronenberger, *The Thread of Laughter*, 34–38.

Leinwand, *The City Staged*, 124–28.

Barbara C. Millard, " 'An Acceptable Violence': Sexual Contest in Jonson's *Epicoene*," *MRDE* 1 (Summer 1984): 143–58.

Karen Newman, "City Talk: Women and Commodification in Jonson's *Epicoene*," *ELH* 56 (Fall 1989): 503–18.

Newman, *Fashioning Feminity*, 134–44.

Marianna da Vinci Nichols, "Truewit and Sir Epicure Mammon: Jonson's Creative Accidents," *ArielE* 7 (January 1976): 4–21.

Edward B. Partridge, "The Allusiveness of *Epicoene*," *ELH* 22 (June 1955): 93–107.

Partridge, *The Broken Compass*, 161–77.

Arnold W. Preussner, "Language and Society in Jonson's *Epicoene*," *Thoth* 15, no. 2 (1975): 9–20.

Julita Rydlewska, "*Epicoene* and the Craft of Comedy," *SAP* 18 (1986): 223–30.

L. G. Salingar, "Farce and Fashion in *The Silent Woman*," *E&S* 20 (1967): 29–46.

Michael Shapiro, "Audience vs. Dramatist in Jonson's *Epicoene* and Other Plays of the Children's Troups," *ELR* 3 (Winter 1973): 400–17.

William W. E. Slights, "*Epicoene* and the Prose Paradox," *PQ* 49 (Winter 1970): 178–87.

Thayer, *Ben Jonson*, 66–84.

Townsend, *Apologie for Bartholomew Fayre*, 62–66.

Watson, *Ben Jonson's Parodic Strategy*, 98–112.

Womack, *Ben Jonson*, 103–07.

Yumiko Yamada, "Classics That Revolt: Modernizing Factors in *Sejanus*, *Epicoene* and *Cataline*," *ShStud* 24 (1985–1986): 31–51.

Every Man in His Humour

Altman, *Tudor Play of Mind*, 179–95.

Barish, *Ben Jonson and the Language of Prose Comedy*, 98–104, 130–41.

Boas, *Introduction to Stuart Drama*, 49–55.

J. A. Bryant, Jr., "Jonson's Revision of *Every Man in His Humour*," *SP* 59 (October 1962): 641–50.

Sheon Joo Chin, "Jonson's Comedy of Humours and *Every Man in His Humour*," *JELL* 31 (May 1990): 85–94.

Ralph Allen Cohen, "The Importance of Setting in the Revision of *Every Man in His Humour*," *ELR* 8 (Summer 1978): 183–96.

John S. Colley, "Opinion, Poetry, and Folly in *Every Man in His Humour*," *SAB* 39 (November 1974): 3–9.

Harrison, *Elizabethan Plays and Players*, 184–88.

Martin Kallich, "Unity of Time in *Every Man in His Humour* and *Cynthia's Revels*," *MLN* 57 (June 1942): 445–48.

JONSON, BEN, *Every Man Out of His Humour*

Leinwand, *The City Staged*, 115–19.

Lawrence L. Levin, "Clement Justice in *Every Man in His Humour*," *SEL* 12 (Spring 1972): 291–307.

Kathryn A. McEuen, "Jonson and Juvenal," *RES* 21 (1945): 93–94.

Mann, *The Elizabethan Player*, 208–09.

Marx, *The Enjoyment of Drama*, 147–49.

J. C. Maxwell, "Comic Mispunctuation in *Every Man in His Humour*," *ES* 33 (October 1952): 218–19.

Barbara C. Millard, and D. Heyward Brock, "Ben Jonson's Humor Plays and the Dramatic Adaptation of the Pastoral," *EM* 28–29 (1979–80): 125–55.

Dave Rankin, "Ben Jonson: Semanticist," *Etc.* 19 (October 1962): 289–97.

Alexander H. Sackton, "The Rhymed Couplet in Ben Jonson's Plays," *Studies in English* 30 (1951): 89–90.

James E. Savage, "Ben Jonson in Ben Jonson's Plays," *UMSE* 3, no. 1 (1962): 1–5, 16–17.

Shapiro, *Rival Playwrights*, 137–45.

Henry L. Snuggs, "The Comic Humours: A New Interpretation," *PMLA* 62 (March 1947): 114–22. Reprinted and abridged in Bluestone and Rabkin, *Shakespeare's Contemporaries*, 172–77.

Stoll, *Shakespeare and Other Masters*, 98–104.

Watson, *Ben Jonson's Parodic Strategy*, 19–46.

Williams, *Unity in Ben Jonson's Early Plays*, 92–120.

Every Man Out of His Humour

Wallace A. Bacon, "The Magnetic Field: The Structure of Jonson's Comedies," *HLQ* 19 (February 1956): 129–32.

Barish, *Ben Jonson and the Language of Prose Comedy*, 104–13.

Beaurline, *Jonson and Elizabethan Comedy*, 103–20.

Boyce, *Theophrastan Character in England to 1642*, 99–101.

Cope, *Theater and the Dream*, 226–36.

Terrance Dunford, "Consumption of the World: Reading, Eating, and Imitation in *Every Man Out of His Humour*," *ELR* 14 (Spring 1984): 131–47.

Edwards, *Threshold of a Nation*, 141–44.

Enck, *Jonson and the Comic Truth*, 43–59.

Allan H. Gilbert, "The Italian Names in *Every Man Out of His Humour*," *SP* 44 (April 1947): 195–208.

Harrison, *Elizabethan Plays and Players*, 198–201.

Frank Kerins, " 'The Crafty Enchaunter': Ironic Satires and Jonson's *Every Man Out of His Humour*," *RenD* 14 (1983): 125–150.

Leggatt, *Ben Jonson*, 190–98.

Kathryn A. McEuen, "Jonson and Juvenal," *RES* 21 (1945): 94–99.

Barbara C. Millard, and D. Heyward Brock, "Ben Jonson's Humor Plays and the Dramatic Adaptation of the Pastoral," *EM* 28–29 (1979–80): 125–55.

Alice Rayner, *Comic Persuasion: Moral Structure in British Comedy from Shakespeare to Stoppard* (Berkeley, Los Angeles, and London: University of California Press, 1987), 41–48.

Rhodes, *Elizabethan Grotesque*, 131–40.

Alexander H. Sackton, "The Paradoxical Encomium in Elizabethan Drama," *Studies in English* 28 (1949): 96–97.

James E. Savage, "Ben Jonson in Ben Jonson's Plays," *UMSE* 3, no. 1 (1962): 5–8, 16–17.

Shapiro, *Rival Playwrights*, 142–44.

Snuggs, *The Comic Humours*, 114–19.

Snuggs, "The Comic Humours: A New Interpretation," *PMLA* 62 (March 1947): 114–22.

Talbert, *Elizabethan Drama and Shakespeare's Early Plays*, 55–57.

Watson, *Ben Jonson's Parodic Strategy*, 47–79.

Wells, *Elizabethan and Jacobean Playwrights*, 196–98.

For the Honour of Wales

Hassel, *Renaissance Drama*, 127–30.

The Fortunate Isles and Their Union

Brooks-Davies, *The Mercurian Monarch*, 93–95.

Alice S. Miskimim, "Ben Jonson and Captain Cox: Elizabethan Gothic Reconsidered," *RenD* 8 (1977): 173–202.

Sweeney, *Jonson and the Psychology of Public Theatre*, 196–206.

Traister, *Heavenly Necromancers*, 163–67.

The Golden Age Restored

W. Todd Furniss, "Ben Jonson's Masques," in *Three Studies in the Renaissance*, 119–24.

Leah Sinanoglou Marcus, "City Metal and Country Mettle: The Occasion of Ben Jonson's Golden Age Restored," in Bergeron, *Pageantry in the Shakespearean Theater*, 26–47.

Alice S. Miskimim, "Ben Jonson and Captain Cox: Elizabethan Gothic Reconsidered," *RenD* 8 (1977): 173–202.

The Gypsies Metamorphosed

W. Todd Furniss, "Ben Jonson's Masques," in *Three Studies in the Renaissance*, 141–51.

McPeek, *The Black Book of Knaves*, 281–84.

Dick Taylor, Jr., "Clarendon and Ben Jonson as Witnesses for the Earl of Pembroke's Character," in Bennett, Cargill, and Hall, *Studies in the English Renaissance*, 326–31.

Haddington Masque (A Masque at Lord Haddington's Marriage)

D. J. Gordon, "Ben Jonson's *Haddington Masque*: The Story and the Fable," *MLR* 42 (April 1947): 180–87.

Carol Marsh-Lockett, "Ben Jonson's *Haddington Masque* and *The Masque of Queenes*: Stuart England and the Notion of Order," *CLAJ* 30 (March 1987): 362–78.

Meagher, *Method and Meaning in Jonson's Masques*, 133–36.

Hymenaei

D. J. Gordon, "*Hymenaei*: Ben Jonson's Masque of Union," *JWCI* 8 (March 1945): 107–45.

Leah Sinanoglou Marcus, "Masquing Occasions and Masque Structure," *RORD* 24 (1981): 7–16.

King James, His Royal and Magnificent Entertainment
(with Dekker)

Erskin-Hill, *The Augustan Idea in English Literature*, 123–33.

Goldberg, *James I and the Politics of Literature*, 50–54.

Graham, *The Golden Age Restor'd*, 1–21.

Love Freed from Ignorance and Folly

Chan, *Music in the Theatre of Ben Jonson*, 241–72.

Hassel, *Renaissance Drama*, 106–07.

James E. May, "Ben Jonson's Use of Petrarchan Materials in His Masque *Love Freed from Ignorance and Folly*," *SPWVSRA* 7 (Spring 1982): 1–7.

Love Restored

Barish, *Ben Jonson and the Language of Prose Comedy*, 251–60.

Jeffrey Fischer, "*Love Restored*: A Defense of Masquing," *RenD* 8 (1977): 231–44.

Hassel, *Renaissance Drama*, 65–69.

Marcus, *The Politics of Mirth*, 27–38.

Orgel, *The Jonsonian Masque*, 72–77.

Love's Triumph Through Callipolis

Kogan, *The Hieroglyphic King*, 111–17.

Parry, *The Golden Age Restor'd*, 184–87.

Love's Welcome at Bolsover

W. Todd Furniss, "Ben Jonson's Masques," in *Three Studies in the Renaissance*, 164–67.

Lovers Made Men

Ronald Heubert, "A Shrew Yet Honest: Manliness in Jonson," *RenD* 15 (1985): 31–68.

Leggatt, *Ben Jonson*, 165–67.

The Magnetic Lady; or, Humours Reconciled

Champion, *Ben Jonson's "Dotages,"* 104–30.

Larry S. Champion, "*The Magnetick Lady*: The Close of Jonson's Circle," *SHR* 2 (1968): 104–21.

Ronald E. McFarland, "Jonson's *Magnetic Lady* and the Reception of Gilbert's *De Magnete*," *SEL* 11 (Spring 1971): 283–93.

Partridge, *The Broken Compass*, 205–12.

Thayer, *Ben Jonson*, 232–46.

The Masque of Augurs

Phyllis N. Braxton, "Jonson's *Masque of Augurs*," *Expl* 45 (Winter 1987): 10–12.

Ernest W. Talbert, "Current Scholarly Work and the 'Erudition' of Jonson's *Masque of Augers*," *SP* 44 (October 1947): 605–24.

The Masque of Beautie

D. J. Gordon, "The Imagery of Ben Jonson's *Masque of Blackness* and *Masque of Beautie*," *JWCI* 6 (March 1943): 122–41.

Richard S. Peterson, "Icon and Mystery in Jonson's *Masque of Beautie*," *JDJ* 5, no. 1–2 (1986): 169–99.

The Masque of Blackness

Anne Burley, "Courtly Personages: The Lady Masquers in Ben Jonson's *Masque of Blackness*," *SPWVSRA* 10 (Spring 1985): 49–61.

D'Amico, *The Moor in English Renaissance Drama*, 53–58.

D. J. Gordon, "The Imagery of Ben Jonson's *Masque of Blackness* and *Masque of Beautie*," *JWCI* 6 (March 1943): 122–41.

Jones, *Othello's Countrymen*, 31–33.

Ann Clive Kelly, "The Challenge of the Impossible: Ben Jonson's *Masque of Blackness,*" *CLAJ* 20 (March 1977): 341–55.

Joseph Lowenstein, *Responsive Readings: Versions of Echo in Pastoral, Epic, and the Jonsonian Masque* (New Haven: Yale University Press, 1984), 93–101.

Meagher, *Method and Meaning in Jonson's Masques*, 107–12.

Orgel, *The Jonsonian Masque*, 113–28.

The Masque of Owls

Alice S. Miskimin, "Ben Jonson and Captain Cox: Elizabethan Gothic Reconsidered," *RenD* 8 (1977): 173–202.

The Masque of Queens

W. Todd Furness, "The Annotation of Ben Jonson's *Masque of Queenes,*" *RES* 5 (October 1954): 344–60.

Harris, *Night's Black Agents*, 67–77.

Carol Marsh-Lockett, "Ben Jonson's *Haddington Masque* and *The Masque of Queenes*: Stuart England and the Notion of Order," *CLAJ* 30 (March 1987): 362–78.

Meagher, *Method and Meaning in Jonson's Masques*, 152–57.

Orgel, *The Jonsonian Masque*, 129–46.

Mercury Vindicated from the Alchemists

Barish, *Ben Jonson and the Language of Prose Comedy*, 261–66.

Edgar H. Duncan, "The Alchemy in Jonson's *Mercury Vindicated,*" *SP* 39 (October 1942): 625–37.

Goldberg, *James I and the Politics of Literature*, 60–61.

Hawkins, *Likeness of Truth in Elizabethan and Restoration Drama*, 8–9.

Nicholl, *The Chemical Theatre*, 100–02.

JONSON, BEN, *Mortimer, His Fall*

Mortimer, His Fall

Leo Kirschbaum, "Jonson, Seneca, and *Mortimer*," in Wallace, *Studies in Honor of John Wilcox*, 9–13, 18–21.

Shapiro, *Rival Playwrights*, 45–48.

Neptune's Triumph for the Return of Albion

W. Todd Furniss, "Ben Jonson's Masques," in *Three Studies in the Renaissance*, 152–58.

Patricia Fumerton, *Cultural Aesthetics: Renaissance Literature and the Practice of Social Ornament* (Chicago: University of Chicago Press, 1991), 195–201.

Loftis, *Renaissance Drama in England and Spain*, 163–64, 225–26.

Orgel, *The Jonsonian Masque*, 91–99.

The New Inn; or, The Light Heart

Barton, *Ben Jonson, Dramatist*, 258–84.

Anne Barton, "*The New Inn* and the Problem of Jonson's Late Style," *ELR* 9 (Winter 1979): 417–18.

Champion, *Ben Jonson's "Dotages,"* 76–103.

Larry S. Champion, "The Comic Intent of Jonson's *The New Inn*," *WHR* 18 (Winter 1964): 66–74.

Chan, *Music in the Theatre of Ben Jonson*, 332–52.

Patrick Cheney, "Jonson's *The New Inn* and Plato's Myth of the Hermaphrodite," *RenD* 14 (1983): 173–94.

Harriett Hawkins, "The Idea of a Theatre in Jonson's *The New Inn*," *RenD* 9 (1966): 205–26.

Jon S. Lawry, "A Prospect of Jonson's *The New Inn*," *SEL* 23 (Spring 1983): 311–27.

Rayburn S. Moore, "Some Notes on the 'Courtly Love' System in Jonson's *The New Inn*," in *Essays in Honor of Walter Clyde Curry, Vanderbuilt Studies in Humanities 2* (Nashville, TN: Vanderbuilt University Press, 1954), 133–42.

Partridge, *Broken Compass*, 189–205,

Edward B. Partridge, "A Crux in Jonson's *The New Inn*," *MLN* 71 (March 1956): 168–69.

Edward B. Partridge, "The Symbolism of Clothes in Jonson's Last Plays," *JEGP* 56 (July 1957): 401–06.

Thayer, *Ben Jonson*, 198–232.

Watson, *Ben Jonson's Parodic Strategy*, 210–28.

News from the New World Discovered in the Moon

Paul R. Sellin, "The Politics of Ben Jonson's *Newes from the New World Discover'd in the Moone*," *Viator* 17 (December 1986): 321–37.

Oberon, The Faery Prince

David Fuller, "The Jonsonian Masque and Its Magic," *M&L* 54 (January 1973): 440–52.

Goldberg, *James I and the Politics of Literature*, 123–36.

Orgel, *The Jonsonian Masque*, 89–91.

Pan's Anniversity; or, The Shepherd's Holiday

W. Todd Furniss, "Ben Jonson's Masques," in *Three Studies in the Renaissance*, 128–37.

Pleasure Reconciled to Virtue

W. Todd Furniss, "Ben Jonson's Masques," in *Three Studies in the Renaissance*, 169–76.

Goldberg, *James I and the Politics of Literature*, 62–64.

Kogan, *The Hieroglyphic King*, 96–107.

Leggatt, *Ben Jonson*, 155–58.

Marcus, *The Politics of Mirth*, 108–27,

Orgel, *The Jonsonian Masque*, 147–85.

Richard S. Peterson, "The Iconography of Jonson's *Pleasure Reconciled to Virtue*," *JMRS* 5 (Fall 1975): 123–53.

Poetaster; or, The Arraignment

Wallace A. Bacon, "The Magnetic Field: The Structure of Ben Jonson's Comedies," *HLQ* 19 (February 1956): 133–34.

Barish, *Ben Jonson and the Language of Prose Comedy*, 121–30.

Beaurline, *Jonson and Elizabethan Comedy*, 132–55.

Joseph A. Dane, "The Ovids of Ben Jonson in *Poetaster* and in *Epicoene*," in Davidson, Giankaris, and Stroup, *Drama in the Renaissance*, 103–15.

Erskin-Hill, *The Augustan Idea in English Literature*, 108–21.

Henry D. Gray, "*The Chamberlain's Men* and *The Poetaster*," *MLR* 42 (April 1947): 173–79.

Harrison, *Elizabethan Plays and Players*, 261–71.

Jackson, *Vision and Judgement*, 20–30.

Kathryn A. McEuen, "Jonson and Juvenal," *RES* 21 (April 1945): 99–102.

James D. Mulvihill, "Jonson's *Poetaster* and the Ovidian Debate," *SEL* 22 (Spring 1982): 235–55.

Ralph Nash, "The Parting Scene in *Poetaster* (IV,ix)," *PQ* 31 (January 1952): 54–62.

Abbie Findlay Potts, "*Cynthia's Revels, Poetaster*, and *Troilus and Cressida*," *SQ* 5 (Summer 1954): 300–02.

Alexander H. Sackton, "The Rhymed Couplet in Ben Jonson's Plays," *Studies in English* 30 (1951): 91–94.

James E. Savage, "Ben Jonson in Ben Jonson's Plays," *UMSE* 3, no. 1 (1962): 11–17.

Shapiro, *Rival Playwrights*, 58–61.

Percy Simpson, "A Modern Fable of Aesop," *MLR* 43 (January 1948): 403–05.

William E. Talbert, "The Purpose and Technique of Jonson's *Poetaster*," *SP* 42 (April 1945): 225–52.

Leonard B. Terr, "Ben Jonson's *Ars Poetica*: A Reinterpretation of *Poetaster*," *Thoth* 11, no. 2 (1971): 3–16.

Eugene M. Waith, "The Poet's Morals in Jonson's *Poetaster*," *MLQ* 12 (April 1951): 13–19.

The Sad Shepherd; or, A Tale of Robin Hood

Barton, *Ben Jonson, Dramatist*, 338–51.

Chan, *Music in the Theatre of Ben Jonson*, 352–65.

T. P. Harrison, "Jonson's *Sad Shepherd* and Spenser," *MLN* 58 (April 1943): 257–62.

Lawrence Lerner, *The Uses of Nostalgia: Studies in Pastoral Poetry* (London: Chatto & Windus, 1972), 163–80.

Marcus, *Politics of Mirth*, 135–39.

Thayer, *Ben Jonson*, 247–66.

Sejanus His Fall

Francis Berry, "Stage Perspective and Elevation in *Coriolanus* and *Sejanus*," in Donaldson, *Jonson and Shakespeare*, 163–78.

Daniel C. Boughner, "Sejanus and Machiavelli," *SEL* 1 (Spring 1961): 81–100.

Daniel C. Boughner, "Jonson's Use of Lipsius in *Sejanus*," *MLN* 73 (April 1958): 247–55.

Daniel C. Boughner, "Juvenal, Horace, and *Sejanus*," *MLN* 75 (November 1960): 545–50.

Bredbeck, *Sodomy and Interpretation*, 78–80.

K. M. Burton, "The Political Tragedies of Chapman and Jonson," *EiC* 2 (October 1952): 401–04, 409–11.

Champion, *Tragic Patterns*, 62–76.

Ellen M. T. Duffy, "Ben Jonson's Debt to Renaissance Scholarship in *Sejanus* and *Cataline*," *MLR* 42 (January 1947): 24–30.

Enck, *Jonson and the Comic Truth*, 89–109.

Wilson F. Engel, III, "The Iron World of *Sejanus*: History in the Crucible of Art," *RenD* 11 (1980): 95–114.

W. Evans, "*Sejanus* and the Ideal Prince Tradition," *SEL* 11 (Spring 1971): 249–64.

Allan Gilbert, "The Eavesdroppers in Jonson's *Sejanus*," *MLN* 69 (March 1954): 164–66.

Gary D. Hamilton, "Irony and Fortune in *Sejanus*," *SEL* 11 (Spring 1971): 265–81.

G. R. Hibbard, "Goodness and Greatness: An Essay on the Tragedies of Ben Jonson and George Chapman," *RMS* 11 (1968): 5–54.

Geoffrey Hill, "The World's Proportion: "Jonson's Dramatic Poetry in *Sejanus* and *Cataline*," *Stratford-Upon-Avon-Studies* 1 (1960: 113–32.

Leigh Holt, "Language and Knowledge in Jonson's *Sejanus*," in Hogg, *Recent Research in Ben Jonson*, 108–30.

Edwin Honig, "*Sejanus* and *Coriolanus*: A Study in Alienation," *MLQ* 12 (December 1951): 408–21.

Frederick Kiefer, "Pretense in Ben Jonson's *Sejanus*," *ELWIU* 4 (Spring 1976): 19–26.

Leo Kirschbaum, "Jonson, Senneca, and *Mortimer*," in Wallace, *Studies in Honor of John Wilcox*, 14–16.

Arthur F. Marotti, "The Self-Reflexive Art of Ben Jonson's *Sejanus*," *TSLL* 12 (Summer 1970): 197–220.

Anthony Miller, "The Roman State in *Julius Caesar* and *Sejanus*," in Donaldson, *Jonson and Shakespeare*, 179–201.

Ralph Nash, "Ben Jonson's Tragic Poems," *SP* 55 (April 1958): 164–86.

Ornstein, *Moral Vision of Jacobean Tragedy*, 86–97.

Norbert H. Platz, " 'By oblique glance of his licentious pen': Ben Jonson's Christian Humanist Protest against the Counter-Renaissance Conception of the State in *Sejanus*," in Hogg, *Recent Research in Ben Jonson*, 71–107.

Prior, *Language of Tragedy*, 113–19.

Christopher Ricks, "*Sejanus* and Dismemberment, *MLN* 76 (April 1961): 301–08.

Alexander H. Sackton, "The Rhymed Couplet in Ben Jonson's Plays," *Studies in English* 30 (1951): 94–100.

Sweeney, *Jonson and the Psychology of Public Theater*.

John Gordon Sweeney, "*Sejanus* and the People's Beastly Rage," *ELH* 48 (Spring 1981): 61–82.

J. I. de Villiers, "Ben Jonson's Tragedies," *English Studies* 45 (December 1964): 433–40.

Wells, *Elizabethan and Jacobean Playwrights*, 53–57.

Matthew H. Wikander, "'Queasy to Be Touched': The World of Ben Jonson's *Sejanus*," *JEGP* 78 (October 1979): 345–57.

Yumiko Yamada, "Classics That Revolt: Modernizing Factors in *Sejanus*, *Epicoene* and *Cataline*," *ShStud* 24 (1985-1986): 31–51.

The Speeches at Prince Henry's Barriers

W. Todd Furniss, "Ben Jonson's Masques," in *Three Studies the Renaissance*, 124–27.

Leggatt, *Ben Jonson*, 74–77.

Alice S. Miskimim, "Ben Jonson and Captain Cox: Elizabethan Gothic Reconsidered," *RenD* 8 (1977): 173–202.

Roy Strong, *Henry, Prince of Wales and England's Lost Renaissance* (London: Thames and Hudson, 1986), 138–53.

Mary C. Williams, "Merlin and the Prince: *The Speeches at Prince Henry's Barriers*," *RenD* 8 (1977): 221–30.

The Staple of News

Barton, *Ben Jonson, Dramatist*, 237–57.

Champion, *Ben Jonson's "Dotages,"* 45–75.

Alan Dessen, "Jonson's 'Knave of Clubs' and *The Play of Cards*," *MLR* 62 (January 1967): 584–85.

Robert C. Jones, "Jonson's *Staple of News* Gossips and Fulwell's *Like Will to Like*: 'The Old Way' in a 'New' Morality Play," *YES* 3 (1973): 74–77.

Devra Rowland Kifer, "*The Staple of News*: Jonson's Festive Comedy," *SEL* 12 (Spring 1972): 329–44.

Douglas M. Lanier, "The Prison-House and the Canon : Allegorical Form and Posterity in Ben Jonson's *The Staple of News*," *MRDE* 2 (Summer 1985): 253–67.

Richard Levin, "*The Staple of News*, The Society of Jeerers, and Canter's College," *PQ* 44 (October 1965): 445–53. Reprinted in Levin, *Multiple Plot*, 184–91.

Loftis, *Renaissance Drama in England and Spain*, 165–66.

Helen Ostovich, "'Jeered by Confederacy': Group Agression in Jonson's Comedies," *MRDE* 3 (Spring 1986): 115–28.

JONSON, BEN, *A Tale of a Tub*

Johnstone Parr, "A Note on Jonson's *The Staple of News*," *MLN* 60 (February 1945): 117.

Partridge, *Broken Compass*, 179–89.

Edward B. Partridge, "The Symbolism of Clothes in Jonson's Last Plays," *JEGP* 56 (July 1957): 396–400.

Keith Salter, "Of the Right to Use Riches," *E&S* 16 (1963): 101–14.

Thayer, *Ben Jonson*, 177–98.

Yumiko Yamada, "*The Staple of News*, Kings and Kingdoms," *SEL* 30 (Spring 1990): 32–38.

A Tale of a Tub

Barton, *Ben Jonson, Dramatist*, 321–37.

Beaurline, *Jonson and Elizabethan Comedy*, 274–86.

J. A. Bryant, *The Compassionate Satirist: Ben Jonson and His Imperfect World* (Athens: University of Georgia Press, 1972), 160–80.

J. A. Bryant, "*A Tale of a Tub*: Jonson's Comedy of the Human Condition," *RenP* 1962 (1963): 95–105.

Edwards, *Threshold of a Nation*, 156–58.

Alexander H. Sackton, "The Rhymed Couplet in Ben Jonson's Plays," *Studies in English* 30 (1951): 88–89.

Mary C. Williams, "*A Tale of a Tub*: Ben Jonson's Folk Play," *NCarF* 22 (Spring 1974): 161–68.

Time Vindicated to Himself and to His Honours

W. Todd Furniss, "Ben Jonson's Masques," in *Three Studies in the Renaissance*, 109–19.

The Vision of Delight

Harriett Hawkins, "Jonson's Use of Traditional Dream Theory in *The Vision of Delight*," *MP* 64 (November 1967): 285–92.

Marcus, *The Politics of Mirth*, 66–77.

Volpone; or, The Fox

Mami Adachi, "Song as Device: Ben Jonson's Use of Seduction Songs in *Volpone* and *The Devil Is an Ass*," *ShStud* 25 (1986–87): 1–24.

Mark A. Anderson, "Structure and Response in *Volpone*," *RMS* 19 (1975): 47–71.

Judd Arnold, "The Double Plot in *Volpone*: A Note on Jonsonian Dramatic Structure," *SCN* 23 (Winter 1965): 47–52.

Wallace A. Bacon, "The Magnetic Field: The Structure of Jonson's Comedies," *HLQ* 19 (February 1956): 139–49.

Jonas A. Barish, "The Double Plot in *Volpone*," *MP* 51 (August 1953): 83–92. Reprinted in Bluestone and Rabkin, *Shakespeare's Contemporaries*, 177–89.

Baum, *The Satiric and Didactic in Ben Jonson's Comedies*, 165–82.

L. A. Beaureline, "Volpone and the Power of Gorgeous Speech," *SLitI* 6, no. 1 (1973): 61–75.

David M. Bergeron, "'Lend Me Your Dwarf': Romance in *Volpone*," *MRDE* (Spring 1986): 99–113.

Thora Balstev Blatt, "Who Was Volpone's 'Danish Gonswart,'" *ES* 56 (December 1975): 393–95.

Boas, *Introduction to Stuart Drama*, 106–10.

Douglas Brooks-Davis, "Jonson's Volpone and Antinous Once More," *N&Q* 30 (April 1983): 145–47.

Canfield, *Word as Bond*, 90–104.

Carol A. Carr, "Volpone and Mosca: Two Styles of Roguery," *CollL* 8 (Spring 1981): 144–57.

Frank N. Clary, Jr., "The Vol and the Pone: A Reconsideration of Jonson's *Volpone*," *ELN* 10 (September 1972): 102–09.

Ralph A. Cohen, The Setting of *Volpone*," *RenP 1977* (1978): 64–75.

Jackson I. Cope, "*Volpone* and the Authorship of *Eastward Ho*," *MLN* 72 (April 1957): 253–56.

John Creaser, "The Popularity of Jonson's Tortoise," *RES* 27 (1976): 38–46.

John Creaser, "A Vindication of Sir Politic Would-Be," *ES* 57 (December 1976): 502–14.

John Creaser, "*Volpone*: The Mortifying of the Fox," *EIC* 25 (July 1975): 329–56.

JONSON, BEN, *Volpone; or, The Fox*

P. H. Davidson, "*Volpone* and the Old Comedy," *MLQ* 24 (March 1963): 154–57.

Leonard F. Dean, "Three Notes on Comic Morality: Celia, Bobadill, and Falstaff," *SEL* 16 (Spring 1976): 263–71.

Sharon M. Deats, "Jonson's *Volpone*," *Expl* 39 (Spring 1981): 32–33.

Dessen, *Jonson's Moral Comedy*, 70–104.

Alan C. Dessen, "*Volpone* and the Late Morality Tradition," *MLQ* 25 (December 1964): 383–99.

Frances Dolan, "'We Must Here Be Fixed': Discovering a Self behind the Mask in *Volpone*," *ISJR* 60 (February 1986): 355–67.

Ian Donaldson, "Jonson and Anger," *YES* 14 (1984): 56–71.

Ian Donaldson, "Jonson's Tortoise," *RES* 19 (1968): 162–66.

Ian Donaldson, "*Volpone*, III.vii.193–4 and Il marescalo," *N&Q* 29 (April 1982): 139–40.

Ian Donaldson, "*Volpone*: Quick and Dead," *EIC* 21 (December 1974): 121–34.

R. P. Draper, "The Golden Age and Volpone's Address to His Gold," *N&Q* 3 (April 1956): 191–92.

Douglas Duncan, "Audience Manipulation in *Volpone*," *WasR* 5, no. 2 (1970): 23–37.

A. Richard Dutton, "*Volpone* and *The Alchemist*: A Comparison in Satiric Techniques," *RMS* 18 (1974): 36–62.

Enck, *Jonson and the Comic Truth*, 110–31.

Dennis J. Enright, "Poetic Satire and Satire in Verse: A Consideration of Jonson and Massinger," *Scrutiny* 18 (Winter 1952): 211–17. Reprinted in Enright, *The Apothecary's Shop—Essays on Literature* (London: Secker & Warburg, 1957), 54–64.

Garner, *The Absent Voice*, 100–24

Donald Gertmenian, "Comic Experience in *Volpone* and *The Alchemist*," *SEL* 17 (Spring 1977): 247–58.

C. J. Gianakaris, Identifying Ethical Values in *Volpone*," *HLQ* 32 (April 1968): 45–57.

C. J. Gianakaris, "Jonson's Use of 'Avocatari' in *Volpone*," *ELN* 12 (September 1974): 8–14.

S. L. Goldberg, "Folly into Crime: The Catastrophe of *Volpone*," *MLQ* 20 (September 1959): 233–42.

Stephen J. Greenblatt, "The False Ending in *Volpone*," *JEGP* 79 (April 1980): 90–104.

Charles A. Hallett, "Jonson's Cecilia: A Reinterpretation of *Volpone*," *SP* 68 (July 1971): 50–69.

Charles A. Hallett, "The Satanic Nature of *Volpone*," *PQ* 49 (Winter 1970): 41–55.

Ben Hardman, "The Magnifico and the Unmoved Mover: The Nature of Power in *Volpone*," *SPWVSRA* 6 (Spring 1981): 14–20.

Hartigan, *Within the Dramatic Spectrum*, 160–67.

Margaret Hartine, "Ben Jonson, *Volpone*, and Charterhouse," *N&Q* 38 (March 1991): 79–81.

Harriett Hawkins, "Folly, Incurable Disease, and *Volpone*," *SEL* 8 (Spring 1968): 335–48.

Hawkins, *Poetic Freedom and Poetic Truth*, 108–12.

H. R. Hays, "Satire and Identification: An Introduction to Ben Jonson," *KR* 19 (Spring 1957): 267–72.

Hoy, *The Hyacinth Room*, 127–41, 172–74.

Myles Hurd, "Between Crime and Punishment in Jonson's *Volpone*," *CollL* 10 (Spring 1983): 172–83.

Kernan, *The Plot of Satire*, 121–42.

Knoll, *Ben Jonson's Plays*, 79–104.

Kronenberger, *The Thread of Laughter*, 24–30.

Alexander Leggatt, "The Suicide of *Volpone*," *UTQ* 39 (January 1969): 19–32.

Harry Levin, "Jonson's Metempsychosis," *PQ* 22 (April 1943): 231–39.

Alexander W. Lyle, "Volpone's Two Worlds," *YES* 4 (1974): 70–76.

MacCarthy, *Humanities*, 54–59.

R. E. R. Madelaine, "Parasites and 'Politicians': Some Comic Stage Images in *Volpone*," *AUMLA* 58 (November 1982): 170–77.

C. N. Manlove, "The Double View in *Volpone*," *SEL* 19 (Spring 1979): 239–52.

Howard Marchitell, "Desire and Domination in *Volpone*," *SEL* 31 (Spring 1991): 287–308.

Julie Manzelmann, Jonson's *Volpone*," *Expl* 47 (Summer 1987): 8–9.

JONSON, BEN, *Volpone; or, The Fox*

Joyce Miller, "*Volpone*: A Study of Dramatic Ambiguity," in Shalvi and Mendilow, *Studies in English Language and Literature*, 35–95.

Lloyd L. Mills, "Barish's 'The Double Plot' Supplemented: The Tortoise Symbolism," *Serif* 4, no. 3 (1967): 25–28.

A. K. Nardo, "The Transmigration of Folly: Volpone's Innocent Grotesques," *ES* 58 (April 1977): 105–09.

Ralph Nash, "The Comic Intent of *Volpone*," *SP* 44 (January 1947): 26–40.

Gloria E. Newton, "Dramatic Imagery in *Volpone*," *Manitoba Arts Review* 8 (Winter 1952): 9–17.

Nicholl, *The Chemical Theatre*, 71–2, 113–17.

Martin R. Orkin, "Languages of Deception in *Volpone*," *Theoria* 59 (October 1982): 39–49.

Ornstein, *The Moral Vision of Jacobean Tragedy*, 112–13, 124–25.

Robert Ornstein, "*Volpone* and Renaissance Psychology," *N&Q* 3 (November 1956): 471–72.

George A. E. Parfitt, "Some Notes on the Classical Borrowings in *Volpone*," *ES* 55 (April 1974): 127–32.

R. B. Parker, "*Volpone* and *Reynard the Fox*," *RenD* 7 (1976): 3–42.

R. B. Parker, "Wolfit's Fox: An Interpretation of *Volpone*," *UTQ* 45 (April 1975): 200–20.

Partridge, *The Broken Compass*, 70–113.

Ranier Pineas, "The Morality of Vice in *Volpone*," *Discourse* 5 (Autumn 1962): 451–59.

Ranier Pineas, "*Volpone* and Renaissance Psychology," *N&Q* 201 (November 1956): 471–72.

Mario Praz, *The Flaming Heart* (Garden City, NY: Anchor, 1950): 170–85.

Rufus Putney, "Jonson's Poetic Comedy," *PQ* 41 (January 1962): 188–204.

Brian Richardson, "Words Made Flesh: Imagery and Causality in Drama," in Hartigan, *Within the Dramatic Spectrum*, 160–67.

James A. Riddell, "Volpone's Fare," *SEL* 21 (Spring 1981): 307–18.

Alexander H. Sackton, "The Paradoxical Encomium in Elizabethan Drama," *Studies in English* 28 (1949): 97–100.

Leo Salinger, "Comic Form in Ben Jonson: *Volpone* and the Philosopher's Stone," in Axton and Williams, *English Drama*, 48–68.

Schell, *Strangers and Pilgrims*, 113–50.

D. A. Scheve, "Jonson's *Volpone* and Traditional Fox Lore," *RES* 1 (July 1950): 242–44.

Scott, *Renaissance Drama*, 47–60.

Joseph L. Simmons, "Volpone as Antinous: Jonson and 'Th' Overthrow of Stage Players,'" *MLR* 70 (January 1975): 13–19.

Harold Skulsky, "Cannibals vs. Demons in *Volpone*," *SEL* 29 (Spring 1989): 291–308.

William W. E. Slights, "The Play of Conspiracies in *Volpone*," *TSLL* 27 (Winter 1985): 369–89.

Malcolm H. South, "Animal Imagery in *Volpone*," *TSL* 10 (Spring 1965): 141–50.

Frederick S. Sternfield, "Song in Jonson's Comedy: A Gloss on Volpone," in Bennett, Cargill, and Hall, *Studies in the English Renaissance Drama*, 310–21.

Stoll, *Shakespeare and Other Masters*, 106–10.

John Sweeney, "*Volpone* and the Theatre of Self-Interest," *ELR* 12 (Spring 1982): 220–41.

Talbert, *Elizabethan Drama and Shakespeare's Early Plays*, 46–47.

Tokson, *The Popular Image of the Blackman in English Drama*, 91–93.

Townsend, *Apologie for Bartholomew Fayre*, 58–72.

Michael J. Warren, "A Note on Jonson's *Volpone*, I,i.76-8," *N&Q* 27 (March 1980): 143–46.

Watson, *Ben Jonson's Parodic Strategy*, 80–97.

John S. Weld, "Christian Comedy: *Volpone*," *SP* 51 (April 1954): 172–93.

Wells, *Elizabethan and Jacobean Playwrights*, 198–200.

Robert Wescott, "Volpone? Or the Fox?" *CR* 17 (1974): 82–96.

Womack, *Ben Jonson*, 66–75.

Yumiko Yamada, "*Volpone* and *The Devil Is an Ass*: Damnation and Salvation through Metamorphosis," *SEL* 18 (December 1978): 195–211.

KILLIGREW, THOMAS

The Parson's Wedding

Gagen, *The New Woman*, 104–06.

KYD, THOMAS

The Spanish Tragedy

Frank R. Ardolino, "The Hangman's Noose and the Empty Box: Kyd's Use of Dramatic and Mythological Sources in *The Spanish Tragedy* (III.iv–vii)," *RenQ* 30 (1977): 334–40.

Frank R. Ardolino, "'Veritas Filia Temporis': Time, Perspective, and Justice in *The Spanish Tragedy*," *SIcon* 3 (1977): 57–69.

Jonas A. Barish, "*The Spanish Tragedy*, or the Pleasures and Perils of Rhetoric," in *Elizabethan Theatre*, ed. John Russell Brown and Bernard Harris (London: Arnold, 1966), 59–85.

Greg Bentley, "Kyd's *The Spanish Tragedy*," *Expl* 39 (Fall 1981): 17–19.

Scavan Bercovitch, "Love and Strife in Kyd's *Spanish Tragedy*," *SEL* 9 (Spring 1969): 215–29.

Keen C. Burrows, "The Dramatic and Structural Significance of the Portuguese Sub-plot in *The Spanish Tragedy*," *RenP* 1968 (1969): 25–35.

Charles K. Cannon, "The Relation of Additions of *The Spanish Tragedy* to the Original Play," *SEL* 2 (Spring 1962): 229–40.

Joe L. Cash, "A Source and Symbolic Function for the Hawk and the Nightingale in *The Spanish Tragedy*," *McNR* 21 (Winter 1969): 67–71.

Clemen, *English Tragedy Before Shakespeare*, 100–12, 267–77.

John S. Colley, "*The Spanish Tragedy* and the Theatre of God's Judgements," *PLL* 10 (Summer 1974): 241–53.

Herbert R. Coursen, "The Unity of *The Spanish Tragedy*," *SP* 65 (December 1968): 768–82.

Ernest de Chickera, "Divine Justice and Private Revenge in *The Spanish Tragedy*," *MLR* 57 (April 1962): 228–32.

William Empson, "*The Spanish Tragedy*," *Nimbus* 3 (Summer 1956): 16–29.

Donna B. Hamilton, "*The Spanish Tragedy*: A Speaking Picture," *ELR* 4 (Summer 1974): 203–17.

Roger Hapgood, "The Judge in the Firie Tower: Another Virgilian Passage in *The Spanish Tragedy*," *N&Q* 13 (July 1966): 287–88.

Harrison, *Elizabethan Plays and Players*, 64–68.

Hawkins, *Likeness of Truth*, 28–31.

Rebecca M. Howard, "The Ironic Consolation of *The Spanish Tragedy*," *SPWVS-RA* 4 (Spring 1979): 9–15.

Hunter, *Dramatic Identities and Cultural Tradition*, 214–29.

Hunter, "Ironies of Justice in *The Spanish Tragedy*," *RenD* 8 (1965): 89–104.

S. F. Johnson, "*The Spanish Tragedy*," in Hosley, *Essays on Shakespeare and Elizabethan Drama*, 23–38.

R. C. Johnston, "Divine Justice and Private Revenge in *The Spanish Tragedy*," *MLR* 57 (April 1962): 232–35.

Margaret Lamb, "Beyond Revenge: *The Spanish Tragedy*," *Mosaic* 9 (Winter 1975): 33–40.

Harry Levin, "An Echo from *The Spanish Tragedy*," *MLR* 57 (May 1949): 297–302.

Michael Henry Levin, " 'Vindicta mihi!': Meaning, Morality, and Motivation in *The Spanish Tragedy*," *SEL* 4 (Spring 1964): 307–24.

Carol McGinnis Kay, "Deception Through Words: A Reading of *The Spanish Tragedy*," *SP* 74 (Spring 1977): 20–38.

Scott McMillin, "The Book of Seneca in *The Spanish Tragedy*," *SEL* 14 (Spring 1974): 201–08.

Mann, *The Elizabethan Player*, 142–43.

Prior, *The Language of Tragedy*, 46–58.

Deborah Rubin, "Justice, Revenge and Villainy in Kyd's *Spanish Tragedy*," *Thoth* 16, no. 2 (1976): 3–13.

Simpson, *Studies in Elizabethan Drama*, 145–50.

Pierre Spriet, "Antisocial Behavior and the Code of Love in Kyd's *The Spanish Tragedy*," *CahiersE* 17 (April 1981): 1–9.

William L. Stull, " 'This Metamorphosde Tragoedie': Thomas Kyd, Cyril Tourneur, and the Jacobean Theatre of Cruelty," *ArielE* 14 (July 1983): 35–49.

Talbert, *Elizabethan Drama and Shakespeare's Early Plays*, 62–64, 72–79, 138–40.

Wells, *Elizabethan and Jacobean Playwrights*, 21–24.

William H. Wiatt, "The Dramatic Function of the Alexandre-Villuppo Episode in *The Spanish Tragedy*," *N&Q* 203 (August 1958): 327–29.

Wiggins, *Journeymen in Murder*, 52–57, 103–07, 131–35.

Donald R. Wineke, "Hieronimo's Garden and 'the Fall of Babylon': Culture and Anarchy in *The Spanish Tragedy*," in *Aeolian Harps: Essays in Honor of Maurice Browning Cramer*, ed. Donna G. Fricke and Douglas C. Fricke (Bowling Green, OH: Bowling Green University Press, 1976), 65–79.

LEGGE, THOMAS

Richardus Tertius

Robert S. Lordi, "The Relationship of *Richard Tertius* to the Main Richard III Plays," *BUSE* 5 (Autumn 1961): 139–53.

McDonnell, *The Aspiring Mind*, 90–94.

Ribner, *The English History Play*, 68–70.

Wiggins, *Journeymen in Murder*, 34–6.

LODGE, THOMAS

A Looking Glass for London and England

Maurice Hunt, "A Looking Glass for Pericles," *ELWIU* 13 (Spring 1986): 3–11.

The Wounds of Civil War

Altman, *The Tudor Play of Mind*, 283–88.

Kiefer, *Fortune and Elizabethan Tragedy*, 122–33.

LUPTON, THOMAS

All For Money

Bevington, *From "Mankind" to Marlowe*, 165–69.

Mann, *The Elizabethan Player*, 24–26, 231–33.

LYLY, JOHN

Alexander, Campaspe, and Diogenes

David M. Bevington, "John Lyly and Queen Elizabeth: Royal Flattery in *Campaspe* and *Sapho and Phao*," *RenP 1965* (1966): 57–67.

Hawkins, *Poetic Freedom and Poetic Truth*, 125–26.

Joseph W. Houppert, *John Lyly* (Boston: Twayne, 1975), 55–71.

Hereward T. Price, "Shakespeare and His Young Contemporaries," *PQ* 41 (January 1962): 40–41.

Saccio, *The Court Comedies of John Lyly*, 26–-4.

Jeff Shulman, "Lyly's Use of Aelian in *Campaspe*," *N&Q* 29 (October 1982): 417–18.

Sybil Truchet, "*Campaspe*: A Brave New World?" *CahiersE* 15 (April 1979): 17–28.

Joseph Westlund, "The Theme of Tact in *Campaspe*," *SEL* 16 (Spring 1976): 213–21.

Endymion, The Man in the Moon

Altman, *The Tudor Play of Mind*, 93–113.

J. A. Bryant, Jr., "The Nature of the Allegory in Lyly's *Endymion*," *RenP 1955* (1956): 4–11.

Sara Deats, "The Disarming of the Knight: Comic Parody in Lyly's *Endymion*," *SAB* 40 (November 1975): 67–75.

Donald Edge, " 'Philadelphi in Argos': A Crux in Lyly's *Endymion*," *N&Q* 25 (October 1978): 439–40.

C. C. Gannon, "Lyly's *Endimion*: From Myth to Allegory," *ELR* 6 (Summer 1976): 220–43.

Bernard F. Huppé, "Allegory of Love in Lyly's Court Comedies," *ELH* 14 (March 1947): 93–113.

Robert S. Knapp, "The Monarchy of Love in Lyly's *Endimion*," *MP* 73 (January 1976): 353–67.

Carolyn Ruth Swift Lenz, "The Allegory of Wisdom in Lyly's *Endimion*," *CompD* 10 (Fall 1976): 235–57.

Saccio, *The Court Comedies of John Lyly*, 169–86.

Saccio, "The Oddity of Lyly's *Endimion*," in Hibbard, *The Elizabethan Theatre V*, 92–111.

Kurt Tetzeli von Rosador, "The Power of Magic: From *Endimion* to *The Tempest*," *ShS* 43 (1991): 1–13.

Peter Weltner, "The Antinomic Vision of Lyly's *Endymion*," *ELR* 3 (Spring 1973): 5–29.

Gallathea

Altman, *The Tudor Play of Mind*, 207–16.

David M. Bergeron, "The Education of Rafe in Lyly's *Gallathea*," *SEL* 23 (Spring 1983): 197–206.

Edwards, *Threshold of a Nation*, 49–52.

Susan C. Kemper, "Dramaturgical Design in Lyly's *Gallathea*," *Thoth* 16, no. 3 (1976): 19–31.

Robert J. Meyer, " 'Pleasure Reconciled to Virtue': The Mystery of Love in Lyly's *Gallathea*," *SEL* 21 (Spring 1981): 193–208.

Saccio, *The Court Comedies of John Lyly*, 95–160.

Love's Metamorphosis

Michael R. Best, "Lyly's Static Drama," *RenD* 1 (1968): 75–86.

Donald J. Edge, " 'Salamints' in John Lyly's *Love's Metamorphosis*," *N&Q* 21 (April 1974): 286.

Bernard F. Huppé, "Allegory of Love in Lyly's Court Comedies," *ELH* 14 (March 1947): 93–113.

Paul E. Parnell, "Moral Allegory in Lyly's *Love's Metamorphosis*," *SP* 52 (January 1955): 1–16.

Saccio, *The Court Comedies of John Lyly*, 161–65.

Jeff Shulman, "Ovidian Myth in Lyly's Courtship Comedies," *SEL* 25 (Spring 1985): 249–69.

David Lloyd Stevenson, "The Love-Game Comedy," *CUSECL* 164 (1946): 168–71.

Midas

Paul Dean, "Edwardes's *Damon and Pithias* and Lyly's *Midas*," *N&Q* 30 (April 1983): 130-–32.

Stephen S. Hilliard, "Lyly's *Midas* as an Allegory of Tyranny," *SEL* 12 (Spring 1972): 243–58.

Carolyn Ruth Lenz, "John Lyly's *Midas*: An Allegory of Epiphany," *SMC* 12 (1980): 133–39.

Mother Bombie

Weld, *Meaning in Comedy*, 125–28.

Sappho and Phao

Beaurline, *Jonsonian and Elizabethan Comedy*, 66–85.

David M. Bevington, "John Lyly and Queen Elizabeth: Royal Flattery in *Campaspe* and *Sapho and Phao*," *RenP 1965* (1966): 57–7.

Jeff Shulman, "Ovidian Myth in Lyly's Courtship Comedies," *SEL* 25 (Spring 1985): 249–69.

The Woman in the Moon

Michael R. Best, "Lyly's Static Drama," *RenD* 1 (1968): 75–86.

Bernard F. Huppé, "Allegory of Love in Lyly's Court Comedies," *ELH* 14 (March 1947): 93–113.

LYNDSAY, SIR DAVID, *A Satire of the Three Estates*

Anne Lancashire, "John Lyly and Pastoral Entertainment," in *The Elizabethan Theatre VIII*, ed. G. R. Hibbard (Port Credit, Ont.: P. D. Meany, 1982), 22–50.

LYNDSAY, SIR DAVID

A Satire of the Three Estates, in Commendation of Virtue and Vituperation of Vice

Vernon Harward, "*Ane Satyre of the Thrie Estaitis* Again," *SSL* 7 (March 1970): 139–46.

Joanne Spencer Kantrowitz, "Allegory," in Happé, *Medieval English Drama*, 144–51.

John MacQueen, "*Ane Satyre of the Thrie Estaitis*," *SSL* 3 (March 1966): 129–43.

E. S. Miller, "The Christening in *Satire of the Three Estates*," *MLN* 60 (January 1945): 42–45.

MALORY, SIR THOMAS

Fair Maid of Ascolat

Earl E. Anderson, "Malory's 'Fair Maid of Ascolat,'" *NM* 87 (June 1986): 237–54.

Flecity Riddy, "Structure and Meaning in Malory's 'The Fair Maid of Ascolat,'" *FMLS* 12 (October 1976): 354–66.

MARLOWE, CHRISTOPHER

Dido, Queen of Carthage

Don Cameron Allen, "Marlowe's *Dido* and the Tradition," in Hosley, *Essays on Shakespeare and Elizabethan Drama*, 64–68.

Asibong, *Comic Sensibility*, 67–69, 71–78, 134–40,

Brandt, *Christopher Marlowe*, 15–49.

Francis J. Chivers, "*Dido, Queen of Carthage* and the Marlovian 'Aspirer,'" *SPWVSRA* 8 (Spring 1983): 49–56.

Clemen, *English Tragedy Before Shakespeare*, 161–62.

Cope, *Dramaturgy of the Daemonic*, 62–71.

Jackson I. Cope, "Marlowe's 'Dido' and the Titillating Children," *ELR* 4 (Summer 1974): 315–25. Reprinted in Bloom, *Christopher Marlowe*, 137–46.

Cutts, *Left Hand of God*, 1–28.

George L. Geckle, "The Wind or the Wound: Marlowe's *Dido, Queen of Carthage*, II.i.253–54," *PBSA* 71 (June 1977): 194–99.

Brian Gibbons, "Unstable Proteus: Marlowe's *The Tragedy of Dido Queen of Carthage*," in Morris, *Christopher Marlowe*, 27–46.

Roma Gill, "Marlowe's Virgil: *Dido, Queen of Carthage*," *RES* 28 (1977): 141–55.

Godshalk, *The Marlovian World Picture*, 38–58.

Thomas P. Harrison, "Shakespeare and Marlowe's *Dido, Queen of Carthage*," *Studies in English* 35 (March 1956): 57–63.

Kuriyama, *Hammer or Anvil*, 53–76.

Clifford Leech, "Marlowe's Humor," in Hosley, *Essays on Shakespeare and Elizabethan Drama*, 71–75.

Richard A. Martin, "Fate, Seneca, and Marlowe's *Dido, Queen of Carthage*," *RenaD* 11 (1980): 45–66.

Jocelyn Powell, "Marlowe's Spectacle," *TDR* 8 (Summer 1964): 195–210.

Matthew N. Proser, "*Dido Queene of Carthage* and the Evolution of Marlowe's Dramatic Style," in Friedenreich, Gill, and Kuriyama, *"A poet and a filthy playmaker,"* 83–97.

Irving Ribner, "Marlowe's 'Tragicke Glassé,'" in Hosley, *Essays on Shakespeare and Elizabethan Drama*, 96–99.

David M. Rogers, "Love and Honor in Marlowe's *Dido, Queen of Carthage*," *Greyfriar* 6 (1963): 6–7.

G. S. Rousseau, "Marlowe's *Dido* and the Rhetoric of Love," *EM* 19 (Spring 1968): 25–49.

Rowse, *Christopher Marlowe*, 43–48.

Shapiro, *Rival Playwrights*, 126–32.

Smith, *Homosexual Desire in Shakespeare's England*, 205–08.

MARLOWE, CHRISTOPHER, *Doctor Faustus*

Stilling, *Love and Death in Renaissance Tragedy*, 41–55.

W. Craig Turner, "Love and the Queen of Carthage: A Look at Marlowe's *Dido*," *ELWIU* 11 (Spring 1984): 3–9.

Doctor Faustus

Doris Adler, "The Acts of *Doctor Faustus* as Monuments of the Moment," *SPWVSRA* 10 (Spring 1985): 1–24.

Asibong, *Comic Sensibility*, 42–47, 84–88, 114–17, 120–26.

C.L. Barber, "The Form of Faustus' Fortunes Good or Bad," *TDR* 8 (Summer 1964): 92–119.

Emily C. Bartels, "Authorizing Subversion: Strategies of Power in Marlowe's *Doctor Faustus*," *RenP* 1988 (1989): 65–74.

Charles N. Beall, "Definition of Theme by Unconsecutive Event: Structure as Induction in Marlowe's *Dr. Faustus*," *RenP* 1961 (1962): 53–62.

Bernard Beckerman, "Scene Patterns in *Doctor Faustus* and *Richard III*," in Honigmann, *Shakespeare and His Contemporaries*, 31–41.

William Blackburn, " 'Heavenly Words': Marlowe's Faustus as a Renaissance Magician," *ESC* 4 (Spring 1978): 1–14.

Herbert Blau, "Language and Structure in Poetic Drama," *MLQ* 18 (March 1957): 29–32.

Michael Boccia, "Faustus Unbound: A Reconsideration of the Fate of Faustus in Christopher Marlowe's *Doctor Faustus*," *LangQ* 25 (Fall–Winter 1986): 8–12.

Muriel C. Bradbrook, "Marlowe's *Dr. Faustus* and the Eldritch Tradition," in Hosley, *Essays on Shakespeare and Elizabethan Drama*, 83–90.

Brandt, *Christopher Marlowe*, 174–98.

Nicholas Brooke, "The Moral Tragedy of *Dr. Faustus*," The *Cambridge Journal* 5 (August 1952): 662–87. Reprinted in O'Neill, *Critics on Marlowe*, 93–114.

Brooks and Heilman, *Understanding Drama*, 529–42.

Paul Budra, "*Doctor Faustus*: Death of a Bibliophile," *Connotations* 1 (March 1991) 1–11.

Mark Thornton Burnett, "*Doctor Faustus* and the Form and Function of the Chorus: Marlowe's Beginnings and Endings," *CIEFLB* 1 (June 1989): 33–45.

Mark Thornton Burnett, "Two Notes on Metre and Rhyme in *Doctor Faustus*," *N&Q* 33 (September 1986): 337–38.

Lily B. Campbell, "*Doctor Faustus*: A Case of Conscience," *PMLA* 67 (March 1952): 219–39.

Nan Cooke Carpenter, " 'Miles' Versus 'Clericus' in Marlowe's *Faustus*," *N&Q* 197 (March 1952): 91–93.

Patrick Cheney, "Love and Magic in *Doctor Faustus*: Marlowe's Indictment of Spenserian Idealism," *Mosaic* 17 (Fall 1984): 93–109.

King-Kok Cheung, "The Dialectic of Despair in *Doctor Faustus*," in Frieden-reich, Gill, and Kuriyama, "*A poet and a filthy play-maker*," 193–201.

Clay, *The Role of Anxiety*, 107–13.

Clemen, *English Tragedy before Shakespeare*, 147–54.

Cornelius, *Marlowe's Use of the Bible*, 19–21, 39–40, 48–50, 96–107.

Francis Dolores Covella, "The Choral Nexus in *Doctor Faustus*," *SEL* 26 (Spring 1986): 201–15.

John H. Crabtree, Jr., "The Comedy in Marlowe's *Dr. Faustus*," *FurmS* 9 (November 1961): 1–9.

Cutts, *Left Hand of God*, 108–48.

C. Davidson, "Faustus of Wittenberg," *SP* 59 (July 1962): 514–23.

Sara Munson Deats, "*Doctor Faustus*: From Chapbook to Tragedy," *ELWIU* 3 (Spring 1976): 3–16.

Sara Munson Deats, "Ironic Biblical Allusion in Marlowe's *Doctor Faustus*," *M&H* 10 (1981): 203–16.

G. I. Duthie, "Some Observations on Marlowe's *Doctor Faustus*," *Archiv* 203 (1966): 81–96.

Una Ellis-Fermor, *The Frontiers of Drama*, 22–24, 139–43.

Roy T. Eriksen, "The Misplaced Clownage-Scene in *The Tragedie of Doctor Faustus* (1616) and Its Implications for the Play's Total Structure," *ES* 62 (June 1981): 249–58.

Roy T. Eriksen, "What Resting Place is This?: Aspects of Time and Place in *Doctor Faustus*," *RenD* 16 (1985): 49–74.

Bernhard Fabian, "Marlowe's *Dr. Faustus*," *N&Q* 201 (February 1956): 56–57.

Bernhard Fabian, "A Note on Marlowe's *Faustus*," *ES* 41 (December 1960): 365–68.

Frederic E. Faverty, *Your Literary Heritage* (Philadelphia: Lippincott, 1959), 64–66.

Maurice S. Friedman, *Problematic Rebel—An Image of Modern Man* (New York: Random House, 1963), 37–41.

Roland M. Frye, "Marlowe's *Doctor Faustus*: The Repudiation of Humanity," *SAQ* 55 (July 1956): 322–28.

Helen Gardener, "Milton's 'Satan' and the Theme of Damnation in Elizabethan Tragedy," *E&S* 1 (1948): 48–53.

Roma Gill, "'Such Conceits as Clownage Keeps in Pay': Comedy and *Dr. Faustus*," in Williams, *The Fool and the Trickster*, 55–63.

Godshalk, *The Marlovian World Picture*, 169–202.

Kenneth L. Golden, "Myth, Psychology, and Marlowe's *Doctor Faustus*," *CL* 12 (Fall 1985): 202–10.

Gomez, *The Alienated Figure in Drama*, 15–22.

Clarence Green, "*Dr. Faustus*: Tragedy of Individualism," *S&S* 10 (Summer 1946): 275–83.

W. W. Greg, "The Damnation of Faustus," *MLR* 41 (April 1946): 97–107. Reprinted in Leech, *Marlowe*, 92–107.

Anne Hargrove, "'Lucifer Prince of the East' and the Fall of Marlowe's Dr. Faustus," *NM* 84 (June 1983): 206–13.

Harrison, *Elizabethan Plays and Players*, 114–16.

Jeffrey P. Hart, "Prospero and Faustus," *BUSE* 2 (Winter 1956): 197–206.

Harry Hatfield, "Can One Sell One's Soul?" in McIver, *Great Moral Dilemmas*, 83–88.

Hawkins, *Likeness of Truth*, 2–3, 5–6.

Hawkins, *Poetic Freedom and Poetic Truth*, 91–97.

Sherman Hawkins, "The Education of Faustus," *SEL* 6 (Spring 1966): 193–209.

Robert B. Heilman, "A Critical Method for Poetic Drama," *Perspective* 1 (Winter 1948): 106–07.

Robert B. Heilman, "The Cult of Personality: Hell's Spells," *CE* 23 (November 1961): 97–98.

Erich Heller, "Faust's Damnation: The Morality of Knowledge," *ChiR* 15 (Summer–Autumn 1962): 1–10.

Sidney R. Homan, Jr., "*Doctor Faustus*, Dekker's *Old Fortunatus*, and the Morality Plays," *MLQ* 26 (December 1965): 497–505.

Raymond A. Houk, "*Doctor Faustus* and *A Shrew*," *PMLA* 62 (December 1947): 950–57.

Hoy, *The Hyacinth Room*, 226–30.

Hoy, "Ignorance in Knowledge: Marlowe's Faustus and Ford's Giovanni," *MP* 57 (February 1960): 145–54.

G. K. Hunter, "Five-Act Structure in *Doctor Faustus*," *TDR* 8 (Summer 1964): 77–91.

R. W. Ingram, " 'Pride in Learning goeth before a fall': Dr. Faustus' Opening Soliloquy," *Mosaic* 13 (Winter 1980): 73–80.

Hobart S. Jarret, "Verbal Ambiguities in Marlowe's *Dr. Faustus*," *CE* 25 (March 1964): 339–40.

Gregory K. Jember, "Shadows and Substance: Some Comments on Marlowe's *Doctor Faustus*," *USSE* 18 (March 1990): 1–13.

Francis R. Johnson, "Marlowe's Astronomy and Renaissance Skepticis," *ELH* 13 (December 1946): 241–54.

Francis R. Johnson, "Marlowe's 'Imperial Heaven,'" *ELH* 12 (March 1945): 35–44.

Hartford Jones, "*Dr. Faustus*," *The Use of English* 13 (Autumn 1961): 25–29.

David Kaula, "Time in *Everyman* and *Dr. Faustus*," *CE* 22 (October 1960): 9–14.

Nicolas Kiessling, "Doctor Faustus and the Sin of Demoniality," *SEL* 15 (Spring 1975): 205–11.

Leo Kirschbaum, "Marlowe's *Faustus*: A Reconsideration," *RES* 19 (March 1943): 225–41. Reprinted in O'Neill, *Critics on Marlowe*, 80–93.

Paul H. Kirschbaum, "Mephistopheles and the Lost 'Dragon,'" *RES* 18 (July 1942): 312–15.

Edgar C. Knowlton, " 'Indian Moors' and *Doctor Faustus*," *CahiersE* 23 (April 1983): 93–97.

Leah S. Marcus, "Textual Indeterminacy and Ideological Difference: The Case of *Doctor Faustus*," *RenD* 20 (1989): 1–29.

Masington, *Marlowe's Tragic Vision*, 124–25, 133–35, 155–56.

T. McAlindon, "Classical Mythology and Christian Tradition in Marlowe's *Doctor Faustus*," *PMLA* 81 (March 1966): 214–23.

T. McAlindon, "The Ironic Vision; Diction and Theme in Marlowe's *Doctor Faustus*," *RES* 32 (May 1981): 129–141

John C. McCloskey, "The Theme of Dispair in Marlowe's *Faustus*," *CE* 4 (November 1942): 110–13.

J. T. McCullen, "Dr. Faustus and Renaissance Learning," *MLR* 51 (January 1956): 6–16.

McDonnell, *The Aspiring Mind*, 123–28.

Mahood, *Poetry and Symbolism*, 64–74.

J. C. Maxwell, "Notes on *Dr. Faustus*," *N&Q* 209 (July 1964): 262.

J. C. Maxwell, "The Sins of Faustus," *Wind and Rain* 4 (March 1947): 49–52.

Arthur Mizener, "The Tragedy of Marlowe's *Dr. Faustus*," *CE* 5 (November 1943): 70–74.

Gerald Morgan, "Harlequin Faustus: Marlowe's Comedy of Hell," *HAB* 18, no. 1 (1967): 22–34.

Harry Morris, "Marlowe's Poetry," *TDR* 8 (Summer 1964): 149–54.

John Norton-Smith, "Marlowe's *Faustus* (I.iii,1–4)," *N&Q* 25 (October 1978): 436–37.

James M. Nosworthy, "Macbeth, Doctor Faustus, and the Juggling Fiends," in Gray, *Mirror up to Shakespeare*, 208–22.

Robert Ornstein, "The Comic Synthesis in *Doctor Faustus*," *ELH* 22 (September 1955): 165–72.

Robert Ornstein, "Marlowe and God: The Tragic Theology of *Dr. Faustus*," *PMLA* 83 (December 1968): 1378–85.

Witold Ostrowski, "The Interplay of the Subjective and the Objective in Marlowe's *Dr. Faustus*," in *Studies in Language and Literature in Honor of Margaret Schlauch*, ed. Mieczyslaw Brahmer, Stanislaw Helstynski, and Julian Krzyzanowski (Warsaw: Panstwowe Wydawnictwo Naukowe, 1966), 293–305.

D. J. Palmer, "Magic and Poetry in *Dr. Faustus*," *CritQ* 6 (Spring 1964): 56–67.

T. J. Parrott, and R. H. Bale, *A Short View of Elizabethan Drama*, 83–89.

Thomas Pettitt, "The Folk-Play in Marlowe's *Doctor Faustus*," *Folklore* 91, no. 1 (1980): 72–77.

Thomas Pettitt, "Formulaic Dramaturgy in *Doctor Faustus*," in Friedenreich, Gill, and Kuriyama, "*A poet and a filthy play-maker*," 167–191.

Martin Puhvel, "Marlowe's *Doctor Faustus*, V.i.," *Expl* 46 (Summer 1988): 3–5.

James A. Reynolds, "Faustus' Flawed Learning," *ES* 57 (October 1976): 329–36.

Irving Ribner, "Marlowe's 'Tragicke Glassé'," in Hosley, *Essays on Shakespeare and Elizabethan Drama*, 108–13.

Christopher Ricks, "*Doctor Faustus* and Hell on Earth," *EIC* 35 (April 1985): 101–20.

Wolfgang Riehle, "Marlowe's *Doctor Faustus* and Renaissance Italy: Some Observations and Suggestions," in *Medieval Studies Conference Aachen 1983: Language and Literature*, ed. Wolf-Dietrich Bald and Horst Weinstock (Frankfurt: Peter Lang, 1984), 185–95.

Rowse, *Christopher Marlowe*, 147–64.

Ariel Sachs, "The Religious Dispair of Doctor Faustus," *JEGP* 63 (October 1964): 625–47.

Scott, *Renaissance Drama*, 18–30.

Shapiro, *Rival Playwrights*, 64–67.

Ghanshiam Sharma, "Psychodrama in Marlowe's *Doctor Faustus*," *AJES* 12 (April 1987): 121–34.

Shaw, *Plays and Players*, 105–12.

Simpson, *Studies in Elizabethan Drama*, 95–111.

Susan Snyder, "Marlowe's *Doctor Faustus* as an Inverted Saint's Life," *SP* 63 (December 1966): 565–77.

Phoebe S. Spinrad, "The Dilettante's Lie in *Doctor Faustus*," *TSLL* 24 (Fall 1982): 243–54.

Lorraine Kochanske Stock, "Medieval Gula in Marlowe's *Doctor Faustus*," *BRH* 85 (Winter 1982): 372–85.

David F. Stover, "The Individualism of Doctor Faustus," *NDQ* 57 (Fall 1989): 146–61.

Philip J. Traci, "Marlowe's Faustus as Artist: A Suggestion about a Theme in the Play," *RenP* 1965 (1966): 3–9.

Traiser, *Heavenly Necromancers*, 89–107.

K. Tetzeli von Rosador, " 'Supernatural Soliciting': Temptation and Imagination in *Doctor Faustus* and *Macbeth*," in Honigmann, *Shakespeare and His Contemporaries*, 42–59.

Michael J. Warren, "*Doctor Faustus*: The Old Man the Text," *ELR* 11 (Spring 1981): 111–47.

Butler Waugh, "Deep and Surface Structure in Traditional and Sophisticated Literature: *Faust*," *SAB* 30 (August 1968): 14–17.

Joseph Westlund, "The Orthodox Christian Framework of Marlowe's *Faustus*," *SEL* 3 (Spring 1963):191–206.

Colin Wilcockson, " 'Come Away' or 'Fetch Them In'? A Note on Marlowe's *Doctor Faustus*," *N&Q* 38 (December 1991): 470–71.

G. W. Wolthius, "Marlowe's *Dr. Faustus* II, ii, 172," *ES* 30 (February 1949): 14–15.

Rowland Wymer, " 'When I Behold the Heavens': A Reading of *Doctor Faustus*," ES 67 (December 1986): 505–10.

David Young, "Where the Bee Sucks: A Triangular Study of *Doctor Faustus*, *The Alchemist*, and *The Tempest*," in Kay and Jacobs, *Shakespeare's Romances Reconsidered*, 149–66.

Edward II

Frank R. Ardolino, "Severed and Brazen Heads: Headhunting in Elizabethan Drama," *JEP* 4 (August 1983): 169–81.

Asibong, *Comic Sensibility*, 28–34, 66–71, 78–84.

Debra Belt, "Anti-Theatricalism and Rhetoric in Marlowe's *Edward II*," *ELR* 21 (Spring 1991): 134–60

Sunesen Bent, "Marlowe and the Dumb Show," *ES* 35 (December 1954): 241–53.

Bevington, *From "Mankind" to Marlowe*, 234–44.

David M. Bevington, and James Shapiro, " 'What are kings, when regiment is gone?' The Decay of Ceremony in *Edward II*," in Friedenreich, Gill, and Kuriyama, *"A poet and a filthy play-maker,"* 263–278.

Purvis E. Boyette, "Wanton Humor and Wanton Poets: Homosexuality in Marlowe's *Edward II*," *TSE* 22 Spring 1974): 33–50.

Brandt, *Christopher Marlowe*, 153–73.

Bredbeck, *Sodomy and Interpretation*, 56–77.

Leonora Leet Brodwin, *"Edward II*: Marlowe's Culminating Treatment of Love," *ELH* 31 (June 1964): 139–55.

Cartelli, *Marlowe, Shakespare*, 121–35.

Clemen, *English Tragedy Before Shakespeare*, 154–61. Reprinted in Leech, *Marlowe*, 138–43.

Cornelius, *Marlowe's Use of the Bible*, 92–96.

Arnold W. Cushner, "Some Observations on Marlowe's *Edward II*," in *Renaissance and Modern: Essays in Honor of Edwin M. Mosley*, ed. Murray J. Levith (Saratoga Springs, NY: Skidmore College, 1976), 11–20.

Cutts, *Left Hand of God*, 196–238.

Sara Munson Deats, "Marlowe's Fearful Symmetry in *Edward II*," in Friedenreich, Gill, and Kuriyama, "*A poet and a filthy play-maker*," 241–62.

Sara Munson Deats, "Myth and Metamorphosis in Marlowe's *Edward II*," *TSLL* 22 (Winter 1980): 304–21.

Elizabeth S. Donno, "'Admiration' and 'Commiseration' in Marlowe's *Edward II*," *NM* 79 (June 1978): 372–83.

Bette H. Duff, "Marlowe's *Edward II*, I,iv.41," *Expl* 39 (Spring 1980): 3–4

Edwards, *Threshold of a Nation*, 60–65.

Elam, *Semiotics of Theatre and Drama*, 159–63.

Robert Fricker, "The Dramatic Structure of *Edward II*," *ES* 34 (October 1953): 204–17.

Robert Fricker, *The Unacknowledged Legislators* (Bern: Francke, 1979), 9–24.

Stephen Guy-Bray, "Homophobia and the Depoliticizing of *Edward II*," *ESC* 17 (June 1991): 125–33.

S. F. Johnson, "Marlowe's *Edward II*," *Expl* 10 (June 1952): 53.

Kuriyama, *Hammer or Anvil*, 175–211.

Clifford Leech, "Marlowe's *Edward II*: Power and Suffering," *CritQ* 1 (Autumn 1959): 181–96. Reprinted in O'Neill, *Critics on Marlowe*, 69–79.

Mark J. Lidman, "Marlowe's *Edward II*: A Study in Kingship," *PMPA* 9 (1984): 111–124.

Masington, *Marlowe's Tragic Vision*, 86–99, 106–12.

Susan McCloskey, "The World's of *Edward II*," *RenD* 16 (1985): 35–48.

McDonnell, *The Aspiring Mind*, 128–39.

John F. McElroy, "Repetition, Contrariety, and Individualization in *Edward II*," *SEL* 24 (Spring 1984): 205–24.

Mahood, *Poetry and Symbolism*, 81–86.

Robert P. Merrix, and Carole Levin, "*Richard II* and *Edward II*: The Structure of Deposition," *ShY* 1 (1990): 1–13.

Marion Perret, "*Edward II*: Marlowe's Dramatic Technique," *REL* 7 (October 1966); 87–91.

Ribner, *The English History Play*, 127–36.

Ribner, "Marlowe's *Edward II* and the Tudor History Play," *ELH* 22 (December 1955): 243–53.

Ribner, "Marlowe's 'Tragicke Glassé,'" in Hosley, *Essays on Shakespeare and Elizabethan Drama*, 106–08.

Rowse, *Christopher Marlowe*, 128–41.

Shapiro, *Rival Playwrights*, 45–48, 91–95.

Smith, *Homosexual Desire in Shakespeare's England*, 209–23.

Steane, *Marlowe*, 204–35.

Claude J. Summers, "Sex, Politics, and Self-Realization in *Edward II*," in Friedenreich, Gill, and Kuriyama, "*A poet and a filthy play-maker*," 221–240.

Ben Taggie, "Marlowe and Shakespeare: *Edward II* and *Richard II*," *PMPA* 13 (1988): 16–21

Talbert, *Elizabethan Drama*, 95–110.

David H. Thurn, "Sovereignty, Disorder, and Fetishism in Marlowe's *Edward II*," *RenD* 21 (1990): 115–41.

Sharon Tyler, "Bedfellows Make Strange Politics: Christopher Marlowe's *Edward II*," in *Drama, Sex and Politics*, ed. James Redmond (Cambridge: Cambridge University Press, 1985), 55–68.

S. Viswanathan, "King Edward II's 'Two Bodies': A Perspective on Marlowe's Play," *LCrit* 16, no. 4 (1981): 76–93.

James Voss, "*Edward II*: Marlowe's Historical Tragedy," *ES* 63 (December 1982): 517–530.

Eugene M. Waith, "*Edward II*: the Shadow of Action," *TDR* 8 (Summer 1964): 59–76.

Michael J. Warren, "Welsh Hooks in *Edward II*," *N&Q* 25 (April 1978): 109–10.

R. A. Watson, "*Edward II*: A Study in Evil," *DUJ* 37 (December 1976): 162–67.

Wells, *Elizabethan and Jacobean Playwrights*, 98–103.

Wiggins, *Journeymen in Murder*, 58–62, 122–28.

F. P. Wilson, *Marlowe and Early Shakespeare*, 90–103. Reprinted in O'Neill, *Critics on Marlowe*, 62–68, and in Leech, *Marlowe*, 128–37.

David Hard Zucker, *Stage and Image in the Plays of Christopher Marlowe*, 114–42.

The Jew of Malta

Asibong, *Comic Sensibility*, 47–54, 128–29.

Howard S. Babb, "Policy in *The Jew of Malta*," *ELH* 24 (June 1957): 85–94.

Emily C. Bartels, "Malta, the Jew, and the Fictions of Difference: Colonialist Discourse in Marlowe's *The Jew of Malta*," *ELR* 20 (Winter 1990): 1–16.

N. W. Bawcutt, "Marlowe's *Jew of Malta* and Foxe's *Acts and Monuments*," *N&Q* 15 (October 1968): 250.

Don Beecher, "*The Jew of Malta* and the Ritual of Inverted Moral Order," *CahiersE* 12 (April 1972): 45–58.

Bevington, *From "Mankind" to Marlowe*, 218–33. Reprinted in Leech, *Marlowe*, 144–58. Reprinted in Bloom, *Christopher Marlowe*, 31–44.

Luc Borot, "Machiavellian Diplomacy and Dramatic Developments in Marlowe's *Jew of Malta*," *CahiersE* 28 (April 1988): 1–11.

Brandt, *Christopher Marlowe*, 129–33, 144–52.

Thomas Cartelli, "Endless Play: The False Starts of Marlowe's *Jew of Malta*," in Friedenreich, Gill, and Kuriyama, *"A poet and a filthy play-maker,"* 117–128.

Thomas Cartelli, *Rival Playwrights*, 162–80.

Clemen, *English Tragedy Before Shakespeare*, 104–09.

Cornelius, *Marlowe's Use of the Bible*, 19–21, 77–89.

Cutts, *Left Hand of God*, 149–69.

Sara M. Deats, "Biblical Parody in Marlowe's *The Jew of Malta*: A Re-Examination," *C&L* 37 (Winter 1988): 27–48.

Fisch, *The Dual Image*, 25–30.

Coburn Freer, "Lies and Lying in *The Jew of Malta*," in Friedenreich, Gill, and Kuriyama, *"A poet and a filthy play-maker,"* 143–165.

Alan Warren Friedman, "The Shackling of Accidents in Marlowe's *Jew of Malta*," *TSLL* 8 (Summer 1966): 155–167.

Godshalk, *The Marlovian World Picture*, 203–22.

Carol F. Heffernan, "*The Jew of Malta*: Barabas's 'Fine Madness,'" *DQR* 8 (1978): 94–107.

MARLOWE, CHRISTOPHER, *The Jew of Malta*

Margaret Hotine, "The Politics of Anti-Semitism: *The Jew of Malta* and *The Merchant of Venice*," *N&Q* 38 (March 1991): 35–38.

Bill G. Hulsopple, "Barabas and Shylock Against a Background of Jewish History in England," *Central States Speech Journal* 12 (Autumn 1960): 38–50.

Arthur Humphreys, "*The Jew of Malta* and *The Merchant of Venice*: Two Readings of Life," *HLQ* 50 (Summer 1987): 279–93.

Hunter, *Dramatic Ideas and Cultural Tradition*, 60–102.

Hunter, "The Theology of Marlowe's *The Jew of Malta*," *JWCI* 27 (1964): 211–40.

Leo Kirschbaum, "Some Light on *The Jew of Malta*," *MLQ* 7 (March 1946): 53–56.

Paul H. Kocher, "English Legal History in Marlowe's *Jew of Malta*," *HLQ* 26 (February 1963): 147–54.

Landa, *The Jew in Drama*, 59–69.

Levin, *The Overreacher*, 56–80. Reprinted in O'Neill, *Critics on Marlowe*, 50–61.

Jean-Marie Maguin, "*The Jew of Malta*: Marlowe's Ideological Stance and the Play-World's Ethos," *CahiersE* 27 (April 1985): 17–26.

Mahood, *Poetry and Symbolism*, 74–81.

J. C. Maxwell, "The Assignment of Speeches in *The Jew of Malta*," *MLR* 43 (October 1948): 510–12.

T. M. Pearce, "Marlowe's *The Jew of Malta*, IV [vi], 7–10," *Expl* 9 (April 1951): 40.

Charles E. Peavy, "*The Jew of Malta*—Antisemitic or Anti-Catholic?" *McNR* 11 (Winter 1959–1960): 57–60.

H, D. Purcell, "Whetstone's *Englysh Myrror* and Marlowe's *Jew of Malta*," *N&Q* 13 (July 1966): 288–290.

Edward L. Rocklin, "Marlowe as Experimental Dramatist: The Role of the Audience in The Jew of Malta," in Friedenreich, Gill, and Kuriyama, *"A poet and a filthy play-maker,"* 129–42.

Eric Rotlistein, "Structure as Meaning in *The Jew of Malta*," *JEGP* 65 (July 1966): 260–73.

Rowse, *Christopher Marlowe*, 81–99.

Shapiro, *Rival Playwrights*, 62–64, 104–10, 119–21.

Sharma, *Christopher Marlowe*, 71–98.

Talbert, *Elizabethan Drama and Shakespeare's Early Plays*, 79–87.

Jeremy Tambling, "Abigail's Party: 'The Difference of Things' in *The Jew of Malta*," in Kehler and Baker, *In Another Country*, 95–112.

Catherine Brown Tkacz, "*The Jew of Malta* and the Pit," *SoAR* 53 (May 1988): 47–57.

Weil, *Christopher Marlowe*, 22–49.

Zucker, *Stage and Image in the Plays of Christopher Marlowe*, 80–98.

The Massacre at Paris

Asibong, *Comic Sensibility*, 16–28.

Brandt, *Christopher Marlowe*, 133–43.

Julia Briggs, "Marlowe's *Massacre at Paris*: A Reconsideration," *RES* 34 (August 1983): 257–78.

Cornelius, *Marlowe's Use of the Bible*, 89–92.

Roy T. Eriksen, "Construction in Marlowe's *The Massacre at Paris*," in *Papers from the First Nordic Conference for English Studies*, Oslo, 17–19 September, 1980, ed. Stig Johansson and Bjorn Tysdahl (Oslo: University of Oslo, 1981), 41–54.

David Gallaway, "The Ramus Scene in Marlowe's *The Massacre at Paris*," *N&Q* 198 (April 1953): 146–47.

Godshalk, *The Marlovian World Picture*, 79–101.

Loftis, *Renaissance Drama in England and Spain*, 84–87, 219–20.

James A. Reynolds, *Repentence and Retribution in Early English Drama* (Salzburg: University of Salzburg, 1982), 53–82.

Irving Ribner, "Marlowe's 'Tragicke Glassé,'" in Hosley, *Essays on Shakespeare and Elizabethan Drama*, 101–06.

Rowse, *Christopher Marlowe*, 99–107.

Shapiro, *Rival Playwrights*, 123–25.

Steane, *Marlowe*, 236–46.

Talbert, *Elizabethan Drama and Shakespeare's Early Plays*, 87–90.

MARLOWE, CHRISTOPHER, *Tamburlaine the Great, Parts I & II*

Weil, *Christopher Marlowe*, 82–104.

Zucker, *Stage and Image in the Plays of Christopher Marlowe*, 99–113.

Tamburlaine the Great, Parts I & II

Altman, *The Tudor Play of Mind*, 338–52.

Asibong, *Comic Sensibility*, 13–16, 34–42, 94–102, 117–19, 140–48.

C. L. Barber, "The Death of Zenocrate: 'Conceiving and Subduing Both' in Marlowe's *Tamburlaine*," *L&P* 16, no. 1 (1966): 15–26.

Kimberly Benston," "Beauty's Just Applause: Dramatic Form and the Tamburlainian Sublime," in Bloom, *Christopher Marlowe*, 207–27.

Bevington, *From "Mankind" to Marlowe*, 199–217.

Johannes H. Birringer, "Marlowe's Violent Stage: 'Mirrors' of Honor in *Tamburlaine*," *ELH* 51 (Summer 1984): 219–39.

Guy Boas, "Tamburlaine and the Horrific," *English* 8 (Autumn 1951): 275–77.

Rick Bowers, "Marlowe's *Tamburlaine the Great*, Part One, IV.i. 47–63," *Expl* 48 (Fall 1989): 4–6.

Brandt, *Christopher Marlowe*, 50–116.

Bruce Edward Brandt, "Marlowe's *Il Tamburlaine*, V.i.86, 103," *Expl* 42 (Fall 1983): 9–10.

Charles Brooks, "*Tamburlaine* and Attitudes Toward Women," *ELH* 24 (March 1957): 1–11.

William J. Brown, "*Henry V* and *Tamburlaine*: The Structural and Thematic Relationship," *ISJR* 57 (November 1982): 113–22.

Mark Thornton Burnett, "*Tamburlaine* and the Body," *Criticism* 33 (Winter 1991): 31–47.

Mark Thornton Burnett, "Tamburlaine: An Elizabethan Vagabond," *SP* 84 (Summer 1987): 308–23.

Mark Thornton Burnett, "*Tamburlaine* and the Renaissance Concept of Honour," *SN* 59 (Summer 1987): 201–06.

Cartelli, *Marlowe, Shakespeare*, 67–93.

Chandhuri, *Infirm Glory*, 113–17.

Frances J. Chivers, "Marlowe's *Tamburlaine*: Ironic Portrait of Fortune's Fool," *SPWVSRA* 7 (Spring 1982): 22–27.

Clay, *The Role of Anxiety*, 89–106.

Clemen, *English Tragedy Before Shakespeare*, 113–43, 238–40, 247–49, 278–83.

Robert Cockroft, "Emblematic Irony: Some Possible Significances of Tamburlaine's Chariot," *RMS* 12 (1968): 33–55.

Cornelius, *Marlowe's Use of the Bible*, 63–77.

Cunningham, *Woe or Wonder*, 93–95.

Cutts, *Left Hand of God*, 29–107

John P. Cutts, "Tamburlaine 'as fierce *Achilles* was,'" *CompD* 1 (Summer 1967): 105–09.

D'Amico, *The Moor in English Renaissance Drama*, 45–49.

Antonio D'Andrea, "The Aspiring Mind: A Study of the *Machiavellian* Element in Marlowe's *Tamburlaine*," *YIS* (1972): 51–77.

Audrey Ekdahl Davidson, and Clifford Davidson, "The Function of Rhetoric, Marlowe's *Tamburlaine*, and 'Reciprocal Illumination,'" *BSUF* 22, no. 1 (1981): 20–29.

G. I. Duthie, "The Dramatic Structure of Marlowe's *Tamburlaine the Great, Parts I and II*," *E&S* 1 (1948): 101–26.

Edwards, *Threshold of a Nation*, 56–60.

B. P. Fisher, "'Phyteus' in Marlowe's *Tamburlaine*," *N&Q* 22 (July 1975): 247–48.

B. P. Fisher, "Pylades and Orestes in Marlowe's *Tamburlaine*," *N&Q* 34 (June 1987): 190–91.

Helen S. Gardner, "The Second Part of *Tamburlaine the Great*," *MLR* 37 (January 1942): 18–24. Reprinted in O'Neill, *Critics on Marlowe*, 37–43.

Ian Gaskell, "*2 Tamburlaine*: Marlowe's 'War against the Gods,'" *ESC* 11 (June 1985): 178–92.

Harrison, *Elizabethan Plays and Players*, 71–73.

Hawkins, *Poetic Freedom and Poetic Truth*, 90–91.

A. D. Hope, *The Cave and the Spring: Essays on Poetry* (Chicago: University of Chicago Press, 1970), 27–44. Reprinted in Bloom, *Christopher Marlowe*, 45–54.

MARLOWE, CHRISTOPHER, *Tamburlaine the Great, Parts I & II*

Francis R. Johnson, Marlowe's 'Imperial Heaven,'" *ELH* 12 (March 1945): 35–44.

Jones, *Othello's Countrymen*, 38–40.

Paul H. Kocher, "Marlowe's Art of War," *SP* 39 (April 1942): 207–25.

Knight, *Golden Labyrinth*, 54–56.

Clifford Leech, "The Structure of *Tamburlaine*," *TDR* 8 (Summer 1964): 32–46.

Jill L. Levenson, " 'Working words': The Verbal Dynamic of *Tamburlaine*," in Friedenreich, Gill, and Kuriyama, *"A poet and a filthy play-maker*," 99–115.

Katherine Lever, "The Image of Man in *Tamburlaine I*," *PQ* 35 (October 1956): 421–26.

Levin, *The Overreacher*, 29–54.

Richard Levin, "The Contemporary Perception of Marlowe's *Tamburlaine*," *MRDE* 1 (Spring 1984): 51–70.

J. Y.Lin, "The Interpretation of Three Lines in Marlowe's *Tamburlaine Part I*," *N&Q* 195 (April 1950): 137–38.

Thomas McAlindon, "*Tamburlaine the Great* and *The Spanish Tragedy*: The Genesis of a Tradition," *HLQ* 45 (Winter 1982): 59–81.

McDonnell, *The Aspiring Mind*, 98–122.

Mahood, *Poetry and Symbolism*, 54–64.

Richard A. Martin, "Marlowe's *Tamburlaine* and the Language of Romance," *PMLA* 93 (March 1978): 248–64.

J. C. Maxwell, "*Tamburlaine, Part I*, IV, iv, 77-79," *N&Q* 197 (October 1952): 444.

Stephen X. Mead, "Marlowe's *Tamburlaine* and the Idea of Empire," *W&D* 7 (Fall 1989): 91–103.

W. M. Merchant, "Marlowe and Machiavelli," *CLS* 13 (January 1944): 1–7.

Robert S. Miola, "Marlowe's *Tamburlaine the Great*," *Expl* 37 (Summer 1979): 21–22

Johnstone Parr, "The Horoscope of Mycetes in Marlowe's *Tamburlaine I*," *PQ* 25 (October 1946): 371–77.

Johnstone Parr, "Tamburlaine's Malady," *PMLA* 59 (September 1944): 696–714.

T. M. Pearce, "Tamburlaine's 'Discipline to Three Sonnes': An Interpretation of *Tamburlaine, Part II*," *MLQ* 15 (March 1954): 18–27.

Donald Peet, "The Rhetoric of *Tamburlaine*," *ELH* 26 (June 1959): 137–55.

Prior, *The Language of Tragedy*, 33–46.

Matthew N. Proser, "*Tamburlaine* and the Art of Destruction," *HSL* 20, no. 1 (1988): 37–51.

Michael Quinn, "The Freedom of Tamburlaine," *MLQ* 21 (June 1960): 315–20.

Ribner, *The English History Play*, 63–67, 89–91, 129–36.

Ribner, "The Idea of History in Marlowe's *Tamburlaine*," *ELH* 20 (December 1953): 251–66.

Ribner, "*Tamburlaine* and *The Wars of Cyprus*," *JEGP* 53 (October 1954): 569–73.

Susan Richards, "Marlowe's *Tamburlaine II*: A Drama of Death," *MLQ* 26 (September 1965): 375–87.

Mary Ellen Rickey, "Astronomical Imagery in *Tamburlaine*," *RenP* 1953 (1954): 63–70.

Rowse, *Christopher Marlowe*, 50–80.

Samuel Schuman, "Minor Characters and the Thematic Structure of Marlowe's *Tamburlaine II*," *MLS* 8 (Spring 1978): 27–33.

Sewell, *The Vision of Tragedy* (New Haven: Yale University Press, 1959), 69–70.

Shapiro, *Rival Playwrights*, 28–37, 86–91, 95–97, 99–101.

Talbert, *Elizabethan Drama and Shakespeare's Early Plays*, 110–21.

Robert T. Taylor, "Maximinus and Tamburlaine," *N&Q* 202 (October 1957): 417–18.

Leonnard Tennhouse, "Balaam and the Soul and the World of *II Tamburlaine*," *NM* 78 (March 1977): 115–17.

J. Oliver Thomson, "Marlowe's 'River Araris,'" *MLR* 48 (July 1953): 323–24.

David H. Thurn, "Sights of Power in *Tamburlaine*," *ELR* 19 (Winter 1989): 3–21.

John W. Velz, "Episodic Structure in Four Tudor Plays: A Virtue of Necessity," *CompD* 6 (Summer 1972): 87–102.

Waith, *The Herculean Hero*, 60–87. Reprinted in Leech, *Marlowe*, 69–91.

Mary M. Wehling, "Marlowe's Mnemonic Nominology with Special Reference to *Tamburlaine*," *MLN* 73 (April 1958): 243–47.

MARSTON, JOHN, *Antonio and Mellida*

Wells, *Elizabethan and Jacobean Playwrights*, 80–83.

Zucker, *Stage and Image in the Plays of Christopher Marlowe*, 20–54.

MARSTON, JOHN

Antonio and Mellida

Ellen Berland, "The Function of Irony in Marston's *Antonio and Mellida*," *SP* 66 (Winter 1969): 739–55.

Allen Bergson, "Dramatic Style as Parody in Marston's *Antonio and Mellida*," *SEL* 11 (Spring 1971): 307–25.

Colley, *John Marston's Theatrical Drama*, 55–80.

Marie Cornelia, "Dramatic Style and Dramatic Language in Marston's *Antonio and Mellida*," *ArielE* 9 (October 1978): 21–29.

R. A. Foakes, "John Marston's Fantastical Plays: *Antonio and Mellida* and *Antonio's Revenge*," *PQ* 41 (January 1962): 229–39.

Geckle, *John Marston's Drama*, 61–80.

Harrison, *Elizabethan Plays and Players*, 208–13.

Donald K. Hedrick, Marston's *Antonio & Mellida* V.i.54 (Rope Verse)," *Expl* 35 (Winter 1977): 15–16.

Michael Higgins, "The Convention of the Stoic Hero as Handled by Marston," *MLR* 39 (October 1944): 339–46.

G. K. Hunter, "English Folly and Italian Vice: The Moral Landscape of John Marston," *Stratford-Upon-Avon Studies* 1 (1960): 81–102.

Cynthia Lewis, "'Wise Men, Folly-Fall'n': Characters Named Antonio in *English Renaissance Drama*," *RenD* 20 (1989): 197–236.

Mann, *The Elizabethan Player*, 113–15.

Nicoll, *English Drama*, 4–11.

Ronald J. Palumbo, "Emblematic Characters in Marston's *Antonio* Plays," *N&Q* 18 (March 1971): 35–37.

Samuel Schoenbaum, "The Precious Balance of John Marston," *PMLA* 67 (December 1952): 1069–78.

Rolf Soellner, "The Madness of Hercules and the Elizabethans," *CL* 10 (Fall 1958): 319–20.

Stilling, *Love and Death in Renaissance Tragedy*, 82–89.

Adrian Weiss, "A Pill to Purge Parody: Marston's Manipulation of the Paul's Environment in the *Antonio* Plays," in Redmond, *The Theatrical Space*, 81–97.

Wells, *Elizabethan and Jacobean Playwrights*, 26–29.

T. F. Wharton, "Old Marston or New Marston: The *Antonio* Plays," *EIC* 25 (October 1975): 357–69.

Antonio's Revenge

Altman, *The Tudor Play of Mind*, 292–302.

Philip J. Ayers, "Marston's *Antonio's Revenge*: The Morality of the Revenging Hero," *SEL* 12 (Spring 1972): 359–74.

Barbara J. Baines, "*Antonio's Revenge*: Marston's Play on Revenge Plays," *SEL* 23 (Spring 1983): 277–94.

Colley, *John Marston's Theatrical Drama*, 80–90.

Gustav Cross, "The Retrograde Genius of John Marston," *REL* 2 (October 1961): 21–27.

Finkelpearl, *John Marston of the Middle Temple*, 150–61.

R. A. Foakes, "John Marston's Fantastical Plays: *Antonio and Mellida* and *Antonio's Revenge*," *PQ* 41 (January 1962): 229–39.

Geckle, *John Marston's Drama*, 81–92.

Charles A. Hallett, and Elaine S. Hallett, "*Antonio's Revenge* and the Integrity of the Revenge Tragedy Motifs," *SP* 76 (Summer 1979): 366–86.

Hallett, and Hallett, *The Revenger's Madness*, 161–80.

Harrison, *Elizabethan Plays and Players*, 214–21.

Clifford Leech, *Shakespeare's Tragedies and Other Studies*, 29–31.

Cynthia Lewis, "'Wise Men, Folly-Fall'n': Characters Named Antonio in English Renaissance Drama," *RenD* 20 (1989): 197–236.

Nicoll, *English Drama*, 8–10.

Ornstein, *Moral Vision of Jacobean Tragedy*, 155–58.

Ronald J. Palumbo, "Emblematic Characters in Marston's *Antonio* Plays," *N&Q* 18 (March 1971): 35–37.

Karen Robertson, "*Antonio's Revenge*: The Tyrant, the Stoic, and the Passionate Man," *MRDE* 4 (Spring 1989): 91–106.

Samuel Schoenbaum,"The Precious Balance of John Marston," *PMLA* 67 (December 1952): 1069–78.

Scott, *John Marston's Plays*, 5–25.

Simpson, *Studies in Elizabethan Drama*, 154–58.

Stilling, *Love and Death in Renaissance Tragedy*, 89–96.

Adrian Weiss, "A Pill to Purge Parody: Marston's Manipulation of the Paul's Environment in the *Antonio* Plays," in Redmond, *The Theatrical Space*, 81–97.

T. F. Wharton, "Old Marston or New Marston: The *Antonio* Plays," *EIC* 25 (October 1975): 357–69.

The Dutch Courtesan

Susan Baker, "Sex and Marriage in *The Dutch Courtezan*," in Kehler and Baker, *In Another Country*, 218–32.

Bliss, *The World's Perspective*, 22–28, 37–41.

Gustav Cross, "Marston, Montaigne, and Morality: *The Dutch Courtesan* Reconsidered," *ELH* 27 (March 1960): 30–43.

Gustav Cross, "The Retrograde Genius of John Marston," *REL* 2 (October 1961): 21–27.

Finkelpearl, *John Marston of the Middle Temple*, 195–219.

Geckle, *John Marston's Drama*, 148–76.

Donna B. Hamilton, "Language and Theme in *The Dutch Courtesan*," *RenD* 5 (1972): 75–87.

Haselkorn, *Prostitution in Elizabethan and Jacobean Drama*, 56–65.

Richard Horwich, "Wives, Courtesans, and the Economics of Love in Jacobean City Comedy," in Davidson, Gianakaris, and Stroupe, *Drama in the Renaissance*, 255–73.

Hoy, *The Hyacinth Room*, 192–98.

Jensen, *John Marston, Dramatist*, 87–103.

Coppelia Kahn, "Whores and Wives in Jacobean Drama," in Kehler and Baker, *In Another Country*, 246–60.

Harry Keyishian, "Dekker's Whore and Marston's *Courtesan*," *ELN* 4 (January 1967): 261–66.

Lacy, *The Jacobean Problem Play*, 84–104.

Leinwand, *The City Staged*, 61–63, 110–13, 178–80, 187–90.

John J. O'Connor, "The Chief Source of Marston's *The Dutch Courtesan*," *SP* 54 (October 1957): 509–15.

Ornstein, *Moral Vision*, 159–63.

Carol W. Pollard, "Immoral Morality: Combinations of Morality Types in *All's Well That Ends Well* and *The Dutch Courtesan*," *CahiersE* 25 (April 1984): 53–59.

Robert K. Presson, "Marston's *The Dutch Courtezan*: The Study of an Attitude in Adaptation," *JEGP* 55 (July 1956): 406–13.

Alexander H. Sackton, "The Paradoxical Encomium in Elizabethan Drama," *Studies in English* 28 (March 1949): 91–92.

Samuel Schoenbaum,"The Precious Balance of John Marston," *PMLA* 67 (December 1952): 1069–78.

Eastward Ho
(with Chapman and Jonson)

Bradbrook, *Growth and Structure of Elizabethan Comedy*, 149–51.

Ralph A. Cohen, "The Function of Setting in *Eastward Ho*," *RenP* 1972 (1973): 83–86.

Richard Horwich, "*Hamlet* and *Eastward Ho!*," *SEL* (Spring 1971): 223–33.

Histriomastix

James P. Bednarz, "Representing Jonson: *Histriomastix* and the Origin of the Poets' War," *HLQ* 54 (Winter 1991): 1–30.

Geckle, *John Marston's Drama*, 34–50.

Alvin Kernan, "John Marston's Play *Histriomastix*," *MLQ* 19 (June 1958): 134–40.

Mann, *The Elizabethan Player*, 148–77.

MARSTON, JOHN, *Jack Drum's Entertainment*

Jack Drum's Entertainment; or, The Comedy of Pasquill and Katherine

Michael C. Andrews, "*Jack Drum's Entertainment* as Burlesque," *RenQ* 24 (1971): 226–31.

Colley, *John Marston's Theatrical Drama*, 94–96.

Geckle, *John Marston's Drama*, 51–60.

Jensen, *John Marston, Dramatist*, 18–31.

A Knack to Know a Knave

Mary Adkins, "The Genius of Dramatic Satire Against the Puritan as Illustrated in *A Knack to Know a Knave*," *RES* 22 (April 1946): 81–95.

Paul E. Bennett, "The Word 'Goths' in *A Knack to Know a Knave*," *N&Q* 20 (November 1955): 462–63.

David J. Houser, "Purging the Commonwealth: Marston's Disguised Dukes and *A Knack to Know a Knave*," *PMLA* 89 (May 1974): 993–1066.

The Malcontent

William Babula, "The Avenger and the Satirist: John Marston's Malvole," in *The Elizabethan Theatre VI*, ed. G. R. Hibbard (Hamden, CT: Shoe String Press, 1977), 48–58.

Robert Beale Bennett, "The Royal Ruse: Malcontentedness in John Marston's *The Malcontent*," *MRDE* 1 (Spring 1984): 71–84.

G. W. S. Brodsky, "Fortune's Bawd: Symbolism of the Maquarelle Episode in *The Malcontent*," *SCN* 41 (Spring–Summer 1983): 9–11.

Larry S. Champion, "*The Malcontent* and the Shape of Elizabethan-Jacobean Comedy," *SEL* 25 (Spring 1985): 361–79.

Ira Clark, "Character and Cosmos in Marston's *Malcontent*," *MLS* 13 (Spring 1983): 80–96.

Curry, *Deception in Elizabethan Drama*, 115–18.

Eliot, *Essays on Elizabethan Drama*, 186–89.

Finkelpearl, *John Marston of the Middle Temple*, 178–94.

Geckle, *John Marston's Drama*, 108–24.

Christine Gomez, "The Malcontent Outsider in British Drama—Jacobean and Modern," *AJES* 12 (April 1987): 53–74.

David J. Greenman, "Atmosphere, Contrast, and Control in Marston's *The Malcontent*," *SJW* 101 (Spring 1975): 134–44.

Hawkins, *Likeness of Truth in Elizabethan and Restoration Drama*, 52–54, 56–57, 75–77.

Donald K. Hedrick, "The Masquing Principle in Marston's *The Malcontent*," *ELR* 8 (Spring 1978): 24–42.

G. K. Hunter, "English Folly and Italian Vice: The Moral Landscape of John Marston," *Stratford-Upon-Avon Studies* 1 (1960): 81–102.

Jensen, *John Marston, Dramatist*, 65–86.

D. J. Lake, "Webster's Additions to *The Malcontent*: Linguistic Evidence," *N&Q* 28 (April 1981): 153–58.

Mann, *The Elizabethan Player*, 116–17.

Brownell Salomon, "The 'Doubleness' of *The Malcontent* and Fairy-Tale Form," *Connotations* 1 (July 1991): 150–63.

Brownell Salomon, "The Theological Basis of Imagery and Structure in *The Malcontent*," *SEL* 14 (Spring 1974): 271–84.

Samuel Schoenbaum,"The Precious Balance of John Marston," *PMLA* 67 (December 1952): 1069–78.

T. F. Wharton, "*The Malcontent* and 'Dreams, Visions, Fantasies,'" *EIC* 24 (Summer 1974): 261–74.

Parasitaster; or, The Fawn

Curry, *Deception in Elizabethan Drama*, 78–81.

Finkelpearl, *John Marston of the Middle Temple*, 220–37.

Finkelpearl, "The Use of the Middle Temple's Christmas Revels in *The Fawn*," *SP* 64 (July 1967): 199–209.

Geckel, *John Marston's Drama*, 125–47.

Joel Kaplan, "John Marston's *The Fawn*: A Saturnalian Satire," *SEL* 9 (Spring 1969): 335–50.

MARSTON, JOHN, *What You Will*

Lacy, *The Jacobean Problem Play*, 104–14.

Scott, *John Marston's Plays*, 72–77.

What You Will

Colley, *John Marston's Theatrical Drama*, 104–16.

Finkelpearl, *John Marston of the Middle Temple*, 162–77.

Geckle, *John Marston's Drama*, 93–107.

Harrison, *Elizabethan Plays and Players*, 241–44, 259–61.

Jensen, *John Marston, Dramatist*, 18–36.

The Wonder of Women; or, The Tragedy of Sophonisba

Gustav Cross, "The Retrograde Genius of John Marston," *REL* 2 (October 1961): 21–27.

Eliot, *Essays in Elizabethan Drama*, 191–94.

Finkelpearl, *John Marston of the Middle Temple*, 238–53.

Geckle, *John Marston's Drama*, 177–201.

Jensen, *John Marston, Dramatist*, 104–22.

Jones, *Othello's Countrymen*, 72–78.

Ribner, *Jacobean Tragedy*, 13–14.

Gareth Roberts, "The 'Beasts of Death' in Marston's *Sophonisba*," *N&Q* 22 (June 1975): 248.

Tokson, *The Popular Image of the Blackman in English Drama*, 84–85.

Peter Ure, "John Marston's *Sophonisba*: A Reconsideration," *DUJ* 10 (December 1949): 81–90. Reprinted in Maxwell, *Elizabethan and Jacobean Drama*, 75–92.

MASON, JOHN

The Turke

Frank W. Wadsworth, "The Relation of *Lust's Dominion* and John Mason's *The Turke*," *ELH* 20 (September 1953): 194–99.

Gordon Williams, Image Patterns in Mason's *The Turke*," *Trivium* 9 (1974): 54–69.

MASSINGER, PHILIP

The Bashful Lover

Butler, *Theatre and Crisis*, 49–54.

Believe As You List

David Bradley, "The Ignorant Elizabethan Author and Massinger's *Believe as You List*," *SSEng* 2 (1976–1977): 98–125.

Edwards, *Threshold of a Nation*, 180–82.

Martin Garrett, "*A Diamond, Though Set in Horn,*" 217–24.

Roma Gill, "'Necessitie of State': Massinger's *Believe as You List*," *ES* 46 (January 1965): 407–16.

A. P. Hogan, "Massinger as a Tragedian: *Believe as You List*," *TSLL* 13 (Winter 1971): 407–19.

Douglas Howard, "Massinger's Political Tragedies," in Howard, *Philip Massinger*, 117–37.

Loftis, *Renaissance Drama in England and Spain*, 145–46, 171–73.

Wells, *Elizabethan and Jacobean Playwrights*, 106–10.

The Bondsman: An Ancient Story

Loftis, *Renaissance Drama in England and Spain*, 168–69.

The City Madam

Michael D. Bliss, "Massinger's *City Madam* and the Lost *City Honest Man*," *ELR* 7 (Autumn 1977): 368–81.

Martin Butler, "Massinger's *The City Madam* and the Caroline Audience," *RenD* 13 (1982): 157–87.

Robert A. Fothergill, "The Dramatic Experience of Massinger's *The City Madam* and *A New Way to Pay Old Debts*," *UTQ* 43 (January 1974): 68–86.

Alan Gerald Gross, "Social Change and Philip Massinger," *SEL* 7 (Spring 1967): 329–42.

Knights, *Drama and Society in the Age of Jonson*, 280–92.

John O. Lyons, "Massinger's Imagery," *RenP* 1954 (1955): 47–54.

Michael Neill, " 'The Tongues of Angels': Charity and the Social Order in *The City Madam*," in Howard, *Philip Massinger* 193–220.

Paul Werstein, "Massinger's *The City Madam* III.i.46-51," *Expl* 38 (Winter 1980): 18–20.

The Custom of the Country
(with Fletcher)

W. D. Howarth, "Cervantes and Fletcher: A Theme with Variations," *MLR* 56 (October 1961): 564–66.

Carolyn Prager, "The Problem of Slavery in *The Custom of the Country*," *SEL* 28 (Spring 1988): 301–17.

Sherbo, *English Sentimental Drama*, 22–24.

The Double Marriage
(with Fletcher)

Wells, *Elizabethan and Jacobean Playwrights*, 141-43.

The Duke of Milan

Don Beecher, "The Courtier as Trickster in Massinger's *The Duke of Milan*," *CahiersE* 23 (April 1983): 73–82.

Ronald Heubert, "'An Artificial Way to Grieve': The Forsaken Woman in Beaumont and Fletcher, Massinger and Ford," *ELH* 44 (December 1977): 601–21.

John O. Lyons, "Massinger's Imagery," *RenP* 1954 (1955): 47–54.

S. Gorley Putt, "The Complacency of Philip Massinger, Gent," *English* 30 (Summer 1981): 99–114.

Wells, *Elizabethan and Jacobean Playwrights*, 65–67.

The Emperor of the East

Garrett, "*A Diamond, Though Set in Horn*," 111–21.

The Fatal Dowery
(with Field)

Swapan Chakravorty, "Court, City and Country: Social and Political Themes in Philip Massinger," *JDECU* 18, no. 1 (1982): 59–86.

William M. Clements, and Frances M. Malpezzi, "Rationalization of Folklore in *The Fatal Dowry*," *SCB* 41 (Winter 1981): 97–98.

The Great Duke of Florence

Garrett, "*A Diamond, Though Set in Horn*," 102–10.

John O. Lyons, "Massinger's Imagery," *RenP* 1954 (1955): 47–54.

Wells, *Elizabethan and Jacobean Playwrights*, 178–82.

The Guardian

Butler, *Theatre and Crisis*, 254–58.

The Knight of Malta
(with Field and Fletcher)

Jones, *Othello's Countrymen*, 80–82.

Wells, *Elizabethan and Jacobean Playwrights*, 150–52.

The Little French Lawyer
(with Fletcher)

N. J. Rigaud, "Mental Cruelty in Fletcher's *The Little French Lawyer*," *CahiersE* 22 (October 1982): 35–39.

Love's Cure; or, The Martial Maid
(with Fletcher)

Jonathan Dollimore, "Subjectivity, Sexuality, and Transgression: The Jacobean Connection," *RenD* 17 (1986): 53–81.

The Maid of Honour

Swapan Chakravorty, "Court, City and Country: Social and Political Themes in Philip Massinger," *JDECU* 18, no. 1 (1982): 59–86.

MASSINGER, PHILIP, *A New Way to Pay Old Debts*

Loftis, *Renaissance Drama in England and Spain*, 145–49.

Russ McDonald, "High Seriousness and Popular Form: The Case of *The Maid of Honour*," in Howard, *Philip Massinger*, 83–116.

Peter F. Mullany, "Religion in Massinger's *The Maid of Honour*," *RenD* 2 (1969): 143–56.

A New Way to Pay Old Debts

R. H. Bowers, "A Note on Massinger's *New Way*," *MLR* 53 (April 1958): 214–15.

Frederick M. Burelbach, "*A New Way to Pay Old Debts*: Jacobean Morality," *CLAJ* 12 (December 1969): 205–13.

D. J. Enright, "Poetic Satire and Satire in Verse: A Consideration of Jonson and Massinger," *Scrutiny* 18 (Winter 1952): 219–23.

C. A. Gibson, "*A New Way to Pay Old Debts* V.i. 321–3: A Proposed Emendation," *N&Q* 29 (December 1982): 490–91.

Knights, *Drama and Society in the Age of Jonson*, 273–80.

Nancy S. Leonard, "Overreach at Bay: Massinger's *A New Way to Pay Old Debts*," in Howard, *Philip Massinger*, 171–92.

John O. Lyons, "Massinger's Imagery," *RenP* 1954 (1955): 47–54.

Michael Neill, "Massinger's Patriarchy: The Social Vision of *A New Way to Pay Old Debts*," *RenD* 10 (1979): 185–213.

Patricia Thompson, "The Old Way and the New Way in Dekker and Massinger," *MLR* 51 (April 1956): 168–78.

Albert H. Tricomi, "*A New Way To Pay Old Debts* and the Country-House Poetic Tradition," *MRDE* 3 (Summer 1986): 177–87.

The Renegado

D'Amico, *The Moor in English Renaissance Drama*, 119–32.

Garrett, "*A Diamond, Though Set in Horn*," 90–102.

Loftis, *Renaissance Drama in England and Spain*, 170–71, 256–57.

Peter F. Mullany, "Massinger's *The Renegado*: Religion in Stuart Tragicomedy," *Genre* 5 (Spring 1972): 138–52.

The Roman Actor

Martin Butler, "Romans in Britain: *The Roman Actor* and the Early Stuart Classical Play," in Howard, *Philip Massinger*, 139–70.

John H. Crabtree, Jr., "Philip Massinger's Use of Rhetoric in *The Roman Actor*," *FurmS* 7 (May 1960): 40–58.

Peter H. Davidson, "The Theme and Structure of *The Roman Actor*," *AUMLA* 39 (May 1963): 39–56.

A. P. Hogan, "Imagery of Acting in *The Roman Actor*," *MLR* 66 (July 1971): 273–81.

Douglas Howard, "Massinger's Political Tragedies," in Howard, *Philip Massinger*, 117–37.

Mann, *The Elizabethan Player*, 193–97, 202–06, 221–23.

Patricia Thomson, "World Stage and Stage in Massinger's *Roman Actor*," *Neophil* 54 (January 1970): 409–26.

Rod Wilson, "Massinger's *The Roman Actor*," *Expl* 40 (Summer 1982): 16–17.

Thierry, King of France, and His Brother Theodoret
(with Fletcher)

Wells, *Elizabethan and Jacobean Playwrights*, 139–41.

The Unnatural Combat

M. Garrett, "Massinger's Belgarde," *N&Q* 30 (April 1983): 154–56.

Colin Gibson, "Massinger's Theatrical Language," in Howard, *Philip Massinger*, 9–38.

A Very Woman; or, The Prince of Tarent
(with Fletcher)

Roma Gill, "Collaboration and Revision in Massinger's *A Very Woman*," *RES* 18 (1967): 136–48.

MASSINGER, PHILIP, *The Virgin Martyr*

The Virgin Martyr
(with Dekker)

Larry S. Champion, "'Disaster with my so many joys': Structure and Perspective in Massinger and Dekker's *The Virgin Martyr*," *MRDE* 1 (Summer 1984): 199–209.

Larry S. Champion, *Thomas Dekker and the Traditions of English Drama*, 105–15.

Peter F. Mullany, "Religion in Massinger and Dekker's *The Virgin Martyr*," *Komos* 2, no. 1 (1970): 89–97.

MAY, THOMAS

Cleopatra Queen of Egypt

J. Wilkes Barry, "Thomas May's *The Tragedy of Cleopatra*," *Discourse* 11, no. 1 (1968): 67–75.

MEDWALL, HENRY

Fulgens and Lucres

John S. Colley, "*Fulgens and Lucres*: Politics and Aesthetics," *ZAA* 15 (1975): 322–30.

Merle Fifield, "Medwell's [sic] Play and No-Play," *SMC* 6 (1974): 531–36.

Robert C. Jones, "The Stage World and the 'Real' World in Medwall's *Fulgens and Lucres*," *MLQ* 32 (June 1971): 131–42.

Peter Meredith, and Meg Twycross, " 'Farte Pryke in Cule' and Cock-Fighting," *METh* 6 (July 1984): 30–39.

Robert P. Merrix, "The Function of the Comic Plot in *Fulgens and Lucrece*," *MLS* 7 (Spring 1977): 16–26.

Interlude of Nature

Charles W. Crupi, "Christian Doctrine in Henry Medwall's *Nature*," *Renascence* 34 (Winter 1982): 100–12.

Merle Fifield, "Medwell's [sic] Play and No-Play," *SMC* 6 (1974): 531–36.

MERBURY, FRANCIS

The Marriage of Wit and Wisdom

Hanna Scolnicov, "To Understand a Parable: The Mimetic Mode of *The Marriage of Wit and Wisdom*," *CahiersE* 29 (April 1986): 1–11.

MIDDLETON, THOMAS

Blurt, Master Constable

Yashdip Singh Bains, "Thomas Middleton's *Blurt, Master Constable* as a Burlesque of Love," in *Essays Presented to Amy G. Stock*, ed. R. K. Kaul (Jaipur: Rajastan University Press, 1965), 41–57.

David M. Holmes, "Thomas Middleton's *Blurt Master Constable*, or *The Spaniard's Night Walk*," *MLR* 64 (December 1969): 1–10.

Rhodes, *Elizabethan Grotesque*, 82–85.

The Changeling
(with Rowley)

Michael C. Andrews, " 'Sweetness' in *The Changeling*," *YES* 1 (1971): 63–67.

Thomas L.Berger, "The Petrarchan Fortress of *The Changeling*," *RenP 1968* (1969): 37–46.

Normand Berlin, "The 'Finger' Image and Relationship of Character in *The Changeling*," *ESA* 12 (June 1969): 162–66.

Lois E. Bueler, "The Rhetoric of Change in *The Changeling*," *ELR* 14 (Spring 1984): 95–113.

Frederick M. Burelbach, Jr., "Middleton and Rowley's *The Changeling*, I.i.52–56," *Expl* 26 (July 1968): 60.

Clay, *The Role of Anxiety*, 220–34.

Dennis, *Dramatic Essays*, 133–40.

Penelope B. R. Doob, "A Reading of *The Changeling*," *ELR* 3 (Summer 1973): 183–206.

Joseph M. Duffy, "Madhouse Optics: *The Changeling*," *CompD* 8 (Summer 1974): 184–98.

MIDDLETON, THOMAS, *The Changeling*

Eliot, *Essays on Elizabethan Drama*, 89–95.

E. Engleberg, "Tragic Blindness in *The Changeling* and *Women Beware Women*," *MLQ* 23 (March 1962): 20–28.

Hawkins, *Poetic Freedom and Poetic Truth*, 2–3, 100–01.

Catherine A. Hébert, "A Note on the Significance of the Title of Middleton's *The Changeling*," *CLAJ* 12 (September 1968): 66–69.

Tinsley Helton, "Middleton and Rowley's *The Changeling*, V,iii,175–77," *Expl* 21 (May 1963): 74.

Karl L. Holzknecht, "The Dramatic Structure of *The Changeling*," *RenP 1953* (1954): 77–87.

Henry E. Jacobs, "The Constancy of Change: Character and Perspective in *The Changeling*," *TSLL* 16 (Winter 1975): 651–74.

Paula Johnson, "Dissimulation Anatomized: *The Changeling*," *PQ* 56 (Summer 1977): 329–38.

Robert Jordan, "Myth and Psychology in *The Changeling*," *RenD* 3 (1970): 157–66.

Dorothea Kehler, "Middleton and Rowley's *The Changeling*, V.iii.175–77," *Expl* 26 (December 1968): Item 44.

Dorothea Kehler, "Rings and Jewels in *The Changeling*," *ELN* 5 (October 1967): 15–17.

Levin, *The Multiple Plot in English Renaissance Drama*, 34–48.

Cynthia Lewis, "'Wise Men, Folly-Fall'n': Characters Named Antonio in English Renaissance Drama," *RenD* 20 (1989): 197–236.

Ornstein, *Moral Vision of Jacobean Tragedy*, 179–90.

Raymond J. Pentzell, "*The Changeling*: Notes on Mannerisms in Dramatic Form," *CompD* 9 (Spring 1975): 3–28.

Dale B. J. Randall, "Some Observations on the Theme of Chastity in *The Changeling*," *ELR* 14 (March 1984): 347–66.

Robert R. Reed, Jr., "A Factual Interpretation of *The Changeling*'s Madhouse Scenes," *N&Q* 195 (June 1950): 247–48.

Ribner, *Jacobean Tragedy*, 126–37.

Christopher Ricks, "The Moral and Poetic Structure of *The Changeling*," *EIC* 10 (July 1960): 290–306.

Emil L. Roy, "Sexual Paradox in *The Changeling*," *L&P* 25, no. 1 (1975): 124–32.

Samuel Schoenbaum, "Middleton's Tragedies—A Critical Study," *CUSECL* 168 (1955): 132–50.

Scott, *Renaissance Drama*, 76–88.

J. L. Simmons, "Diabolical Realism in Middleton and Rowley's *The Changeling*, *RenD* 11 (1980): 135–70.

Stoll, *From Shakespeare to Joyce*, 309–12.

J. Chesley Taylor, "Metaphores of the Moral World: Structure in *The Changeling*," *TSE* 20 (Spring 1972): 41–56.

T. B. Tomlinson, "Poetic Naturalism—*The Changeling*," *JEGP* 63 (October 1964): 648–59.

Wells, *Elizabethan and Jacobean Playwrights*, 39–41.

A Chaste Maid in Cheapside

Joanne Altieri, "Against Moralizing Jacobean Comedy: Middleton's *Chaste Maid*," *Criticism* 30 (Spring 1988): 171–87.

David M. Bergeron, "Middleton's Moral Landscape: *A Chaste Maid in Cheapside* and *The Triumphs of Truth*," in Friedenreich, *"Accompaninge the players,"* 133–46.

Harry R. Burke, "The Kaleidoscopic Vision: Multiple Perspectives in Middleton's *A Chaste Maid in Cheapside*," *ISJR* 57 (November 1982): 123–29.

Ruby Chatterji, "Theme, Imagery, and Unity in *A Chaste Maid in Cheapside*," *RenD* 8 (1965): 105–26.

Charles A. Hallett, "Middleton's Allwit: the urban cynic," *MLQ* 30 (December 1960): 498–507.

R. V. Holdsworth, "*A Chaste Maid in Cheapside* V.ii.49–50," *N&Q* 24 (March 1977): 136.

Ingrid Hotz-Davies, "*A Chaste Maid in Cheapside* and *Women Beware Women*: Feminism, Anti-Feminism and the Limitations of Satire," *CahiersE* 39 (April 1991): 29–39.

Coppelia Kahn, "Whores and Wives in Jacobean Drama," in Kehler and Baker, *In Another Country*, 246–60.

D. J. Lake, " 'Waltering' in *A Chaste Maid in Cheapside*," *N&Q* 30 (April 1983): 154.

Richard Levin, "The Four Plots of *A Chaste Maid in Cheapside*," *RES* 16 (1965): 14–24.

Levin, *The Multiple Plot in English Renaissance Drama*, 192–202.

Arthur F. Marotti, "Fertility and Comic Form in *A Chaste Maid in Cheapside*," *CompD* 3 (Spring 1969): 65–74.

R. B. Parker, "Middleton's Experiments with Comedy and Judgement," *Stratford-Upon-Avon Studies* 1 (1960): 179–99.

Rowe, *Thomas Middleton & the New Comedy Tradition*, 130–52.

Samuel Schoenbaum, "*A Chaste Maid in Cheapside* and Middleton's City Comedy," in Bennett, Cargill, and Hall, *Studies in the English Renaissance Drama*, 287–309. Reprinted in *Shakespeare and Others*, 203–17.

Stephen Wigler, "Thomas Middleton's *A Chaste Maid in Cheapside*: The Delightful and the Disgusting," *AI* 33 (Summer 1976): 197–215.

Robert I. Williams, "Machiavelli's *Mandragola*, Touchwood Senior, and the Comedy of Middleton's *A Chaste Maid in Cheapside*," *SEL* 10 (Spring 1970): 385–96.

A Fair Quarrel
(with Rowley)

Asp, *A Study of Thomas Middleton's Tragicomedies*, 103–47.

Farr, *Thomas Middleton and the Drama of Realism*, 38–49.

R. V. Holdsworth, "The Medical Jargon in *A Fair Quarrel*," *RES* 23 (1972): 448–54.

Kistner and Kistner, *Middleton's Tragic Themes*, 29–41.

A.L. Kistner and M. K. Kistner, "The Themes and Structures of *A Fair Quarrel*," *TSL* 23 (Spring 1977): 31–46.

Levin, *The Multiple Plot in English Renaissance Drama*, 66–75.

Levin, "The Three Quarrels of *A Fair Quarrel*," *SP* 61 (April 1964): 219–31.

Michael E. Mooney, " 'The Common Sight' and Dramatic Form: Rowley's Embedded Jig in *A Fair Quarrel*," *SEL* 20 (Spring 1980): 305–23.

Samuel Schoenbaum, "Middleton's Tragi-Comedies," *MP* 54 (August 1956): 16–19.

The Family of Love

Joanne Altieri, "Pregnant Puns and Sectarian Rhetoric: Middleton's *Family of Love*," *Mosaic* 22 (Fall 1989): 45–57.

Clifford Davidson, "Middleton and *The Family of Love*," *EM* 20 (Spring 1969): 81–92.

A. L. Kistner, and M. K. Kistner, "*The Family of Love* and *The Phoenix*: Early Development of a Theme," *ELWIU* 7 (Spring 1980): 179–90.

Leinwand, *The City Staged*, 67–68, 121–23, 169–70.

Richard Levin, "The Family of Lust and *The Family of Love*," *SEL* 6 (Spring 1966): 309–22.

John F. McElroy, "Middleton, Entertainer or Moralist? An Interpretation of *The Family of Love* and *Your Five Gallants*," *MLQ* 37 (March 1976): 35–46.

Arthur F. Marotti, "The Purgations of Middleton's *The Family of Love*," *PLL* 7 (Spring 1971): 80–84.

Baldwin Maxwell, " 'Twenty Good Nights'—*The Knight of the Burning Pestle* and Middleton's *Family of Love*," *MLN* 63 (April 1948): 233–37.

W. J. Olive, "Imitation of Shakespeare in Middleton's *Family of Love*," *PQ* 29 (January 1950): 75–78.

W. J. Olive, " 'Twenty Good Knights'—*The Knight of the Burning Pestle*, *The Family of Love*, and *Romeo and Juliet*," *SP* 47 (April 1950): 182–89.

Rowe, *Thomas Middleton & the New Comedy Tradition*, 34–52.

A Game at Chess

Martin Butler, "William Prynne and the Allegory of Middleton's *Game at Chess*," *N&Q* 30 (April 1983): 153–54.

Thomas Cogswell, "Thomas Middleton and the Court, 1624: *A Game at Chess* in Context," *HLQ* 47 (Autumn 1984): 273–88.

Richard A. Davies, and Alan R. Young, " 'Strange Cunning' in Thomas Middleton's *A Game at Chess*," *UTQ* 45 (July 1976): 236–45.

Farr, *Thomas Middleton and the Drama of Realism*, 98–124.

Margot C. Heinemann, "Middleton's *A Game at Chess*: Parliamentary-Puritans and Opposition Drama," *ELR* 5 (Summer 1975): 232–50.

T. H. Howard-Hill, "The Author as Scribe or Reviser? Middleton's Intentions in *A Game at Chess*," *Text* 3 (1987): 305–18. Reprinted as "Political Interpretations of Middleton's *A Game at Chess*," in *YES* 21 (1991): 274–85.

Loftis, *Renaissance Drama in England and Spain*, 166–67, 173–75, 177–83, 228–29.

George R. Price, "Latin Oration in *A Game of Chesse*," *HLQ* 23 (August 1960): 389–93.

Roussel Sargent, "Theme and Structure in Middleton's *A Game at Chess*," *MLR* 66 (October 1971): 721–30.

Jane Sherman, "The Pawns' Allegory in Middleton's *A Game at Chesse*," *RES* 29 (1978): 147–59.

Wells, *Elizabethan and Jacobean Playwrights*, 209–11.

Paul Yachnin, "*A Game at Chess* and Chess Allegory," *SEL* 22 (Spring 1982): 316–30.

Paul Yachnin, "*A Game at Chess*: Thomas Middleton's 'Praise of Folly,'" *MLQ* 48 (March 1987): 107–23.

The Honest Whore
(with Dekker)

Blow, *Rhetoric in the Plays of Thomas Dekker*, 18–21, 31–32, 36–39, 46–48, 51–52, 57–58, 60–62, 98–100, 119–20.

Normand Berlin, "Thomas Dekker: A Reappraisal," *SEL* 6 (Spring 1966): 263–77.

Arthur Brown, "Citizen Comedy and Domestic Drama," *Stratford-Upon-Avon-Studies* 1 (1960): 69–73.

Larry S. Champion, "From Melodrama to Comedy: A Study of Dramatic Perspective in Dekker's *The Honest Whore*, Parts I and II," *SP* 69 (Summer 1972): 192–209.

Viviana Comensoli, "Gender and Eloquence in Dekker's *The Honest Whore, Part II*," *ESC* 15 (Fall 1989): 249–62.

Haselkorn, *Prostitution in Elizabethan and Jacobean Drama*, 116–36.

R. L. Horn, "Thematic Structure of *The Honest Whore*, Part I," *DUJ* 46 (December 1984): 7–10.

A. L. Kistner, and M. K. Kistner, "*I Honest Whore*: A Comedy of Blood," *HAB* 23, no. 4 (1972): 23–27.

Kistner, and Kistner, *Middleton's Tragic Themes*, 103–11.

Lacy, *Jacobean Problem Play*, 60–84.

Leinwand, *The City Staged*, 70–73, 131–33, 175–78

McPeek, *The Black Book of Knaves*, 82–89.

Michael Manheim, "The Thematic Structure of Dekker's *2 Honest Whore*," *SEL* 5 (Spring 1965): 356–81.

Anne Parten, "Masculine Adultery and Feminine Rejoinders in Shakespeare, Dekker and Sharpham," *Mosaic* 17 (Winter 1984): 9–18.

Neill Rhodes, *Elizabethan Grotesque*, 77–80.

Charlotte Spivack, "Bedlam and Bridewell: Ironic Design in *The Honest Whore*," *Komos* 3, no. 1 (1973): 10–16.

Peter Ure, "Patient Madman and Honest Whore: The Middleton-Dekker Oxymoron," *E&S* 19 (1966): 18–40. Reprinted in Maxwell, *Elizabethan and Jacobean Drama*.

The Inner Temple Masque; or, Masque of Heroes

Hassel, *Renaissance Drama*, 107–10.

A Mad World, My Masters

P. K. Ayers, "Plot, Subplot, and the Uses of Dramatic Discord in *A Mad World, My Masters* and *A Trick To Catch the Old One*," *MLQ* 47 (March 1986): 3–18.

Farley-Hills, *The Comic in Renaissance Comedy*, 81–107.

Hallett, *Middleton's Cynics*, 63–92.

Hallett, "Penitent Brothel, the Succubus and Parson's Resolution: A Reappraisal of Penitent's Position in Middleton's Canon," *SP* 69 (October 1972): 72–86.

Hallett, "Volpone as the Source of the Sickroom Scene in Middleton's *Mad World*," *N&Q* 18 (March 1971): 24–25.

Haselkorn, *Prostitution in Elizabethan and Jacobean Drama*, 83–95.

Leanore Leiblein, "The Lessons of Feigning in *A Mad World, My Masters*," *MLS* 8 (Winter 1978): 23–32.

Leanore Leiblein, "Thomas Middleton's Prodigal Play," *CompD* 10 (Spring 1976): 54–60.

MIDDLETON, THOMAS, *The Mayor of Queenborough*

Leinwand, *The City Staged*, 56–59, 103–07, 174–75.

Levin, *The Multiple Plot in English Renaissance Drama*, 168–73.

Mann, *The Elizabethan Player*, 76–77.

Arthur F. Marotti, "The Method in the Madness of *A Mad World, My Masters*," *TSL* 15 (Spring 1970): 99–108.

Robert L. Root, Jr., "The Troublesome Reformation of Penitent Brothel: Middletonian Irony and *A Mad World, My Masters*," *CLAJ* 25 (September 1981): 82–90.

Rowe, *Thomas Middleton & the New Comedy Tradition*, 93–114.

William W. E. Slights, "The Trickster-Hero and Middleton's *A Mad World, My Masters*," *CompD* 3 (Spring 1969): 87–98.

Fumiko Takase, "Thomas Middleton's Antifeminist Sentiment in *A Mad World, My Masters*," in *Playing with Gender: A Renaissance Pursuit*, ed. Jean R. Brink, Maryanne C. Horowitz, and Allison P. Coudert (Urbana: University of Illinois Press, 1991), 19–31.

Michael Taylor, "Realism and Morality in Middleton's *A Mad World, My Masters*," *L&P* 18, no. 2 (1968): 166–78.

Stephen Wigler, "Penitent Brothel Reconsidered: The Place of The Grotesque in Middleton's *A Mad World, My Masters*," *L&P* 25, no. 1 (1975): 17–26.

The Mayor of Queenborough; or, Hengest, King of Kent

Kistner and Kistner, *Middleton's Tragic Themes*, 59–71.

Anne Lancashire, "The Emblematic Castle in Shakespeare and Middleton," in Gray, *Mirror Up to Shakespeare*, 223–41.

Mann, *The Elizabethan Player*, 74–91.

Samuel Schoenbaum, "*Hengist, King of Kent* and Sexual Preoccupation in Jacobean Drama," *PQ* 29 (April 1950): 182–98.

Samuel Schoenbaum, "Middleton's Tragedies—A Critical Study," *CUSECL* 168 (1955): 69–101.

Michaelmas Term

Ruby Chatterji, "Unity and Disparity: *Michaelmas Term*," *SEL* 8 (Spring 1968): 349–63.

Anthony Covatta, *Thomas Middleton's City Comedies*, (Lewisburg, PA: Bucknell University Press, 1973), 79–98.

Curry, *Deception in Elizabethan Drama*, 46–52.

Hallett, *Middleton's Cynics*, 24–44.

Haselkorn, *Prostitution in Elizabethan and Jacobean Drama*, 95–107.

R. V. Holdsworth, "Middleton's *Michaelmas Term* V.i.70," *Expl* 35 (Fall 1977): 13–14.

A. L. Kistner, and M. K. Kistner, "Heirs and Identity: The Bases of Social Order in *Michaelmas Term*," *MLS* 16 (Fall 1986): 61–71.

W. Nicholas Knight, "Sex and Law Language in Middleton's *Michaelmas Term*," in Friedenreich, *"Accompaninge the Players,"* 89–108.

John Lehr, "Two Names in Middleton's *Michaelmas Term*," *ELN* 18 (September 1980): 15–19.

Leinwand, *The City Staged*, 51–56, 99–103, 164–65.

Levin, *The Multiple Plot in English Renaissance Drama*, 168–70, 173–82.

Baldwin Maxwell, "Middleton's *Michaelmas Term*," *PQ* 22 (January 1943): 29–35.

George E. Rowe, Jr., "Prodigal Sons, New Comedy, and Middleton's *Michaelmas Term*," *ELR* 7 (Spring 1977): 90–107. Reprinted in Rowe, *Thomas Middleton and the New Comedy Tradition*, 53–72.

Paul Yachnin, "Social Competition in Middleton's *Michaelmas Term*," *EIRC* 13 (1987): 87–99.

More Dissemblers Besides Women

Lila Geller, "Widows' Vows and *More Dissemblers Beside Women*," *MRDE* 5 (1991): 287–308.

McElroy, *Parody and Burlesque*, 106–54.

Kenneth Muir, "Two Plays Reconsidered: *More Dissemblers Besides Women* and *No Wit, No Help Like a Woman's*," in Friedenreich, *"Accompaninge the players,"* 147–59.

Rowe, *Thomas Middleton & the New Comedy Tradition*, 153–75.

Samuel Schoenbaum, "Middleton's Tragi-Comedies," *MP* 54 (August 1956): 13–16.

No Wit, No Help Like a Woman

David M. Bergeron, "Middleton's *No Wit, No Help* and Civic Pagentry," in Bergeron, *Pagentry in the Shakespearean Theatre*, 65–80.

Mark Eccles, "Middleton's Comedy The Almanac; Or, *No Wit, No Help like a Woman's*," *N&Q* 34 (September 1987): 296–97.

Leinwand, *The City Staged*, 162–64, 184–86.

Kenneth Muir, "Two Plays Reconsidered: *More Dissemblers Besides Women and No Wit, No Help Like a Woman's*," in Friedenreich, *"Accompaninge the players,"* 147–59.

Rowe, *Thomas Middleton & the New Comedy Tradition*, 114–30.

Wells, *Elizabethan and Jacobean Playwrights*," 227–29.

The Old Law; or, A New Way to Please You
(with Rowley)

Asp, *A Study of Thomas Middleton's Tragicomedies*, 148–210.

A. A. Bromham, "The Contemporary Significance of *The Old Law*," *SEL* 24 (Spring 1984): 327–39.

George E. Rowe, Jr., "*The Old Law* and Middleton's Comic Vision," *ELH* 42 (June 1975): 189–202.

George E. Rowe, Jr., *Thomas Middleton & the New Comedy Tradition*, 175–89.

The Phoenix

Clifford Davidson, "*The Phoenix*: Middleton's Didactic Comedy," *PLL* 4 (Spring 1968): 121–30.

Alan C. Dessen, "Middleton's *The Phoenix* and the Allegorical Tradition," *SEL* 6 (Spring 1966): 291–308.

A. L. Kistner, and M. K. Kistner, "The Family of Love and *The Phoenix*: Early Development of a Theme," *ELWIU* 7 (Spring 1980): 179–90.

R. B. Parker, "Middleton's Experiments with Comedy and Judgement," *Stratford-Upon-Avon Studies* 1 (1960): 179–99.

Rowe, *Thomas Middleton & the New Comedy Tradition*, 26–34.

Paul Yachnin, "The Significance of Two Allusions in Middleton's *Phoenix*," *N&Q* 33 (September 1986): 375–77.

The Roaring Girl; or, Moll Cut-Purse
(with Dekker)

Bradbrook, *Growth and Structure of Elizabethan Comedy*, 172–74.

Patrick Cheney, "Moll Cutpurse as Hermaphrodite in Dekker and Middleton's *The Roaring Girl*," *Ren&R* 7 (May 1983): 120–34.

Viviana Comensoli, "Play-Making, Domestic Conduct, and the Multiple Plot in *The Roaring Girl*," *SEL* 27 (Spring 1987): 249–66.

Mark Eccles, "Mary Frith, the *Roaring Girl*," *N&Q* 32 (March 1985): 65–66.

Marjorie Garber, "The Logic of the Transvestite: *The Roaring Girl* (1608)," in Kastan, and Stallybrass, *Staging the Renaissance*, 221–34.

Jo E. Miller, "Women and the Market in *The Roaring Girl*," *Ren&R* 14 (Winter 1990): 11–23.

Mary Beth Rose, "Women in Men's Clothing: Apparel and Social Stability in *The Roaring Girl*," *ELR* 14 (Autumn 1984): 367–91.

The Spanish Gipsy
(with Rowley)

Frederick M. Burelbach, Jr., "Theme and Structure in *The Spanish Gipsy*," *HAB* 19, no. 2 (1968): 37–41.

A. L. Kistner, and M. K. Kistner, *Middleton's Tragic Themes*, 13–26.

A. L. Kistner, and M. K. Kistner, "*The Spanish Gipsy*," *HAB* 25 (Summer 1974): 211–24.

A Trick to Catch the Old One

P. K. Ayers, "Plot, Subplot, and the Uses of Dramatic Discord in *A Mad World, My Masters* and *A Trick to Catch the Old One*," *MLQ* 47 (March 1986): 3–18.

Signi Falk, "Plautus' Persa and Middleton's *A Trick to Catch the Old One*," *MLN* 66 (January 1951): 19–21.

J. George, "Millipood," *N&Q* 193 (April 1948): 149–50.

Haselkorn, *Prostitution in Elizabethan and Jacobean Drama*, 76–83.

Robert Bechtold Heilman, *The Ways of the World: Comedy and Society* (Seattle: University of Washington Press, 1978), 163–66.

MIDDLETON, THOMAS, *The Triumphs of Love and Antiquity*

Izumi Kadono, "The Prodigal in *A Trick to Catch the Old One*," *SES* 7 (1982): 33–46.

Knight, *Drama and Society in the Age of Jonson*, 262–63.

Leinwand, *The City Staged*, 59–61, 107–09.

Richard Levin, "The Dampit Scenes in *A Trick to Catch the Old One*," *MLQ* 25 (June 1964): 140–52.

Richard Levin, *The Multiple Plot in English Renaissance Drama*, 127–37.

Joseph Messina, "The Moral Design of *A Trick to Catch the Old One*," in Friedenreich, *"Accompaninge the players*," 109–32.

David B. Mount, "The '(Un)Reclaymed Forme' of Middleton's *A Trick to Catch the Old One*," *SEL* 31 (Spring 1991): 259–72.

R. B. Parker, "Middleton's Experiments with Comedy and Judgment," *Stratford-Upon-Avon Studies* 1 (1960): 179–99.

Rowe, *Thomas Middleton & the New Comedy Tradition*, 72–91.

Scott Cutler Shershow, "The Pit of Wit: Subplot and Unity in Middleton's *A Trick to Catch the Old One*," *SP* 88 (Summer 1991): 363–81.

The Triumphs of Love and Antiquity: An Honourable Solemnity

Theodore B. Leinwand, "London's Triumphing: The Jacobean Lord Mayor's Show," *CLIO* 11 (Winter 1982) 137–53.

The Triumphs of Truth: A Solemnity

Bergeron, *English Civic Pagentry*, 179–86.

Bergeron, "Middleton's Moral Landscape: A Chaste Maid in Cheapside and *The Triumphs of Truth*," in Friedenreich, *"Accompaninge the players,"* 133–46.

D'Amico, *The Moor in English Renaissnce Drama*, 58–62.

Theodore B. Leinwand, "London's Triumphing: The Jacobean Lord Mayor's Show," *CLIO* 11 (Winter 1982) 137–53.

The Widow

Renu Juneja, "The Widow as Paradox and Paradigm in Middleton's Plays," *JGE* 34 (Spring 1982): 3–19.

Kenneth Friedenreich, "Introduction: How to Read Middleton," in Friedenreich *"Accompaninge the Players,"* 1–14.

Robert T. Levine, "Middleton's *The Widow*," *Expl* 44 (Winter 1986): 18–20.

The Witch

Asp, *A Study of Thomas Middleton's Tragicomedies*, 211–57.

David George, "The Problem of Middleton's *The Witch* and Its Sources," *N&Q* 14 (April 1967): 209–11.

Kistner and Kistner, *Middleton's Tragic Themes*, 73–83.

Anne Lancashire, *"The Witch*: Stage Flop or Political Mistake?" in Friedenreich, *"Accompaninge the players,"* 161–81.

McElroy, *Parody and Burlesque*, 155–215.

Samuel Schoenbaum, "Middleton's Tragi-Comedies," *MP* 54 (August 1956): 8–10.

Women Beware Women

J. B. Batchelor, "The Pattern of *Women Beware Women*," *YES* 2 (1972): 78–88.

A. A. Bromham, "The Tragedy of Peace: Political Meaning in *Women Beware Women*," *SEL* 26 (Spring 1986): 309–29.

Laura Bromley, "Men and Women Beware: Social, Political, and Sexual Anarchy in *Women Beware Women*," *ISJR* 61 (February 1987): 311–21.

Champion, *Tragic Patterns in Jacobean and Caroline Drama*, 152–67.

Larry S. Champion, "Tragic Vision in Middleton's *Women Beware Women*," *ES* 57 (January 1977): 410–24.

J. A. Cole, "Sunday Dinners and Thursday Suppers: Social and Moral Contexts of the Food Imagery in *Women Beware Women*," in Hogg, *Jacobean Miscellany* 4, 86–98.

Anthony B. Dawson, *"Women Beware Women* and the Economy of Rape," *SEL* 27 (Spring 1987): 303–20.

Daniel Dodson, "Middleton's Livia," *PQ* 27 (October 1948): 376–81.

E. Engleberg, "Tragic Blindness in *The Changeling* and *Women Beware Women*," *MLQ* 23 (March 196): 20–28.

Inga-Stina Ewbank, "Realism and Morality in *Women Beware Women*," *E&S* 22 (1969): 57–70.

Verna Ann Foster, "The Dead's Creature: The Tragedy of Bianca in *Women Beware Women*," *JEGP* 78 (October 1979): 508–21.

Huston D. Hallahan, "The Thematic Juxtaposition of the Representational and the Sensational in Middleton's *Women Beware Women*," *SIcon* 2 (1976): 66–84.

Charles A. Hallett, "The Psychological Drama of *Women Beware Women*," *SEL* 12 (Autumn 1972): 375–89.

Anne M. Hasselkorn, "Sin and the Politics of Penitence: Three Jacobean Adultresses," in Hasselkorn and Travitsky, *The Renaissance Englishwoman in Print*, 119–36.

R. V. Holdsworth, "Two Proverbs in Middleton and Some Contemporaries," *N&Q* 28 April 1981): 172–73.

Ingrid Hotz-Davies, "*A Chaste Maid in Cheapside* and *Women Beware Women*: Feminism, Anti-Feminism and the Limitations of Satire," *CahiersE* 39 (April 1991): 29–39.

Izumi Kadono, "The Inserted Masque in *Women Beware Women*," *SES* 9 (1984): 19–31.

Laura Severt King, "Violence and the Masque: A Ritual Sabotaged in Middleton's *Women Beware Women*," *PCP* 21 (November 1986): 42–47.

Kistner and Kistner, *Middleton's Tragic Themes*, 85–100.

Kistner and Kistner, "Will, Fate and the Social Order in *Women Beware Women*," *ELWIU* 3 (Spring 1976): 17–31.

Dorothea Krook, "Tragedy and Satire: Middleton's *Women Beware Women*," in Shalvi and Mendilow, *Studies in English Language and Literature*, 96–120.

McAlindon, *English Renaissance Tragedy*, 209–35.

Michael McCanles, "The Moral Dialectic of Middleton's *Women Beware Women*," in Friedenreich, *"Accompaninge the players,"* 203–18.

Kenneth Muir, "The Role of Livia in *Women Beware Women*," in Coleman and Hammond, *Poetry and Drama, 1570–1700*, 76–89.

Ornstein, *Moral Vision of Jacobean Tragedy*, 190–99.

R. B. Parker, "Middleton's Experiments with Comedy and Judgement," *Stratford-Upon-Avon Studies* 1 (1960): 179–99.

John Potter, " 'In Time of Sports': Masques and Masking in Middleton's *Women Beware Women*," *PLL* 18 (Winter 1982): 368–83.

Ribner, *Jacobean Tragedy*, 137–52.

Ribner, "Middleton's *Women Beware Women*: Poetic Imagery and the Moral Visions," *TSE* 9 (Spring 1959): 19–34.

Christopher Ricks, "Word-Play in *Women Beware Women*," *RES* 12 (August 1961): 238–50.

Jennifer Strauss, "Dance in Thomas Middleton's *Women Beware Women*," *Parergon* 29 (April 1991): 37–43.

Neil Taylor, and Bryan Loughrey, "Middleton's Chess Strategies in *Women Beware Women*," *SEL* 24 (Spring 1984): 341–54.

Albert H. Tricomi, "Middleton's *Women Beware Women* as Anticourt Drama," *MLS* 19 (Spring 1989): 65–77.

Wells, *Elizabethan and Jacobean Playwrights*, 41–44.

Stephen Wigler, "Parent and Child: The Pattern of Love in *Women Beware Women*," in Friedenreich, *"Accompaninge the players,"* 183–201.

Your Five Gallants

Alan G. Cross, "Middleton's *Your Five Gallants*: The Fifth Act," *PQ* 44 (Spring 1965): 124–29.

Leinwand, *The City Staged*, 109–10.

John F. McElroy, "Middleton, Entertainer or Moralist? An Interpretation of *The Family of Love* and *Your Five Gallants*," *MLQ* 37 (1976): 35–46.

Baldwin Maxwell, Thomas Middleton's *Your Five Gallants*," *PQ* 30 (January 1951): 30–39.

MILTON, JOHN

Arcades

Brown, *John Milton's Aristocratic Entertainments* (Cambridge: Cambridge University Press, 1985), 41–56.

John G. Demaray, "*Arcades* as a Literary Entertainment," *PLL* 8 (Spring 1972): 15–26.

Mary Ann McGuire, "Milton's *Arcades* and the Entertainment Tradition," *SP* 75 (1978): 451–71.

MILTON, JOHN, *Comus: A Masque Presented at Ludlow Castle*

John Malcolm Wallace, "Milton's *Arcades*," *JEGP* 58 (October 1959): 627–36.

Comus: A Masque Presented at Ludlow Castle

Don C. Allen, "Milton's *Comus* as a Failure in Artistic Compromise," *ELH* 16 (June 1949): 104–19.

John Arthos, "The Realms of Being in the Epilogue of *Comus*," *MLN* 76 (April 1961): 321–24.

Marc Beckwith, "*Comus* and the Zodiacus Vitae," *MiltonQ* 20 (December 1986): 145–47.

Joan S. Bennett, "Virgin Nature in *Comus*," *MiltonS* 23 (1987): 21–32.

Purvis E. Boyette, Milton's Abstracted Sublimities: The Structure and Meaning in *A Mask*," *TSE* 18 (Spring 1970): 35–58.

Fredelle Bruser, "*Comus* and the Rose Song," *SP* 44 (October 1944): 625–44.

Thomas O. Calhoun, "On John Milton's *A Mask at Ludlow*," *MiltonS* 6 (1974): 165–79.

Jean F. Camé, "Myths and Myths in Milton's *Comus*," *CahiersE* 15 (April 1974): 3–24.

John Creaser, "Milton's *Comus*: The Irrelevance of the Castlehaven Scandal," *N&Q* 31 (September 1984): 307–17.

John Creaser, "'The present aid of this occasion': The Setting of *Comus*," in Lindley, *The Court Masque*, 111–34.

E. H. Dye, "Milton's *Comus* and Boethius' *Consolation*," *MiltonQ* 19 (March 1985): 1–7.

Robert L. Entzminger, "The Politics of Love in Tasso's Aminta and Milton's *Comus*," in Milton in *Italy: Contexts, Images, Contradictions*, ed. Mario A. Di Cesare (Binghamton, NY: Medieval and Renaissance Texts and Studies; 1991), 463–76.

Donald M. Friedman, "*Comus* and the Truth of the Ear," in *"The muses commonweale": Poetry and Politics in the Seventeenth Century*, ed. Claude J. Summers and Ted-Larry Pebworth (Columbia: University of Missouri Press, 1988), 119–34.

Thomas P. Harrison, "The 'Haemony' Passage in *Comus* Again," *PQ* 22 (July 1943): 251–54.

L. W. Hyman, "*Comus* and the Limits of Interpretation," *Structuralist Rev.* 2 (1981): 68–77.

Richard Kell, "Theme and Action in Milton's *Comus*," *EIC* 24 (April 1974): 48–54.

Christopher Kendrick, "Milton and Sexuality: A Symptomatic Reading of *Comus*," *Criticism* 25 (Fall 1983): 293–327.

Philip C. Kolin, "Milton's *Samson Agonistes*, 393–412," *Expl* 30 (December 1972): Item 30.

William Leahy, "Polltion and *Comus*," *EIC* 11 (January 1961): 111.

Edward S. LeCompt, "New Light on the 'Haemony' Passage in *Comus*," *PQ* 21 (July 1942): 283–98.

William G. Madsen, "The Idea of Nature in Milton's Poetry," *Yale Studies in English* 138 (1958): 185–218.

John M. Major, "*Comus* and *The Tempest*," *SQ* 10 (Spring 1959): 177–84.

Anthony Mortimer, "*Comus* and Michaelmas," *ES* 65 (April 1984): 111–19.

Bruce Morton, "Milton's *Comus*, Lines 60–67, 422–25," *Expl* 49 (Summer 1991): 209–12.

Richard Neuse, "Metamorphosis and Symbolic Action in *Comus*," *ELH* 34 (March 1967): 49–64.

James Obertino, "Milton's Use of Aquinas in *Comus*," *MiltonS* 22 (1986): 21–43.

Willaim A. Oram, "The Invocation of Sabrina," *SEL* 24 (Spring 1984): 121–39.

Violet O'Valle, "Milton's *Comus* and Welsh Oral Tradition," *MiltonS* 18 (1983): 25–44.

T. S. K. Scott-Craig, "Miltonic Tragedy and Christian Vision," in Scott *The Tragic Vision and the Christian Faith*, 99–109.

Catherine M. Shaw, "The Unity of *Comus*," *XUS* 10, no. 1 (1971): 33–43.

George William Smith, Jr., "Milton's Revisions and the Design of *Comus*," *ELH* 46 (March 1979): 56–80.

B. J. Sokol, " 'Tilted Lees,' Dragons, Haemony, Menarche, Spirit, and Matter in *Comus*," *RES* 41 (August 1990): 309–24.

Paul Stevens, "Magic Structures: *Comus* and the Illusions of Fancy," *MiltonQ* 17 (October 1983): 84–89.

Shigeo Suzuki, "A Three-Step Study of Milton's *Comus*," *SES* 3 (1978): 99–112.

Traister, *Heavenly Necromancers*, 169–78.

Mindele Anne Treip, "*Comus* as 'Progress,'" *MiltonQ* 20 (March 1986): 1–13.

Rosamund Tuve, *Images and Themes in Five Poems by Milton* (Cambridge: Cambridge University Press, 1957), 112–61.

Wells, *Elizabethan and Jacobean Playwrights*, 173–75.

Robert A. White, "The Cup and the Wand as Archetypes in *Comus*," *MiltonQ* 25 (March 1991): 22–25.

Michael Wilding, "Milton's 'A Masque Presented at Ludlow Castle, 1634': Theatre and Politics on the Border," *Trivium* 20 (1985): 147–79. Reprinted in *MiltonQ* 21 (December 1987): 35–51.

Roger B. Wilkenfield, "A Seat at the Center: An Interpretation of *Comus*," *ELH* 33 (Spring 1966): 170–79.

David Wilkinson, "The Escape from Pollution: A Comment on *Comus*," *EIC* 10 (January 1960): 32–43.

A. S. P. Woodhouse, "*Comus* Once More," *UTQ* 19 (April 1950): 218–23.

Samson Agonistes

Joan S. Bennet, "A Reading of *Samson Agonistes*," in *The Cambridge Companion to Milton*, ed. Dennis Danielson (Cambridge: Cambridge University Press, 1989), 225–41.

Robert Beum, "The Rhyme in *Samson Agonistes*," *TSLL* 4 (Summer 1962): 177–82.

Steven Blakemore, "Milton's *Samson Agonistes*, Lines 80–82," *Expl* 42 (Spring 1984): 17–18.

D. F. Bouchard, "Samson as 'Medicine Man': Ritual Function and Symbolic Structure in *Samson Agonistes*," *Genre* 5 (Summer 1972): 257–70.

A. B. Chambers, "Wisdom and Fortitude in *Samson Agonistes*," *PMLA* 78 (September 1963): 315–20.

Lee S. Cox, "The 'Evening Dragon' in *Samson Agonistes*: A Reappraisal," *MLN* 76 (November 1961): 577–84.

Clay Daniel, "Lust and Violence in *Samson Agonistes*," *SCRev* 6 (Spring 1989): 6–31.

Jackie DiSalvo, "'The Lord's Battells': *Samson Agonistes* and the Puritan Revolution," *MiltonS* 4 (1972): 39–62.

John D. Ebbs, "Milton's Treatment of Poetic Justice in *Samson Agonistes*," *MLQ* 22 (December 1961): 377–89.

Ellis-Fermor, *Frontiers of Drama*, 17–34, 148–53.

Robert L. Entzminger, "*Samson Agonistes* and the Recovery of Metaphor," *SEL* 22 (Winter 1982): 137–56.

Kenneth Fell, "From Myth to Martyrdom: Towards a View of *Samson Agonistes*," *ES* 34 (August 1953): 144–55.

Fisch, *The Dual Image*, 40–41.

Stanley Fish, "Spectacle and Evidence in *Samson Agonistes*," *CritI* 15 (Spring 1989): 556–86.

Wendy Furman, "*Samson Agonistes* as Christian Tragedy: A Corrective View," *PQ* 60 (Spring 1981): 169–81.

David Gay, "John 10:18 and the Typology of *Samson Agonistes*," *ELN* 27 (December 1989): 49–52.

David Gay, " 'Sinews, Joints and Bones': Milton's *Samson Agonistes* and Psalm 139," *StHum* 17 (June 1990): 49–62.

Allan H. Gilbert, "Is *Samson Agonistes* Finished?" *PQ* 28 (January 1949): 98–106.

Christopher Gilles, "*Samson Agonistes*," *The Use of English* 5 (Summer 1954): 223–30.

William O. Harris, "Despair and 'Patience' as the Truest Fortitude in *Samson Agonistes*," *ELH* 30 (June 1963): 107–20.

Frank Kermode, "*Samson Agonistes* and Hebrew Prosody," *DUJ* 45 (March 1953): 49–63.

William Kerrigan, "The Irrational Coherence of *Samson Agonistes*," *MiltonS* 22 (1986): 217–32.

Laura Lunger Knoppers, " 'Sung and Proverb'd for a Fool': *Samson Agonistes* and Solomon's Harlot," *MiltonS* 26 (1991): 239–51.

Laura Lunger Knoppers, " 'This So Horrid Spectacle': *Samson Agonistes* and the Execution of the Regicides," *ELR* 20 (Autumn 1990): 487–504.

Anthony Low, "*Samson Agonistes* and the 'Pioneers of Aphasia,' " *MiltonQ* 25 (December 1991): 143–48.

K. R. Srinivasa Lyengar, "*Samson Agonistes*," in *The Laurel Bough: Essays Presented in Honour of Professor M. V. Rama Sarma*, ed. G. Nageswara Rao (Bombay: Blackie, 1983), 65–73.

William G. Madsen, "From Shadowy Types to Truth," *English Institute Essays* (1964): 95–114.

Mahood, *Poetry and Symbolism*, 237–39.

E. L. Marilla, "*Samson Agonistes*: Interpretation," *SN* 29 (Spring 1957): 67–76.

B. Eugene McCarthy, "Metaphor and Plot in *Samson Agonistes*," *MiltonQ* 6 (March 1972): 86–92.

Raven I. McDavid, "*Samson Agonistes* 1096: A Re-examination," *PQ* 33 (January 1954): 86–89.

Martin E. Miller, " 'Pathos' and 'Katharsis' in *Samson Agonistes*," *ELH* 31 (June 1964): 156–74.

Laurie P. Morrow, "The 'Meet and Happy Conversation': Dalila's Role in *Samson Agonistes*," *MiltonQ* 17 (May 1983): 38–42.

Judith A. Moses, "*Samson Agonistes*: Love, Authority and Guilt," *AI* 44 (Winter 1987): 331–45.

John Mulryan, "The Heroic Tradition of Milton's *Samson Agonistes*," *MiltonS* 15 (1983): 217–34.

Leonard Mustazza, "The Verbal Plot of *Samson Agonistes*," *MiltonS* 23 (1987): 241–58.

Ralph Nash, "Chivalric Themes in *Samson Agonistes*," in Wallace and Ross, *Studies in Honor of John Wilcox*, 23–38.

Mary Ann Radzinowicz, "The Distinctive Tragedy of *Samson Agonistes*," *MiltonS* 17 (1983): 249–80.

Christopher Ricks, "Milton, III: Paradise Regained and *Samson Agonistes*," in *New History of Literature, II: English Poetry and Prose, 1540–1674*, ed. Christopher Ricks (New York: Bedrick, 1987), 293–309.

D. M. Rosenberg, "*Samson Agonistes*: 'Proverb'd for a fool,' " *CentR* 32 (Winter 1988): 65–78.

Roston, *Biblical Drama*, 152–64.

Charles T. Samuels, "Milton's *Samson Agonistes* and Rational Christianity," *DR* 43 (Winter 1963–1964): 495–506.

Samuel S. Stollmann, "Milton's Understanding of the 'Hebraic' in *Samson Agonistes*," *SP* 69 (July 1972): 334–47.

Chauncey B. Tinker, "*Samson Agonistes*," in Brooks, *Tragic Themes in Western Literature*, 59–76.

Darryl Tippens, "The Kenotic Experience of *Samson Agonistes*," *MiltonS* 22 (1986): 173–94.

Darryl Tippens, "'Race of Glory, Race of Shame': Kenotic Thought in *Samson Agonistes*," *MiltonQ* 19 (December 1985): 96–100.

John C. Ulreich, Jr., "'Beyond the Fifth Act': *Samson Agonistes* as Prophecy," *MiltonS* 17 (1983): 281–318.

John C. Ulreich, Jr., "Samson's 'Fiery Virtue': The Typological Problem in *Samson Agonistes*," *Cithara* 30 (May 1991): 26–33.

George R. Waggoner, "The Challange to Single Combat in *Samson Agonistes*," *PQ* 39 (January 1960): 82–91.

Julia Waggoner, "*Samson Agonistes*: Milton's Use of Syntax to Define Character," in *Literary Computing and Literary Criticism: Theoretical and Practical Essays on Theme and Rhetoric*, ed. Rosanne G. Potter (Philadelphia: University of Pennsylvania Press, 1989), 145–65.

G. A. Wilkes, "The Interpretation of *Samson Agonistes*," *HLQ* 26 (October 1963): 363–80.

Arnold Williams, "A Note on *Samson Agonistes, LL* 90–94," *MLN* 63 (December 1948); 537.

A. S. P. Woodhouse, "Tragic Effects in *Samson Agonistes*," *UTQ* 28 (April 1959): 205–22.

MONTAGUE, WALTER

The Shepherd's Paradise

Hassel, *Renaissance Drama*, 90–92.

MUNDAY, ANTHONY

The Book of Sir Thomas More

Charles R. Forker, and Joseph Candido, "Wit, Wisdom, and Theatricality in *The Book of Sir Thomas Moore*," *ShakS* 13 (1980): 85–104.

Alistair Fox, "The Paradoxical Design of *The Book of Sir Thomas Moore*," *Ren&R* 5 (August 1981): 162–73.

MUNDAY, ANTHONY, *Chryso-Thriambos: The Triumphs of Gold*

MacD. P. Jackson, "Anthony Munday and the Play of *Thomas More*," *Moreana* 22 (April 1985): 83–84.

Mann, *The Elizabethan Player*, 14–40.

Scott McMillin, "*The Book of Sir Thomas Moore*: A Theatrical View," *MP* 68 (August 1970): 10–24.

Thomas Merriam, "Did Munday Compose *Sir Thomas More?*" *N&Q* 37 (June 1990): 175–78.

Thomas Merriam, "Was Munday the Author of *Sir Thomas More?*" *Moreana* 24 (June 1987): 25–30.

Judith Doolin Spikes, "*The Book of Sir Thomas Moore*: Structure and Meaning," *Moreana* 11 (June 1974): 25–39.

Chryso-Thriambos: The Triumphs of Gold, at the Inauguration of Sir John Pemberton in the Dignity of Lord Mayor

Leah Sinanoglou Marcus, "City Metal and Country Mettle: The Occasion of Ben Jonson's *Golden Age Restored*," in Bergeron, *Pageantry in the Shakespearean Theater*, 26–47.

Death of Robert, Earl of Huntingdon
(with Chettle)

J. M. R. Margeson, "Dramatic Form: The Huntingdon Plays," *SEL* 14 (Spring 1974): 223–38.

Downfall of Robert, Earl of Huntingdon
(with Chettle)

J. M. R. Margeson, "Dramatic Form: The Huntingdon Plays," *SEL* 14 (Spring 1974): 223–38.

John a Kent and John a Cumber

E. A. J. Honigmann, "*John a Kent*," *YES* 13 (1983): 288–93.

Roslyn L. Knutson, "Play Identifications: *The Wise Man of West Chester* and *John a Kent and John a Cumber*; *Longshanks* and *Edward I*," *HLQ* 47 (Winter 1984): 1–11.

William B. Long, "*John a Kent and John a Cumber*: An Elizabethan Playbook and Its Implications; Essays in Honor of S. F. Johnson," in Elton and Long, *Shakespeare and Dramatic Tradition*, 125–43.

Traister, *Heavenly Necromancers*, 43–47.

Metropolis Coronata: The Triumphs of Ancient Drapery in a Second Year's Entertainment in Honour of Sir John Jolles, Lord Mayor

Theodore B. Leinwand, "London's Triumphing: The Jacobean Lord Mayor's Show," *CLIOI* 11 (Winter 1982) 137–53.

Sir John Oldcastle

Larry S. Champion, "'Havoc in the Commonwealth': Perspective, Political Ideology, and Dramatic Strategy in *Sir John Oldcastle* and the English Chronicle Plays," *MRDE* 5 (Spring 1991): 165–79.

The Triumphs of Re-United Britannia; Performed in Honor of Sir Leonard Holliday, Lord Mayor

Richard Dutton, "*King Lear, The Triumphs of Reunited Britannia*, and 'The Matter of Britain,'" *L&H* 12 (Autumn 1986): 139–51.

Zelauto

William Chester Jordan, "Approaches to the Court Scene in the Bond Story: Equity and Mercy or Reason and Nature," *SQ* 33 (Spring 1982): 49–59.

NABBES, THOMAS

Hannibal and Scipio

R. W. Vince, "Thomas Nabbes' *Hannibal and Scipio*: Sources and Theme," *SEL* 11 (Spring 1971): 327–43.

Microcosmus: A Moral Masque

R. W. Vince, "Morality and Masque: The Context for Thomas Nabbes' *Microcosmus*," *ES* 53 (October 1972): 328–34.

NASHE, THOMAS

An Almond for a Parrat

Mann, *The Elizabethan Player*, 69–70.

Summer's Last Will and Testament

Barber, *Shakespeare's Festive Comedy*, 58–86.

Peter Berek, "Artifice and Realism in Lyly, Nashe, and *Love's Labor's Lost*," *SEL* 23 (Spring 1983): 207–21.

Elizabeth Cook, "'Death proves them all but toyes': Nashe's Unidealising Show," in Lindley, *The Court Masque*, 17–32.

McPeek, *The Black Book of Knaves*, 73–77.

J. J. M. Tobin, "More on 'Nothing,'" *N&Q* 32 (December 1985): 479–80.

NORTON, THOMAS

The Tragedy of Gorboduc; or, The Tragedy of Ferrex and Porrex
(with Sackville)

Mark Breitenberg, "Reading Elizabethan Iconicity: *Gorboduc* and the Semiotics of Reform," *ELR* 18 (Spring 1988): 194–217.

Clemen, *English Tragedy Before Shakespeare*, 56–74, 253–57.

McDonnell, *The Aspiring Mind*, 70–86.

Franco Moretti, "'A huge Eclipse': Tragic Form and the Deconsecration of Sovereignty," in Greenblatt, *The Power of Forms*, 7–40.

Prior, *The Language of Tragedy*, 31–33.

Ribner, *The English History Play in the Age of Shakespeare*, 41–52.

Robert Y. Turner, "Pathos and the *Gorboduc* Tradition, 1560–1590," *HLQ* 25 February 1962): 97–120.

PEELE, GEORGE

The Arraignment of Paris: A Pastoral

Clemen, *English Tragedy Before Shakespeare*, 163–67.

Inga-Stina Ewbank, "'What words, what looks, what wonders?': Language and Spectacle in the Theatre of George Peele," in Hibbard, *The Elizabethan Theatre V*, 124–54.

Henry G. Lesnick, "The Structural Significance of Myth and Flattery in Peele's *Arraignment of Paris*," *SP* 65 (April 1968): 163–70.

Louis Adrian Montrose, "Gifts and Reasons: The Context of Peele's *Araygnement of Paris*," *ELH* 47 (September 1980): 433–61.

Susan T. Viguers, "Art and Reality in George Peele's *The Araygnement of Paris* and *David and Bethsabe*," *CLAJ* 30 (June 1987): 481–500.

Andrew Von Hendy, "The Triumph of Chastity: Form and Meaning in *The Arraignment of Paris*," *RenD* 1 (1968): 87–101.

Battle of Alcazar

Bevington, *From "Mankind" to Marlowe*, 104–07.

Clemen, *English Tragedy Before Shakespeare*, 171–73.

D'Amico, *The Moor in English Renaissance Drama*, 81–83.

Inga-Stina Ewbank, "'What words, what looks, what wonders?': Language and Spectacle in the Theatre of George Peele," in Hibbard, *The Elizabethan Theatre V*, 124–54.

Jones, *Othello's Countrymen*, 40–49.

McDonnell, *The Aspiring Mind*, 150–52.

M. K. Nellis, "Peele's Night: Dumb or Divine Architect?," *N&Q* 30 (April 1983): 132–33.

Tokson, *The Popular Image of the Blackman in English Drama*, 117–18.

Susan T. Viguers, "Peele's *The Battle of Alcazar*," *Expl* 43 (Winter 1985): 9–12.

The Hunting of Cupid

John P. Cutts, "Peele's *Hunting of Cupid*," *SRen* 5 (1958): 121–29.

King Edward the First, Surnamed Edward Longshankes

Braunmuller, *George Peele*, 87–106.

Clemen, *English Tragedy Before Shakespeare*, 167–73.

PEELE, GEORGE, *The Love of King David and Fair Bethsabe*

Roslyn L. Knutson, "Play Identifications: *The Wise Man of West Chester* and *John a Kent and John a Cumber*; *Longshanks* and *Edward I*," *HLQ* 47 (Winter 1984): 1–11.

J. C. Maxwell, "Peele, *Edward I*, 1238–9," *N&Q* 22 (April 1975): 248.

Marilyn K. Nellis, "Peele's *Edward I*," *Expl* 44 (Winter 1986): 5–8

John D. Reeves, "Two Perplexities in Peele's *King Edward the First*," *N&Q* 201 (August 1956): 328–29.

John D. Reeves, "Persus and the Flying Horse in Peele and Heywood," *RES* 6 (November 1955): 397.

Ribner, *The English History Play in the Age of Shakespeare*, 89–94.

William Tydeman, "Peele's *Edward I* and the Elizabethan View of Wales," in *The Welsh Connection: Essays by Past and Present Members of the Department of English Language and Literature, University College of North Wales, Bangor*, ed. William Tydeman (Llandysul: Gower, 1986), 24–53.

The Love of King David and Fair Bethsabe

Blackburn, *Biblical Drama*, 171–82.

Carolyn Blair, "On the Question of Unity in George Peele's *David and Bathsabe*," in *Studies in Honor of John C. Hodges and Alwin Thaler*, ed. R. B. Davis and J. L. Lievsay (Knoxville: University of Tennessee Press, 1961), 35–41.

Braunmuller, *George Peele*, 107–25.

Clemen, *English Tragedy Before Shakespeare*, 173–76, 262–67.

T. W. Craike, "Some Notes on the Text of Peele's *David and Bethsabe*," *N&Q* 23 (April 1977): 208–10.

I. S. Ekeblad, "*The Love of King David and Fair Bethsabe*: A Note on George Peele's Biblical Drama," *ES* 39 (April 1958): 57–62.

Inga-Stina Ewbank, "The House of David in Renaissance Drama: A Comparative Study," *RenD* 8 (1965): 3–40.

Inga-Stina Ewbank, "'What words, what looks, what wonders?': Language and Spectacle in the Theatre of George Peele," in Hibbard, *The Elizabethan Theatre V*, 124–54.

Knight, *Golden Labyrinth*, 60–61.

McDonnell, *The Aspiring Mind*, 148–50.

Roston, *Biblical Drama*, 100–09.

Stilling, *Love and Death in Renaissance Tragedy*, 56–66.

Susan T. Viguers, "Art and Reality in George Peele's *The Araygnement of Paris* and *David and Bethsabe*," *CLAJ* 30 (June 1987): 481–500.

Carolyn Whitney-Brown, "'A Farre More Worthy Wombe': Reproductive Anxiety in Peele's *David and Bethsabe*," in Kehler and Baker, *In Another Country*, 181–204.

The Old Wives' Tale

Frank R. Ardolino, "Severed and Brazen Heads: Headhunting in Elizabethan Drama," *JEP* 4 (August 1983): 169–81.

M. C. Bradbrook, Peele's *The Old Wives' Tale*, in *Aspects of Dramatic Form*, 3–16.

M. C. Bradbrook, "Peele's *Old Wives' Tale*: A Play of Enchantment," *ES* 43 (October 1962): 323–30.

Cope, *Dramaturgy of the Daemonic*, 50–60.

Jackson I. Cope, "Peele's *Old Wives' Tale*: Folk Stuff into Ritual Form," *ELH* 49 (Summer 1982): 326–38.

John D. Cox, "Homely Matter and Multiple Plots in Peele's *Old Wives' Tale*," *TSLL* 20 (Fall 1978): 330–46.

Philip Edwards, "'Seeing Is Believing': Action and Narration in *The Old Wives' Tale* and *The Winter's Tale*," in Honigman, *Shakespeare and His Contemporaries*, 79–93.

Mary G. Free, "Audience within Audience in *The Old Wives' Tale*," *RenP 1982* (1983): 53–61.

Herbert Goldstone, "Interplay in Peele's *The Old Wives' Tale*," *BUSE* 4 (Winter 1960): 202–13.

Thomas N. Grove, "Some Observations on the 'Marvelous' *Old Wives' Tale*," *SAP* 11 (1979): 201–02.

Leanore Lieblein, "Doubling as a Language of Transformation: The Case of *The Old Wives' Tale*," in Jones-Davies, *Du Texte à la scene*, 225–43.

Sylvia Lyons-Render, "Folk Motifs in George Peele's *The Old Wives Tale*," *TFSB* 26 (September 1960): 62–71.

Joan C. Marx, "'Soft, Who Have We Here?' The Dramatic Technique of *The Old Wives*' Tale," *RenD* 12 (1981): 117–43.

PICKERING, JOHN, *Horestes*

Roger de V. Renwick, "The Mummers' Play and *The Old Wives' Tale*," *JAF* 94 (October–December 1981): 433–55.

Laurilyn J. Rockey, "*The Old Wives' Tale* as Dramatic Satire," *ETJ* 22 (June 1970): 268–75.

Traister, *Heavenly Necromancers*, 40–43.

Susan T. Viguers, "The Hearth and the Cell: Art in *The Old Wives' Tale*," *SEL* 21 (Spring 1981): 209–21.

PICKERING, JOHN

Horestes

P. Happé, "Tragic Themes in Three Tudor Moraliteies," *SEL* 5 (Spring 1965): 207–27.

James E. Phillips, "A Revaluation of *Horestes* (1567)," *HLQ* 18 (May 1955): 227–44.

Karen Robertson, "The Body Natural of a Queen: Mary, James, *Horestes*," *Ren&R* 14 (Winter 1990): 25–36.

Michael Shapiro, "John Pikeryng's *Horestes*: Auspices and Theatricality; Essays in Honor of S. F. Johnson," in Elton and Long, *Shakespeare and Dramatic Tradition*, 211–26.

Rosemary Woolf, "The Influence of Mystery Plays upon the Popular Tragedies of the 1560's," *RenD* 6 (1973): 89–105.

PRESTON, THOMAS

Cambises, King of Persia

William A. Armstrong, "The Authorship and Political Meaning of *Cambises*," *ES* 36 (June 1955): 289–99.

Bevington, *From "Mankind" to Marlowe*, 81–89, 183–89, 211–16.

Clemen, *English Tragedy Before Shakespeare*, 193–94.

Abraham Feldman, "King Cambises' Vein," *N&Q* 196 (March 1951): 98–100.

P. Happé, "Tragic Themes in Three Tudor Moralities," *SEL* 5 (Spring 1965): 207–27.

Harrison, *Elizabethan Plays and Players*, 5–9.

G. R. Hibbard, "From 'Iygging Vaines of Riming Mother Wits' to 'the Spacious Volubilitie of a Drumming Decasillabon': Papers Given at Eleventh Internat. Conf. on Elizabethan Theatre Held at Univ. of Waterloo, Waterloo, Ont., in July 1985," in Magnusson and McGee, *The Elizabethan Theatre, XI*, 55–73.

Joel H. Kaplan, "Reopening King Cambises' Vein," *Essays in Theatre* 5 (May 1987): 103–14.

McDonnell, *The Aspiring Mind*, 99–100.

Mann, *The Elizabethan Player*, 234–35.

Ribner, *English History Play in the Time of Shakespeare*, 53–60.

Rossiter, *English Drama from Early Times to the Elizabethans*, 142–44.

Karl P. Wentersdorf, "The Allegorical Role of the Vice in Preston's *Cambises*," *MLS* 11 (Spring 1981): 54–69.

Rosemary Woolf, "The Influence of Mystery Plays upon the Popular Tragedies of the 1560's," *RenD* 6 (1973): 89–105.

RANDOLPH, THOMAS

Hey for Honesty, Down with Knavery

Martin Butler, "The Auspices of Thomas Randolph's *Hey for Honesty, Down with Knavery*," *N&Q* 35 (December 1988): 491–92.

The Muses' Looking-Glass

Jonas Barish, "Three Caroline 'Defenses' of the Stage ; Essays in Honor of Eugene M. Waith," in Braunmuller and Bulman, *Comedy from Shakespeare to Sheridan*, 194–212.

John Cutts, "Thomas Randolph's *The Muse's Looking-Glass* and *The Battle of the Vices against the Virtues*," *N&Q* 32 (June 1985): 161–62.

RASTELL, JOHN

The Nature of the Four Elements

Bevington, *From "Mankind" to Marlowe*, 45–47.

RASTALL, JOHN, *Calisto and Melibea*

Hiroshi Ozawa, "The Structural Innovations of the More Circle Dramatists," *ShStud* 19 (1980–1981): 1–23.

Calisto and Melibea

Albert J. Geritz, "*Calisto and Melebea* (ca. 1530)," *Celestinesca* 4 (May 1980): 17–29.

Johan Johan

Howard B. Norland, "Formalizing English Farce: *Johan Johan* and Its French Connection," *CompD* 17 (Summer 1983): 141–52.

REDFORD, JOHN

Wyt and Science

Edgar T. Schell, "*Scio Ergo Sum*: The Structure of *Wit and Science*," *SEL* 16 (Spring 1976): 179–99. Reprinted in *Strangers and Pilgrims*, 55–76.

John W. Velz, and Carl P. Dow, Jr., "Tradition and Originality in *Wyt and Science*," *SP* 65 (October 1968): 631–46.

Thomas Ramey Watson, "Redford's *Wyt and Science*," *Expl* 39 (Summer 1981): 3–5.

RIGHTWISE, JOHN

Cardinalis Pacificus

W. R. Streitberger, "The Play Called 'Heretic Luther' (1527)," *TA* 44 (1989–90): 21–36.

ROWLEY, SAMUEL

When You See Me You Know Me

Ribner, *The English History Play in the Age of Shakespeare*, 278–84.

ROWLEY, WILLIAM

All's Lost by Lust

D'Amico, *The Moor in English Renaissance Drama*, 98–119.

Tokson, *The Popular Image of the Blackman in English Drama*, 78–79.

The Changeling
(with Middleton)

Michael C. Andrews, " 'Sweetness' in *The Changeling*," *YES* 1 (1971): 63–67.

Thomas L. Berger, "The Petrarchan Fortress of *The Changeling*," *RenP 1968* (1969): 37–46.

Normand Berlin, "The 'Finger' Image and Relationship of Character in *The Changeling*," *ESA* 12 (June 1969): 162–66.

Lois E. Bueler, "The Rhetoric of Change in *The Changeling*," *ELR* 14 (Spring 1984): 95–113.

Frederick M. Burelbach, Jr., "Middleton and Rowley's *The Changeling*, I.i.52–56," *Expl* 26 (July 1968): 60.

Clay, *The Role of Anxiety*, 220–34.

Dennis, *Dramatic Essays*, 133–40.

Penelope B. R. Doob, "A Reading of *The Changeling*," *ELR* 3 (Summer 1973): 183–206.

Joseph M. Duffy, "Madhouse Optics: *The Changeling*," *CompD* 8 (Summer 1974): 184–98.

Eliot, *Essays on Ellizabethan Drama*, 89–95.

E. Engleberg, "Tragic Blindness in *The Changeling* and *Women Beware Women*," *MLQ* 23 (March 1962): 20–28.

Hawkins, *Poetic Freedom and Poetic Truth*, 2–3, 100–01.

Catherine A. Hébert, "A Note on the Significance of the Title of Middleton's *The Changeling*," *CLAJ* 12 (September 1968): 66–69.

Tinsley Helton, "Middleton and Rowley's *The Changeling*, V,iii,175–77," *Expl* 21 (May 1963): 74.

Karl L. Holzknecht, "The Dramatic Structure of *The Changeling*," *RenP 1953* (1954): 77–87.

Henry E. Jacobs, "The Constancy of Change: Character and Perspective in *The Changeling*," *TSLL* 16 (Winter 1975): 651–74.

Paula Johnson, "Dissimulation Anatomized: *The Changeling*," *PQ* 56 (Summer 1977): 329–38.

Robert Jordan, "Myth and Psychology in *The Changeling*," *RenD* 3 (1970): 157–66.

Dorothea Kehler, "Middleton and Rowley's *The Changeling*, V.iii.175–77," *Expl* 26 (December 1968): Item 44.

Dorothea Kehler, "Rings and Jewels in *The Changeling*," *ELN* 5 (October 1967): 15–17.

Levin, *The Multiple Plot in English Renaissance Drama*, 34–48.

Ornstein, *Moral Vision of Jacobean Tragedy*, 179–90.

Raymond J. Pentzell, "*The Changeling*: Notes on Mannerisms in Dramatic Form," *CompD* 9 (Spring 1975): 3–28.

Dale B. J. Randall, "Some Observations on the Theme of Chastity in *The Changeling*," *ELR* 14 (March 1984): 347–66.

Robert R. Reed, Jr., "A Factual Interpretation of *The Changeling*'s Madhouse Scenes," *N&Q* 195 (June 1950): 247–48.

Ribner, *Jacobean Tragedy*, 126–37.

Christopher Ricks, "The Moral and Poetic Structure of *The Changeling*," *EIC* 10 (July 1960): 290–306.

Emil L. Roy, "Sexual Paradox in *The Changeling*," *L&P* 25, no. 1 (1975): 124–32.

Samuel Schoenbaum, "Middleton's Tragedies—A Critical Study," *CUSECL* 168 (1955): 132–50.

Scott, *Renaissance Drama*, 76–88.

J. L. Simmons, "Diabolical Realism in Middleton and Rowley's *The Changeling*, *RenD* 11 (1980): 135–70.

Stoll, *From Shakespeare to Joyce*, 309–12.

J. Chesley Taylor, "Metaphores of the Moral World: Structure in *The Changeling*," *TSE* 20 (Spring 1972): 41–56.

T. B. Tomlinson, "Poetic Naturalism—*The Changeling*," *JEGP* 63 (October 1964): 648–59.

Wells, *Elizabethan and Jacobean Playwrights*, 39–41.

A Cure for a Cuckold
(with Webster)

Inga-Stina Ekeblad, "Webster's Constructional Rhythm," *ELH* 24 (September 1957): 165–76.

Forker, *The Skull Beneath the Skin*, 171–89.

Mina Irgat, "Disease Imagery in the Plays of J. Webster," *Litera* 2 (1955): 2–24.

Murray, *A Study of John Webster*, 215–36.

Pearson, *Tragedy and Tragicomedy in the Plays of John Webster*, 115–32.

A Fair Quarrel
(with Middleton)

Asp, *A Study of Thomas Middleton's Tragicomedies*, 103–47.

Farr, *Thomas Middleton and the Drama of Realism*, 38–49.

R. V. Holdsworth, "The Medical Jargon in *A Fair Quarrel*," *RES* 23 (1972): 448–54.

Kistner and Kistner, *Middleton's Tragic Themes*, 29–41.

A. L. Kistner, and M. K. Kistner, "The Themes and Structures of *A Fair Quarrel*," *TSL* 23 (Spring 1977): 31–46.

Levin, *The Multiple Plot in English Renaissance Drama*, 66–75.

Levin, "The Three Quarrels of *A Fair Quarrel*," *SP* 61 (April 1964): 219–31.

Michael E. Mooney, "'The Common Sight' and Dramatic Form: Rowley's Embedded Jig in *A Fair Quarrel*," *SEL* 20 (Spring 1980): 305–23.

Samuel Schoenbaum, "Middleton's Tragi-Comedies," *MP* 54 (August 1956): 16–19.

The Maid in the Mill
(with Fletcher)

Klaus P. Steiger, "'May a Man be Caught with Faces?': The Convention of 'Heart' and 'Face' in Fletcher and Rowley's *The Maid in the Mill*," *E&S* 20 (1967): 47–63.

195

ROWLEY, WILLIAM, *The Old Law; or, A New Way to Please You*

The Old Law; or, A New Way to Please You
(with Middleton)

Asp, *A Study of Thomas Middleton's Tragicomedies*, 148–210.

A. A. Bromham, "The Contemporary Significance of *The Old Law*," *SEL* 24 (Spring 1984): 327–39.

George E. Rowe, Jr., "*The Old Law* and Middleton's Comic Vision," *ELH* 42 (June 1975): 189–202.

George E. Rowe, Jr., *Thomas Middleton & the New Comedy Tradition*, 175–89.

A Shoemaker and a Gentleman

R. V. Holdsworth, "Two Proverbs in Middleton and Some Contemporaries," *N&Q* 28 (April 1981): 172–73.

The Spanish Gipsy
(with Middleton)

Frederick M. Burelbach, Jr., "Theme and Structure in *The Spanish Gipsy*," *HAB* 19, no. 2 (1968): 37–41.

A. L. Kistner, and M. K. Kistner, *Middleton's Tragic Themes*, 13–26.

A. L. Kistner, and M. K. Kistner, "*The Spanish Gipsy*," *HAB* 25 (Summer 1974): 211–24.

The Travels of the Three English Brothers, Sir Thomas, Sir Anthony, Mr. Robert Shirley
(with Day and Wilkins)

H. Neville Davies, "*Pericles* and the Sherley Brothers," in Honigmann, *Shakespeare and His Contemporaries*, 94–113.

Mann, *The Elizabethan Player*, 68–73.

Samuel Schoenbaum, "John Day and Elizabethan Drama," *BPLQ* 5 (July 1953): 142–45.

A Wit at Several Weapons
(with Fletcher and Middleton)

James E. Savage, "The Effects of Revision in the Beaumont and Fletcher Play, *Wit at Several Weapons*," *UMSE* 1, no. 1 (1960): 32–50.

The Witch of Edmonton
(with Dekker and Ford)

Adams, *English Domestic or Homiletic Tragedies*, 132–42.

J. V. Ashton, "Dekker's Use of Folklore in *Old Fortunatus, If This Be Not A Good Play*, and *The Witch of Edmonton*," *PQ* 41 (January 1962): 240–41, 245–51.

David Atkinson, "Moral Knowledge and the Double Action of *The Witch of Edmonton*," *SEL* 25 (Spring 1985): 419–37.

David Atkinson, "The Two Plots of *The Witch of Edmonton*," *N&Q* 31 (June 1984): 229–30.

Leonora L. Brodwin, "The Domestic Tragedy of Frank Thorney in *The Witch of Edmonton*," *SEL* 7 (Spring 1967): 311–28.

Viviana Comensoli, "Witchcraft and Domestic Tragedy in *The Witch of Edmonton*," in *The Politics of Gender in Early Modern Europe*, ed. Jean R. Brink, Allison P. Coudert, and Maryanne C. Horowitz (Kirksville, MO: Sixteenth Century Journal Publications; 1989) 43–60.

Anthony B. Dawson, "Witchcraft/Bigamy: Cultural Conflict in *The Witch of Edmonton*," *RenD* 20 (1989): 77–98.

Harris, *Night's Black Agents*, 90–108.

Michael Hattaway, "Women and Witchcraft: The Case of *The Witch of Edmonton*," *Trivium* 20 (1985): 49–68.

Edward Sackville West, "The Significance of *The Witch of Edmonton*," *Criterion* 17, no. 1 (1973): 23–32.

Wells, *Elizabethan and Jacobean Playwrights*, 71–75.

SACKVILLE, THOMAS

The Tragedy of Gorboduc; or, The Tragedy of Ferrex and Porrex
(with Norton)

Mark Breitenberg, "Reading Elizabethan Iconicity: *Gorboduc* and the Semiotics of Reform," *ELR* 18 (Spring 1988): 194–217.

Clemen, *English Tragedy Before Shakespeare*, 56–74, 253–57.

McDonnell, *The Aspiring Mind*, 70–86.

Franco Moretti, "'A huge Eclipse': Tragic Form and the Deconsecration of Sovereignty," in Greenblatt, *The Power of Forms*, 7–40.

Prior, *The Language of Tragedy*, 31–33.

Ribner, *The English History Play in the Age of Shakespeare*, 41–52.

Robert Y. Turner, "Pathos and the *Gorboduc* Tradition, 1560–1590," *HLQ* 25 February 1962): 97–120.

SHAKESPEARE, WILLIAM

All's Well That Ends Well

John F. Adams, "*All's Well That Ends Well*: The Paradox of Procreation," *SQ* 12 (Summer 1961): 261–70.

Janet Adelman, "Bed Tricks: On Marriage as the End of Comedy in *All's Well That Ends Well* and *Measure for Measure*," in Holland, Homan, and Paris, *Shakespeare's Personality*, 151–74.

Carolyn Asp, "Subjectivity, Desire and Female Friendship in *All's Well That Ends Well*," *L&P* 32, no. 4 (1986): 48–63.

Susan Bassnett-McGuire, "An Ill Marriage in an Ill Government: Patterns of Unresolved Conflict in *All's Well That Ends Well*," *ShJE* 120 (1984): 97–102.

Tita French Baumlin, " 'All yet Seems Well, and if It Ends so Meet': Ambiguity and Tragic Language in *All's Well That Ends Well*," *EIRC* 17 (1991): 125–43.

Josephine W. Bennett, "New Techniques of Comedy in *All's Well That Ends Well*," *SQ* 18 (Autumn 1967): 337–62.

J. Scott Bentley, "Helena's Paracelsian Cure of the King: *Magia Naturalis* in *All's Well That Ends Well*," *CaudaP* 5 (Spring 1986): 1–4.

David M. Bergeron, "The Mythical Structure of *All's Well That Ends Well*," *TSLL* 14 (Winter 1973): 559–68.

David M. Bergeron, "The Structure of Healing in *All's Well That Ends Well*," *SAB* 34 (November 1972): 25–34.

David S. Berkeley, and Donald Keesee, "Bertram's Blood-Consciousness in *All's Well That Ends Well*," *SEL* 31 (Spring 1991): 247–58.

Werner Berthoff, "'Our Means Will Make Us Means': Character as Virtue in *Hamlet* and *All's Well*," *NLH* 5 (1974): 319–51.

E. M. Blistein, "The Object of Scorn: An Aspect of the Comic Antagonist," *WHR* 14 (Spring 1960): 210–12.

M. C. Bradbrook, "Shakespeare's Hybrid: *All's Well That Ends Well*," in *Aspects of Dramatic Form*, 40–54.

M. C. Bradbrook, "Virtue is the True Nobility: A Study of the Structure of *All's Well That Ends Well*," *RES* 1 (October 1950): 289–301.

Anthony Brennan, "Helena versus Time's Winged Chariot in *All's Well That Ends Well*," *MQ* 21 (1980): 391–411.

Brockbank, *On Shakespeare*, 250–56.

James L. Calderwood, "The Mingled Yarn of *All's Well*," *JEGP* 62 (January 1963): 61–76.

James L. Calderwood, "Styles of Knowing in *All's Well*," *MLQ* 25 (September 1964): 272–94.

Thomas Cartelli, "Shakespeare's 'Rough Magic': Ending as Artifice in *All's Well That Ends Well*," *CentR* 27 (Spring 1983): 117–34.

Cecil Williamson Cary, "Burlesque as a Method of Irony in Shakespeare's *Troilus* and *All's Well That Ends Well*," *SMC* 5 (1973): 203–14.

Eileen Z. Cohen, " 'Virtue Is Bold': The Bed-Trick and Characterization in *All's Well That Ends Well* and *Measure for Measure*," *PQ* 65 (Spring 1986): 171–86.

Cox, *Shakespeare and the Dramaturgy of Power*, 82–103.

Dawson, *Indirections*, 88–108.

Carl Dennis, "*All's Well That Ends Well* and the Meaning of *Agape*," *PQ* 50 (Winter 1971): 75–84.

Christy Desmet, "Speaking Sensibly: Feminine Rhetoric in *Measure for Measure* and *All's Well That Ends Well*," *RenP 1986* (1987): 43–51.

Foakes, *Shakespeare*, 7–17.

French, *Shakespeare's Division of Experience*, 165–82.

Gerard J. Gross, "The Conclusion to *All's Well That Ends Well*," *SEL* 23 (Spring 1983): 257–76.

Grudin, *Mighty Opposites*, 89–98.

Jay L. Halio, "*All's Well That Ends Well*," *SQ* 15 (Winter 1964): 33–44.

Jay L. Halio, "Traitor in *All's Well* and *Troilus and Cressida*," *MLN* 72 (June 1957): 408–09.

Edward L. Hart, "A Mixed Consort: Leontes, Angeto, Helena," *SQ* 15 (Winter 1964): 80–83.

Haselkorn, *Prostitution in Elizabethan and Jacobean Drama*, 54–55.

Robert H. Hethmon, "The Case for *All's Well*; What's Wrong With the King?" *Drama Critique* 7 (Winter 1964): 26–31.

W. Speed Hill, "Marriage as Destiny: An Essay on *All's Well That Ends Well*," *ELR* 5 (Autumn 1975): 344–59.

Barbara Hodgedon, "The Making of Virgins and Mothers: Sexual Signs, Substitute Scenes and Doubled Presences in *All's Well That Ends Well*," *PQ* 66 (Winter 1987): 47–71.

Maurice Hunt, "*All's Well That Ends Well* and the Triumph of the Word," *TSLL* 30 (Fall 1988): 388–411.

Maurice Hunt, "Words and Deeds in *All's Well That Ends Well*," *MLQ* 48 (December 1987): 320–38.

G. K. Hunter, "Atavism and Anticipation in Shakespeare's Style," *EIC* 7 (October 1957): 451–53.

Nicolas Jacobs, "Saffron and Syphilis: *All's Well That Ends Well*, IV.v.1–3," *N&Q* 22 (April 1975): 171–72.

H. W. Jones, "*All's Well*, IV, ii, 38 Again," *MLR* 55 (April 1960): 241–42.

David Scott Kastan, "*All's Well That Ends Well* and the Limits of Comedy," *ELH* 52 (Fall 1985): 575–89.

Walter N. King, "Shakespeare's 'Mingled Yarn,'" *MLQ* 21 (March 1960): 33–44.

Knight, *Sovereign Flower*, 95–160.

Eric La Guardia, "Chastity, Regeneration, and World Order in *All's Well That Ends Well*," in Slote, *Myth and Symbol*, 119–32.

Clifford Leech, "The Theme of Ambition in *All's Well That Ends Well*," *ELH* 21 (March 1954): 17–29.

Alexander Leggatt, "*All's Well That End's Well*: The Testing of Romance," *MLQ* 32 (March 1971): 21–41.

Richard A. Levin, "*All's Well That Ends Well*, and 'All Seems Well,'" *ShakS* 13 (1980): 131–44.

Richard A. Levin, "The Two French Lords of *All's Well That Ends Well*," *N&Q* 26 (April 1979): 122–25.

Cynthia Lewis, "'Derived Honesty and Achieved Goodness': Doctrines of Grace in *All's Well That Ends Well*," *Ren&R* 14 (Spring 1990): 147–70.

Paul J. Marcotte, "Shakespeare's *All's Well That Ends Well*, Lines 2017–2018," *Expl* 41 (Fall 1982): 6–9.

James McKenzie, "A Shakespearean Emendation," *N&Q* 197 (April 1952): 160.

Ruth Nevo, "Motive and Meaning in *All's Well That Ends Well*," in Mahon, and Pendleton, *"Fanned and winnowed opinions,"* 26–51.

Nicholl, *The Chemical Theatre*, 74–75.

Barbara D. Palmer, "'The Eagles are gone': Soliloquies in the Tragi-Comedies," *ISJR* 54 (November 1980): 441–48.

David J. Palmer, "Comedy and the Protestant Spirit in Shakespeare's *All's Well That Ends Well*," *BJRL* 71 (Spring 1989): 95–107.

R. B. Parker, "War and Sex in *All's Well That Ends Well*," *ShS* 37 (1984): 99–113.

Frances M. Pearce, "A Quest for Unity: A Study of Failure and Redemption in *All's Well That Ends Well*," *SQ* 25 (Winter 1974): 71–88.

Helen P. Pettigrew, "The Young Count Rousillon," *WVUBPL* 4 (1943): 22–30.

Carol W. Pollard, "Immoral Morality: Combinations of Morality Types in *All's Well That Ends Well* and *The Dutch Courtesan*," *CahiersE* 25 (April 1984): 53–59.

Alan W. Powers, "'Meaner Parties': Spousal Conventions and Oral Culture in *Measure for Measure* and *All's Well That Ends Well*," *UCrow* 8 (1988): 28–41.

John Edward Price, "Anti-Marralistic Moralism in *All's Well That Ends Well*," *ShakS* 12 (1979): 95–111.

Joseph G. Price, "From Farce to Romance: *All's Well That Ends Well*," *ShJE* 99 (1963): 57–71.

Margaret L. Ranald, "The Bethrothals in *All's Well That Ends Well*," *HLQ* 26 (February 1963): 179–92.

A. P. Riemer, "On Not Being Reconciled to Bertram: *All's Well That Ends Well* and the Conventions of Renaissance Comedy," *SSEng* 1 (1975–76): 46–68.

Christopher Roark, "Lavatch and Service in *All's Well That Ends Well*," *SEL* 28 (Spring 1988): 241–58.

W. Ronald Runyan, "The Healing of Hierarchy in *All's Well That Ends Well*," *SPWVSRA* 5 (Spring 1980): 49–55.

Lynn Veach Sadler, "Eye Imagery in *All's Well That Ends Well*: A Neglected Problem," *LWU* 10 (June 1977): 156–68.

Ernest Schanzer, "Atavism and Anticipation in Shakespeare's Style," *EIC* 7 (July 1957): 252–55.

Francis G. Schoff, "Claudio, Bertram, and a Note on Interpretation," *SQ* 10 (Winter 1959): 11–23.

Willem Schrickx, "*All's Well That Ends Well* and Its Historical Relevance; Essays in Honour of Irene Simon," in Maes-Jelinek, Michel, and Michel-Michot, *Multiple Worlds, Multiple Words*, 257–74.

Alice Shalvi, "The Pursuit of Honor in *All's Well That Ends Well*," in Shalvi and Mendilow, *Studies in English Language and Literature*, 9–34.

Michael Shapiro, "'The Web of Our Life': Human Cruelty and Mutual Redemption in *All's Well That Ends Well*," *JEGP* 71 (January 1973): 514–26.

Shaw, *Plays and Players*, 9–16.

Paul N. Siegel, "Shakespeare and the Neo-Chivalric Cult of Honor," *CentR* 8 (Winter 1964): 56–60.

Peggy Munoz Simonds, "Sacred and Sexual Motifs in *All's Well That Ends Well*," *RenQ* 42 (Spring 1989): 33–59.

J. M. Silverman, "Two Types of Comedy in *All's Well That Ends Well*," *SQ* 24 (Winter 1973): 25–34.

Eliot Slater, "Word Links with *All's Well That Ends Well*," *N&Q* 24 (February 1977): 109–12.

Susan Snyder, "*All's Well That Ends Well* and Shakespeare's Helens: Text and Subtext, Subject and Object," *ELR* 18 (Winter 1988): 66–77.

Gary Taylor, "'*Praestat difficilior lectio*': *All's Well That Ends Well* and *Richard III*," *RenS* 2 (March 1988): 27–46.

Michael Taylor, "Persecuting Time with Hope: The Cynicism of Romance in *All's Well That Ends Well*," *ESC* 11 (September 1985): 282–94.

Alexander Welsh, "The Loss of Men and Getting of Children: *All's Well That Ends Well* and *Measure for Measure*," *MLR* 73 (January 1978): 17–28.

G. A. Wilkes, "*All's Well That Ends Well* and 'The Common Stock of Narrative Tradition,'" *LeedsSE* 20 (Summer 1989): 207–16.

Harold S. Wilson, "Dramatic Emphasis in *All's Well That Ends Well*," *HLQ* 13 (May 1950): 217–40.

Antony and Cleopatra

Lyndall Abraham, "Alchemical Reference in *Antony and Cleopatra*," *SSEng* 8 (1982–1983); 100–04.

John Alvis, "The Religion of Eros: A Re-Interpretation of *Antony and Cleopatra*," *Renascence* 30 (Autumn 1978): 185–98.

Donald K. Anderson, Jr., "A New Gloss for the 'Three-Nook'd World' of *Antony and Cleopatra*," *ELN* 17 (September 1979): 103–06.

A. A. Ansari, "Antony and Cleopatra: An Image of Liquifaction," *AJES* 8 (April 1983): 79–93.

Wallace A. Bacon, "The Suicide of Antony," *ShAB* 24 (July 1949): 193–202.

Sylvan Barnet, "Recognition and Reversal in *Antony and Cleopatra*," *SQ* 9 (Summer 1957): 331–34.

J. Leeds Barroll, "Antony and Pleasure," *JEGP* 57 (October 1959): 709–20.

J. Leeds Barroll, "Scarrus and the Scarred Soldier," *HLQ* 22 (October 1959): 31–40.

J. Leeds Barroll, "Shakespeare and the Art of Character: A Study of Anthony," *ShakS* 5 (1969): 159–235.

Ralph Behrens, "Cleopatra Exonerated," *ShN* 9 (November 1959): 36.

Arthur H. Bell, "Time and Convention in *Antony and Cleopatra*," *SQ* 24 (Spring 1973): 253–64.

Raymond Benoit, "The Prophecy in the Play: *Antony and Cleopatra*," *Greyfriar* 17 (1974): 3–7.

Peter Berek, "Doing and Undoing: The Value of Action in *Antony and Cleopatra*," *SQ* 32 (Autumn 1981): 295–304.

David S. Berkeley, "On Desentimentalizing Antony," *N&Q* 209 (April 1964): 139–42.

J. Wilkes Berry, "Two Hoops in Shakespeare's *Antony and Cleopatra*," *CEA* 35, no. 3 (1973): 29–30.

William Blisset, "Dramatic Irony in *Antony and Cleopatra*," *SQ* 18 (Summer 1967): 151–66.

David-Everett Blythe, "Shakespeare's *Antony and Cleopatra*," *Expl* 49 (Winter 1991): 77–79.

Adrien Bonjour, "From Shakespeare's Venus to Cleopatra's Cupids," *ShS* 15 (1962): 73–90.

Adrien Bonjour, "Shakespeare and the Toil of Grace," in Bloom, *Shakespeare 1564–1964*, 88–94.

Lawrence Edward Bowling, "Antony's Internal Disunity," *SEL* 4 (Spring 1964): 239–46.

Lawrence Edward Bowling, "Duality in the Minor Characters in *Antony and Cleopatra*," *CE* 18 (February 1957): 251–55.

Thomas D. Bowman, "Antony and the 'lass unparalled'd," *ShN* 7 (December 1957): 47.

Bradley, *Oxford Lectures on Poetry*, 279–310.

Bradshaw, *Shakespeare's Skepticism*, 32–37.

Nielson das Neves Brandaô, "Defeat in *Antony and Cleopatra*," *Signal* 1, no. 1 (1978): 101–16.

Anthony S. Brennan, "Excellent Dissembling: Antony and Cleopatra Playing at Love," *MQ* 19 (1978): 313–29.

Joa~o Batista B. de Brito, "Duality," *Signal* 1, no. 1 (1978): 32–46.

Brooks, and Heilman, *Understanding Drama*, 673–74.

Mercedes Broussard, "Mother and Child: Cleopatra and the Asp," *CEA* 37, no. 1 (1974): 25–26.

Brown, *Dramatis Personae*, 227–35.

Andrew S. Cairncross, "*Antony and Cleopatra*, III.x.10," *N&Q* 22 (April 1975): 173.

Canfield, *Word as Bond in English Literature*, 291–300.

Cecil, *Poets and Story Tellers*, 3–24.

Chandhuri, *Infirm Glory*, 184–92.

Maurice Charney, "Shakespeare's Antony: A Study of Image Themes," *SP* 54 (April 1957): 149–61.

Maurice Charney, "Shakespeare's Style in *Julius Caesar* and *Antony and Cleopatra*," *ELH* 26 (September 1959): 355–67.

Thomas Clayton, " 'Mysterious by this Love': The Unregenerate Resurrection of *Antony and Cleopatra*," in *Jadavpur University Essays and Studies III: A Festschrift in Honor of S. C. Sengupta*, ed. Jagannath Chakravorty (Calcutta: Jadavpur University, 1981), 95–116.

John Coates, " 'The Choice of Hercules' in *Antony and Cleopatra*," *ShS* 31 (1978): 45–52.

Albert Cook, "Shakespeare's *Antony and Cleopatra*, V, ii, 338–341," *Expl* 6 (November 1947): 9.

Coombe, *Literature and Criticism*, 97–99, 129–131.

Walter R. Coppedge, "The Joy of the Worm: Dying in *Antony and Cleopatra*," *RenP* 1987 (1988): 41–50.

Maria Glaucia de V. Costa, "The Moon and Cleopatra: A Case of Parallelism in *Antony and Cleopatra*," *Signal* 1, no. 1 (1978): 47–64.

Gordon W. Couchman, "*Antony and Cleopatra* and the Subjective Convention," *PMLA* 76 (September 1961): 420–25.

Graham Cullum, " 'Condemning Shadows Quite': *Antony and Cleopatra*," *P&L* 5 (Fall 1981): 186–203.

Delora G. Cunningham, "The Characterization of Shakespeare's Cleopatra," *SQ* 6 (Winter 1955): 9–17.

David Daiches, "Imagery and Meaning in *Anthony and Cleopatra*," *ES* 43 (October 1962): 343–58.

D'Amico, *The Moor in English Renaissance Drama*, 149–61.

John F. Danby, "The Shakespearean Dialectic: An Aspect of *Antony and Cleopatra*," *Scrutiny* 16 (September 1949): 196–212. Reprinted in Danby, *Poets on Fortune's Hill*, 128–51.

Maria Luisa Dañobeitia-Fernandez, "Cleopatra's Role Taking: A Study of *Antony and Cleopatra*," *RCEI* 12 (April 1986): 55–73.

Davidson, *The Solace of Literature*, 57–61.

Clifford Davidson, "*Antony and Cleopatra*: Circe, Venus, and the Whore of Babylon," *BuR* 25, no. 1 (1980): 31–55.

H. Neville Davies, "Jacobean *Antony and Cleopatra*," *ShakS* 17 (1985): 123–58.

Timothy C. Davis, "Shakespeare's *Antony and Cleopatra*," *Expl* 48 (Spring 1990): 176–78.

Dawson, *Indirections*, 138–47.

Karen Degenhart, "*Antony and Cleopatra*: Psychic Elements in Conflict," *Lapis* (Homewood, IL) 6 (January 1980): 29–39.

Janette Dillon, " 'Solitariness': Shakespeare and Plutarch," *JEGP* 78 (April 1979): 325–44.

Elizabeth Story Donno, "Cleopatra Again," *SQ* 7 (Spring 1956): 227–33.

Madeleine Doran, "The Language of Hyperbole in *Antony and Cleopatra*," *QQ* 72 (Spring 1965): 26–51. Reprinted in *Shakespeare's Dramatic Language*, 154–81.

Georgia Dunbar, "The Verse Rhythms of *Antony and Cleopatra*," *Style* 5 (Summer 1971): 231–45.

Eagleton, *Shakespeare and Society*, 122–29.

Howard Erskine-Hill, "Antony and Octavius: The Theme of Temperance in *Antony and Cleopatra*," *RMS* 14 (1970): 26–47.

Harold Farmer, " 'I'll give thee leave to play': Theatre Symbolism in *Antony and Cleopatra*," *ESA* 20, no. 2 (1977): 107–20.

Andrew Fichter, "*Antony and Cleopatra*: 'The Time of Universal Peace,'" *ShS* 33 (1980): 99–111.

A. M. I. Fiskin, "*Antony and Cleopatra*: Tangled Skeins of Love and Power," *UDQ* 10, no. 2 (1975): 93–105.

Robert E. Fitch, "No Greater Crack?" *SQ* 19 (Winter 1968): 3–17.

French, *Shakespeare's Division of Experience*, 253–67.

J. Fuzier, "*Antony and Cleopatra*'s Three-Stage Tragic Structure: A Study in Development," *CahiersE* 18 (April 1978): 69–74.

W. L. Godshalk, "Dolabella as Agent Provocateur," *RenP* 1976 (1977): 69–74.

James J. Greene, "*Antony and Cleopatra*: The Birth and Death of Androgyny," *HSL* 19, no. 2–3 (1987): 24–44.

Grudin, *Mighty Opposites*, 165–79.

Charles A. Hallett, "Change, Fortune, and Time: Aspects of the Sub-Lunar World in *Antony and Cleopatra*," *JEGP* 75 (January 1976): 75–89.

Hallett and Hallett, *Analyzing Shakespeare's Action*, 162–63, 175–76.

Robert Hapgood, "Hearing Shakespeare: Sound and Meaning in *Antony and Cleopatra*," *ShS* 24 (1971): 1–12.

Richard C. Harrier, "Cleopatra's End," *SQ* 13 (Winter 1962): 63–65.

Duncan S. Harris, " 'Again for Cydnus': The Dramaturgical Resolutiom of *Antony and Cleopatra*," *SEL* 17 (Spring 1977): 219–31.

Hawkes, *Shakespeare's Talking Animals*, 178–91.

Hawkins, *Poetic Freedom and Poetic Truth*, 73–74, 105–06, 126–31.

Ray L. Heffner, Jr., "The Messengers in Shakespeare's *Antony and Cleopatra,*" *ELH* 43 (June 1976): 154–62.

Henn, *The Harvest of Tragedy*, 47–49, 147–149.

T. Walter Herbert, "A Study of Meaning in *Antony and Cleopatra,*" in Bryan, Morris, Murphee, and Williams, *All These to Teach*, 47–66.

R. P. Hewett, *Reading and Response*, 115–20.

G. R. Hibbard, "Feliciter Audax: *Antony and Cleopatra* I.1.1-24," in Edwards, Ewbank, and Hunter, *Shakespeare's Styles*, 95–109.

Richard Hillman, "Antony, Hercules, and Cleopatra: 'The Bidding of the Gods' and 'The Subtlest Maze of All,'" *SQ* 38 (Winter 1987): 442–51.

Sidney R. Homan, "Divided Response and the Imagination in *Antony and Cleopatra,*" *PQ* 49 (Autumn 1970): 460–68.

Roberta Hooks, "Shakespeare's *Antony and Cleopatra*: Power and Submission," *AI* 44 (Spring 1987): 37–49.

Houston, *Shakespearean Sentences*, 179–97.

Robert D. Hume, "Individuation and Development of Character Through Language in *Antony and Cleopatra,*" *SQ* 24 (Spring 1973): 280–300.

Robert G. Hunter, "Cleopatra and the 'Oestre Junoicque,'" *ShakS* 5 (1969): 236–39.

Cynthia D. Hymel, "Shakespeare's *Antony and Cleopatra,*" *Expl* 37 (Summer 1979): 2–4.

Russell Jackson, "The Triumphs of *Antony and Cleopatra,*" *JDSG* (1984): 128–48.

Max H. James, " 'The Noble Ruin': *Antony and Cleopatra,*" *CollL* 8 (Spring 1981): 127–43.

Laura Jepsen, *Ethical Aspects of Tragedy*, 95–101.

Jones, *Othello's Countrymen*, 23–24.

Gordon P. Jones, "The 'Strumpet's Fool' in *Antony and Cleopatra,*" *SQ* 34 (Spring 1983): 62–68.

William M. Jones, "Protestant Zeal in the Personality of Shakespeare's *Mark Antony,*" *McNR* 18 (1967): 73–85.

Nicholas Jose, "*Antony and Cleopatra*: Face and Heart," *PQ* 62 (Fall 1983): 487–505.

Kastan, *Shakespeare and the Shapes of Time*, 127–31.

David Kaula, "The Time Sense of *Antony and Cleopatra*," *SQ* 15 (Summer 1964): 211–23.

Clare Kinney, "The Queen's Two Bodies and the Divided Emperor: Some Problems of Identity in *Antony and Cleopatra*," in Haselkorn and Travitsky, *The Renaissance Englishwoman in Print*, 177–86.

Leo Kirschbaum, "Shakespeare's Cleopatra," *ShAB* 19 (October 1944): 161–71.

Knight, *Golden Labyrinth*, 91–92, 236–37.

Knight, *Imperial Theme*, 199–350.

L. C. Knights, "On the Tragedy of *Anthony and Cleopatra*," *Scrutiny* 16 (Winter 1949): 318–22.

Stanley J. Kozikowski, "Shakespeare's *Antony and Cleopatra* V.ii.309–11," *Expl* 35 (Winter 1977): 7–8.

Constance Brown Kuriyama, "The Mother of the World: A Psychoanalytic Interpretation of Shakespeare's *Antony and Cleopatra*," *ELR* 7 (Summer 1977): 124–51.

Albert C. Labriola, "Renaissance Neoplatonism and Shakespeare's Characterization of Cleopatra," *HUSL* 3 (1975): 20–36.

Marilyn Larson, "The Fallen World of Shakespeare's *Antony and Cleopatra*," *Encyclia* 66 (1989): 79–86.

Harry Levin, "Two Monumental Death-Scenes: *Antony and Cleopatra*, 4.15; 5.2," in Fabian and von Rosador, *Shakespeare: Text, Language, Criticism*, 147–63.

Michael Lloyd, "Antony and the Game of Chance," *JEGP* 61 (July 1962): 549–54.

Michael Lloyd, "Cleopatra as Isis," *ShS* 12 (1959): 88–94.

Michael Lloyd, "The Roman Tongue," *SQ* 10 (Autumn 1959): 461–69.

John H. Long, "*Antony and Cleopatra*: A Double Critical Reversal," *RenP* 1963 (1964): 28–34.

Joseph A. Longo, "Cleopatra and Octavia: Archetypal Imagery in *Antony and Cleopatra*," *UDR* 10 (Autumn 1974): 29–37.

Ronald R. MacDonald, "Playing Till Doomsday: Interpreting *Antony and Cleopatra*," *ELR* 15 (Winter 1985): 78–99.

Maynard Mack, "*Antony and Cleopatra*: The Stillness and the Dance," in Crane, *Shakespeare's Art*, 79–114.

Clayton G. MacKenzie, "*Antony and Cleopatra*: A Mythological Perspective," *OL* 45, no. 4 (1990): 309–29.

Katherine V. MacMullan, "Death Imagery in *Antony and Cleopatra*," *SQ* 14 (Autumn 1963): 399–410.

J. M. Maguin, "A Note on Shakespeare's Handling of Time and Space Data in *Antony and Cleopatra*," *CahiersE* 18 (April 1978): 61–67.

D. R. C. Marsh, "The Conflict of Love and Responsibility in *Antony and Cleopatra*," *Theoria* 15, no. 1 (1960): 1–27.

McCollom, *Tragedy*, 200–03.

Thomas McFarland, "Antony and Octavius," *YR* 49 (December 1959): 204–29.

Donald J. McGinn, "Cleopatra's Immolation Scene," in Kirk and Main, *Essays in Literary History*, 57–90.

James G. McManaway, "Notes on Act V of *Antony and Cleopatra*," *ShakS* 1 (1962): 1–6.

McPeek, *The Black Book of Knaves*, 278–81.

Peter Meredith, " 'That pannelled me at the heeles': *Antony and Cleopatra* IV. x. 34," *ES* 55 (Summer 1974): 118–26.

L.J. Mills, "Cleopatra's Tragedy," *SQ* 11 (Spring 1960): 147–62.

Dennis S. Mitchell, "Shakespeare's *Antony and Cleopatra* II.ii.811–813," *Expl* 35 (Winter 1957): 22–24.

Margery M. Morgan, " 'Your Crown's Awry': *Antony and Cleopatra* in the Comic Tradition," *Komos* 1, no. 2 (1968): 128–39.

Kenneth Muir, "*Antony and Cleopatra*, III, xiii, 73-8," *N&Q* 206 (April 1961): 142.

Kenneth Muir, "The Imagery of *Antony and Cleopatra*," *KN* 8, no. 3 (1961): 249–64.

J. R. Mulryne, "*Antony and Cleopatra*: Penny Plain or Tuppence Coloured; Soc. Fr. Shakespeare Actes du Congres 1982," in Jones-Davies, *Du Texte à la scene*, 93–109.

Toshio Murakami, "Cleopatra and Volumnia," *ShStud* 9 (1970–71): 28–55.

Norman Nathan, "*Antony and Cleopatra*: IV, vii, 6-10," *N&Q* 200 (July 1955): 293–94.

Ruth Nevo, "The Masque of Greatness," *ShakS* 3 (1968): 111–28.

Richard Nochimson, "The End Crowns All: Shakespeare's Deflation of Tragic Possibility in *Antony and Cleopatra*," *English* 26 (Spring 1977): 99–132.

Arthur M. Z. Norman, "Daniel's *The Tragedy of Cleopatra* and Shakespeare's *Antony and Cleopatra*," *SQ* 9 (Winter 1958): 11–18. Reprinted in *MLR* 54 (January 1959): 1–9.

J. M. Nosworthy, "Symbol and Character in *Antony and Cleopatra*," *ShN* 6 (February 1956): 4.

Herta Maria F. de Q. Nunes, "Enobarbus: 'He is of Note,'" *Signal* 1, no. 1 (1978): 10–32.

Robert Ornstein, "The Ethics of Imagination: Love and Art in *Antony and Cleopatra*," in Brown and Harris, *Later Shakespeare*, 31–48.

Michael Payne, "Erotic Irony and Polarity in *Antony and Cleopatra*," *SQ* 24 (Spring 1973): 265–79.

T. M. Pearce, "Shakespeare's *Antony and Cleopatra*, V, ii, 243–359," *Expl* 12 (December 1953): 17.

N. H. Pearson, "Shakespeare's *Antony and Cleopatra*," *LCrit* 1 (Summer 1959): 53–73.

Marion Perret, "Shakespeare's Use of Messengers in *Antony and Cleopatra*," *DramaS* 5 (May 1966): 67–72.

H. W. Piper, "Shakespeare's *Antony and Cleopatra*," *Expl* 26 (September 1967): Item 10.

Pogson, *In the East My Pleasure Lies*, 107–16.

J. M. Purcell, "*A & C*, I, ii, 42–43," *N&Q* 203 (May 1958): 187–88.

Clifford J. Ronan, "Caesar's Revenge and the Roman Thoughts in *Antony and Cleopatra*," *ShakS* 19 (1991): 171–82.

Gordon N. Ross, "Enobarbus on Horses: *Antony and Cleopatra*, 111.vii.7–9," *SQ* 31 (Autumn 1980): 386–87.

William Rossky, "*Antony and Cleopatra*, I.ii.79: Enobarbus' 'Mistake,'" *SQ* 35 (Autumn 1984): 324–25.

Martha Tuck Rozett, "The Comic Structures of Tragic Endings: The Suicide Scenes in *Romeo and Juliet* and *Antony and Cleopatra*," *SQ* 36 (Summer 1985): 152–64.

Norma M. Schulman, "A 'Motive for Metaphor': Shakespeare's *Antony and Cleopatra*," *HUSL* 4 (1976): 154–74.

Harry M. Schwalb, "Shakespeare's *Antony and Cleopatra*, I, ii, 1–5," *Expl* 8 (May 1950): 53.

Elias Schwartz, "*Antony and Cleopatra*," *CE* 23 (April 1962): 550–58.

Ethel Seaton, "*Antony and Cleopatra* and the *Book of Revelation*," *RES* 22 (July 1946): 219–24.

Michael Shapiro, "Boying Her Greatness: Shakespeare's Use of Coterie Drama in *Antony and Cleopatra*," *MLR* 77 (January 1982): 1–15.

Stephen A. Shapiro, "The Varying Shore of the World: Ambivalence in *Antony and Cleopatra*," *MLQ* 27 (March 1966): 18–32.

Shaw, *Plays and Players*, 187–95.

J. Shaw, "Cleopatra and Seleucus," *REL* 7 (October 1966): 79–86.

J. Shaw, "'In Every Corner of the Stage': *Antony and Cleopatra*, IV. iii," *ShakS* 7 (1974): 277–32.

R. Shaw-Smith, "*Antony and Cleopatra*, II.ii.204," *SQ* 24 (Winter 1973): 92–93.

Paul N. Siegel, "Foreshadowings of Cleopatra's Death," *N&Q* 203 (September 1958): 386–87.

James E. Siemon, "'The Strong Necessity of Time': Dilemma in *Antony and Cleopatra*," *ES* 54 (July 1973): 316–25.

Jyotsna Singh, "Renaissance Antitheatricality, Antifeminism, and Shakespeare's *Antony and Cleopatra*," *RenD* 20 (1989): 99–121.

Gordon R. Smith, "The Melting of Authority in *Antony and Cleopatra*," *CollL* 1 (Spring 1974): 1–18.

J. Oates Smith, "The Alchemy of *Antony and Cleopatra*," *Bucknell University Studies* 12 (March 1964): 37–50.

Smith, *Dualities in Shakespeare*, 189–214.

Maria Selma Ataide Smith, "Last Farewells in *Antony and Cleopatra*," *Signal* 1, no. 1 (1978): 65–77.

Michael Harold Smith, "Men of Ice: The Dehumanizing Effects of Ambition in Shakespeare's *Antony and Cleopatra*," *Signal* 1, no. 1 (1978): 117–26.

S. M. Smith, " 'This Great Solemnity': A Study of the Presentation of Death in *Antony and Cleopatra*," *ES* 45 (April 1964): 163–76.

Stella T. Smith, "Imagery of Union, Division, and Disintegration in *Antony and Cleopatra*," *CCR* 1, no. 2 (1977): 15–28.

Susan Snyder, "Patterns of Motion in *Antony and Cleopatra*," *ShS* 33 (1980): 113–22.

Benjamin T. Spencer, "*Antony and Cleopatra* and the Paradoxical Metaphor," *SQ* 9 (Summer 1958): 373–78.

Madelon Sprengnether, "The Boy Actor and Femininity in *Antony and Cleopatra*," in Holland, Homan, and Paris, *Shakespeare's Personality*, 191–205.

Donald A. Stauffer, *The Nature of Poetry* (New York: Norton, 1946), 253–59.

Arnold Stein, "The Image of Antony's Lyric and Tragic Imagination," *KR* 21 (Autumn 1959): 586–606.

David Stempel, "The Transmigration of the Crocodile," *SQ* 7 (Winter 1956): 59–72.

Brents Stirling, "Cleopatra's Scene with Seleucus: Plutarch, Daniel and Shakespeare," *SQ* 15 (Spring 1964): 299–311. Reprinted in McManaway, *Shakespeare 400*, 299–311.

Joseph S. Stull, "Cleopatra's Magnimity: The Dismissal of the Messenger," *SQ* 7 (Winter 1956): 73–78.

Styan, *The Elements of Drama*, 214–17.

Sutherland and Hurtsfield, *Shakespeare's World*, 116–35.

Jeri Tanner, "The Power of Names in Shakespeare's *Antony and Cleopatra*," *Names* 35 (September–December 1987): 164–74.

John S. Tanner, "'Here Is My Space': The Private Mode in Donne's Poetry and Shakespeare's *Antony and Cleopatra*," *ISJR* 60 (February 1986): 417–30.

Helen S. Thomas, "'Breeze' and 'Bees' 'Sailes' and 'Tailes' *Antony and Cleopatra* III. x. 17–22," *CEA* 37, no. 1 (1974): 23–24.

Mary Olive Thomas, "Cleopatra and the 'Mortal Wretch,'" *ShJE* 99 (1963): 174–83.

Mary Olive Thomas, "The Repetitions in Antony's Death Scene," *SQ* 9 (Spring 1958): 153–57.

Leslie Thomson, "*Antony and Cleopatra*, Act 4, Scene 16: 'A Heavy Sight,'" *ShS* 41 (1989): 77–90.

J. J. M. Torbin, "Apuleius and *Antony and Cleopatra*, Once More," *SN* 51 (Summer 1979): 225–28.

L. W. Tolmie, "'Least cause'/'All cause': Roman Infinite Variety: An Essay on *Antony and Cleopatra*," *SoRA* 11 (1978): 113–31.

Kenneth Tucker, "Psychetypes and Shakespeare's *Antony and Cleopatra*," *JEP* 5 (August 1984): 176–81.

Van Lann, *The Idiom of Drama*, 25–27.

Maurice J. F. Van Woensel, "Revelry and Carousing in Shakespeare's *Antony and Cleopatra*," *Signal* 1, no. 1 (1978): 78–100.

Raymond B. Waddington, "*Antony and Cleopatra*: 'What Venus Did with Mars,'" *ShakS* 2 (1966): 210–27.

Eugene M. Waith, "Manhood and Valor in Two Shakespearean Tragedies," *ELH* 17 (December 1950): 268–73.

Alan Warner, "A Note on *Antony and Cleopatra*," *English* 11 (Spring 1957): 139–44.

Ruth Waterhouse, "Shakespeare's *Antony and Cleopatra* I. iv. 12–13 and 44–47," *Expl* 33 (October 1975): Item 17.

Morris Weitz, "Literature without Philosophy: *Antony and Cleopatra*," *ShS* 28 (1975): 29–36.

Waller B. Wigginton, "'One way like a Gorgon': An Explication of *Antony and Cleopatra*, 2.5.116-17," *PLL* 16 (Autumn 1980): 366–75.

George W. Williams, "Shakespeare's *Antony and Cleopatra*, III, xiii, 26," *Expl* 20 (May 1962): 79.

Williams, *Drama in Performance*, 54–74.

Marilyn L. Williamson, "Fortune in *Anthony and Cleopatra*," *JEGP* 67 (July 1968): 423–29.

Marilyn L. Williamson, "Patterns of Development in *Anthony and Cleopatra*," *TSL* 14 (Spring 1969): 129–39.

Elkin C. Wilson, "Shakespeare's Enobarbus," in McManaway, *Joseph Q. Adams Memorial Studies*, 391–408.

William D. Wolf, "'New Heaven, New Earth': The Escape from Mutability in *Antony and Cleopatra*," *SQ* 33 (Autumn 1982): 328–35.

Paul Yachnin, "'Courtiers of Beauteous Freedom': *Antony and Cleopatra* in Its Time," *Ren&R* 15 (Winter 1991): 1–20.

As You Like It

Susan Baker, "Shakespeare and Ritual: The Example of *As You Like It*," *UCrow* 9 (1989): 9–23.

Barber, *Shakespeare's Festive Comedy*, 222–39.

C. L. Barber, "The Use of Comedy in *As You Like It*," *PQ* 21 (October 1942): 353–67.

Johannes Adam Bastiaenen, *Moral Tone of Jacobean and Caroline Drama*, 18–20.

Michael Bath, "Weeping Stags and Melancholy Lovers: The Iconography of *As You Like It*, II, i," *Emblematica* 1 (Spring 1986): 13–52.

Margaret Boemer Beckman, "The Figure of Rosalind in *As You Like It*," *SQ* 29 (Winter 1978): 44–51.

Robert B. Bennett, "The Reform of a Malcontent: Jacques and the Meaning of *As You Like It*," *ShakS* 9 (1976): 183–204.

Edward L. Berry, "Rosalynde and Rosalind," *SQ* 31 (Spring 1980): 42–52.

David-Everett Blythe, "Shakespeare's *As You Like It*, II.iv.55–56," *Expl* 42 (Spring 1984): 14–15.

Barbara J. Bono, "Mixed Gender, Mixed Genre in Shakespeare's *As You Like It*," in Lewalski, *Renaissance Genres*, 189–212.

Mark Bracher, "Contrary Notions of Identity in *As You Like It*," *SEL* 24 (Spring 1984): 225–40.

Alan Taylor Bradford, "Jacques's Distortion of the Seven Ages Paradigm," *SQ* 27 (Spring 1970): 171–76.

Brown, *Dramatis Personae*, 235–39.

Margie Burns, "Odd and Even in *As You Like It*," *Allegorica* 5 (Summer 1980): 119–40.

David G. Byrd, "Shakespeare's Familaritie between Sir Rowland and Duke Senior in *As You Like It*," *SQ* 26 (Summer 1975): 205–06.

Carol J. Carlisle, "Helen: Faucit's Rosalind," *ShakS* 12 (1979): 65–94.

Susan Carlson, *Women and Comedy: Rewriting the British Theatrical Tradition* (Ann Arbor: University of Michigan Press, 1991), 43–67.

Susan Carlson, "Women in *As You Like It*: Community, Change, and Choice," *ELWIU* 14 (Fall 1987): 151–69.

William G. Carson, "*As You Like It* and the Stars," *QJS* 43 (April 1957): 117–27.

Albert R. Crillo, "*As You Like It*: Pastoralism Gone Awry," *ELH* 38 (March 1971): 19–39.

Howard C. Cole, "The Moral Vision of *As You Like It*," *CollL* 3 (Spring 1976): 17–32.

Judith Dale, "*As You Like It* and Some Medieval Themes," in *Words, Wai-Te-Ata Studies in Literature*, ed. P. T. Hoffman, D. F. McKenzie, and Peter Robb (Wellington, NZ: Wai-Te-Ata Press, 1966), 54–65.

A. Stuart Daley, "The Dispraise of the Country in *As You Like It*," *SQ* 36 (Autumn 1985): 300–14.

A. Stuart Daley, "The Midsummer Deer of *As You Like It*, II.i," *PQ* 58 (Spring 1979): 103–06.

A. Stuart Daley, "To Moralize a Spectacle: *As You Like It*, Act 2, Scene 1," *PQ* 86 (Spring 1986): 147–70.

A. Stuart Daley, "The Triumph of Patience in *As You Like It*," *AJES* 13 (April 1988): 45–66.

A. Stuart Daley, "The Tyrant Duke of *As You Like It*: Envious Malice Confronts Honor, Pity, Friendship," *CahiersE* 34 (October 1988): 39–51.

A. Stuart Daley, "Where Are the Woods in *As You Like It*?" *SQ* 34 (Summer 1983): 172–80.

Dawson, *Indirections*, 20–37.

John Doebler, "Orlando: Athlete of Virtue," *ShS* 26 (1973): 111–17.

Madelein Doran, "'Yet Am I Inland Bred,'" *SQ* 15 (Spring 1964): 99–114.

R. P. Draper, "Shakespeare's Pastoral Comedy," *EA* 11 (January 1959): 1–17.

Macdonald Emslie, "*As You Like It*," *The Use of English* 6 (Winter 1954): 99–104.

Peter B. Erickson, "Sexual Politics and the Social Structure in *As You Like It*," *MR* 23 (Spring 1982): 65–83.

Charles R. Forker, "All the World's a Stage: Multiple Perspectives in Arden," *ISJR* 54 (November 1980): 421–30.

René E. Fortin, "'Tongues in Trees': Symbolic Patterns in *As You Like It*," *TSLL* 14 (Winter 1972): 569–82.

French, *Shakespeare's Division of Experience*, 106–11.

Charles Frey, "The Sweetest Rose: *As You Like It* as Comedy of Reconciliation," *NYLF* 1 (Winter 1978): 167–83.

Brian Gibbons, "Amorous Fictions and *As You Like It*," in Mahon, and Pendleton, *"Fanned and winnowed opinions,"* 52–78.

SHAKESPEARE, WILLIAM, *As You Like It*

Girard, *Theatre of Envy*, 92–105.

Robert H. Goldsmith, "'Touchstone' Critic in Motley," *PMLA* 69 (September 1953): 884–95.

Gomez, *The Alienated Figure in Drama*, 45–46.

Eamon Grennan, "Telling the Trees from the Wood: Some Details of *As You Like It* Re-Examined," *ELR* 7 (Summer 1977): 197–206.

Jay L. Halio, "'No Clock in the Forest': Time in *As You Like It*," *SEL* 2 (Spring 1962): 197–209.

Hallett and Hallett, *Analyzing Shakespeare's Action*, 72–73, 113–14.

Robert Hapgood, "Shakespeare's *As You Like It*, III.iii," *Expl* 24 (June 1966): Item 60.

Marta Powell Harley, "Rosalind, the Hare, and the Hyena in Shakespeare's *As You Like It*," *SQ* 36 (Autumn 1985): 335–37.

Hawkins, *Likeness of Truth in Elizabethan and Restoration Drama*, 11–12.

Nancy K. Hayles, "Sexual Disguise in *As You Like It* and *Twelfth Night*," *ShS* 32 (1979): 63–72.

Donald K. Hedrick, "Merry and Weary of Conversation: Textual Uncertainty in *As You Like It*, II.iv," *ELH* 46 (March 1979): 21–34.

Michael Hennessy, "'Had I Kingdoms to Give': Place in *As You Like It*," *ELWIU* 4 (Spring 1977): 143–51.

Elaine Hobby, "'My Affection Hath an Unknown Bottom': Homosexuality and the Teaching of *As You Like It*," in Aers and Wheale, *Shakespeare in the Changing Curriculum*, 125–42.

Maurice Hunt, "Words and Deeds in *As You Like It*," *ShY* 2 (1991): 23–48.

W. Hutchings, "'Exits and Entrances': Ways in and out of Arden," *CritQ* 21 (Autumn 1979): 3–13.

Wolfgang Iser, "The Dramatization of Double Meaning in Shakespeare's *As You Like It*," *TJ* 35 (October 1983): 307–32.

Robert C. Johnson, "To Understand Love: The Statements of *As You Like It* and *Twelfth Night*," *AJES* 4 (April 1979): 156–64.

J. T. Jones, "What's That 'Ducdame,'" *MLN* 62 (December 1947): 563–64.

David Scott Kastan, and Nancy J. Vickers. "Shakespeare, Scéve and 'A Woeful Ballad,'" *N&Q* 27 (April 1980): 165–66.

Gilchrist Keel, "'Like Juno's Swans': Rosalind and Celia in *As You Like It*," *CCTEP* 56 (September 1991): 5–11.

Knight, *The Golden Labyrinth*, 68–70.

Richard A. Knowles, "Ducdame," *SQ* 18 (Autumn 1967): 438–41.

Richard A. Knowles, "Myth and Type in *As You Like It*," *ELH* 33 (January 1966): 1–22.

Helge Kokeritz, "Touchstone in Arden: *As You Like It*, II,iv,16," *MLQ* 7 (March 1946): 61–65.

Judy Z. Kronenfield, "Shakespeare's Jacques and the Pastoral Cult of Solitude," *TSLL* 18 (Winter 1976): 451–73.

Judy Z. Kronenfield, "Social Rank and the Pastoral Ideals of *As You Like It*," *SQ* 29 (Summer 1978): 333–48.

François Laroque, "'No Assembly but Horn-Beasts': A Structural Study of Arden's Animal Farm," *CahiersE* 11 (April 1977): 55–62.

François Laroque, "Ovidian Transformations and Folk Festivities in *A Midsummer Night's Dream*, *The Merry Wives of Windsor*, and *As You Like It*," *CahiersE* 25 (April 1984): 23–36.

Maura Slattery Kuhn, "Much Virtue in 'If,'" *SQ* 28 (Spring 1977): 40–50.

Kevin Margarey, "The Touchstone and the Toilet: Nature as Shakespeare's Irreducible in *As You Like It*," in Brissenden, *Shakespeare and Some Others*, 44–64.

Marx, *The Enjoyment of Drama*, 141–44.

William McCollom, "Form and Attitude in Comedy," *DramaS* 3 (May 1963): 60–68.

Frank McCombie, "Medium and Message in *As You Like It* and King Lear," *ShS* 33 (1980): 67–80.

Angus McIntosh, "*As You Like It*: A Grammatical Clue to Character," *REL* 4 (April 1963): 68–81.

John McQueen, "*As You Like It* and Medieval Literary Tradition," *FMLS* 1 (July 1965): 216–29.

William E. Miller, "All the World's a Stage," *N&Q* 208 (March 1963): 99–101.

Marco Mincoff, "What Shakespeare Did to Rosalynde," *ShJE* 96 (1960): 78–89.

Louis Adrian Montrose, "'The Place of a Brother' in *As You Like It*: Social Process and Comic Form," *SQ* 32 (Spring 1981): 28–54.

Harry Morris, *"As You Like It"* Et in Arcadia Ego," *SQ* 26 (Summer 1975): 269–75.

H. J. Oliver, "An Alleged Variant in *As You Like It*," *N&Q* 14 (December 19967): 136.

Martin R. Orkin, "Shakespeare's *As You Like It*," *Expl* 42 (Winter 1984): 5–7.

Dale G. Priest, "Oratio and Negotium: Manipulative Modes in *As You Like It*," *SEL* 28 (Spring 1988): 273–86.

Dale G. Priest, "Rosalind's Child's Father," *N&Q* 27 (April 1980): 166.

Mary Ellen Rickey, "Rosalind's Gentle Jupiter," *SQ* 13 (Summer 1962): 365–66.

Winfried Schleiner, "Jaques and the Melancholy Stag," *ELN* 17 (January 1980): 175–79.

Winfried Schleiner, " 'Tis Like the Howling of Irish Wolves Against the Moone': A Note on *As You Like It*, V. ii. 109," *ELN* 12 (January 1974): 5–8.

Robert Schwartz, "Rosalynde among the Familists: *As You Like It* and an Expanded View of Its Sources," *SCJ* 20 (Spring 1989): 69–76.

Alice-Lyle Scoufos, "The Paradiso Terrestre and the Testing of Love in *As You Like It*," *ShakS* 14 (1981): 215–27.

Peter J. Seng, "The Foresters' Song in *As You Like It*," *SQ* 10 (Spring 1969): 246–49.

Cecil C. Seronsy, "The Seven Ages of Man Again," *SQ* 4 (Summer 1953): 364–65.

Shapiro, *Rival Playwrights*, 102–04, 115–17.

John Shaw, "Fortune and Nature in *As You Like It*," *SQ* 6 (Winter 1955): 45–50.

Kola Shittu, *"As You Like It*—No Absolutism Here," *Legacy* 3, no. 1 (1976): 39–44.

Jeff Shulman, "'The Recuyell of the Historyes of Troye' and the Tongue-Tied Ortando," *SQ* 31 (Autumn 1980): 390.

Sarup Singh, "A Note on *As You Like It*," *IJES* 4, no. 1 (1963): 162–68.

Smith, *Homosexual Desire in Shakespeare's England*, 151–55.

Smith, *Shakespeare's Romances*, 71–94.

J. A. B. Somerset, *"As You Like It*, III.iii.10–13, and *King Lear*, II.iv.125: Analogues from Robert Wilson's Three Ladies of London," *N&Q* 29 (April 1982): 116–18.

Warren Staebler, "Shakespeare's Play of Atonement," *ShAB* 24 (April 1949): 91–105.

Kay Stanton, "The Disguises of Shakespeare's *As You Like It*," *ISJR* 59 (February 1985): 295–305.

Kay Stanton, "Shakespeare's Use of Marlowe in *As You Like It*," in Friedenreich, Gill, and Kuriyama, *"A poet and a filthy play-maker,"* 23–35.

David Lloyd Stevenson, "The Love-Game Comedy," *CUSECL* 164 (1946): 199–207.

Styan, *The Elements of Drama*, 153–54.

Donn Ervin Taylor, "'Try in Time in Despite of a Fall': Time and Occasion in *As You Like It*," *TSLL* 24 (Summer 1982): 121–36.

Michael Taylor, "*As You Like It*: The Penalty of Adam," *CritQ* 15 (Spring 1973): 76–80.

E. Michael Thron, "Jaques: Emblems and Morals," *SQ* 30 (Spring 1979): 84–89.

Philip Traci, "*As You Like It*: Homosexuality in Shakespeare's Play," *CLAJ* 25 (September 1981): 91–105.

Kent Talbot van den Berg, "Theatrical Fiction and the Reality of Love in *As You Like It*," *PMLA* 90 (October 1975): 885–93.

S. Viswanathan, "The Medlar in the Forest of Arden," *NM* 77 (April 1976): 93–94.

Raymond B. Waddington, "Moralizing the Spectacle: Dramatic Emblems in *As You Like It*," *SQ* 33 (Summer 1982): 155–63.

Helen M. Whall, "*As You Like It*: The Play of Analogy," *HLQ* 47 (Winter 1984): 33–46.

Paul J. Willis, "'Tongues in Trees': The Book of Nature in *As You Like It*," *MLS* 18 (Summer 1988): 65–74.

Rawdon Wilson, "The Way to Arden: Attitudes toward Time in *As You Like It*," *SQ* 26 (Spring 1975): 16–24.

Young, *The Heart's Forest*, 39–72.

The Comedy of Errors

Glyn Austen, "Ephesus Restored: Sacramentalism and Redemption in *The Comedy of Errors*," *L&T* 1 (March 1987): 54–69.

SHAKESPEARE, WILLIAM, *The Comedy of Errors*

William Babula, "If I Dream Not: Unity in *The Comedy of Errors*," *SAB* 38 (November 1973): 26–33.

T. W. Baldwin, "Errors and Marprelate" in *Studies in Honor of DeWitt T. Starnes*, ed. Thomas P. Harrison, Archibald A. Hill, Ernest C. Mossner, and James Sledd (Austin: University of Texas Press, 1967), 9–23.

C. L. Barber, "Shakespearian Comedy," *CE* 25 (April 1964): 493–97.

Charles Brooks, "Shakespeare's Romantic Shrews," *SQ* 11 (Summer 1960): 351–56.

Brooks, and Heilman, *Understanding Drama*, 22–24.

Harold Brooks, "Themes and Structure in *The Comedy of Errors*," *Stratford-Upon-Avon Studies* 3 (1961): 55–72.

Joseph Candido, "Dining Out in Ephesus: Food in *The Comedy of Errors*," *SEL* 30 (Spring 1990): 217–41.

Thomas Clayton, "The Text, Imagery, and Sense of the Abbess's Final Speech in *The Comedy of Errors*," *Anglia* 91, no. 4 (1973): 479–84.

Louise G. Clubb, "Italian Comedy and *The Comedy of Errors*," *CL* 19 (Summer 1977): 240–51.

Jonathan V. Crewe, "God or The Good Physician: The Rational Playwright in *The Comedy of Errors*," *Genre* 15 (Spring–Summer 1982): 203–23. Reprinted in Greenblatt, *The Power of Forms*, 203–24.

A. Bronson Feldman, "Portals of Discovery," *AI* 16 (Spring 1959): 77–107.

A. Bronson Feldman, "Shakespeare's Early Errors," *International Journal of Psychoanalysis* 36 (March–April 1955): 114–33.

Francis Fergusson, "*The Comedy of Errors* and *Much Ado About Nothing*," *SR* 62 (Winter 1954): 24–37. Reprinted in *The Human Image*, 144–160.

Barbara Freedman, "Egeon's Doubt: Self-Division and Self-Redemption in *The Comedy of Errors*," *ELR* 10 (Autumn 1980): 360–83.

Barbara Freedman, "Errors in Comedy: A Psychoanalytic Theory of Farce," *NYLF* 5–6 (Winter 1980): 233–43.

French, *Shakespeare's Division of Experience*, 71–76.

René Girard, "Comedies of Errors: Plautus-Shakespeare-Moliere," in *American Criticism in the Poststructuralist Age*, ed. Ira Konigsberg (Ann Arbor: University of Michigan Press, 1981), 66–86.

Eamon Grennan, "Arm and Sleeve: Nature and Custom in *The Comedy of Errors*," *PQ* 59 (Spring 1980): 150–64.

Gurewitch, *Comedy*, 89–92.

Charles Haines, "Some Notes on Love and Money in *The Comedy of Errors*," in *Critical Dimensions: English, German, and Comparative Literature Essays in Honour of Aurelio Zanco*, ed Mario Curelli and Alberto Martino (Cuneo: SASTE, 1978), 107–16.

Thomas P. Hennings, "The Anglican Doctrine of the Affectionate Marriage in *The Comedy of Errors*," *MLQ* 47 (June 1986): 91–107.

Richard Henze, "*The Comedy of Errors*: A Freely Binding Chain," *SQ* 22 (Winter 1971): 35–41.

Hibbard, *Making of Shakespeare's Dramatic Poetry*, 89–92.

Terry Humby, "Illusions, Isaiah, and 'Owles' in *The Comedy of Errors*," *N&Q* 38 (December 1991): 472–73.

Dorothea Kehler, "*The Comedy of Errors* as Problem Comedy," *RMRLL* 47, no. 4 (1987): 229–40.

Arthur F. Kinney, "Shakespeare's *Comedy of Errors* and the Nature of Kinds," *SP* 85 (Winter 1988): 29–52.

W. Thomas MacCary, "*The Comedy of Errors*: A Different Kind of Comedy," *NLH* 9 (1978): 525–36.

Paul J. Marcotte, "Eros in *The Comedy of Errors*," *RUO* 38 (1968): 642–67.

Paul J. Marcotte, "Shakespeare's *The Comedy of Errors*, V.i.400–402," *Expl* 41 (Fall 1982): 9–12.

J. C. Maxwell, "'Fat and Scant of Breath' Again—*Comedy of Errors*, III, i, 64–65," *ES* 32 (February 1951): 29–30.

Patricia Parker, "Elder and Younger: The Opening Scene of *The Comedy of Errors*," *SQ* 34 (Autumn 1983): 325–27.

Vincent F. Petronella, "Structure and Theme Through Separation and Union in Shakespeare's *The Comedy of Errors*," *MLR* 69 (October 1974): 481–88.

J. M. Purcell, "*Comedy of Errors*, 11 ii, 57," *N&Q* 203 (April 1958): 180.

Robert A. Ravich, "A Psychoanalytic Study of Shakespeare's Early Plays," *Psychoanalytic Quarterly* 33 (July 1964): 396–99.

Robert A. Ravich, "Shakespeare and Psychiatry," *L&P* 14 (Summer–Fall 1964): 99–101.

Gareth Roberts, "*The Comedy of Errors* II.ii.190: 'Owls' or 'Elves?'" *N&Q* 34 (June 1987): 202–04.

Gamini Salgado, "'Time's Deformed Hand': Sequence, Consequence, and Inconsequence in *The Comedy of Errors*," *ShS* 25 (1972): 81–91.

Scott, *Renaissance Drama*, 1–17.

Catherine M. Shaw, "The Conscious Art of *The Comedy of Errors*," *NYLF* 5–6 (Winter 1980): 17–28.

Shaw, *Plays and Players*, 50–57.

Simpson, *Percy Studies in Elizabethan Drama*, 13–17.

Camille Wells Slights, "Time's Debt to Season: *The Comedy of Errors*, IV.ii.58," *ELN* 24 (September 1986): 22–25.

Soellner, *Shakespeare's Patterns*, 62–77.

Gary Taylor, "Textual and Sexual Criticism: A Crux in *The Comedy of Errors*," *RenD* 19 (1988): 195–225.

K. Tetzeli Von Rosador, "Plotting the Early Comedies: *The Comedy of Errors*, *Love's Labour's Lost*, *The Two Gentlemen of Verona*," *ShS* 37 (1984): 13–22.

Roger Warren, "*The Comedy of Errors* and *Frederick of Jennen*," *N&Q* 35 (March 1988): 44.

John S. Weld, "Old Adam New Apparelled," *SQ* 7 (Autumn 1956): 453–56.

Stanley Wells, "Reunion Scenes in *The Comedy of Errors* and *Twelfth Night*: Festschrift fur Siegfried Korninger," in *A Yearbook of Studies in English Language and Literature 1985/86*, ed. Otto Rauchbauer (Vienna: Braumuller, 1986), 267–76.

Paul Werstine, " 'Urging of her wracke' in *The Comedy of Errors*," *SQ* 31 (Summer 1980): 392–94.

Gwyn Williams, "*The Comedy of Errors* Rescued from Tragedy," *REL* 5 (October 1964): 63–71.

Deborah Baker Wyrick, "The Ass Motif in *The Comedy of Errors* and *A Midsummer Night's Dream*," *SQ* 33 (Winter 1982): 432–48.

Coriolanus

Janet Adelman, "'Anger's My Meat': Feeding, Dependency, and Aggression in *Coriolanus*," in Bevington and Halio, *Shakespeare, Pattern of Excelling Nature*, 108–24.

John Alvis, "*Coriolanus* and Aristotle's Magnanimous Man Reconsidered," *IJPP* 7 (Fall 1978): 4–28.

A. A. Ansari, "*Coriolanus*: The Roots of Alienation," *AJES* 6 (April 1981): 14–34.

Simon A. Barker, "Shakespeare's *Coriolanus*: Texts and Histories," *Assays* 4 (1987): 109–28.

David B. Barron, "*Coriolanus*: Portrait of the Artist as an Infant," *AI* 19 (Summer 1962): 171–93.

Anne Barton, "*Julius Caesar* and *Coriolanus*: Shakespeare's Roman World of Words," in *Shakespeare's Craft: Eight Lectures*, ed. Philip H. Highfill, Jr. (Carbondale: Southern Illinois University Press for George Washington University, 1982), 24–47.

Arthur H.Bell, "*Coriolanus* III.ii.72–80: 'Cryptic' and 'Corrupt'?" *ELN* 9 (September 1971): 18–20.

Ralph Berry, "The Metamorphoses of *Coriolanus*," *SQ* 26 (Winter 1975): 172–83.

Ralph Berry, "Sexual Imagery in *Coriolanus*," *SEL* (Spring 1973): 301–16.

John Bligh, "The Mind of Coriolanus," *ESC* 13 (September 1987): 256–70.

William Blissett, "*Coriolanus* and the Helms of State," in *Familiar Colloquy: Essays Presented to Arthur Edward Baker*, ed. Patricia Brückmann (Ontario: Oberon Press, 1973), 144–62.

W. F. Bolton, "Meneius's 'Scale't': A New Defense," *ELN* 10 (December 1972): 110–11.

Michael D. Bristol, "Lenten Butchery: Legitimation Crisis in *Coriolanus*," in Howard and O'Connor, *Shakespeare Reproduced*, 207–24.

Brockbank, *On Shakespeare*, 147–51.

I. R. Browning, "Coriolanus: Boy of Tears," *EIC* 5 (January 1955): 18–31.

Margaret B. Bryan, "Volumnia—Roman Matron or Elizabethan Huswife," *RenP 1972* (1973): 43–58.

James C. Bulman, "*Coriolanus* and the Matter of Troy," in Gray, *Mirror up to Shakespeare*, 242–60.

Kenneth Burke, "*Coriolanus*—and the Delights of Faction," *HudR* 19 (Summer 1966): 185–202.

Winifred Burns, "The Character of Marcius *Coriolanus*," *Poet Lore* 52 (Spring 1946): 31–48.

Dolores M. Burton, "Odds beyond Arithmetic: Comparative Clauses in *Coriolanus*," *Style* 14 (Fall 1980): 299–317.

F. G. Butler, "Vestures and Gestures of Humility: *Coriolanus* Acts II and III," *ESA* 25, no. 2 (1982): 79–108.

James L. Calderwood, "*Coriolanus*: Wordless Maenings and Meaningless Words," *SEL* 6 (Spring 1966): 211–24.

Jane Carducci, "Shakespeare's *Coriolanus*: 'Could I Find Out/The Woman's Part in Me,'" *L&P* 33, no. 2 (1987): 11–20.

Stanley Cavell, "'Who Does the Wolfe Love?' *Coriolanus* and the Interpretations of Politics," in Parker and Hartman *Shakespeare and the Question of Theory*, 145–272. Reprinted in Greenblatt, *Representing the English Renaissance,* 197–216.

Maurice Charney, "The Dramatic Use of Imagery in Shakespeare's *Coriolanus*," *ELH* 23 (September 1956): 183–93.

Maurice Charney, "The Imagery of Food and Eating in *Coriolanus*," in Kirk and Main, *Essays in Literary History*, 37–56.

Thomas Clayton, "'Balancing at Work': (R)evoking the Script in Performance and Criticism," in Thompson and Thompson, *Shakespeare and the Sense of Performance*, 228–49.

E. A. Colman, "The End of *Coriolanus*," *ELH* 34 (March 1967): 1–20.

Combes, *Literature and Criticism*, 28–30.

David Z. Crookes, "'Small as a Eunuch': A Problem in 'Coriolanus,' Act III Scene 2," *M&L* 67 (April 1986): 159–61.

Lawrence N. Danson, "Metonymy and *Coriolanus*," *PQ* 52 (Winter 1973): 30–42.

Leonard F. Dean, "Voice and Deed in *Coriolanus*," *UR* 11 (March 1955): 177–83.

Elizabeth Story Donno, "*Coriolanus* and a Shakespearean Motif; Essays in Honor of S. F. Johnson," in Elton and Long, *Shakespeare and Dramatic Tradition*, 47–68.

Doran, *Shakespeare's Dramatic Language*, 182–217.

Eagleton, *Shakespeare and Society*, 98–122.

Una Ellis-Fermor, "Some Functions of Verbal Music in Drama," *ShJE* 90 (1954): 43–48.

Dennis J. Enright, "*Coriolanus*: Tragedy or Debate?" *EIC* 4 (January 1954): 1–19.

Stanley Fish, "How to do Things with Austin and Searle: Speech Act Theory and Literary Criticism," *MLN* 91 (December 1976): 983–1025.

Foakes, *Shakespeare*, 87–93.

French, *Shakespeare's Vision of Experience*, 270–79.

D. G. Gillham, "*Coriolanus*," *ESA* 20, no. 1 (1977): 43–52.

Christopher Givan, "Shakespeare's *Coriolanus*: The Premature Epitaph and the Butterfly," *ShakS* 12 (1979): 143–58.

Barry Goldfarb, "The Socratic Paradigm in Shakespeare's *Coriolanus*," *T&P* 11 (1991): 39–48.

Michael Goldman, "Characterizing *Coriolanus*," *ShS* 34 (1981): 73–84.

D. J. Gordon, "Name and Fame: Shakespeare's *Coriolanus*," in *Papers Mainly Shakespearean*, ed. G. I. Duthie (Edinburgh: Oliver and Boyd, 1966), 40–57.

Harley Granville-Barker, "Verse and Speech in *Coriolanus*," *RES* 23 (January 1947): 1–15.

Andrew Gurr, "*Coriolanus* and the Body Politic," *ShS* 28 (1975): 63–69.

Jay L. Halio, "*Coriolanus*: Shakespeare's 'Drama of Reconcilliation,'" *ShakS* 6 (1970): 289–303.

Hallett and Hallett, *Analyzing Shakespeare's Action*, 51–54, 73–74, 154–61, 164–65, 191–93, 201–03.

H. George Han, "The Orchard and the Street: The Political Mirror of the Tragic in *Julius Caesar* and *Coriolanus*," *CLAJ* 27 (December 1983): 169–86.

G. B. Harrison, "A Note on *Coriolanus*," in McManaway, *Joseph Q. Adams Memorial Studies*, 239–52.

Frances Helphinstine, "Volumnia: The Life of Rome," *SPWVSRA* 4 (Spring 1979): 55–63.

R. F. Hill, "*Coriolanus*: Violentest Contrariety," *E&S* 17 (1964): 12–23.

Clifford Chalmers Hoffman, "*Coriolanus* and His Poor Host: A Note," *EA* 35 (April–June 1982): 173–76.

Chrles K. Hofling, "An Interpretation of Shakespeare's *Coriolanus*," *AI* 14 (Winter 1957): 407–35.

Holloway, *The Story of the Night*, 121–30.

James Holstun, "Tragic Superfluity in *Coriolanus*," *ELH* 50 (1983): 485–507.

Edwin Honig, "Sejanus and *Coriolanus*: A Study in Alienation," *MLQ* 12 (December 1951): 407–21.

Houston, *Shakespearean Sentences*, 159–78.

Howarth, *The Tiger's Heart*, 16–19.

Maurice Hunt, "'Violent'st' Complementarity: The Double Warriors of *Coriolanus*," *SEL* 31 (Spring 1991): 309–25.

W. Hutchings, "Beast or God: The *Coriolanus* Controversy," *CritQ* 24 (Summer 1982): 35–50.

R. W. Ingram, "'Their noise be our instruction': Listening to *Titus Andronicus* and *Coriolanus*," in Gray, *Mirror up to Shakespeare*, 277–94.

Zvi Jagendorf, "*Coriolanus*: Body Politic and Private Parts," *SQ* 41 (Winter 1990): 455–69.

Robert C. Johnson, "Silence and Speech in *Coriolanus*," *AJES* 5 (April 1980): 190–210.

Vernon E. Johnson, "Shakespeare's *Coriolanus* IV. vii. 27–57," *Expl* 33 (October 1974): Item 21.

Paul A. Jorgensen, "Shakespeare's *Coriolanus*: Elizabethan Soldier," *PMLA* 64 (March 1949): 231–35.

Paul A. Jorgensen, "Divided Command in Shakespeare," *PMLA* 70 (September 1955): 750–61.

Knight, *The Golden Labyrinth*, 145–46.

Knight, *Imperial Theme*, 154–98.

L. C. Knights, "Shakespeare and Political Wisdom: A Note on the Personalism of *Julius Caesar* and *Coriolanus*," *SR* 61 (Winter 1953): 43–55.

Jean Lepley, "Should Rome Burn? The Morality of Vengeance in *Coriolanus* (and Beyond)," *Soundings* 64 (Winter 1983): 404–21.

J. C. F. Littlewood, "*Coriolanus*," *CQ* 2 (1967): 339–57.

Lisa Lowe, "'Say I Play the Man I Am': Gender and Politics in *Coriolanus*," *KR* 48 (Fall 1986): 86–95.

Jean MacIntyre, "Words, Acts, and Things: Visual Language in *Coriolanus*," *ESC* 10 (March 1984): 1–10.

Michael McCanles, "The Dialectic of Transcendence in Shakespeare's *Coriolanus*," *PMLA* 82 (January 1967): 44–53.

Millar MacLure, "Shakespeare and the Lonely Dragon," *UTQ* 24 (January 1955): 114–18.

J. C. Maxwell, "Animal Imagery in *Coriolanus*," *MLR* 42 (October 1947): 417–21.

McCollum, *Tragedy*, 47–48, 126–29, 145–46.

Stanley D. McKenzie, "'Unshout the Noise That Banish'd Martius': Structural Paradox and Dissembling in *Coriolanus*," *ShakS* 18 (1986): 189–204.

Patricia K. Mezaros, "'There is a world elsewhere': Tragedy and History in *Coriolanus*," *SEL* 16 (Spring 1976): 273–85.

Nancy Carolyn Michael, "Shakespeare's *Coriolanus*, His Metamorphosis from Man to Monster," *BSUF* 19, no. 2 (1978): 12–19.

Anthony Miller, "*Coriolanus*: The Tragedy of Virtus," *SSEng* 9 (1983–1984): 37–60.

Virgil Nemoianu, "*Coriolanus*, or the Secondary as Hero," in Alphonse Juilland, *D'une passion l'autre*, ed. Brigitte Cazelles (Saratoga, CA: Anma Libri, 1987), 63–83.

Peter F. Neumeyer, "*Coriolanus*: Ingratitude is Monstrous," *CE* 26 (December 1964): 192–97.

Peter F. Neumeyer, "Not Local Habitation Nor a Name: *Coriolanus*," *UR* 22 (1966): 195–98.

Nuttall, *A New Mimesis*, 114–20.

H. J. Oliver, "Coriolanus as Tragic Hero," *SQ* 10 (Winter 1959): 53–60.

R. B. Parker, "*Coriolanus* and 'th'interpretation of the time,'" in Gray, *Mirror up to Shakespeare*, 261–76.

Gail Kern Paster, "To Starve with Feeding: The City in *Coriolanus*," *ShakS* 11 (1978): 123–44.

Edward Pechter, "Shakespeare's Roman Plays as History," *RPLit* 2 (1979): 233–41.

Matthew Prosser, "*Coriolanus*: The Constant Warrior and the State," *CE* 24 (April 1963): 507–12.

A. Luis Pujante, "'No Sense Nor Feeling': A Note on *Coriolanus*, 4.1," *SQ* 41 (Winter 1990): 489–90.

J. M. Purcell, "Shakespeare's *Coriolanus* III,i,101," *Expl* 15 (March 1957): 36.

Rufus Putney, "Coriolanus and His Mother," *Psychoanalytic Quarterly* 31 (July 1962): 364–81.

Michael Quinn, "Caius Marcius Coriolanus: The Self as Art," *ShakB* 5–6 (November–December 1986, January–February 1987): 5–8.

Norman Rabkin, "*Coriolanus*: The Tragedy of Politics," *SQ* 17 (Summer 1966): 195–212.

Phyllis Rackin, "*Coriolanus*: Shakespeare's Anatomy of Virtus," *MLS* 13 (Spring 1983): 68–79.

Constance C. Relihan, "Appropiation of the 'Thing of Blood': Absence of Self and the Struggle for Ownership in *Coriolanus*," *ISJR* 62 (February 1988): 407–20.

W. Riehle, "*Coriolanus*, I.i.217 'Unroofd,'" *N&Q* 27 (April 1980): 174.

Irving Ribner, "The Tragedy of *Coriolanus*," *ES* 34 (February 1953): 1–9.

F. H. Ronda, "*Coriolanus*—A Tragedy of Youth," *SQ* 12 (Spring 1961): 103–06.

Rossiter, *Angel with Horns*, 235–52.

Anselm Schlosser, "Reflections on Shakespeare's *Coriolanus*," *PP* 1 (1963): 11–21.

Peggy Munoz Simonds, "*Coriolanus* and the Myth of Juno and Mars," *Mosaic* 18 (Spring 1985): 33–50.

Victor Skretkowicz, "*Coriolanus* (1.iii.44): An Alternative Emendation," *N&Q* 25 (April 1978):153–54

William W. E. Slights, "Bodies of Text and Textualized Bodies in Sejanus and *Coriolanus*," *MRDE* 5 (Summer 1991): 181–93.

Smith, *Homosexual Desire in Shakespeare's England*, 33–35.

Gordon Ross Smith, "Authoritarian Patterns in Shakespeare's *Coriolanus*," *L&P* 9 (Summer–Fall 1959): 45–51.

Peter J. Smith, "*Coriolanus*," *CahiersE* 39 (April 1991): 82–84.

Thomas Sorge, "The Failure of Orthodoxy in *Coriolanus*," in Howard and O'Connor, *Shakespeare Reproduced*, 225–41.

Madelon Sprengnether, "Annihilating Intimacy in *Coriolanus*," in *Women in the Middle Ages and the Renaissance: Literary and Historical Perspectives*, ed. Mary Beth Rose (Syracuse, NY: Syracuse University Press, 1986), 89–111.

G. Thomas Tanselle, and Florence W. Dunbar, "Legal Language in *Coriolanus*," *SQ* 13 (Spring 1962): 231–38.

Michael Taylor, "Playing the Man He Is: Role-Playing in Shakespeare's *Coriolanus*," *ArielE* 15 (January 1984): 19–28.

Fran Teague, "Headgear in *Coriolanus*," *ShakB* 4 (July–August 1986): 5–7.

Leonard Tennenhouse, "*Coriolanus*: History and the Crisis in Semantic Order," *CompD* 10 (Fall 1976): 328–46. Reprinted in Davidson, Gianakaris, and Stroupe, *Drama in the Renaissance*, 217–35.

Traversi, D. A. "*Coriolanus*," in Stallman, *Critiques and Essays in Criticism*, 141–53.

Joyce Van Dyke, "Making a Scene: Language and Gesture in *Coriolanus*," *ShS* 30 (1977): 135–46.

John W. Velz, "Cracking Strong Curbs Asunder: Roman Destiny and the Roman Hero in *Coriolanus*," *ELR* 13 (Winter 1983): 58–69.

Robert N. Watson, "*Coriolanus*: An Exercise in Psychoanalysis," *Tri-Q* 2 (Spring 1960): 41–43.

Watson, *Shakespeare and the Hazards of Ambition*, 149–221.

Hans-Jurgen Weckermann, "*Coriolanus*: The Failure of the Autonomous Individual," in Fabian and von Rosador, *Shakespeare: Text, Language, Criticism*, 334–50.

Joseph Weixlmann, " '. . . action may/Conveniently the rest convey . . .': Some Key Presentational Images in Shakespeare's *Coriolanus*," *ForumH* 12, no. 2 (1974): 9–13.

Gwyn Williams, "The Oedipus Complex in *Coriolanus*," *Bulletin of the Faculty of Arts* 4 (1948): 61–66.

Marilyn L. Williamson, "Violence and Gender Ideology in *Coriolanus* and *Macbeth*," in Kamps, *Shakespeare Left and Right*, 147–66.

Richard Wilson, "Against the Grain: Representing the Market in *Coriolanus*," *SCen* 6 (Autumn 1991): 111–48.

Gordon W. Zeevald, "*Coriolanus* and Jacobean Politics," *MLR* 57 (July 1962): 321–34.

Cymbeline

A. A. Ansari, "*Cymbeline*: The Design of Harmony," *AJES* 12 (April 1987): 9–26.

David M. Bergeron, "*Cymbeline*: Shakespeare's Last Roman Play," *SQ* 31 (Winter 1980): 31–41.

David M. Bergeron, "Sexuality in *Cymbeline*," *ELWIU* 10 (Fall 1983): 159–68.

J. P. Brockbank, "History and Histronics in *Cymbeline*," *ShS* 11 (1958): 42–49.

SHAKESPEARE, WILLIAM, *Cymbeline*

Brockbank, *On Shakespeare*, 272–82.

Douglas Bruster, "*Cymbeline* and the Sudden Blow," *UCrow* 10 (1990) 101–12.

John S. Colley, "Disguise and New Guise in *Cymbeline*," *ShakS* 7 (1974): 233–52.

F. Corin, "A Note on the Dirge in *Cymbeline*," *ES* 40 (June 1959): 173–79.

John W. Crawford, "Intuitive Knowledge in *Cymbeline*," *UCrow* 1 (1978): 74–81.

John W. Crawford, "Shakespeare's *Cymbeline*," *Expl* 39 (Summer 1980): 4–6.

Danby, *Poets on Fortune's Hill*, 103–05.

Rowena Davies, " 'Alone th'Arabian Bird': Imogen as Elizabeth I?" *N&Q* 26 (April 1979): 137–40.

Hough-Lewis Dunn, "Shakespeare's *Cymbeline*, II, 15-17," *Expl* 30 (March 1972): Item 57.

Edwards, *Threshold of a Nation*, 87–94.

Foakes, *Shakespeare*, 98–118.

French, *Shakespeare's Division of Experience*, 306–312.

Marjorie Garber, "*Cymbeline* and the Languages of Myth," *Mosaic* 10 (Autumn 1977): 105–15.

Lila Geller, "*Cymbeline* and the Imagery of Covenant Theology," *SEL* 20 (Spring 1980): 241–55.

Brian Gibbons, "Fabled Cymbeline," *DSGW* 123 (1987), 78–99.

John Gillies, "The Problem of Style in *Cymbeline*," *SoRA* 15 (November 1982): 269–90.

Joan F. Gilliland, "*Cymbeline* as Folk Tale," *BWVACET* 6 (Spring 1981): 13–18.

Bernard Harris, "'What's past is prologue': *Cymbeline* and *Henry VIII*," in Brown and Harris, *Later Shakespeare*, 203–34.

Jonathan Hart, "Alienation, Double Signs with a Difference: Conscious Knots in *Cymbeline* and *The Winter's Tale*," *CIEFLB* 1 (June 1989): 58–78.

Joan Hartwig, "Cloten, Autolycus, and Caliban: Bearers of Parodic Burdens," in Kay and Jacobs, *Shakespeare's Romances Reconsidered*, 91–103.

Nancy K. Hayles, "Sexual Disguise in *Cymbeline*," *MLQ* 41 (June 1980): 231–47.

A. K. Hieatt, "*Cymbeline* and the Intrusion of Lyric into Romance Narrative: Sonnets, 'A Lover's Complaint,' Spenser's Ruins of Rome," in Logan and Teskey, *Unfolded Tales*, 98–118.

A. K. Hieatt, T. G. Bishop, and E. A. Nicholson, "Shakespeare's Rare Words: 'Lover's Complaint,' *Cymbeline*, and Sonnets," *N&Q* 34 (June 1987): 219–24.

F. D. Hoeniger, "Irony and Romance in *Cymbeline*," *SEL* 2 (Spring 1962): 219–28.

F. D. Hoeniger, "Two Notes on *Cymbeline*," *SQ* 8 (Winter 1957): 132–33.

Houston, *Shakespearean Sentences*, 198–213.

Maurice Hunt, "Perspectivism in *King Lear* and *Cymbeline*," *StHum* 14 (June 1987): 18–31.

Maurice Hunt, "Shakespeare's Empirical Romance: *Cymbeline* and Modern Knowledge," *TSLL* 22 (Autumn 1980): 322–42.

Henry E. Jacobs, "Rewriting Shakespeare: The Framing of *Cymbeline*," *RenP 1982* (1983): 79–87.

Kastan, *Shakespeare and the Shapes of Time*, 145–61.

Carol McGinnis Kay, "Generic Sleight of Hand in *Cymbeline*," *SAB* 46 (November 1981): 34–40.

Walter Kluge, " 'Fidele's Dirge' in Shakespeare's *Cymbeline*," *ShJE* 102 (1966): 211–22.

G. Wilson Knight, *The Crown of Life* (New York: Oxford University Press, 1947), 129–202.

Knight, *The Golden Labyrinth*, 83–84.

Knight, *The Sovereign Flower*, 73–80.

D. E. Landry, "Dreams as History: The Strange Unity of *Cymbeline*," *SQ* 33 (Spring 1982): 68–79.

Judiana Lawrence, "Natural Bonds and Artistic Coherence in the Ending of *Cymbeline*," *SQ* 35 (Winter 1984): 440–60.

J. S. Lawry, "'Perishing Root and Increasing Vine' in *Cymbeline*," *ShakS* 12 (1979): 179–93.

Leavis, *The Common Pursuit*, 173–79.

Alexander Leggatt, "The Island of Miracles: An Approach to *Cymbeline*," *ShakS* 10 (1977): 191–209.

Cynthia Lewis, "'With Simular Proof Enough': Modes of Misperception in *Cymbeline*," *SEL* 31 (Spring 1991): 343–64.

W. W. Main, "Shakespeare's 'Fear no More the Heat O' Th' Sun,'" *Expl* 9 (March 1951): 36.

P. Marudanayagam, "Shakespeare's *Cymbeline*," *Expl* 39 (Fall 1980): 32–33.

Joan C. Marx, "The Encounter of Genres: *Cymbeline*'s Structure of Juxtaposition," in Pope, *Analysis of Literary Texts*, 138–44.

J. Paul McRoberts, " 'What Dear Sir, Thus Raps You?' *Cymbeline* I, vii, 50–51," *LangQ* 22 (Fall–Winter 1983): 22, 26, 29.

Barbara Melchiori, "'Still Harping on My Daughter,'" *English Miscellany* 11 (1960): 64–65.

Robert S. Miola, "*Cymbeline*: Shakespeare's Valediction to Rome," in *Roman Images*, ed. Annabel Patterson (Baltimore: Johns Hopkins University Press, 1984), 51–62.

Robin Moffit, "*Cymbeline* and the Nativity," *SQ* 13 (Spring 1962): 207–18.

Barbara A. Mowat, "*Cymbeline*: Crude Dramaturgy and Aesthetic Distance," *RenP 1966* (1967): 39–47.

Kenneth Muir, "A Trick of Style and Some Implications," *ShakS* 6 (1970): 305–10.

Nicholl, *The Chemical Theatre*, 227–36.

Edward F. Nolan, "Shakespeare's 'Fear no More The Heat O' Th' Sun,'" *Expl* 11 (October 1952): 4.

J. M. Nosworthy, "The Integrity of Shakespeare: Illustrated from *Cymbeline*," *ShS* 8 (1955): 52–56.

Patricia Parker, "Romance and Empire: Anachronistic *Cymbeline*," in Logan and Teskey, *Unfolded Tales*, 189–207.

George L. Phillip, "Shakespeare's 'Fear no More The Heat O' Th' Sun,'" *Expl* 12 (October 1953): 2.

Beryl Pogson, "Esoteric Significance of *Cymbeline*," *Baconiana* 32 (Autumn 1948): 192–98, 228.

Beryl Pogson, *In the East My Pleasure Lies*, 47–57.

H. L. Rogers, "The Prophetic Label in *Cymbeline*," *RES* 11 (August 1960): 296–99.

R. J. Schork, "Allusion, Theme, and Characterization in *Cymbeline*," *SP* 69 (July 1972): 210–16.

Shaw, *Plays and Players*, 114–24.

James E. Simon, "Noble Virtue in *Cymbeline*," *ShS* 29 (1976): 51–61.

Peggy Munoz Simonds, "The Marriage Topos in *Cymbeline*: Shakespeare's Variations on a Classical Theme," *ELR* 19 (Winter 1989): 94–117.

Peggy Munoz Simonds, " 'No More . . . Offend Our Hearing': Aural Imagery in *Cymbeline*," *TSLL* 24 (Summer 1982): 137–54.

Peggy Munoz Simonds, "Some Emblematic Courtier Topoi in *Cymbeline*," *RenP 1980* (1981): 97–112.

Meredith Skura, "Interpreting Posthumus' Dream from Above and Below: Families, Psychoanalysts, and Literary Critics," in Schwartz and Kahn, *Representing Shakespeare*, 203–16.

A. A. Stephenson, "The Significance of *Cymbeline*," *Scrutiny* 10 (April 1942): 185–94.

Homer Swander, "*Cymbeline* and the 'Blameless Hero,' " *ELH* 31 (September 1964): 259–70.

Homer Swander, "*Cymbeline* and the Woman Falsely Accused," *ShN* 4 (December 1954): 50.

Homer Swander, "*Cymbeline*: Religious Idea and Dramatic Design," in McNeir and Greenfield, *Pacific Coast Studies in Shakespeare*, 248–62.

Michael Taylor, "The Pastoral Reckoning of *Cymbeline*," *ShS* 36 (1983): 97–106.

Brook Thomas, "*Cymbeline* and the Perils of Interpretation," *NOR* 10 (Summer–Fall 1983): 137–45.

Ann Thompson, and John O. Thompson, "The Syntax of Metaphor in *Cymbeline*: Proceedings of Third Congress of International Shakespeare Association," in Habicht, Palmer, and Pringle, *Images of Shakespeare*, 80–97.

Robert Y. Turner, "Slander in *Cymbeline* and Other Jacobean Tragicomedies," *ELR* 13 (Spring 1983): 182–202.

Roger Warren, "Theatrical Virtuosity and Poetic Complexity in *Cymbeline*," *ShS* 29 (1976): 41–49.

Glynne Wickham, "Riddle and Emblem: A Study in the Dramatic Structure of *Cymbeline*," in Carey, *English Renaissance Studies*, 94–113.

Martin Wiggins, *Journeymen in Murder*, 99–101.

Hamlet

Lionel Abel, *Metatheatre* (New York: Hill & Wang, 1963), 1–59.

Nicolas Abraham, and Nicholas Rand, "The Phantom of Hamlet or the Sixth Act: Preceded by the Intermission of 'Truth,'" *Diacritics* 18 (Winter 1988): 2–19.

Lionel Adey, "Enjoyment, Contemplation, and Hierarchy in *Hamlet*," in *Evolution of Consciousness: Studies in Polarity: Essays in Honor of Owen Barfield*, ed. Shirley Sugarman (Middletown, CT: Wesleyan University Press, 1976), 149–67.

Geoffrey Aggeler, "*Hamlet* and the Stoic Sage," *HSt* 9 (Summer–Winter 1987): 21–33.

Deborah T. Curren Aquino, "A Note on *Hamlet* I.4.36–38," *HSt* 3 (Summer 1981): 48–52.

Amin al-Ayouty, "The Mask of *Hamlet*," *JEn* 5 (Spring 1978): 55–61.

Nigel Alexander, "Critical Disagreement About Oedipus and Hamlet," *ShS* 20 (1967): 33–40.

N. B. Allen, "Polonius's Advice to Laertes," *ShAB* 19 (October 1943): 187–90.

Richard D. Alticke, "*Hamlet* and the Odor of Morality," *SQ* 5 (Spring 1954): 167–76.

Donald K. Anderson, Jr., "The King's Two Rouses and Providential Revenge in *Hamlet*," *ISJR* 56 (August 1981): 23–29.

Mary Anderson, "*Hamlet*: The Dialectic Between Eye and Ear," *Ren&R* 15 (Fall 1991): 299–313.

Michael Cameron Andrews, "'Excellent Well. You Are a Fishmonger!'" *RenP* 1977 (1978): 59–68.

Michael Cameron Andrews, "*Hamlet* and the Satisfactions of Revenge," *HSt* 3 (Winter 1981): 83–102.

Michael Cameron Andrews, "His Mother's Closet: A Note on *Hamlet*," *MP* 80 (November 1982): 164–66.

Michael Cameron Andrews, "*Hamlet*: Revenge and the Critical Mirror," *ELR* 8 (Spring 1978): 9–23.

Michael Cameron Andrews, "'Remember Me': Memory and Action in *Hamlet*," *JGE* 33 (Winter 1981): 261–70.

Michael Cameron Andrews, "Shakespeare's *Hamlet*," *Expl* 49 (Summer 1991): 208–09.

Niels L. Anthonisen, "The Ghost in *Hamlet*," *AI* 22 (Autumn 1966): 232–49.

Alex Aronson, "A Note on Shakespeare's Dream Imagery," *Visuabharati Quarterly* 19 (August–October 1952): 190–91.

Paul M. Arriola, "Two Baroque Heroes: Segismundo and Hamlet," *Hispania* 43 (December 1960): 537–40.

Heather Asals, "'Should' and 'Would': *Hamlet* and the Idioms of the Father," *Genre* 13 (Winter 1980): 431–39.

Leonard R. N. Ashley, "'Now Might I Doe It Pat': *Hamlet* and the Despicable Non-Act in the Third Act," *HSt* 13 (Summer–Winter 1991): 85–91.

C. Thomas Ault, "Shakespeare's *Hamlet*," *Expl* 49 (Summer 1991): 204–07.

Lawrence Babb, "Hamlet, Melancholy, and the Devil," *MLN* 59 (February 1944): 120–22.

Lawrence Babb, *The Elizabethan Malady*, 106–10.

William B. Bache, "Hamlet, Macbeth, and Lear Offstage: The Significance of Absence," *DR* 59 (Autumn 1979): 308–20.

Margery Bailey, "Shakespeare in Action," *CE* 15 (March 1954): 311–14.

Jonathan Baldo, "'He That Plays the King': The Problem of Pretending in *Hamlet*," *Criticism* 25 (Winter 1983): 13–26.

Conrad A. Balliet, "'To Sleep, To Die . . .'Tis a Consummation,'" *RS* 36 (1968): 26–36.

Bamborough, *The Little World of Man*, 34–35, 91–92, 112–14.

Francis Barker, "The Essex Symposia: Literature/Politics/Theory; Which Dead? *Hamlet* and the Ends of History," in Barker, Hulme, and Iversen, *Uses of History*, 47–75.

David Barrett, "Take Him for all in all," *NM* 62 (March 1961): 164–69.

Jackson G. Barry, *Dramatic Structure: The Shaping of Experience* (Berkeley, Los Angeles, and London: University of California Press, 1970), 207–12.

Lucy Bate, "Which Did or Did Not Go to the Grave?" *SQ* 17 (Summer 1966): 163–64.

Battenhouse, *Poets of Christian Thought*, 34–39.

Roy W. Battenhouse, "The Ghost in *Hamlet*: A Catholic Linchpin?" *SP* 48 (April 1951): 161–92.

Roy W. Battenhouse, "Hamlet's Apostrophe on Man: Clue to the Tragedy," *PMLA* 66 (December 1951): 1073–113.

Denver E. Baughan, "The Very Cause of Hamlet's Lunacy," *ShN* 9 (September 1959): 30.

Andria Beacock, "Notes on Melancholia/Schizophrenia as a Social Disease: Robert Burton, R. D. Laing, and Hamlet," *MSE* 6, no. 1–2 (1977): 1–14.

Beardsley, *Aesthetics*, 245–46.

Catherine Beasley, "The Case of Hamlet's Conscience," *SP* 76 (Spring 1979): 127–48.

Josephine Waters Bennett, "Characterization in Polonius' Advice to Laertes," *SQ* 4 (January 1953): 3–9.

Josephine Waters Bennett, "These Few Precepts," *SQ* 7 (Spring 1956): 275–76.

Robert B. Bennett, "The Dramatic Function of Hamlet's Cloud," *Archiv* 215 (1978): 89–92.

Robert B. Bennett, "*Hamlet* and the Burden of Knowledge," *ShakS* 15 (1982): 77–97.

William E. Bennett, "The Gravediggers' Scene: A Unifying Thread in *Hamlet*," *UCrow* 5 (Fall 1984): 160–65.

Greg Bentley, "Melancholy, Madness and Syphilis in *Hamlet*," *HSt* 6 (Summer–Winter 1984): 75–80.

Edmund Bergler, "The Seven Paradoxes in Shakespeare's *Hamlet*," *AI* 16 (Winter 1959): 379–405.

Craig A. Bernthal, "'Self' Examination and Readiness in *Hamlet*," *HSt* 7 (Summer–Winter 1985): 38–51.

E. G. Berry, "Hamlet and Suetonius," *The Phoenix* 2 (Autumn 1948): 73–81.

Francis Berry, "Young Fortinbras," *Life and Letters Today* 52 (February 1947): 94–103.

Ralph Berry, "Hamlet: Nationhood and Identity," *UTQ* 49 (June 1980): 283–303.

Berry, *Shakespearean Structures*, 24–46.

Ralph Berry, "'To Say One': An Essay on *Hamlet*," *ShS* 28 (1975): 107–15.

Werner Berthoff, "'Our Means Will Make Us Means': Character as Virtue in *Hamlet* and *All's Well*," *NLH* 5 (1974): 319–51.

Harvey Birenbaum, "To Be and Not to Be: The Archetypal Form of *Hamlet*," *PCP* 16 (June 1981): 19–28.

W. H. Bizley, "The Stars Over Denmark—Some Metaphysical Considerations for a Reading of *Hamlet*," *Theoria* 41 (April 1973): 31–44.

Robert E. Bjork, "Reverberations from Hamlet's Solid Flesh," *Comitatus* 10 (Winter 1979–80): 116–22.

James Black, "Hamlet's Vows," *Ren&R* 2 (February 1978): 33–48

David-Everett Blythe, "Shakespeare's *Hamlet*," *Expl* 44 (Winter 1986): 9–10.

Bodkin, *Archetypal Patterns in Poetry*, 9–13, 59–60.

N. Bogholm, "The Hamlet Drama," *OL* 4, no. 2 (1946): 157–228.

Piero Boitani, "Anagnorisis and Reasoning: Electra and Hamlet," *REALB* 7 (1990): 99–136.

Adrien Bonjour, "*Hamlet* and the Phantom Clue," *ES* 35 (December 1954): 253–59.

Adrien Bonjour, "The Question of Hamlet's Grief," *ES* 43 (October 1962): 336–43.

Adrien Bonjour, "The Test of Poetry," *ShJE* 100 (1964): 149–58.

Lynda E. Boose, "The Fashionable Polonius," *HSt* 1 (Spring 1979): 67–77.

E. Kerr Borthwick, "'So Capital a Calf': The Pun in *Hamlet*, III.ii.105," *SQ* 35 (Summer 1984): 203–04.

Fredson Bowers, "The Death of Hamlet: A Study in Plot and Character," in Bennett, Cargill, and Hall, *Studies in the English Renaissance Drama*, 29–42.

Fredson Bowers, "Dramatic Structure and Criticism: Plot in *Hamlet*," *SQ* 15 (Spring 1964): 207–18.

Fredson Bowers, "Hamlet as Minister and Scourge," *PMLA* 70 (September 1955): 741–49.

Fredson Bowers, "The Moment of Final Suspense in *Hamlet*: 'We Defy Augury,'" in Bloom, *Shakespeare 1564–1964*, 50–55.

Fredson Bowers, "A Note on *Hamlet* I, v, 33 and II, ii, 191," *SQ* 4 (January 1953): 51–56.

Fredson Bowers, "Shakespeare's Art: The Point of View," in *Literary Views*, ed. Carroll Camden (Chicago: University of Chicago Press, 1964), 49–50.

R. H. Bowers, "Polonius: Another Postscript," *SQ* 4 (Summer 1953): 362–64.

Benjamin Boyce, "Shakespeare's *Hamlet*, II, ii, 198–208," *Expl* 7 (October 1948): 2.

Robert Bozanich, "The Eye of the Beholder: Hamlet to Ophelia, II.ii.109–24," *SQ* 31 (Winter 1980): 90–93.

Bradshaw, *Shakespeare's Skepticism*, 6–13.

Bredbeck, *Sodomy and Interpretation*, 181–85.

Anthony S. Brennan, "Shakespeare's *Hamlet* III.iv.22–26," *Expl* 38 (Fall 1980): 43–44.

Horst Breuer, "Three Notes on *Hamlet*," *ES* 56 (April 1975): 20–28.

Horst Breuer, "Shakespeare's *Hamlet*, III.i.56–88," *Expl* 40 (Spring 1982): 14–15.

Howard Bridgewater, "The Character of Hamlet," *Baconiana* 36 (November 1952): 143–45.

J. Philip Brockbank, "Hamlet the Bonesetter," *ShS* 30 (1977): 103–15.

Brockbank, *On Shakespeare*, 167–84.

Jules Brody, "Freud, *Hamlet*, and the Metaphysics of Tragedy," *Lang&S* 10 (Summer 1977): 248–61.

Bertrand H. Bronson, "Costly Thy Habit," *SQ* 7 (Spring 1956): 280–81.

Brown, *Dramatis Personae*, 219–26.

John M. Brown, "The Setting for *Hamlet*," *Stratford-Upon-Avon Studies* 5 (1963): 163–84.

John M. Brown, "Shakespeare's Subtext: II," *TDR* 8 (Winter 1963): 86–95, 99–101.

Richard T. Brucher, "Fantasies of Violence: *Hamlet* and *The Revenger's Tragedy*," *SEL* 21 (Spring 1981): 257–70.

Neal H. Bruss, "Lacan and Literature: Imaginary Objects and Social Order," *MR* 22 (Spring 1981): 62–92.

Bullough, *Mirror of Minds*, 80–83.

Barbara Burge, "*Hamlet*: The Search for Identity," *REL* 5 (April 1964): 59–71.

Robert E. Burkhart, "Hamlet: Is He Still Delaying?" *HSt* 6 (Summer–Winter 1984): 81–86.

Bernard Burkom, "Hamlet as Activist," *SJS* 5 (Fall 1979): 68–79.

J. Anthony Burton, "Hamlet, Osric, and the Duel," *ShakB* 2 (July–August 1984): 5–7, 22–25.

J. Anthony Burton, "'His Quarry Cries on Hauocke': Is It Shakespeare's Own Judgement on the Meaning of *Hamlet*?" *UCrow* 11 (1991): 62–81.

Andrew S. Cairncross, "Two Notes on *Hamlet*," *SQ* 9 (Autumn 1958): 586–88.

James L. Calderwood, "Hamlet: The Name of Action," *MLQ* 39 (September 1978): 331–62.

Mark L. Caldwell, "*Hamlet* and the Senses," *MLQ* 40 (June 1979): 135–54.

Carroll Camden, "On Ophelia's Madness," *SQ* 15 (Spring 1964): 247–55. Reprinted in McManaway, *Shakespeare 400*, 247–55.

Lily B. Campbell, "Polonius: The Tyrant's Ears," in McManaway, *Joseph Q. Adams Memorial Studies*, 295–313.

Oscar J. Campbell, "What Is the Matter with Hamlet?" *YR* 32 (December 1942): 309–22.

E. Frank Candlin, "Hamlet's Successor," *The Norseman* 7 (September–October 1949): 348–55.

Canfield, *Word as Bond in English Literature*, 222–34.

Charles K. Cannon, " 'As in a Theatre': *Hamlet* in Light of Calvin's Doctrine of Predestination," *SEL* 11 (Spring 1971): 203–22.

Carol J. Carlisle, "Hamlet's 'Cruelty' in the Nunnery Scene: The Actors' Views," *SQ* 18 (Spring 1967): 129–40.

Ricks Carson, "Shakespeare's *Hamlet*," *Expl* 49 (Winter 1991): 76.

Larry S. Champion, " 'By Indirections Find Directions Out': The Soliloquies in *Hamlet*," *JGE* 27 (Winter 1975): 265–80.

Larry S. Champion, "Laertes' Return to Elsinore," *SQ* 17 (Winter 1966): 81–83.

Chandhuri, *Infirm Glory*, 134–46.

Josephine Chandler, "Some Notes on the Problem of Hamlet," *SJS* 1 (Spring 1975): 81–85.

Maurice Charney, "Analogy and Infinite Regress in *Hamlet*," in Charney and Reppen, *Psychoanalytic Approaches to Literature and Film*, 156–67.

Maurice Charney, "Hamlet's O-Groans and Textual Criticism," *RenD* 9 (1978): 109–19.

Maurice Charney, "The 'Now Could I Drink Hot Blood' Soliloquy and the Middle of *Hamlet*," *Mosaic* 10 (Fall 1977): 77–86.

Maurice Charney, "Reading *Hamlet*: Text, Context, and Subtext," in Quinn, *How to Read Shakespearean Tragedy*, 89–134.

Una Chaudhuri, "Seeing, Saying, Knowing: *Hamlet* and the Tenuous Project of Drama Semiotics," *NOR* 11 (Fall–Winter 1984): 119–27.

B. D. Cheadle, "Hamlet at the Graveside: A Leap into Hermeneutics," *ESA* 22, no. 1 (1979): 83–90.

David R. Cheney, "Hamlet-Complex Oedipus Complex," *ShN* 17 (September 1967): 58.

Livia Ciulei, "*Hamlet* and the Taste of Time," *RoR* 33 (July 1979): 127–34.

John A. Clair, "Shakespeare's *Hamlet*, III, i, 92," *Expl* 14 (October 1955): 5.

C. C. Clarke, "A Note on 'To be or not to be,'" *EIC* 10 (January 1960): 18–23.

Silvia Mussi da Silva Claro, "The Dramatic Function of 'Aeneas' Tale to Dido' in *Hamlet*," *EAA* 1 (1977): 95–112.

Clay, *The Role of Anxiety*, 118–38.

Thomas Clayton, "A Crux in *Hamlet* I.iii: *Safty:Sanctity* (21) and *Beguide:Beguile* (131)," *ShakS* 3 (1968): 43–61.

Thomas Clayton, "The Quibbling Polonius and the Pious Bonds: The Rhetoric of *Hamlet* I.iii," *ShakS* 2 (1966): 59–94.

Clemen, *Shakespeare's Dramatic Art*, 60–68, 175–77.

Charles H. Clifton, "Hamlet Ludens: The Importance of Playing in *Hamlet*," *SPWVSRA* 6 (1981): 35–41.

Ruth H. Cline, "A Note on *Hamlet*," *MLN* 66 (January 1951): 40.

Louise George Clubb, "The Arts of Genre: *Torrismondo* and *Hamlet*," *ELH* 47 (December 1980): 657–69.

Karin S. Coddon, "'Suche Strange Desygns': Madness, Subjectivity, and Treason in *Hamlet* and Elizabethan Culture," *RenD* 20 (1989): 51–75.

Brent M. Cohen, "'What Is It You Would See?' *Hamlet* and the Conscience of the Theatre," *ELH* 44 (March 1977): 222–47.

Michael M. Cohen, "The Deceitful Hamlet," *UCrow* 1 (1978): 41–52.

Michael Cohen, "*Hamlet*" in *My Mind's Eye* (Athens: University of Georgia Press, 1989): 1–173, passim.

Michael Cohen, "'To what base uses we may return': Class and Mortality in *Hamlet* (5.1)," *HSt* 9 (Summer–Winter 1987): 78–85.

John Scott Colley, "Drama, Fortune, and Providence in *Hamlet*," *CollL* 5 (Spring 1978): 48–56.

David Collins, "The Extent of Negation in Shakespearean Tragedy: Some Reflections on *Hamlet*," *PMPA* 3 (1978): 16–23.

E. A. M. Colman, "*Hamlet*: The Poem or the Play?" *SSEng* 1 (1975–76): 3–12.

Confrey, *The Moral Mission of Literature*, 175–200.

Raymond Conlon, "*Hamlet*: A Movement Towards the Divine," *MSE* 3, no. 1 (1971): 27–33.

Thomas F. Connolly, "Shakespeare and the Double Man," *SQ* 1 (January 1950): 30–33.

William Cooke, "Shakespeare's *Hamlet*," *Expl* 36 (Winter 1978): 10–11.

H. R. Coursen, "Ophelia's Doubtful Death," *C&L* 27 (Spring 1978): 28–31.

H. R. Coursen, "That Within: *Hamlet* and Revenge," *Bucknell University Studies* 11 (May 1963): 19–34.

Catherine I. Cox, "Saturnalian Sacrifice: Comic-Tragic Blending in *Hamlet*," *EIRC* 12 (1986): 87–104.

Roger L. Cox, "*Hamlet's Hamatia*: Aristotle or St. Paul?" *YR* 55 (March 1966): 347–64.

Martin Coyle, "Shakespeare's *Hamlet*," *Expl* 40 (Spring 1982): 13.

Martin Coyle, "Shakespeare's *Hamlet*," *Expl* 43 (Fall 1984): 12–13.

Hardin Craig, "Hamlet as a Man of Action," *HLQ* 27 (May 1964): 222–38.

Hardin Craig, "Shakespeare and the Normal World: The Range of Action," *Rice Institute Pamphlets* 31 (January 1944): 15–32.

Craig, *The Written Word*, 32–48.

Jane Crawford, "*Hamlet*, III.ii.146," *RES* 18 (April 1967): 40–45.

Clifford Mortimer Crist, "Hamlet Maledictum," *Maledicta* 3 (Summer 1979): 185–92.

Lester G. Crocker, "*Hamlet, Don Quixote*, and *La Vida es Suena*," *PMLA* 69 (March 1954): 278–313.

Patrick Cruttwell, "The Morality of Hamlet—'Sweet Prince' or 'Arrant Knight'?" *Stratford-Upon-Avon Studies* 5 (1963): 110–28.

Peter Cummings, "Hearing in *Hamlet*: Poisoned Ears and the Psychopathology of Flawed Audition," *ShY* 1 (Spring 1990): 81–92.

Cunningham, *Woe or Wonder*, 11–13, 17–23, 28–30, 32–37, 43–44, 109–11.

Joost Daalder, "'Hamlet,' Art and Practicality," *English* 39 (Spring 1990): Daiches, *Critical Approaches to Literature*, 195–96, 236–37.

R. Balfour Daniels, "Ophelia Reconsidered," *NDQ* 28 (Winter 1960): 30–32.

A. Datta, "*Hamlet*: A Study and an Interpretation," *Journal of the University of Saugar* 7, no. 7 (1958): 34–54.

Davidson, *The Solace of Literature*, 75–78.

Joe Lee Davis, "Something of What Happens in *Hamlet*," *UTQ* 12 (July 1943): 426–34.

O. B. Davis, "A Note on the Function of Polonius' Advice," *SQ* 9 (Winter 1958): 85–86.

Dawson, *Indirections*, 38–61.

Charles A. Dawson, "Hamlet the Actor," *SAQ* 47 (October 1948): 522–33.

Sara M. Deats, "The Once and Future Kings: Four Studies of Kingship in *Hamlet*," *ELWIU* 9 (Spring 1982): 15–30.

Sara M. Deats, "Shakespeare' *Hamlet*," *Expl* 39 (Spring 1981): 31–32.

R. W. Dent, "Hamlet: Scourge and Minister," *SQ* 29 (Winter 1978): 82–84.

Alan C. Dessen, "Hamlet's Poisoned Sword: A Study in Dramatic Imagery," *ShakS* 5 (1969): 53–69.

George Detmold, "Hamlet's 'All But Blunted Purpose,'" *ShAB* 24 (January 1949): 23–36.

Donald Hugh Dickinson, "The Two Queens in *Hamlet*," *Drama Critique* 2 (November 1959): 106–19.

Carole T. Diffey, " 'Such Large Discourse': The Role of 'Godlike Reason' in *Hamlet*," *HSt* 11 (Summer–Winter 1989): 22–33.

John Doebler, "The Play Within the Play: The Muscipula Diaboli in *Hamlet*," *SQ* 23 (Summer 1972): 161–69.

Frank A. Doggett, "Repetitions of a Young Prince: Note on Thematic Recurrence in *Hamlet*," in Bryan, et al., *All These to Teach*, 33–46.

Frank A. Doggett, "Shakespeare's *Hamlet*, II, ii, 116–119," *Expl* 16 (January 1958): 25.

Cay Dollerup, "'Enquire me first what Danskers are in Paris': A Note on Shakespeare's Use of the Word 'Dansker' in *Hamlet*," *Lang&L* 1, no. 2 (1972) 92–94.

Steven Doloff, "Divinity and the Danish Throne in *Hamlet*," *ShakB* 9 (Summer 1991): 12.

J. Lyle Donaghy, "Hamlet and Ophelia," *Dublin Magazine* 24 (January–March 1949): 23–28.

Denis Donoghue, "Shakespeare's Rhetoric," *Studies* 47 (Winter 1958): 431–36.

Madeleine Doran, "That Undiscovered Country," in Maxwell, *Renaissance Studies in Honor of Hardin Craig*, 221–30.

Madeleine Doran, "The Language of *Hamlet,*" *HLQ* 27 (May 1964): 259–78. Reprinted in *Shakespeare's Dramatic Language*, 33–62.

Charles Clay Doyle, "Blow below the Belt: Hamlet's Crude Insult," *Maledicta* 2 (Summer 1978): 177–81.

N. N. Dracoulides, "Psychoanalytical Investigation of Shakespeare's *Hamlet,*" *Transactional Mental Health Research Newsletter* 19 (January 1977): 2–9.

John W. Draper, "Subjective Conflict in Shakespearean Tragedy," *NM* 62 (March 1960): 214–16.

John W. Draper, "The Tempo of Hamlet's Role," *RMLC* 2 (September–December 1947): 193–203.

Amaresh Dutta, "A Note on *Hamlet,*" in *Modern Studies and Other Essays in Honour of Dr. R. K. Sinha*, ed. R. C. Prasad and A. K. Sharma (New Delhi: Vikas, 1987), 147–51.

Robert D. Eagleson, "Eschatological Speculations and the Use of the Infinitive," *SQ* 26 (Summer 1975): 206–08.

Eagleton, *Shakespeare and Society*, 39–65.

Richard Eberhart, "Tragedy as Limitations: Comedy as Control and Resolution," *TDR* 6 (June 1962): 3–9.

Charles W. Eckert, "The Festival Structure of the *Orestes-Hamlet* Tradition," *CL* 15 (Fall 1963): 321–37.

Philip Edwards, "Tragic Balance in *Hamlet,*" *ShS* 36 (1983): 43–52.

Martha Egan, "Metaphysics, Shadows, and Non-Action," *Topic* 23 (Spring 1972): 58–63.

Elam, *Semiotics of Theatre and Drama*, 185–207.

Eliot, *Essays on Elizabethan Drama*, 55–63.

T. S. Eliot, "Hamlet and His Problems," in Schorer, *Criticism*, 266–68. Reprinted in Stallman, *Critiques and Essays in Criticism*, 384–88.

Ellis-Fermor, *The Frontiers of Drama*, 88–93.

Una Ellis-Fermor, "Shakespeare and the Dramatic Mode," *Neophil* 37 (April 1953): 104–12.

Eugene England, "*Hamlet* against Revenge," *L&B* 7 (March 1987): 49–62.

Juan Estraellas, "*Don Quixote* and *Hamlet* as Symbols of Contrasting Cutural and Educational Patterns," *Topic* 13 (Spring 1962): 15–23.

G. Blakemore Evans, "My Tables, Meet it is I Set it Down," *MLR* 42 (April 1947): 235–36.

G. Blakemore Evans, "Two Notes on *Hamlet*: II. 2. 357–58; III. 1. 121–31," *MLR* 81 (January 1986): 34–36.

Barbara Everett, "Hamlet: A Time to Die," *ShS* 30 (1977): 117–23.

Inga-Stina Ewbank, "Hamlet and the Power of Words," *ShS* 30 (1977): 85–102.

A. L. Faber, "Hamlet, Sarcasm and Psychoanalysis," *PsyR* 55, no. 1 (1968): 79–90.

M. D. Faber, "The Conscience of the King," *L&P* 14 (Summer–Fall 1964): 80–85.

M. D. Faber, "Ophelia's Doubtful Death," *L&P* 16 (Fall 1966): 103–08.

Arthur H. R. Fairchild, "*Hamlet* as a Tragedy of Transition," *University of Missouri Studies* 19, no. 2 (1944): 11–27.

Doris V. Falk, "Proverbs and the Polonius Destiny," *SQ* 18 (Winter 1967): 23–36.

W. Edward Farrison, "Ophelia's Reply Concerning Her Father," *CLAJ* 1 (March 1958): 53–57.

W. Edward Farrison, "Horatio's Report to Hamlet," *MLN* 72 (June 1957): 406–08.

John P. Farrell, "Hamlet's Final Role: Symbolism in the Duel Scene," *BuR* 14, no. 2 (1966): 19–37.

James Feibleman, "The Theory of *Hamlet*," *JHI* 7 (April 1946): 131–50.

A. Bronson Feldman, "The March of *Hamlet*," *ShN* 13 (December 1963): 55.

Francis Fergusson, "*Hamlet*: The Analogy of Action," *HudR* 2 (Summer 1949): 165-10. Reprinted in *The Idea of a Theatre: A Study of Ten Plays* (Princeton: Princeton University Press, 1949), 98–142.

Margaret W. Ferguson, "*Hamlet*: Letters and Spirits," in Parker and Hartman, *Shakespeare and the Question of Theory*, 292–309.

Lois Feuer, "The Unnatural Mirror: Bend Sinister and *Hamlet*," *Critique: Studies in Contemporary Fiction* 30 (Fall 1988): 3–12.

Philip Fisher, "Thinking about Killing: *Hamlet* and the Paths among the Passions," *Raritan* 11 (Summer 1991): 43–77

Sandra K. Fischer, "Hearing Ophelia: Gender and Tragic Discourse in *Hamlet*," *Ren&R* 14 (Winter 1990): 1–10.

Richard Flatter, "The Climax of the Play-Scene in *Hamlet*," *ShJE* 87 (1951): 26–42.

Robert F. Fleissner, "Hamlet's Flesh Alchemically Considered," *ES* 59 (September 1978): 508–09.

Robert F. Fleissner, "*Princeps Arte Ambulandi*: The Pace of *Hamlet*," *HSt* 6 (Summer–Winter 1984): 23–29.

Richard Fly, "Accommodating Death: The Ending of *Hamlet*," *SEL* 24 (Spring 1984): 257–74.

R. A. Foakes, "Character and Speech in *Hamlet*," *Stratford-Upon-Avon Studies* 5 (1963): 148–62.

R. A. Foakes, "Hamlet and the Court of Elsinore," *ShS* 9 (1956): 35–43.

Foakes, *Shakespeare*, 82–84.

Charles R. Forker, "Shakespeare's Theatrical Symbolism and Its Function in *Hamlet*," *SQ* 14 (Summer 1963): 215–29.

Richard Foster, "Hamlet and the Word," *UTQ* 30 (April 1961): 229–45.

Elizabeth Foulds, "Enter Ophelia Distracted," *Life and Letters Today* 36 (January 1943): 36–41.

Alastair Fowler, "The Plays within the Play of *Hamlet*," in Mahon and Pendleton, *"Fanned and winnowed opinions,"* 166–83.

Louis Fraiberg, *Psychoanalysis and American Literary Criticism* (Detroit: Wayne State University Press, 1960), 47–63, 208–12.

Neil Freidman, "On the Mutability of the Oedipus Complex: Note on the Hamlet Case," *AI* 20 (Summer 1963): 107–31.

A. L. French, "Hamlet and the Sealed Commission," *ES* 47 (April 1966): 28–30.

A. L. French, "Hamlet's Nunnery," *ES* 48 (April 1967): 141–45.

French, *Shakespeare's Division of Experience*, 140–54.

Sigmund Freud, "Psychopathic Characters on the Stage," *Psychoanalytic Quarterly* 11 (October 1942): 463–64.

Roland Mushat Frey, "'Looking before and after': The Use of Visual Evidence and Symbolism for Interpreting *Hamlet*," *HLQ* 45 (Winter 1982): 1–19.

SHAKESPEARE, WILLIAM, *Hamlet*

Ellis Fridner, "A Textual Puzzle in *Hamlet*," *ES* 47 (October 1966): 431.

Alan Warren Friedman, "Hamlet the Unready," *MLQ* 37 (March 1976): 15–34.

William Frossberg, "Shakespeare's *Hamlet*, III, iii, 36–72," *Expl* 25 (May 1976): Item 74.

Dean Frye, "Custom and Utterance in *Hamlet*: Essays Presented to A. E. Malloch," in *Literature and Ethics*, ed. Gary Wihl and David Williams (Kingston: McGill-Queen's University Press, 1988), 18–31.

Prosser H. Frye, *Romance and Tragedy* (Lincoln: University of Nebraska Press, 1961), 292–93.

Roland Mushat Frye, "Ladies, Gentlemen, and Skulls: *Hamlet* and the Iconographic Traditions," *SQ* 30 (Winter 1979): 15–28.

Donald R. Fryxell, "The Significance of Hamlet's Delay," *Discourse* 6 (Autumn 1963): 270–94.

Katharine Garvin, "Slings and Arrows," *REL* 8 (July 1967): 96–98.

Paul Gaudet, " 'He Is Justly Served': The Ordering of Experience in *Hamlet*," *HSt* 7 (Summer–Winter 1985): 52–68.

M. Teresa Gertude, "*Hamlet, Prince of Denmark*: Allusions to Music," *Horizontes* 7 (April 1964): 48–51.

Alan H. Gilbert, *The Principles and Practice of Criticism*, 95–147.

Lisa Gim, "*Hamlet* and Matthew X: Providence in the Fall of a Sparrow," *UMSE* 4, no. 1 (1963): 56–61.

Avram Gimbel, "A Congruence of Personalities—Hamlet and Claudius," *HSt* 9 (Summer–Winter 1987): 90–92.

A. Andre Glaz, "*Hamlet*, or the Tragedy of Shakespeare," *AI* 19 (Summer 1961): 129–59.

Ronald J. Goba, "A Reading of *Hamlet*: An Experiment in Personalized 'New Criticism,' " *Virginia English Bulletin* 36 (Winter 1986): 40–48.

Harold C. Goddard, "Hamlet to Ophelia," *CE* 16 (April 1955): 403–15.

Harold C. Goddard, "In Ophelia's Closet," *YR* 34 (March 1946): 462–74.

D. R. Godfrey, "The Player's Speech in *Hamlet*: A New Approach," *Neophil* 34 (July 1950): 162–69.

William L. Godshalk, "Hamlet's Dream of Innocence," *ShakS* 9 (1976): 221–32.

Philip Goldstein, "Hamlet: Not a World of His Own," *ShakS* 13 (1980): 71–83.

Gomez, *The Alienated Figure in Drama*, 47–49, 158–70.

Paul Goodman, *The Structure of Literature*, 162–72.

Phyllis Gorfain, "Toward a Theory of Play and the Carnivalesque in *Hamlet*," *HSt* 13 (Summer–Winter 1991): 25–49.

Patricia S. Gourlay, "Guilty Creatures Sitting at a Play: A Note on *Hamlet*, Act II, Scene 2," *RenQ* 24 (1971): 221.

H. H. Anniah Gowda, "*Hamlet* and the Culmination of Poetic Drama," in Rao, *The Laurel Bough*, 35–48.

Michael Graves, "Hamlet as Fool," *HSt* 4 (Summer–Winter 1982): 72–88.

Neil Graves, "'Even for an Eggshell': Hamlet and the Problem of Fortinbras," *UCrow* 2 (1979): 51–63.

Andrew J. Green, "The Cunning of the Scene," *SQ* 4 (October 1953): 395–404.

Andrew J. Green, "Exit Horatio," *PQ* 30 (April 1951): 220–21.

Richard Leighton Greene, "Hamlet's Skimmington" in Weellek and Ribeiro *Evidence in Literary Scholarship*, 1–11.

Thomas Greene, "The Postures of Hamlet," *SQ* 11 (Summer 1960): 357–66.

Dennis Grunes, "The King's Caught Conscience," *BSUF* 19, no. 2 (1978): 3–11.

Cherrell Guilfoyle, "'Ower Swete Sokor': The Role of Ophelia in *Hamlet*," *CompD* 14 (Spring 1980): 3–17. Reprinted in Davidson, Gianakaris, and Stroupe, *Drama in the Renaissance*, 163–77.

Cherrell Guilfoyle, "The Beginning of *Hamlet*," *CompD* 14 (Summer 1980): 137–58.

David Haley, "Gothic Armaments and King Hamlet's Poleaxe," *SQ* 29 (Autumn 1978): 407–13.

Jay L. Halio, "Hamlet's Alternatives," *TSLL* 8 (Spring 1966): 169–88.

Hallett and Hallett, *Analysing Shakespeare's Action*, 23–26, 35–36, 41–42, 54–57, 68–69, 71–72, 90–91, 112–13, 123–27, 135–36, 139–41, 183–84, 204–05.

Ralph J. Hallman, *Psychology of Literature* (New York: Philosophical Library, 1961), 140–43, 150–51.

John Halverson, "*Hamlet*: Ethos and Transcendence," *Anglia* 106, no. 1–2 (1988): 44–73.

Paul Hamill, "Death's Lively Image: The Emblematic Significance of the Closet Scene in *Hamlet*," *TSLL* 16 (Summer 1974): 249–62.

R. W. Hamilton, "The Instability of Hamlet," *CrSurv* 3, no. 2 (1991): 170–77.

William Hamilton, "*Hamlet* and Providence," *ChS* 47 (Fall 1964): 193–207.

James P. Hammersmith, "*Hamlet* and the Myth of Memory," *ELH* 45 (December 1978): 597–605.

John E. Hankins, "Hamlet's 'God-Kissing Carrion': A Theory of the Generation of Life," *PMLA* 64 (June 1949): 507–16.

John E. Hankins, "*Hamlet* and *Oedipus* Reconsidered," *ShN* 6 (April 1956): 11.

O. B. Hardison, Jr. "The Dramatic Triad in *Hamlet*," *SP* 57 (April 1960): 144–64.

Barbara Hardy, "The Figure of Narration in *Hamlet*," in *A Centre of Excellence: Essays Presented to Seymour Betsky*, ed. Robert Druce (Amsterdam: Rodopi, 1987), 1–14.

Barbara Hardy, "The Figure of Narration in *Hamlet*," *DQR* 16, no. 1 (1986): 2–15.

Walter Morris Hart, "Shakespeare's Use of Verse and Prose," in *Five Gayley Lectures, 1947–1954*, ed. L. B. Benniou and G. R. Potter (Berkeley: University of California Press, 1954), 2–6.

G. F. Hartford, "Once More Delay," *ESA* 20 (March 1977): 1–9.

William T. Hastings, "Is *Hamlet* a Hoax?" in Bloom, *Shakespeare 1564–1964*, 38–49.

Terence Hawkes, "Hamlet's Apprehension," *MLR* 55 (April 1960): 238–41.

Hawkes, *Shakespeare's Talking Animals*, 105–26.

Hawkins, *Likeness of Truth in Elizabethan and Restoration Drama*, 57–58.

Hawkins, *Poetic Freedom and Poetic Truth*, 1–2, 83–89, 92–93.

Hawthorne, *Tragedy, Myth, and Mystery*, 143–73.

Tetsumaro Hayashi, "Hamlet's Satori: 'The Readiness Is All' and 'Let It Be,'" *BSUF* 16, no. 3 (1975): 67–69.

Althea Hayter, "'The Murder of Gonzago,'" *ArielE* 3 (January 1972): 29–33.

Alison G. Hayton, "'The King my father?' Paternity in *Hamlet*," *HSt* 9 (Summer–Winter 1987): 53–64.

Donald K. Hedrick, "'It is No Novelty for a Prince to be a Prince': An Enantiomorphous Hamlet," *SQ* 35 (Spring 1984): 62–76.

Carolyn Heilbrun, "The Character of Hamlet's Mother," *SQ* 8 (Spring 1957): 201–06.

Robert B. Heilman, "Twere Best not Know Myself: *Othello, Lear, Hamlet,*" *SQ* 15 (Spring 1964): 89–98.

Robert B. Heilman, "To Know Himself: An Aspect of Tragic Structure," *REL* 5 (April 1964): 43–57.

Richard Helgerson, "What Hamlet Remembers," *ShakS* 10 (1977): 67–97.

Agnes Heller, "Shakespeare and Human Nature," *New Hungarian Quarterly* 5 (Spring 1964): 16–20.

Lora Heller, and Abraham Heller, "Hamlet's Parents: The Dynamic Formulation of a Tragedy," *AI* 17 (Winter 1960): 413–21.

Ann Louise Hentz, "*Hamlet*: The Anatomy of a Task," *CE* 27 (March 1966): 523–28.

T. Walker Herbert, "Shakespeare Announces a Ghost," *SQ* 1 (October 1950): 251–54.

T. Walker Herbert, "Dramatic Characters Viewed by Others in the Same Play," *ShN* 7 (April 1957): 12.

Highet, *The Powers of Poetry*, 286–92, 306–07.

Richard Hilliman, "*Hamlet* and Death: A Recasting of the Play within the Player," *Essays in Literature* 13 (Fall 1986): 201–18.

Raymond Himelick, "*Hamlet* and the Contempt of the World," *SAQ* 48 (Spring 1949): 167–75.

Julian Hilton, "Dissecting the Body of *Hamlet,*" *New Comparison: A Journal of Comparative and General Literary Studies* 2 (Autumn 1986): 148–55.

Pearl Hogrefe, "Artistic Unity in *Hamlet,*" *SP* 46 (April 1949): 184–95.

Norman N. Holland, "Freud on Shakespeare," *PMLA* 75 (July 1960): 163–67.

James V. Holleran, "Maimed Funeral Rites in *Hamlet,*" *ELR* 19 (Winter 1989): 65–93.

John Holloway, "Dramatic Irony in Shakespeare," *Northern Miscellany of Literary Criticism* 1 (Autumn 1953): 10–13.

Holloway, *The Story of the Night*, 21–36.

Michael E. Holstein, "'Actions that a man might play': Dirty Tricks at Elsinore and the Politics of Play," *PQ* 55 (Spring 1976): 323–39.

S. Homchaudhuri, "*Hamlet* and *Samson Agonistes,*" *HSt* 8 (Summer–Winter 1986): 52–64.

E. A. J. Honigmann, "The Politics in *Hamlet*, and the World of the Play," *Stratford-Upon-Avon Studies* 5 (1963): 129–47.

R. L. Horn, "*Hamlet*, III.ii.376: A Defense of Q2's 'The Bitter Day,'" *SQ* 33 (Summer 1982): 179–81.

Kimiko Hotta, "The Garden Imagery in Shakespeare's *Hamlet*," *SES* 1 (1976): 1–4.

Houston, *Shakespearean Sentences*, 76–101.

Percy H. Houston, "There's Nothing Either Good or Bad But Thinking Makes It So," *ShAB* 24 (January 1949): 48–53.

D. R. Howard, "*Hamlet* and the Contempt of the World," *SAQ* 58 (Spring 1959): 167–75.

Howarth, *The Tiger's Heart*, 63–67.

Mark Howell, "Shakespeare's *Hamlet* IV.ii.24–29," *Expl* 38 (Spring 1979): 26–27.

Cyrus Hoy, "Comedy, Tragedy, Tragicomedy," *VQR* 36 (Winter 1960): 108–10.

Arthur P. Hudson, "Romantic Apologiae for Hamlet's Treatment of Ophelia," *ELH* 9 (March 1942): 59–70.

Geoffrey Hughes, "The Tragedy of a Revenger's Loss of Conscience: A Study of *Hamlet*," *ES* 57 (October 1976): 395–409.

Max Huhner, "Polonius's Advice to Laertes," *ShAB* 19 (January 1944): 29–35.

Arthur Humphreys, "The Poetry of *Hamlet*," *The Literary Half-Yearly* 5 (July 1964): 37–48.

Arthur Humphreys, "Style and Expression in *Hamlet*," in Crane, *Shakespeare's Art*, 29–52.

Edward B. Hungerford, "*Hamlet*: The World at the Center," *TriQ* 8 (1967): 69–89.

John Hunt, "A Thing of Nothing: The Catastrophic Body in *Hamlet*," *SQ* 39 (Spring 1988): 27–44.

aurice Hunt, "Art of Judgment, Art of Compassion: The Two Arts of *Hamlet*," *ELWIU* 18 (Spring 1991): 3–20.

Maurice Hunt, "Hamlet, the Gravedigger, and Indecorous Decorum," *CollL* 11 (Spring 1984): 141–50.

G. K. Hunter, "The Heroism of Hamlet," *Stratford-Upon-Avon Studies* 5 (1963): 90–109.

G. K. Hunter, "Socrates' Precepts and Polonius' Character," *SQ* 8 (Autumn 1957): 501–06.

Harold R. Hutcheson, "Hamlet's Delay," *ShN* 1 (October 1951): 19.

George Hyde, "Hamlet the Pole," *NewComp* 5 (Summer 1988): 111–22.

Rudiger Imhof, "*Fortinbras Ante Portas*: The Role and Significance of Fortinbras in *Hamlet*," *HSt* 8 (Summer–Winter 1986): 8–29.

R. W. Ingram, "*Hamlet, Othello*, and *King Lear*: Music and Tragedy," *ShJE* 100 (1964): 159–67.

Richard Jacobs, "Sex and Money: A Note on *Hamlet* I.iii.108–09," *SQ* 31 (Winter 1980): 88–90.

Zvi Jagendorf, " 'Fingers on Your Lips, I Pray': On Silence in *Hamlet*," *English* 27 (Summer 1978): 121–28.

James, *The Dream of Learning*, 33–68.

Richard Paul Janaro, "Dramatic Significance in *Hamlet*," *UMPEAL* 1 (March 1953): 107–15.

Lisa Jardine, "The Essex Symposia: Literature/Politics/Theory; 'No offence i' th' world': *Hamlet* and Unlawful Marriage," in Barker, Hulme, and Iversen, *Uses of History*, 123–39.

Lloyd N. Jeffrey, "Polonius: A Study in Ironic Characterization," *CEA* 33, no. 2 (1971): 3–7.

Harold Jenkins, "How Many Grave-Diggers has *Hamlet*?" *MLR* 51 (October 1956): 562–65.

Harold Jenkins, "The Tragedy of Revenge in Shakespeare and Webster," *ShS* 14 (1961): 45–48.

Harold Jenkins, "Two Readings in *Hamlet*," *MLR* 50 (July 1959): 393–95.

Harold Jenkins, "Hamlet and Ophelia," *PBA* 49 (1963): 135–52.

Jespen, *Ethical Aspects of Tragedy*, 68–74.

W. T. Jewkes, "Stratford-upon-Avon Studies 20: 'To tell my story': The Function of Framed Narrative and Drama in *Hamlet*," in Bradbury and Palmer, *Shakespearian Tragedy*, 31–46.

Jean Jofen, "Two Mad Heroines," *L&P* 11 (Summer 1961): 70–77.

Barbara A. Johnson, "The Fabric of the Universe Rent: Hamlet as an Inversion of The Courtier," *HSt* 9 (Summer–Winter 1987): 34–52.

Edgar Johnson, "The Dilemma of Hamlet," in McIver, *Great Moral Dilemmas*, 99–112.

Jerah Johnson, "The Concept of the 'King's Two Bodies' in *Hamlet*," *SQ* 18 (Autumn 1967): 430–34.

S. F. Johnson, "The Regeneration of Hamlet," *SQ* 3 (July 1952): 197–207.

Arthur Johnston, "The Player's Speech in *Hamlet*," *SQ* 13 (Winter 1962): 21–30.

Mark Johnston, " 'One Word More': An Analysis of *Hamlet*, III.iv.180–196," *EAS* 9 (April 1980): 19–23.

Ernest Jones, "The Death of Hamlet's Father," *International Journal of Psychoanalysis* 29 (March–April 1948): 174–76. Reprinted in *Yearbook of Psychoanalysis* 6 (1950): 276–90; *Essays in Applied Psychoanalysis* (London: Hogarth, 1951), 323–29; *Psychoanalysis and Literature*, ed. Hendrik M. Ruitenbeek (New York: Dutton, 1964), 14–19.

Hoover H. Jordan, "Shakespeare's *Hamlet*, III, i, 56–97," *Expl* 9 (December 1949): 29.

Paul A. Jorgensen, "Hamlet's Therapy," *HLQ* 27 (May 1964): 239–59.

Paul A. Jorgensen, "Hamlet's World of Words," *ShN* 12 (February 1962): 3.

Miriam Joesph, "Discerning the Ghost in *Hamlet*," *PMLA* 76 (December 1961): 493–502.

Miriam Joesph, "*Hamlet*: A Christian Tragedy," *SP* 59 (April 1962): 119–40.

David Kaula, "*Hamlet* and the 'Sparing Discovery,' " *ShS* 24 (1971): 71–77.

Maqbool H. Khan, "The Fare in *Hamlet*," *AJES* 11, no. 1 (1986): 33–42.

David Scott Kastan, " 'His Semblable Is His Mirror': *Hamlet* and the Imitation of Revenge," *ShS* 19 (1991): 111–24.

Norman Kelvin, "Fortinbras' Links With Hamlet," *BNYPL* 66 (December 1962): 657–60.

Lysander Kemp, "Understanding *Hamlet*," *CE* 13 (October 1951): 9–13.

Alvin B. Kernan, "Politics and Theatre in *Hamlet*," *HSt* 1 (Spring 1979): 1–12.

Alvin B. Kernan, "Shakespeare and the Rhetoric of Politics: 'This must be so,' Act I, Scene 2 of *Hamlet*," in *Politics, Power, and Shakespeare*, ed. Frances McNeely Leonard (Arlington: Texas Humanities Resource Center, University of Texas at Arlington Library, 1981), 47–62.

Arnold Kettle, "*Hamlet*," *ZAA* 10, no. 2 (1962): 117–27.

Sarvar Khambatta, "'Foul and Most Unnatural Murder': *Hamlet* and *Macbeth*," *HSt* 10 (Summer–Winter 1988): 130–36.

Arthur Noel Kincaid, "Hamlet's Cue for Passion in the Nunnery Scene," *ShakS* 10 (1977): 99–113.

Leo Kirshbaum, "Hamlet and Ophelia," *PQ* 35 (October 1956): 376–93.

H. D. Kitto, *Form and Meaning in Drama—A Study of Six Greek Plays and Hamlet* (London: Methuen, 1956), 246-339.

Holger Klein, "Preface: Receiving *Hamlet* Reception," *NewComp* 2 (Autumn 1986): 5–13.

Joan Larson Klein, "'Angels and Ministers of Grace': *Hamlet*, IV.v–vii," *Allegorica* 1 (Autumn 1976): 156–76.

Joan Larson Klein, "The Bait of Falsehood: *Hamlet*," *CollL* 4 (Summer 1977): 220–24.

Joan Larson Klein, "'What Is't to Leave Betimes?' Proverbs and Logic in *Hamlet*," *ShS* 32 (1979): 163–76.

Knight, *Explorations*, 92–93, 101–07.

Knight, *The Golden Labyrinth*, 7–9, 75–79, 91–94, 222–24, 256–57.

Knight, *The Imperial Theme*, 96–124.

Knight, *The Olive and the Sword*, 41–44.

Knight, *The Sovereign Flower*, 47–51.

G. W. Knight, "Two Notes on the Text of *Hamlet* (1947)," in *The Wheel of Fire* (1962 ed.), 17–46, 299–325, 326–43.

L. C. Knights, "Shakespearean Tragedy: *Hamlet*," *DQR* 10, no. 1 (1980): 2–18.

Jan Kott, "Hamlet and Orestes," *PMLA* 82 (March 1967): 303–13.

P. H. Kocher, "The Exchange of Weapons in *Hamlet*," *MLN* 57 (January 1942): 50–55.

Alexandra V. Krinkin "The Romantic Revolution of the Ego: Ego as Hamlet," *Hopkins Review* 1 (Summer 1948): 13–24.

Masakazu Kurikoma, "The Language of *Hamlet*," *Anglica* 6 (March–June 1966): 135–60.

Robin Lampson, "Should It Have Been Called Shakespeare's 'Hoist with His Own Petard'?" *CEA* 36, no. 3 (1974): 12–13.

Hilton Landry, "The Leaven of Wickedness: *Hamlet*, I.iv.1–38," in McNeir and Greenfield, *Pacific Coast Studies in Shakespeare*, 122–33.

Robert Langenfeld, "Imagery and Its Relationship to the Ethos of *Hamlet*," in *Jacobean Miscellany 3*, ed. James Hogg (Salzburg: University of Salzburg, 1983), 120–30.

Gosta Langenfelt, "Shakespeare's Danskers (*Hamlet* II, i, 7.)," *ZAA* 12, no. 3 (1964): 266–77.

J. J. Lawlor, "The Tragic Conflict in *Hamlet*," *RES* 1 (April 1950): 97–113.

W. W. Lawrence, "Ophelia's Heritage," *MLR* 42 (October 1947): 409–16.

W. W. Lawrence, "Ophelia's Heritage: A Correction," *MLR* 44 (April 1949): 236.

W. W. Lawrence, "Hamlet and Fortinbras," *PMLA* 61 (September 1946): 673–99.

W. W. Lawrence, "Hamlet's Sea Voyage," *PMLA* 59 (March 1944): 45–70.

Leaska, *The Voice of Tragedy*, 96–109, 216–17.

Edward S. Le Comte, "The Ending of *Hamlet* as a Farewell to Essex," *ELH* 17 (June 1950): 97–114.

Nancy M. Lee-Riffe, "What Fortinbras and Laertes Tell Us about Hamlet," *HSt* 3 (Winter 1981): 103–09.

Lagretta T. Lenker, "Insight Books: Suicide and the Dialectic of Gender in Hamlet," in Deats and Lenker, *Youth Suicide Prevention*, 93–114.

T. Lennan, "The Happy Hunting Ground," *UTQ* 29 (April 1960): 388–97.

Lesser, *Fiction and the Unconscious*, 73–75, 107–10, 199–200.

Simon O. Lesser, "Freud and Hamlet Again," *AI* 12 (Fall 1955): 207–20.

Jill L. Levenson, "Dramatists at (Meta) Play: Shakespeare's *Hamlet*, II, ii, ll.410–591 and Pirandello's *Henry IV*," *MD* 24 (September 1981): 330–37.

J. W. Lever, "Three Notes on Shakespeare's Plants," *RES* 3 (April 1952): 123–29,

David Leverenz, "The Woman in *Hamlet*: An Interpersonal View," *Signs* 4 (Autumn 1978): 291–308.

Albert William Levi, *Literature, Philosophy and the Imagination* (Bloomington: Indiana University Press, 1962), 274–92.

Levich, *Aesthetics and the Philosophy of Criticism*, 221–22, 225–26.

Harry Levin, "The Antic Disposition," *ShJE* 94 (1959): 175–90.

Harry Levin, "An Explication of the Player's Speech," *KR* 12 (Spring 1950): 273–96.

Richard A. Levine, "The Tragedy of Hamlet's World View," *CE* 23 (April 1962): 539–46.

Roger Lewis, "The Hortatory Hamlet," *PBSA* 72 (March 1978): 59–60.

Luther J. Link, "A Remarkable Feature of Two *Hamlet* Soliloquies," *TCEL* 54 (1981): 1–9.

William Liston, "Laertes' Advice to Ophelia in *Hamlet*, I.iii.12–14," *ColIL* 12 (Spring 1985): 187–89.

Andre Lorant, "*Hamlet* and Mythical Thought," *Diogenes* 118 (Summer 1982): 49–76.

Lucas, *Literature and Psychology*, 27–61.

Julia Lupton, "Truant Dispositions: Hamlet and Machiavelli," *JMRS* 17 (Spring 1987): 59–82.

Robert Luyster, "The Phenomenology of *Hamlet* and the Evolution of Consciousness," *IR* 41 (Spring 1984): 5–19.

Bridget Gellert Lyons, "The Iconography of Ophelia," *ELH* 44 (March 1977): 60–74.

Jean MacIntyre, "*Hamlet* and the Comic Heroine," *HSt* 4 (Summer–Winter 1982): 6–18.

Maynard Mack, "The Jacobean Shakespeare: Some Observations on the Construction of the Tragedies," *Stratford-Upon-Avon Studies* 1 (1960): 11–42.

Maynard Mack, "The World of *Hamlet*," in *YR* 41 (June 1952): 502–23. Reprinted in Brooks, *Tragic Themes in Western Literature*, 30–59.

Michael L. Magie, "Tact, or Hamlet's Bastards," *YR* 69 (March 1980): 234–55.

François Maguin, "The Breaking of Time: *Richard II*, *Hamlet*, and *Macbeth*," *CahiersE* 7 (April 1965): 25–41.

John W. Mahon, "Providential Visitations in *Hamlet*," *HSt* 8 (Summer–Winter 1986): 40–51.

John M. Major, "The 'Letters Seal'd' in *Hamlet* and the Character of Claudius," *JEGP* 57 (July 1959): 512–21.

P. Malekin, "Death's Dialectic in *Hamlet*," *SN* 48 (Summer 1976): 283–89.

Elizabeth Malsen, "Yorick's Place in *Hamlet*," *E&S* 36 (1983): 1 13.

Frank Manley, "The Cock Crowing in *Hamlet*," *PQ* 45 (October 1966): 442–47.

Mann, *The Elizabethan Player*, 41–53, 206–07.

F. H. Mares, "The Equivocations of *Hamlet*," in Alan Brissenden, ed., *Shakespeare and Some Others*, 65–82.

Derick R. C. Marsh, "Hal and Hamlet: The Loneliness of Integrity," in Donaldson, *Jonson and Shakespeare*, 18–34.

Elizabeth Maslen, "Scenes Unseen in *Hamlet*," *NewComp* 2 (Autumn 1986): 14–30.

Kurian Mattam, "The Concept of Sin in the Shakespearian Tragedies: *Hamlet, King Lear, Macbeth* and *Othello*: An Exploration," *Unitas* 64 (June 1991): 165–230.

Baldwin Maxwell, "Hamlet's Mother," *SQ* 15 (Spring 1964): 235–46. Reprinted in McManaway, *Shakespeare 400*, 235–46.

J. C. Maxwell, " 'Fat and Scant of Breath' Again," *ES* 32 (February 1951): 29–30.

J. C. Maxwell, "The Ghost From the Grave: A Note on Shakespeare's Apparitions," *DUJ* 18 (March 1956): 57–58.

Jerome Mazzaro, "Madness and Memory: Shakespeare's *Hamlet* and *King Lear*," *CompD* 19 (Summer 1985): 97–116.

Ronald J. McCaig, "Further Speculation on 'Solid' in *Hamlet*," *ShN* 16 (January 1966): 32.

Ralph A. McCanse, "Hamlet's Lack of Balance," *CE* 10 (May 1949): 476–79.

Howard McCord, "Sad Jackself Hamlet," *RS* 36 (1968): 166–68.

David J. McDonald, "*Hamlet* and the Mimesis of Absence: A Post–Structuralist Analysis," *ETJ* 30 (March 1978): 36–53.

D. McElroy, " 'To Be, or Not to Be'—Is That the Question?" *CE* 25 (April 1964): 543–45.

William M. McKim, "The Tongue and the Heart: A Pattern of Speech as Action in *Hamlet*," *KPAB* 12 (January 1985): 40–49.

Juliet McLauchlan, "The Prince of Denmark and Claudius's Court," *ShS* 27 (1974): 43–57.

Peter McLaughlin, "The Elements of Tragedy," *QQ* 71 (Spring 1964): 104–07.

C. F. Menninger, "The Insanity of Hamlet," *Menninger Quarterly* 6, no.1 (1952): 1–8.

W. M. Merchant, "Shakespeare's Theology," *REL* 5 (October 1964): 81–84.

Daniel Meyer-Dinkgrafe, " 'My Thoughts Be Bloody or Be Nothing Worth'— 'The Readiness Is All . . . Let Be': Hamlet at the Crossroads," *HSt* 8 (Summer–Winter 1986): 77–82.

Walter L. Meyers, "Shakespeare's *Hamlet*," *Expl* 9 (November 1950): 10.

Laurence Michel, "Hamlet: Superman, Subchristian," *CentR* 6 (Spring 1962): 230–44.

Anthony Miller, "*Hamlet*, II.ii-III.iv: Mirrors of Revenge," *SSEng* 11 (1985–1986): 3–22.

Anthony Miller, "A Reminiscence of Erasmus in *Hamlet*, III.ii.92–95," *ELN* 24 (September 1986): 19–22.

David L. Miller, "*Hamlet*: The Lie as an Image of the Fall," *RenP 1978* (1979): 1–8.

William E. Miller, " 'Little Eyases,' " *SQ* 28 (Winter 1977): 86–88.

Peter Milward, "The Horizon of *Hamlet*," *ELLS* 13 (1976): 5–18.

M. Mincoff, "Shakespeare and Hamartia," *ES* 45 (April 1964): 130–36.

M. Mincoff, "The Structural Pattern of Shakespeare's Tragedies," *ShS* 3 (1950): 58–65.

Harvey Mindess, "If Hamlet Had Had a Sense of Humour," in *It's a Funny Thing, Humor*, ed. Anthony J. Chapman and Hugh C. Foote (Oxford: Pergamon, 1977), 3–5.

J. M. Moloney, and L. Rockelin, "A New Interpretation of *Hamlet*," *International Journal of Psychoanalysis* 30 (March–April 1949): 92–107.

Gary. V. Monitto, " 'Sallied Flesh' (Q1, Q2): *Hamlet* I.ii.129," *SB* 36 (1983): 177–78.

Gary. V. Monitto, "Shakespeare's *Hamlet*," *Expl* 46 (Winter 1988): 6.

David C. H. Morgan, " 'When Mercy Seasons Justice': How (and Why) Hamlet Does Not Kill Claudius," *HSt* 10 (Summer–Winter 1988): 47–78.

Mikhail M. Morozov, "The Individualization of Shakespeare's Characters Through Imagery," *ShS* 2 (1949): 83–84; 93–106.

Harry Morris, "Ophelia's 'Bonny Sweet Robin,' " *PMLA* 73 (December 1958): 601–03.

Barbara Mowat, "The Form of Hamlet's Fortunes," *RenD* 19 (1988): 97–126.

Kenneth Muir, "Four Notes on *Hamlet*," *AJES* 6, no. 2 (1981): 115–21.

Kenneth Muir, "Imagery and Symbol in *Hamlet*," *EA* 17 (October–December 1964): 352–63.

Kenneth Muir, "Some Freudian Interpretations of Shakespeare," *PLPLS* 7 (July 1952): 43–46.

Muller, *The Spirit of Tragedy*, 171–81.

Gilbert Murry, "Hamlet and Orestes," in *Five Approaches of Literary Criticism— An Arrangement of Contemporary Critical Essays*, ed. Wilbur S. Scott (New York: Collier, 1962), 254–57, 260–61, 279–80.

John M. Murry, "The Doctrine of Will in Shakespeare," *Aryan Path* 35 (August 1964): 339–42.

Silvia Mussi da Silva Carlo, "The Dramatic Function of 'Aeneas' Tale to Dido' in *Hamlet*," *EAA* 1 (1977): 95–112.

Leonard Mustazza, "Language as Poison, Plague, and Weapon in Shakespeare's *Hamlet* and *Othello*," *PE* 11 (Spring 1985): 5–14.

Milton C. Nahm, *Aesthetic Experience and Its Presuppositions* (New York: Harper, 1946), 373–86, 414–17.

Anna K. Nardo, "Hamlet, 'A Man to Double Business Bound,'" *SQ* 34 (Summer 1983): 181–99.

Joseph Natoli, "Dimensions of Consciousness in *Hamlet*," *Mosaic* 19 (Winter 1986): 91–98.

Michael Neill, "Remembrance and Revenge: *Hamlet*, *Macbeth* and *The Tempest*," in Donaldson, *Jonson and Shakespeare*, 35–56.

C. E. Nelson, "Power and Politics in *Hamlet*," *WCSC* 32 (September 1964): 217–27.

Nelson, *Play Within a Play*, 17–30.

Alex Newell, "The Dramatic Context and Meaning of Hamlet's 'To Be or not to be' Soliloquy," *PMLA* 80 (March 1965): 38–50.

Nicholl, *The Chemical Theatre*, 121–22, 238–39.

Thomas Nollet, " 'Nothing Either Good or Bad': Sophistry and Self-Delusion in *Hamlet*," *ACM* 2, no. 1 (1989): 1–25.

Don Parry Norford, "'Very Like a Whale': The Problem of Knowledge in *Hamlet*," *ELH* 46 (September 1979): 559–76.

J. M. Nosworthy, "The Death of Ophelia," *SQ* 15 (Autumn 1964): 345–48.

J. M. Nosworthy, "*Hamlet* and the Player Who Could not Keep Counsel," *ShS* 3 (1950): 74–82.

J. M. Nosworthy, "The Structural Experiment in *Hamlet*," *RES* 22 (August 1946): 282–88.

Winifred Nowottny, "The Application of Textual Theory to *Hamlet*'s Dying Words," *MLR* 52 (June 1957): 161–67.

Elizabeth Thompson Oakes, "'Killing the Calf' in *Hamlet*," *SQ* 34 (Summer 1983): 215–16.

Gordon W. O'Brien, "*Hamlet* IV.v.156-157," *SQ* 10 (Spring 1959): 249–51.

John O'Meara, "*Hamlet* and the Fortunes of Sorrowful Imagination: A Re-Examination of the Genesis and Fate of the Ghost," *CahiersE* 35 (April 1989): 15–25.

John O'Meara, "*Hamlet* and the Tragedy of Sexuality," *HSt* 10 (Summer–Winter 1988): 117–25.

Francis R. Olley, "Claudius at Prayer: The Problem of Motivation in *Hamlet*," *Drama Critique* 7 (Winter 1964): 22–25.

Elder Olson, "*Hamlet* and the Hermaneutics of Drama," *MP* 61 (February 1964): 225–37.

L. E. Orange, "Hamlet's Mad Soliloquy," *SAQ* 64 (Winter 1965): 60–71.

Ornstein, *Moral Vision of Jacobean Tragedy*, 234–40.

Robert Ornstein, "The Mystery of *Hamlet*: Notes Toward an Archetypal Solution," *CE* 21 (October 1959): 30–36.

Charlotte F. Otten, "Ophelia's 'Long Purples' or 'Dead Men's Fingers,'" *SQ* 30 (Autumn 1979): 397–402.

Toshikazu Oyama, "The Cloud Theme in *Hamlet*," *ShStud* 1 (1962): 47–60.

Bernard J. Paris, "Hamlet and His Problems: A Horneyan Analysis," *CentR* 21 (Winter 1977): 36–66.

Bernard J. Paris, "Third Force Psychology and the Study of Literature," in *Psychological Perspectives on Literature: Freudian Dissidents and Non-Freudians: A Casebook*, ed. Joseph Natoli (Hamden, CT: Archon, 1984), 155–80.

T. M. Parrott, "Fullness of Bread," *SQ* 3 (October 1952): 379–80.

John Paterson, "The Word in *Hamlet*," *SQ* 2 (January 1951): 47–55.

M. Christopher Pecheux, "Another Note on 'This fell sergeant, Death,'" *SQ* 26 (Winter 1975): 74–75.

Thomas A. Pendleton, "Hamlet's Ears," *Mid-Hudson Lang. Studies* (Poughkeepsie, NY) 1 (Spring 1978): 51–61.

Vincent F. Petronella, "Hamlet's 'To be or not to be' Soliloquy: Once More unto the Breach," *SP* 71 (February 1974): 72–88.

Vincent F. Petronella, "Shakespeare's *Hamlet,*" *Expl* 25 (May 1967): Item 56.

Manfred Pfister, "Germany Is *Hamlet*: The History of a Political Interpretation," *NewComp* 2 (Autumn 1986): 106–26.

Peter G. Phialas, "Hamlet and the Grave-Maker," *JEGP* 63 (April 1964): 226–34.

John A. S. Phillips, "Why Does Hamlet Delay? Hamlet's Subtle Revenge," *Anglia* 98, no. 1 (1980): 34–50.

Timothy Dayne Pinnow, "Toward a New *Hamlet*: Breathing New Life into an Old Character," *T&P* 11 (1991): 83–87.

W. B. Piper, "Of Hamlet's Transformation," *SHR* 2 (December 1968): 324–42.

Seymour M. Pitcher, "Two Notes on Shakespeare," *PQ* 21 (April 1942): 239–40.

David L. Pollard, "Belatedness in *Hamlet,*" *HSt* 11 (Summer–Winter 1989): 49–59.

Beryl Pogson, *In the East My Pleasure Lies*, 92–106.

Karl Polyani, "*Hamlet,*" *YR* 43 (March 1954): 336–50.

Moody E. Prior, "The Play Scene in *Hamlet,*" *ELH* 9 (September 1942): 188–97.

Matthew N. Proser, "Madness, Revenge, and the Metaphor of the Theater in Shakespeare's *Hamlet* and Pirandello's *Henry IV,*" *MD* 24 (September 1981): 338–52.

Richard Proudfoot, "'The play's the thing': Hamlet and the Conscience of the Queen," in Mahon and Pendleton, *"Fanned and winnowed opinions,"* 160–65.

Martin Puhvel, "The Background of 'Shards, Flints, and Pebbles,' *Hamlet*, V.i," *ELN* 15 (December 1978): 164–67.

Rufus Putney, "What 'Praise to Give'?" *PQ* 23 (October 1944): 312–13.

Thomas Pyles "Ophelia's 'Nothing,'" *MLN* 64 (May 1949): 322–23.

Maurice T. Quinlan, "Shakespeare and the Catholic Burial Services," *SQ* 5 (Summer 1954): 302–03.

Dale B. J. Randall, "Ecce Signum! Hamlet's Handsaw Again," *RenP* 1965 (1966): 47–50.

Alur Janaki Ram, "Arjuna and Hamlet: Two Moral Dilemmas," *PE&W* 18 (February 1968): 11–28.

N. M. Rao, "Hawk and Handsaw: A Study of *Hamlet*," in Sharma, *Essays on Shakespeare*, 231–42.

Gideon Rappaport, "*Hamlet*: Revenge and Readiness," *UCrow* 7 (1987): 80–95.

Eric Rasmussen, "Fathers and Sons in *Hamlet*," *SQ* 35 (Winter 1984): 463.

Eric Rasmussen, "'Pollux' for 'Pollax': An Emendation of *Hamlet* 1.1.66," *HSt* 6 (Summer–Winter 1984): 72–74.

Robert R. Reed, Jr., "Hamlet, the Pseudo-Procrastinator," *SQ* 9 (Spring 1958): 177–86.

John Rees, "*Hamlet*: A Note on Structure," *HSt* 3 (Winter 1981): 112–16.

B. L. Reid, "The Last Act and Action of *Hamlet*," *YR* 54 (October 1964): 59–80.

Kenneth Reinhard, and Julia Lupton, "Shapes of Grief: Freud, Hamlet, and Mourning," *Genders* 4 (March 1989): 50–67.

Raymond H. Reno, "Hamlet's Quintessence of Dust," *SQ* 12 (Spring 1961): 107–13.

Carter Revard, "*Hamlet* I.iv.36-38: *Of a Doubt* and *OED Adulterer v*," *ELN* 17 (September 1979): 106–08.

Michael R. Richards, "Hamlet: Divine Physician," *UCrow* 1 (1978): 53–63.

William Robbins, "*Hamlet* as Allegory," *UTQ* 21 (April 1952): 217–23.

W. R. Robinson, "The Visual Powers Denied and Coupled: *Hamlet* and *Fellini-Satyricon* as Narratives of Seeing," in *Shakespeare's "More than words can witness": Essays on Visual and Non-verbal Enactment in the Plays*, ed. Sidney Homan (Lewisburg, PA: Bucknell University Press, 1980). 177–206.

Leo Rockas, "'Stick Fiery Off': Foils in *Hamlet*," *DR* 58 (Winter 1978–79): 647–60.

Joseph J. Romm, "Why Hamlet Dies," *HSt* 10 (Summer–Winter 1988): 79–94.

Clifford J. Ronan, "*Homo Multiplex* and the 'Man' Equivocation in *Hamlet*," *HSt* 4 (Summer-Winter 1982): 33–53.

Jacqueline Rose, "*Hamlet*: The Mona Lisa of Literature," *CritQ* 28 (Spring–Summer 1986): 35–49.

Jacqueline Rose, "New Accents: Sexuality in the Reading of Shakespeare: *Hamlet* and *Measure for Measure*," in Drakakis, *Alternative Shakespeares*, 95–118.

Mark Rose, "*Hamlet*," in *Homer to Brecht: The European Epic and Dramatic Traditions*, ed. Michael Seidel and Edward Mendelson (New Haven: Yale University Press, 1977), 238–54.

Jason P. Rosenblatt, "Aspects of the Incest Problem in *Hamlet*," *SQ* 29 (Summer 1978): 349–64.

Daniel W. Ross, and Brooke K. Horvath, "Inaction in *Othello* and *Hamlet*," *UCrow* 11 (1991): 52–61.

Ross, *Philosophy in Literature*, 255–63.

Rossiter, *Angel with Horns*, 171–88.

William Rossky, "Hamlet as Jeremiah," *HSt* 1 (Spring 1979): 101–08.

Roston, *Biblical Drama*, 123–26.

Nicholas Royle, "Nuclear Piece: Memoires of *Hamlet* and the Time to Come," *Diacritics* 20 (Spring 1990): 39–55.

James Ruoff, "Shakespeare's Elegy in a Country Churchyard: Stoic or Christian?" *Wichita State University Bulletin* 41, no. 1 (1965): 3–10.

Jon R. Russ, " 'Old Mole' in *Hamlet*, I.v.162," *ELN* 12 (December 1975): 163–68.

Andrew J. Sacks, "Shakespeare's *Hamlet* III.ii.338–41," *Expl* 35 (Fall 1977): 18.

Pierre Sahel, "The Cease of Majesty in *Hamlet*," *HSt* 1 (Spring 1979): 109–16.

Pierre Sahel, "War in *Hamlet*," *AJES* 6, no. 2 (1981): 184–95.

Arthur H. Sampley, "Hamlet Among the Mechanists," *ShAB* 17 (July 1942): 134–49.

London A. Sanders, "Horatio—Friend to the Dane," *Madison Quarterly* 2 (March 1942): 77–88.

Hade Saunders, " 'Who Would Fardels Bear?': *Hamlet*, III.i.76," *CentR* 8 (Winter 1964): 71–76.

D. S. Savage, "Heraldry and Alchemy in Shakespeare's *Hamlet*," *UR* 17 (Spring 1961): 231–40.

Francis G. Schoff, "Horatio: A Shakespearian 'Confidant,'" *SQ* 7 (Winter 1956): 53–57.

Elliot M. Schrero, "A Misinterpretation of Freud," *CE* 10 (May 1949): 476.

Elias Schwartz, "The Possibilities of Christian Tragedy," *CE* 21 (January 1960): 210–12.

Robert Schwartz, "Coming Apart at the 'Seems': More on the Complexity of *Hamlet*," *PCP* 17 (November 1982): 40–49.

Dietrich Schwanitz, "The Time Is Out of Joint, but Life Goes On: *Hamlet* or the Ephesian Matron," *JAAR* 51 (March 1983): 37–53.

Charles P. Segal, "Oedipus Rex: Tragic Heroism and Sacral Kingship in Five Oedipus Plays and *Hamlet*," *Helios* 5, no. 1 (1977): 1–10.

Ronald G. Shafer, "Hamlet: Christian or Humanist?" *StHum* 17 (June 1990): 21–35.

Shapiro, *Rival Playwrights*, 126–32.

Ghanshiam Sharma, "The Function of Horatio in *Hamlet*," *HSt* 8 (Summer–Winter 1986): 30–39.

Shaw, *Plays and Players*, 265–74, 285–90.

Michael Shelden, "The Imagery of Constraint in *Hamlet*," *SQ* 28 (Summer 1977): 355–58.

Warren Shepard, "Hoisting the Enginer With His Own Petar," *SQ* 7 (Spring 1956): 281–85.

Edward J. Shoben, Jr. "A Clinical View of Tragedy," *ColQ* 11 (Spring 1963): 352–63. Reprinted in *L&P* 14 (Winter 1964): 23–34.

Francis Shocmaker, *Aesthetic Experience and the Humanities* (New York: Columbia University Press, 1943), 192–227.

Elaine Showalter, "Representing Ophelia: Women, Madness, and the Responsibilities of Feminist Criticism," in Parker and Hartman, *Shakespeare and the Question of Theory*, 77–94.

Paul N. Siegel, "Discerning the Ghost in *Hamlet*," *PMLA* 78 (March 1963): 148–49.

Kaja Silverman, "*Hamlet* and the Common Theme of Fathers," *enclitic* 3, no. 2 (1979): 106–21.

Percy Simpson, *Studies in Elizabethan Drama*, 150–54.

Harold Skulsky, "'I know my course': Hamlet's Confidence," *PMLA* 89 (June 1974): 477–86.

Harry Slochower, "Shakespeare's *Hamlet*: The Myth of Modern Sensibility," *AI* 7 (November 1950): 197–238.

Kristian Smidt, "The 'Mobled Queen' and the 'Sweet Prince': Observations on the Composition of Shakespeare's *Hamlet*," *Edda* 4 (Autumn 1987): 347–60.

Kristian Smidt, "Notes on *Hamlet*," *ES* 31 (August 1950): 136–41.

Kristian Smidt, "Politics, Courtiers, Soldiers, and Scholars: Type Characters in *Hamlet*," *ES* 57 (January 1976): 337–47.

James Smith, "The Funeral of Ophelia," *Irish Monthly* 79 (February 1951): 60–66.

Rebecca Smith, "A Heart Cleft in Twain: The Dilemma of Shakespeare's Gertrude," in Lenz, et al., *The Woman's Part*, 194–210.

Roland M. Smith, "Hamlet said 'Pajock,'" *JEGP* 44 (July 1945): 392–95.

Stella T. Smith, "On the Language of *Hamlet*," *CCR* 3, no. 2 (1979): 2–10.

George Soule, "Hamlet's Quietus," *CE* 26 (December 1964): 231.

J. Duncan Spaeth, "Horatio's Hamlet," *ShAB* 24 (January 1949): 37–47.

Theodore Spencer, "The Isolation of the Shakespearean Hero," *SR* 52 (Summer 1944): 317–21, 323–25.

Stephen Spender, *The Making of a Poem* (New York: Norton, 1962), 119–23.

Marvin Spevack, "Hamlet and Imagery: The Mind's Eye," *NS* 15 (1966): 203–12.

Soellner, *Shakespeare's Patterns*, 172–94.

Michael Srigley, "'Rightly to be Great': A Note on *Hamlet* IV.iv.53–56," *SN* 56 (Summer 1984): 163–68.

Tony J. Stafford, "Hamlet's House of Death," *PLL* 10 (Spring 1974): 15–20.

Bert O. States, "Horatio—Our Man in Elsinore: An Essay on Dramatic Logic," *SAQ* 78 (Winter 1979): 46–56.

Melvin Stephens, "Shakespeare's *Hamlet* II.i," *Expl* 35 (Fall 1977): 20–21.

Brents Sterling, "Theme and Character in *Hamlet*," *MLQ* 13 (December 1952): 323–32.

Sanford Sternlicht, "Hamlet: The Actor as Prince," *HSt* 4 (Summer–Winter 1982): 19–32.

Martin Stevens, "Hamlet and the Pirates: A Critical Reconsideration," *SQ* 26 (Spring 1975): 276–84.

G. H. Stevenson, "Social Pychiatry and *Hamlet*," *RSCPT* 43 (June 1949): 143–51.

Charles D. Stewart, "Four Shakesperean Cruxes," *CE* 9 (January 1948): 187–88.

Kay Stockholder, "Sex and Authority in *Hamlet*, *King Lear* and *Pericles*," *Mosaic* 18 (Summer 1985): 17–29.

Victor H. Strandberg, "The Revenger's Tragedy: Hamlet's Costly Code," *SAQ* 65 (Winter 1966): 95–103.

Ernest A. Strathman, "The Devil Can Cite Scripture," *SQ* 15 (Spring 1964): 20–22.

Henri Suhamy, "The Metaphorical Fallacy: Some Remarks on the Sickness Imagery in *Hamlet*," *CahiersE* 24 (October 1983): 27–32.

Goro Suzuki, "*Hamlet*: An Essay in Reconstruction," *RenB* 13 (1986): 47–65.

Jim Swan, "*Hamlet* and the Technology of the Mind's Eye; Urbino: July 6–9, 1990," in *Seventh International Conference on Literature and Psychology* (Lisbon: Instituto Superior de Psicologia Aplicada, 1991), 87–102.

J. Swart, "I Know not 'Seems': A Study of *Hamlet*," *REL* 2 (October 1961): 60–76.

Samuel A. Tannenbaum, "Claudius Not a Patchock," *ShAB* 20 (October 1945): 156–59.

Marion A, Taylor, "Ophelia Exonerated," *ShN* 10 (May 1960): 27.

Myron Taylor, "Tragic Justice and the House of Polonius," *SEL* 8 (Spring 1968): 273–81.

Alwin Thaler, "In My Mind's Eye, Horatio," *SQ* 7 (Autumn 1956): 351–54.

C. G. Thayer, "*Hamlet*: Drama as Discovery and as Metaphor," *SN* 28 (Summer 1956): 118–29.

Gordon K. Thomas, "Speaking of Reason to the Danes," *UCrow* 1 (1978): 69–73.

Thompson, and Thompson, *Shakespeare: Meaning and Metaphor*, 89–131.

Lee Thorn, "Kyd Caps Revenge: *Hamlet* as Rite of Passage," *HSt* 10 (Summer–Winter 1988): 126–29.

John J. M. Tobin, "Apuleius and Ophelia," *Classical Bulletin* 56 (Spring 1980): 69–70.

Robert Tracy, "The Owl and the Baker's Daughter: A Note on *Hamlet* IV.v.42–43," *SQ* 17 (Winter 1966): 83–86.

E. M. Trehern, "'Dear, They Durst Not,'" *English* 10 (Summer 1954): 59–60.

E. M. Trehern, "Notes on *Hamlet*," *MLR* 40 (July 1945): 213–16.

Roger J. Trienens, "The Symbolic Cloud in *Hamlet*," *SQ* 5 (Spring, 1954): 211–13.

Lionel Trilling, "Freud and Literature," *Horiron* 16 (September 1943): 191–96.

Charles Turek, "Shakespeare's *Hamlet*," *Expl* 44 (Winter 1986): 8–9.

Charles Turek, "Shakespeare's *Hamlet*," *Expl* 48 (Summer 1990): 239–41.

Van Lann, *The Idiom of Drama*, 99–105, 124–29, 168–73, 194–206, 226–29, 247–50, 305–15, 340–54.

Thomas F. Van Lann, "Ironic Reversal in *Hamlet*," *SEL* 6 (Spring 1966): 247–62.

Gene Edward Veith, Jr. "'Wait upon the Lord': David, Hamlet, and the Problem of Revenge," in *The David Myth in Western Literature*, ed. Raymond-Jean Frontain and Jan Wojcik (West Lafayette, IN: Purdue University Press, 1980), 70–83.

Marguerite M. Vey-Miller, and Ronald J. Miller, "Degrees of Psychopathology in *Hamlet*," *HSt* 7 (Summer–Winter 1985): 81–87.

John Virtue, "Shakespeare's *Hamlet*, I, iii, 79–90," *Expl* 16 (June 1959): 55.

R. Viswanathan, "Shakespeare's *Hamlet*," *Expl* 46 (Winter 1988): 6–8.

S. Viswanathan, "The Door in *Hamlet*, That Janus of Plays," *AJES* 12 (April 1987): 1–8.

S. Viswanathan, "'This Fell Sergeant, Death' Once More," *SQ* 29 (Winter 1978): 84–85.

Raymond B. Waddington, "Lutheran *Hamlet*," *ELN* 27 (December 1989): 27–42.

Frank W. Wadsworth, "*Hamlet* and the Methods of Literary Analysis: A Note," *AI* 19 (Spring 1962): 90–95.

Linda W. Wagner, "Ophelia: Shakespeare's Pathetic Plot Device," *SQ* 14 (Winter 1963): 94–97.

Julia Grace Wales, "Horatio's Commentary," *ShAB* 17 (January 1942): 40–56.

Julia G. Wales, "Horatio's Commentary: A Study on the Warp and Woof of *Hamlet*," *SAB* 17 (March 1952): 40–56.

J. W. Walter, "The Dumb Show and the 'Mouse Trap,'" *MLR* 39 (July 1944): 286–87.

James Walter, "Memoria, Faith and Betrayal in *Hamlet*," *C&L* 37 (Winter 1988): 11–26.

J. K. Walton, "The Structure of *Hamlet*," *Stratford-Upon-Avon Studies* 5 (1963): 44–89.

Sidney Warhaft, "Hamlet's Solid Flesh Resolved," *ELH* 28 (March 1961): 21–30.

Sidney Warhaft, "The Mystery of *Hamlet*," *ELH* 30 (September 1963): 193–208.

Robert N. Watson, "Giving up the Ghost in a World of Decay: Hamlet, Revenge, and Denial," *RenD* 21 (1990): 199–223.

Joan Webber, "*Hamlet* and the Freeing of the Mind," in Henning, Kimbrough, and Knowles, *English Renaissance Drama*, 76–99.

Peter Dow Webster, "Arrested Individuation or the Problem of Joseph K. and Hamlet," *AI* 5 (November 1948): 225–45.

Robert Weimann, "Mimesis in *Hamlet*," in Parker and Hartman, *Shakespeare and the Question of Theory*, 275–91.

Karl P. Wentersdorf, "Animal Symbolism in Shakespeare's *Hamlet*," *CompD* 17 (Winter 1983–1984): 348–82.

Karl P. Wentersdorf, "*Hamlet*: Notes on Three Cruxes," *SN* 50 (Spring 1978): 179–83.

Karl P. Wentersdorf, "*Hamlet*: Ophelia's Long Purples," *SQ* 29 (Summer 1978): 413–17.

Robert H. West, "King Hamlet's Ambiguous Ghost," *PMLA* 70 (December 1955): 1107–17.

Joseph Westlund, "Ambivalence in the Player's Speech in *Hamlet*," *SEL* 18 (Spring 1978): 245–56.

James L. Wheeler, "Existence and *Hamlet*," *SJS* 4, no. 2 (1978): 23–31.

Beatrice White, "Two Notes on Hamlet," *NM* 65 (March 1964): 92–96.

R. S. White, "The Spirit of Yorick; Or, The Tragic Sense of Humour in *Hamlet*," *HSt* 7 (Summer–Winter 1985): 9–26.

R. S. White, "The Tragedy of Ophelia," *ArielE* 9 (April 1978): 41–53.

Robert B. White, Jr., "*Hamlet*, V.ii: The Gemlore of the Wineglass," *NCarF* 20 (Spring 1972): 159–62.

G. A. Wilkes, "'An Understanding Simple and Unschooled': The 'Immaturity'of Hamlet," *SSEng* 1 (1975–76): 69–75.

John S. Wilks, "The Discourse of Reason: Justice and the Erroneous Conscience in *Hamlet*," *ShakS* 18 (1986): 117–44.

George Walton Williams, "Antique Romans and Modern Danes in *Julius Caesar* and *Hamlet*," in Newey and Thompson, *Literature and Nationalism*, 41–55.

George W. Williams, "Sleep in *Hamlet*," *RenP* 1963 (1964): 17–20.

Gwyn Williams, "'The Pale Cast of Thought," *MLR* 45 (April 1950): 216–18.

Williams, *Drama in Performance*, 75–79.

Robert F. Willson, Jr., "Hamlet: Man of the Theater," *CahiersE* 28 (October 1985): 37–44.

Robert F. Willson, Jr., "*Hamlet*: The Muddled Mouse-Trap," *CLAJ* 22 (June 1978): 160–66.

Robert F. Willson, Jr., "The Hatless Hamlet," *HSt* 3 (Winter 1981): 117–18.

Robert F. Willson, Jr., "Shakespeare's *Hamlet* II.ii.603–04," *Expl* 35 (Winter 1977): 2–3.

Mathew Winston, "Misreading *Hamlet*," *HSt* 3 (Summer 1981): 53–54.

M. R. Woodhead, "Deep Plots and Indescretions in 'The Murder of Gonzago,'" *ShS* 32 (1979): 151–61.

William R. Wray, "You, Claudius: An Anatomy of a Name," *PAPA* 6 (Spring 1980): 78–94.

George T. Wright, "Hendiadys and *Hamlet*," *PMLA* 96 (March 1981): 168–93.

Young, *Immortal Shadows*, 8–14, 211–14.

Lois Ziegelman, "*Hamlet*: Shakespeare's Mannerist Tragedy: Coll. of Essays from the Ohio Shakespeare Conf., 1981, Wright State Univ., Dayton, Ohio," in Cary and Limouze, *Shakespeare and the Arts*, 57–71.

Henry IV, Parts I & II

Richard Abrams, "Rumor's Reign in *2 Henry IV*: The Scope of a Personification," *ELR* 16 (Autumn 1986): 467–95.

Henry Hitch Adams, "Falstaff's Instinct," *SQ* 5 (Spring 1954): 208–09.

Henry Hitch Adams, "Two Notes on *I Henry IV*," *SQ* 3 (July 1952): 292–93.

Paul J. Aldus, "Analogical Probability in Shakespeare's Plays," *SQ* 6 (Autumn 1955): 402–09.

Alex Aronson, "A Note on Shakespeare's Dream Imagery," *Visuabharati Quarterly* 19 (August–October 1952): 174–75.

Robin Atthill, "*Henry IV, Part II*," *The Use of English* 9 (Summer 1958): 253–58.

Barbara J. Baines, "Kingship of the Silent King: A Study of Shakespeare's Bolingbroke," *ES* 61 (1980): 24–36.

Christopher Baker, "The Iconography of Falstaff's Judgement: The Parliament of Heaven in *Henry IV, Part II*," *CCETP* 52 (September 1987): 13–19.

C. L. Barber, "From Ritual to Comedy: An Examination of *Henry IV*," *English Institute Essays* (1954): 22–51.

Barber, *Shakespeare's Festive Comedy*, 192–221.

Jonas A. Barish, "The Turning Away of Prince Hal," *ShakS* 1 (1965): 9–17.

Eben Bass, "Falstaff and the Succession," *CE* 24 (April 1963): 502–06.

Roy Battenhouse, "Falstaff as Parodist and Perhaps Holy Fool, *PMLA* 90 (January 1975): 32–52.

Gorman Beauchamp, "Falstaff and Civilization's Discontents," *CollL* 3 (Winter 94–101.

Robert B. Bennett, "Prince Hal's Crisis of Timing in the Tavern Scene of *Henry IV, Part 1*," *CahiersE* 23 (April 1978): 15–23.

William E. Bennett, "Shakespeare's *Henry IV, Part I*, IV.i. (98–99)," *Expl* 27 (September 1968): Item 1.

Harry Berger, Jr. "Sneak's Noise or Rumor and Detextualization in *2 Henry IV*," *KR* 46 (Fall 1984): 58–78.

David M. Bergeron, "Shakespeare Makes History: *2 Henry IV*," *SEL* 31 (Spring 1991): 231–45.

David Berkeley, and Donald Edison, "The Theme of *Henry IV, Part I*," *SQ* 19 (Winter 1968): 25–31.

Ronald Berman, "The Nature of Guilt in the *Henry IV* Plays," *ShakS* 1 (1965): 18–28.

Edward I. Berry, "The Rejection Scene in *2 Henry IV*," *SEL* 17 (Spring 1977): 201–18.

Berry, *Poet's Grammar*, 62–64.

Berry, *Shakespearean Structures*, 1–11.

S. L. Bethel, "The Comic Element in Shakespeare's Histories," *Anglia* 61, no. 1 (1952): 92–101.

James Black, "'Anon, Anon, Sir': Discourse of Occasion in *Henry IV*," *CahiersE* 37 (April 1990): 27–42.

D. S. Bland, "Justice Shallow's 'Hem, boys!,'" *N&Q* 25 (April 1978): 132.

John W. Blanpied, "'Unfathered heirs and loathly births of Nature': Bringing History to Crisis in *2 Henry IV*," *ELR* 5 (Summer 1975): 212–31.

Samuel Bogard, "*I King Henry the Fourth*, II, iv, 315ff," *SQ* 1 (April 1950): 76–77.

Fredson Bowers, "Hal and Francis in *King Henry IV, Part I*," *RenP 1964* (1965): 15–20.

Thomas D. Bowman, "A Further Note on the Mother Reference in *Henry IV, Part 1*," *SQ* 1 (October 1950): 295.

Thomas D. Bowman, "Two Addenda to Hotspur's Tragic Behavior," *Journal of General Education* 16 (April 1964): 69–71.

David Boyd, "The Player Prince: Hal in *Henry IV Part I*," *SSEng* 6 (1980–81): 3–16.

A. C. Bradley, *Oxford Lectures on Poetry*, 247–75.

Bradshaw, *Shakespeare's Skepticism*, 50–66.

Ernest Brennecke, "Shakespeare's 'Singing Man of Windsor,'" *PMLA* 66 (December 1951): 1188–92.

Brooks, and Heilman, *Understanding Drama*, 317–19; 376–99.

Margaret B. Bryan, "'Sir Walter Blunt. There's honor for you!,'" *SQ* 26 (Summer 1975): 292–98.

Bullough, *Mirror of Minds*, 69–71.

James B. Burleson, Jr., "The Infamous Victory of Falstaff," *UCrow* 1 (1978): 36–40.

H. Edward Cain, "Further Light on the Relation of *1* and *2 Henry IV*," *SQ* 3 (January 1952): 21–39.

Truman W. Camp, "Shakespeare's *Henry IV, Part 1*, and the Ballad 'Chevy Chase,'" *N&Q* 13 (April 1966): 131–32.

Josie P. Campbell, "Farce as a Function in Medieval and Shakespearean Drama," *UCrow* 3 (1980): 11–18.

Chanduri, *Infirm Glory*, 124–33.

Frank Chapman, "*Henry IV, Part 1*," *The Use of English* 5 (Autumn 1953): 12–15.

Raymond Chapman, "The Wheel of Fortune in Shakespeare's Historical Plays," *RES* 1 (January 1950): 1–3, 67.

F. Nick Clary, "Reformation and Its Counterfeit: The Recovery of Meaning in *Henry IV, Part One*: Selected Papers from Seventh Annual Florida State University Conference on Literature & Film," in *Ambiguities in Literature and Film*, ed. Hans P. Braendlin (Tallahassee: Florida State University Press, 1988), 76–94.

Clemen, *Shakespeare's Dramatic Art*, 107–08.

Seymour B. Connor, "The Role of Douglas in *Henry IV, Part One*," *Studies in English* 27 (June 1948): 215–21.

R. P. Corballis, "'Buzz, Buzz': Bee-Lore in *2 Henry IV*," *N&Q* 28 (April 1981): 127–28.

Norman Council, "Prince Hal: Mirror of Success," *ShakS* 7 (1974): 125–46.

Gerard H. Cox, "'Like a Prince Indeed': Hal's Triumph of Honor in *1 Henry IV*," in Bergeron, *Pageantry in the Shakespearean Theater*, 130–49.

Jonathan Crewe, "Reforming Prince Hal: The Sovereign Inheritor in *2 Henry IV*," *RenD* 21 (1990): 225–42.

Neva Daniel, "Looking at Shakespeare With an 'Existential' Eye," *Journal of Communication* 7 (Winter 1957): 176–78.

Jo Ann Davis, "*Henry IV*: From Satirist to Satiric Butt," in *Aeolian Harps: Essays in Honor of Maurice Browning Cramer*, ed. Donna G. Fricke and Douglas C. Fricke (Bowling Green, OH: Bowling Green University Press, 1976), 89–93.

Norman Davis, "Falstaff's Name," *SQ* 28 (Autumn 1977): 513–15.

Timothy C. Davis, "Shakespeare's *1 Henry IV*," *Expl* 49 (Spring 1991): 137–39.

Alan C. Dessen, "The Intemperate Knight and the Politic Prince: Late Morality Structure in *1 Henry IV*," *ShakS* 7 (1974): 147–72.

Hugh Dickinson, "The Reformation of Prince Hal," *SQ* 12 (Winter 1961): 33–46.

Jane Donaworth, "Shakespeare's *Henry IV, Part I*," *Expl* 36 (Fall 1978): 33–34.

Madeleine Doran, "Imagery in *Richard II* and in *Henry IV*," *MLR* 37 (April 1942): 113–22. Reprinted in *Shakespeare's Dramatic Language*, 221–33.

R. J. Dorius, "A Little More Than a Little," *SQ* 11 (Winter 1960): 22–26.

John W. Draper, "Falstaff, 'A Fool and Jester,'" *MLQ* 17 (December 1946): 453–62.

Annette Drew-Bear, "'The Strangest Tale That Ever I Heard': Embellished Report in *1 Henry IV*," *ISJR* 61 (May 1987): 333–45.

E. E. Duncan-Jones, "'Forlorn' in *Cymbeline* and *1 Henry IV*," *N&Q* 202 (February 1957): 64.

Richard M. Eastman, "Political Values in *Henry IV, Part One*: A Demonstration of Liberal Humanism," *CE* 33 (April 1972): 901–07.

V. J. Emmett, Jr., "*1 Henry IV*: Structure, Platonic Psychology, and Politics," *MQ* 19 (1978): 355–69.

Gareth Lloyd Evans, "The Comical-Tragical-Historical Method: *Henry IV*," *Stratford-Upon-Avon Studies* 3 (1961): 145–64.

John X. Evans, "Shakespeare's 'Villainous Salt-Peter': The Dimensions of an Allusion," *SQ* 15 (Autumn 1964): 451–54.

Willard Farnham, "The Medieval Comic Spirit in the English Renaissance," in McManaway, *Joseph Q. Adams Memoral Studies*, 435–37.

Robert J. Fehrenbach, "The Characterization of the King in *1 Henry IV*," *SQ* 30 (Winter 1979): 42–50.

Kristen Figg, "A 'Sober-blooded boy': The Role of John Lancaster in *1* and *2 Henry IV*," *SPWVSRA* 8 (1983): 9–14.

C. Overbury Fox, "The 'Haunch of Winter,'" *N&Q* 199 (January 1954): 21.

Leslie Freeman, "Shakespeare's Kings and Machiavelli's Prince," *CCP* 1 (September 1964): 25–42.

French, *Shakespeare's Division of Experience*, 37–69.

Elizabeth Freund, "Strategies of Inconclusiveness in *Henry IV, Part I*," *NYLF* 5–6 (1980): 207–16.

Colin Gardner, "Hotspur," *SoRA* 3 (1968): 34–51.

Anthony Gash, "Shakespeare's Comedies of Shadow and Substance: Word and Image in *Henry IV* and *Twelfth Night*," *W&I* 4 (January 1988): 626–62.

Bridget Gellert, "The Melancholy of Moor-Ditch: A Gloss of *1 Henry IV*, I.ii.87–88," *SQ* 18 (Winter 1967): 70–71.

Paul Goodman, *The Structure of Literature*, 103–16.

P. A. Gottschalk, "Hal and the 'Play Extempore' in *1 Henry IV*," *TSLL* 15 (Winter 1974): 605–14.

Stephen Greenblatt, "Invisible Bullets: Renaissance Authority and Its Subversion, *Henry IV* and *Henry V*," in Dollimore and Sinfield, *Political Shakespeare*, 18–47.

C. A. Greer, "Falstaff a Coward?" *N&Q* 200 (April 1955): 176–77.

C. A. Greer, "Falstaff's Diminuation of Wit," *N&Q* 199 (November 1954): 468.

C. A. Greer, "Shakespeare and Prince Hal," *N&Q* 198 (November 1953): 424–26.

Alan G. Gross, "The Justification of Prince Hal," *TSLL* 10 (Spring 1968): 27–35.

Hallett and Hallett, *Analyzing Shakespeare's Action*, 3–5, 61–67, 84–86, 136–37.

C. G. Harlow, "Shakespeare, Nashe, and the Ostrich Crux in *I Henry IV*," *SQ* 17 (Spring 1966): 171–74.

Haselkorn, *Prostitution in Elizabethan and Jacobean Drama*, 45–48.

Sherman H. Hawkins, "*Henry IV*: The Structural Problem Revisited," *SQ* 33 (Autumn 1982): 278–301.

Sherman H. Hawkins, "Virtue and Kingship in Shakespeare's *Henry IV*," *ELR* 5 (1975): 313–43.

Hewett, *Reading and Response*, 106–10.

G. B. Hibbard, "An Emmendation in *2 Henry VI* I.iv," *N&Q* 12 (October 1965): 332.

G. B. Hibbard, "*Henry IV* and *Hamlet*," *ShS* 30 (1977): 1–12.

Hibbard, *Making of Shakespeare's Dramatic Poetry*, 162–92.

Christopher Highley, "Wales, Ireland, and *Henry IV*," *RenD* 21 (1990): 91–114.

Susan Hills, "Shakespeare's *I Henry IV*, II.iv (468–98)," *Expl* 39 (Summer 1981): 7–9.

Richard S. M. Hirsch, "A Second Echo of *Edward II* in I.iii of *1 Henry IV*," *N&Q* 22 (April 1975): 168.

Houston, *Shakespearean Sentences*, 22–25, 33–34.

Arthur Humphreys, "Shakespeare's Political Justice in *Richard II* and *Henry IV*," *Stratford Papers on Shakespeare* 5 (1964): 30–50.

Arthur Humphreys, "A Note on *2 Henry IV*, II iv (362–63)," *N&Q* 208 (March 1963): 98.

Arthur Humphreys, "Two Notes on *2 Henry IV*," *MLR* 59 (April 1964): 171–72.

Maurice Hunt, "Time and Timelessness in *1 Henry IV*," *EIRC* 10 (1984): 56–66.

Gregory K. Jember, "Glory, Jest, and Riddle: The Three Deaths of Falstaff," *Thoth* 12, no. 3 (1972): 30–38.

Paul A. Jorgensen, "The 'Dastardly Treachery' of Prince John of Lancaster," *PMLA* 76 (December 1961): 488–92.

Paul A. Jorgensen, "Divided Command in Shakespeare," *PMLA* 70 (September 1955): 750–61.

Paul A. Jorgensen, "My Name is Pistol Call'd," *SQ* 1 (April 1950): 73–75.

Paul A. Jorgensen, " 'Redeeming Time' in Shakespeare's *Henry IV*," *TSL* 5 (Spring 1960): 101–10.

Walter J. Kaiser, *Praisers of Folly*, (Cambridge, MA: Harvard University Press, 1963), 14–16, 195–275.

Seiya Kasahara, "The Tudor Myth and *Henry IV*," *SES* 5 (1980): 29–44.

Dorothea Kehler, "'And Nothing Pleaseth but Rare Accidents': Suspense and Peripety in *1 Henry IV*," *UCrow* 7 (1987): 58–67.

John Kerrigan, "*Henry IV* and the Death of Old Double," *EIC* 40 (January 1990): 24–53.

Razia Khan, "The Hero in Shakespeare's *Henry IV*," *DUS* 12 (June 1964): 35–40.

Arthur H. King, "Some Notes on Ambiguity in *Henry IV Part 1*," *SN* 14 (1941–1942): 161–83.

Leo Kirschbaum, "The Demotion of Falstaff," *PQ* 41 (January 1962): 58–60.

Knight, *The Golden Labyrinth*, 71–74, 77–78, 82–84.

Knight, *The Olive and the Sword*, 25–29.

Knight, *The Sovereign Flower*, 33–37.

U. C. Knoepflmacher, "The Humors in *Henry IV Part I*," *CE* 24 (April 1963): 497–501.

Richard Knowles, "Unquiet and the Double Plot of *2 Henry IV*," *ShakS* 2 (1966): 133–40.

E. Kris, "Prince Hal's Conflict" *Psychoanalytic Quarterly* 17 (October 1948): 487–506.

Anthony La Branche, "'If Thou Wert Sensible of Courtesy': Private and Public Virtue in *Henry IV, Part One*," *SQ* 17 (Autumn 1966): 371–82.

Eric La Guardia, "Ceremony and History: The Problem of Symbol from *Richard II* to *Henry V*," in McNeir and Greenfield, *Pacific Coast Studies in Shakespeare*, 68–88.

Mary Lascelles, "Shakespeare's Comic Insight," *PBA* 48 (1962): 180–85.

Leech, Clifford. "The Unity of *2 Henry IV*," *ShS* 6 (1953): 16–24.

Harry Levin, "Falstaff Uncolted," *MLN* 61 (April 1946): 305–10.

Lawrence L. Levin, "Hotspur, Falstaff, and the Emblem of Wrath in *I Henry IV*," *ShakS* 10 (1977): 43–65.

Ruth M. Levitsky, "Shakespeare's *2HIV*, II.iv," *Expl* 35 (Winter 1977): 23–24.

Rebecca Liebowitz, "*King Henry IV Part I*: The Education of a Prince," *CRUX* 10 (April 1973): 21–22.

Warren J. Macisac, " 'A Commodity of Good Names' in the *Henry IV* Plays," *SQ* 29 (Autumn 1978): 417–19.

Frank Manley, "The Unity of Betrayal in *II Henry IV*," *SLitI* 5, no. 1 (1972): 91–110.

Louis Marder, "Shakespeare's 'Lincolnshire Bagpipe,' " *N&Q* 195 (September 1950): 383–85.

John T. Marvin, "The Nature of Causation in the History Plays," in Margery Bailey, *Ashland Studies for Shakespeare 1962*, 67–77.

J. C. Maxwell, "*2 Henry IV*, II.iv.91ff," *MLR* 42 (October 1947): 485.

William G. McCollom, "Formalism and Illusion in Shakespeare's Drama," *QJS* 31 (December 1945): 450–52.

C. E. McGee, "*2 Henry IV*: The Last Tudor Royal Entry," in Gray, *Mirror up to Shakespeare*, 149–58.

Richard L. McGuire, "The Play-Within-the-Play in *I Henry IV*," *SQ* 18 (Winter 1967): 47–52.

J. McLaverty, "No Abuse: The Prince and Falstaff in the Tavern Scenes of *Henry IV*," *ShS* 34 (1981): 105–10.

Herbert Marshall McLuhan, "*Henry IV*, A Mirror for Magistrates," *UTQ* 17 (January 1948): 152–60.

Anne Marie McNamara, "*Henry IV*: The King as Protagonist," *SQ* 10 (Summer 1959): 423–31.

Waldo F. McNeir, "Shakespeare, *Henry IV, Part I*, II, i, 76–85," *Expl* 10 (April 1952): 37.

Waldo F. McNeir, "Structure and Theme in the First Tavern Scene (II.iv) of *I Henry IV*," in McNeir and Greenfield, *Pacific Coast Studies in Shakespeare*, 89–105.

McPeek, *The Black Book of Knaves*, 171–80.

Robert P. Merrix and Arthur Palacas. "Gadshill, Hotspur, and the Design of Proleptic Parody," *CompD* 14 (1980–81): 299–311.

Walter E. Meyers, "Hal: The Mirror of All Christian Kings," in Durant and Hester, *A Fair Day in the Affections*, 67–77.

Charles Mitchell, "The Education of a True Prince," *TSL* 12 (Spring 1967): 13–21.

Harry Morris, "Prince Hal: Apostle to the Gentiles," *ClioI* 7 (Spring 1978): 227–46.

S. Musgrove, "The Birth of Pistol," *RES* 10 (February 1959): 56–58.

Nuttall, *A New Mimesis*, 144–61.

Martin R. Orkin, "After a Collar Comes a Halter in *1 Henry IV*," *N&Q* 31 (June 1984): 188–89.

Martin R. Orkin, "'He Shows a Fair Pair of Heels' in *1 Henry IV* and Elsewhere," *ELN* 23 (September 1985): 19–23.

Martin R. Orkin, "A Proverb Allusion and Proverbial Association in *1 Henry IV*," *N&Q* 30 (April 1983): 120–21.

Martin R. Orkin, "Shakespeare's *Henry IV, I*," *Expl* 42 (Summer 1984): 11–12.

Martin R. Orkin, "Sir John Falstaff's Taste for Proverbs in *Henry IV, Part 1*," *ES* 65 (October 1984): 392–404.

T. M. Pearce, "Shakespeare's 'Mother Reference', *1 Henry IV* (II, iv, 265f)," *N&Q* 197 (January 1952): 25–26.

Leslie E. F. Pearsall, "Pike and Jacks in *Henry IV, Part 1*," *N&Q* 13 (April 1966): 132–33.

Edward Pechter, "Falsifying Men's Hopes: The Ending of *1 Henry IV*," *MLQ* 41 (June 1973): 211–30.

Ruth S. Perot, "Shakespeare's *1 Henry IV*, III, iii, 91–97," *Expl* 20 (December 1961): 36.

G. M. Pinciss, "The Old Honor and the New Courtesy: *1 Henry IV*," *ShS* 31 (1978): 85–91.

Robert H. Ray, "'By God's Liggens' in *2 Henry IV*: An Explanation," *ELN* 15 (March 1978): 268–71.

Raymond H. Reno, "Hotspur: The Integration of Character and Theme," *RenP 1961* (1962): 17–26.

Irving Ribner, "Bolingbroke, A True Machiavellian," *MLQ* 9 (April 1948): 177–84.

Ribner, *The English History Play*, 169–82.

Irving Ribner, "The Political Problem in Shakespeare's Lancatrian Tetralogy," *SP* 49 (April 1952): 182–84.

A. P. Riemer, "'A World of Figures': Language and Character in *Henry IV Part 1*," *SSEng* 6 (1980-81): 62–74.

Martin Robbins, "The Musical Meaning of 'Mode' in *Henry IV*," *ELN* 8 (March 1971): 252–57.

Henri Roddier, "A Freudian Detective's Shakespeare," *MP* 48 (November 1950): 130–31.

Norman Sanders, "The True Prince and the False Thief: Prince Hal and the Shift of Identity," *ShS* 30 (1977): 29–34.

James L. Sanderson, "'Buff Jerkin': A Note to *I Henry IV*," *ELN* 4 (September 1966): 92–95.

James Schevill, "Towards a Rhythm of Comic Action," *Western Speech* 20 (Winter 1956): 5–8.

Elizabeth Schafer, "Falstaff's 'Singing-Man of Windsor': *2 Henry IV*, II.1," *SQ* 39 (Winter 1988): 58–59.

Daniel Seltzer, "Prince Hal and Tragic Style," *ShS* 30 (1977): 13–27.

Peter J. Seng, "Songs, Time and the Rejection of Falstaff," *ShS* 15 (1962): 31–40.

M. A. Shaaber, "Pistole Quotes St. Augustine?" *ELN* 14 (September 1977): 90–92.

M. A. Shaaber, "The Unity of *Henry IV*," in McManaway, *Joseph Q. Adams Memorial Studies*, 217–27.

Shapiro, *Rival Playwrights*, 82–84.

Shaw, *Plays and Players*, 85–95.

John Shaw, "The Staging of Parody and Parallels in *I Henry IV*," *ShS* 20 (1967): 61–73.

J. D. Shuchter, "Prince Hal and Francis: The Imitation of an Action," *ShakS* 3 (1968): 129–37.

Carol Marks Sicherman, "'King Hal': The Integrity of Shakespeare's Portrait," *TSLL* 21 (Winter 1979): 503–21.

Paul N. Siegal, "Falstaff and His Social Milieu," in *Weapons of Criticism: Marxism in America and Literary Tradition*, ed. Norman Reich (Palo Alto, CA: Ramparts, 1976), 163–72.

Paul N. Siegal, "Shakespeare's *King Henry IV, Part II*," *Expl* 9 (November 1950): 9.

John P. Sisk, "Prince Hal and the Specialists," *SQ* 28 (Autumn 1977): 520–24.

Kristian Smidt, "Openings and Unfoldings: Structural Faults in *Richard II* and *Henry IV*," *ShN* 30 (April 1980): 13–14.

J. A. B. Somerset, "Falstaff, the Prince, and the Pattern of *2 Henry IV*," *ShS* 30 (1977): 35–45.

Benjamin T. Spencer, "The Stasis of *Henry IV, Part II*," *TSL* 6 (Spring 1961): 61–70.

Benjamin T. Spencer, "*2 Henry IV* and the Theme of Time," *UTQ* 13 (July 1944): 394–99.

Oliver L. Steele, Jr., "Shakespeare's *I Henry IV*, II, iii, 64," *Expl* 14 (June 1956): 59.

Steiner, *The Death of Tragedy*, 253–55.

Douglas J. Stewart, "Falstaff the Centaur," *SQ* 28 (Winter 1977): 5–21.

E. E. Stoll, "A Falstaff for the 'Bright,'" *MP* 51 (February 1954): 145–59.

Jack R. Sublette, "The Distorted Time in *2 Henry IV*," in Sharma, *Essays on Shakespeare in Honour of A. A. Ansari*, 195–210.

Jack R. Sublette, "Shakespeare's *1 Henry IV*: A Topsy-Turvy World," in *Elizabethan Miscellany 3*, ed. James Hogg (Salzburg: University of Salzburg, 1981), 47–61.

Jack R. Sublette, "Time's Fool: A Reading of *I Henry IV*," *AJES* 8 (April 1983): 68–78.

Edmund M. Taft, IV, "The Crown Scene in *Henry IV, Part 2*," *ISJR* 59 (May 1985): 307–17.

Leonard Tennenhouse, "Strategies of State and Political Plays: *A Midsummer Night's Dream, Henry IV, Henry V, Henry VIII*," in Dollimore and Sinfield, *Political Shakespeare*, 109–28.

Mary O. Thomas, "The Elevation of Hal in *I Henry IV*," *SLitI* 5, no. 1 (1972): 73–89.

E. M. W. Tillyard, "Shakespeare's Historical Cycle: Organism or Compilation," *SP* 51 (January 1954): 37–38.

Dain A. Trafton, "Shakespeare's *Henry IV*: A New Prince in a New Principality," in *Shakespeare as Political Thinker*, ed. John Alvis and Thomas G. West (Durham, NC: Carolina Academic Press, 1981), 83–94.

D. A. Traversi, "*Henry IV-Part I*," *Scrutiny* 15 (December 1947): 24–35.

D. A. Traversi, "*Henry IV-Part II*," *Scrutiny* 15 (Spring 1948): 117–27.

William John Tucker, "Irish Aspects of Shakespeare," *Catholic World* 156 (March 1943): 702–04.

Saxon Walker, "Mime and Heraldry in *Henry IV, Part I*," *English* 11 (Autumn 1956): 91–96.

Watson, *Shakespeare and the Hazards of Ambition*, 48–73.

Henry J. Webb, "Falstaff's Clothes," *MLN* 59 (March 1944): 162–64.

Henry J. Webb, "Falstaff's Tardy Tricks," *MLN* 58 (May 1943): 377–79.

Karl P. Wentersdorf, "Shakespeare and Carding: Notes on Cruxes in *1 Henry IV* and in *Twelfth Night*," *SQ* 36 (Spring 1985): 215–19.

Gilian West, "'Estridges that with the wind': A Note on *1 Henry IV*, IV.i., 97–100," *ES* 58 (April 1977): 20–22.

Gilian West, "A Glossary to the Language of Debt at the Climax of *1 Henry IV*," *N&Q* 36 (September 1989): 323–24.

Gilian West, "Scroop's Quarrel: A Note on *2 Henry IV*. IV.i., 88–96," *ELN* 18 (December 1981): 174–75.

Gilian West, "'Titan,' 'Onyers,' and Other Difficulties in the Text of *1 Henry IV*," *SQ* 3 (Summer 1983): 330–33.

V. Whitcombe, "*Henry IV, Part 1*," *The Use of English* 13 (Spring 1962): 178–83.

Reed Whitemore, "Shakespeare Yet," *Poetry Magazine* 92 (June 1958): 189–95.

Gayle Whittier, "Falstaff as a Welshwoman: Uncomic Androgyny," *BSUF* 20, no. 3 (1979): 23–35.

Michele Willems, "Misconstruction in *1 Henry IV*," *CahiersE* 37 (April 1990): 43–57.

Williams, *The Image of the City*, 40–42.

George Walton Williams, "Second Thoughts on Falstaff's Name," *SQ* 30 (Winter 1979): 82–84.

Robert F. Willson, Jr., "Falstaff in *1 Henry IV*: What's in a Name?" *SQ* 27 (Spring 1976): 199–200.

Elkin C. Wilson, "Falstaff—Clown and Man," in Bennett, Cargill and Hall, *Studies in the English Renaissance*, 345–56.

Paul Yachnin, "History, Theatricality, and the 'Structural Problem' in the *Henry IV* Plays," *PQ* 70 (Spring 1991): 163–79.

W. Gordon Zeeveld, "'Food for Powder'—'Food for Worms,'" *SQ* 3 (July 1952): 249–53.

S. P. Zitner, "Anon, Anon: Or a Mirror for a Magistrate," *SQ* 19 (Winter 1968): 63–70.

Henry V

Joanne Altieri, "Romance in *Henry V*," *SEL* 21 (Spring 1981): 223–40.

Joel B. Altman, "'Vile Participation': The Amplification of Violence in the Theatre of *Henry V*," *SQ* 42 (Winter 1991): 1–32.

William Babula, "Whatever Happened to Prince Hal? An Essay on *Henry V*," *ShS* 30 (1977): 47–59.

John Barnard, "The Murder of Falstaff, David Jones, and the 'Disciplines of War,'" Wellek and Ribeiro, *Evidence in Literary Scholarship*, 13–27.

F. W. Bateson, "A Table of Green Fields," *EIC* 7 (April 1957): 222–26.

Thomas L. Berger, "The Disappearance of Macmorris in Shakespeare's *Henry V*," *RenP* 1984 (1985): 13–26.

Edward I. Berry, "'True Things and Mock'ries': Epic and History in *Henry V*," *JEGP* 78 (1979): 1–16.

Philip Birkinshaw, "'A Little Touch of Harry in the Night': An Essay of Patriotism in *Henry V*," *ShSA* 3 (1989): 33–44.

James Black, "Shakespeare's *Henry V* and the Dreams of History," *ESC* 1 (Spring 1975): 13–30.

Philip E. Blank, Jr., "Pistol's 'taste of much correction' (*Henry V*, V.i.)," in Durant and Hester, *A Fair Day in the Affections*, 79–85.

Edyth Blumert, "Antechamber to Agincourt (A Study of Tempo in *Henry V*)," *WVUPP* 6 (January 1949): 22–30.

Haldeen Braddy, "The Flying Horse in *Henry V*," *SQ* 5 (Spring 1954): 205–07.

Phyllis N. Braxton, "Shakespeare's Merry Wives of Windsor and *Henry V*," *Expl* 48 (Fall 1989): 8–10.

Anthony S. Brennan, "That Within Which Passes Show: The Function of the Chorus in *Henry V*," *PQ* 58 (January 1979): 40–52.

Keith Brown, "Historical Context and *Henry V*," *CahiersE* 29 (April 1986): 77–81.

William J. Brown, "*Henry V* and Tamburlaine: The Structural and Thematic Relationship," *ISJR* 57 (December 1982): 113–22.

Cartelli, *Marlowe, Shakespeare*, 140–46.

Raymond Chapman, "The Wheel of Fortune in Shakespeare's Historical Plays," *RES* 1 (January 1950): 1–3, 5–6.

David Collins, "On Re-Interpreting *Henry V*," *UCrow* 4 (1982): 18–34.

Dorothy Cook, "*Henry V*: Maturing Man and Majesty," *SLitI* 5, no. 1 (1972): 111–28.

Krystian Czerniecki, "The Jest Digested: Perspectives on History in *Henry V*," in *On Puns: The Foundation of Letters*, ed. Jonathan Culler (Oxford: Blackwell, 1988), 62–82.

Jack D'Amico, "Moral and Political Conscience: Machiavelli and Shakespeare's *Macbeth* and *Henry V*," *IQ* 27 (Summer 1986): 31–41.

Lawrence Danson, "*Henry V*: King, Chorus, and Critics," *SQ* 34 (Winter 1983): 27–43

Davidson, *The Solace of Literature*, 102–05.

Jonathan Dollimore, and Alan Sinfield, "History and Ideology: The Instance of *Henry V*," in *Alternative Shakespeares*, ed. John Drakakis (London: Methuen, 1985), 206–27.

John W. Draper, "Falstaff, A Fool and Jester," *MLQ* 17 (December 1946): 453–62.

John W. Draper, "Falstaff's Death," *Baconiana* 40 (November 1956): 91–93.

Ellis-Fermor, *The Frontiers of Drama*, 42–47.

Peter B. Erickson, "'The Fault/My Father Made': The Anxious Pursuit of Heroic Fame in Shakespeare's *Henry V*," *MLS* 10 (Winter 1979–80): 10–25.

Robert F. Fleissner, "Falstaff's Green Sickness Unto Death," *SQ* 12 (Winter 1961): 47–55.

Allan Gilbert, "Patriotism and Satire in *Henry V*," *UMPEAL* 1 (March 1953): 40–64.

W. L. Godshalk, "*Henry V*'s Politics of Non-Responsibility," *CahiersE* 17 (April 1980): 11–20.

Stephen Greenblatt, "Invisible Bullets: Renaissance Authority and Its Subversion, *Henry IV* and *Henry V*," in Dollimore and Sinfield, *Political Shakespeare*, 18–47.

Andrew Gurr, "Why Captain Jamy in *Henry V*?" *Archiv* 226 (1989): 365–73.

Antony Hammond, "'It must be your imagination then': The Prologue and the Plural Texts in *Henry V* and Elsewhere," in Mahon and Pendleton, *"Fanned and winnowed opinions,"* 133–50.

Hawkins, *Likeness of Truth*, 63–64.

Highet, *The Powers of Poetry*, 13–14.

Martin Holmes, "A Heraldic Allusion in *Henry V*," *N&Q* 195 (August 1950): 333.

Leslie Hotson, "Ancient Pistol," *YR* 38 (September 1948): 51–66.

Houston, *Shakespeare's Sentences*, 72–75.

Hilda Hulme, "The 'Table of Green Fields,'" *EIC* 7 (January 1957): 117–19.

William B. Hunter, "Falstaff," *SAQ* 50 (January 1951): 86–95.

MacD. P. Jackson, "*Henry V* III.vi,181: An Emendation," *N&Q* 13 (April 1966): 133–34.

Paul A. Jorgensen, "The Courtship Scene in *Henry V*," *MLQ* 11 (June 1950): 180–88.

Paul A. Jorgensen, "Divided Command in Shakespeare," *PMLA* 70 (September 1955): 750–61.

Paul A. Jorgensen, "My Name is Pistol Call'd," *SQ* 1 (April 1950): 73–75.

J. Kleinstuck, "The Problem of Order in Shakespeare's Histories," *Neophil* 38 (October 1954): 268–73.

Knight, *The Olive and the Sword*, 29–40.

Koller, Katherine, "Falstaff and the Art of Dying," *MLN* 60 (June 1945): 383–86.

Ernst Kris, "Prince Hal's Conflict," *Psychoanalytic Quarterly* 17 (October 1948): 487–506.

John Laird, *Philosophical Incursions Into English Literature* (New York: Russell & Russell, 1946), 4–5, 18–20.

Eric La Guardia, "Ceremony and History: The Problem of Symbol from *Richard II* to *Henry V*," in McNeir and Greenfield, *Pacific Coast Studies in Shakespeare*, 68–88.

Robert Adger Law, "The Choruses in *Henry The Fifth*," *Studies in English* 35 (March 1956): 11–21.

Amy Lynch, "*Henry V*: Majesty and the Man," *UCrow* 4 (1982): 35–40.

Gina MacDonald, and Andrew MacDonald, "*Henry V*: A Shakespearean Definition of Politic Reign," *StHum* 9 (September 1982): 32–39.

Jean-Marie Maguin, "A Note on a Further Biblical Parallel with the Death of Falstaff (*Henry V*, II.3.23–7)," *CahiersE* 10 (April 1968): 65–66.

Jean-Marie Maguin, "Shakespeare's Structural Craft and Dramatic Technique in *Henry V*," *CahiersE* 7 (April 1965): 51–67.

J. C. Maxwell, "*Henry V*, II, ii, 17–29," *N&Q* 199 (May 1954): 195.

William G. McCollom, "Formalism and Illusion in Shakespeare's Drama," *QJS* 31 (December 1945): 446–47, 450–53.

A. A. Mendilow, "Falstaff's Death of a Sweat," *SQ* 9 (Autumn 1958): 479–83.

Peter Milward, "The Function of the Chorus in *Henry V*," *ShStud* 22 (1983–1984): 1–9.

John Robert Moore, "Shakespeare's *Henry V*," *Expl* 1 (June 1943): 61.

Muir, *Essays on Literature and Society*, 166–81.

Norman Nathan, "A Table of Green Fields," *N&Q* 204 (March 1959): 92–94.

Franklin B. Newman, "The Rejection of Falstaff and the Rigorous Charity of the King," *ShakS* 2 (1966): 153–61.

Newman, *Fashioning Feminity*, 95–108.

Nicholl, *The Chemical Theatre*, 236–38.

T. M. Parrott, "Fullness of Bread," *SQ* 3 (October 1952): 379–81.

Annabel Patterson, "Back by Popular Demand: The Two Versions of *Henry V*," *RenD* 19 (1988): 29–62.

Michael Platt, "Falstaff in the Valley of the Shadow of Death,"

Interpretations 8, no. 1 (1979): 5–29.

Jerrold Plotnick, "'Imaginary Puissance': The New Historicism and *Henry V*," *ESC* 17 (September 1991): 249–67.

Joseph A. Porter, "More Echoes from Eliot's Ortho-Epia Gallica, in *King Lear* and *Henry V*," *SQ* 37 (Winter 1986): 486–88.

Moody E. Prior, "Comic Theory and the Rejection of Falstaff," *ShakS* 9 (1976): 159–76.

Pye, *Royal Phantasm*, 13–42.

Norman Rabkin, "Rabbits, Ducks, and *Henry V*," *SQ* 28 (Summer 1977): 279–96.

E. A. Rauchut, "'Guilty in Defence': A Note on *Henry V*, 3.3.123," *SQ* 42 (Winter 1991): 55–57.

E. A. Rauchut, "The Traitor-Sentencing Scene (2.2) in Shakespeare's *Henry V*," *EA* 43 (September 1990): 414–17.

Ribner, *English History Play*, 181–91.

W. M. Richardson, "The Brave New World of Shakespeare's *Henry V* Revisited," *Allegorica* 6 (Winter 1981): 149–54.

Brownell Salomon, "Thematic Contraries and the Dramaturgy of *Henry V*," *SQ* 31 (Autumn 1980): 343–56.

James Schevill, "Towards a Rhythm of Comic Action," *Western Speech* 20 (Winter 1956): 5–8.

Helen J. Schwartz, "The Comic Scenes in *Henry V*," *HUSL* 4 (1976): 18–26.

Alice L. Scoufos, "The 'Martyrdom'of Falstaff," *ShakS* 2 (1966): 174–91.

Shapiro, *Rival Playwrights*, 84–86, 99–102.

Soellner, *Shakespeare's Patterns*, 113–28.

Monroe M. Stearns, "Shakespeare's *Henry V*," *Expl* 2 (December 1943): 19.

John M. Stedman, "Falstaff's 'Facies Hippocratica': A Note on Shakespeare and Renaissance Medical Theory," *SN* 29 (Summer 1957): 130–35.

Gary Taylor, "Shakespeare's Leno: *Henry V*, IV.v.14," *N&Q* 26 (January 1979): 117–18.

Mark Taylor, "Imitation and Perspective in *Henry V*," *CLIO* 16 (Fall 1986): 35–47.

Terrell L. Tebbetts, "Shakespeare's *Henry V*: Politics and the Family," *SCRev* 7 (Spring 1990): 8–19.

Leonard Tennenhouse, "Strategies of State and Political Plays: *A Midsummer Night's Dream, Henry IV, Henry V, Henry VIII*," in Dollimore and Sinfield, *Political Shakespeare*, 109–28.

Barbara H. Traister, "'I Will . . . Be Like a King': Henry V Plays Richard II," *CLQ* 26 (June 1990): 112–21.

E. M. Trehern, "The Death of Falstaff (*Henry V*, II.3.18f)," *CahiersE* 27 (April 1985): 83.

Tuckey John S. "'Table of Greene Fields' Explained," *EIC* 6 (October 1956): 486–91.

Peter Ure, "A Table of Green Fields," *EIC* 7 (April 1957): 223–24.

Van Lann, *The Idiom of Drama*, 156–58, 237–38.

Ayne C. Venanzio, "Pistol, the Mirror Image of *Henry V*," *SPWVSRA* 6 (1981): 21–26.

J. H. Walter, "With Sir John in it," *MLR* 41 (July 1946): 237–45.

Watson, *Shakespeare and the Hazards of Ambition*, 75–81.

Karl P. Wentersdorf, "The Conspiracy of Silence in *Henry V*," *SQ* 27 (Spring 1976): 264–87.

Allan Wilkinson, "A Note on *Henry V* Act IV," *RES* 1 (October 1950): 345–46.

Williams, *The Image of the City*, 40–42.

George W. Williams, "The Unity of Act V of *Henry V*," *SAB* 40 (March 1975): 3–9.

Philip Williams, "The Birth and Death of Falstaff Reconsidered," *SQ* 8 (Summer 1957): 359–65.

E. C. Wilson, "Falstaff-Clown and Man," in Bennett, Cargill, and Hall, *Studies in the English Renaissance Drama*, 345–56.

Rose A. Zimbardo, "The Formalism of *Henry V*," *CCP* 1 (1964): 16–24.

Henry VI Parts I, II, & III

David M. Bergeron, "The Play-within-the-Play in *3 Henry VI*," *TSL* 22 (Spring 1977): 37–45.

Ronald S. Berman, "Fathers and Sons in the *Henry VI* Plays," *SQ* 13 (Autumn 1962): 487–97.

Ronald S. Berman, "Power and Humility in Shakespeare," *SAQ* 60 (Fall 1961): 412–15.

Ronald S. Berman, "Shakespeare's Conscious Histories," *DR* 41 (Winter 1961/62): 485–95.

Berry, *Shakespearean Structures*, 15–17.

David M. Bevington, "The Domineering Female in *I Henry VI*," *ShakS* 2 (1966): 51–58.

Wayne L. Billings, "Ironic Lapses: Plotting in *Henry VI*," *SLitI* 5, no. 1 (1972): 27–49.

N. F. Blake, "Fume/Fury in *2 Henry VI*," *N&Q* 38 (March 1991): 49–51.

John W. Blanpied, "'Art and Baleful Sorcery': The Counterconsciousness of *Henry VI, Part I*," *SEL* 15 (Spring 1975): 213–27.

John W. Blanpied, "The *Henry VI* Plays: In Pursuit of the Ground," *SUS* 10 (1978): 197–209.

J. P. Brockbank, "The Frame of Disorder: *Henry VI*," *Stratford-Upon-Avon Studies* 3 (1961): 73–100.

Brockbank, *On Shakespeare*, 80–103.

Bullough, *Mirror of Minds*, 51–53.

Sigurd Burckhardt, "'I Am But Shadow of Myself': Ceremony and Design in *I Henry VI*," *MLQ* 28 (March 1967): 139–58.

Andrew S. Cairncross, "An Inconsistency in *3 Henry VI*," *MLR* 50 (October 1955): 492–94.

James L. Calderwood, "Shakespeare's Evolving Imagery: *2 Henry VI*," *ES* 48 (December 1968): 481–93.

Virginia M. Carr, "Animal Imagery in *2 Henry VI*," *ES* 53 (October 1972): 408–12.

Larry S. Champion, "'Prologue to Their Play': Shakespeare's Structural Progress in *2 Henry VI*," *TSLL* 19 (Summer 1977): 294–312.

Wolfgang H. Clemen, "Anticipation and Foreboding in Shakespeare's Early Histories," *ShS* 6 (1953): 25–26.

Clemen, *Shakespeare's Dramatic Art*, 18–25.

Wolfgang H. Clemen, "Some Aspects of Style in the *Henry VI* Plays," in Edwards, Ewbank, and Howard, *Shakespeare's Style*, 9–24.

Cox, *Shakespeare and the Dramaturgy of Power*, 82–103.

John D. Cox, "*3 Henry VI*: Dramatic Convention and the Shakespearean History Play," *CompD* 12 (Spring 1978): 42–60.

Cunningham, *Woe or Wonder*, 54–55.

Paul Dean, "Shakespeare's *Henry VI* Trilogy and Elizabethan 'Romance' Histories: The Origins of a Genre," *SQ* 33 (Winter 1982): 34–48.

John W. Draper, "The 'Turk' in *Henry VI, Part 1*," *WVUPP* 10 (January 1956): 37–39.

Arthur Freeman, "Notes on the Text of *2 Henry VI*, and the 'Upstart Crow,'" *N&Q* 15 (April 1968): 128–30.

Stephen Greenblatt, "Murdering Peasants: Status, Genre, and the Representation of Rebellion," in *Representing the English Renaissance*, 1–29.

Michael Hattaway, "Rebellion, Class Consciousness, and Shakespeare's *2 Henry VI*," *CahiersE* 33 (April 1988): 13–22.

Hibbard, *Making of Shakespeare's Dramatic Poetry*, 62–71, 78–82.

Houston, *Shakespearean Sentences*, 22–27.

John E. Jordan, "The Reporter of *Henry VI, Part 2*," *PMLA* 66 (December 1949): 1089–113.

Kastan, *Shakespeare and the Shapes of Time*, 12–25.

Carol McG. Kay, "Traps, Slaughter, and Chaos: A Study of Shakespeare's *Henry VI* Plays," *SLitI* 5, no. 1 (1972): 1–26.

Knight, *The Olive and the Sword*, 4–11.

Knight, *The Sovereign Flower*, 14–23.

Ronald Knowles, "The Farce of History: Miracle, Combat, and Rebellion in *2 Henry VI*," *YES* 21 (1991): 168–86.

Michael Manheim, "Duke Humphrey and the Machiavels," *ABR* 23 (September 1972): 249–57.

John T. Marvin, "The Nature of Causation in the History Plays," in Bailey, *Ashland Studies for Shakespeare 1962*, 43–50.

McDonnell, *The Aspiring Mind*, 176–87.

Thomas H. McNeal, "Margaret of Anjou: Romantic Princess and Troubled Queen," *SQ* 9 (Winter 1958): 1–10.

Waldo F. McNeir, "Comedy in Shakespeare's Yorkist Tetralogy," *PCP* 9 (March 1974): 48–55.

Giorgio Melchiori, "The Role of Jealousy: Restoring the Q Reading of *2 Henry VI*, Induction, 16," *SQ* 34 (Summer 1983): 327–30.

M. Mincoff, "The Composition of *Henry VI, Part 1*," *SQ* 16 (Spring 1965): 279–87.

M. Mincoff, "*Henry VI, Part Three* and *The True Tragedy*," *ES* 42 (October 1961): 273–88.

P. G. Nilsson, "The Upstart Crow and Henry VI," *Moderna Sprak* 58 (1964): 293–303.

Betty G. Norvell, "The Dramatic Portrait of Margaret in Shakespeare's *Henry VI* Plays," *BWVACET* 8 (Spring 1983): 38–44.

Robert A. Ravich, "A Psychoanalytic Study of Shakespeare's Early Plays," *Psychoanalytic Quarterly* 33 (July 1964): 393–95.

Ribner, *The English History Play in the Age of Shakespeare*, 96–116.

James A. Riddell, "Talbot and the Countess of Auvergne," *SQ* 28 (1977): 51–57.

Nicole Rowan, "Shakespeare's *Henry VI*-Trilogy: A Reconsideration: Presented to Professor Willem Schrickx on the Occasion of His Retirement," in *Elizabethan and Modern Studies*, ed. J. P. Vander Motten (Ghent: Rijksuniversiteit Gent, 1985), 191–202.

Peter Saccio, "Images of History in *3 Henry VI*," *ShakB* 2 (March–April 1984): 13–20.

Shapiro, *Rival Playwrights*, 86–95.

Alan R. Smith, and Karen T. Morris, "Shakespeare's *Henry VI, Part III*," *Expl* 41 (Summer 1983): 3–5.

Tillyard, *Essays Literary and Educational*, 39–46.

E. M. W. Tillyard, "Shakespeare's Historical Cycle: Orqanism or Compilation?" *SP* 51 (January 1954): 34–39.

J. J. M. Tobin, "Shakespeare and Apuleius," *N&Q* 25 (April 1978): 120–21.

Raymond V. Utterback, "Public Men, Private Wills, and Kingship in *Henry VI, Part III*," *RenP* 1977 (1978): 47–54.

Roger Warren, "'Contrarieties Agree': An Aspect of Dramatic Technique in *Henry VI*," *ShS* 37 (1984): 75–83.

Donald G. Watson, "The Dark Comedy of the *Henry VI* Plays," *Thalia* 1 (Fall–Winter 1978): 11–21.

Gwyn Williams, "Suffolk and Margaret: A Study of Some Sections of Shakespeare's *Henry VI*," *SQ* 25 (Summer 1974): 310–22.

Marilyn L. Williamson, "The Courtship of Katherine and the Second Tetralogy," *Criticism* 17 (1975): 326–34.

Donald R. Wineke, "The Relevance of Machiavelli to Shakespeare: A Discussion of *1 Henry VI*," *CLIO* 13 (Fall 1983): 17–36.

D. J. Womersley, "*3 Henry VI*: Shakespeare, Tacitus, and Parricide," *N&Q* 32 (December 1985): 468–73.

Henry VIII
(with Fletcher)

Iska Alter, "'To reform and make fitt': *Henry VIII* and the Making of 'Bad' Shakespeare," in Charney, *"Bad" Shakespeare*, 176–86.

Eckhard Auberlen, "*King Henry VIII*: Shakespeare's Break with the 'Bluff-King-Harry' Tradition," *Anglia* 98, no. 3 (1980): 319–47.

William M. Baillie, "*Henry VIII*: A Jacobean History," *ShakS* 12 (1979): 247–66.

Ronald Berman, "*King Henry the Eighth*: History and Romance," *ES* 48 (February 1967): 112–21.

Paul Bertram, "*Henry VIII*: The Conscience of the King," in Bower, *In Defense of Reading*, 153–73.

Lee Bliss, "The Wheel of Fortune and the Maiden Phoenix of Shakespeare's *King Henry VIII*," *ELH* 42 (1975): 1–25.

Rick Bowers, "Shakespeare's *Henry VIII*, II.i.62–68, 124–31," *Expl* 44 (Winter 1986): 10–12.

Robin Bowers, "'The merciful construction of good women': Katherine of Aragon and Pity in Shakespeare's *King Henry*," *C&L* 37 (Spring 1988): 29–51.

Joseph Candido, "Katherine of Aragon and Female Greatness: Shakespeare's Debt to Dramatic Tradition," *ISJR* 54 (July 1980): 491–98.

Frank V. Cespedes, "'We are one in fortunes': The Sense of History in *Henry VIII*," *ELR* 10 (1980): 413–38.

Janct Clare, "Beneath Pomp and Circumstance in *Henry VIII*," *ShStud* 21 (1982–1983): 65–81.

John D. Cox, "*Henry VIII* and the Masque," *ELH* 45 (1978): 390–409.

Cunningham, *Woe or Wonder*, 52–54.

John P. Cutts, "Shakespeare's Song and Masque Hand in *Henry VIII*," *ShJE* 99 (1963): 184–95.

Paul Dean, "Dramatic Mode and Historical Vision in *Henry VIII*," *SQ* 37 (1986): 175–89.

E. E. Duncan-Jones, "Queen Katherine's Vision and Queen Margaret's Dream," *N&Q* 206 (April 1961): 142–43.

Howard Felperin, "Shakespeare's *Henry VIII*: History as Myth," *SEL* 6 (Spring 1966): 225–46,

Foakes, *Shakespeare*, 173–83.

Bernard Harris, "'What's past is prologue': *Cymbeline* and *Henry VIII*," in *Later Shakespeare*, ed. John R. Brown and Bernard Harris (London: Arnold; New York: St. Martin's, 1966), 203–34.

Mary E. Hazard, "'Order Gave Each Thing View': 'Shows, Pageants and Sights of Honour' in *King Henry VIII*," *W&I* 3 (January 1987): 95–103.

Howarth, *The Tiger's Heart*, 159–63.

Kastan, *Shakespeare and the Shapes of Time*, 133–41.

Knight, *The Crown of Life*, 256–336.

Knight, *The Olive and the Sword*, 76–85.

Knight, *The Sovereign Flower*, 80–87:

Stuart M. Kurland, "*Henry VIII* and James I: Shakespeare and Jacobean Politics," *ShS* 19 (1991): 203–18.

John Loftis, "*Henry VIII* and Calderon's *La cisma de Inglaterra*," *CL* 34 (Summer 1982): 208–22.

John Loftis, *Renaissance Drama in England and Spain*, 8–11, 20–24.

Tom McBride, "*Henry VIII* as Machiavellian Romance," *JEGP* 76 (1977): 26–39.

Thomas Merriam, "New Light on *Henry VIII*," *ShN* 30 (May 1980): 20.

Linda McJ. Micheli, "'Sit by Us': Visual Imagery and the Two Queens in *Henry VIII*," *SQ* 38 (Winter 1987): 452–66.

Kim H. Noling, "Grubbing Up the Stock: Dramatizing Queens in *Henry VIII*," *SQ* 39 (1988): 291–306.

Ants Oras, "'Extra Monosyllables' in *Henry VIII* and the Problem of Authorship," *JEGP* 52 (April 1953): 198–213.

Alexander A. Parker, "*Henry VIII* in Shakespeare and Calderone," *MLR* 43 (July 1948): 327–52.

Hugh M. Richmond, "The Feminism of Shakespeare's *Henry VIII*," *ELWIU* 6 (Spring 1979): 11–20.

Peter L. Rudnytsky, "*Henry VIII* and the Deconstruction of History," *ShS* 43 (1991): 43–57.

F. Schreiber-McGee, "'The view of earthly glory': Visual Strategies and the Issue of Royal Prerogative in *Henry VIII*," *ShakS* 20 (1987): 191–200.

Anne Shaver, "Structure and Ceremony: A Case for Unity in *King Henry VIII*," *SPWVSRA* 2 (1977): 1–23.

Camille Wells Slights, "The Politics of Conscience in All Is True (or *Henry VIII*)," *ShS* 43 (1991): 59–68.

Leonard Tennenhouse, "Strategies of State and Political Plays: A *Midsummer Night's Dream, Henry IV, Henry VI, Henry VIII*," in Dollimore and Sinfield, *Political Shakespeare*, 109–28.

Tillyard, *Essays Literary and Educational*, 47–54.

Robert W. Uphaus, "History, Romance, and *Henry VIII*," *ISJR* 53 (February 1979): 177–83.

White, *Antiquity Forgot*, 74–87.

Glynne Wickham, "The Dramatic Structure of Shakespeare's *King Henry the Eighth*: An Essay in Rehabilitation," *PBA* 70 (1984): 149–66.

H. R. Woudhuysen, "*King Henry VIII* and 'All Is True,'" *N&Q* 31 (June 1984): 217–18.

Alan R. Young, "Shakespeare's *Henry VIII* and the Theme of Conscience," *ESC* 7 (Spring 1981): 38–53.

Julius Caesar

Paul J. Aldus, "Analogical Probability in Shakespeare's Plays," *SQ* 6 (Autumn 1955): 401–02.

John Alvis, "A Probable Platonic Allusion and Its Significance in Shakespeare's *Julius Caesar*," *UCrow* 2 (1979): 64–73,

John Anson, "*Julius Caesar*: The Politics of the Hardened Heart," *ShakS* 2 (1966): 11–33.

Arthos, *Shakespeare's Use of Dream and Vision*, 111–35.

Barbara J. Baines, "Political and Poetic Revisionism in *Julius Caesar*," *UCrow* 10 (1990): 42–54.

J. Leeds Barroll, "The Characterization of Otavius," *ShakS* 6 (1970): 231–88.

Anne Barton, "*Julius Caesar* and *Coriolanus*: Shakespeare's Roman World of Words," in Highfill, *Shakespeare's Craft*, 24–47.

A. Jonathan Bate, "The Cobbler's Awl: *Julius Caesar*, I.i.21–24," *SQ* 35 (1984): 461–62.

Ralph Berry, "*Julius Caesar*: A Roman Tragedy," *DR* 61 (Autumn 1981): 325–36.

John Bligh, "Cicero's Choric Comment in *Julius Caesar*," *ESC* 8 (1982): 391–408.

Jan H. Blits, "Manliness and Friendship in Shakespeare's *Julius Caesar*," *IJPP* 9 (September 1981): 155–67.

William R. Bowden, "The Mind of Brutus," *SQ* 17 (1966): 57–67.

Brockbank, *On Shakespeare*, 122–39, 143–47.

Bernard R. Breyer, "A New Look at *Julius Caesar*," *VSH* 2 (1954): 161–80.

J. A. Bryant, Jr. "*Julius Ceasar* from a Euripidean Perspective," *CompD* 16 (Summer 1982): 97–111.

John Russell Brown, "Shakespeare's Subtext: 1," *TDR* 8 (Fall 1963): 78–94.

Sigurd Burckhardt, "How Not to Murder Caesar," *CentR* 11 (1967): 141–56.

Burke, *Perspectives by Incongruity*, 64–75.

Kenneth Burke, "Antony in Behalf of the Play," in *The Philosophy of Literary Form*, 279–90. Reprinted in Schorer, *Criticism*, 533–38.

Richard A. Burt, "'A Dangerous Rome': Shakespeare's *Julius Caesar* and the Discursive Determinism of Cultural Politics," in *Contending Kingdoms: Historical, Psychological and Feminist Approaches to the Literature of Sixteenth-Century England and France*, ed. Marie-Rose Logan and Peter L. Rudnytsky (Detroit: Wayne State University Press, 1991), 109–27.

Alex Capelle, "The Misadventures of Julius Caesar," *CahiersE* 24 (October 1983): 33–45.

David L. Carson, "The Dramatic Importance of Prodigies in *Julius Caesar*, Act II, Scene 1," *ELN* 2 (March 1965): 177–80.

Maurice Charney, "Shakespeare's Style in *Julius Caesar* and *Antony and Cleopatra*," *ELH* 26 (September 1959): 355–67.

Thomas Clayton, "'Should Brutus Never Taste of Portia's Death But Once?' Text and Performance in *Julius Caesar*," *SEL* 23 (Spring 1983): 237–55.

Clemen, *Shakespeare's Dramatic Art*, 49–60.

John W. Crawford, "The Religious Question in *Julius Caesar*," *SoQ* 15 (June 1977): 297–302.

E. L. Dachslager, "'The Most Unkindest Cut': A Note on *Julius Caesar* III.ii.187," *ELN* 11 (March 1974): 258–59.

Lynn de Gerenday, "Play, Ritualization, and Ambivalence in *Julius Caesar*," *L&P* 24, no. 1 (1974): 24–33.

Doran, *Shakespeare's Dramatic Language*, 120–53.

John Roland Dove, and Peter Gamble, "'Lovers in Peace,' Brutus and Cassius: A Re-Examination," *ES* 60 (1979): 543–54.

John W. Draper, "The Speech Tempo of Brutus and Cassius," *Neophil* 30 (October 1946): 184–86.

Mildred O. Durham, "Drama of the Dying God in *Julius Caesar*," *HSL* 11, no. 1 (1979): 49–57.

Henry Ebel, "Caesar's Wounds: A Study of William Shakespeare," *PsyR* 62, no. 2 (1975): 107–30.

Ellis-Fermor, *The Frontiers of Drama*, 48–50.

Roy T. Eriksen, "Extant and in Choice Italian: Possible Italian Echoes in *Julius Caesar* and Sonnet 78," *ES* 69 (1988): 224–37.

Harold Feldman, "Unconscious Envy in Brutus," *AI* 9 (Fall–Winter 1952): 307–35.

Robert F. Fleissner, "'Non sanz droirt': Law and 'Heraldry' in *Julius Caesar*," *HSL* 9, no. 3 (1977): 196–212.

Robert F. Fleissner, "That Philosophy in *Julius Caesar* Again," *Archiv* 222 (1985): 344–45.

P. Jeffrey Ford, "Bloody Spectacle in Shakespeare's Roman Plays: The Politics and Aesthetics of Violence," *ISJR* 54 (1980): 481–89.

Roland M. Frye, "Rhetoric and Poetry in *Julius Caesar*," *QJS* 37 (February 1951): 41–48.

Jean A. Fuzier, "Rhetorio versus Rhetoric: A Study of Shakespeare's *Julius Caesar*," *CahiersE* 25 (April 1974): 25–65.

René Girard, "Collective Violence and Sacrifice in Shakespeare's *Julius Caesar*," *Salmagundi* 88–89 (1990–1991): 399–419.

Gayle Greene, "The Language of Brutus' Soliloquy: Similitude and Self-Deception in Shakespeare's *Julius Caesar*," in *Humanitas: Essays in Honor of Ralph Ross*, ed. Quincey Howe, Jr. (Claremont, CA: Scripps College 1977), 74–86.

Gayle Greene, "'The Power of Speech to Stir Men's Blood': The Language of Tragedy in Shakespeare's *Julius Caesar*," *RenD* 11 (1980): 67–93.

James J. Greene, "A Contemporary Approach to Two Shakespearean Tragedies," in Quinn, *How to Read Shakespearean Tragedy*, 355–85.

Augusto Guidi, "'Creature' in Shakespeare," *N&Q* 197 (October 1952): 443–44.

Hager, *Shakespeare's Political Animal*, 51–63.

Alan Hager, "'The Teeth of Emulation': Failed Sacrifice in Shakespeare's *Julius Caesar*," *UCrow* 8 (1988): 54–68.

Jay L. Halio, "Hamartia, Brutus, and the Failure of Personal Confrontation," *Person* 48, no. 1 (1967): 42–55.

Vernon Hall, Jr., "*Julius Caesar*: A Play Without Political Bias," in Bennett, Cargill, and Hall, *Studies in English Renaissance Drama*, 106–24.

Hallett and Hallett, *Analyzing Shakespeare's Action*, 42–46, 127–28, 171–75, 196–97, 310–34.

H. George Han, "The Orchard and the Street: The Political Mirror of the Tragic in *Julius Caesar* and *Coriolanus*," *CLAJ* 27 (June 1983): 169–86.

Robert Hapgood, "Speak Hands for Me: Gesture as Language in *Julius Caesar*," *DramS* 5 (August 1966): 162–70.

Mildred E. Hartsock, "The Complexity of *Julius Caesar*," *PMLA* 81 (January 1966): 56–62.

Burton Hatlen, "A World without Absolutes: Dialectic in Shakespeare's *Julius Caesar*," *PPMRC* 3 (1978): 167–82.

Harriet Hawkins, "Likeness with Difference: Patterns of Action in *Romeo and Juliet, Julius Caesar*, and *Macbeth*," *MEJ* 6, no. 2 (1968): 1–13

Hawkins, *Likeness of Truth*, 144–51.

Hawkins, *Poetic Freedom and Poetic Truth*, 12–13.

Richard M. Haywood, "Shakespeare and the Old Roman," *CE* 16 (November 1954): 98–101, 151.

Robert B. Heilman, "To Know Himself: An Aspect of Tragic Structure," *REL* 5 (April 1964): 39–43.

Norman N. Holland, "The 'Anna' and 'Cynicke' Episodes in *Julius Caesar*," *SQ* 11 (Autumn 1960): 439–44.

Joseph W. Houppert, "Fatal Logic in *Julius Caesar*," *SAB* 39 (November 1974): 10–21.

F. C. Hunt, "Shakespeare's Delineation of the Passion of Anger," *Baconiana* 29 (October 1945): 136–41.

Jepsen, *Ethical Aspects of Tragedy*, 111–16.

R. T. Jones, "Shakespeare's *Julius Caesar*," *Theoria* 12 (1959): 41–50.

Paul A. Jorgensen, "Divided Command in Shakespeare," *PMLA* 70 (September 1955): 750–61.

Mark Kanzer, "Shakespeare's Dog Images: Hidden Keys to *Julius Caesar*," *AI* 36 (Spring 1979): 2–31.

David Kaula, " 'Let Us Be Sacrificers': Religious Motifs in *Julius Caesar*," *ShakS* 14 (1981): 197–14.

John R. Kayser, and Ronald J. Lettieri, " 'The Last of All the Romans': Shakespeare's Commentary on Classical Republicanism," *CLIO* 9 (Spring 1980): 197–227.

Leo Kirschbaum, "Shakespere's Stage Blood and its Critical Significance," *PMLA* 64 (June 1949): 519–24.

Knight, *The Imperial Theme*, 32–95.

G. W. Knight, "Brutus and Macbeth," in *The Wheel of Fire*, 120–39.

L. C. Knights, "Shakespeare and Political Wisdom: A Note on the Personalism of *Julius Caesar* and *Coriolanus*," *SR* 61 (Winter 1953): 43–55.

Naomi Conn Liebler, " 'Thou Bleeding Piece of Earth': The Ritual Ground of *Julius Caesar*," *ShakS* 14 (1981): 175–96.

Thomas McAlindon, "The Numbering of Men and Days: Symbolic Design in The Tragedy of *Julius Caesar*," *SP* 81 (1984): 372–93.

McDonnell, *The Aspiring Mind*, 232–46.

G. Harold Metz, "A Stylometric Comparison of Shakespeare's *Titus Andronicus*, *Pericles*, and *Julius Caesar*," *ShN* 29 (January 1979): 42.

Anthony Miller, "The Roman State in *Julius Caesar* and Sejanus," in Donaldson, *Jonson and Shakespeare*, 179–201.

Robert S. Miola, "*Julius Caesar* and the Tyrannicide Debate," *RenQ* 38 (1985): 271–89.

Ann Molan, "*Julius Caesar*: The General Good and the Singular Case," *CR* 26 (1984): 84–100.

Nancy Moore, "The Stoicism of Brutus and the Structure of *Julius Caesar*," *SPWVSRA* 8 (1983): 29–37.

Edward Tetsuya Motatashi, " 'The Suburbs of Your Good Pleasure': Theatre and Liberties in *Julius Caesar*," *ShakS* 26 (1988): 41–75.

Robert D. Moynihan, "Stars, Portents, and Order in *Julius Caesar*," *MLS* 7 (Spring 1977): 26–31.

Norman Nathan, "Flavius Leases his Audience," *N&Q* 1 (April 1954): 149–50.

Nuttall, *A New Mimesis*, 105–13.

Yasuhiro Ogawa, " 'Sacred Blood': An Essay on *Julius Caesar*," *Lang&C* 20 (1991): 17–32.

Martin R. Orkin, "A Cluster of Proverb Allusions in *Julius Caesar*," *N&Q* 31 June 1984): 195–96.

Avraham Oz, "*Julius Caesar* and the Prophetic Mind," *Assaph* 1, no. 1, part C (1984): 28–39.

Barbara L. Parker, " 'This Monstrous Apparition': The Role of Perception in *Julius Caesar*," *BSUF* 16, no. 3 (1975): 70–77.

Gail Kern Paster, " 'In the Spirit of Men There Is No Blood': Blood as Trope of Gender in *Julius Caesar*," *SQ* 40 (Spring 1989): 284–98.

Vincent F. Petronella, "Dramatic Conjuring in Shakespeare's *Julius Caesar*," *DR* 57 (1977): 130–40.

G. M. Pinciss, "Rhetoric as Character: The Forum Speeches in *Julius Caesar*," *UCrow* 4 (1982): 113–21.

Beryl Pogson, *In the East My Pleasure Lies*, 119–20.

Thomas Pughe, " 'What should the wars do with these jigging fools?' The Poets in Shakespeare's *Julius Caesar*," *ES* 69 (1988)): 313–22.

Norman Rabkin, "Structure, Convention, and Meaning in *Julius Caesar*," *JEGP* 63 (April 1964): 240–54.

Carmen Rogers, "Heavenly Justice in the Tragedies of Shakespeare," *UMPEAL* 1 (March 1953): 116–28.

Clifford J. Ronan, "Shakespeare's *Julius Caesar*, I.i.51," *Expl* 42 (Fall 1983): 11–12.

James U. Rundle, "Shakespeare's *Julius Caesar*, IV.iii.21–24," *Expl* 41 (Fall 1983): 5–6.

Mark Sacharoff, "Suicide and Brutus' Philosophy in *Julius Caesar*," *JHI* 33 (April 1972): 115–22.

Norman Sanders, "The Shift of Power in *Julius Caesar*," *REL* 5 (April 1964): 24–35.

Ernest Schanzer, "The Problem of *Julius Caesar*," *SQ* 6 (Summer 1955): 297–308.

Ernest Schanzer, "The Tragedy of Shakespeare's Brutus," *ELH* 22 (March 1955): 1–15.

Elias Schwartz, "On the Quarrel Scene in *Julius Caesar*," *CE* 19 (January 1958): 169–70.

Shapiro, *Rival Playwrights*, 122–25.

Shaw, *Plays and Players*, 290–99.

Carol Marks Sicherman, "Short Lines and Interpretation: The Case of *Julius Caesar*," *SQ* 35 (1984): 180–95.

Alan R. Smith, "Shakespeare's *Julius Caesar*," *Expl* 42 (Fall 1984): 9–10.

Gordon Ross Smith, "Brutus, Virtue, and Will," *SQ* 10 (Summer 1959): 367–79.

Warren D. Smith, "The Duplicate Revelation of Portia's Death," *SQ* 4 (April 1953): 153–61.

Soellner, *Shakespeare's Patterns*, 150–71.

Michael G. Southwell, "Dawn in Brutus' Orchard," *ELN* 5 (September 1967): 91–98.

G. A. Starr, "Caesar's Just Cause," *SQ* 17 (Winter 1966): 77–79.

J. I. M. Stewart, "*Julius Caesar* and *Macbeth*: Two Notes on Shakespearean Technique," *MLR* 40 (July 1945): 166–71.

Brents Stirling, "Brutus and the Death of Portia," *SQ* 10 (Spring 1959): 211–17.

Shigeki Takada, "Calls and Silence: Style of Distance in *Julius Caesar*," *ShStud* 23 (1984–1985): 1–37.

Terrence N. Tice, "Calphurnia's Dream and Communication with the Audience in Shakespeare's *Julius Caesar*," *ShY* 1 (1990): 37–49.

J. J. M. Tobin, "Apuleius and the Proscription Scene in *Julius Caesar*," *Archiv* 216 (1979): 348–50.

William B. Toole, "The Cobbler, the Disrobed Image and the Motif of Movement in *Julius Caesar*," *UCrow* 4 (1982): 41–55.

Peter Ure, "Character and Role from *Richard III* to *Hamlet*," *Stratford-Upon-Avon Studies* 5 (1963): 9–13.

Marvin L. Vawter, "'After Their Fashion': Cicero and Brutus in *Julius Caesar*," *ShakS* 9 (1976): 205–20.

Marvin L. Vawter, "'Division 'tween Our Souls': Shakespeare's Stoic Brutus," *ShakS* 7 (194): 173–96.

John W. Velz, "Episodic Structure in Four Tudor Plays: A Virtue of Necessity," *CompD* 6 (Summer 1972): 87–102.

John W. Velz, "Orator and Imperator in *Julius Caesar*: Style and the Process of Roman History," *ShakS* 15 (1982): 55–75.

John W. Velz, and Sarah C. Velz. "Publius, Mark Anthony's Sister's Son," *SQ* 26 (Winter 1975): 69–74.

Alexnader Welsh, "Brutus Is an Honorable Man," *YR* 64 (December 1975): 496–513.

Andrew M. Wilkinson, "A Psychological Approach to *Julius Caesar*," *REL* 7 (October 1966): 65–78.

George Walton Williams, "Antique Romans and Modern Danes in *Julius Caesar* and *Hamlet*," in Newey and Thompson, *Literature and Nationalism*, 41–55.

Robert F. Willson, Jr. "*Julius Caesar*: The Forum Scene as Historic Play-Within," *ShY* 1 (1990): 14–27.

King John

Dean R. Baldwin, "Style in Shakespeare's *King John*," *Lang&S* 16 (Winter 1983): 64–76.

Jonas Barish, "*King John* and Oath Breach," in Fabian and von Rosador, *Shakespeare: Text, Language, Criticism*, 1–18.

Roy Battenhouse, "*King John*: Shakespeare's Perspective and Others," *NDEJ* 14 (Summer 1982): 191–215.

Roy Battenhouse, "Religion in *King John*: Shakespeare's View," *Connotations* 1 (July 1991): 140–49.

Ronald Berman, "Anarchy and Order in *Richard III* and *King John*," *ShS* 20 (1967): 51–59.

E. G. Bierhaus, Jr., "Shakespeare's *King John*," *Expl* 38 (Spring 1979):19.

Gunnar Boklund, "The Troublesome Ending to *King John*," *SN* 40 (Summer 1968): 175–84.

Adrien Bonjour, "Bastinado for the Bastard?" *ES* 45 (Supplement) (1964): 169–76.

Adrien Bonjour, "The Road to Swinstead Abbey: A Study of the Sense and Structure of *King John*," *ELH* 18 (December 1951): 253–74.

Sigurd Burckhardt, "*King John*: The Ordering of This Present Time," *ELH* 33 (1966): 133–15.

Sidney C. Burgoyne, "Cardinal Pandulph and the 'Curse of Rome,'" *ColL* 4 (Summer 1977): 232–40.

James L. Calderwood, "Commodity and Honour in *King John*," *UTQ* 29 (April 1960): 341–56.

Wolfgang H. Clemen, "Anticipation and Foreboding in Shakespeare's Early Histories," *ShS* 6 (1953): 31–33.

Clemen, *Shakespeare's Dramatic Art*, 104–05.

Edwards, *Threshold of a Nation*, 115–22.

Eamon Grennan, "Shakespeare's Satirical History: A Reading of *King John*," *ShakS* 11 (1978): 21–37.

Hibbard, *Making of Shakespeare's Dramatic Poetry*, 133–43.

David P. Hirvela, "Structural Unity in *King John*: A State History Perspective," *ISJR* 58 (April 1984): 289–98.

David P. Hirvela, "What the Gardener Knew: Pruning and Power in *The Troublesome Raigne of King John* and *Richard II*," *JRMMRA* 9 (January 1988): 117–29.

Houston, *Shakespearean Sentences*, 52–55.

Kastan, *Shakespeare and the Shapes of Time*, 51–54.

Knight, *The Olive and the Sword*, 12–16.

Knight, *The Sovereign Flower*, 25–29.

Alexander Leggatt, "Dramatic Perspective in *King John*," *ESC* 3 (1977): 1–17.

Carole Levin, " 'I Trust I May Not Trust Thee': Women's Visions of the World in Shakespeare's *King John*," in Levin and Watson, *Ambiguous Realities*, 219–34.

Loftis, *Renaissance Drama in England and Spain*, 74–80.

John Trumbell Marvin, "The Nature of Causation in the History Plays," in Bailey, *Ashland Studies for Shakespeare 1962*, 56–61.

J. C. Maxwell, "*King John*—Textual Notes," *N&Q* 195 (October 1950): 473–74.

James E. May, "Imagery of Disorderly Motion in *King John*: A Thematic Gloss," *ELWIU* 10 (Spring 1983): 17–28.

William G. McCollom, "Formalism and Illusion in Shakespeare's Drama," *QJS* 31 (December 1945): 446–50.

R. W. McConchie, "Shakespeare's *King John*, I.i.231," *Expl* 40 (Fall 1981): 7–9.

E. C. Pettet, "Hot Irons and Fever: A Note on Some of the Imagery of *King John*," *EIC* 4 (April 1954): 128–44.

John Sibly, "The Anonmalous Case of *King John*," *ELH* 33 (1966): 415–21.

Robert D. Stevick, "'Repentant Ashes': The Matrix of Shakespearian Poetic Language," *SQ* 13 (Summer 1962): 366–70.

Sidney Thomas, "'Enter a Sheriff': Shakespeare's King John and *The Troublesome Raigne*," *SQ* 37 (1986): 98–100.

Jacqueline Trace, "Shakespeare's Bastard Faulconbridge: An Early Tudor Hero," *ShakS* 13 (1980): 59–69.

Julia C. Van de Water, "The Bastard in *King John*," *SQ* 11 (Spring 1960): 137–46.

White, *Antiquity Forgot*, 44–73.

Wiggins, *Journeymen in Murder*, 92–94.

Douglas C. Wixson, "'Calm Words Folded Up in Smoke': Propaganda and Spectator Response in Shakespeare's *King John*," *ShakS* 14 (1981): 111–27.

David Womersley, "The Politics of Shakespeare's *King John*," *RES* 40 (December 1989): 497–515.

King Lear

K. M. Abenheimer, "On Narcissism - Including an Analysis of *King Lear*," *BJMP* 20 (1945): 322–29.

Robert P. Adams, "King Lear's Revenges," *MLQ* 21 (1960): 223–27.

Doris Adler, "The Half-Life of Tate in *King Lear*," *KR* 47 (Summer 1985): 52–56.

Sohail Ahsan, "*King Lear*—the Unresolved Tension," *AJES* 13 (July 1988): 125–51.

D. M. Anderson, "A Conjecture on *King Lear* IV, ii, 57," *N&Q* 199 (August 1954): 331.

Judith H. Anderson, "The Conspiracy of Realism: Impasse and Vision in *King Lear*," *SP* 84 (Winter 1987): 1–23.

Michael Cameron Andrews, "Lear's Wheel of Fire and Centaur Daughters," *RenP 1964* (1965): 21–24.

A. A. Ansari, "*King Lear*: The Vision of Horror," *AJES* 8 (October 1983): 205–22.

Iffat Ara, "Edmund the Bastard in *King Lear*," *AJES* 13 (July 1988): 152–70.

Carolyn Asp, "'The Clamor of Eros': Freud, Aging, and *King Lear*," in *Memory and Desire: Aging - Literature - Psychoanalysis*, ed. Kathleen Woodward and Murray M. Schwartz (Bloomington: Indiana University Press, 1986), 192–204.

Norman R. Atwood, "Cordelia and Kent: Their Fateful Choice of Style," *Lang&S* 9 (Winter 1974): 42–54.

William B. Bache, "Lear as Old Man—Father—King," *CLAJ* 19 (March 1975): 1–9.

James V. Baker, "Existential Examination of *King Lear*," *CE* 23 (April 1962): 46–50 .

R. C. Bald, "'Thou, Nature, Art My Goddess': Edmund and Renaissance Free-Thought," in McManaway, *Joseph Q. Adams Memorial Studies*, 337–49.

Bamborough, *The Little World of Man*, 17–19, 77–78.

Jonas A. Barish, and Marshall Waingrow "'Service' in *King Lear*," *SQ* 9 (Summer 1958): 347–55.

A. D. Barnes, "Kent's 'Holy Cords': A Biblical Allusion in *King Lear* II.ii.74–76," *ELN* 22 (December 1984): 20–22.

Jonathan Bate, "Ovid and the Mature Tragedies: Metamorphosis in *Othello* and *King Lear*," *ShS* 41 (1989): 133–44.

Roy W. Battenhouse, "Shakespearean Tragedy as Christian: Some Confusions in the Debate," *CentR* 8 (Winter 1964): 77–84.

Josephine Waters Bennett, "The Storm Within: The Madness of Lear," *SQ* 13 (Spring 1962): 137–55.

Harry Berger, Jr., "*King Lear*: The Lear Family Romance," *CentR* 23 (1979): 348–76.

Ronald S. Berman, "Power and Humility in Shakespeare," *SAQ* 60 (Fall 1961): 416–19.

Ronald S. Berman, "Sense and Substance in *King Lear*," *NM* 65 (March 1964): 96–103.

David Bevington, "'Is This the Promised End?': Death and Dying in *King Lear*," *PAPS* 133 (September 1989): 404–15.

Jyoti Bhattacharya, "*King Lear*: The Last Four Lines," *JDECU* 18, no. 1 (1981–1982): 1–27.

Geoffrey L. Bickersteth, "The Golden World of *King Lear*," *PBA* 32 (1946): 147–72.

Peter Bilton, "The Lack of Accommodation in *King Lear*," *DSGW* 121 (1985): 94–105.

Harvey Birenbaum, "The Art of Our Necessities: The Softness of *King Lear*," *YR* 72 (Summer 1983): 581–99.

James Black, "*King Lear*: Art Upside-Down," *ShS* 33 (1980): 35–42.

Herbert Blau, "A Subtext Based on Nothing," *TDR* 8 (Winter 1963): 122–32.

Herbert Blau, "Language and Structure in Poetic Drama," *MLQ* 18 (1957): 27–28.

Sophia B. Blaydes, "Cordelia: Loss of Insolence," *StHum* 5 (September 1976): 15–21.

Mark J. Blechner, "*King Lear*, *King Leir*, and Incest Wishes," *AI* 45 (Fall 1988): 309–25.

Edward A. Block, "*King Lear*: A Study in Balanced and Shifting Sympathies," *SQ* 10 (Autumn 1959): 499–512.

David Everett Blythe, "Lear's Soiled Horse," *SQ* 31 (Winter 1980): 86–88.

Bodkin, *Archetypal Patterns in Poetry*, 280–84.

Bruce Thomas Boehrer, "*King Lear* and the Royal Progress: Social Display in Shakespearean Tragedy," *RenD* 21 (1990): 243–61.

Fredson Bowers, "The Structure of *King Lear*," *SQ* 31 (Winter 1980): 7–20.

Bradshaw, *Shakespeare's Skepticism*, 85–95.

Norman A. Brittin, "Shakespeare's Dramaturgical Foresight in *King Lear*," *SUS* 21 (1989): 85–90.

Brockbank, *On Shakespeare*, 220–43.

J. P. Brockbank, "'Upon Such Sacrifices,'" *PBA* 62 (1976): 109–34.

Nicholas Brooke, "The Ending of *King Lear*," in Bloom, *Shakespeare 1564–1964*, 71–87.

Brooks, and Heilman, *Understanding Drama*, 650–61.

Huntington Brown, "Lear's Fool: A Boy, Not a Man," *EIC* 13 (April 1963): 164–71.

Jack R. Brown, "Shakespeare's *King Lear*, III, vi, 47," *Expl* 23 (December 1964): 32.

Stephen J. Brown, "Shakespeare's King and Beggar," *YR* 64 (March 1975): 370–95.

Peter Bryant, "Nuncle Lear," *ESA* 20, no. 1 (1977): 27–41.

Bullough, *Mirror of Minds*, 84–86.

Sigurd Burckhardt, "*King Lear*: The Quality of Nothing," *The Minnesota Review* 2 (October 1961): 33–50.

Sigurd Burckhardt, "On Reading Ordinary Prose," *APSR* 54 (June 1960): 468–70.

Frederick M. Burelbach, "Names of Supporting Characters in *Hamlet, King Lear*, and *Macbeth*," *Names* 35 (September–December 1987): 127–38.

F. G. Butler, "Blessing and Cursing in *King Lear*," *UES* 24 (May 1986): 7–11.

James L. Calderwood, "Creative Uncreation in *King Lear*," *SQ* 37 (Spring 1986): 5–19.

Oscar James Campbell, "The Salvation of Lear," *ELH* 15 (June 1948): 93–109.

Peter Carpenter, "*King Lear, Macbeth*, and the Use of Memory," *CrSurv* 3, no. 2 (1991): 194–207.

William C. Carroll, "'The Base Shall Top th'Legitimate': The Bedlam Beggar and the Role of Edgar in *King Lear*," *SQ* 38 (Winter 1987): 426–41.

I. B. Cauthen, Jr., "'The Foule Flibbertigibbet' *King Lear*, III. iv. 113, IV. i. 60," *N&Q* 203 (March 1958): 98–99.

Dermot Cavanagh, "'Bereaved Sense': Problems of Definition in *King Lear*," *CrSurv* 3, no. 2 (1991): 157–62.

Chandhuri, *Infirm Glory*, 164–73.

Clay, *The Role of Anxiety*, 139–50.

Thomas Clayton, "Old Light on the Text of *King Lear*," *MP* 78 (May 1981): 347–67.

Cleman, *Shakespeare's Dramatic Art*, 177–83.

Walter Cohen, "*King Lear* and the Social Dimensions of Shakespearean Tragic Form, 1603–1607," *BuR* 25, no. 1 (1980): 106–18.

Confrey, *The Moral Mission of Literature*, 165–74.

H. R. Coursen, "'Age Is Unnecessary': A Jungian Approach to *King Lear*," *UCrow* 55 (1984): 75–92.

H. R. Coursen, "The Death of Cordelia: A Jungian Approach," *HUSL* 8 (1980): 1–12.

Paul M. Cubeta, "Lear's Comic Vision: 'Come, let's away to prison,'" in Edens, et al., *Teaching Shakespeare*, 138–52.

Thomas J. Cummings, "In Search of Goneril's Mew," *CEA* 31, no. 1 (1968): 4–5.

Cunningham, *Woe or Wonder*, 9–14.

John Cunningham, "*King Lear*, the Storm, and the Liturgy," *C&L* 34 (Fall 1984): 9–30.

John F. Danby, "*King Lear* and Christian Patience," *Cambridge Journal* 1 (February 1948): 305–20. Reprinted in *Poets on Fortune's Hill*, 105–07; 118–27.

John F. Danby, "The Fool in *King Lear*," *DUJ* 8 (December 1946): 17–24.

Neva Daniel, "Looking at Shakesepeare with an 'Existential' Eye," *Journal of Communication* 7 (Winter 1957): 180–82.

Mario L. D'Avanzo, "'He Mildews the White Wheat': *King Lear* III.iv.120–24," *SQ* 28 (1977): 88–89.

Clifford Davidson, "The Iconography of Wisdom and Folly in *King Lear*," *AUS—Papers in English and American Studies* 3 (1984): 189–214.

Dawson, *Indirections*, 132–38.

Andrew Dillon, "Edgar's Journey: Shame, Anger, and Maturity in *King Lear*," *NDQ* 57 (Spring 1989): 81–91.

Steven Doloff, "'Let Me Talk with This Philosopher': The Alexander/Diogenes Paradigm in *King Lear*," *HLQ* 54 (Summer 1991): 253–55.

Jane Donawerth, "Diogenes the Cynic and Lear's Definition of Man, *King Lear* III.iv.101–109," *ELN* 15 (September 1977): 10–14.

John Donnelly, "Incest, Ingratitude and Insanity—Aspects of the Psychopathology of *King Lear*," *Psychoanalytic Review* 40 (April 1953): 149–55.

Madeline Doran, "Command Question and Assertion in *King Lear*," in Crane, *Shakespeare's Art*, 53–79. Revised and reprinted in *Shakespeare's Dramatic Language*, 92–119.

Philip Drew, "'Run, Run, O Run': Drama and Melodrama in *King Lear*," *English* 28 (Summer 1979): 109–15.

James P. Driscoll, "The Vision of *King Lear*," *ShakS* 10 (1977): 159–89.

Alan Dundes, "'To Love My Father All: A Psychoanalytic Study of the Folktale Source of *King Lear*," *SFQ* 40 (September 1976): 353–66.

E. Catherine Dunn, "The Storm in *King Lear*," *SQ* 3 (October 1952): 329–33.

Richard Dutton, "*King Lear, The Triumphs of Reunited Britannia*, and 'The Matter of Britain,'" *L&H* 12 (Autumn 1986): 139–51.

Harriet Dye, "Appearance-Reality Theme in *King Lear*," *CE* 25 (April 1964): 514–17.

Arthur M. Eastnan, "King Lear's 'Poor Fool,'" *MichA* 49 (1964): 531–40.

Fred Eastman, *Christ in the Drama*, 28–35.

M. J. C. Echerou, "Dramatic Intensity and Shakespeare's *King Lear*," *ESA* 6 (March 1963): 44–50.

R. S. Edgecombe, "Out-Heroding Herod: Hyper-Hyperbole in *King Lear* and Donne's 'Nocturnal,'" *Theoria* 63 (October 1984): 67–72.

Egan, *Drama within Drama*, 16–55.

G. R. Elliott, "The Initial Contrast in Lear," *JEGP* 58 (April 1959): 251–63.

William Elton, "Lear's 'Good Years,'" *MLR* 59 (April 1964): 177–78.

William Elton, " 'Our Means Secure Us' (*King Lear*, IV, i, 20)," *Neophil* 47 (July 1963): 225–27.

John X. Evans, "Erasmian Folly and Shakespeare's *King Lear*: A Study in Humanist Intertextuality," *Moreana* 27 (September 1990): 3–23.

[Explicator Editors] "Shakespeare's *King Lear*, V, iii," *Expl* 3 (December 1944): 21.

M. D. Faber, "Some Remarks on the Suicide of King Lear's Eldest Daughter," *UR* 23 (Winter 1967): 313–17.

Harold Fisch, "*King Lear* and the Blessing of Jacob," in *KM* 80, 49–50.

Robert F. Fleissner, "Lear's Learned Name," *Names* 22 (June 1974): 183–84.

Robert F. Fleissner, "Lear's 'Poor Fool' as the Poor Fool," *EIC* 13 (October 1963): 425–27.

Robert F. Fleissner, "The 'Nothing' Element in *King Lear*," *SQ* 13 (Winter 1962): 67–70.

R. A. Foakes, "Textual Revision and the Fool in *King Lear*," *Trivium* 20 (1985): 33–47.

Rene F. Fortin, "Hermeneutical Circularity and Christian Interpretations of *King Lear*," *ShakS* 12 (1979): 113–25.

Duncan Fraser, "Much Virtue in 'Nothing': Cordelia's Part in the First Scene of *King Lear*," *CQ* 8 (1978): 1–10.

Winifred Frazer, "King Lear's 'Good Block,'" *SQ* 28 (Summer 1977): 354–55.

Sanford Freedman, "Character in a Coherent Fiction: On Putting King Lear Back Together Again," *P&L* 7 (October 1983): 196–212.

French, *Shakespeare's Division of Experience*, 219–42.

Kenneth Friedenreich, "The Albany Subplot and the Emotional Impact of *King Lear*," *SHR* 13 (September 1979): 293–307.

Dean Frye, "The Context of Lear's Unbuttoning," *ELH* 32 (March 1965): 17–31.

Gottlieb Gaiser, "The Fool's Prophecy as a Key to His Function in *King Lear*," *Anglia* 104, no. 1–2 (1986): 115–17.

Marjorie Garson, "Imagery in *King Lear*," *Manitoba Arts Review* (1958/59): 12–17.

Marilyn Gaull, "Love and Order in *King Lear*," *ETJ* 19 (September 1967): 333–42.

Gauri Prasad Ghosh, "*King Lear*: A Dark Synthesis Leading Nowhere," *JDECU* 18, no. 2 (1982–1983): 33–54.

C. Herbert Gilliland, "*King Lear* III.ii.25–36: The Fool's 'Codpiece' Song," *ELN* 22 (December 1984): 16–19.

Charles H. Gold, "A Variant Reading in *King Lear*," *N&Q* 206 (April 1961): 141–42.

Jonathan Goldberg, "Dover Cliff and the Conditions of Representation: *King Lear* 4:6 in Perspective," *PoT* 5 (1984): 537–47.

Jonathan Goldberg, "Textual Properties," *SQ* 37 (1986): 213–17.

Robert H. Goldsmith, "Kent: Plain Blunt Englishman," *ShN* 7 (April 1957): 12.

Phyllis Gorfain, "Contest, Riddle, and Prophecy: Reflexivity through Folklore in *King Lear*," *SFQ* 41 (June 1977): 239–54.

Kenneth J. E. Graham, "'Without the Form of Justice': Plainness and the Performance of Love in *King Lear*," *SQ* 42 (Autumn 1991): 438–61.

Stephen Greenblatt, "The Cultivation of Anxiety: King Lear and His Heirs," *Raritan* 2 (Summer 1982): 92–114.

Stephen Greenblatt, "*King Lear* and Harsnett's 'Devil-Fiction,'" in *The Power of Forms*, 239–42.

Thelma Nelson Greenfield, "The Clothing Motif in *King Lear*," *SQ* 5 (Summer 1954): 281–86.

Thomas A. Greenfield, "Excellent Things in Women: The Emergence of Cordelia," *SAB* 42 (February 1977): 44–52.

Grudin, *Mighty Opposites*, 137–53.

Hazel Sample Guyol, "A Temperance of Language: Goneril's Grammar and Rhetoric," *EJ* 55 (1966): 316–19.

Hallett and Hallett, *Analyzing Shakespeare's Action*, 80–82, 90–91, 106–08, 149–51, 184–85, 199–201.

Peter Halter, "The Endings of *King Lear*," in Bridges, *On Strangeness*, 85–98.

John E. Hankins, "Lear and the Psalmist," *MLN* 61 (February 1946): 88–90.

John E. Hankins, "Shakespeare's *King Lear*, V, iii," *Expl* 3 (April 1945): 48.

O. B. Hardison, Jr., "Myth and History in *King Lear*," *SQ* 26 (Spring 1975): 227–42.

Barbara Hardy, "Aspects of Narration in *King Lear*," *SHJW* (1987): 100–08.

Duncan S. Harris, "The End of *Lear* and a Shape for Shakespearean Tragedy," *ShakS* 9 (1976): 253–68.

Charles T. Harrison, "The Everest of Poems," *SR* 75 (Winter 1967): 662–71.

Richmond Y. Hathorn, "Lear's Equations," *CentR* 4 (Winter 1960): 51–69.

Richmond Y. Hathorn, *Tragedy, Myth, and Mystery*, 174–94.

Terry Hawkes, "'Love' in *King Lear*," *RES* 1O (May 1959): 178–81.

Hawkes, *Shakespeare's Talking Animals*, 167–78.

Hawkins, *Likeness and Truth*, 160–71.

Michael Hays, "Reason's Rhetoric: King Lear and the Social Uses of Irony," *Boundary* 7, no. 2 (1979): 97–118.

A. T. Hazen, "Shakespeare's *King Lear*, IV, i," *Expl* 2 (November 1943): 10.

Robert B. Heilman, "'Poor Naked Wretches and Proud Array': The Clothes Pattern," in *The Modern Critical Spectrum*, ed. Gerald J. Goldberg (Englewood Cliffs, NJ: Prentice-Hall, 1962), 18–31.

Robert B. Heilman, "Shakespeare's *King Lear*, IV, vi, 169," *Expl* 6 (November 1947): 10.

Robert B. Heilman, "Twere Best Not Know Myself: Othello, Lear, Macbeth," *SQ* 15 (Spring 1964): 89–98.

Robert B. Heilman, "The Two Natures in *King Lear*," *Accent* 8 (Autumn 1947): 51–58.

Robert B. Heilman, "The Unity of *King Lear*," *SR* 56 (Winter 1948): 58–68. Reprinted in R. W. Stallman, *Critiques and Essays in Criticism*, 154–61.

S. K. Heninger, Jr., "Shakespeare's *King Lear*, III, ii, 1–9," *Expl* 15 (October 1956): 1.

Hugh L. Hennedy, "'King Lear'" Recognizing the Ending," *SP* 71 (Winter 1974): 137–84.

Catherine A. Herbert, "Shakespeare's *King Lear* III.iv.161," *Expl* 34 (May 1976): Item 72.

Mathilda M. Hills, "Shakespeare's *King Lear* IV.vi.205–208," *Expl* 35 (Fall 1977): 31–32.

Michael Hinchliffe, "The Error of *King Lear*: A Reading of the Love Game in Act I Scene 1," in *L'Errur dans la littérature en la pensée anglaises: Actes du Centre Aixios de Recherches Anglais*, ed. F. J. Rigaud (Aix-en-Provence: Université de Provence, 1980), 27–51.

Hideo Hiramatsu, "The Structure and Theme of *King Lear*," *ShStud* 12 (1974): 31–45.

Dorothy C. Hockey, "The Trial Pattern in King Lear," *SQ* 10 (Summer 1959): 389–95.

R. I. V. Hodge, and Gunther Kress, "The Semiotics of Love and Power: *King Lear* and a New Stylistics," *SoRA* 15 (July 1982): 143–56.

Devon Leigh Hodges, "Cut Adrift and 'Cut to the Brains': The Anatomized World of *King Lear*," *ELR* 11 (Spring 1981): 194–212.

Theodore C. Hoepfner, "We That are Young," *N&Q* 199 (March 1954): 110.

Patrick Colm Hogan, "*King Lear*: Splitting and Its Epistemic Agon," *AI* 36 (Spring 1979): 32–44.

Sandra Hole, "The Background of Divine Action in *King Lear*," *SEL* 8 (Spring 1968): 217–33.

Holloway, *The Story of the Night*, 75–98.

Claudette Hoover, "'The Lusty Stealth of Nature': Sexuality and Antifeminism in *King Lear*," *Atlantis* 11 (Autumn 1985): 87–106.

J. W. Houppert, "Love and Death in *King Lear*," in Quinn, *How to Read Shakespearean Tragedy*, 179–228.

Houston, *Shakespearean Sentences*, 102–23.

Skiles Howard, "Attendants and Others in Shakespeare's Margins: Doubling in the Two Texts of *King Lear*," *ThS* 32 (November 1991): 187–213.

Howarth, *The Tiger's Heart*, 170–73.

Ronald Huebert, "Paganism in *King Lear*," *DR* 56 (Winter 1976): 429–47.

Hilda Hulme, "Three Shakespearean Glosses," *N&Q* 202 (September 1957): 237–38.

Maurice Hunt, "Perspectivism in *King Lear* and *Cymbeline*," *StHum* 14 (June 1987): 18–31.

Eleanor N. Hutchens, "The Transfer of Power in *King Lear* and *The Tempest*," *REL* 4 (April 1963): 82–93.

Lawrence W. Hyman, "Is There a Moral in *King Lear?*" *Greyfriar* 18 (1977): 19–28.

Von R. W. Ingram, "*Hamlet, Othello*, and *King Lear*: Music and Tragedy," *ShJE* 100 (1964): 159–61, 170–72.

Arnold Isenberg, "Cordelia Absent," *SQ* 2 (July 1951): 185–94.

Soji Iwasaki, "Time and Truth in *King Lear*," *ShStud* 5 (1967): 1–42.

Soji Iwasaki, "The World Upside Down in *King Lear*," in Anzai Milward, *Poetry and Drama in the Age of Shakespeare*, 139–55.

Esther Merle Jackson, "*King Lear*: The Grammar of Tragedy," *SQ* 17 (Winter 1966): 25–40.

James L. Jackson, "'These same crosses': *King Lear*, V.iii.279," *SQ* 31 (Autumn 1980): 387–90.

MacD. P. Jackson, " 'The Gods Deserve Your Kindness!': *King Lear*, III.vi.5," *N&Q* 208 (March 1963): 101.

Howard Jacobson, "Shakespeare's *King Lear*, I.i.181," *Expl* 34 (September 1975): Item 10.

Harry V. Jaffa, "The Limits of Politics: An Interpretation of *King Lear*, Act 1, Scene 1," *APSR* 51 (June 1957): 405–27.

James, *The Dream of Learning*, 69–126.

Sears Jayne, "Charity in *King Lear*," *SQ* 15 (Spring 1964): 277–88. Reprinted in McManaway, *Shakespeare 400*, 277–88.

Raymond Jenkins, "The Socratic Imperative and *King Lear*," *RenP 1962* (1963): 85–94.

Jepsen, *Ethical Asperts of Tragedy*, 58–63.

S. F. Johnson, "Attitudes Towards Justice in *King Lear*," *ShN* 4 (February 1954): 8.

Evan Jones, "Daring Wind and Rain: Twelfth Night and *King Lear*," *SoRA* 8 (1975): 125–37.

Graham Jones, "The Goose in *Lear*," *N&Q* 195 (July 1950): 295.

James Land Jones, "*King Lear* and the Metaphysics of Thunder," *Xavier University Studies* 3 (June 1964): 51–80.

Coppelia Kahn, "The Absent Mother in *King Lear*," in *Rewriting the Renaissance: The Discourse of Sexual Difference in Early Modern Europe*, ed. Margaret W. Ferguson, Maureen Quilligan, and Nancy J. Vickers (Chicago: University of Chicago Press, 1986), 33–49.

Sholom J. Kahn, "'Enter Lear Mad,'" *SQ* 8 (Summer 1957): 311–29.

Mark Kanzer, "Imagery in *King Lear*," *AI* 22 (Spring 1965): 3–13.

Kastan, *Shakespeare and the Shapes of Time*, 86–89, 102–22.

David Kaula, "Edgar on Dover Cliff: An Emblematic Reading," *ESC* 5 (Autumn 1979): 377–87.

Michael H. Keefer, "Accommodation and Synecdoche: Calvin's God in *King Lear*," *ShakS* 20 (1987): 147–68.

Alvin B. Kernan, "Formalism and Realism in Elizabethan Drama: The Miracles in *King Lear*," *RenD* 9 (1966): 59–66.

Alvin B. Kernan, "Meaning and Emptiness in *King Lear* and *The Tempest*," *RenD* 18 (1987): 225–36.

Ian J. Kirby, "The Passing of King Lear," *ShS* 41 (1989): 145–57.

Kathy L. Kirik, "An Inquiry into Misogyny in *King Lear*: The Making of an Androgyny," *JEP* 1 (June 1979): 13–28.

Arthur Kirsch, "The Emotional Landscape of *King Lear*," *SQ* 39 (1988): 154–70.

Leo Kirschbaum, "Albany," *ShS* 13 (196O): 20–29.

Leo Kirschbaum, "A Detail in *King Lear*," *RES* 25 (April 1949): 153–54.

Leo Kirschbaum, "Banquo and Edgar: Character or Function?" *EIC* 7 (January 1957): 8–21.

Carol Knight, "Animal Imagery in *King Lear*," *Mantitoba Arts Review* 8 (Winter 1954): 11–22.

G. Wilson Knight, "Gloucester's Leap," *EIC* 22 (July 1972): 279–88.

Knight, *The Golden Labyrinth*, 75–77.

Knight, *The Olive and the Sword*, 51–54.

G. W. Knight, "*King Lear* and the Comedy of the Grotesque," in *The Wheel of Fire*, 160–76.

G. W. Knight, "The *Lear* Universe," in *The Wheel of Fire*, 177–206.

L. C. Knights, "*King Lear* as Metaphor," in Slote, *Myth and Symbol*, 21–38.

Mark Koch, "The Shaking of the Superflux: *King Lear*, Charity, Value, and the Tyranny of Equivalence," *UCrow* 10 (1990): 86–100.

S. G. Kossick, "*King Lear*: Act 1, Scene ii: The Character of Edmund," *CRUX* 16 (January 1982): 29–35.

S. G. Kossick, "*King Lear*: The Closing Scenes," *CRUX* 20 (May 1986): 54–63.

S. G. Kossick, "*King Lear*: A Commentary on the Opening Scene," *CRUX* 17 (May 1983): 37–46.

James H. Lake, "Shakespeare's *King Lear*, V.iii.311–326," *Expl* 41 (Summer 1983): 9–10.

Antony Landon, "Icon, Word and Paradox in *King Lear* and *Macbeth*," in *Papers from the First Nordic Conference for English Studies, Oslo, 17–19 September, 1980*, ed. Stig Johansson and Bjorn Tysdahl (Oslo: University of Oslo, 1981), 109–133.

Berel Lang, "Nothing Comes of All: Lear-Dying," *NLH* 9 (1978): 537–59.

Robert Langenfeld, "The Role of Suffering in *King Lear*," in *Elizabethan Miscellany 3*, ed. James Hogg (Salzburg: University of Salzburg, 1981), 74–85.

Jacqueline E. M. Latham, "Unconscious Self-Revelation by Goneril and Regan," *DSGW* 113 (1977): 164–67.

Leaska, *The Voice of Tragedy*, 117–31.

Adrienne Lockhart, "The Cat Is Grey: King Lear's Mad Trial Scene," *SQ* 26 (Autumn 1975): 469–71.

Philip W. London, "The Stature of Lear," *UWR* 1 (January 1965): 173–86.

Robert Loper, "*King Lear*," *ShN* 8 (September 1958): 28.

John B. Lord, "Comic Scenes in Shakespearean Tragedy," *WSCS* 32 (September 1964): 236–38.

Frank L. Lucas, *Literature and Psychology*, 62–71.

Timothy J. Lukes, "Marcuse and Lear: The Politics of Motley," *MQ* 22 (1980): 32–45.

Jean MacIntyre, "Shakspeare's *King Lear* III.vi.8," *Expl* 21 (November 1962): 24.

Jean MacIntyre, "Truth, Lies, and Poesie in *King Lear*," *Ren&R* 6 (February 1982): 34–45.

Maynard Mack, "'We Came Crying Hither': An Essay on Some Characteristics of *King Lear*," *YR* 54 (December 1964): 161–86.

Hugh Maclean, "Disguise in *King Lear*: Kent and Edgar," *SQ* 11 (Winter 1960): 49–54.

Norman Maclean, "Episode, Scene, Speech, and Word: The Madness of Lear," in *Critics of Criticism, Ancient and Modern*, ed. Ronald S. Crane (Chicago: University of Chicago Press, 1964), 595–615.

Jean-Marie Maguin, "Imagination and Image Types in *King Lear*," *CahiersE* 9 (April 1968): 9–28.

Molly Mahood, "Minimal Characters in *King Lear*," in Nagarajan and Viswanathan, *Shakespeare in India*, 18–34.

John M. Major, "Shakespeare's *King Lear*, IV, ii, 62," *Expl* 17 (November 1958): 13.

Julian Markels, "*King Lear*, Revolution, and the New Historicism," *MLS* 21 (Spring 1991): 11–26.

Julian Markels, "Shakespeare's Confluence of Tragedy and Comedy: *Twelfth Night* and *King Lear*," *SQ* 15 (Winter 1964): 75–88.

Herbert Martey, "Shakespeare's *King Lear*, IV, vi, 1–80," *Expl* 11 (November 1952): 10.

William F. Martin, "*King Lear* and the Seven Deadly Sins," *TAIUS* 2 (January 1969) 46–57.

Marx, *The Enjoyment of Drama*, 105–12.

H. A. Mason, "*King Lear*: The Central Stream," *CQ* 2 (1967): 23–48.

H. A. Mason, "*King Lear* (II): Manipulating Our Sympathies," *CQ* 2 (1967): 148–66.

H. A. Mason, "*King Lear* (III): Radical Incoherence?" *CQ* 2 (1967): 212–35.

Kurian Mattam, "The Concept of Sin in the Shakespearian Tragedies: *Hamlet, King Lear, Macbeth* and *Othello*: An Exploration," *Unitas* 64 (June 1991): 165–230.

Richard Matthews, "Edmund's Redemption in *King Lear*," *SQ* 26 (1975): 25–29.

J. C. Maxwell, "The Technique of Invocation in *King Lear*," *MLR* 45 (April 1950): 142–47.

Jerome Mazzaro, "Madness and Memory: Shakespeare's *Hamlet* and *King Lear*," *CompD* 19 (Summer 1985): 97–116.

John C. McCloskey, "The Emotive Use of Animal Imagery in *King Lear*," *SQ* 13 (Summer 1962): 321–25.

McDonnell, *The Aspiring Mind*, 246–64.

Angus McIntosh, and Colin Williamson, "*King Lear*, Act 1, scene 1. A Stylistic Approach," *RES* 14 (February 1963): 54–58.

James J. McKenzie, "Edgar's 'Persian Attire,'" *N&Q* 201 (March 1956): 98–99.

John J. McLaughlin, "The Dynamics of Power in *King Lear*: An Adlerian Interpretation," *SQ* 29 (Winter 1978): 37–43.

Kathleen McLuskie, "The Patriarchal Bard: Feminist Criticism and Shakespeare: *King Lear* and *Measure for Measure*," in Dollimore and Sinfield, *Political Shakespeare*, 88–108.

Waldo F. McNeir, "The Last Lines of *King Lear*: v.iii. 320-27," *ELN* 4 (March 1966): 183–88.

Waldo F. McNeir, "The Role of Edmund in *King Lear*," *SEL* 18 (Spring 1968): 187–216.

McPeek, *The Black Book of Knaves*, 217–36.

Barbara Melchiori, "Still Harping on my Daughter," *EM* 11 (1960): 72–74.

Giorgio Melchiori, "Degrees of Metaphor: *King Lear*: Proceedings of Third Congress of the International Shakespeare Association," in *Images of Shakespeare*, ed. Werner Habicht, D. J. Palmer, and Roger Pringle (Newark: University of Delaware Press, 1988), 73–79.

W. M. Merchant, "Shakespeare's Theology," *REL* 5 (October 1966): 75–78.

Laurence Michel, "Shakespearean Tragedy: Critique of Humanism From the Inside," *MR* 2 (Summer 1961): 645–46.

Linda Micheli, "'The Thing Itself': Literal and Figurative Language in *King Lear*," *PQ* 60 (Summer 1981): 343–56.

Barbara C. Millard, "Virago with a Soft Voice: Cordelia's Tragic Rebellion in *King Lear*," *PQ* 68 (Winter 1989): 143–65.

Ronald F. Miller, "*King Lear* and the Comic Form," *Genre* 8 (Winter 1975): 1–25.

Evander Milne, "On the Death of Cordelia," *English* 6 (Summer 1947): 244–48.

Peter Milward, "'Nature' in Hooker and *King Lear*," *ShStud* 13 (1974–75): 25–43.

Peter Milward, "Notes on the Religious Dimension of *King Lear*," *ELLS* 23 (1986): 5–27.

Peter Milward, "A Philosophy of Nature in *King Lear*?: Essays in Honour of Professor Toyohiko Tatsumi's Seventieth Birthday," in Milward, *Poetry and Faith in the English Renaissance*, 111–20.

Ivor Morris, "Cordelia and Lear," *SQ* 8 (Spring 1957): 141–58.

Leonard Moss, "Rhetorical Addition in *King Lear*, I," *Lang&S* 20 (Winter 1986): 16–29.

Leonard Moss, "Rhetorical Addition in *King Lear*, II," *Lang&S* 20 (Spring 1987): 171–84.

Muir, *Essays on Literature and Society*, 33–49.

Kenneth Muir, "*King Lear*, II, iv, 170," *N&Q* 196 (April 1951): 170.

Kenneth Muir, "Madness in *King Lear*," *ShS* 13 (1960): 30–40.

Asim Kumar Mukherjee, "Nature in *King Lear*," *OJES* 17 (1981): 1–17.

Muller, *The Spirit of Tragedy*, 185–93.

John M. Munro, "The Problem of Choice in *King Lear*," *SAQ* 63 (Spring 1964): 240–44.

S. Musgrove, "*King Lear* I.i.170," *RES* 8 (May 1957): 170–71.

S. Musgrove, "The Nomenclature of *King Lear*," *RES* 7 (August 1956): 294–98.

S. Musgrove, "Thieves' Cant in *King Lear*," *ES* 62 (January 1981): 5–13.

Kenneth Myrick, "Christian Pessimism in *King Lear*," in Bloom, *Shakespeare 1564–1964*, 56–70.

Dorothy E. Nameri, "Shakespeare's Use of Language as Exemplified in *King Lear*," *CdlL* 14, no. 1–2 (1988): 217–21.

William Nelson, "'Complement of Leave-Taking' Between Lear and the King of France," *RenQ* 27 (1974): 193–95.

Nicholl, *The Chemical Theatre*, 143–224,

August Nigro, "*King Lear* and the Via Negativa," *SPWVSRA* 10 (1985): 62–67.

Winifred M. T. Nowottny, "Lear's Questions," *ShS* 10 (1957): 90–97.

Winifred M. T. Nowottny, "Some Aspects of the Style of *King Lear*," *ShS* 13 (1960): 49–57.

Marianne Novy, "Patriarchy, Mutuality, and Foregiveness in *King Lear*," *SHR* 13 (September 1979): 281–92.

Yasuhiro Ogawa, "'Things Which Are Not': The Problematics of 'Nothing' in *King Lear*," *EFLL* 29 (1981): 115–53.

James Ogden, "The Ending of *King Lear*," *AJES* 8 (July 1983): 180–85.

Olson, *Tragedy and the Theory of Drama*, 195–215.

Horst Oppel, "The Phenomenon of Acceleration in *King Lear*," *AJES* 3 (October 1978): 215–27.

Michael Orange, "Coherence and Incoherence in *King Lear*," *SSEng* 10 (1984–1985): 3–16.

Ornstein, *Moral Vision of Jacobean Tragedy*, 121–25, 260–73.

Toshikazu Oyama, "*King Lear* and Its Tragic Pattern," *ShStud* 5 (1967): 43–71.

Toshiko Oyama, "The World of Lear's Fool-The Dramatic Mode of His Speech," *ShS* 17 (1963): 10–30.

Douglas H. Parker, "The Third Suitor in *King Lear* Act 1, Scene I," *ES* 72 (April 1991): 136–45.

Paul Parnell, "Is There a Case for Goneril and Regan?" *ShN* 2 (May 1952): 20.

Phillip Parotti, "A New Dimension to Goneril's Depravity: Shakespeare's Amazonian Allusion in *King Lear*," *PAPA* 8 (Spring 1982): 33–41.

Johnstone Parr, "Edmund's Nativity in *King Lear*," *ShAB* 21 (October 1946): 181–85.

Johnstone Parr, "A Note on the 'Late Eclipses' in *King Lear*," *ShAB* 20 (January 1945): 46–48.

T. M. Parrott, "'Gods' or 'gorls' in *King Lear*, V, iii, 17," *SQ* 4 (October 1953): 427–32.

Morriss Henry Partee, "Edgar and the Ending of *King Lear*," *SN* 63 (Summer 1991): 175–80.

Morriss Henry Partee, "The Function of Cordelia," *ISJR* 54 (July 1980): 449–59.

Peter Pauls, "The True Chronicle History of *King Leir* and Shakespeare's *King Lear*: A Reconsideration," *UCrow* 5 (1984): 93–107.

Arpad Pauncz, "Psychopathology of Shakespeare's *King Lear*," *AI* 9 (April 1952): 57–78.

Derek Peat, "'And that's true too': *King Lear* and the Tension of Uncertainty," *ShS* 33 (1980): 43–53.

Derek Peat, "Responding Blindly: A Reading of a Scene in *King Lear*," *SSEng* 10 (1984–1985): 103–08.

Edward Pechter, "On the Blinding of Gloucester," *ELH* 45 (June 1978): 181–200.

Russell A. Peck, "Edgar's Pilgrimage: High Comedy in *King Lear*," *SEL* 7 (Spring 1967): 219–37.

Mike Pedretti, "*King Lear*: The Fool and the Paradox of the Universe," *SPWVS-RA* 4 (1979): 44–55.

Vincent F. Petronella, "*King Lear*, II.iv 128–35," *Expl* 39 (Summer 1981): 9–10.

Robert B. Pierce, "Shakespeare's *King Lear*," *Expl* 37 (Summer 1979): 7–8.

David Pirie, "Lear as King," *CritQ* 22 (Summer 1980): 5–20.

Pogson, *In the East My Pleasure Lies*, 23–46.

Joseph A. Porter, "More Echoes from Eliot's *Ortho-Epia Gallica*, in *King Lear* and *Henry VI*," *SQ* 37 (Autumn 1986): 486–88.

Laurel Porter, "*King Lear* and the Crisis of Retirement," in *Aging in Literature*, ed. Laurel Porter and Laurence M. Porter (Troy, MI: International Book Publishers, 1984), 59–71.

Alan Price, "The Blinding of Gloucester," *N&Q* 197 (July 1952): 313–14.

Prior, *The Language of Tragedy*, 180–85.

David Pugh, "From the Static to the Progressive Order of Nature: *King Lear* and *Gotz von Berlichingen*," *CRCL* 17 (September–December 1990): 255–79.

Lawrence Raab, "And We Were Left Darkling: Notes on *King Lear*," *ASch* 36 (1967): 657–59.

Phyllis Rackin, "Delusion as Resolution in *King Lear*," *SQ* 21 (Winter 1970): 29–34.

Ragini Ramachandra, "*King Lear* in the Light of Indian Poetics," *LCrit* 26, no. 1 (1991): 30–39.

D. D. Raphael, *Paradox of Tragedy* (Bloomington: Indiana University Press, 1959), 52–57.

Robert A. Ravich, "Shakespeare and Psychiatry," *L&P* 14 (Summer–Fall 1964): 102–05.

Ribner, *The English History Play*, 247–53.

Irving Ribner, "The Gods are Just: A Reading of *King Lear*," *TDR* 2 (May 1958): 34–54

Julian C. Rice, "The Empathic Edgar: Creativity as Redemption in *King Lear*," *SMy* 7 (Winter 1984): 50–60.

Val Richards, "'His Majesty the Baby': A Psychoanalytic Approach to *King Lear*," in Aers and Wheale, *Shakespeare in the Changing Curriculum*, 162–79.

William Ringler, "Exit Kent," *SQ* 11 (Summer 1960): 311–17.

Josephine A. Roberts, "*King Lear* and the Prefixes of Inversion," *NM* 79 (June 1978): 384–90.

James E. Robinson, "*King Lear* and the Space Between," *NDEJ* 12 (Spring 1979): 27–54.

Henri Roddier, "A Freudian Detective's Shakespeare," *MP* 48 (November 1950): 132.

Carmen Rogers, "Heavenly Justice in the Tragedies of Shakespeare," *UMPEAL* 1 (March 1953): 116–28.

John D. Rosenberg, "King Lear and His Comforters," *EIC* 16 (April 1966): 135–46.

Lawrence Rosinger, "Shakespeare's *King Lear*, I.iv.226–230," *Expl* 41 (Summer 1983): 8–9.

Gordon N. Ross, "Shakespeare's *King Lear*, 1.i.16," *Expl* 36 (Fall 1978): 5.

Gordon N. Ross, "Shakespeare's *King Lear*, 1.i.306," *Expl* 36 (Winter 1978): 25–26.

Grant C.Roti, "Shakespeare's *King Lear* I.i.56," *Expl* 32 (November 1974): Item 32.

Kathleen G. Rousseau, "Captain Ahab and King Lear: Their Kingship," *SPWVS-RA* 9 (1984): 69–76.

Martha Tuck Rozett, "Tragedies within Tragedies: Kent's Unmasking in *King Lear*," *RenD* 18 (1987): 237–58.

Leo Salingar, "Romance in *King Lear*," *English* 27 (1978): 5–21.

Lino Falzon Santucci, "Multiple Codes and Alternative Performances in *King Lear*, I.i.23–265," in *Dialoganalyse, III: Referate der 3. Arbeitstagung Bologna 1990*, I & II, ed. Sorin Stati, Edda Weigand, and Franz Hundsnurscher (Tubingen: Niemeyer, 1991), II: 49–58.

Joseph Satin, "The Symbolic Role of Cordelia in *King Lear*," *ForumH* 9, no. 3 (1971–1972): 14–17.

SHAKESPEARE, WILLIAM, *King Lear*

Melita Schaum, "The Social Dynamic: Liminality and Reaggregation in King Lear," *AJES* 9 (July 1984): 148–54.

Lawrence R. Schehr, "*King Lear*: Monstrous Mimesis," *SubStance* 36 (1982): 51–63.

Schell, *Strangers and Pilgrims*, 151–95.

Winfried Schleiner, "Justifying the Unjustifiable: The Dover Cliff Scene in *King Lear*," *SQ* 36 (Autumn 1985): 337–43.

Gary Schmidgall, *Shakespeare and the Courtly Aesthetic* (Berkeley, Los Angeles, and London: University of California Press, 1981), 162–64.

Francis G. Schoff, "*King Lear*: Moral Example or Tragic Protagonist," *SQ* 13 (Spring 1962): 157–72.

Max F. Schulz, "*King Lear*," *TSE* 7 (Spring 1957): 83–90.

Raman Selden, "*King Lear* and True Need," *ShakS* 19 (1991): 143–70.

Cecil C. Seronsy, "Shakespeare's *King Lear*, I, i, 159–63," *Expl* 17 (December 1958): 21.

Sewall, *The Vision of Tragedy*, 68–79.

Mohan Lal Sharma, "Shakespeare's *King Lear*, III, 65–79," *Expl* 30 (March 1972): Item 46.

Allan R. Shickman, "The Fool's Mirror in *King Lear*," *ELR* 21 (Winter 1991): 75–86.

Sister Scholastica Schuster, "The Redemptive Pattern in *King Lear*," *ABR* 18 (December 1967): 492–503.

Melvin Seiden, "The Fool and Edmund: Kin and Kind," *SEL* 19 (Spring 1979): 197–214.

Roger D. Sell, "Two Types of Style Contrast in *King Lear*: A Literary-Critical Appraisal," in *Style and Text: Studies Presented to Nils Erik Enkvist*, ed. Hakan Ringbom, Alfhild Ingberg, Ralf Norrman, Kurt Nyholm, Rolf Westman, and Kay Wikberg (Stockholm: Sprakforlaget Skriptor, 1975), 158–71.

John Shaw, "*King Lear*: The Final Lines," *EIC* 26 (July 1966): 260–67.

Paul N. Siegel, "Adversity and the Miracle of Love in *King Lear*," *SQ* 6 (Summer 1955): 325–36.

Dorothy Skriletz, "The Rhetoric: An Aid to the Study of Drama," *Southern Speech Journal* 25 (Spring 1960): 217–22.

Harold Skulsky, "*King Lear* and the Meaning of Chaos," *SQ* 17 (Winter 1966): 3–17.

Donald M. Smith, " 'And I'll go to bed at noon': The Fool in *King Lear*," *EAS* 5 (April 1976): 37–45.

Gerald Smith, "A Note on the Death of Lear," *MLN* 70 (June 1955): 403–04.

Ronald M. Smith, "*King Lear* and the Merlin Tradition," *MLQ* 17 (1946): 153–74.

Susan Snyder, "*King Lear* and the Prodigal Son," *SQ* 17 (Summer 1966): 361–69.

Susan Snyder, "*King Lear* and the Psychology of Dying," *SQ* 33 (Autumn 1982): 449–60.

Rolf Soellner, "*King Lear* and the Magic of the Wheel," *SQ* 35 (Spring 1984): 274–89.

Soellner, *Shakespeare's Patterns*, 281–326.

J. Fisher Solomon, "King in *Lear*: A Semiotic for Communal Adaptation," *AJS* 3, no. 2 (1984): 56–76.

Benjamin T. Spencer, "*King Lear*: A Prophetic Tragedy," *CE* 5 (March 1944): 302–07.

Theodore Spencer, "The Isolation of the Shakespearean Hero," *SR* 52 (Summer 1944): 324–26.

Marvin Spevack, "Shakespeare's *King Lear*, IV, vi, 152," *Expl* 17 (October 1958): 4.

J. Stampfer, "The Catharsis of *King Lear*," *ShS* 13 (1960): 1–10.

Bert O. States, "Standing on the Extreme Verge in *King Lear* and Other High Places," *GaR* 36 (Summer 1982): 417–25.

Steiner, *The Death of Tragedy*, 256–59, 276–80.

Jeffrey Stern, "*King Lear*: The Transference of the Kingdom," *SQ* 41 (Summer 1990): 299–308.

Warren Stevenson, "Albany as Archetype in *King Lear*," *MLQ* 26 (June 1965): 257–63.

Charles D. Stewart, "Four Shakespearean Cruxes," *CE* 9 (January 1948): 188–91.

Katherine Stockholder, "The Multiple Genres of *King Lear*: Breaking the Archetypes," *BuR* 16, no. 1 (1968): 40–63.

Katherine Stockholder, "Sex and Authority in *Hamlet, King Lear* and *Pericles*," *Mosaic* 18 (Summer 1985): 17–29.

L. M. Storozynsky, "*King Lear* and Chaos," *CrSurv* 3, no. 2 (1991): 163–69.

Ernest A. Strathmann, "The Devil Can Quote Scripture," *SQ* 15 (Spring 1964): 19–20.

Thomas B. Stroup, "Cordelia and the Fool," *SQ* 12 (Spring 1961): 127–32.

Betty K. Stuart, "Truth and Tragedy in *King Lear*," *SQ* 18 (Spring 1967): 167–80.

Styan, *The Elements of Drama*, 107–17, 121–22.

Claude J. Summers, "'Stand Up for Bastards!' Shakespeare's Edmund and Love's Failure," *CollL* 4 (Summer 1977): 225–31.

Joseph H. Summers, "'Look there, look there!' The Ending of *King Lear*," in Carey, *English Renaissance Studies Presented to Dame Helen Gardner*, 74–93.

Masahiko Sunohara, "*King Lear* as a Tragedy of Love, with Special Regard to Passive Love," *ShStud* 20 (1981–1982): 59–89.

Edward W. Tayler, "*King Lear* and Negation," *ELR* 20 (Winter 1990): 17–39.

E. M. M. Taylor, "Lear's Philosopher," *SQ* 6 (Summer 1955): 364–65.

Gary Taylor, "A New Source and an Old Date for *King Lear*," *RES* 33 (July 1982): 396–413.

Gary Taylor, "The War in *King Lear*," *ShS* 33 (1980): 27–34.

Taylor, *To Analyze Delight*, 172–236.

Warren Taylor, "Lear and the Lost Self," *CE* 25 (April 1964): 509–13.

Alwin Thaler, "The Gods and God in *King Lear*," *RenP* 1954 (1955): 32–39.

Ann Thompson, "Are There Any Women in *King Lear*?" in Wayne, *The Matter of Difference*, 117–28.

Ann Thompson, "*King Lear*" (Atlantic Highlands, NJ: Humanities, 1988).

Leslie M. Thompson, "Shakespeare's *King Lear*," *Expl* 23 (March 1965): Item 57.

Thompson, and Thompson, *Shakespeare*, 47–88.

L. W. Tolmie, "'No Seconds? All Myself?' An Essay on King Lear," *SoRA* 12 (1979): 38–62.

Isadore Traschen, "The Elements of Tragedy," *CentR* 6 (Spring 1962): 215–29.

Darwin T. Turner, "*King Lear* Re-examined," *CLAJ* 3 (September 1959): 27–39.

Steven Urtowitz, "Interrupted Exits in *King Lear*," *ETJ* 30 (October 1978): 203–10.

Z. A. Usmani, "*King Lear*: Nothing and the Thing Itself," in Sharma, *Essays on Shakespeare in Honour of A. A. Ansari*, 253–83.

Van Lann, *The Idiom of Drama*, 117–18, 285–86.

John W. Velz, "Division, Confinement, and the Moral Structure of *King Lear*," *RUS* 51 (January 1965): 97–108.

Eliseo Vivas, *The Artistic Transaction, and Other Essays on Theory of Literature* (Columbus: Ohio State University Press, 1963), 127–29.

Kathleen Wales, "An Aspect of Shakespeare's Dynamic Language: A Note on the Interpretation of *King Lear* III.vii.113: 'He childed as I father'd!,'" *ES* 59 (October 1978): 395–404.

Mick Wallis, "Emblem, Psychology and Feeling: Playing and Reading *King Lear*," *CrSurv* 3, no. 3 (1991): 229–39.

J. K. Walton, "Lear's Last Speech," *ShS* 13 (1960): 11–19.

Michael Warren, "*King Lear*, IV. vi.83: The Case for 'Crying,'" *SQ* 35 (Summer 1984): 319–21.

Michael Warren, "*King Lear*, V.iii.265: Albany's 'Fall and Cease,'" *SQ* 33 (Spring 1982): 178–79.

Jerry Wasserman, "'And Every One Have Need of Other': Bond and Relationship in *King Lear*," *Mosaic* 9 (Spring 1976): 15–30.

Jean Anne Waterstradt, "Making the World a Home: The Family Portrait in Drama," *BYUS* 19 (1979): 501–21.

W. B. C. Watkins, "The Two Techniques in *King Lear*," *RES* 18 (April 1967): 1–26.

Sandra A. Wawrytko, "Meaning and Merging: The Hermeneutics of Reinterpreting *King Lear* in the Light of the *Hsiao-ching*," *PE&W* 36 (October 1986): 393–408.

Manfred Weidhorn, "Lear's Schoolmasters," *SQ* 13 (Summer 1962): 305–16.

Robert Weimann, "The Authority of Emblems versus the Emblems of Authority in *King Lear*," *ACM* 3, no. 1 (1990): 1–16.

Weisinger, *The Agony and the Triumph*, 109–10.

Herbert Weisinger, "A Shakespeare all too Modern," *ArQ* 20 (Winter 1964): 304–08.

Stanley Wells, "The Taming of the Shrew and *King Lear*: A Structural Comparison," *ShS* 33 (1980): 55–66.

Gilian West, " 'My Father, Poorly Led?' A Suggested Emendation to *King Lear*, IV.i.10," *ELN* 23 (March 1986): 22–23.

Robert H. West, "Sex and Pessimism in *King Lear*," *SQ* 11 (Winter 1960): 55–60.

Jonathan White, "*King Lear*, Suffering, and Character Deconstruction: The Case of Edgar/Poor Tom," *QFG* 3 (1984): 305–21.

Gayle Whittier, "Cordelia as Prince: Gender and Language in *King Lear*," *Exemplaria* 1 (Fall 1989): 367–39.

George W. Williams, "The Poetry of Storm in *King Lear*," *SQ* 2 (January 1951): 57–71.

George Walton Williams, "Petitionary Prayer in *King Lear*," *SAQ* 85 (Autumn 1986): 360–73.

George Walton Williams, "Second Thoughts on Lear's 'Good Block,'" *SQ* 29 (Autumn 1978): 421–22.

Robert F. Wilson, Jr. "Shakespeare's *King Lear* I.i.312," *Expl* 38 (Spring 1979): 7.

Joseph Wittreich, "'Image of That Horror': The Apocalypse in *King Lear*," in *The Apocalypse in English Renaissance Thought and Literature: Patterns, Antecedents, and Repercussions*, ed. C. A. Patrides and Joseph Wittreich (Ithaca, NY: Cornell University Press, 1984), 175–206.

Chester L. Wolford, "*King Lear* and an End of Tragedy," *SPWVSRA* 5 (1980): 37–41.

Samuel Yellen, "The Two Kneelings of King Lear," *VQR* 60 (Winter 1984): 453–64.

Alan R. Young, "The Written and Oral Sources of *King Lear* and the Problem of Justice in the Play," *SEL* 15 (Spring 1975): 309–19.

Young, *The Heart's Forest*, 73–103.

R. A. Zimbardo, "The King and the Fool: *King Lear* as Self-Deconstructing Text," *Criticism* 32 (Winter 1990): 1–29.

Sheldon P. Zitner, "The Fool's Prophecy," *SQ* 18 (Winter 1967): 76–80.

Love's Labour's Lost

Geoffrey Ashe, "Several Worthies," *N&Q* 195 (November 1950): 492–93.

Carolyn Asp, "*Love's Labour's Lost*: Language and the Deferral of Desire," *L&P* 35, no. 3 (1989): 1–21.

Weston Babcock, "Fools, Fowles, and Perttaunt-Like in *Love's Labour's Lost*," *SQ* 2 (July 1951): 211–19.

Barber, *Shakespeare's Festive Comedy*, 87–118.

G. Beiner, "Endgame in *Love's Labour's Lost*," *Anglia* 103, no. 1 (1985): 48–70.

Thomas L. Berger, "The Lack of Song in *Love's Labours Lost*," *SQ* 26 (1975): 53–55.

Ronald Berman, "Shakespeare Comedy and the Uses of Reason," *SAQ* 63 (Winter 1964): 1–4.

Francis Berry, *Poetry and the Physical Voice* (London: Routledge, 1962), 135–37, 144–45.

Christine M. Bird, "Games Courtiers Play in *Love's Labours Lost*," *HSL* 11, no. 1 (1979): 41–48.

William Blisset, "'Strange Without Heresy' (*Love's Labour's Lost*, 5.1.6)," *ES* 38 (October 1957): 209–11.

Alan Brissenden, "Shakespeare's Use of Dance: *Love Labour's Lost*, *Much Ado about Nothing*, and *The Merry Wives of Windsor*," in *Shakespeare and Some Others*, 30–43.

Bertrand H. Bronson, "Daisies Pied and Icicles," *MLN* 63 (January 1948): 35–38.

Kevan Brown, "Telltale Poetry: A Study of the Four Courtiers in *Love's Labour's Lost*," *SoQ* 13 (April 1974): 83–92.

Bullough, *Mirror of Minds*, 62–64.

James L. Calderwood, "*Love's Labour's Lost*: A Wantoning with Words," *SEL* 5 (Spring 1965): 317–22.

Harry Curtis, Jr., "Four Woodcocks in a Dish: Shakespeare's Humanization of the Comic Perspective in *Love's Labours Lost*," *SHR* 13 (March 1979): 115–24.

John W. Draper, "Tempo in *Love's Labour's Lost*," *ES* 29 (October 1948): 129–37.

Manfred Draudt, "Holofernes and Mantuanus: How Stupid Is the Pedant of *Love's Labour's Lost*?" *Anglia* 109, no. 4 (1991): 443–51.

Manfred Draudt, "Katherine's 'Mask' and 'Cap' in *Love's Labour's Lost*: Act III, Scene 1, Lines 124 and 209," in *A Yearbook in English Language and Literature*, ed. Max Gauna (Vienna: Braumuller, n.d.), 1–6.

Malcolm Evans, "Mercury versus Apollo: A Reading of *Love's Labour's Lost*," *SQ* 26 (Winter 1975): 113–27.

French, *Shakespeare's Division of Experience*, 87–91.

Northrop Frye, "Shakespeare's Experimental Comedy," *Stratford Papers on Shakespeare* 2 (1961): 1–14.

Tahita Fulkerson, "The Sweet Smoke of Rhetoric: *Love's Labour's Lost*," *CCTEP* 53 (September 1988): 7–14.

Sister M. Teresa Gertrude, "*Love's Labour's Lost*," *Horizontes* 7 (October 1963): 47–52.

Neal L. Goldstein, "*Love's Labour's Lost* and the Renaissance Vision of Love," *SQ* 25 (Summer 1974): 335–50.

R. Chris Hassel, Jr., "Love versus Charity in *Love's Labor's Lost*," *ShakS* 10 (1977): 17–41.

Hawkes, *Shakespeare's Talking Animals*, 53–72.

Hawkins, *Likeness of Truth*, 6–7.

Mary E. Hazard, "Shakespeare's 'living art': A Live Issue from *Love's Labour's Lost*: Collection of Essays from the Ohio Shakespeare Conference, 1981, Wright State Univ., Dayton, Ohio," in *Shakespeare and the Arts*, ed. Cecile Williamson Cary and Henry S. Limouze (Washington, DC: University Press of America, 1982), 181–98.

Tinsley Helton, "Shakespeare's *Love's Labour's Lost*, V, ii, 940–941," *Expl* 22 (December 1963): 25.

S. K. Henninger, "The Pattern of *Love's Labour's Lost*," *ShakS* 7 (1974): 25–54.

Hibbard, *Making of Shakespeare's Dramatic Poetry*, 92–95, 105–13.

Cyrus Hoy, "*Love's Labour's Lost* and the Nature of Comedy," *SQ* 13 (Winter 1962): 31–40. Reprinted in *The Hyacinth Room*, 22–38.

G. K. Hunter, "Poem and Context in *Love's Labour's Lost*," in Edwards, Ewbank, and Hunter, *Shakespeare's Styles*, 25–38.

Robert G. Hunter, "The Function of the Songs at the End of *Love's Labour's Lost*," *ShakS* 7 (1974): 55–64.

M. Jackson, "A Shakespeare Quibble," *N&Q* 207 (September 1962): 331–32.

John Kerrigan, "*Love's Labour's Lost* and the Circling Seasons," *EIC* 28 (July 1978): 269–87.

John Kerrigan, "Shakespeare at Work: The Katharine-Rosaline Tangle in *Love's Labour's Lost*," *RES* 33 (July 1982): 129–36.

Pankaj Khanna, "*Love's Labour's Lost*: Shakespeare's Satiric Mode," *RUSEng* 11 (January 1978): 17–26.

Anthony J. Lewis, "Shakespeare's Via Media in *Love's Labour's Lost*," *TSLL* 16 (Summer 1974): 243–48.

T. T. Low, "*Love's Labour's Lost*," *The Use of English* 12 (Summer 1961): 242–44.

William Matthews, "Language in *Love's Labour's Lost*," *E&S* 17 (1964): 1–11.

Catherine M. McLay, "The Dialogues of Spring and Winter: A Key to the Unity of *Love's Labour's Lost*," *SQ* 18 (Winter 1967): 119–27.

J. M. Nosworthy, "The Importance of Being Marcade," *ShS* 32 (1979): 105–14.

J. H. Pafford, "Schoole of Night (*L. L. L.* 4.3252)," *N&Q* 202 (December 1957): 143.

Howard Parsoni, "Cruxes in *Love's Labour's Lost*," *N&Q* 200 (July 1955): 287–89.

Judith C. Perryman, "A Tradition Transformed in *Love's Labour's Lost*," *EA* 37 (April–June 1984): 156–62.

Judith C. Perryman, "'The Words of Mercury': Alchemical Imagery in *Love's Labour's Lost*," in *The Spirit of the Court: Selected Proceedings of the Fourth Congress of the International Courtly Literature Society (Toronto 1983)*, ed. Glyn S. Burgess (Dover, NH: Brewer, 1985), 246–53.

Anthony G. Petti, "The Fox, the Ape, the Humble Bee and the Goose," *Neophil* 44 (July 1960): 208–13.

Richard Proudfoot, "*Love's Labour's Lost*: Sweet Understanding and the Five Worthies," *E&S* 37 (1984): 16–30.

Robert A. Ravich, "A Psychoanalytic Study of Shakespeare's Early Plays," *Psychoanalytic Quarterly* 33 (July 1964): 400–02.

Bobbyann Roesen, "*Love's Labour's Lost*," *SQ* 4 (October 1953): 411–26.

Mats Ryden, "Shakespeare's Cuckoo-Buds," *SN* 49 (Spring 1977): 25–27.

W. Schrickx, *Shakespeare's Early Contemporaries* (Antwerp: De Nederlandsche Boekhandel, 1956), 235–66.

H. D. Siler, "A French Pun in *Love's Labour's Lost*," *MLN* 60 (February 1945): 124–25.

Kristian Smidt, "Shakespeare in Two Minds: Unconformities in *Love's Labour's Lost*," *ES* 65 (June 1984): 205–19.

Soellner, *Shakespeare's Patterns*, 78–96.

Karl F. Thompson, "Shakespeare's Romantic Comedies," *PMLA* 67 (December 1952): 1079–85, 1091–93.

Albert H. Tricomi, "The Witty Idealization of the French Court in *Love's Labour's Lost*," *ShakS* 12 (1979): 25–33.

Gustav Ungerer, "Two Items of Spanish Pronunciations in *Love's Labour's Lost*," *SQ* 14 (Summer 1963): 245–51.

K. Tetzeli Von Rosador, "Plotting the Early Comedies: *The Comedy of Errors, Love's Labour's Lost, The Two Gentlemen of Verona*," *ShS* 37 (1984): 13–22.

E. J. West, "On the Essential Theatricality of *Love's Labour's Lost*," *CE* 9 (May 1948): 427–29.

Joseph Westlund, "Fancy and Achievement in *Love's Labour's Lost*," *SQ* 18 (Winter 1967): 37–46.

R. S. White, "Oaths and the Anticomic Spirit in *Love's Labour's Lost*," in Brissenden, *Shakespeare and Some Others*, 11–29.

John Wilders, "The Unresolved Conflicts of *Love's Labour's Lost*," *EIC* 27 (December 1977): 20–33.

Macbeth

Michael J. B. Allen, "Macbeth's Genial Porter," *ELR* 4 (Autumn 1974): 326–36.

Daniel Amneus, "The Cawdor Episode in *Macbeth*," *JEGP* 63 (April 1964): 185–90.

Daniel Amneus, "Macbeth's 'Greater Honor,'" *ShakS* 6 (1970): 223–30.

Ruth L. Anderson, "The Pattern of Behavior Culminating in *Macbeth*," *SEL* 3 (Spring 1963): 151–74.

A. A. Ansari, "Fools of Time in *Macbeth*," *AJES* 2 (April 1977): 45–59.

Seiko Aoyama, "The Metaphysics of Poetry in *Macbeth*: Essays in Honour of Professor Toyohiko Tatsumi's Seventieth Birthday," in Milward, *Poetry and Faith in the English Renaissance*, 97–104.

William A. Armstrong, "Torch, Cauldron and Taper: Light and Darkness in *Macbeth*," in Coleman and Hammond, *Poetry and Drama, 1570–1700*, 47–59.

Aerol Arnold, "The Recapitulation Dream in *Richard III* and *Macbeth*," *SQ* 6 (Winter 1955): 57–62.

Alex Aronson, "A Note on Shakespeare's Dream Imagery," *Visuabharati Quarterly* (August–October 1952): 175–80.

John Arthos, "The Naive Imagination and the Destruction of Macbeth," *ELH* 14 (March 1947): 114–26. Reprinted in *The Art of Shakespeare* (New York: Barnes & Noble, 1964), 36–52.

Carolyn Asp, "'Be bloody, bold and resolute': Tragic Action and Sexual Stereotyping in *Macbeth*," *SP* 78 (Spring 1981): 153–69.

Weston Babcock, "Macbeth's 'Cream-Fac'd Loone," *SQ* 4 (April 1953): 199–202.

M. M. Badawi, "Euphemism and Circumlocution in Macbeth," *CairoSE* (1960): 25–46.

R. C. Bald, "Macbeth's 'Baby of a Girl,'" *ShAB* 24 (October 1949): 220–22.

David B. Barron, "The Babe That Milks: An Organic Study of *Macbeth*," *AI* (Summer 1960): 133–61.

H. W. Bateson, "Banquo and Edgar–Character or Function?" *EIC* 7 (July 1957): 324–25.

B. J. Bedard, "The Thane of Glamis Had a Wife," *UDR* 14 (Spring 1979–80): 39–43.

Harry Berger, Jr., "The Early Scenes of *Macbeth*: Preface to a New Interpretation," *ELH* 47 (March 1980): 1–31.

Berry, *Poet's Grammar*, 48–57.

Francis Berry, "Macbeth: Tense and Mood," *Orpheus* 6, no.1 (1959): 43–50.

Berry, *Shakespearean Structures*, 87–100.

Wilkes Berry, and Steven Gerson, "From Tree to Weed: Macbeth's Degeneration," *McNR* 23 (1976–77): 21–24.

Sukamari Bhattacharji, "The Banquet in *Macbeth* and Folk Beliefs," *JDECU* 17, no. 2 (1981–1982): 79–84.

Dennis Biggins, "'Appal' in *Macbeth* III.iv.60," *ELN* 4 (September 1967): 259–61.

Dennis Biggins, "Full of Scorpions," *TSL* 10 (February 1966): 110.

Dennis Biggins, "Scorpions, Serpents, and Treachery in *Macbeth*," *ShakS* 1 (Spring 1965): 29–36.

Dennis Biggins, "Sexuality, Witchcraft, and Violence in *Macbeth*," *ShakS* 8 (1977): 255–77.

Harvey Birenbaum, "Consciousness and Responsibility in *Macbeth*," *Mosaic* 15 (June 1982): 17–32.

James Black, "*Macbeth*: The Arming of the Hero," *ESQ* 3 (Summer 1977): 253–66.

Herbert Blau, "Language and Structure in Poetic Drama," *MLQ* 18 (March 1957): 33–34.

William Blissett, "The Secret'st Man of Blood: A Study of Dramatic Irony in *Macbeth*," *SQ* 10 (Summer 1959): 379–408.

David-Everett Blythe, "Shakespeare's *Macbeth*," *Expl* 48 (Sprinq 1990): 178–80.

Joan H. Blythe, "'His Horses Go About': The Circumstance of Banquo's Death and the Escape of Fleance," *N&Q* 21 (January 1974): 131–32.

Wayne C. Booth, "Macbeth as Tragic Hero," *JGE* 6 (October 1951): 17–25.

Robert Bossler, "Was Macbeth a Victim of Battle Fatigue?" *CE* 8 (May 1947): 436–38.

Rick Bowers, "*Macbeth* and Death: Paranoia and Primogeniture," *UCrow* 10 (1990): 55–68.

Robert R. Boyle, "The Imagery of *Macbeth*, I, vii, 21–28," *MLQ* 16 (June 1955): 130–36.

Bradley, *Oxford Lectures on Poetry*, 87–90.

Wallace R. Brandon, "The Moment of Tragedy in *Le Cid/Macbeth*," *LangQ* 23 (Spring–Summer 1985): 20–22.

Lucy Brashear, "'My dearest partner in greatness': A Reappraisal of Lady Macbeth," *SPWVSRA* 5 (Spring 1980): 14–24.

Horst Breuer, "Disintegration of Time in Macbeth's Soliloquy 'Tomorrow, and tomorrow, and tomorrow,'" *MLR* 71 (April 1976): 256–71.

D. J. Brindley, "*Macbeth* as Evidence of Shakespeare's Dramatic Genius," *CRUX* 15 (March 1981): 34–41.

D. J. Brindley, "Reversal of values in *Macbeth*," *ESA* 6 (September 1963): 137–43.

F. H. Cecil Brock, "Oedipus, Macbeth and the Christian Tradition," *ConR 1950* (March 1950) : 176–81.

Nicholas Brooke, "Language Most Shows a Man . . .? Language and Speaker in *Macbeth*," in Edwards, Ewbank, and Howard, *Shakespeare's Styles*, 67–77.

Nicholas Brooke, "The Songs for *Macbeth*," in *KM 80*, 23–24.

Cleanth Brooks, "The Naked Babe and the Cloak of Manliness," in *The Well Wrought Urn: Studies in the Structure of Poetry* (New York: Reynal & Hitchcock, 1947), 21–46.

Cleanth Brooks, "Shakespeare as a Symbolist Poet," *YR* 34 (December 1945): 642–65.

Brooks and Heilman, *Understanding Drama*, 668–73.

Hans Broszinski, "Christian Reality in 'Macbeth,'" *Theology* 50, no. 4 (1947): 456–64.

Joseph A. Bryant, Jr. "*Macbeth* and the Meaning of Tragedy," *KRev* 8 (Summer 1988): 3–17.

Frederick M. Burelbach, "Names of Supporting Characters in *Hamlet, King Lear*, and *Macbeth*," *Names* 35 (September–December 1987): 127–38.

Margaret D. Burrell, "*Macbeth*: A Study in Paradox," *ShJE* 9O (1954): 167–SO.

Rebecca Weld Bushnell, "Oracular Silence in *Oedipus the King* and *Macbeth*," *CML* (Summer 1982): 195–204.

Joan M. Byles, "*Macbeth*: Imagery of Destruction," *AI* 39 (Summer 1982): 149–64.

James L. Calderwood, "*Macbeth*: Counter-*Hamlet*," *ShakS* 17 (1985): 103–21.

James L. Calderwood, "'More Than What You Were': Augmentation and Increase in *Macbeth*," *ELR* 14 (Winter 1984): 70–82.

Lily B. Campbell, "Political Ideas in *Macbeth*, IV, iii," *SQ* 2 (October 1951): 281–86.

Canfield, *Word as Bond in English Literature*, 19O–98.

Leon Cantrell, "The Irony of *Macbeth*," *Balcony* 3, no. 1 (1965): 36–39.

Mario Carlisky, "Primal Scene, Procereation and The Number 13," *AI* 19 (Spring 1962): 19–2O.

Peter Carpenter, "*King Lear, Macbeth*, and the Use of Memory," *CrSurv* 3, no. 2 (1991): 194–207.

Cartelli, *Marlowe, Shakespeare*, 94–118.

Chandhuri, *Infirm Glory*, 173–84.

King-Kok Cheung, "Shakespeare and Kierkegaard: 'Dread' in *Macbeth*," *SQ* 35 (Autumn 1984): 430–39.

C. C. Clark, "Darkened Reason in *Macbeth*," *DUJ* 23 (December 1960): 11–18.

Clay, *The Role of Anxiety*, 153–64.

Clemen, *Shakespeare's Dramatic Art*, 76–87.

Karin S. Goddon, "'Unreal Mockery': Unreason and the Problem of Spectacle in *Macbeth*," *ELH* 56 (December 1989): 485–501.

Robert G. Collmer, "An Existentialist Approach to *Macbeth*," *Person* 41 (Autumn 1960): 484–91.

H. Coombes, *Literature and Criticism*, 50–52.

L. A. Cormican, "Medieval Idiom in Shakespeare," *Scrutiny* 17 (October 1950): 186–202.

Judith Cossons, "*Macbeth*, I, vii," *N&Q* 196 (August 1951): 368.

Herbert P. Coursen, Jr., "In Deepest Consequence: *MacBeth*," *SQ* 18 (Summer 1967): 375–88.

Herbert R. Coursen, Jr., "A Jungian Approach to Characterization: *Macbeth*," in Erickson, and Kahn, *Shakespeare's 'Rouqh Magic*,' 230–44.

Herbert R. Coursen, Jr., "Malcolm and Edgar," *Discourse* 11, no. 4 (1968) 430–38.

Hardin Craig, "Morality Plays and Elizabethan Drama," *SQ* 1 (Winter 1950): 64–72.

Hardin Craig, "Three Great Political Tragedies," in *An Interpretation of Shakespeare* (New York: Dryden, 1948), 254–301.

Craig, *The Written Word*, 49–61.

Delora G. Cunningham, "*Macbeth*: The Tragedy of a Hardened Heart," *SQ* 14 (Winter 1963): 39–48.

Joost Daalder, "Shakespeare's Attitude to Gender in *Macbeth*," *AUMLA* 70 (December 1988): 366–85.

Muhammad M. Dadawi, "Euphemism and Circumlocution in *Macbeth*," *Bulletin of the Faculty of Arts* (Alexandria University) 13 (1959): 101–122.

Daiches, *Critical Approaches to Literature*, 270–75.

Peter M. Daly, "Of Macbeth, Martlets and Other 'Fowles of Heauen,'" *Mosaic* 12 (Winter 1978): 23–46.

Jack D'Amico, "Moral and Political Conscience: Machiavelli and Shakespeare's *Macbeth* and *Henry V*," *IQ* 27 (Summer 1986): 31–41.

Arun Kumar Dasgupta, "A Note on *Macbeth* II, ii, 61–63," *N&Q* 205 (September 1960): 332–33.

Davidson, *The Solace of Literature*, 70–74.

Clifford Davidson, "'Full of Scorpions Is My Mind," *TLS* 4 (November 1965): 988.

Clifford Davidson, "The Witches' Dances in *MacBeth*," *ShN* 18 (Spring 1968): 37.

Cecil W. Davies, "Action and Soliloquy in *Macbeth*" *EIC* 8 (October 1958): 451–53.

Nick Davis, "Finding the Centre of *Macbeth*," in *KM 80*, 36–38.

Thomas De Quincey, "On the Knicking at the Gate in *Macbeth*," in *Schorer, Criticism*, 471–73.

Huston Diehl, "Horrid Image, Sorry Sight, Fatal Vision: The Visual Rhetoric of *Macbeth*," *ShakS* 16 (1983): 191–203.

H. W. Donner, "She Would Have Died Hereafter," *ES* 40 (October 1959): 385–89.

Madeleine Doran, "The *Macbeth* Music," *ShakS* 16 (1983): 153–73.

Toni Dorfman, and Will Valk, "That Sansing Bell: An Ironic Borrowing in *Macbeth*," *ShakB* 4 (January–February 1986): 22.

Alan S. Downer, "The Life of Our Design," *HudR* (Summer 1949): 242–63.

John W. Draper, "Patterns of Humor and Tempo in *Macbeth*," *Neophil* 31 (July 1947): 202–07.

John W. Draper, "Subjective Conflict in Shakespearean Tragedy," *NM* 61, no. 1 (1960): 216–17.

G. I. Duthie, "Antithesis in *MacBeth*," *ShS* 19 (1966): 25–33.

Peter Dyson, "The Structural Function of the Banquet Scene in *Macbeth*," *SQ* 14 (Autumn 1963): 369–78.

J. C. Eade, "Shakespeare's *Macbeth* I.ii.2508," *Expl* 38 (Fall 1980): 31–32.

Eagleton, *Shakespeare and Society*, 130–38.

Eastman, *Christ in the Drama*, 15–28, 31 35.

Joseph J. Egan, "'Of Kernes and Gallowglasses': An Error in *Macbeth*," *ELN* 15 (June 1978): 167–71.

Kier Elam, *Semiotics of Theatre and Drama*, 123–26, 128–30.

Norman E. Eliason, "Shakespeare's Purgative Drug *Cyme*," *MLN* 57 (December 1942): 663–65.

Ellis-Fermor, *The Frontiers of Drama*, 50–52, 88–89.

Adel Ata Elyas, "Two Ambitious Devils: Satan and Macbeth," *JKSUA* 11, no.1 (1984): 71–81.

Inga-Stina Ewbank, "The Fiend–like Queen: A Note on *Macbeth* and Seneca's *Medea*," *ShS* 18 (1966): 82–94.

A. H. R. Fairchild, "Shakespeare and the Tragic Theme," *University of Missouri Studies* 19, no. 2 (1944): 58–72, 105–40.

Paul Fatout, "Shakespeare's *Macbeth*, II, ii, 40," *Expl* 9 (December 1950): 22.

Ann D. Ferguson, "A Brief Comparison of Supernatural Elements in *Richard III* and *Macbeth*, *GorR* 9 (Summer 1966): 184–92.

Ferguson, *Trope and Allegory*, 26–31, 33–37, 44–47.

Francis Fergusson, *The Human Image in Dramatic Literature*, 115–25.

Francis Fergusson, "*Macbeth* as the Imitation of an Action," *English Institute Essays* (1951): 31–43. Reprinted in *The Art of the Theatre*, ed. Robert W. Corrigan (San Francisco: Chandler, 1964), 200–08.

Richard Flatter, "The Question of Free Will, and Other Observations on *Macbeth*," *EM* 10 (Spring 1959): 87–106.

Robert F. Fleissner, "'The Secret'st Man of Blood': Foreshadowings of *Macbeth* in *Arden of Feversham*," *UDR* 14 (Spring 1979–80): 7–14.

R. A. Foakes, "Contrasts and Connections: Some Notes on Style in Shakespeare's Comedies and Tragedies," *ShJE* 90 (1954): 74–81.

R. A. Foakes, "Macbeth," *Stratford Papers on Shakespeare* (1962): 150–74.

Jean Fosse, "The Lord's Anointed Temple: A Study of Some Symbolic Patterns in *Macbeth*," *CahiersE* 6 (April 1974): 15–22.

Alice Fox, "How Many Pregnancies Had Lady Macbeth?" *UDR* 14 (Spring 1979–80): 33–37.

Alice Fox, "Obstetrics and Gynecology in *Macbeth*," *ShakS* 12 (1979): 127–41.

Bernard Frank, "Shakespeare's *Macbeth*, V.v.17–28," *Expl* 43 (Spring 1985): 5–7.

William J. Free, "Shakespeare's *Macbeth*, III.iv.122–26 and IV.i.90–94," *Expl* 19 (April 1961): 50.

William W. French, "What 'May Become a Man': Image and Structure in *Macbeth*," *CollL* 12 (Spring 1985): 191–201.

French, *Shakespeare's Division of Experience*, 242–53.

Roland M. Frye, "Launching the Tragedy of *Macbeth*: Temptation, Deliberation, and Consent in Act I," *HLQ* 50 (Autumn 1987): 249–61.

Roland M. Frye, "*Macbeth* and the Powers of Darkness," *EUQ* 8 (October 1952): 164–74.

Roland M. Frye, "'Out, Out, Brief Candle' and the Jacobean Understanding," *N&Q* 200 (April 1955): 143–45.

Steven H. Gale, "Analysis of Passages form *Macbeth*," *Horizontes* 36 (April 1975): 5–7.

Kay Gallwey, "*Macbeth*: Two Kinds of Hero," *CRUX* 22 (April 1988): 34–41.

Guari Prasad Ghosh, "*Macbeth*: Struggle and Defeat of the Moral Will," *JDECU* 19, no. 1–2 (1983–1984): 1–20.

C. G. Gilbert, "*Macbeth*, V, iii, 22," *N&Q* 205 (September 1960): 33–34.

Christopher Gillie, "Banquo and Edgar—Character or Function?" *EIC* 7 (July 1957): 322–24.

A. F. Glencross, "Christian Tragedy," in *A Christian Approach to Western Literature*, ed. Aloysius Norton (Westminster, MD: Newman, 1961), 66–68.

Jonathan Goldberg, "Speculations: *Macbeth* and Source," in *Post-Structuralist Readings of English Poetry*, ed. Richard Machin and Christopher Norris (Cambridge: Cambridge University Press, 1987), 38–58. Reprinted in *Shakespeare Reproduced: The Text in History and Ideology*, ed. Jean E. Howard and Marion F. O'Connor (New York: Methuen, 1987), 242–64.

Gomez, *The Alienated Figure in Drama*, 28–34.

Bill Goode, "How the Lady Knew Her Lord: A Note on *Macbeth*," *AI* 20 (Winter 1963): 349–56.

Randolf Goodman, *Drama on Stage*, 116–42.

Phyllis Gorfain, "Riddles and Tragic Structure in *Macbeth*," *MissFR* 10, no. 2 (1976): 187–209.

James J. Greene, "*Macbeth*: Masculinity as Murder," *AI* 41 (Summer 1984): 155–80.

M. E. Grenander, "*Macbeth* IV.i.44–45 and Convulsive Ergotism," *ELN* 15 (June 1977): 102–03.

M. E. Granander, "*Macbeth* as Diaphthorody: Notes toward the Definition of a Form," *YCC* 10 (1983): 224–48.

T. N. Grove, "The Cauldron of Hell-Broth: An Imagistic Analysis of *Macbeth*," *GyS* 1, no. 2 (1974): 24–39.

Grudin, *Mighty Opposites*, 153–65.

Luisa Guj, "*Macbeth* and the Seeds of Time," *ShakS* 18 (1986): 175–88.

Hager, *Shakespeare's Political Animal*, 105–14.

Jay L. Halio, "Bird Imagery in *Macbeth*," *ShN* 13 (February 1963): 7.

Hallett and Hallett, *Analyzing Shakespeare's Action*, 6–7, 88–89.

John B. Harcourt, "I Pray You, Remember the Porter," *SQ* 12 (Autumn 1961): 393–402.

Edith Harnett, "Look, How Our Partner's Rapt," *RLMC* 30 (1977): 105–20.

D. Harrington-Lueker, "Imagination versus Introspection: *The Cenci* and *Macbeth*," *KSJ* 32 (Summer 1983): 172–89.

Walter M. Hart, "Shakespeare's Use of Verse and Prose," *University of California Publications English Studies* 10 (1954): 8–17.

R. Chris Hassel, Jr., "'All Hail Macbeth!'" *LangQ* 12 (Spring–Summer 1974): 43.

Hawkes, *Shakespeare's Talking Animals*, 142–57.

Harriet Hawkins, "Likeness with Difference: Patterns of Action in *Romeo and Juliet*, *Julius Caesar*, and *Macbeth*," *MEJ* 6, no. 2 (1968): 1–13.

Hawkins, *Likeness of Truth*, 151–60.

Hawkins, *Poetic Freedom and Poetic Truth*, 4–5, 20–21, 99–104.

Robert B. Heilman, "The Criminal as Tragic Hero: Dramatic Methods," *ShS* 19 (1966): 12–24.

Robert B. Heilman, "'Twere Best not Know Myself: *Othello*, *Lear*, *Macbeth*," *SQ* 15 (Spring 1964): 89–98.

Olive Henneberger, "Banquo, Loyal Subject," *CE* 8 (October 1946): 18–22.

Hewett, *Reading and Response*, 110–15.

Highet, *The Powers of Poetry*, 304–05.

Theodore C. Hoepfner, "Shakespeare's *Macbeth*, I, vii, 1–28," *Expl* 7 (March 1949): 34.

Patrick Colm Hogan, "*Macbeth*: Authority and Progenitorship," *AI* 40 (Winter 1983): 385–95.

Norman N. Holland, "Macbeth as Hibernal Giant," *L–P* 10 (Spring 1960): 37–38.

John Holloway, "Dramatic Irony in Shakespeare," *Northern Miscellany of Literary Criticism* 1 (Autumn 1953): 3–10.

Holloway, *The Story of the Night*, 57–74.

Richard Horwich, "Intergrity in *Macbeth*: The Search for the 'Single State of Man,'" *SQ* 29 (Autumn 1978): 365–73.

Houston, *Shakespearean Sentences*, 142–50.

Alan Hughes, "Lady MacBeth: A Fiend Indeed?" *SoRA* 11 (August 1978): 107–12.

William B. Hunter, Jr., "A Decorous *Macbeth*," *ELN* 8 (September 1981): 169–73.

Isabel Hyde, "*Macbeth*: A Problem," *English* 13 (Autumn 1960): 91–94.

Laurence W. Hyman, "*Macbeth*: The Hand and the Eye," *TSL* 5 (Spring 1960): 97–100.

Richard S. Ide, "The Theatre of the Mind: An Essay on *Macbeth*," *ELH* 42 (Fall 1975): 338–61.

Richard S. Ide, "The Tragedy of Banquo (By William Shakespeare)," *L&P* 17, no. 1 (1967): 87–94.

William Ingram, "'Enter Macduffe; with Macbeth's Head,'" *TN* 26 (January 1972): 75–77.

Jane H. Jack, "*Macbeth*, King James, and the Bible," *ELH* 22 (September 1955): 173–93.

Howard Jacobson, "*Macbeth*, I.vii.7–10," *SQ* 35 (Summer 1984): 321–32.

Pierre Janton, "Sonship and Fatherhood in *Macbeth*," *CahiersE* 35 (April 1989): 47–58.

Ludwig Jekels, "The Riddle of Shakespeare's *Macbeth*," *Psychoanalytic Review* 30 (October 1943): 361–85. Reprinted in *Selected Papers*, 105–30.

Archibald Jenderson, "MacBeth as Underdog: Central Villain, Tragic Hero," *ForumH* 4 (December 1967): 14–17.

Jepson, *Ethical Aspects of Tragedy*, 27–31.

Anthony L. Johnson, "Number Symbolism in *Macbeth*," *Analysis* 4 (Spring 1986): 25–41.

Clarence O. Johnson, "'Hoboyes' and Macbeth: A Note on *Macbeth* I.vi," *EIRC* 5 (1979): 33–39.

Francis R. Johnson, "Shakespearean Imagery and Senecan Imitation," in McManaway, *Joseph Q. Adams Memorial Studies*, 43–53.

Bertram L. Joseph, "Character and Plot," *DramS* 4 (Fall 1964): 541–46.

V. Y. Kantak, "An Approach to Shakespearian Tragedy: The 'Actor' Image in *Macbeth*," *ShS* 16 (1963): 42–52.

Kastan, *Shakespeare and the Shapes of Time*, 91–101.

Mary Kavanagh, "The Weird Sisters of *Macbeth*," *Baconiana* 32 (October 1948): 72–74.

Sarvar Khambatta, "'Foul and Most Unnatural Murder': *Hamlet* and *Macbeth*," *HSt* 10 (Summer–Winter 1988): 130–36.

Robert M. Kimbrough, "*Macbeth*: The Prisoner of Gender," *ShakS* 16 (1983): 175–90.

Arthur F. Kinney, "Shakespeare's *Macbeth* and the Question of Nationalism," in Newey and Thompson, *Literature and Nationalism*, 56–75.

Leo Kirschbaum, "Banquo and Edgar: Character or Function?" *EIC* 7 (January 1957): 1–8.

Joan Larsen Klein, "Lady Macbeth: 'Infirm of purpose,'" in Lenz, et al., *The Women's Part*, 240–55.

Bernice W. Kliman, "Thanes in the Folio *Macbeth*," *ShakB* 9 (Winter 1991): 5–8.

G. Wilson Knight, "Brutus and Macbeth," in *The Wheel of Fire*, 120–39.

G. Wilson Knight, *The Christian Renaissance* (New York: Norton, 1962), 45–47, 186–87.

Knight, *Explorations*, 31–54.

Knight, *The Golden Labyrinth*, 75–77, 231–33.

G. Wilson Knight, "Macbeth and the Metaphysics of Evil," *The Wheel of Fire*, 140–59.

G. Wilson Knight, "The Milk of Concord: An Essay on the Life Themes in *Macbeth*," in *The Imperial Theme*, 125–53, 327–42. Reprinted in Stallman, *Critiques and Essays in Criticism*, 119–40.

Knight, *The Olive and the Sword*, 54–58.

Knight, *The Sovereign Flower*, 58–64, 280–86.

John Knoepfle, "*Macbeth*: Despair in Seven Stages," *ShN* 9 (September 1959): 26.

Paul H. Kocher, "Lady Macbeth and the Doctor," *SQ* 5 (Autumn 1954): 341–50.

Philip C. Kolin, "Macbeth, Malcolm, and the Curse of the Serpent," *SCB* 34 (Summer 1974): 159–60.

Dorothea Krook, "The Naked New-Born Babe Again: Perhaps an Art Image," *CritQ* 21 (Fall 1979): 46–47.

Jenijoy La Belle, "'A Strange Infirmity': Lady Macbeth's Amenorrhea," *SQ* 31 (Autumn 1980): 381–86.

Charles G. Labrizzi, "*Macbeth* and the 'Milk of Human Kindness': A Note," *MSE* 5, no. 4 (1978): 29–31.

Antony Landon, "*Macbeth* and the Folktale 'The Fisher and His Wife': Hanasaari/Hansholmen, 19–21 May 1983," in *Proceedings from the Second Nordic Conference for English Studies*, ed. Haken Ringbom and Matti Rissanen (Abo: Abo Akademi, 1984), 423–35.

François Laroque, "Magic in *Macbeth*," *CahiersE* 35 (April 1989): 59–84.

Jacqueline E. Lawson, "The Inferna; *Macbeth*," *ACM* 1, no. 1 (1988): 33–43.

Leaska, *The Voice of Tragedy*, 108–17.

F. N. Lees, "A Biblical Connotation in *Macbeth*," *N&Q* 195 (December 1950): 534.

Alexander Leggatt, "*Macbeth* and the Last Plays," in Gray, *Mirror up to Shakespeare*, 189–207.

Laurence Lerner, "Tragedy: Religious, Humanist," *REL* 2 (October 1961): 28–33.

Harry Levin, "Two Scenes from *Macbeth*," in *Shakespeare's Craft: Eight Lectures*, ed. Philip H. Highfill, Jr. (Carbondale: Southern Illinois University Press for George Washington University, 1982), 48–68.

William T. Liston, "'Male and Female Created He Them': Sex and Gander in *Macbeth*," *CollL* 16 (Summer 1989): 232–39.

E. A. Loomis, "Master of the Tiger," *SQ* 7 (Winter 1956): 457.

John B. Lord, "Comic Scenes in Shakespearean Tragedy," *WCSC* 32 (September 1964): 238.

Robert J. Lordi, "Macbeth and His 'dearest partner of greatness,' Lady Macbeth," *UCrow* 4 (1982): 94–106.

H. W. Love, "Seeing the Difference: Good and Evil in the World of *Macbeth*," *Aumla* 72 (July 1989): 203–28.

David Lowenthal, "*Macbeth*: Shakespeare Mystery Play," *IJPP* 16 (Spring 1989): 311–57.

Lucas, *Literature and Psychology*, 76–77.

E. B. Lyle, "The 'Twofold Balls and Treble Scepters' in *Macbeth*," *SQ* 28 (Winter 1977): 516–19.

E. B. Lyle, "Macduff's Reception of Macbeth's Messenger: A Suggestion That the Episode at *Macbeth* III.vi.37b–45a Has Been Displaced From Earlier in the Scene," *AUMLA* 41 (January 1974): 75–78.

Maynard Mack, "The Jacobean Shakespeare: Some Observations on the Construction of the Tragedies," *Stratford-Upon-Avon Studies* 1 (1960): 11–42.

Francois Maguin, "The Breaking of Time: *Richard II*, *Hamlet*, and *Macbeth*," *CahiersE* 7 (April 1975): 25–41.

J. M. Maguin, "Bell, Book, and Candle in *Macbeth*: A Note on I.5.61–2; II.1.5, 31–2 and 62," *CahiersE* 12 (April 1977): 65–68.

H. O. Makey, "In the Literature Class: Study of the Opening Scenes of *Macbeth*," *EJ* 39 (September 1950): 360–66

A. E. Malloch, "Equivocation: A Cicuit of Reasons," in *Familiar Colloquy: Essays Presented to Arthur Edward Braker*, ed. Patricia Brückmann (Ontario: Oberon Press, 1978), 132–43.

John Margetts, "A Note on *Macbeth* I.ii.22.," *KM 80*, 92–97.

Julian Markels, "The Spectacle of Deterioration: *Macbeth* and the 'Manner' of Tragic Imitation," *SQ* 12 (Summer 1961): 293–303.

Kurian Mattam, "The Concept of Sin in the Shakespearean Tragedies: *Hamlet*, *King Lear*, *Macbeth* and *Othello*: An Exploration," *Unitas* 64 (June 1991): 165–230.

B. Maxwell, "That Undiscovered Country," in *Renaissance Studies in Honor of Hardin Craig*, 230–35.

J. C. Maxwell, "That Ghost From the Grave: A Note on Shakespeare's Apparitions," *DUJ* 18 (March 1956): 58.

J. C. Maxwell, "*Macbeth*, 4, ii, 107," *MLR* 51 (January 1956): 73.

John C. McCloskey, "Why Not Fleance?" *ShAB* 20 (April 1945): 118–20.

McCollum, *Tragedy*, 51–56.

J. Wilson McCutchan, "He Has No Children," *McNR* 8 (Spring 1956): 41–52.

Dana Sue McDermott, "The Void in *Macbeth*: A Symbolic Design," in Redmond, *Drama and Symbolism*, 113–25.

McDonnell, *The Aspiring Mind*, 265–93.

Arthur R. McGee, "*Macbeth* and the Furies," *ShS* 19 (1966): 55–67.

McPeek, *The Black Book of Knaves*, 80–82.

Ninian Mellamphy, "The Ironic Catastrophe in *Macbeth*," *ArielE* 11 (October 1980): 3–19.

W. Moelwyn Merchant, "'His Fiend-like Queen,'" *ShS* 19 (1966): 75–81.

Marco Mincoff, "The Structural Pattern of Shakepeare's Tragedies," *ShS* 3 (1950): 63–65.

Lee Mitchell, "Shakespeare's Legerdemain," *Speech Monographs* 16 (August 1949): 144–52, 154–57, 160–61.

Bernard Moro, and Michele Willems, "Death and Rebirth in *Macbeth* and *The Winter's Tale*," *CahiersE* 21 (April 1982): 35–48.

Mikhail M. Morozov, "The Individualization of Shakespeare's Characters Through Imagery," *ShS* 2 (1949): 83–84, 88–93.

Harry Morris, "*Macbeth*, Dante, and the Greatest Evil," *TSL* 12 (Spring 1967): 22–38.

Kenneth Muir, "Image and Symbol in *Macbeth*," *ShS* 19 (1966): 45–54.

Kenneth Muir, "The Uncomic Pun," *Cambridge Journal* 3 (1950): 472–85. Reprinted in *The Singulatrity of Shakespeare and Other Essays* (Liverpool: Liverpool University Press, 1977), 20–37.

W. A. Murray, "Why Was Duncan's Blood Golden?" *ShS* 19 (1966): 34–44.

Myers, *Tragedy: A View of Life*, 13–15, 105–09.

V. C. Nag, "*Macbeth*: A Character Study," in *The Moving Finger*, ed. V. N. Bhushan (Bombay: Padma, 1945), 194–212.

S. Nagarajan, "A Note of Banquo," *SQ* 7 (Autumn 1956): 371–76.

Michael Neill, "Rememberance and Revenge: *Hamlet*, *Macbeth* and *The Tempest*," in Donaldson, *Jonson and Shakespeare*, 35–56.

Newman, *Fashioning Femininity*, 53–70.

David Norbrook, "*Macbeth* and the Politics of Historiography," in *Politics of Discourse: The Literature and History of Seventeenth-Century England*, ed.

Kevin Sharpe and Steven N. Zwicker (Berkeley: University of California Press, 1987), 78–116.

J. M. Nosworthy, "The Bleeding Captain Scene in *Macbeth*," *RES* 22 (April 1946): 126–30.

J. M. Nosworthy, "The Hecate Scenes in *Macbeth*," *RES* 24 (April 1948): 138–39.

James M. Nosworthy, "*Macbeth, Doctor Faustus*, and the Juggling Fiends," in Gray, *Mirror up to Shakespeare*, 208–22.

Richard O'Dea, "Vehicle and Tenor in *MacBeth*," *Coranto* 5, no. 1 (1967): 26–28.

Yasuhiro Ogawa, "'Fair Is Foul, and Foul Is Fair': The 'Ambivalent' Fiction in *Macbeth*," *Lang&C* 2 (1982): 17–54.

Olson, *Tragedy and the Theory of Drama*, 45–46, 113–25.

Flemming Olsen, "The Banquet Scene in *Macbeth*: Variation upon a Topos," in *A Literary Miscellany Presented to Eric Jacobsen*, ed. Graham D. Caie and Holger Norgaard (Copenhagen: University of Copenhagen, 1988), 108–32.

Ornstein, *Moral Vision of Jacobean Tragedy*, 230–34.

Robert Pack, "*Macbeth*: The Anatomy of Loss," *YR* 45 (September 1956): 533–48.

Bernard J. Paris, "Bargains with Fate: The Case of *Macbeth*," *AJP* 42 (Spring 1982): 7–20.

Ann Parker, "*Macbeth*—Two Notes: 2. 'Thou sour and firm-set earth,'" *SSEng* 5 (1979–80): 102–04.

Graham Parry, "A Theological Reading of *Macbeth*," *Caliban* 21 (1984): 133–40.

Howard Parsons, "*Macbeth*: Emendations," *N&Q* 199 (August 1954): 331–33.

Howard Parsons, "*Macbeth*: Some Emendations," *N&Q* 197 (September 1952): 403.

Henry N. Paul, "The Imerial Theme in *Macbeth*," in McManaway, *Joseph Q. Adams Memorial Studies*, 253–68.

Vincent F. Petronella, "The Role of Macduff in *Macbeth*," *EA* 32 (January 1979): 11–19.

Pogson, *In the East My Pleasure Lies*, 85–91.

David L. Pollard, "'O Scotland, Scotland': The Anti-Heroic Play of *Macbeth*," *UCrow* 8 (1988): 69–76.

Pye, *Regal Phantasm*, 142–72.

P. Ramamoorthy, "'The Banquet is the Thing . . .' A Note on *Macbeth*," *AJES* 14 (April 1989): 1–8.

John Crowe Ransom, "On Shakespeare's Language," *SR* 55 (Spring 1947): 181–98.

Margie Rauls, "The Image of Echo and Reverberation in *Macbeth*," *CLAJ* 32 (December 1989): 361–72.

Fr. Robert R. Reed, "The Fatal Elizabethan Sisters in *Macbeth*," *N&Q* 200 (October 1955): 425–27.

B. L. Reid, "*Macbeth* and the Play of Absolutes," *SR* 73 (Winter 1965): 19–46.

Irving Ribner, "*Macbeth*: The Pattern of Idea and Action," *SQ* 10 (Spring 1959): 147–59.

Irving Ribner, "Political Doctrine in *Macbeth*," *SQ* 4 (April 1953): 202–05. Reprinted in *The English History Play*, 254–59.

Irving Ribner, "Shakespeare's Christianity and the Problem of Belief," *CentR* 8 (Winter 1964): 103–06.

Brian Richardson, "'Hours Dreadful and Things Strange': Inversions of Chronology and Casuality in *Macbeth*," *PQ* 68 (Summer 1989): 283–94.

Barbara Riebling, "Virtue's Sacrifice: A Machiavellian Reading of *Macbeth*," *SEL* 31 (Spring 1991): 273–86.

A. P. Riemer, "*Macbeth*—Two Notes: 1. 'The bank and school of time,'" *SSEng* 5 (1979–80): 96–101.

Henri Roddier, "A Freudian Detective's Shakespeare," *MP* 47 (November 1950): 122–25.

Marvin Rosenberg, "Lady Macbeth's Indispensable Child," *ETJ* 26 (March 1974): 14–19.

Rossiter, *Angel with Horns*, 209–34.

Robert Roth, "Another World of Shakespeare," *MP* 49 (August 1951): 55–58.

Lynn Veach Sadler, "The Three Guises of Lady Macbeth," *CLAJ* 19 (March 1975): 10–19.

Ernest Schanzer, "Four Notes on Macbeth," *MLR* 52 (April 1957): 223–27.

James Schiffer, "*Macbeth* and the Bearded Women," in Kehler and Baker, *In Amother Country*, 204–17.

Daniel E. Schneider, "On How to Write a Play—Analysis of Shakespeare's *Macbeth*," in *The Psychological and the Artist* (New York: Farrar, Straus, 1950), 257–92.

S. Schoenbaum, "Enter a Porter (*Macbeth*, 2.3)" in Fabian and von Rosador, *Shakespeare: Text, Language, Criticism*, 246–53.

F. G. Schoff, "Shakespeare's 'Fair is Foul,'" *N&Q* 199 (June 1954): 241–43.

S. C. Sen Gupta, *Shakespearian Comedy* (Calcutta: Oxford University Press, 1950), 201–14.

Lyndon Shanley, "*Macbeth*: The Tragedy of Evil," *CE* 22 (February 1961): 305–11.

Paul N. Siegel, "Echoes of the Bible Story in *Macbeth*," *N&Q* 200 (April 1955): 142–43.

Stuart Sillars, "Shakespeare's *Macbeth*," *Expl* 41 (Spring 1983): 17–18.

Edward Silling, "Another Meaning for 'breech'd': *Macbeth* II, iii, 116," *MSE* 4, no. 3 (1974): 56.

Alan Sinfield, "*Macbeth*: History, Ideology and Intellectuals," *CritQ* 28 (Spring–Summer 1986): 63–77.

Regina Smit, "*Macbeth* and the Sanctity of the Guest," *Standpunte* 36 (October 1983): 46–52.

Grover Smith, "The Naked New-Born Babe in *Macbeth*: Some Iconographical Evidence," *RenP 1963* (1964): 21–27.

R. M. Smith, "Macbeth's 'Cyme' Once More," *MLN* 60 (January 1945): 33–38.

Smith, *Dualities in Shakespeare*, 160–88.

Soellner, *Shakespeare's Patterns*, 327–54.

Theodore Spencer, "*Macbeth* and *Antony and Cleopatra*, in *Shakespeare and the Nature of Man* (New York: Macmillan, 1942), 153–76.

A. C. Sprague, "A *Macbeth* of Few Words," in Bryan, Morris, Murphee, and Williams, *All These to Teach*, 80–101.

John Stachniewski, "Calvinist Psychology in *Macbeth*," *ShakS* 20 (1987): 169–89.

Bert O. States, "The Horses of *Macbeth*," *KR* 47 (Spring 1985): 52–66.

Kay Stockholder, "*Macbeth*: A Dream to Love," *AI* 44 (Summer 1987): 85–105.

Donald A. Stauffer, "The Dark Tower," in *Shakespeare's World of Images: The Development of His Moral Ideas* (New York: Norton, 1949), 163–200.

Arnold Stein, "Macbeth and Word Magic," *SR* (Spring 1951): 271–84.

Brents Sterling, "The Unity of *Macbeth*," *SQ* 4 (October 1953): 385–94.

John S. Tanner, "The Syllables of Time: An Augustinian Context for *Macbeth* 5.5," *JRMMRA* 8 (January 1987): 131–46.

Mark Taylor, "Letters and Readers in *Macbeth*, *King Lear*, and *Twelfth Night*," *PQ* 69 (Winter 1990): 31–53.

J. J. M. Tobin, "*Macbeth* and Christ's Teares over Jerusalem," *AJES* 7 (April 1982): 72–78.

Michio Tokumi, "Manhood in *Macbeth*," *SELL* 33 (January 1983): 1–14.

T. B. Tomlinson, "Action and Soliloquy in *Macbeth*," *EIC* 8 (April 1958): 147–55.

Frederic B. Tromly, "Macbeth and his Porter," *SQ* 26 (Winter 1975): 151–56.

Rachel Trubowitz, "'The Single State of Man': Androgyny in *Macbeth* and *Paradise Lost*," *PLL* 26 (Summer 1990): 305–33.

Carol Strongin Tufts, "Shakespeare's Conception of Moral Order in *Macbeth*," *Renascence* 39 (Winter 1987): 340–53.

Edith Slosson Tyson, "Shakespeare's *Macbeth* and Dante's *Inferno*: A Comparison of the Images of Hell, Damnation and Corruption," *ISJR* 54 (December 1980): 461–68.

Z. A. Usmani, "The Drama of Values in *Macbeth*," *AJES* 3 (April 1978): 63–79.

S. Viswanathan, "*Macbeth* in the Tiring House: The Clothes and Actor Motifs in the Play," *Anglia* 100, no. 1 (1982): 18–35.

K. Tetzeli von Rosador, "'Supernatural Soliciting': Temptation and Imagination in *Doctor Faustus* and *Macbeth*," in Honigmann, *Shakespeare and His Contemporaries*, 42–59.

Eugene M. Waith, "Manhood and Valor in Two Shakespearean Tragedies," *ELH* 17 (December 1950): 265–68.

A. J. A. Waldock, "*Macbeth*," *SSEng* 0 (1983–1984): 3–20.

Richard Waswo, "Damnation Puritan Style: Macbeth, Faustus, and Christian Tragedy," *JMRS* 4 (Autumn 1974): 63–99.

Watson, *Shakespeare and the Hazards of Ambition*, 88–134.

Karl Wentersdorf, "Witchcraft and Politics in *Macbeth*; Proceedings of the Centenary Conference of the Folklore Society," in *Folklore Studies in the Twentieth Century*, ed. Venetia J. Newall (Woodbridge, UK, and Totowa, NJ: Brewer, Rowman & Littlefield, 1978, 1980), 431–37.

Albert Wertheim, "'Things climb upward to what they were before': The Reteaching and Regreening of *Macbeth*," in Edens, et. al., *Teaching Shakespeare*, 114–37.

Robert H. West, "Night's Black Agents in *Macbeth*," *RenP 1955* (1956): 17–24.

Perry D. Westbrook, "A Note on *Macbeth*, Act II, Scene 1," *CE* 7 (January 1946): 219–20.

Bart Westerweel, "*Macbeth*, Time, and Prudence; Seventeen Papers Read at Centenary Conference, Groningen, 15–16 Jan. 1986," in *One Hundred Years of English Studies in Dutch Universities*, ed. G. H. V. Bunt, E. S. Cooper, J. L. Mackenzie, and D. R. M. Wilkinson (Amsterdam: Rodopi, 1987), 199–210.

White, *Antiquity Forgot*, 31–43.

Glynne Wickham, "Hell-Castle and Its Door-Keeper," *ShS* 19 (1966): 68–74.

Martin Wiggins, "*Macbeth* and Premeditation," in *The Arts, Literature, and Society*, ed. Arthur Marwick (London: Routledge, 1990), 23–47.

David Willbern, "Phantasmagoric *Macbeth*," *ELR* 16 (Autumn 1986): 68–74.

Raymond Williams, "Monologue in *Macbeth*," in Kappler and Bryson, *Teaching the Text*, 180–202.

Marilyn L. Williamson, "Violence and Gender Ideology in *Coriolanus* and *Macbeth*," in *Shakespeare Left and Right*, ed. Ivo Kamps (New York: Routledge, 1991), 147–66.

Robert F. Wilson, Jr., "Fearful Punning: the Name Game in *Macbeth*," *CahiersE* 15 (April 1979): 29–34.

Robert F. Wilson, Jr., "Macbeth the Player King: The Banquet Scene as Frustrated Play Within the Play," *SJW* 114 (Spring 1978): 107–14.

Sarah Wintle and Rene Weis, "*Macbeth* and the Barren Sceptre," *EIC* 41 (April 1991): 128–46.

Nicholas Wolterstoriff, "Was Macduff of Woman Born? The Onotolgy of Characters," *NDEJ* 12 (Spring 1979): 123–39.

James O. Wood, "Hecate's 'Vap'rous' Drop, Profound," *N&Q* 209 (July 1964): 262–64.

James O. Wood, "Two Notes on *Macbeth*," *N&Q* 209 (April 1964): 137–38.

William R. Wray, and Mary Rohrberger, "Shakespeare's *Macbeth* I.iii.116–117," *Expl* 38 (Fall 1980): 19–20.

Robert M. Wren, "The 'Hideous Trumpet' and Sexual Transformation in *Macbeth*," *ForumH* 4 (October 1967): 18–21.

Bruce W. Young, "The Language of *Macbeth*: A Comparison of Shakespeare's and Davenant's Versions," *ISJR* 60 (December 1986): 431–43.

Young, *Immortal Shadows*, 96–100.

Karl F. Zender, "The Death of Young Siward: Providential Order and Tragic Loss in *MacBeth*," *TSLL* 17 (Winter 1975): 415–25.

Zaixin Zhang, "Shakespeare's *Macbeth*," *Expl* 47 (Winter 1989): 11–13.

Sheldon P. Zitner, "*Macbeth* and the Oral Scale of Tragedy," *JGE* 16 (April 1964): 20–28.

Measure for Measure

Janet Adelman, "Bed Tricks: On Marriage as the End of Comedy in *All's Well That Ends Well* and *Measure for Measure*," in Holland, Homan, and Paris, *Shakespeare's Personality*, 151–74.

David Aers, and Gunther Kress, "The Politics of Style: Discourses of Law and Authority in *Measure for Measure*," *Style* 16 (Winter 1982): 22–37.

Joanne Altieri, "Style and Social Disorder in *Measure for Measure*," *SQ* 25 (Winter 1974): 6–16.

A. A. Ansari, "*Measure for Measure* and the Masks of Death," *AJES* 2 (July 1977): 231–46.

Babb, *The Elizabethan Malady*, 148–49.

Barbara J. Baines, "Assaying the Power of Chastity in *Measure for Measure*," *SEL* 30 (Spring 1990): 283–301.

Battenhouse, *Poets of Christian Thought*, 39–42.

Roy W. Battenhouse, "*Measure for Measure* and Christian Doctrine of the Atonement," *PMLA* 61 (December 1946): 1029–59.

N. W. Bawcutt, "'He Who the Sword of Heaven Will Bear': The Duke versus Angelo in *Measure for Measure*," *ShS* 37 (1984): 89–97.

Beardsley, *Aesthetics*, 56–57.

Ralp Berry, "Language and Structure in *Measure for Measure*," *UTQ* 46 (June 1977):147–61.

Berry, *Shakespearean Structures*, 47–63.

David Bevington, "Shakespeare's Development: *Measure for Measure* and *Othello*," in Gedo, Pollock, *Psychoanalysis: The Vital Issues*, 277–96.

D. S. Brewer, "*Measure for Measure*, I, I, 3–9," *N&Q* 200 (October 1955): 425.

Carolyn E. Brown, "Erotic Religious Flagellation and Shakespeare's *Measure for Measure*," *ELR* 16 (Winter 1986): 139–65.

Carolyn E. Brown, "*Measure for Measure*: Isabella's Beating Fantasies," *AI* 43 (Spring 1986): 67–80.

Carolyn E. Brown, "*Measure for Measure*: Duke Vincentio's 'Crabbed' Desires," *L&P* 35, no. 1–2 (1989): 66–88.

Robert D. Callahan, "The Theme of 'Government' in *Measure for Measure*," *Paunch* 25, no. 1 (1966): 31–52.

Susan Carlson, "'Fond Fathers' and Sweet Sisters: Alternative Sexualities in *Measure for Measure*," *ELWIU* 16 (Spring 1989): 13–31.

Arnold Cassola, "On the Meaning of 'Enciel'd' in *Measure for Measure*," *ELN* 27 (June 1990): 22–27.

Chambers, *Man's Unconquerable Mind*, 277–310.

Chandhuri, *Infirm Glory*, 154–64.

Clemen, *Shakespeare's Dramatic Art*, 174–75.

Nevill Coghill, "Comic Form in *Measure for Measure*," *ShS* 8 (1955): 14–27.

Eileen Z. Cohen, "'Virtue Is Bold': The Bed-Trick and Characterization in *All's Well That Ends Well* and *Measure for Measure*," *PQ* 65 (Spring 1986): 171–86.

Howard E. Cole, "The 'Christian' Context of *Measure for Measure*," *JEGP* 64 (October 1965): 425–51.

Michael J. Collins, "*Measure for Measure*: Comedy in the Rag and Bone Shop," *CrSurv* 1, no. 1 (1989): 24–32.

Albert Cook, "Metaphysical Poetry and *Measure for Measure*," *Accent* 13 (Spring 1953): 122–27.

H. Coombes, *Literature and Criticism*, 71–72.

Cox, *Shakespeare and the Dramaturgy of Power*, 151–61.

John V. Curry, *Deception in Elizabethan Comedy*, 63–64, 152–54.

John P. Cutts, "Perfect Contrition: A Note on *Measure for Measure*," *N&Q* 205 (November 1960): 416–19.

Daiches, *Critical Approaches to Literature*, 349–55.

Edgar F. Daniels, "Shakespeare's *Measure for Measure*, III.i.13–15," *Expl* 46 (Fall 1987): 5.

Dawson, *Indirections*, 110–28.

Anthony B. Dawson, "*Measure for Measure*, New Historicism, and Theatrical Power," *SQ* 39 (Spring 1988): 328–41.

Christy Desmet, "'Neither Maid, Widow, nor Wife': Rhetoric of the Woman Controversy in *Measure for Measure* and *All's Well That Ends Well*," *RenP* 1985 (1986): 43–51.

John W. Dickinson, "Renaissance Equity and *Measure for Measure*," *SQ* 13 (Summer 1962): 287–97.

Carolee T. Diffey, "The Last Judgement in *Measure for Measure*," *DUJ* 35 (March 1974): 231–37.

W. M. T. Dodds, "The Character of Angelo in *Measure for Measure*," *MLR* 41 (July 1946): 246–55.

Dennis Dodge, "Life and Death in *Measure for Measure*," *RecL* 4, no. 1 (1975): 43–58.

Jonathan Dollimore, "Transgression and Surveillance in *Measure for Measure*," in Dollimore and Sinfield, *Political Shakespeare*, 72–87.

John W. Draper, "*Measure for Measure* and the London Stews," *WVUPP* 23 (January 1977): 5–17.

John W. Draper, "Patterns of Tempo in *Measure for Measure*," *WVUPP* 9 (1953): 11–19.

Katherine Duncan-Jones, "Stoicism in *Measure for Measure*: A New Source," *RES* 28 (1977): 441–46.

Wilbur Dunkel, "Law and Equity in *Measure for Measure*," *SQ* 13 (Summer 1962): 275–85.

Eagleton, *Shakespeare and Society*, 66–97.

Anthony S. G. Edwards, and Anthony W. Jenkins, "'Prenzie': *Measure for Measure* III.i," *SQ* 27 (Summer 1976): 333–34.

Charles S. Felver, "A Proverb Turned Jest in *Measure for Measure*," *SQ* 11 (Summer 1960): 385–87.

Ferguson, *Trope and Allegory*, 60–70.

Francis Fergusson, "Philosophy and Theatre in *Measure for Measure*," *KR* 14 (Winter 1952): 103–20. Reprinted in *The Human Image in Dramatic Literature*, 126–43.

Robert F. Fleissner, "Shakespeare's *Measure for Measure*, II.iv.136," *Expl* 32 (December 1974): Item 42.

Foakes, *Shakespeare*, 17–31.

James E. Ford, "Barnardine's Nominal Nature in *Measure for Measure*," *PLL* 18 (Winter 1982): 77–81.

William A. Freedman, "The Duke in *Measure for Measure*," *TSL* 9 (Spring 1964): 31–38.

French, *Shakespeare's Division of Experience*, 182–196.

Brian Gibbons, "'Bid Them Bring the Trumpets to the Gate': Staging Questions for *Measure for Measure*," *HLQ* 54 (Spring 1991): 31–42.

William L. Godshalk, "'The Devil's Horn': Appearance and Reality," *SQ* 23 (Summer 1972): 202–05.

William L. Godshalk, "*Measure for Measure*: Freedom and Restraint," *ShakS* 6 (1970): 137–50.

Phyllis Gorfain, "'Craft Against Vice': Riddling as Ritual in *Measure for Measure*," *Assaph* 5, no. 3 (1989): 91–107.

Anne Greco, "A Due Sincerity," *ShakS* 6 (1970): 151–73.

Robin Grove, "A Measure for Magistrates," *CR* 19 (1977): 3–23.

Grudin, *Mighty Opposites*, 98–114.

Jay L. Halio, "The Metaphor of Conception and Elizabethan Theories of Imagination," *Neophil* 50 (October 1966): 454–61.

Lawrence S. Hall, "Isabella's Angry Ape," *SQ* 15 (Summer 1964): 157–60.

Hallett and Hallett, *Analyzing Shakespeare's Action*, 30–31, 141–44.

Donna B. Hamilton, "The Duke in *Measure for Measure*: 'I Find an Apt Remission in Myself,'" *ShakS* 6 (1970): 175–83.

Paul Hammond, "The Argument of *Measure for Measure*," *ELR* 16 (Autumn 1986): 496–519.

John E. Hankins, "Pains of the Afterworld in Milton and Shakespeare," *PMLA* 71 (June 1956): 487–95.

Robert Hapgood, "The Provost and Equity in *Measure for Measure*," *SQ* 15 (Winter 1964): 114–15.

Alfred Harbage, "Shakespeare and the Myth of Perfection," *SQ* 15 (Spring 1964): 7–10.

Davis P. Harding, "Elizabethan Bethrothals and *Measure for Measure*," *JEGP* 49 (April 1950): 139–48.

John L. Harrison, "The Convention of Heart and Tongue and the Meaning of *Measure for Measure*," *SQ* 5 (January 1954): 1–10.

Edward L. Hart, "A Mixed Consort: Leontes, Angelo, Helena," *SQ* 15 (Winter 1964): 79–80.

Haselkorn, *Prostitution in Elizabethan and Jacobean Drama*, 48–51.

Dayton Haskin, S. J., "Mercy and the Creative Process in *Measure for Measure*," *TSLL* 19 (Winter 1977): 348–62.

Harriet Hawkins, "'The Devil's Party': Virtues and Vices in *Measure for Measure*," *Shs* 31 (1978): 105–13.

Hawkins, *Likeness of Truth*, 21–25, 49–78.

Norman L. Holland, "'Do' or 'Die' in *Measure for Measure*, I.iii.43," *N&Q* 202 (March 1957): 52.

Norman L. Holland, "*Measure for Measure*: The Duke and the Prince," *CL* 11 (Winter 1959): 16–20.

John Holloway, "Dramatic Irony in Shakespeare," *Northern Miscellany of Literary Criticism* 1 (Autumn 1953): 13–16.

E. A. J. Honigman, "Shakespeare's Mingled Yarn and *Measure for Measure*," *PBA* 67 (1981): 101–21.

Houston, *Shakespearean Sentences*, 153–57.

Jean E. Howard, "*Measure for Measure* and the Restraints of Convention," *ELWIU* 10 (Fall 1983): 149–58.

Herbert Howarth, "Shakespeare's Flattery in *Measure for Measure*," *SQ* 16 (Winter 1965): 29–37.

Howarth, *The Tiger's Heart*, 123–35.

Patricia Howe, "'Morality and Mercy in Vienna': Moral Relativism in Shakespeare's *Measure for Measure* and Schnitzler's *Das weite Land*: Essays in Honor of Ronald Peacock," in *Patterns of Change: German Drama and the European Tradition*, ed. Dorothy James and Sylvia Ranawake (New York: Peter Lang, 1990), 215–27.

Hoy, *The Hyacinth Room*, 11–15.

Cyrus L. Hoy, "Comedy, Tragedy, Tragicomedy," *VQR* 36 (Winter 1960): 110–14.

Ronald Huebert, "Taking the Measure of Manliness," *DR* 63 (Summer 1983): 125–34.

Hilda Hulme, "Three Notes: *Troilus and Cressida*, V.vii.11; *Midsummer Night's Dream*, II.i.54; *Measure for Measure*, II.i.39," *JEGP* 57 (October 1958): 724–25.

Maurice Hunt, "Comfort in *Measure for Measure*," *SEL* 27 (Spring 1987): 213–32.

G. K. Hunter, "Six Notes on *Measure for Measure*," *SQ* 15 (Summer 1964): 167–72.

Lawrence W. Hyman, "Mariana in *Measure for Measure*," *UR* 31 (December 1964): 123–27.

Lawrence W. Hyman, "*Measure for Measure*: Moral Attitudes and the Comic Spirit," *Greyfriar* 25 (1984): 16–24.

Lawrence W. Hyman, "Mariana and Shakespeare's Theme in *Measure for Measure*," *UR* 31 (1964): 123–27.

Lawrence W. Hyman, "The Unity of *Measure for Measure*," *MLQ* 36 (March 1975): 3–20.

Richard S. Ide, "Shakespeare's Revisionism: Homiletic Tragicomedy and the Ending of *Measure for Measure*," *ShakS* 20 (1987): 105–27.

R. L. P. Jackson, "Necessary Ambiguity: The Last Act of *Measure for Measure*," *CR* 26 (1984): 114–29.

Harry V. Jaffa, "Chastity as Political Principle: An Interpreation of Shakespeare's *Measure for Measure*," in Alvis and West, *Shakespeare as Political Thinker*, 181–213.

R. B. Jenkins, "Shakespeare's *Measure for Measure*," *Expl* 39 (Summer 1981): 11–14.

M. Lindsay Kaplan, "Slander in *Measure for Measure*," *RenD* 21 (1990): 23–54.

Helen A. Kaufman, "Trappolin Supposed a Prince and *Measure for Measure*," *MLQ* 18 (March 1957): 113–24.

R. J. Kaufman, "Bond Slaves and Counterfeits: Shakespeare's *Measure for Measure*," *ShakS* 3 (1968):85–97.

Arthur C. Kirsch, "The Integrity of *Measure for Measure*," *ShS* 28 (1975): 89–105.

Bernice W. Kliman, "Isabella in *Measure for Measure*," *ShakS* 15 (1982): 137–48.

Knight, *The Olive and the Sword*, 44–47.

G. W. Knight, "*Measure for Measure* and the Gospels," in *The Wheel of Fire*, 73–96.

L. C. Knights, "The Ambiguity of *Measure for Measure*," *Scrutiny* 10 (January 1942): 222–32. Reprinted in Bentley, *The Importance of Scrutiny*, 141–49.

Jan Kott, "Head for Maidenhead, Maidenhead for Head: The Structure of Exchange in *Measure for Measure*," in Conejero, *En torno a Shakespeare*, 93–113.

Gregory W. Lanier, "Physic That's Bitter to Sweet End: The Tragicomic Structure of *Measure for Measure*," *ELWIU* 14 (Spring 1987): 15–36.

Mary Lascelles, "'Glassie Essence,' *Measure for Measure*, II.ii.120," *RES* 2 (April 1951): 140–42.

W. W. Lawrence, "*Measure for Measure* and Lucio," *SQ* 9 (Autumn 1958): 443–54.

J. S. Lawry, "Imitations and Creation in *Measure for Measure*: Collection of Essays from the Ohio Shakespeare Conference, 1981, Wright State University, Dayton, Ohio," in Cary and Limouze, *Shakespeare and the Arts*, 217–29.

F. R. Leavis, "The Greatness of *Measure for Measure*," *Scrutiny* 10 (January 1942): 234–46. Reprinted in *The Common Pursuit*, 160–72. Reprinted in Bentley, *The Importance of Scrutiny*, 150–62.

Clifford Leech, "The 'Meaning' of *Measure for Measure*," *ShS* 3 (1950): 66–73.

Clifford Leech, "Shakespeare's Comic Dukes," *REL* 5 (April 1964): 110–13.

Alexander Leggatt, "Substitution in *Measure for Measure*," *SQ* 39 (Summer 1988): 342–59.

Jacques Lezra, "Pirating Reading: The Appearance of History in *Measure for Measure*," *ELH* 56 (July 1989): 255–92.

Lee Ligon-Jones, "Be Absolute: Death and Sex in *Measure for Measure* and *Edward III*," *CCTEP* 55 (September 1990): 7–15.

Julia Reinhard Lupton, "Afterlives of the Saints: Hagiography in *Measure for Measure*," *Exemplaria* 2 (Fall 1990): 375–401.

Cynthia Lewis, "'Dark Deeds Darkly Answered': Duke Vincentio and Judgement in *Measure for Measure*," *SQ* 34 (Spring 1983): 271–89.

Ronald R. Macdonald, "*Measure for Measure*: The Flesh Made Word," *SEL* 30 (Spring 1990): 265–82.

Eleen Mackay, "*Measure for Measure*," *SQ* 14 (Spring 1963): 109–14.

Toshio Maeda, "Truth and Grace in Measure for Measure: Essays in Honour of Professor Toyohiko Tatsumi's Seventieth Birthday," in Milward, *Poetry and Faith in the English Renaissance*, 85–95.

Jean-Marie Maguin, "The Anagogy of *Measure for Measure*," *CahiersE* 16 (April 1979): 19–26.

Darrle Mansell, Jr., " 'Seemers' in *Measure for Measure*," *MLQ* 27 (June 1966): 270–84.

D. R. C. Marsh, "The Mood of *Measure for Measure*," *SQ* 14 (Winter 1963): 31–38.

J. C. Maxwell, "*Measure for Measure*: The Play and the Themes," *PBA* 60 (1974): 199–218.

J. C. Maxwell, "*Measure for Measure*: 'vain pity' and 'compelled sins,'" *EIC* 16 (April 1966): 253–55.

Tom McBride, "*Measure for Measure* and the Unreconciled Virtues," *CompD* 8 (Summer 1974): 264–74.

McCollum, *Tragedy*, 13–14, 105–06, 126–27, 197–99.

Donald J. McGinn, "The Precise Angelo," in McManaway, *Joseph Q. Adams Memorial Studies*, 129–39.

Philip C. McGuire, "Silence and Genre: The Example of *Measure for Measure*," *ISJR* 59 (March 1985): 241–51.

Kathleen McLuskie, "The Patriarchal Bird: Feminist Criticism and Shakespeare: *King Lear* and *Measure for Measure*," in Dollimore and Sinfield, *Political Shakespeare*, 88–108.

McPeek, *The Black Book of Knaves*, 271–73.

Dieter Mehl, "Corruption, Retribution and Justice in *Measure for Measure* and *The Revenger's Tragedy*," in Honigmann, *Shakespeare and His Contemporaries*, 114–28.

Robert S. Mikkelsen, "To Catch a Saint: Angelo in *Measure for Measure*," *WHR* 12 (Summer 1958): 261–75.

Stanton Millet, "The Structure of *Measure for Measure*," *BUSE* 2 (Winter 1956): 207–17.

Paul Mills, "Brothers and Enemies in *Measure for Measure*," in Jowitt and Taylor, *Self and Society*, 96–109.

Marco Mincoff, "*Measure for Measure*: A Question of Approach," *ShakS* 2 (1966): 141–52.

Susan Moore, "Virtue and Power in *Measure for Measure*," *ES* 63 (August 1982): 308–17.

S. Musgrave, "Some Composite Scenes in *Measure for Measure*," *SQ* 15 (Winter 1964): 67–74.

Leonard Mustazza, "Shakespeare's *Measure for Measure*," *Expl* 47 (Fall 1988): 2–4.

S. Nagarajan, "*Measure for Measure* and Elizabethan Bethrothals," *SQ* 14 (Spring 1963): 115–20.

Norman Nathan, "The Marriage of Duke Vincentio and Isabella," *SQ* 7 (Winter 1956): 43–45.

A. D. Nutall, "*Measure for Measure*: The Bed Trick," *ShS* 28 (1975): 51–56.

Orestein, *The Moral Vision of Jacobean Tragedy*, 250–60. Reprinted in *UR* 24 (Autumn 1957): 15–22.

Lucy Owen, "Mode and Character in *Measure for Measure*," *SQ* (Winter 1974): 17–32.

Christopher Palmer, "Selfishness in *Measure for Measure*," *EIC* 28 (April 1978): 187–207.

Bernard J. Paris, "The Inner Conflicts of *Measure for Measure*: A Psychological Approach," *CentR* 25 (Spring 1981): 266–76.

Thomas A. Pendleton, "Shakespeare's Disguised Duke Play: Middleton, Marston, and the Sources of *Measure for Measure*," in Mahon and Pendleton, *"fanned and winnowed opinions,"* 79–98.

Douglas L. Petterson, "*Measure for Measure* and the Anglican Doctrine of Contrition," *N&Q* 209 (April 1964): 135–37.

G. M. Pinciss, "The 'Heavenly Comforts of Despair' and *Measure for Measure*," *SEL* 30 (Spring 1990): 303–13.

Beryl Pogson, "A Psychological Study of *Measure for Measure*," *Baconiana* 33 (January 1949): 35–42.

Pogson, *In the East My Pleasure Lies*, 58–69.

E. M. Pope, "Shakespeare on Hell," *SQ* 1 (July 1950): 162–64.

A. M. Potter, "The Problem of Form and the Role of the Duke in *Measure for Measure*," *Theoria* 69 (May 1987): 41–52.

Alan W. Powers, "'Meaner Parties': Spousal Conventions and Oral Culture in *Measure for Measure* and *All's Well That Ends Well*," *UCrow* 8 (1988): 28–41.

Gideon Rappaport, "Measuring *Measure for Measure*," *Renascence* 39 (Summer 1987): 502–13.

Marcia Riefer, "'Instruments of Some More Mightier Member': The Constriction of Female Power in *Measure for Measure*," *SQ* 35 (Winter 1984) 157–69.

Hugh Robertson, "*Troilus and Cressida* and *Measure for Measure* in Their Age: Shakespeare's Thought in Its Context," in Jowitt and Taylor, *Self and Society*, 3–26.

William John Roscelli, "Isabella, Sin and Civil Law," *UR* 28 (Spring 1962): 215–27.

Brian Rose, "Friar-Duke and Scholar-King," *ESA* 9 (March 1966): 72–82.

Jacqueline Rose, "Sexuality in the Reading of Shakespeare: *Hamlet* and *Measure for Measure*," in Drakakis, *Alternative Shakespeares*, 95–118.

David Rosenbaum, "Shakespeare's *Measure for Measure* I.ii," *Expl* 33 (February 1975): Item 57.

Judith Rosenheim, "*Measure for Measure*, II.i 37–40: Souding 'Breaks of Ice,'" *SQ* 35 (Spring 1984): 87–91.

Judith Rosenheim, "The Stoic Meaning of the Friar in *Measure for Measure*," *ShakS* 15 (1982): 171–215.

Gordon N. Ross, "The Balance of *Measure for Measure*," *SPWVSRA* 6 (Spring 1981): 1–7.

Rossiter, *Angel With Horns*, 152–70.

Douglas F. Rutledge, "The Structural Parallel Between Rituals of Reversal, Jacobean Political Theory, and *Measure for Measure*," *ISJR* 62 (July 1988): 421–41.

Roger Sale, "The Comic Mode of *Measure for Measure*," *SQ* 19 (Spring 1968): 55–61.

Ernest Schanzer. "The Marriage Contracts in *Measure for Measure*," *ShS* 13 (1960): 81–89.

Margaret Scott, "'Our City's Institutions': Some Further Reflections on the Marriage Contracts in *Measure for Measure*," *ELH* 49 (December 1982): 790–804.

Scott, *Renaissance Drama*, 61–75.

Paul N. Siegel, "*Measure for Measure*: The Significance of the Title," *SQ* 4 (July 1953): 317–20.

Paul N. Siegel, "Angelo's Precise Guards," *PQ* 29 (October 1950): 442–43.

K. B. Sitaramayya, "Ape and Essence: An Approach to Shakespeare's *Measure for Measure*," *JEngS* 2 (March 1979): 52–57.

Meredith Skura, "New Interpretations for Interpretation in *Measure for Measure*," *Boundary* 7, no. 2 (1979): 39–59.

Don Smith, "Truth and Seeming Truth: The Language of *Measure for Measure* and *Troilus and Cressida*," in Jowitt and Taylor, *Self and Society*, 45–60.

Gordon Ross Smith, "Renaissance Political Realities and Shakespeare's *Measure for Measure*," *PPMRC* 7 (1982): 83–92.

Smith, *Dualities in Shakespeare*, 123–59.

Robert M. Smith, "Interpretations of *Measure for Measure*," *SQ* 1 (October 1950): 208–18.

W. D. Smith, "More Light on *Measure for Measure*," *MLQ* 23 (December 1962): 309–22.

Soellner, *Shakespeare's Patterns*, 215–36.

Raymond Southall, "*Measure for Measure* and the Protestant Ethic," *EIC* 11 (January 1961): 10–33.

Phoebe S. Spinrad, "*Measure for Measure* and the Art of Not Dying," *TSLL* 26 (Spring 1984): 74–93.

David L. Stevenson, "Design and Structure in *Measure for Measure*: A New Appraisal," *ELH* 23 (December 1956): 256–78.

David Sundelson, "Misogyny and Rule in *Measure for Measure*," *WS* 9, no. 1 (1981): 83–91.

Wylie Sypher, "Shakespeare as Casuist: *Measure for Measure*," *SR* 58 (Spring 1950): 262–80.

Gary Taylor, "*Measure for Measure*, IV.ii.41–46," *SQ* 29 (Summer 1978): 419–21.

Terrell L. Tebbetts, "Talking Back to the King: *Measure for Measure* and the *Basilicon Doron*," *CollL* 12 (Winter 1985): 122–34.

Leonard Tennenhouse, "Representing Power: *Measure for Measure* in Its Time," *Genre* 15 (Spring–Summer 1982): 139–56.

Alwin Thaler, "The 'Devil's Crest' in *Measure for Measure*," *SP* 50 (April 1953): 188–94.

David Thatcher, "A Crux in *Measure for Measure*, II.3.40–2," *CahiersE* 37 (April 1990): 69–72.

Paul James Toscano, "*Measure for Measure*" Tragedy and Redemption," *BYUS* 16 (1976): 277–89.

D. A. Traversi, "*Measure for Measure*," *Scrutiny* 11 (Summer 1942): 40–58.

James Trombetta, "Versions of Dying in *Measure for Measure*," *ELR* 6 (Spring 1976): 60–76.

John H. Velz, "Copiousness in *Measure for Measure*," *CahiersE* 15 (April 1979): 65–67.

Sarah C. Velz, "Man's Need and God's Plan in *Measure for Measure* and *Mark IV*," *ShS* 25 (1972): 37–44.

John Wasson, "*Measure for Measure*: A Play of Incontinence," *ELH* 27 (December 1960): 262–75.

Robert N. Watson, "False Immortality in *Measure for Measure*: Comic Means, Tragic Ends," *SQ* 41 (Winter 1990): 411–32.

Alice Walker, "The Text of *Measure for Measure*," *RES* 9 (Spring 1958): 1–20.

David K. Weiser, "The Ironic Hierarchy in *Measure for Measure*," *TSLL* 19 (Winter 1977): 323–47.

Herbert Weisinger, "Myth, Method, and Shakespeare," *JGE* 16 (April 1964): 45–48.

Herbert Weisinger, "A Shakespeare All Too Modern," *ArQ* 20 (Winter 1964): 308–13.

Alexander Welsh, "The Loss of Men and Getting of Children: *All's Well That Ends Well* and *Measure for Measure*," *MLR* 73 (December 1978): 17–28.

Karl P. Wenterdorf, "The Marriage Contracts in *Measure for Measure*: A Reconsideration," *ShS* 32 (1979): 129–44.

West, *The Court and the Castle*, 44–48.

Charles W. Whitworth, Jr., "Why Saint Luke's? A Note on *Measure for Measure*," *SQ* 36 (Spring 1985): 214–15.

Gary A. Wiener, "Shakespeare's *Measure for Measure*," *Expl* 41 (Summer 1983): 7.

H. S. Wilson, "Action and Symbol in *Measure for Measure* and *The Tempest*," *SQ* 4 (October 1953): 375–84.

Mathew Winston, "'Craft against Vice': Morality Play Elements in *Measure for Measure*," *ShakS* 14 (1981): 229–48.

The Merchant of Venice

Douglas Anderson, "The Old Testament Presence in *The Merchant of Venice*," *ELH* 52 (June 1985): 119–32.

A. A. Ansari, "*The Merchant of Venice*: An Existential Comedy," *AJES* 11 (April 1986): 18–32.

Russell Astley, "Through a Looking Glass, Darkly: Judging the Hazards of *The Merchant of Venice*," *ArielE* 10 (April 1979): 17–34.

David Bady, "The Sum of Something: Arithmetic in *The Merchant of Venice*," *SQ* 36 (Winter 1985): 10–30.

Christoper P. Baker, "Salerio, Solanio, Salarino and Salario," *Names* 23 (March 1975): 56–57.

Martin Banham, "*The Merchant of Venice* and the Implicit Stage Direction," *CrSurv* 3, no. 3 (1991): 269–74.

Barber, *Shakespeare's Festive Comedy*, 163–91.

Sylvan Barnet, "Prodigality and Time in *The Merchant of Venice*," *PMLA* 87 (January 1972): 26–30.

David N. Beauregard, "Sidney, Aristotle, and *The Merchant of Venice*: Shakespeare's Triadic Images of Liberality and Justice," *ShakS* 20 (1987): 33–51.

Alan W. Bellringer, "The Expression of Trust in *The Merchant of Venice*," *FMLS* 19 (October 1983): 331–47.

Mark R. Benbow, "The Merchant Antonio, Elizabethan Hero," *CLQ* 12 (June 1976): 156–70.

Alice N. Benston, "Portia, the Law and the Tripartite Structure of *The Merchant of Venice*," *SQ* 30 (Summer 1979): 367–85.

Harry Berger, Jr. "Marriage and Mercifixion in *The Merchant of Venice*: The Casket Scene Revisited," *SQ* 32 (Spring 1981): 155–62.

Ralph Berry, "Discomfort in *The Merchant of Venice*," *Thalia* 1 (Winter 1978–79): 9–16.

Murray Biggs, "A Neurotic Portia," *ShS* 25 (1972): 153–59.

Harvey Birenbaum, "A View From the Rialto: Two Pyschologies in *The Merchant of Venice*," *SJS* 9 (Spring 1983): 68–80.

David H. Bishop, "Shylock's Humor," *ShAB* 23 (October 1948): 174–80.

SHAKESPEARE, WILLIAM, *The Merchant of Venice*

Allan Bloom, "Shakespeare on Jew and Christian: An Interpreation of *The Merchant of Venice*," *Social Research* 30 (Spring 1963): 1–22.

Bradshaw, *Shakespeare's Skepticism*, 21–32, 80–84.

Brockbank, *On Shakespeare*, 13–19, 71–74.

Paula Brody, "Shylock's Omophagia: A Ritual Approach to *The Merchant of Venice*," *L&P* 17, no. 3 (1967): 229–34.

Bullough, *Mirror of Minds*, 65–68.

Sigurd Burckhardt, "*The Merchant of Venice*: The Gentle Bond," *ELH* 29 (September 1962): 239–62.

Charles D. Cannon, "'Know Him I Shall' in *The Merchant of Venice*," *ELN* 26 (September 1988): 8–11.

Paul A. Cantor, "Religion and the Limits of Community in *The Merchant of Venice*," *Soundings* 70 (Spring–Summer 1987): 239–58.

Morris Carnousky, "Mirror of Shylock," *TDR* 3 (October 1958): 35–45.

Neil Carson, "Hazarding and Cozening in *The Merchant of Venice*," *ELN* 9 (March 1972): 168–72.

Cartelli, *Marlowe, Shakespeare*, 152–56.

Chambers, *Man's Unconquerable Mind*, 407–08.

Birendranath Chowdhury, "*The Merchant of Venice* and the World of Commerce," *JDECU* 18, no. 1 (1982–1983): 33–53.

Clemen, *Shakespeare's Dramatic Art*, 163–65.

Clurman, *Lies Like Truth*, 151–53.

D. M. Cohen, "The Jew and Shylock," *SQ* 31 (Spring 1980): 53–63.

Hening Cohen, "Shakespeare's *Merchant of Venice* II.vii.8–79," *SQ* 2 (January 1951): 79.

Walter Cohen, "*The Merchant of Venice* and the Possibilities of Historical Criticism," *ELH* 49 (December 1982): 765–89.

John Scott Colley, "Launcelot, Jacob, and Esau: Old and New Law in *The Merchant of Venice*," *YES* 10 (1980): 181–89.

John S. Coolidge, "Law and Love in *The Merchant of Venice*," *SQ* 27 (Summer 1976): 243–63.

Raphalle Costa de Beauregard, "Interpreting *The Merchant of Venice*," *CahiersE* 39 (April 1991): 1–16.

Lester G. Crocker, "*The Merchant of Venice* and Christian Conscience," *Diogenes* 118 (Summer 1982): 77–102.

D'Amico, *The Moor in English Renaissance Drama*, 162–77.

K. B. Danks, "The Case of Antonio's Melancholy," *N&Q* 199 (March 1954): 111.

Dawson, *Indirections*, 3–19.

M. G. Deshpande, "Loneliness in *The Merchant of Venice*," *EIC* 11 (July 1961): 368–69.

William B. Dillingham, "Antonio and Black Bile," *N&Q* 202 (October 1957): 419.

Austin C. Dobbins and Roy W. Battenhouse, "Jessica's Morals: A Theological View," *ShakS* 9 (1976): 107–20.

John W. Draper, "Shakespeare's Antonio and the Queen's Finance," *Neophil* 51 (July 1967): 178–85.

John W. Draper, "Usury in *The Merchant of Venice*," *MP* 50 (August 1953): 37–47.

Manfred Draudt, "The Unity of *The Merchant of Venice*: Festschrift fur Siegfried Korninger," in Rauchbauer, *A Yearbook of Studies in English Language and Literature 1985/86*, 5–26.

Walter F. Eggers, Jr. "Love and Likeness in *The Merchant of Venice*," *SQ* 28 (Summer 1977): 327–33.

Anita Engle, "New Thesis on Origin of *The Merchant of Venice*: Was Shylock a Jew?" *Jewish Quarterly* 1 (Summer 1953): 13–18.

Lars Engle, "'Thrift Is Blessing': Exchange and Explanation in *The Merchant of Venice*," *SQ* 37 (Spring 1986): 20–37.

Michael Ferber, "The Ideology of *The Merchant of Venice*," *ELR* 20 (Autumn 1990): 431–64.

Sidney Finklestein, "Shakespeare's Shylock," *Mainstream* 15 (June 1962): 26–42.

Harold Fisch, *The Dual Image*, 24–25, 29–35.

A. Fodor, "Shakespeare's Portia," *AI* 16 (Spring 1959): 49–64.

René E. Fortin, "Launcelot and the Uses of Allegory in *The Merchant of Venice*," *SEL* 14 (Spring 1974): 259–70.

French, *Shakespeare's Division of Experience*, 96–101.

Thomas H. Fujimura, "Mode and Structure in *The Merchant of Venice*," *PMLA* 81 (July 1966): 499–511.

David Galloway, "Alcides and His 'Rage': A Note on *The Merchant of Venice*," *N&Q* 201 (August 1956): 330–31.

Sand M. Gamal, "The Function of Song in Shakespeare's Comedies," *CairoSE* (1961–1962): 115–17.

John Garrett, "*The Merchant of Venice*," *ShN* 6 (September 1956): 31.

Keith Geary, "The Nature of Portia's Victory: Turning to Men in *The Merchant of Venice*," *ShS* 37 (1984): 55–68.

René Girard, "'To Entrap the Wisest': A Reading of *The Merchant of Venice*," in *Literature and Society*, ed. Edward W. Said (Baltimore: Johns Hopkins University Press, 1974), 100–19.

Cary B. Graham, "Standards of Value in *The Merchant of Venice*," *SQ* 4 (April 1953): 145–51.

William Green, "The Two Faces of *The Merchant of Venice*," *Yiddish* 4 (Winter 1982): 86–99.

Robert P. Griffin, "*The Merchant of Venice*: Time and Change," *CollL* 9 (Winter 1982): 39–43.

Grudin, *Might Opposites*, 51–74.

Gary R. Grund, "The Fortunate Fall and Shakespeare's *Merchant of Venice*," *SN* 55 (Summer 1983): 153–65.

Hallett and Hallett, *Analyzing Shakespeare's Action*, 37–38.

Monica Joyce Hamill, "Poetry, Law, and the Pursuit of Perfection: Portia's Role in *The Merchant of Venice*," *SEL* 18 (Spring 1978): 229–43.

Robert Hapgood, "Portia and *The Merchant of Venice*: The Gentle Bond," *MLQ* 28 (March 1967): 19–32.

R. Chris Hassel, Jr., "Antonio and the Ironic Festivity of *The Merchant of Venice*," *ShakS* 6 (1970): 67–74.

R. Chris Hassel, Jr., "Frustrated Communion in *The Merchant of Venice*," *Cithera* 13 (May 1974): 19–33.

Burton Hatlen, "Feudal and Bourgeois Concepts of Value in *The Merchant of Venice*," *BuR* 25, no. 1 (1980): 91–105.

Hawkins, *Poetic Freedom and Poetic Truth*, 9–10.

Richard Henze, " 'Which Is the Merchant Here? And Which the Jew?' " *Criticism* 16 (Autumn 1974): 287–300.

Hibbard, *Making of Shakespeare's Dramtic Poetry*, 153–61.

R. F. Hill, "*The Merchant of Venice* and the Pattern of Romantic Comedy," *ShS* 28 (1975): 75–87.

Jan Lawson Hinely, "Bond Priorities in *The Merchant of Venice*," *SEL* 20 (Spring 1980): 217–39.

Allan Holaday, "Shakespeare, Richard Edwards, and the Virtues Reconciled," *JEGP* 66 (July 1967): 200–06.

Joan Ozark Holmer, "Loving Wisely and the Casket Test: Symbolic and Structural Unity in *The Merchant of Venice*," *ShakS* 11 (1978): 53–76.

Richard Horwich, "Riddle and Dilemma in *The Merchant of Venice*," *SEL* 17 (Spring 1977): 191–200.

Houston, *Shakespearean Sentences*, 55–57.

Howarth, *The Tiger's Heart*, 50–63.

Wayne A. Howitt, "Shylock's Own Language and Reality," *GyS* 2, no. 1 (1975): 13–20.

G. I. Hughes, "Generosity and Alienation in *The Merchant of Venice*," *Crux* 40 (February 1973): 5–12.

Hilde M. Hulme, "Three Notes on *The Merchant of Venice*," *Neophil* 41 (January 1957): 46–50.

Arthur Humphreys, "*The Jew of Malta* and *The Merchant of Venice*: Two Readings of Life," *HLQ* 50 (Summer 1987): 279–93.

Maurice Hunt, "Ways of Knowing in *The Merchant of Venice*," *SQ* 30 (Spring 1979): 89–93.

J. D. Hurrell, "Love and Friendship in *The Merchant of Venice*," *TSLL* 3 (Autumn 1961): 328–41.

Lawrence W. Hyman and Thomas H. Fujimara, "Antonio in *The Merchant of Venice*," *PMLA* 82 (October 1967): 649–50.

Masaaki Imanishi, "What Happened to Belmont as the 'Green World'? An Essay on *The Merchant of Venice*," in Milward and Anzai, *Poetry and Drama*, 118–38.

Cary F. Jacob, "Reality and *The Merchant of Venice*," *QJS* 28 (October 1942): 307–14.

Vera M. Jiji, "Portia Revisted: The Influence of Unconscious Factors upon Theme and Characterization in *The Merchant of Venice*," *L&P* 26, no. 1 (1977): 5–15.

Jones, *Othello's Countrymen*, 68–71.

Coppelia Kahn, "The Cuckoo's Note: Male Friendship and Cuckoldry in *The Merchant of Venice*," in Erickson and Kahn, *Shakespeare's 'Rough Magic,'* 104–12.

John S. Kenyon, "Shakespeare's Pronunciation of Stephano: *The Merchant of Venice* V. I. 28, 51," *PQ* 37 (Winter 1958): 504–06.

Frank Kermode, "The Mature Comedies," *Stratford-Upon-Avon Studies* 3 (1961): 220–24.

Leo Kirshbaum, "Shakespeare 'God' and 'Bad,'" *RES* 23 (April 1945): 139–42.

Leo Kirshbaum, "Shylock in the City of God," *ShN* 4 (September 1954): 33.

Seymour Kleinberg, "*The Merchant of Venice*: The Homosexual and Anti-Semite in Nascent Capitalism," in *Literary Visions of Homosexuality*, ed. Stuart Kellogg (New York: Haworth, 1983), 113–26.

Dennis R. Klinck, "Shylock and 'Neschech,'" *ELN* 17 (September 1979): 18–22.

Ron Klingspon, "Play and Interplay in the Trial Scene of *The Merchant of Venice*," *Thalia* 9 (Spring–Summer 1986): 36–47.

Knight, *The Golden Labyrinth*, 69–71, 83–84.

Sarah Kofman, "Conversions: *The Merchant of Venice* under the Sign of Saturn," in *Literary Theory Today*, ed. Peter Collier and Helga Geyer-Ryan (Ithaca, NY: Cornell University Press, 1990), 142–66.

Dorothea Kohler, "*The Merchant of Venice*: A Lesson in Deconstruction," *EngR* 41, no. 1 (1990): 27–29.

Stanley J. Kozikowsik, "The Allegory of Love and Fortune: The Lottery in *The Merchant of Venice*," *Renascence* 32 (Winter 1980): 105–15.

E. E. Krapf, "A Psychoanalytic Study of Shakespeare and Antisemitism: Shylock and Antonio," *Psychoanalytic Review* 42 (April 1955): 113–30.

Landa, *The Jew in Drama*, 255–59.

M. J. Landa, *The Shylock Myth* (London: Allen, 1942), 32–45.

Clifford Leech, "Shakespeare's Comic Dukes," *REL* 5 (April 1964): 104–05.

Carol Leventen, "Patrimony and Patriarchy in *The Merchant of Venice*," in Wayne, *The Matter of Difference*, 59–79.

Harry Levin, "A Garden in Belmont: *The Merchant of Venice*, 5.1; Essays in Honor of S. F. Johnson," in Elton and Long, *Shakespeare and Dramatic Tradition*, 13–31.

Ruth M. Levitsky, "Shylock as Unregenerate Man," *SQ* 28 (Spring 1977): 58–64.

Milton A. Levy, "Did Shakespeare Join the Casket and Bond Plots in *The Merchant of Venice*?" *SQ* 11 (Summer 1960): 388–91.

Barbara K. Lewalski, "Biblical Allusion and Allegory in *The Merchant of Venice*," *SQ* 13 (Summer 1962): 327–43.

Cynthia Lewis, "Antonio and Alienation in *The Merchant of Venice*," *SAB* 48 (November 1983): 19–31.

David Lucking, "Standing for Sacrifice: The Casket and Trial Scenes in *The Merchant of Venice*," *UTQ* 58 (October 1989): 355–75.

Desmond McCarthy, *Humanities*, 49–53.

Maxine McKay, "*The Merchant of Venice*: A Reflection of Early Conflict Between Courts of Law and Courts of Equity," *SQ* 15 (Autumn 1964): 371–76.

Hugh Maclean, "Bassanio's Name and Nature," *Names* 25 (March 1977): 55–62.

M. M. Mahood, "Golden Lads and Girls," *AJES* 4 (July 1979): 108–23.

Mary S. Mathis, "Portia's Role-Playing in *The Merchant of Venice*: Yes, Nerissa, We Shall Turn to Men," *CCTEP* 53 (September 1988): 42–51.

William G. McCollon, "Formalism and Illusion in Shakespearian Drama," *QJS* 31 (December 1945): 446–47, 450.

Robert McMahon, "'Some There Be That Shadows Kiss': A Note on *The Merchant of Venice*, II.ix.65," *SQ* 37 (1986): 371–73.

Horst Meller, "A Pound of Flesh and the Economics of Christian Grace: Shakespeare's *The Merchant of Venice*," in Sharma, *Essay on Shakespeare in Honour of A. A. Ansari*, 150–74.

Graham Midgley, "*The Merchant of Venice*: A Reconsideration," *EIC* 10 (April 1960): 121–33.

Charles Mitchell, "The Conscience of Venice: Shakespeare's Merchant," *JEGP* 63 (April 1964): 214–25.

Thomas Moisan, "'Which is the merchant here? And which the Jew?' Subversion and Recuperation in *The Merchant of Venice*," in Howard and O'Connor, *Shakespeare Reproduced*, 188–206.

Harry Morris, "The Judgement Theme in *The Merchant of Venice*," *Renascence* 39 (Fall 1986): 292–311.

SHAKESPEARE, WILLIAM, *The Merchant of Venice*

Ralph Nash, "Shylock's Wolfish Spirit," *SQ* 10 (Winter 1959): 125–28.

Norman Nathan, "Belmont and the Monte di Pieta in *The Merchant of Venice*," *CahiersE* 18 (April 1980): 69–70.

Norman Nathan, "Everyone Loves Money in *The Merchant of Venice*," *SJS* 10 (Fall 1984): 31–39.

Norman Nathan, "Shylock, Jacob and God's Judgement," *SQ* 1 (October 1950): 255–59.

Norman Nathan, "Three Notes on *The Merchant of Venice*," *ShAB* 23 (October 1948): 152–73.

Karen Newman, "Portia's Ring: Unruly Women and the Structures of Exchange in *The Merchant of Venice*," *SQ* 38 (Spring 1987): 19–33.

Lawrence Normand, "Reading the Body in *The Merchant of Venice*," *TexP* 5 (Spring 1991): 55–73.

Marianne L. Novy, "Giving, Taking, and the Role of Portia in *The Merchant of Venice*," *PQ* 58 (Winter 1979): 137–54.

Marianne L. Novy, "Sex, Reciprocity, and Self-Sacrifice in *The Merchant of Venice*," in *Human Sexuality in the Middle Ages and Renaissance*, ed. Douglas Radcliffe-Ulmstead (Pittsburgh: University of Pittsburgh Press, 1978), 153–66.

Nuttall, *A New Mimesis*, 121–29.

James O'Hara, "Shakespeare's *The Merchant of Venice*," *Expl* 37 (Spring 1979): 11–13.

Avraham Oz, "The Egall Yoke of Love: Prophetic Unions in *The Merchant of Venice*," *Assaph* 2, no. 3 (1985): 56–72.

Bernard J. Paris, "The Not So Noble Antonio: A Horneyan Analysis of Shakespeare's *Merchant of Venice*," *AJP* 49 (September 1989): 189–200.

Morriss Henry Partee, "Love and Responsibility in *The Merchant of Venice*," *Greyfriar* 29 (1988): 15–23.

Morriss Henry Partee, "Sexual Testing in *The Merchant of Venice*," *McNR* 32 (1988–1989): 64–79.

Anne Parten, "Re-establishing Sexual Order: The Ring Episode in *The Merchant of Venice*," *SPWVSRA* 6 (Spring 1981): 27–34. Reprinted in *WS* 9, no. 2 (1982): 145–55.

Richard H. Popkin, "A Jewish Merchant of Venice," *SQ* 40 (Autumn 1989): 329–31.

Eric Rasmussen, "Shakespeare's *The Merchant of Venice*, III.ii.63–68," *Expl* 44 (Winter 1986): 12–13.

Theodor Reik, "Jessica, My Child," *AI* 8 (March 1951): 3–27. Reprinted in *The Secret Self*, 33–56.

Irving Ribner, "Marlowe and Shakespeare," *SQ* 15 (Spring 1964): 44–49.

Kiernan Ryan, "*The Merchant of Venice*: Past Significance and Present Meaning" *ShJE* 117 (1981): 49–54.

Anselm Schlosser, "Dialectic in *The Merchant of Venice*," *ZAA* 23, no. 1 (1975): 5–11.

Amiel Schotz, "The Law That Never Was: A Note on *The Merchant of Venice*," *ThR* 16 (1991): 249–52.

Peter J. Seng, "The Riddle Song in *The Merchant of Venice*," *N&Q* 203 (May 1958): 191–93.

John B. Shackford, "The Bond of Kindness: Shylock's Humanity," *UR* 21 (Winter 1954): 85–91.

Shapiro, *Rival Playwrights*, 103–12.

Ronald A. Sharp, "Gift Exchange and the Economies of Spirit in *The Merchant of Venice*," *MP* 83 (February 1986): 250–65.

Marc Shell, "The Wether and the Ewe: Verbal Usury in *The Merchant of Venice*," *KR* 41 (Fall 1979): 65–92.

Michael W. Shurgot, "The Gobbos and Christian 'Seeing' in *The Merchant of Venice*," *UCrow* 4 (1982): 56–60.

Michael W. Shurgot, "Gobbo's Gift and the 'Muddy Vesture of Decay' in *The Merchant of Venice*," *ELWIU* 10 (Fall 1983): 139–48.

Paul N. Siegel, "Shylock and the Puritan," *Columbia University Forum* 5 (Fall 1962): 14–19.

Paul N. Siegel, "Shylock and the Puritan Usurers," *UMPEAL* 1 (March 1953): 129–38.

Elizabeth S. Sklar, "Bassanio's Golden Fleece," *TSLL* 18 (Winter 1976): 500–09.

Camille Slights, "In Defense of Jessica: The Runaway Daughter in *The Merchant of Venice*." *SQ* 31 (Autumn 1980): 357–68.

Kristian Smidt, "Unconformities in *The Merchant of Venice*," in *Historical and Editorial Studies in Medieval and Early Modern English for Johan Gerritsen*, ed. Mary-Jo Arn, Hanneke Wirtjes, and Hans Jansen (Groningen: Wolters-Noordhoff, 1985), 15–35.

Smith, *Homosexual Desire in Shakespeare's England*, 67–69.

Fred Manning Smith, "Shylock on the Right of Jews and Emilia on the Rights of Women," *WVUPP* 5 (January 1947): 32–33.

John Hazel Smith, "Shylock: 'Devil Incarnation' or 'Poor Man . . . Wronged'?" *JEGP* 60 (January 1961): 1–21.

Lewis W. Smith, "Shakespeare and the Speaking Line," *Poet Lore* 48 (Spring 1942): 69–70.

Warren D. Smith, "Shakespeare's Shylock," *SQ* 15 (Summer 1964): 193–99.

Ernest A. Strathmann, "The Devil Can Quote Scripture," *SQ* 15 (Spring 1964): 17.

Vivian Summers, "*The Merchant of Venice*," *The Use of English* 12 (Spring 1961): 161–66.

David Sundelson, "The Dynamics of Marriage in *The Merchant of Venice*," *HIS* 4 (Spring–Summer 1981): 245–62.

James Sutherland, "How the Characters Talk," in Sutherland and Hurtsfield, *Shakespeare's World*, 116–35.

Leonard Tennenhouse, "The Counterfeit Order of *The Merchant of Venice*," in Schwartz and Kahn, *Representing Shakespeare*, 54–69.

John B. Thompson, "The Modification of Stereotypes in *The Merchant of Venice*," *ESA* 26, no. 1 (1983): 1–11.

E. M. W. Tillyard, "The Trial Scene in *The Merchant of Venice*," *REL* 2 (October 1961): 51–59. Reprinted in *Essays Literary and Educational*, 30–38.

E. M. W. Tillyard, "Loneliness in *The Merchant of Venice*," *EIC* 11 (October 1961): 487–88.

Barbara Tovey, "The Golden Casket: An Interpretation of *The Merchant of Venice*," in Alvis and West, *Shakespeare as Political Thinker*, 215–37.

E. F. J. Tucker, "The Letter of the Law in *The Merchant of Venice*," *ShS* 29 (1976): 93–101.

Raymond B. Waddington, "*The Merchant of Venice* III.i.108–113: A Transformation Emblem," *ELN* 14 (September 1976): 92–98.

Sidney Warhalft, "Anti-Semitism in *The Merchant of Venice*," *Manitoba Arts Review* 10 (Winter 1956): 3–15.

Michael J. Warren, "A Note on *The Merchant of Venice*, II.i.31," *SQ* 32 (Winter 1981): 104–05.

Albert Wertheim, "The Treatment of Shylock in *The Merchant of Venice*," *ShakS* 6 (1970): 75–87.

E. J. West, "The Use of Contrast in *The Merchant of Venice*," *ShAB* 21 (October 1946): 172–76.

Richard P. Wheeler, "'. . . And my loud crying still': The Sonnets, *The Merchant of Venice*, and *Othello*," in Erickson and Kahn, *Shakespeare's 'Rough Magic*,' 193–209.

Frank Whigham, "Ideology and Class Conduct in *The Merchant of Venice*," *RenD* 10 (1979): 93–115.

Catherine T. Wildermuth, "Rings around Venice: Love in *The Merchant of Venice*," *CCTEP* 47 (September 1982): 6–13.

Leah W. Wilkins, "Shylock's Pound of Flesh and Laban's Sheep," *MLN* 62 (January 1947): 28–30.

F. Lyman Windolph, *Revelations of the Law in Literature* (Philadelphia: University of Pennsylvania Press, 1956), 44–58.

Young, *Immortal Shadows*, 41–44.

The Merry Wives of Windsor

G. Beiner, "The Libido as Pharmakos, or: The Triumph of Love: *The Merry Wives of Windsor* in the Context of Comedy," *OL* 43, no. 3 (1988): 195–216.

Frederick G. Blair, "Shakespeare's Bear 'Sackerson," *N&Q* 198 (December 1953): 514–15.

Phyllis N. Braxton, "Shakespeare's *Merry Wives of Windsor* and *Henry V*," *Expl* 48 (Fall 1989): 8–10.

William Carroll, "'A Received Belief': Imagination in *The Merry Wives of Windsor*," *SP* 74 (Spring 1977): 186–215.

Sandra Clark, "'Wives may be merry and yet honest too': Women and Wit in *The Merry Wives of Windsor* and Some Other Plays," in Mahon and Pendleton, *"Fanned and winnowed opinions,"* 249–67.

Nancy Cotton, "Castrating (W)itches: Impotence and Magic in *The Merry Wives of Windsor*," *SQ* 38 (Autumn 1987): 321–26.

John P. Cutts, "Falstaff's 'Heavenlie Jewel': Incidental Music for *The Merry Wives of Windsor*," *SQ* 11 (Winter 1960): 89–92.

Charles L. Draper, "Falstaff's Bardolf," *Neophil* 33 (October 1949): 222–26.

John W. Draper, "Falstaff, 'A Fool and Jester,'" *MLQ* 17 (December 1946): 453–62.

Peter Erickson, "The Order of the Garter, the Cult of Elizabeth, and Class-Gender Tension in *The Merry Wives of Windsor*," in Howard and O'Connor, *Shakespeare Reproduced*, 116–40.

Marvin Felheim, and Philip Traci, "Realism in *The Merry Wives of Windsor*," *BSUF* 22, no. 1 (1981): 52–59.

Robert F. Fleissner, "The Malleable Knight and the Unfettered Friar: *The Merry Wives of Windsor* and Boccaccio," *ShakS* 11 (1978): 77–93.

Barbara Freedman, "Falstaff's Punishment: Buffoonery as Defensive Posture in *The Merry Wives of Windsor*," *ShakS* 14 (1981): 163–74.

French, *Shakespeare's Division of Experience*, 101–05.

John Gall, "'O you panderly rascals': Plot and Characterization in *The Merry Wives of Windsor*," *SPWVSRA* 9 (Spring 1984): 1–7.

Christiane Gallenca, "Ritual and Folk Custom in *The Merry Wives of Windsor*," *Cahiers* 27 (April 1985): 27–41.

C. J. Gianakaris, "Folk Ritual as Comic Catharsis and *The Merry Wives of Windsor*," *MissFR* 10, no. 2 (1976): 138–53.

William L. Godshalk, "An Apology for *The Merry Wives of Windsor*," *RenP 1972* (1973): 97–108.

Leonard Goldstein, "Some Aspects of Marriage and Inheritance in Shakespeare's *The Merry Wives of Windsor* and Chapman's *All Fools*," *ZAA* 12, no. 3 (1964): 375–86.

C. A. Greer, "Falstaff's Diminution of Wit," *N&Q* 199 (November 1954): 468.

Richard F. Hardin, "Honor Revenged: Falstaff's Fortunes and *The Merry Wives of Windsor*," *ELWIU* 5 (Fall 1978): 143–52.

Dorothy B. Hart, "*The Merry Wives* and Two Brethren," *SP* 39 (April 1942): 261–78.

Jan Lawson Hinely, "Comic Scapegoats and the Falstaff of *The Merry Wives of Windsor*," *ShakS* 15 (1982): 37–54.

Ronald Huebert, "Levels of Parody in *The Merry Wives of Windsor*," *ESC* 3 (Summer 1977): 136–52.

William B. Hunter, "Falstaff," *SAQ* 50 (January 1951): 86–95.

Frederick B. Jonassen, "The Meaning of Falstaff's Allusion to the Jack-a-Lent in *The Merry Wives of Windsor*," *SP* 88 (Winter 1991): 46–68.

Dorothea Kehler, "Shakespeare's *The Merry Wives of Windsor*," *Expl* 49 (Winter 1991): 76–77.

Judith J. Kollmann, "'Ther is noon oother uncabus but he': *The Canterbury Tales*, *Merry Wives of Windsor*, and Falstaff," in Donaldson and Kollmann, *Chaucerian Shakespeare*, 43–68.

François Laroque, "Ovidian Transformations and Folk Festivities in *A Midsummer Night's Dream*, *The Merry Wives of Windsor*, and *As You Like It*," *CahiersE* 25 (April 1984): 23–36.

McPeek, *The Black Book of Knaves*, 180–86.

Roy F. Montgomery, "A Fair House Built on Another Man's Ground," *SQ* 5 (Spring 1954): 207–08.

Muir, *Essays on Literature and Society*, 166–81.

Nicholl, *The Chemical Theatre*, 78–80.

Anne Parten, "Falstaff's Horns: Masculine Inadequacy and Feminine Mirth in *The Merry Wives of Windsor*," *SP* 82 (Spring 1985): 184–99.

Theodor Reik, "Comedy of Intrigue," in *The Secret Self*, 63–75.

Jeanne Addison Roberts, "The Merry Wives: Suitable Shallow, But Neither Simple Nor Slender," *ShakS* 6 (1970): 102–23.

Shapiro, *Rival Playwrights*, 112–14.

Camille Wells Slights, "Pastoral and Parody in *The Merry Wives of Windsor*," *ESC* 11 (March 1985): 12–25.

Robert A. H. Smith, "*Doctor Faustus* and *The Merry Wives of Windsor*," *RES* 23 (1972): 395–97.

John M. Steadman, "Falstaff as Actaeon: A Dramatic Emblem," *SQ* 14 (Summer 1963): 231–44.

Alice Walker, "*The Merry Wives of Windsor*, III. Iii. 176," *RES* 9 (May 1958): 173.

E. J. West, "On Master Slender," *CE* 8 (February 1947): 228–30.

David M. White, "An Explanation of the 'Brook-Broome' Question in Shakespeare's *The Merry Wives of Windsor*," *PQ* 21 (July 1946): 280–83.

Williams, *The Image of the City*, 40–42.

A Midsummer Night's Dream

John A. Allen, "Bottom and Titania," *SQ* 18 (Winter 1967): 44–62.

A. A. Ansari, "Shakespeare's Allegory of Love," *AJES* 3 (April 1978): 44–62.

Alex Aronson, "A Note on Shakespeare's Dream Imagery," *Visuabharati Quarterly* 19 (August–October 1952): 169–70.

Arthos, *Shakespeare's Use of Dream and Vision*, 85–109.

Barber, *Shakespeare's Festive Comedy*, 119–62.

James P. Bednarz, "Imitations of Spenser in *A Midsummer Night's Dream*," *RenD* 14 (1983): 79–102.

Alan W. Bellringer, "The Act of Change in *A Midsummer Night's Dream*," *ES* 64 (June 1983): 201–17.

Dorothy Bethurum, "Shakespeare's Comment on Mediaeval Romance in *A Midsummer Night's Dream*," *MLN* 60 (February 1945): 85–94.

David Bevington, "'But we are spirits of another sort': The Dark Side of Love and Magic in *A Midsummer Night's Dream*," in *Medieval and Renaissance Studies*, ed. Seigfried Wenzel (Chapel Hill: University of North Carolina Press, 1978), 80–92.

Dale M. Blount, "Modifications in Occult Folklore as a Comic Device in Shakespeare's *A Midsummer Night's Dream*," *FCS* 9 (1984): 1–17.

Max Bluestone, "An Anti-Jewish Pun in *A Midsummer Night's Dream*, III. I. 97," *N&Q* 198 (August 1953): 325–29.

George A. Bonnard, "Shakespeare's Purpose in *Midsummer Night's Dream*," *ShJE* 92 (1956): 268–79.

Bradshaw, *Shakespeare's Skepticism*, 39–47, 66–72.

Jane K. Brown, "Discordia Concors: On the Order of *A Midsummer Night's Dream*," *MLQ* 48 (March 1987): 20–41.

James L. Calderwood, "*A Midsummer Night's Dream*: Anamorphism and Theseus' Dream," *SQ* 42 (Autumn 1991): 409–30.

James L. Calderwood, "*A Midsummer Night's Dream*: The Illusion of Drama," *MLQ* 26 (December 1965): 506–22.

Josie P. Campbell, "Farce as Function in Medieval and Shakespearean Drama," *UCrow* 3 (1980): 11–18.

Hanne Carlsen, "'What fools these mortals be!': Ovid in *A Midsummer Night's Dream*," in Caie and Norgaard, *A Literary Miscellany*, 94–107.

Thomas Clayton, "'Fie What a Question's That If Thou Wert Near a Lewd Interpreter': The Wall Scene in *A Midsummer Night's Dream*," *ShakS* 7 (1974): 101–14.

Ralph Alan Cohen, "The Strategy of Misdirection in *A Midsummer Night's Dream* and *Bartholomew Fair*," *RenP 1981* (1982): 65–75.

M. E. Comtois, "The Comedy of the Lovers in *A Midsummer Night's Dream*," *ELWIU* 12 (Spring 1985): 15–25.

Naomi Conn, "The Promise of Arcadia: Nature and Natural Man in Shakespeare's Comedies," *CCP* 1 (1964): 120–22.

D. H. Craig, "The Idea of the Play in *A Midsummer Night's Dream* and *Bartholomew Fair*," in Donaldson, *Jonson and Shakespeare*, 89–100.

John P. Cutts, "The Fierce Vexations of a *Midsummer Night's Dreame*," *SQ* 14 (Spring 1963): 183–85.

Dawson, *Indirections*, 63–70.

Leo Paul S. De Alvarez, "Poetry and Kingship: Shakespeare's *A Midsummer Night's Dream*," *BuR* 29, no. 1 (1984): 158–84.

Luis Alberto de Miranda, "*A Midsummer Night's Dream* as a Foreshadowing of Shakespeare's Vision of Reality," *EAA* 5–6 (1981–1982): 172–82.

R. V. Dent, "Imagination in *A Midsummer Night's Dream*," *SQ* 15 (Spring 1964): 115–29. Reprinted in McManaway, *Shakespeare 400*, 115–29.

William B. Dillingham, "Bottom: The Third Ingredient," *EUQ* 12 (December 1956): 230–37.

Madeline Doran, "*A Midsummer Night's Dream*: A Metamorphosis," *Rice Institute Pamphlets* 46 (January 1960): 113–35.

Allen Dunn, "The Indian Boy's Dream Wherein Every Mother's Son Rehearses His Part: Shakespeare's *A Midsummer Night's Dream*," *ShakS* 20 (1987): 15–32.

M. D. Faber, "Hermia's Dream: Royal Road to *A Midsummer Night's Dream*," *L&P* 22, no. 2 (1972): 179–90.

Florence Falk, "Dream and Ritual Process in *A Midsummer Night's Dream*," *ComD* 14 (Autumn 1980): 263–79.

Peter F. Fisher, "The Argument of *A Midsummer Night's Dream*," *SQ* 8 (Summer 1957): 307–10.

Donald W. Foster, "Shakespeare's *A Midsummer Night's Dream*," *Expl* 43 (Fall 1984): 14–16.

Wolfgang Franke, "The Logic of Double Entendre in *A Midsummer Night's Dream*," *PQ* 58 (Spring 1979): 282–97.

French, *Shakespeare's Division of Experience*, 91–94.

Saad M. Gamal, "*A Midsummer Night's Dream* and *Romeo and Juliet*, Some Parallels," *CairoSE* (1963–64): 109–17.

Shirley Nelson Garner, "*A Midsummer Night's Dream*: 'Jack Shall Have Jill/Nought Shall Go Ill,'" *WS* 9, no. 1 (1981): 47–63.

René Girard, "Bottom's One Man Show," in *The Current in Criticism: Essays on the Present and Future in Literary Theory*, ed. Clayton Koelb and Virginia Lokke (West Lafayette, IN: Purdue University Press, 1987), 99–122.

Reneé Girard, "Myth and Ritual in Shakespeare: *A Midsummer Night's Dream*," in *Textual Strategies: Perspectives in Post-Structuralist Criticism*, ed. Joseph V. Harari (Ithaca, NY: Cornell University Press, 1979), 189–212.

Girard, *Theatre of Envy*, 29–79.

Weston A. Gui, "Bottom's Dream," *AI* 9 (Fall–Winter 1952): 251–305.

Jay L. Halio, "Nightingales That Roar: The Language of *A Midsummer Night's Dream*," in Allen and White, *Traditions and Innovations*, 137–49.

Jay L. Halio, "Nightingales That Roar, Morrises Filled With Mud: The Dramatic Language of *A Midsummer Night's Dream*," *ShN* 26 (Winter 1976): 35.

Vicki Shahly Hartman, "*A Midsummer Night's Dream*: A Gentle Concord to the Oedipal Problem," *AI* 40 (Winter 1983): 355–69.

Terence Hawkes, "Comedy, Orality, and Duplicity: *A Midsummer Night's Dream* and *Twelfth Night*," *NYLF* 5–6 (Winter 1980): 155–63.

Hawkins, *Likeness of Truth*, 27–29, 31–35.

S. K. Heninger, Jr., "'Wondrous Strange Snow'—*A Midsummer Night's Dream* V. I. 66," *MLN* 68 (November 1953): 481–83.

T. Walter Herbert, "Dislocation and the Modest Demand in *A Midsummer Night's Dream*," *RenP 1960* (1961): 31–36.

Charles Hertel, "Shakespeare's *A Midsummer Night's Dream* I.ii.113," *Expl* 33 (December 1975): Item 39.

Hewett, *Reading and Response*, 102–06.

Hibbard, *Making of Shakespeare's Dramatic Poetry*, 145–53.

Jan Lawson Hinely, "Expounding the Dream: Shaping Fantasies in *A Midsummer Night's Dream*," in Charney and Reppen, *Psychoanalytic Approaches to Literature and Film*, 120–38.

Norman H. Holland, "Hermia's Dream," in Schwartz and Kahn, *Representing Shakespeare*, 1–20.

Peter Holland, "Dreaming the *Dream*," in Iselin and Moreau, *Le Songe d'une nuit d'été*, 9–27.

James V. Holleran, "The Pyramus-Thisbe Theme in *A Midsummer Night's Dream*," *CEJ* 3, no. 1 (1967): 20–26.

Hilda Hulme, "Three Notes: *Troilus and Cressida*, V. Vii. 11; *Midsummer Night's Dream*, II. I. 54; *Measure for Measure*, II. I. 39," *JEGP* 57 (October 1958): 722–24.

Maurice Hunt, "Individualism in *A Midsummer Night's Dream*," *SCB* 46 (Summer 1986): 1–13.

Biodun Iginla, "Woman and Metaphor," *enclitic* 2, no. 1 (1978): 27–37.

Gerald F. Jacobson, "A Note on Shakespeare's *Midsummer Night's Dream*," *AI* 19 (Spring 1962): 21–26.

Frank Kermode, "The Mature Comedies," *Stratford-Upon-Avon Studies* 3 (1961): 214–20.

Knight, *The Golden Labyrinth*, 69–70.

M. E. Lamb, "*A Midsummer Night's Dream*: The Myth of Theseus and the Minotaur," *TSLL* 21 (Winter 1979): 478–91.

Larry Langford, "The Story Shall Be Changed: The Senecan Sources of *A Midsummer Night's Dream*," *CahiersE* 25 (April 1984): 37–51.

François Laroque, "Ovidian Transformations and Folk Festivities in *A Midsummer Night's Dream, The Merry Wives of Windsor*, and *As You Like It*," *CahiersE* 25 (April 1984): 23–36.

Robert A. Law, "The 'Pre-Conceived Pattern' of *A Midsummer Night's Dream*," *Studies in English* (University of Texas) 22 (March 1943): 5–14.

Ann Lecercle, "Of Mazes, Merry-Go-Rounds and Immaculate Conceptions: The Dream Logic of *A Midsummer Night's Dream*," in Iselin and Moreau, *Le Songe d'une nuit d'été*, 141–54.

Virgil Lee, "Puck's 'Tailor': A Mimic Pun?" *SQ* 26 (Spring 1975): 55–57.

Clifford Leech, "Shakespeare's Comic Dukes," *REL* 5 (April 1964): 103–04.

Theodore B. Leinwand, "'I Believe We Must Leave the Killing Out': Deference and Accommodation in *A Midsummer Night's Dream*," *RenP 1985* (1986): 11–30.

SHAKESPEARE, WILLIAM, *A Midsummer Night's Dream*

Ishrat Lindblad, "The Autotelic Function of *A Midsummer Night's Dream*," in Johansson and Tysdahl, *Papers from the First Nordic Conference for English Studies*, 134–47.

Joseph A. Longo, "Myth in *A Midsummer Night's Dream*," *CahiersE* 18 (April 1980): 17–27.

M. M. Mahood, "*A Midsummer Night's Dream*: The Dialectic of Eros-Thanatos," *AI* 38 (Fall 1981): 269–78.

Philip C. McGuire, "Egeus and the Implications of Silence," in Thompson and Thompson, *Shakespeare and the Sense of Performance*, 103–15.

Philip C. McGuire, "Intentions, Options, and Greatness: An Example from *A Midsummer Night's Dream*," in Homan, *Shakespeare and the Triple Play*, 177–86.

D. F. McKenzie, "Shakespeare's Dream of Knowledge," *Landfall* 18 (March 1964): 41–48.

McPeek, *The Black Book of Knaves*, 132–33

James S. McPeek, "The Psyche Myth and *A Midsummer Night's Dream*," *SQ* 23 (Winter 1972): 69–79.

Mann, *The Elizabethan Player*, 42–43, 206–07.

John S. Mebane, "Structure, Source, and Meaning in *A Midsummer Night's Dream*," *TSLL* 24 (Fall 1982): 255–70.

Raeburn Miller, "The Persons of Moonshine: *A Midsummer Night's Dream* and the 'Disfigurement' of Realities," in *Explorations of Literature*, ed. Rima D. Reck (Baton Rouge: Louisiana State University Press, 1966), 25–31.

Ronald F. Miller, "*A Midsummer Night's Dream*: The Fairies, Bottom, and the Mystery of Things," *SQ* 26 (Spring 1975): 254–68.

Louis Adrian Montrose, "*A Midsummer Night's Dream* and the Shaping Fantasies of Elizabethan Culture: Gender, Power, Form," in Ferguson, Quilligan, and Vickers, *Rewriting the Renaissance*, 65–87.

Kenneth Muir, "Pyramus and Thisbe: A Study in Shakespeare's Method," *SQ* 5 (Spring 1954): 141–53.

H. A. Myers, "*Romeo and Juliet* and *A Midsummer Night's Dream*: Tragedy and Comedy," in Barnet, *Aspects of the Drama*, 35–39, 43–49. Reprinted in *Tragedy: A View of Life*, 110–28.

Nelson, *Play Within a Play*, 12–15.

Howard Nemerov, "The Marriage of Theseus and Hippolyta," *KR* 18 (Autumn 1956): 633–41. Reprinted in *Poetry and Fiction*, 17–24.

William A. Nitze, "*A Midsummer Night's Dream*, V, I, 4–17," *MLR* 50 (October 1955): 495–97.

Paul A. Olson, "*A Midsummer Night's Dream* and the Meaning of Court Marriage," *ELH* 24 (June 1957): 95–119.

David Ormerod, "*A Midsummer Night's Dream*: The Monster in the Labyrinth," *ShakS* 11 (1978): 39–52.

Anne Paolucci, "The Lost Days in *A Midsummer Night's Dream*," *SQ* 28 (Summer 1977): 317–26.

Douglas H. Parker, "'Limander' and 'Helen' in *A Midsummer Night's Dream*," *SQ* 33 (Spring 1982): 99–101.

Annabel Patterson, "Bottom's Up: Festive Theory in *A Midsummer Night's Dream*," *RenP 1987* (1988): 25–39.

D'Orsay W. Pearson, "Male Sovereignty, Harmony and Irony in *A Midsummer Night's Dream*," *UCrow* 7 (1987): 24–35.

T. M. Pearce, "Shakespeare's *A Midsummer Night's Dream*, IV, I, 214–15," *Expl* 18 (October 1959): 8.

Vincent F. Petronella, "Shakespeare's *A Midsummer Night's Dream*," *Expl* 37 (Spring 1978): 5–6.

Pogson, *In the East*, 70–77.

Arthur Quiller-Couch, *Cambridge Lectures* (London: Dent, 1943), 123–36.

Clifford Earl Ramsey, "*A Midsummer Night's Dream*," in *Homer to Brecht: The European Epic and Dramatic Traditions*, ed. Michael Seidel and Edward Mendelson (New Haven: Yale University Press, 1977), 214–37.

Robert A. Ravich, "A Psychoanalytic Study of Shakespeare's Early Plays," *Psychoanalytic Quarterly* 33 (July 1964): 405–07.

Robert A. Ravich, "Shakespeare and Psychiatry," *L&P* 14 (Summer/Fall 1964): 98.

Lou Agnes Reynolds and Paul Sawyer, "Folk Medicine, and the Four Fairies of *A Midsummer Night's Dream*," *SQ* 10 (Autumn 1959): 513–21.

James E. Robinson, "The Ritual and Rhetoric of *A Midsummer Night's Dream*," *PMLA* 83 (January 1968): 380–91.

T. V. Robinson, "Palpable Hot Ice: Dramatic Burlesque in *A Midsummer Night's Dream*," *SP* 61 (April 1964): 192–204.

James E. Savage, "Notes on *A Midsummer Night's Dream*," *UMSE* 2, no. 1 (1961): 65–78.

Ernest Schanzer, "The Central Theme of *A Midsummer Night's Dream*," *UTQ* 20 (April 1951): 233–38.

Ernest Schanzer, "The Moon and the Fairies in *A Midsummer Night's Dream*," *UTQ* 24 (April 1955): 234–46.

Ernest Schanzer, "Atavism and Anticipation in Shakespeare's Style," *EIC* 7 (July 1957): 245–49.

Leah Scragg, "Shakespeare, Lyly and Ovid: The Influence of *Gallathea* on *A Midsummer Night's Dream*," *ShS* 30 (1977): 125–34.

Jeffrey Shulman, "Bottom Is Up: The Role of Illusion in *A Midsummer Night's Dream*," *EAS* 16 (May 1987): 9–21.

Paul N. Siegel, "*A Midsummer Night's Dream* and the Wedding Guests," *SQ* 4 (April 1953): 139–44.

Hallett Smith, "The Poetry of the Lyric Group: *Richard II, Romeo and Juliet, A Midsummer Night's Dream*," in Highfill, *Shakespeare's Craft*, 69–93.

Smith *Shakespeare's Romances*, 120–33.

Jonathan C. Smith, "*A Midsummer Night's Dream* and the Allegory of Theologians," *C&L* 28 (Winter 1979): 15–23.

Stephen L. Smith, "*A Midsummer Night's Dream*: Shakespeare, Play and Metaplay," *CentR* 21 (Spring 1977): 194–209.

Joan Stansbury, "Characterization of the Four Young Lovers in *A Midsummer Night's Dream*," *ShS* 35 (1982): 57–63.

Walter F. Staton, Jr., "Ovidian Elements in *A Midsummer Night's Dream*," *HLQ* 26 (February 1963): 165–78.

Thomas B. Stroup, "Bottom's Name and His Epiphany," *SQ* 29 (Spring 1978): 79–82.

Styan, *The Elements of Drama*, 178–80. Reprinted in *The Context and Craft of Drama*, ed. Robert W. Corrigan and James L. Rosenberg (San Fransisco: Chandler, 1964), 113–15.

Homer Swander, "Editors vs. Text: The Scripted Geography of *A Midsummer Night's Dream*," *SP* 87 (Winter 1990): 83–108.

Leonard Tennenhouse, "Strategies of State and Political Plays: *A Midsummer Night's Dream, Henry IV, Henry V, Henry VIII*," in Dollimore and Sinfield, *Political Shakespeare*, 107–28.

Sidney Thomas, "The Bad Weather in *A Midsummer Night's Dream*," *MLN* 64 (May 1949): 319–22.

William J. Tucker, "Irish Aspects of Shakespeare," *Catholic World* 156 (March 1943): 698–99.

Anca Vlasopolos, "The Ritual of Midsummer: A Pattern for *A Midsummer Night's Dream*," *RenQ* 31 (1978): 21–29.

Raymond B. Waddington, "Two Notes Iconographic on *A Midsummer Night's Dream*: I, Hermia's Dream; II, Peter Quince: 'What's in a name?,'" *ELN* 26 (September 1988): 12–17.

Barry Weller, "Identity Dis-Figured: *A Midsummer Night's Dream*," *KR* 47 (Summer 1985): 66–78.

Stanley Wells, *A Midsummer Night's Dream* Revisited," *CrSurv* 3, no. 1 (1991): 14–29.

Stanley Wells, "A Note on Demetrius's *Vile Name*," *CahiersE* 10 (April 1972): 67–68.

E. T. West, "Hypothosis Concerning *A Midsummer Night's Dream*," *CE* 9 (February 1948): 247–49.

Robert F. Willson, Jr., "Burlesque Tone in *A Midsummer Night's Dream*, or the Play from Bottom Up," *LHR* 13, no. 1 (1972): 115–27.

Robert F. Willson, Jr., "The Chink in the Wall: Anticlimax and Dramatic Illusion in *A Midsummer Night's Dream*," *ShJE* 117 (1981): 85–90.

Deborah Baker Wyrick, "The Ass Motif in *The Comedy of Errors* and *A Midsummer Night's Dream*," *SQ* 33 (Autumn 1982): 432–48.

Rose A. Zimbardo, "Regeneration and Reconciliation in *A Midsummer Night's Dream*," *ShakS* 6 (1970): 35–50.

Sheldon Zitner, "The Worlds of *A Midsummer Night's Dream*," *SAQ* 59 (Summer 1960): 397–403.

Much Ado About Nothing

A. A. Ansari, "*Much Ado About Nothing* and the Masks of Reality," *AJES* 5 (July 1980): 175–89.

William B. Bache, "The 'Eye of Love' in *Much Ado About Nothing*," *Discourse* 11, no. 3 (1968): 224–29.

F. Bastian, "George Vargis, Constable," *N&Q* 202 (January 1957): 11.

Harry Berger, Jr., "Against the Sink-a-Pace: Sexual and Family Politics in *Much Ado About Nothing*," *SQ* 33 (Summer 1982): 302–13.

Andrew S. Cairncross, "Shakespeare and Ariosto: *Much Ado About Nothing*, *King Lear*, and *Othello*," *RenQ* 29 (1976): 178–82.

Richard Coates, "Dogberry and Verges as a Pair in *Much Ado About Nothing*," *Names* 34 (June 1986): 236–37.

Naomi Conn, "The Promise of Arcadia: Nature and the Natural Man in Shakespeare's Comedies," *CCP* 1 (1964): 119–20.

Carol Cook, "'The Sign and Semblance of Her Honor': Reading Gender Difference in *Much Ado About Nothing*," *PMLA* 101 (January 1986): 186–202.

David Cook, "'The very temple of delight': The Twin Plots of *Much Ado About Nothing*," in Coleman and Hammond, *Poetry and Drama, 1570–1700*, 32–46.

T. W. Craik, "*Much Ado About Nothing*," *Scrutiny* 19 (October 1953): 297–316.

Alan E. Craven, "Compositor Analysis to Edited Text: Some Suggested Readings in *Richard II* and *Much Ado About Nothing*," *PBSA* 76, no. 1 (1982): 43–62.

Andrew B. Crighton, "Hercules Shaven: A Centering Mythic Metaphor in *Much Ado About Nothing*," *TSLL* 16 (Winter 1975): 619–26.

Leonard F. Dean, "Shakespeare's *Much Ado About Nothing*, IV, I, 291," *Expl* 2 (May 1944): 51.

Thomas J. Derrick, "Merry Tales in *Much Ado About Nothing*," *Thalia* 8 (Fall–Winter 1985): 21–26.

John Drakakis, "Trust and Transgression: The Discursive Practices of *Much Ado About Nothing*," in Machin and Norris, *Post-Structuralist Readings of English Poetry*, 59–84.

John F. Draper, "Dogberry's Due Process of Law," *JEGP* 42 (October 1943): 563–67.

John W. Draper, "Benedick and Beatrice," *JEGP* 41 (April 1942): 140–49.

Gavin Edwards, "Anticipation and Retrospect in *Much Ado About Nothing*," *EIC* 41 (October 1991): 277–90.

Barbara Everett, "*Much Ado About Nothing*," *CritQ* 3 (Winter 1961): 319–34.

Marvin Felheim, "Comic Realism in *Much Ado About Nothing*," *PP* 3 (1964): 213–25.

Francis Fergusson, "*The Comedy of Errors* and *Much Ado About Nothing*," *SR* 62 (Winter 1954): 24–37. Reprinted in *The Human Image in Dramatic Literature*, 144–60.

French, *Shakespeare's Division of Experience*, 119–32.

Michael D. Friedman, "'Hush'd on Purpose to Grace Harmony': Wives and Silence in *Much Ado About Nothing*," *TJ* 42 (October 1990): 350–63.

C. O. Gardner, "Beatrice and Benedick," *Theoria* 49 (May 1977): 1–17.

Allan Gilbert, "Two Margarets: The Composition of *Much Ado About Nothing*," *PQ* 41 (January 1962): 61–71.

Girard, *Theatre of Envy*, 80–91.

Sidney L. Gulick, Jr., "More Ado About Ado," *ShAB* 23 (April 1948): 55–59.

Hager, *Shakespeare's Political Animal*, 97–104.

James P. Hammersmith, "Villainy upon Record: The Dogberrian Method," *Interpretations* 11 (March 1979): 13–23.

P. Harvey, "*Much Ado About Nothing*," *Theoria* 11 (1958): 32–36.

Terry Hawkes, "The Old and the New in *Much Ado About Nothing*," *N&Q* 203 (December 1958): 524–25.

Ray L. Heffner, Jr., "Hunting for Clues in *Much Ado About Nothing*," in *Literature and Society: Cross-Cultural Perspectives*, ed. Roger J. Bresnahan (Washington, DC: U. S. Information Service, 1977), 177–227.

Dorothy C. Hockey, "Notes, Notes, Forsooth . . .," *SQ* 8 (Summer 1957): 353–58.

Jean E. Howard, "Renaissance Antitheatricality and the Politics of Gender and Rank in *Much Ado About Nothing*," in Howard and O'Connor, *Shakespeare Reproduced*, 163–87.

Harold Jenkins, "The Ball Scene in *Much Ado About Nothing*," in Fabian and von Rosador, *Shakespeare: Text, Language, Criticism*, 98–117.

W. N. King, "Much Ado About Something," *SQ* 15 (Summer 1964): 143–56.

Knight, *The Golden Labyrinth*, 67–68.

Elliot Krieger, "Social Relations and the Social Order in *Much Ado About Nothing*," *ShS* 32 (1979): 49–61.

Margaret Swanson Lacy, *The Jacobean Problem Play*, 7–28.

F. Dean Leonard, "Shakespeare's *Much Ado About Nothing*, IV, I, 291," *Expl* 2 (May 1944): 51.

B. K. Lewalski, "Love, Appearance and Reality: Much Ado About Something," *SEL* 8 (Spring 1968): 235–51.

Robert Loper, "*Much Ado About Nothing*," *ShN* 8 (September 1958): 28.

Margaret Macpherson, "Claudio and the Conventions of Courtly Love," *Makerere Journal* 6 (1962): 38–49.

R. E. R. Madelaine, "Oranges and Lemans: *Much Ado About Nothing*, IV.i.31," *SQ* 33 (Autumn 1982): 491–92.

F. H. Mares, "Comic Procedures in Shakespeare and Jonson: *Much Ado About Nothing* and *The Alchemist*," in Donaldson, *Jonson and Shakespeare*, 101–18.

William G. McCollum, "The Role of Wit in *Much Ado About Nothing*," *SQ* 19 (Spring 1968): 165–74.

McPeek, *The Black Book of Knaves*, 198–216.

James A. S. McPeek, "The Thief 'Deformed' and *Much Ado About Nothing*,'" *BUSE* 4 (Summer 1960): 65–75.

William W. Morgan, "Verse and Prose in *Much Ado About Nothing*: An Analytic Note," *English* 20 (Spring 1971): 89–92.

Paul Mueschke, and Miriam Mueschke, "Illusion and Metamorphosis in *Much Ado About Nothing*," *SQ* 18 (Spring 1967): 53–65.

Jeffrey Rayner Myers, "An Emended *Much Ado About Nothing*, Act V, Scene iii," *PBSA* 84 (December 1990): 413–18.

Kerley Neill, "Much Ado About Claudio: An Acquittal for the Slandered Groom," *SQ* 3 (April 1952): 91–107.

David Omerod, "Faith and Fashion in *Much Ado About Nothing*," *ShS* 25 (1972): 93–105.

Laurie E. Osborne, "Dramatic Play in *Much Ado About Nothing*: Wedding the Italian Novella and English Comedy," *PQ* 69 (Spring 1990): 167–218.

Charles A. Owen, "Comic Awareness, Style, and Dramatic Technique in *Much Ado About Nothing*," *BUSE* 5 (Winter 1961): 193–207.

Anne Parten, "Beatrice's Horns: A Note on *Much Ado About Nothing*, II.i.25–27," *SQ* 35 (Summer 1984): 201–02.

Adam Pasicki, "Some Rhetorical Figures in *Much Ado About Nothing*," *KN* 15, no. 2 (1968): 147–54.

Estus Polk, "The Function of Dogberry and the Watch in *Much Ado About Nothing*," *Descant* 5 (Spring 1961): 33–35.

Abbie F. Potts, "Spenserian 'Courtesy' and 'Temperance' in *Much Ado About Nothing*," *ShAB* 17 (April 1942): 103–11.

Abbie F. Potts, "Spenserian 'Courtesy' and 'Temperance' in *Much Ado About Nothing* (Concluded)," *ShAB* 17 (July 1942): 126–33.

C. T. Prouty, "A Lost Piece of Stage Business in *Much Ado About Nothing*," *MLN* 65 (March 1950): 207–08.

Hugh M. Richmond, "Much Ado About Notables," *ShakS* 12 (1979): 49–63.

Gordon N. Ross, "Shakespeare's *Much Ado About Nothing*," *Expl* 48 (Fall 1989): 6–7.

Rossiter, *Angel with Horns*, 65–81.

Joyce Hengerer Sexton, "The Theme of Slander in *Much Ado About Nothing* and Garter's *Susanna*, " *PQ* 54 (Autumn 1975): 419–33.

Shaw, *Plays and Players*, 312–19.

Denzell S. Smith, "The Command 'Kill Claudio' in *Much Ado About Nothing*," *ELN* 4 (September 1967): 181–83.

James Smith, "*Much Ado About Nothing*," *Scrutiny* 13 (Spring 1946): 242–56.

Henry L. Snuggs, "Act-Division of *Much Ado About Nothing*," *RenP 1954* (1955): 65–74.

Tony J. Stafford, "Benedick's Cure in *Much Ado About Nothing*," *ReAL* 4, no. 2 (1971): 43–56.

David Lloyd Stevenson, "The Love-Game Comedy," *CUSECL* 164 (1946): 208–16.

Ronald St. Pierre, "'God will send you no horns': The Banter of Cuckoldry in *Much Ado About Nothing*," *ShLR* 22 (1988): 129–40.

Eiko Suhara, "Beatrice's Speech and Her Characterization in *Much Ado About Nothing*," in *Gengo to Buntai: Hagiashida Chiaki Kyoju Kanreki Kinen Ronbunshu,* ed. Chiaki Higashida (Osaka: Osaka Kyoiku Tosho, 1975), 50–58.

A. P. Taylor, "The Sick Time," *MLN* 65 (May 1950): 344–45.

Mark Taylor, "Presence and Absence in *Much Ado About Nothing*," *CentR* 33 (Winter 1989): 1–12.

Karl F. Thompson, "Shakespeare's Romantic Comedies," *PMLA* 67 (December 1952): 1076–81, 1088–89, 1091–93.

J. J. M. Tobin, "On the Asininity of Dogberry," *ES* 59 (July 1978): 199–201.

John Traugott, "Creating a Rational Rinaldo: A Study in the Mixture of the Genres of Comedy and Romance in *Much Ado About Nothing*," *Genre* 15 (Spring–Summer 1982: 157–81. Reprinted in Greenblatt, *The Power of Forms*, 157–82.

John Wain, "The Shakespearean Lie-detector: Thoughts on *Much Ado About Nothing*," *CritQ* 9 (Spring 1967): 27–42.

Stanley Wells, "A Crus in *Much Ado About Nothing* III.iii.152–63," *SQ* 31 (Spring 1980): 85–86.

E. J. West, "Much Ado About an Unpleasant Play," *ShAB* 22 (January 1947): 30–34.

James J. Wey, "'To Grace Harmony': Musical Design in *Much Ado About Nothing*," *BUSE* 4 (Autumn 1960):181–88.

Mary C. Williams, "Much Ado About Chastity in *Much Ado About Nothing*," *RenP* 1983 (1984): 37–45.

Othello

W. D. Adamson, "Unpinned or Undone? Desdemona's Critics and the Problem of Sexual Innocence," *ShakS* 13 (1980): 169–86.

Doris Adler, "The Rhetoric of *Black* and *White* in *Othello*," *SQ* 25 (Spring 1974): 248–57.

Charles Altieri, "Criticism as the Situating of Performances; Or, What Wallace Stevens Has to Tell Us About Othello," in *American Critics at Work: Examinations of Contemporary Literary Theory*, ed. Victor A. Kramer (Troy, NY: Whitston, 1984), 265–95.

Joel B. Altman, "'Preposterous conclusions': Eros, Enargeia, and the Composition of *Othello*," *Representations* 18 (Spring 1987): 129–57.

Viola H. Anderson, "Othello and Peregrina, 'Richer Than all his Tribe,'" *MLN* 64 (June 1949): 415–17.

A. A. Ansari, "Solitariness of the Victim in *Othello*," *AJES* 9 (April 1984): 121–47.

Stanford S. Apseloff, "Shakespeare's *Othello*," *Expl* 38 (Fall 1980): 4.

Stanford S. Apseloff, "Shakespeare's *Othello*, I.i.21," *Expl* 40 (Fall 1981): 10–11.

Stanford S. Apseloff, "Shakespeare's *Othello*, II.i.253–58 and *The Winter's Tale*, I.ii.115 and 125–26," *Expl* 42 (Spring 1984): 12–13.

Aerol Arnold, "The Function of Brabantio in *Othello*," *SQ* 8 (Winter 1957): 51–56.

John Arthos, "The Fall of Othello," *SQ* 9 (Spring 1958): 93–104.

Weston Babcock, "Iago—An Extraordinary Honest Man," *SQ* 16 (Spring 1965): 297–301.

William B. Bache, "Tension and Related Strategies in *Othello*," *CollL* 4 (Spring 1977): 257–61.

Steven Baker, "Sight and a Sight in *Othello*," *ISJR* 61 (August 1987): 301–09.

Bamborough, *The Little World of Man*, 18–19.

G. D. Barche, "*Othello*: A Vritti Approach," *LCrit* 25, no. 3 (1990): 13–22.

Emily C. Bartels, "Making More of the Moor: Aaron, Othello, and Renaissance Refashionings of Race," *SQ* 41 (Winter 1990): 433–54.

Jonathan Bate, "Ovid and the Mature Tragedies: Metamorphosis in *Othello* and *King Lear*," *ShS* 41 (1989): 133–44.

John Bayley, *The Characters of Love—A Study in the Literature of Personality* (London: Constable, 1960), 125–202.

John Bayley, "The Fragile Structure of *Othello*," *TLS* 20 (June 1980): 707–09.

Sharon Beehler, "'An Enemy in Their Mouths': The Closure of Language in *SQ*," *UCrow* 10 (1990): 69–85.

Bentley, *The Play*, 372–73, 484–88.

David S. Berkeley, "A Vulgarization of Desdemona," *SEL* 3 (Spring 1963): 233–39.

S. L. Bethel, "Shakespeare's Imagery: The Diabolic Images in *Othello*," *ShS* 5 (1952): 62–80.

David S. Bergeron, "'Let's Talk of Graves': *Othello* V.ii.5," *MissFR* 10, no. 2 (1976): 154–62.

David M. Bergeron, "Othello's Handkerchief: 'The Recognizance and Pledge of Love,'" *ELR* 5 (Autumn 1975): 360–74.

Ralph Berry, "Pattern in *Othello*," *SQ* 23 (Winter 1971): 3–19.

Berry *Shakespearean Structures*, 64–86.

David Bevington, "Shakespeare's Development: *Measure for Measure* and *Othello*," in Gedo and Pollock, *Psychoanalysis: The Vital Issues*, vol. 1, 277–96.

Ann Blake, "The Comedy of *Othello*," *CR* 15 (1972): 46–51.

Allan D. Bloom, "Cosmopolitan Man and the Political Community: An Interpretation of *Othello*," *APSR* 54 (March 1960): 130–57.

Allan D. Bloom, "Political Philosophy and Poetry," *APSR* 54 (June 1960): 458–61.

Bodkin, *Archetypal Patterns in Poetry*, 217–24, 227–29.

G. Bonnard, "Are Othello and Desdemona Innocent or Guilty?" *ES* 30 (October 1949): 175–84.

Thomas D. Bowman, "The Characterization and Motivation of Iago," *CE* 4 (May 1943): 460–68.

Thomas D. Bowman, "In Defense of Emilia," *ShAB* 22 (July 1947): 99–104.

Thomas D. Bowman, "Desdemona's Last Moments," *PQ* 39 (January 1960): 114–17.

Thomas D. Bowman, "An Honorable Murder, if You Will," *ShN* 2 (December 1952): 43.

Graham Bradshaw, "Leavis, *Othello*, and Self-Knowledge," *DQR* 9 (1979): 18–31.

Bradshaw, *Shakespeare's Skepticism*, 12–23.

Phyllis Natalie Braxton, "*Othello*: The Moor and the Metaphor," *SAB* 55 (November 1990): 1–17.

Ernest Brenneckt, "'Nay, That's Not Next!' The Significance of Desdemona's 'Willow Song,'" *SQ* 4 (January 1953): 35–38.

Michael D. Bristol, "Charivari and the Comedy of Abjection in *Othello*," *RenD* 21 (1990): 3–21.

Brockbank, *On Shakespeare*, 198–219.

Brooks and Heilman, *Understanding Drama*, 661–68.

A. D. Fitton Brown, "Two Points of Interpretation," *N&Q* 202 (February 1957): 51.

C. F. Burgess, "Othello's Occupation," *SQ* 26 (Summer 1975): 208–13.

Kenneth Burke, *A Grammar of Motives* (New York: Prentice-Hall, 1945), 413–14.

Kenneth Burke, "*Othello*: An Essay to Illustrate a Method," *HudR* 4 (Summer 1951): 165–203. Reprinted in *Perspectives by Incongruity*, 152–95.

Burke, *The Philosophy of Literary Form*, 64–65.

Philip Butcher, "Othello's Racial Identity," *SQ* 3 (July 1952): 243–47.

Andrew S. Cairncross, "Shakespeare and Ariosto: *Much Ado About Nothing, King Lear*, and *Othello*," *RenQ* (1976): 178–82.

James L. Calderwood, "Appalling Property in *Othello*," *UTQ* 57 (October 1988): 353–75.

James L. Calderwood, "Speech and Self in *Othello*," *SQ* 38 (Summer 1987): 293–303.

Carroll Camden, "Iago on Women," *JEGP* 48 (January 1949): 47–71.

Bert Cardullo, "A Note on *Othello*," *LangQ* 24 (Fall–Winter 1985): 12.

Stanley Cavell, "Epistomology and Tragedy: A Reading of *Othello* (Together with a Cover Letter)," *Daedalus* 108, no. 3 (1979): 27–43.

Ebun Clark, "Othello the Complete Gentleman: An African Folkloric Interpretation," *JCL* 25, no. 1 (1990): 182–98.

Clay, *The Role of Anxiety*, 164–79.

Clemen, *English Tragedy Before Shakespeare*, 245–46.

Clurman, *Lies Like Truth*, 153–56.

Derek Cohen, "Patriarchy and Jealousy in *Othello* and *The Winter's Tale*," *MLQ* 48 (September 1987): 207–23.

Eilleen Z. Cohen, "Mirror of Virtue: The Role of Cassio in *Othello*," *ES* 57 (April 1976): 115–27.

E. A. M. Colman, "*Othello* and the Sense of an Ending," *SSEng* 4 (1978–79): 31–37.

Ann Jennalie Cook, "The Design of Desdemona: Doubt Raised and Resolved," *ShakS* 13 (1980): 187–96.

Ruth Cowhig, "Blacks in English Renaissance Drama and the Role of Shakespeare's *Othello*," in *The Black Presence in English Literature*, ed. David Dabydeen (Manchester: Manchester University Press, 1985), 1–25.

Ruth Cowhig, "The Importance of Othello's Race," *JCL* 12, no. 2 (1977): 153–61.

Edmund H. Creeth, "Moral and Tragic Recognition: the Uniqueness of *Othello, Macbeth*, and *King Lear*," *MichA* 45 (1960): 386–87.

Peter Cummings, "The Making of Meaning: Sex Words and Sex Acts in Shakespeare's *Othello*," *GettR* 3 (Winter 1990): 75–80.

Cunningham, *Woe or Wonder*, 24–27.

Walter Curry, "A Further Study in the Characterization Motivation of Iago," *CE* 4 (May 1943): 460–69.

Jared R. Curtis, "'As Liberall as the North': Emilia's Unruliness—A Study in Context," *SQ* 17 (Spring 1966): 168–71.

John P. Cutts, "Notes on *Othello*," *N&Q* 204 (July–August 1959): 251–52.

Earl L. Dachslager, "The Villiany of Iago: 'What You Know You Know,'" *CEA* 38, no. 3 (1975): 4–10.

Lee Dae-suk, "*Othello*: Black Color as Symbol of Evil," *JELL* 37 (December 1991): 709–17.

D'Amico, *The Moor in English Renaissance Drama*, 177–96.

A. Datta, "*Othello*: A Study of the Poetic Approach to Tragic Problems," *Journal of the University of Saugar* 6, no. 6 (1957): 1–18.

Jacob I. De Villiers, "The Tragedy of *Othello*," *Theoria* 7 (1955): 71–78.

Wayne Dodd, "'But I'll Set down the Pegs that Make this Music,'" *NM* 68, no. 2 (1967): 321–26.

Bettie A. Doebler, "Othello's Angels: The *Ars Moriendi*," *ELH* 34 (June 1967): 156–72.

Denis Donohue, "Shakespeare's Rhetoric," *Studies* 47 (Winter 1958): 436–40.

Madeleine Doran, "Good Name in *Othello*," *SEL* 7 (Spring 1967): 195–217.

Madeleine Doran, "Iago's 'If—': An Essay on the Syntax of *Othello*," in *The Drama of the Renaissance: Essays for Leicester Bradner*, ed. Elmer W. Blistein (Providence, RI: Brown University Press, 1970), 69–99. Revised and reprinted in *Shakespeare's Dramatic Language*, 63–91.

T. S. Dorsch, "The Poor Trash of Venice," *SQ* 6 (Summer 1955): 359–61.

J. W. Draper, "Patterns of Temper and Humor in *Othello*," *ES* 28 (June 1947): 65–74.

J. W. Draper, "Shakespeare and Barbary," *EA* 14 (July–September 1961): 311–13.

J. W. Draper, "Speech Tempo in Act I of *Othello*," *WVUPP*5 (January 1947): 49–58.

J. W. Draper, "Subjective Conflict in Shakespearean Tragedy," *NM* 62, no. 1 (1960): 217–18.

J. W. Draper, "The Tempo of Shylock's Speech," *JEGP* 44 (July 1945): 281–85.

J. W. Draper, "Changes in the Tempo of Desdemona's Speech," *Angelica* 1 (August 1946): 149–53.

Eastman, *Christ in the Drama*, 11–12, 24–25, 31–35.

Michael J. Echeruo, "The Context of Othello's Tragedy," *SoRA* 2 (1967): 299–316.

John P. Emery, "Othello's Epilepsy," *Psychoanalysis and the Psychoanalytic Review* 46 (Winter 1959): 30–32.

Balz Engler, "*Othello*, II.i.155: To Change the Cod's Head for the Salmon's Tale," *SQ* 35 (Summer 1984): 202–03.

Barbara Everett, "Reflections on the Sentimentalist's *Othello*," *CritQ* 3 (Summer 1961): 127–38.

Barbara Everett, "'Spanish' Othello: The Making of Shakespeare's Moor," *SQ* 35 (Spring 1982): 101–12.

M. D. Faber, "*Othello*: Symbolic Action, Ritual, and Myth," *AI* 31 (Summer 1974): 159–205.

M. D. Faber, "Suicidal Patterns in *Othello*," *L&P* 14 (Summer–Fall 1964): 85–96.

M. D. Faber, and Alan F. Dilnot, "On a Line of Iago's," *AI* 25 (Spring 1968): 86–90.

Arthur H. R. Fairchild, "Shakespeare and the Tragic Theme," *University of Missouri Studies* 19, no. 2 (1944): 28–43, 105–40.

Gabriel Fallon, "Some Notes on *Othello*," *Irish Monthly* 73 (May 1945): 204–10.

A. Bronson Feldman, "Othello in Reality," *AI* 11 (Summer 1954): 147–79.

A. Bronson Feldman, "Othello's Obsessions," *AI* 9 (Summer 1952): 147–64.

A. Bronson Feldman, "The Yellow Malady: Short Studies of Five Tragedies of Jealousy," *L&P* 6 (May 1956): 38–40, 51–52.

Joel Fineman, "The Sound of O in *Othello*: The Real Tragedy of Desire," in *Psychoanalysis and . . .*, ed. Richard Feldstein and Henry Sussman (New York: Routledge, 1990), 33–46.

Fineman, *The Subjectivity Effect*, 143–64.

Robert F. Fleissner, "Addendum: Chasing a Ghost," *Names* 24 (March 1976): 75–76.

Robert F. Fleissner, "Othello as the Indigent Indian: Old World, New World, or Third World," *SJW* 114 (Spring 1978): 92–100.

Robert F. Fleissner, "The Moor's Nomenclature," *N&Q* 25 (April 1978): 143.

R. A. Foakes, "The Descent of Iago: Satire, Ben Jonson, and Shakespeare's *Othello*," in Honigmann, *Shakespeare and His Contemporaries*, 16–30.

R. A. Foakes, "Iago, Othello and the Critic," in Durry, Ellrodt, and Jones-Davies, *De Shakespeare à T. S. Eliot: Melanges offerts à Henri Fluchère* (Paris: Didier, 1976), 61–72.

French, *Shakespeare's Division of Experience*, 203–218.

David L. Frost, "Othello and the Democrats," *SSEng* 4 (1978–79): 3–17.

Giles Y. Gamble, "Shakespeare's *Othello* III.ii.482–86," *Expl* 35 (Fall 1977): 35–36.

C. O. Gardner, "Tragic Fission in *Othello*," *ESA* 20, no. 1 (1977): 11–25.

Helen Louise Gardner, "The Noble Moor," *Annual Shakespeare Lecture of the British Academy* (1955): 189–205.

Mary Gardner, "Some Notes on *Othello*," *CRUX* 15 (October 1981): 37–40.

S. N. Garner, "Shakespeare's Desdemona," *ShakS* 9 (1976): 233–52.

Julia Genster, "Lieutenancy, Standing in, and *Othello*," *ELH* 57 (December 1990): 785–809.

Albert Gerard, "Alack, Poor Iago!: Intellect and Action in *Othello*," *ShJE* 94 (1958): 218–32.

Albert Gerard, "'Egregiously An Ass': The Dark Side of the Moor. A View of Othello's Mind," *ShS* 10 (1957): 98–106.

J. Gerritsen, "More Paired Words in *Othello*," *ES* 39 (October 1958): 212–14.

Gauri Prasad Ghosh, "*Othello* and the Problem Plays: A World of Chrysolite Embedded in Chaos," *JDECU* 18, no. 1 (1982–1983): 13–21.

Gilbert, *The Principles and Practice of Criticism*, 27–64.

A. Andre Glaz, "Iago or Moral Sadism," *AI* 19 (Winter 1962): 323–48.

D. R. Godfrey, "Shakespeare and the Green-Eyed Monster," *Neophil* 56 (July 1972): 207–20.

Madelon Gohlke, "'All That Is Spoke Is Marred': Language and Consciousness in *Othello*," *WS* 9, no. 2 (1982): 157–76.

Leon Golden, "*Othello, Hamlet,* and Aristotelian Tragedy," *SQ* 35 (Summer 1984): 142–56.

Alexander G. Gonzalez, "The Infection and Spread of Evil: Some Major Patterns of Imagery and Language in *Othello*," *SAB* 50 (November 1985): 35–49.

Stephen J. Greenblatt, "Improvisation and Power," in Said, *Literature and Society*, 57–99.

Gayle Greene, "'But Words Are Words': Shakespeare's Sense of Language in *Othello*," *EA* 34 (July–September 1981): 270–81.

Gayle Greene, "'This That You Call Love': Sexual and Social Tragedy in *Othello*," *JWSL* 1, no. 1 (1979): 16–32.

Eamon Grennan, "The Women's Voices in *Othello*: Speech, Song, Silence," *SQ* 38 (Autumn 1987): 275–92.

Kenneth Gross, "Slander and Skepticism in *Othello*," *ELH* 56 (December 1989): 819–52.

Grudin, *Mighty Opposites*, 124–37.

Cherrell Guilfoyle, "*Mactacio Desdemonae*: Medieval Scenic Form in the Last Scene of *Othello*," *CompD* 19 (Winter 1985–1986): 305–20.

Nancy Gutierrez, "Witchcraft and Adultery in *Othello*: Strategies of Subversion," in Brink, Horowitz, and Coudert, *Playing with Gender*, 3–18.

John V. Hagopian, "Psychology and the Coherent Form of Shakespeare's *Othello*," *MichA* 45 (1960): 373–80.

Jay L. Halio, "The Metaphor of Conception and Elizabethan Theories of Imagination," *Neophil* 50 (October 1966): 454–61.

Hallett and Hallett, *Analyzing Shakespeare's Action*, 47–48, 58–59, 75–79, 86–87, 94–95, 97–102, 105–06, 121–22, 132–33, 144–48, 168–71, 175–78.

R. N. Hallstead, "Idolatrous Love: A New Approach to *Othello*," *SQ* 19 (Spring 1968): 107–24.

Abby Jane Dubman Hansen, "Shakespeare's *Othello*," *Expl* 35 (Winter 1977): 4–6.

Walter M. Hart, "Shakespeare's Use of Verse and Prose," *University of California Publications English Studies* 10 (1954): 6.

Lodwick Hartley, "Dropping the Handkerchief: Pronoun Reference and Stage Direction in *Othello* III.iii," *ELN* 8 (September 1971): 173–76.

William L. Hastead, "Artifice and Artistry in *Richard II* and *Othello*," *UMPEAL* 7 (March 1964): 19–20, 33–35.

Terence Hawkes, "Iago's Use of Reason," *SP* 58 (April 1961): 160–69.

Hawkes, *Shakespeare's Talking Animals*, 132–42.

Hawkins, *Likeness of Truth*, 11–14.

Hawkins, *Poetic Freedom and Poetic Truth*, 26–27.

Robert Heilman, "Approach to *Othello*," *SR* 64 (Winter 1956): 98–116.

Robert Heilman, "The Economics of Iago and Others," *PMLA* 68 (June 1953): 555–71.

Robert Heilman, "More Fair Than Black: Light and Dark in *Othello*," *EIC* 1 (October 1951): 315–35.

Robert Heilman, "'Twere Best Not Know Myself': Othello, Lear, Macbeth," *SQ* 15 (Spring 1964): 89–98.

Robert Heilman, "Wit and Witchcraft: Thematic Form in *Othello*," *ArQ* 12 (Spring 1956): 5–15.

Robert Heilman, "Dr. Iago and his Potions," *VQR* 28 (Autumn 1952): 568–84.

Henn, *The Harvest of Tragedy*, 23–24, 96–98.

Carolyn Herbert, "Comic Elements in *Othello*," *RenP 1956* (1957): 32–38.

T. Walter Herbert, "Shakespeare and the Craft of Fiction," *EUQ* 20 (Summer 1964): 85–86.

John A. Hodgson, "Desdemona's Handkerchief as an Emblem of Her Reputation," *TSLL* 19 (Autumn 1977): 313–22.

Theodore C. Hoepfner, "Iago's Nationality," *N&Q* 200 (January 1955): 14–15.

Theodore C. Hoepfner, "An *Othello* Gloss," *N&Q* 201 (November 1956): 470.

Peter Hollindale, "Othello and Desdemona," *CrSurv* 1, no. 1 (1989): 43–52.

Holoway, *The Story of the Night*, 37–56, 155–56.

Julia B. Holloway, "Strawberries and Mulberries: *Ulysses* and *Othello*," in *Hypatia: Essays in Classics, Comparative Literature, and Philosophy Presented to Hazel E. Barnes on Her Seventieth Birthday*, ed. William M. Calder, Ulrich K. Goldsmith, and Phyllis B. Kevevan (Boulder, CO: Associated University Press, 1985), 125–36.

Joan Ozark Holmer, "Othello's Threnos: 'Arabian Trees' and 'Indian' versus 'Judean,'" *ShakS* 13 (1980): 145–67.

Wayne Holmes, "*Othello*: Is't Possible?" *UCrow* 1 (1978): 1–23.

Lionel P. Honore, "Othello and Phedre: The Protagonist as Deluded Victim," *CLAJ* 21 (December 1978): 38–55.

Houston, *Shakespearean Sentences*, 122–30.

Edward Hulber, "The Damnation of *Othello*: Some Limitations on the Christian View of the Play," *SQ* 9 (Summer 1958): 295–300.

Bill G. Hulsopple, "Barabas and Shylock Against a Background of Jewish History in England," *Central States Speech Journal* 12 (Autumn 1960): 38–50.

Maurice Hunt, "The Similar Complementarity of *Othello*," *JRMMRA* 11 (January 1990): 101–25,

Grace Hunter, "Notes on Othello's 'Base Indian,'" *ShAB* 19 (January 1944): 26–28.

Geoffrey Hutchings, "Emilia: A Case History in Women's Lib," *ESA* 21, no. 1 (1978): 71–77.

R. W. Von Ingram, "*Hamlet, Othello*, and *King Lear*: Music and Tragedy," *ShJE* 100 (1964): 159–61, 167–70.

Linda V. Itzoe, "Shakespeare's *Othello* IV.i," *Expl* 38 (Winter 1980): 39–40.

Geoffrey S. Ivy, "Othello and the Rose-Lip'd Cherubin: An Old Reading Restored," *SQ* 19 (Spring 1958): 208–12.

Edward C. Jacobs, and Karen R. Jacobs, "'Tis Monstrous': Dramaturgy and Irony in *Othello*," *UCrow* 9 (1989): 52–62.

Pierre Janton, "Othello's Weak Function," *CahiersE* 7 (April 1975): 43–50.

David L. Jeffrey, and Patrick Grant, "Reputation in *Othello*," *ShakS* 6 (1970): 197–208.

Laura Jepsen, *Ethical Aspects of Tragedy*, 46–55.

Rosalind Johnson, "African Presence in Shakespearean Drama: Parallels Between *Othello* and the Historical Leo Africanus," *Journal of African Civilizations* 7 (November 1985): 276–87.

Eldred D. Jones, "The Machiavel and the Moor," *EIC* 10 (April 1960): 234–38.

Jones, *Othello's Countrymen*, 86–109.

Hoover H. Jordan, "Dramatic Illusion in *Othello*," *SQ* 1 (July 1950): 146–52.

Paul A. Jorgensen, "Honesty in *Othello*," *SP* 47 (October 1950): 557–67.

Paul A. Jorgensen, "'Perplex'd in the Extreme': The Role of Thought in *Othello*," *SQ* 15 (Spring 1964): 265–75. Reprinted in McManaway, *Shakespeare 400*, 265–75.

Kastan, *Shakespeare and the Shapes of Time*, 81–88.

David Kaula, "Othello Possessed: Notes on Shakespeare's Use of Magic and Witchcraft," *ShakS* 2 (1966): 112–32.

Dorothea Kehler, "*Othello* and Racism," *ZAA* 36, no. 1 (1988): 124–32.

Rosalind King, "'The murder's out of tune': The Music and Structure of *Othello*," *ShS* 39 (1987): 149–58.

Arthur Kirsch, "The Polarization of Erotic Love in *Othello*," *MLR* 73 (December 1978): 721–40.

Samuel Kliger, "Othello: The Man of Judgement," *MP* 48 (May 1951): 221–24.

Jean Kline, C.S.C., "Othello: 'A fixed figure for the time of scorn,'" *SQ* 26 (Summer 1975): 139–50.

Knight, "The Othello Music," in *The Wheel of Fire*, 97–119.

Philip C. Kolin, "Shakespeare's *Othello*, I.i.8–17; 35–40," *Expl* 38 (Spring 1979): 38–39.

Joel Kovel, "*Othello*," *AI* 35 (Summer 1978): 113–19.

Masakazu Kurikoma, "An Essay on the Dialogues Between Othello and Iago," *Angelica* 4 (October 1959): 83–93.

James H. Lake, "*Othello* and the Comforts of Love," *AI* 45 (Fall 1988): 327–35.

Robert Langbaum, "Character Versus Action in Shakespeare," *SQ* 8 (Winter 1957): 60–62, 68.

François Laroque, "An Additional Note to '*Othello* and Popular Traditions,'" *CahiersE* 33 (April 1988): 57–58.

François Laroque, "An Archaeology of the Dramatic Text: *Othello* and Popular Traditions," *CahiersE* 32 (October 1987): 13–35.

François Laroque, "*Othello, The Tempest* and the Grotesque," *Cycnos* 5 (1989): 45–62.

Leavis, *The Common Pursuit*, 136–59.

Margaret Lenta, "*Othello* and the Tragic Heroine," *CRUX* 21 (May 1987): 26–35.

Laurence Lerner, "The Machival and the Moor," *EIC* 9 (October 1959): 339–60.

Lesser, *Fiction and the Unconscious*, 116–18.

Levich, *Aesthetics and the Philosophy of Criticism*, 174–75.

Harry Levin, "*Othello* and the Motive-Hunters," *CentR* 8 (Winter 1964): 1–16.

Richard Levin, "The Indian/Iudean Crux in *Othello*," *SQ* 33 (Spring 1982): 60–67.

Richard Levin, "The Indian/Iudean Crux in *Othello*: An Addendum," *SQ* 34 (Spring 1983): 72.

Ruth Levitsky, "All-In-All Sufficiency in *Othello*," *ShakS* 6 (1970): 209–21.

Nicholas Linfield, "You and Thou in Shakespeare: *Othello* as an Example," *ISJR* 57 (June 1982): 163–78.

K. I. MacDonald, Shakespeare's *Othello*, V.ii.359–60," *Expl* 26 (March 1968): 65.

Russ MacDonald, "*Othello*, Thorello, and the Problem of the Foolish Hero," *SQ* 30 (Spring 1979): 51–67.

Maynard Mack, "The Jacobean Shakespeare: Some Observations on the Construction of the Tragedies," *Stratford-Upon-Avon Studies* 1 (1960): 11–42.

John M. Major, "Desdemona and Dido," *SQ* 10 (Winter 1959): 123–25.

Derick R. C. Marsh, "*Othello* Re-Read," *SSEng* 14 (1988–1989): 3–12.

P. Marudanayagam, "Shakespeare's *Othello*, IV.i.106–108," *Expl* 40 (Spring 1982): 16.

Philip Mason, "*Othello* and Race Prejudice," *Caribbean Quarterly* 8 (September 1962): 154–62.

Kurian Mattam, "The Concept of Sin in the Shakespearian Tragedies: *Hamlet, King Lear, Macbeth* and *Othello*: An Exploration," *Unitas* 64 (June 1991): 165–230.

Joseph T. McCullen, Jr., "Iago's Use of Proverbs for Persuasion," *SEL* 4 (Spring 1964): 247–62.

Arthur McGee, "Othello's Motive for Murder," *SQ* 15 (Winter 1964): 45–54.

Leo F. McNamara, "Dramic Convention and the Psychological Study of Character in *Othello*," *MichA* 47 (1962): 649–58.

Trevor McNeely, "Supersubtle Shakespeare: *Othello* as a Rhetorical Allegory," *DQR* 19 (1989): 243–63.

James A. S. McPeek, "The 'Arts Inhibited' and the Meaning of *Othello*," *BUSE* 1 (Autumn 1955): 129–47.

McPeek, *The Black Book of Knaves*, 210–15, 273–78.

Giorgio Melchiori, "The Rhetoric of Character Construction: *Othello*," *ShS* 34 (1981): 61–72.

George Meri, "*Othello*," *SJW* 104 (Spring 1968): 85–108.

Lawrence Michel, "Shakespearean Tragedy: Critique of Humanism From the Inside," *MR* 2 (Summer 1961): 638–44.

A. R. Mills, "The Case of *Othello*: Leavis vs. Bradley," *CRUX* 21 (February 1987): 56–67.

Peter Milward, "The Base Judean: Notes on the Interpretation of *Othello*, V. ii. 346," *ShStud* 1 (1962): 7–14.

Marco Mincoff, "The Structural Pattern of Shakespeare's Tragedies," *ShS* 3 (1950): 62–63.

Robert S. Miola, "*SQ* Furens," *SQ* 41 (Spring 1990): 49–64.

John Mooney, "Othello's 'It is the cause . . .': An Analysis," *ShS* 6 (1953): 94–105.

John Robert Moore, "The Character of Iago," *University of Missouri Studies* 21, no. 1 (1946): 37–46.

John Robert Moore, "Othello, Iago, and Cassio as Soldiers," *PQ* 31 (April 1952): 189–94.

P. Rama Moorthy, "*Othello*: The Visionary Tale," in Sharma, *Essays on Shakespeare in Honor of A. A. Ansari*, 243–52.

Meg M. Moring, "The Dark Glass: Mirroring and Sacrifice in Shakespeare's *Othello* and Hardy's *Tess of the D'Urbervilles*," *CCTEP* 56 (September 1991): 12–18.

Mikhail M. Morozov, "The Individualization of Shakespeare's Characters Through Imagery," *ShS* 2 (1949): 83–90.

Timothy Morris, "Shakespeare's *Othello*," *Expl* 48 (Summer 1990): 238.

Kenneth Muir, "Double Time in *Othello*," *N&Q* 197 (February 1952): 76–77.

Kenneth Muir, "Freedom and Slavery in *Othello*," *N&Q* 199 (January 1954): 20–21.

Kenneth Muir, "The Jealousy of Iago," *EM* 2 (Spring 1951): 65–84.

G. N. Murphy, "A Note on Iago's Name," in *Literature and Society*, ed. Bernice Slote (Lincoln: University of Nebraska Press, 1964), 38–43.

Timothy Murray, "*Othello*, an Index and Obscure Prologue to the History of Foul Generic Thoughts," in Atkins and Bergeron, *Shakespeare and Deconstruction*, 213–44.

John M. Murry, "The Doctrine of Will in Shakespeare," *Aryan Path* 35 (August 1964): 338–42.

Leonard Mustazza, "Language as Poison, Plague, and Weapon in Shakespeare's *Hamlet* and *Othello*," *PE* 11 (Spring 1985): 5–14.

W. Nash, "Paired Words in *Othello*: Shakespeare's Use of a Stylistic Device," *ES* 39 (April 1958): 62–67.

Carol Thomas Neely, "Women and Men in *Othello*: 'What should such a fool/Do with so good woman?'" *ShakS* 10 (1977): 133–58. Reprinted in Lenz, et al., *The Woman's Part*, 211–39.

Carol Thomas Neely, "Changing Places in *Othello*," *ShS* 37 (1984): 115–31.

Michael Neill, "Unproper Beds: Race Adultery, and the Hideous in *Othello*," *SQ* 40 (Autumn 1989): 383–412.

Bonnie Nelson, "Much Ado about Something: The Law of Lombardy and the 'Othello Play' Phenomenon," *SN* 58 (Spring 1986): 71–83.

Karen Newman, "'And wash the Ethiop white': Femininity and the Monstrous in *Othello*," in Howard and O'Connor, *Shakespeare Reproduced*, 141–62.

Newman, *Fashioning Femininity*, 70–93.

Fraser Nieman, "Shakespeare's *Othello*, IV, ii, 47–53," *Expl* 6 (June 1948): 54.

Winifred M. T. Nowottny, "Justice and Love in *Othello*," *UTQ* 21 (July 1952): 330–44.

Nuttall, *A New Mimesis*, 131–43.

Yasuhiro Ogawa, "'This Forked Plague': The Meaning of Comedy in *Othello*," *EFLL* 26 (1980): 273–311

Olson, *Tragedy and the Theory of Drama*, 104–07.

Robert C. Olson, "Shakespeare's *Othello* I, I, 25–26," *Expl* 22 (March 1964): 59.

P. A. Onesta, "*Othello*," *Theoria* 15 (1960): 61–63.

Martin Orkin, "Civility and the English Colonial Enterprise: Notes on Shakespeare's *Othello*," *Theoria* 68 (December 1986): 1–14.

Martin Orkin, "*Othello* and the 'Plain Face' of Racism," *SQ* 38 (Summer 1987): 166–88.

Martin Orkin, "Shakespeare's 'clothes of gold & riche veluet weede': Proverb Allusions, Especially in *Othello*," *UES* 17 (May 1979): 18–26.

Ornstein, *Moral Vision of Jacobean Tragedy*, 227–30.

Toshiko Oyama, "The Fate of A Shakespeare Machiavel: A Study of Language and Imagery in *Othello*," *Angelica* 3 (June 1958): 30–50.

Toshikazu Oyama, "The Tragic Fate of Othello's World of Consciousness," *Angelica* 6 (October 1967): 1–24.

B. A. Park, "'Of One That Loved Not Wisely, but Too Well': *Othello* and the *Heroides*," *ELN* 19 (June 1981): 102–04.

Patricia Parker, "Shakespeare and Rhetoric: 'Dialation' and 'Delation' in *Othello*," in Parker and Hartman, *Shakespeare and the Question of Theory*, 54–74.

Morriss Henry Partee, "Marriage and the Responsibility of Othello," *PAPA* 15 (April 1989): 48–58.

Stanley Peskin, "*Othello* and Its Subtitle," *UES* 29 (September 1991): 8–17.

Pogson, *In the East*, 11–22.

Rodney Poisson, "The 'Calumniator Credited' and the Code of Honor in Shakespeare's *Othello*," *ESC* 2 (Fall 1976): 381–401.

Rodney Poisson, "Death for Adultery: A Note on *Othello*, III.iii.394–96," *SQ* 28 (Spring 1977): 89–92.

Rodney Poisson, "*Othello* V.ii.347: 'The Base Indian' Yet Again," *MLR* 62 (July 1967): 209–11.

Rodney Poisson, "'Which Heaven Has Forbid the Ottomites,'" *SQ* 18 (Spring 1967): 67–70.

Leonard Prager, "The Clown in *Othello*," *SQ* 11 (Winter 1960): 94–96.

Moody E. Prior, "Character in Relation to Action in *Othello*," *MP* 44 (May 1947): 225–37.

Moody E. Prior, "A New Reading of *Othello*," *MP* 45 (May 1948): 270–72.

Majorie Pryse, "Lust for Audience: An Interpretation of *Othello*," *ELH* 43 (September 1976): 461–78.

Rufus Putney, "What 'Praise to Give'?" *PQ* 23 (October 1944): 313–19.

Paul Ramsey, "*Othello*: The Logic of Damnation," *UCrow* 1 (1978): 24–35.

Margaret L. Ranald, "The Indiscretions of Desdemona," *SQ* 14 (Spring 1963): 127–40.

Frank P. Rand, "The Over Garrulous Iago," *SQ* 1 (July 1950): 155–61.

William O. Raymond, "Motivation and Character Portrayal in *Othello*," *UTQ* 17 (October 1947): 80–96.

Joan Rees, "*Othello* as Key Play," *RES* 41 (1990): 185–90.

Reik, *The Secret Self*, 57–62.

Irving Ribner, "*Othello* and the Pattern of Shakespearean Tragedy," *TSE* 5 (Spring 1955): 69–82.

Norman Richardson, "Shakespeare's *Othello*, I.ii.62," *Expl* 47 (Spring 1989): 6–7.

Hugh Richmond, "Love and Justice: *Othello*'s Shakespearean Context," in McNeir and Greenfield, *Pacific Coast Studies in Shakespeare*, 148–72.

Christopher Ricks, "The Machiaval and the Moor," *EIC* 10 (January 1960): 117.

Henri Roddier, "A Freudian Detective's Shakespeare," *MP* 48 (November 1950): 122–29.

Stephen Rogers, "Othello and the Ways of Thinking," in Quinn, *How to Read Shakespearean Tragedy*, 135–78.

Marvin Rosenberg, "In Defense of Iago," *SQ* 6 (Spring 1955): 145–58.

Marvin Rosenberg, "Reputation, Oft Lost Without Deserving," *SQ* 9 (Autumn 1958): 502–06.

R. M. Rosetti, "A Crux and No Crux," *SQ* 13 (Summer 1962): 299–303.

Daniel W. Ross, and Brooke K. Horvath, "Inaction in *Othello* and *Hamlet*," *UCrow* 11 (1991): 52–61.

Lawrence J. Ross, "'A Fellow Almost Damn'd in a Fair Wife,'" *ELN* 5 (September 1968): 256–64.

Lawrence J. Ross, "Marble, 'Crocodile,' and 'Turban's Turk' in *Othello*," *PQ* 40 (October 1961): 476–84.

Ross, *Philosophy in Literature*, 64–66, 255–63.

Lawrence J. Ross, "Shakespeare's 'Dull Clown' and Symbolic Music," *SQ* 17 (Summer 1966): 107–28.

Lawrence J. Ross, "Three Readings in the Text of *Othello*," *SQ* 14 (Spring 1963): 121–26.

Lawrence J. Ross, "World and Chrysolite in *Othello*," *MLN* 76 (December 1961): 683–92.

Rossiter, *Angel with Horns*, 189–208.

Felicity Rosslyn, "Nature Erring from Itself: *Othello* Again," *CQ* 18 (1989): 289–302.

Peter L. Rudnytsky, "The Purloined Handkerchief in *Othello*," in *The Psychoanalytic Study of Literature*, ed. Joseph Reppen and Maurice Charney (Hillsdale, NJ: Analytic Press, 1985), 169–90.

Peter L. Rudnytsky, "*A Woman Killed With Kindness* as Subtext of *Othello*," *RenD* 14 (1983): 103–24.

George Rylands, "Shakespeare's Poetic Energy," *Annual Shakespeare Lecture of the British Academy* (1951): 114–18.

John E. Seaman, "Othello's Pearl," *SQ* 19 (Spring 1968): 81–85.

G. G. Sedgewick, *Of Irony* (Toronto: University of Toronto Press, 1948), 41–44, 85–116.

John B. Shackford, "The Motivation of Iago," *ShN* 3 (September 1953): 30.

Brian W. Shaffer, " 'To Manage Private and Domestic Quarrels': Shakespeare's *Othello* and the Genre of Elizabethan Domestic Tragedy," *ISJR* 62 (December 1988): 443–57.

Naseeb Shaheen, " 'Like the Base Judean,' " *SQ* 3 (Spring 1980): 93–95.

Naseeb Shaheen, "The Use of Scripture in *Othello*," *UMSE* 6, no. 1 (1988): 48–62.

Stephen A. Shapiro, "Othello's Desdemona," *L&P* 14 (Spring 1964): 56–61.

Vandana Sharma, "Shakespeare and the 'New' World: *Othello* and Cultural Readings," *T&P* 11 (1991): 97–105.

Catherine M. Shaw, " 'Dangerous Conceits Are Their Natures Poisons': The Language of *Othello*," *UTQ* 49 (October 1980): 304–19.

John Shaw, " 'What is the Matter?' in *Othello*," *SQ* 17 (Summer 1966): 157–61.

Arthur Sherbo, "*Othello*, II.i.303, 'this poor trash of Venice, whom I trace,' " *SQ* 31 (Autumn 1980): 391–92.

Paul N. Siegel, "The Damnation of Othello: An Addendum," *PMLA* 68 (December 1953): 1068–78.

T. Sipahigil, " 'Sagitary/Sagittar' in *Othello*," *SQ* 27 (Summer 1976): 200–01.

John P. Sisk, "The Cybernetics of *Othello*," *NOR* 2 (Spring 1979): 74–77.

Smith, *Homosexual Desire in Shakespeare's England*, 161–64.

Fred Manning Smith, "Shylock on the Rights of Jews and Emilia on the Rights of Women," *WVUPP* 5 (January 1947): 32–33.

Gordon Ross Smith, "Iago the Paranoiac," *AI* 16 (Summer 1959): 155–67.

Gordon Ross Smith, "The Masks of Othello," *L&P* 12 (Summer 1962): 75–77.

Philip A. Smith, "Othello's Diction," *SQ* 9 (Summer 1958): 428–30.

Malvern Van Wyk Smith, "*Othello* and the Narrative of Africa," *ShSA* 4 (1990–1991): 11–30.

Edward A. Snow, "Sexual Anxiety and the Male Order of Things in *Othello*," *ELR* 10 (Winter 1980): 384–412.

Soellner, *Shakespeare's Patterns*, 259–80.

Gunnar Sorelius, "*Othello* and the Language of Cosmos," *SN* 55, no. 1 (1983): 11–17.

Theodore Spencer, "The Isolation of the Shakespearean Hero," *SR* 52 (July/Sept 1944): 321–23.

Rudolph Splitter, "Language, Sexual Conflict and 'Symbiosis Anxiety' in *Othello*," *Mosaic* 15 (September 1982): 17–26.

Evert Sprinchorn, "The Handkerchief Trick in *Othello*," *Columbia University Forum* 7 (Winter 1964): 25–30.

Kezia Vanmeter Sproat, "Rereading *Othello*, II, 1," *KR* 47 (Summer 1985): 44–51.

Albert F. Sproule, "A Time Scheme for *Othello*," *SQ* 7 (Spring 1956): 217–26.

Michael Srigley, "A Note on *Othello* I.iii.288–89," *SN* 52, no. 1 (1980): 61–67.

Janet C. Stavropoulos, "Love and Age in *Othello*," *ShakS* 19 (1991): 125–42.

Douglas Stewart, "*Othello*: Roman Comedy as Nightmare," *EUQ* 22 (Summer 1967): 252–76.

Brents Stirling, "Psychology in *Othello*," *ShAB* 19 (July 1944): 135–44.

Kay Stockholder, "Form as Metaphor: *Othello* and Love-Death Romance," *DR* 64 (Winter 1984–1985): 736–47.

E. E. Stoll, "Iago not a 'Malcontent,'" *JEGP* 51 (April 1952): 163–67.

E. E. Stoll, "Slander in Drama," *SQ* 4 (October 1953): 433–50.

E. E. Stoll, "Mainly Controversy: *Hamlet*, *Othello*," *PQ* 24 (October 1945): 312–16.

E. E. Stoll, "A 'New' Reading of *Othello*," *MP* 45 (February 1948): 208–10.

Earnest A. Strathmann, "The Devil Can Cite Scripture," *SQ* 15 (Spring 1964): 17–19.

June Sturrock, "*Othello*: Women and 'Woman,'" *Atlantis* 9 (Spring 1984): 1–8.

Styan, *The Elements of Drama*, 32–39, 54–55.

J. P. Sullivan, "The Machiaval and the Moor," *EIC* 10 (April 1960): 231–34.

Estelle W. Taylor, "The Ironic Equation on Shakespeare's *Othello*: Appearances Equal Reality," *CLAJ* 21 (June 1977): 202–11.

Frances Teague, "*Othello* and the New Comedy," *CompD* 20 (Spring 1986): 54–64.

Pia Teodorescu-Brinzeu, "The Figurative Language and Its Poetic Function (with Reference to Shakespeare's *Othello*)," *RRL* 25 (January–June 1980): 115–23.

Pia Teodorescu-Brinzeu, "A Systematic Approach to the Theatre," *Poetics* 6 (Autumn 1977): 351–74.

Alwin Thaler, "Delayed Exposition in Shakespeare," *SQ* 1 (July 1950): 140–43.

A. R. Thompson, *Dry Mock*, 31–34.

Ann Thompson, and John Thompson, "'To Look So Low as Where They Are': Hand and Heart Synecdoches in *Othello*," *SoRA* 19 (1986): 53–66.

J. J. M. Tobin, "*Othello* and the Apologia of Apuleius," *CahiersE* 21 (April 1982): 27–33.

William Toole III, "'Iagothello': Psychological Action and the Theme of Transformation in *Othello*," *SAB* 41 (June 1976): 71–77.

Brian F. Tyson, "Ben Jonson's Black Comedy: A Connection between *Othello* and *Volpone*," *SQ* 29 (Spring 1978): 60–66.

Richard Veit, "'Like the Base Judean': A Defense of an Oft-Rejected Reading in *Othello*," *SQ* 26 (Winter 1975): 466–69.

A. E. Voss, "*Othello*: Race and Civilization," *CRUX* 22 (January 1988): 44–49.

John N. Wall, "Shakespeare's Aural Art: The Metaphor of the Ear in *Othello*," *SQ* 30 (Autumn 1979): 358–66.

Y. Walpole, "'And Cassio High in Oath' (*Othello*, II, iii, 227)," *MLR* 40 (January 1945): 47–48.

J. K. Walton, "'Strength's Abundance': A View of *Othello*," *RES* 11 (February 1960): 8–17.

M. Ware, "How was Desdemona Murdered?" *ES* 45 (April 1964): 177–80.

Henry L. Warnken, "Iago as a Projection of Othello," *CCP* 1 (1964): 1–15.

Ivar Watson, "Iago, the Devil's Disciple," *LdD* 9 (1979): 51–61.

Martin Waugh, "*Othello*: The Tragedy of Iago," *Psychoanalytic Quarterly* 19 (April 1950): 202–12.

Valerie Wayne, "Historical Differences: Misogyny and *Othello*," in *The Matter of Difference*, 153–79.

Henry J. Webb, "The Military Background in *Othello*," *PQ* 30 (January 1951): 40–52.

Henry J. Webb, "Rude am I in my Speech," *ES* 30 (April 1958): 67–72.

Everett K. Weedin, Jr., "Love's Reason in *Othello*," *SEL* 15 (Spring 1975): 293–308.

Weisinger, *The Agony and the Triumph*, 20–25, 106–09.

Herbert Weisinger, "A Casebook on *Othello*," *L&P* 12 (Summer 1962): 78–82.

Herbert Weisinger, "Iago's Iago," *UR* 20 (Winter 1953): 83 –89.

Wells, *Elizabethan and Jacobean Playwrights*, 61–63.

Karl P. Wentersdorf, "The Time Problem in *Othello*: A Reconsideration," *DSGW* 121 (1985): 63–77.

Fred West, "Iago the Psychopath," *SAB* 43 (May 1978): 27–35.

Robert H. West, "The Christianness of *Othello*," *SQ* 15 (Autumn 1964): 333–44.

Robert H. West, "Iago and the Mystery of Inequity," *RenP 1960* (1961): 63–69.

Richard P. Wheeler, "'. . . And my loud crying still': The Sonnets, *The Merchant of Venice*, and *Othello*," in Erickson and Kahn, *Shakespeare's 'Rough Magic*,' 193–209.

Henry G. Widdowson, "*Othello* in Person," in *Language and Literature: An Introductory Reader in Stylistics*, ed. Ronald Carter (London: Allen & Unwin, 1982), 41–52.

John Wilcox, "Othello's Crucial Moment," *ShAB* 24 (July 1949): 181–92.

G. A. Wilkes, "The 'Compulsive Course' of *Othello*," *SSEng* 5 (1979–80): 31–37.

Karina Williamson, "'Honest' and 'False' in *Othello*," *SN* 35 (1963): 211–20.

Robert F. Willson, Jr., "Brabantio Seduced: The Opening Scene of *Othello*," *TSL* 22 (Spring 1977): 28–36.

Robert F. Willson, Jr., "Iago's Satanic Marriage," *McNR* 21 (1977–1978): 20–27.

Arthur H. Wilson, "Othello's Racial Identity," *SQ* 4 (Summer 1953): 209.

Rob Wilson, "*Othello*: Jealousy as Mimetic Contagion," *AI* 44 (Fall 1987): 213–33.

Young, *Immortal Shadows*, 230–35.

John Arthos, "*Pericles, Prince of Tyre*: A Study in the Dramatic Use of Romantic Narrative," *SQ* 4 (Summer 1953): 257–70.

Babb, *Elizabethan Malady*, 105–06.

G. A. Barker, "Themes and Variations in Shakespeare's *Pericles*," *ES* 44 (December 1963): 401–14.

Brockbank, *On Shakespeare*, 283–302.

Kwang Soon Cho, "Shakespeare's Control of Audience Response: Dramatic Techniques in *Pericles*," *JELL* 36 (December 1990): 729–48.

Danby, *Poets on Fortune's Hill*, 87–103.

H. Neville Davies, "*Pericles* and the Sherley Brothers," in Honigmann, *Shakespeare and His Contemporaries*, 94–113.

Stephen Dickey, "Language and Role in *Pericles*," *ELR* 16 (Winter 1986): 550–56.

Mary Judith Dunbar, "'To the judgement of your eye': Iconography and the Theatrical Art of Pericles; Proc. of the 2nd Cong. of the Internat. Shakespeare Assn., 1981," in Muir, Halio, and Plamer, *Shakespeare, Man of the Theater*, 86–97.

Philip Edwards, "An Approach to the Problem of *Pericles*," *ShS* 5 (1952): 25–49.

Walter F. Eggers, Jr., "Shakespeare's Gower and the Role of Authorial Presenter," *PQ* 54 (1975): 434–43.

Bertrand Evans, "The Poem of *Pericles*," *University of California Publications English Studies* 11 (1955): 35–56.

Inga-Stina Ewbank, "'My Name Is Marina': The Language of Recognition," in Edwards, Ewbank, and Howard, *Shakespeare's Styles*, 111–30.

Nona Feinberg, "Marina in *Pericles*: Exchange Values and the Art of Moral Discourse," *ISJR* 57 (June 1982): 153–61.

Howard Felperin, "Shakespeare's Miracle Play," *SQ* 18 (Summer 1967): 363–74.

Annette Flowers, "Disguise and Identity in *Pericles, Prince of Tyre*," *SQ* 26 (1975): 30–41.

French, *Shakespeare's Division of Experience*, 297–306.

Elena Glazov-Corrigan, "The New Function of Language in Shakespeare's *Pericles*: Oath Versus 'Holy Word,'" *ShS* 43 (1991): 131–40.

P. Golden, "Antiochus' Riddle in Gower and Shakespeare," *RES* 6 (July 1955): 245, 248–51.

Phyllis Gorfain, "Puzzle and Artifice: The Riddle as Metapoetry in *Pericles*," *ShS* 29 (1976): 11–20.

Sara Hanna, "Christian Vision and Iconography in *Pericles*," *UCrow* 11 (1991): 92–116.

Haselkorn, *Prostitution in Elizabethan and Jacobean Drama*, 51–53.

Richard Hillman, "Shakespeare's Gower and Gower's Shakespeare: The Larger Debt of *Pericles*," *SQ* 36 (Winter 1985): 427–37.

F. David Hoeniger, "Gower and Shakespeare in *Pericles*," *SQ* 33 (Winter 1982): 461–79.

Hilda M. Hulme, "Two Notes on the Interpretation of Shakespeare's Text," *N&Q* 204 (October 1959): 354.

Maurice Hunt, "A Looking Glass for *Pericles*," *ELWIU* 13 (Spring 1986): 3–11.

Maurice Hunt, "'Opening the Book of Monarch's Faults': *Pericles* and Redemptive Speech," *ELWIU* 12 (Fall 1985): 155–70.

Maurice Hunt, "*Pericles* and the Emblematic Imagination" *StHum* 17 (June 1990): 1–20.

Cynthia Marshall, "The Seven Ages of Pericles," *JRMMRA* 8 (January 1987): 147–62.

MacD. P. Jackson, "George Wilkins and the First Two Acts of *Pericles*: New Evidence from Function Words," *L&LC* 6 (1991): 155–63.

Robert J. Kane, "A Passage in *Pericles*," *MLN* 68 (September 1953): 483–84.

Akira Kataoka, "*Pericles*: A Quest of Purity," *SELL* 34 (March 1984): 19–41.

Maqbool H. Kahn, "The Design of Wonder in *Pericles*," *AJES* 3 (April 1978): 80–106.

Knight, *The Crown of Life*, 32–75.

Knight, *The Golden Labyrinth*, 82–84.

Anthony J. Lewis, "'I feed on mother's flesh': Incest and Eating in *Pericles*," *ELWIU* 15 (Fall 1988): 147–63.

John H. Long, "Laying the Ghosts in *Pericles*," *SQ* 7 (Winter 1956): 39–42.

Louis Marder, "Stylometric Analysis and the Pericles Problem," *ShN* 26 (December 1976): 46.

Barbara Melchiori, "Still Harping on My Daughter," *EM* 11 (Spring 1960): 60–63.

Patricia K. Meszaros, "*Pericles*: Shakespeare's Divine Musical Comedy; Collection of Essays from the Ohio Shakespeare Conference, 1981, Wright State University, Dayton, Ohio," in Cary and Limouze, *Shakespeare and the Arts*, 3–20.

G. Harold Metz, "A Stylometric Comparison of Shakespeare's *Titus Andronicus, Pericles*, and *Julius Caesar*," *ShN* 29 (Fall 1979): 42.

Kenneth Muir, "*Pericles*, II, v," *N&Q* 194 (August 1948): 362.

Kenneth Muir, "The Problem of *Pericles*," *ES* 30 (June 1949): 65–83.

J. R. Mulryne, "'To Glad Your Ear and Please Your Eyes': *Pericles* at the Other Place," *CritQ* 24 (Winter 1979): 31–40.

Norman Nathan, "Pericles and Jonah," *N&Q* 201 (January 1956): 10–11.

Gerald J. Schifhorst, "The Imagery of *Pericles* and What It Tells Us," *BSUF* 8, no. 3 (1967): 61–70.

Simpson, *Studies in Elizabethan Drama*, 17–22.

M. W. A. Smith, "The Authorship of Acts I and II of *Pericles*: A New Approach Using the First Words of Speeches," *CHum* 22 (January 1988): 23–41.

M. W. A. Smith, "An Initial Investigation of the Authorship of *Pericles*: Statistics Support Scholars: Shakespeare Did Not Write Acts I & II," *ShN* 33 (Fall 1983): 22.

M. W. A. Smith, "A Procedure to Determine Authorship Using Pairs of Consecutive Words: More Evidence for Wilkin's Participation in *Pericles*," *CHum* 23 (April 1989): 113–29.

Kay Stockholder, "Sex and Authority in *Hamlet, King Lear* and *Pericles*," *Mosaic* 18 (Summer 1985): 17–29.

Michael Taylor, "'Here is a thing too young for such a place': Innocence in *Pericles*," *ArielE* 13 (July 1982): 3–19.

Sidney Thomas, "The Problem of *Pericles*," *SQ* 34 (1983): 448–50.

J. M. Tomkins, "Why Pericles?" *RES* 3 (October 1952): 315–24.

James O. Wood, "The Case of Shakespeare's *Pericles*," *SJS* 6 (Summer 1980): 39–58.

James O. Wood, "Shakespeare, *Pericles*, and the Genevan Bible," *PCP* 12 (January 1977): 82–89.

Alan R. Young, "A Note on the Tournament Impresas in *Pericles*," *SQ* 36 (Autumn 1985): 453–56.

Richard II

R. H. Altick, " 'Conveyers' and Fortune's Buckets in *Richard II*," *MLN* 61 (March 1946): 179–80.

Donald K. Anderson, Jr., "*Richard II* and *Perkin Warbeck*," *SQ* 13 (Spring 1962): 260–63.

Alex Aronson, "A Note on Shakespeare's Dream Imagery," *Visaubharti Quarterly* 18 (August–October 1952): 173.

Richard D. Attick, "Symphonic Imagery in *Richard II*," *PMLA* 62 (June 1947): 399–65.

William Bache, "*Richard II*: Failure in Kinship," *Discourse* 8, no. 2 (1965): 178–84.

Harry Berger, Jr., "*Richard II* 3.2: An Exercise in Imaginary Audition," *ELH* 55 (December 1988): 755–96. Reprinted and expanded in *Imaginary Audition: Shakespeare on Stage and Page* (Berkeley: University Of California Press, 1989), 74–138.

David M. Bergeron, "*Richard II* and Carnival Politics," *SQ* 42 (1991): 33–43.

Ronald Berman, "*Richard II*: The Shapes of Love," *MSpr* 58 (1964): 1–8.

Thomas F. Berninghausen, "Banishing Cain: The Gardening Metaphor in *Richard II* and the Genesis Myth of the Origin of History," *ELWIU* 14 (Spring 1987): 3–14.

Berry, *Poet's Grammar*, 61–62.

Harvey Birenbaum, "Between the Mirror and the Face: Symbolic Reality in *Richard II*," in Homan, *Shakespeare and the Triple Play*, 58–75.

Norman Bisset, "The Historical Pattern from *Richard II* to *Henry V*: Shakespeare's Analysis of Kinship," in Conejero, *En torno a Shakespeare*, 209–39.

James Black, "The Interlude of the Beggar and the King in *Richard II*," in Bergeron, *Pageantry in the Shakespearean Theater*, 104–13.

Allan Bloom, "*Richard II*," in Alvis and West, *Shakespeare as Political Thinker*, 51–61.

W. F. Bolton, "Richardian Law Reports and *Richard II*," *ShakS* 20 (1987): 53–65.

Stephen Booth, "Syntax as Rhetoric in *Richard II*," *Mosaic* 10 (Summer 1977): 87–103.

Diane Bornstein, "Trial by Combat and Official Irresponsibility in *Richard II*," *ShakS* 8 (1975): 131–41.

Brockbank, *On Shakespeare*, 283–302.

J. P. Brockbank. "*Richard II* and the Music of Man's Lives," *LeedsSE* 14 (Spring 1983): 57–73.

Nicholas Brooke, "*Richard II* [1595]," in *Shakespeare's Early Tragedies*, 107–37.

J. A. Bryant, "The Linked Analogies of *Richard II*," *SR* 65 (Summer 1957): 420–33.

Francelia Butler, "The Relationship between Moral Competence and Old Age in *Richard II*, *2 Henry IV*, and *Henry V*," *SQ* 16 (Spring 1965): 236–38.

Virginia M. Carr, "The Power of Grief in *Richard II*," *EA* 31 (January 1978): 145–51.

I. B. Cauthen, Jr., "*Richard II* and the Image of the Betrayed Christ," *RenP 1953* (1954): 45–48.

Larry S. Champion, "The Function of Mowbray: Shakespeare's Maturing Artistry in *Richard II*," *SQ* 26 (Winter 1975): 3–7.

Raymond Chapman, "The Wheel of Fortune in Shakespeare's Historical Plays," *RES* 1 (January 1950): 1–5.

Wolfgang H. Clemen, "Anticipation and Foreboding in Shakespeare's Early Histories," *ShS* 6 (1953): 30–31.

Wolfgang Clemen, "Past and Future in Shakespeare's Drama," *PBA* 52 (1966): 231–52. Reprinted in Clemen, *Shakespeare's Dramatic Art*, 124–46.

John Scott Colley, "The Economics of *Richard II*?" *SJW* 113 (Summer 1977): 158–63.

Louise Cowan, "God Will Save the King: Shakespeare's *Richard II*," in Alcis and West *Shakespeare as Political Thinker*, 63–81.

Ruth Cowhig, "*Richard II* as a Political Tragedy," *Use of English* 18 (Summer 1967): 238–31.

Alan E. Craven, "Compositor Analysis to Edited Text: Some Suggested Readings in *Richard II* and *Much Ado About Nothing*," *PBSA* 76 (March 1982): 43–62.

John P. Cutts, "Christian and Classical Imagery in *Richard II*," *Universitas* 2, no. 2 (1964): 70–76.

Geraldo U. De Sousa, "Semiotics of Kingship in *Richard II*," in Atkins and Bergeron, *Shakespeare and Deconstruction*, 173–92.

Leonard F. Dean, "*Richard II*: The State and the Image of the Theater," *PMLA* 67 (March 1952): 211–18.

Leonard F. Dean, "*Richard II* to *Henry V*: A Closer View," in Harrison, et al., *Studies in Honor of DeWitt T. Starnes*, 37–52.

Madeleine Doran, "Imagery in *Richard II* and *Henry VI*," *MLR* 37 (April 1942): 113–22. Reprinted in *Shakespeare's Dramatic Language*, 221–33.

Madeleine Doran, "Yet I am inland bred," *SQ* 15 (Spring 1964): 99–114. Reprinted in McManaway, *Shakespeare 400*, 99–114.

R. J. Dorius, "A Little More Than a Little," *SQ* 11 (Winter 1960): 13 22.

D. L. Douglas, "'After Such Knowledge, What Forgiveness?' A Critical Interpretation of *Richard II*," *Parergon* 15 (January 1977): 27–36.

Alan S. Downer, "The Like of Our Design," *HudR* 2 (Summer 1949): 249–51, 255–58.

John W. Draper, "The Character of Richard II," *PQ* 21 (April 1942): 228–36.

R. P. Draper, "Wasted Time in *Richard II*," *CrSurv* 1, no. 1 (1989): 33–42.

Arthur M. Eastman, "Shakespeare's Negative Capability," *MichA* 42 (1956): 344–47.

John R. Elliot, Jr., "*Richard II* and the Medieval," *RenP 1965* (1966): 25–34.

Karl Felson, "*Richard II*: Three-Part Harmony," *SQ* 23 (Winter 1972): 107–11.

Ferguson, *Trope and Allegory*, 91–99.

Diane Ferris, "Elizabeth I and Richard II: Portraits in 'Masculine' and 'Feminine' Princes," *IJWS* 4 (January–February 1981): 10–18.

Charles R. Forker, "Shakespeare's Chronical Plays as Historical-Pastoral," *ShakS* 1 (1965): 85–104.

Leslie Freeman, "Shakespeare's Kings and Machiavelli's Prince," *CCP* 1 (1964): 25–42.

Donald M. Friedman, "John of Gaunt and the Rhetoric of Frustration," *ELH* 43 (June 1976): 279–99.

A. L. French, "Who Deposed Richard the Second?" *EIC* 17 (October 1967): 411–33.

Takeo Fujii, "Verb-Adverb Combination in Shakespeare's Language," *Anglica* 5 (March 1965): 54–91.

C. O. Gardner, "The Great Deepening: An Essay on Richard II," in *Generous Converse: English Essays in Memory of Edward Davis*, ed. Brian Green (Cape Town: Oxford University Press, 1980), 37–43.

Grace Mary Garry, "Unworthy Sons: *Richard II*, Phaethon and the Disturbance of Temporal Order," *MLS* 9 (Winter 1978–79): 15–19.

Paul Gaudet, "Northumberland's 'Persuasion': Reflections on *Richard II*, II.i.224–300," *UCrow* 4 (1982): 73–85.

Paul Gaudet, "The 'Parasitical' Counselors in Shakespeare's *Richard II*: Problem in Dramatic Interpretation," *SQ* 33 (Spring 1982): 142–54.

Ernest B. Gilman, "*Richard II* and the Perspectives of History," *RenD* 7 (1976): 85–115.

Jack Benoit Gohn, "*Richard II*: Shakespeare's Legal Brief on the Royal Prerogative and the Succession to the Throne," *Georgetown Law Journal* 70 (1982): 943–73.

Jonathan Goldberg, "Rebel Letters: Postal Effects from *Richard II* to *Henry V*," *RenD* 19 (1988): 3–28.

Paul Goodman, *The Structure of Literature*, 59–66.

George D. Gopen, "Private Grief into Public Action: The Rhetoric of John of Gaunt in *Richard II*," *SP* 84 (Summer 1987): 338–62.

Anne Gould, "Tragedy and the Heroism on Richard II," *Thoth* 1 (Fall 1959): 1–13.

Robert A. Greenberg, "Shakespeare's *Richard II*, IV, I, 244–250," *Expl* 15 (February 1957): 29.

Thelma N. Greenfield, "Nonvocal Music: Added Dimension in Five Shakespeare Plays," in McNeir and Greenfield, *Pacific Coast Studies in Shakespeare*, 106–21.

William Griffin, "Conjectures on a Missing Line in *Richard II*," *TSL* 7 (Spring 1962): 105–12.

Paul V. Hale, "The Castle of Grief in *Richard II*," *LHR* 13, no. 1 (1972): 128–40.

Jay L. Halio, "The Metaphor of Conception and Elizabethan Theories of Imagination," *Neophil* 50 (October 1966): 454–61.

Hallett and Hallett, *Analyzing Shakespeare's Action*, 95–97.

William L. Halstead, "Artifice and Artistry in *Richard II* and *Othello*," *UMPEAL* 7 (March 1964): 19–35.

Robert Hapgood, "Shakespeare's Thematic Modes of Speech: *Richard II* to *Henry V*, *ShS* 20 (1967): 41–49.

Richard Harrier, "Ceremony and Politics in *Richard II*," in Fabian and von Rosador, *Shakespeare: Text, Language, Criticism*, 80–97.

R. Chris Hassel, Jr., "Enjambement and Anarchy in Bolingbroke," *LangQ* 10 (Spring 1972): 48–56.

Hawkes, *Shakespeare's Talking Animals*, 73–104.

Hawkins, *Likeness of Truth*, 2–3.

S. K. Heninger, Jr., "The Sun King Analogy in *Richard II*," *SQ* 11 (Summer 1960): 319–27.

J. H. Hexter, "Property, Monopoly, and Shakespeare's *Richard II*," in *Culture and Politics from Puritanism to the Englightenment*, ed. Perez Zagorin (Berkeley: University of California Press), 1–24.

Hibbard, *Making of Shakespeare's Dramatic Poetry*, 72–74, 113–19.

R. F. Hill, "Dramatic Techniques and Interpreation in *Richard II*," *Stratford-Upon-Avon Studies* 3 (1961): 101–22.

C. H. Hobday, "Why the Sweets Melted: A Study in Shakespeare's Imagery," *SQ* 16 (Winter 1965): 3–17.

Dorothy C. Hockey, "A World of Rhetoric in *Richard II*," *SQ* 15 (Summer 1964): 179–91.

Graham Holderness, "'A Woman's War': Feminist Reading of *Richard II*," in Kamps, *Shakespeare Left and Right*, 167–83.

Sidney Homan, "*Richard II*: The Aesthetics of Judgement," *SLitI* 5, no. 1 (1972): 65–71.

Houston *Shakespearean Sentences*, 57–59.

Arthur Humphreys, "Shakespeare's Political Justice in *Richard II* and *Henry IV*," *Stratford Papers on Shakespeare* 5 (1964): 30–50.

R. W. Ingram, "Musical Pauses and the Vision Scenes in Shakespeare's Last Plays," in McNeir and Greenfield, *Pacific Coast Studies in Shakespeare*, 234–47.

Henry E. Jacobs, "Prophecy and Ideology in Shakespeare's *Richard II*," *SAB* 51 (January 1986): 3–17.

Pamela K. Jensen, "Beggars and Kings: Cowardice and Courage in Shakespeare's *Richard II*," *IJPP* 18 (Fall 1990): 111–43.

Paul A. Jorgensen, "Vertical Patterns in *Richard II*," *ShAB* 23 (July 1948): 119–34.

Dorothea Kehler, "King of Tears: Mortality in *Richard II*," *RMRLL* 39, no. 1 (1985): 7–18.

Dorothea Kehler, "*Richard II*, 5.3: Traditions and Subtext," in Allen and White, *Traditions and Innovations*, 126–36.

Dorothea Kehler, "What the Gardener Knew: Pruning and Power in *The Troublesome Raigne of King John* and *Richard II*," *JRMMRA* 9 (January 1988): 117–29.

J. Kleinstuck, "The Character of Bolingbroke," *Neophil* 41 (January 1957): 51–56.

Samuel Kliger, "The Sun Imagery in *Richard II*," *SP* 45 (April 1948): 196–202.

Knight, *The Golden Labyrinth*, 71–72.

Knight, *The Imperial Theme*, 351–67.

Knight, *The Olive and the Sword*, 20–24.

Knight, *The Sovereign Flower*, 29–33.

Seiei Kobayashi, "An Essay on *King Richard II*," in Milward and Anzai, *Poetry and Drama*, 106–17.

Shirley G. Kossick, "*Richard II*: The Deposition Scene," *UES* (May 1968): 79–85. Reprinted in *Communique* (Pietersburg) 5, no. 2 (1980): 79–84.

Eric LaGuardia, "Ceremony and History: The Problem of Symbol from *Richard II* to *Henry V*," in McNeir and Greenfield, *Pacific Coast Studies in Shakespeare*, 68–88.

Georges Lamoine, "*Richard II* and the Myth of the Fisher King," *CahiersE* 30 (October 1986): 75–78.

Clifford Leech, "Shakespeare and the Idea of the Future," *UTQ* 35 (April 1966): 213–28.

Alexander Leggatt, "A Double Reign: *Richard II* and *Perkin Warbeck*," in Honigmann, *Shakespeare and His Contemporaries*, 129–39.

Lauren Lepow, "Shakespeare's *Richard II*, V.ii 39–40," *Expl* 40 (Fall 1981): 9.

Clayton G. MacKenzie, "Paradise and Paradise Lost in *Richard II*," *SQ* 37 (Autumn 1986): 318–39.

Hugh MacLean, "Time and Horsemanship in Shakespeare's Histories," *UTQ* 35 (April 1966): 229–45.

François Maguin, "The Breaking of Time: *Richard II*, *Hamlet*, and *Macbeth*," *CahiersE* 7 (April 1975): 25–41.

William C. McAvoy, "Form in *Richard II*, II, I, 40–66," *JEGP* 54 (July 1955): 355–61.

McCollum, *Tragedy*, 140–41, 193–96.

William C. McCollum, "Formalism and Illusion in Shakespearian Drama," *QJS* 31 (December 1945): 446–48.

McDonnell, *The Aspiring Mind*, 206–26.

Scott McMillin, "Shakespeare's *Richard II*: Eyes of Sorrow, Eyes of Desire," *SQ* 35 (Spring 1984): 40–52.

James A. S. McPeek, "Richard and His Shadow World," *AI* 15 (Summer 1958): 195–212.

W. Moelwyn Merchant, "Shakespeare's Theology," *RES* 15 (1964): 72–88.

W. Moelwyn Merchant, "The Phaeton Allusion in *Richard II*: The Search for Identity," *ELR* 17 (Summer 1987): 277–87.

Robert P. Merrix, and Carole Levin, "*Richard II* and *Edward II*: The Structure of Deposition," *ShY* 1 (1990): 1–13.

Jeanie Grant Moore, "Queen of Sorrow, King of Grief: Reflections and Perspectives in *Richard II*," in Kehler and Baker, *In Another Country*, 19–35.

Homer Nearing, Jr., "A Three-Way Pun in *Richard II*," *MLN* 62 (January 1947): 31–33.

Faith G. Norris, "Shakespeare's *Richard II*," *Expl* 35 (October 1978): 19–20.

A. D. Nottall, "Ovid's Narcissus and Shakespeare's Richard II: The Reflected Self," in *Ovid Renewed; Ovidian Influences on Literature and Art from the Middle Ages to the Twentieth Century*, ed. Charles Martindale (Cambridge: Cambridge University Press, 1988): 137–50.

Robert Ornstein, "Character and Reality in Shakespeare," in Bloom, *Shakespeare 1564–1964*, 3–18.

Shirley Parry, "*Richard II* Reappraised," *Trivium* 21 (1986): 119–36.

Josephine A. Pearce, "Constituent Elements in Shakespeare's English History Plays," *UMPEAL* 1 (March 1953): 149–50.

Jean-Pierre Petit, "A Note on Performatives in *Richard II*," in *Discourse and Style II*, ed. J. P. Petit (Lyon: Hermès, 1980), 105–07.

Peter G. Phialas, "The Medieval in *Richard II*," *SQ* 12 (Summer 1961): 305–10.

R. Poisson, "*Richard II*: Tudor Orthodoxy or Political Heresy," *HAB* 14 (Fall 1963): 5–11.

Forster Provost, "The Sorrows of Shakespeare's *Richard II*," in McNeir, *Studies in English Renaissance*, 40–51.

Christopher Pye, "The Betrayal of the Gaze: Theatricality and Power in Shakespeare's *Richard II*," *ELH* 55 (December 1988): 575–98.

Michael Quinn, "'The King is not Himself': The Personal Tragedy of *Richard II*," *SP* 56 (April 1959): 169–86.

Phyllis Rackin, "The Role of the Audience in Shakespeare's *Richard II*," *SQ* 36 (Spring 1985): 262–81.

Margaret Loftus Ranald, "The Degradation of *Richard II*: An Inquiry into the Ritual Backgrounds," *ELR* 7 (Summer 1977): 170–96.

Robert R. Reed, Jr., "*Richard II*: Portrait of a Psychotic," *JGE* 16 (April 1964): 55–67.

Donald H. Reiman, "Appearance, Reality, and Moral Order in *Richard II*," *MLQ* 25 (March 1964): 34–45.

Ribner, *The English History Play*, 154–67.

Irving Ribner, "Bolingbroke, a True Machiavellian," *MLQ* 9 (June 1948): 177–84.

Irving Ribner, "The Political Problem in Shakespeare's Lancastrian Tetralogy," *SP* 49 (April 1952): 174–82.

James A. Riddell, "The Admirable Character of York," *TSLL* 21 (Winter 1979): 492–502.

Gordon N. Ross, "Shakespeare's Poetic Gestures: Metaphor and Mimesis in *Richard II*," *SPWVSRA* 3 (Spring 1978): 30–37.

Rossiter, *Angel with Horns*, 23–39.

Samuel Schoenbaum, "*Richard II* and the Realities of Power," *ShS* 28 (1975): 1–13.

Murray M. Schwartz, "Anger, Wounds, and the Forms of Theatre in *King Richard II*: Notes for a Psychoanalytic Interpretation," *Assays* 2 (1982): 115–29.

Raymond C. Shady, "The Goddess Fortuna in Shakespeare's *Richard II*," *Greyfriar* 20 (1979): 5–13.

Alice Shalvi, "Studies in Kingship: *Henry VI*, *Richard III*, *Richard II*, *Henry IV*, and *Henry V*," in Mendilow and Shalvi, *The World and Art of Shakespeare*, 89–118.

Allan Shickman, "The 'Perspective Glass' in Shakespeare's *Richard II*," *SEL* 18 (Spring 1978): 217–28.

Kristian Smidt, "Openings and Unfoldings: Structural Faults in *Richard II* and *Henry IV*," *ShN* 30 (April 1980): 13–14.

Hallett Smith, "The Poetry of the Lyric Group: *Richard II, Romeo and Juliet, A Midsummer Night's Dream*," in Highfall, *Shakespeare's Craft*, 69–93.

Stella T. Smith, "Imagery of Downward Motion in Shakespeare's *King Richard The Second*," *ShN* 4 (February 1954): 8.

Karl E. Snyder, "Kings and Kingship in Four of Shakespeare's History Plays," in *Shakespeare 1964*, ed. Jim W. Corder (Fort Worth: Texas Christian University Press, 1965): 43–58.

Soellner, *Shakespeare's Patterns*, 97–112.

Robert Speaight, "Shakespeare and the Political Spectrum as Illustrated by *Richard II*," in Jackson, *Stratford Papers on Shakespeare* 1964, 135–54.

John Stevens, "Shakespeare and the Music of the Elizabethan Stage," in *Shakespeare in Music*, ed. Phyllis Hartnoll (London: Macmillan, 1964), 3–48.

Brents Stirling, "Bolingbroke's 'Decision,'" *SQ* 2 (January 1951): 27–34.

Zdenek Stribrny, "The Dialectrics of Characterization in *Richard II*," *PP* 24, no. 4 (1981): 177–82.

Jack R. Sublette, "Imagery of Time and Change in *Richard II*," *AJES* 7 (April 1982): 34–54.

Jack R. Sublette, "Order and Power in *Richard II*," *BSUF* 22, no. 1 (1981): 42–51.

James Sutherland, "How the Characters Talk," in Sutherland and Hurtsfield, *Shakespeare's World*, 116–35.

Arthur Suzman, "Imagery and Symbolism in *Richard II*," *SQ* 7 (Autumn 1956): 355–70.

Ben Taggie, "Marlowe and Shakespeare: *Edward II* and *Richard II*," *PMPA* 13 (1988): 16–21.

Karl F. Thompson, "*Richard II*, Martyr," *SQ* 8 (Spring 1957): 159–66.

R. Ann Thompson, "The 'Two Buckets' Image in *Richard II* and *The Isle of Gulls*," *Archiv* 213 (1976): 108.

William B. Toole, III, "Psychological Action and Structure in *Richard II*," *JGE* 30 (January 1978): 165–84.

David Toor, "Shakespeare's *King Richard II*, IV. I. 237–42," *Expl* 31 (October 1972): Item 23.

Barbara H. Traister, "'I Will . . . Be Like a King': *Henry V* Plays *Richard II*," *CLQ* 26 (June 1990): 112–21.

Derek Traversi, "*Richard II*," in Jackson, *Stratford Papers on Shakespeare*, 11–29.

James Tulip, "Dramatic Representation in Shakespeare's *Richard II*," *SSEng* 1 (1975–76): 32–45.

Parker Tyler, "Phaeto: The Metaphysical Tension Between the Ego and the Universe in English Poetry," *Accent* 16 (Spring 1956): 29–44.

Peter Ure, "Character and Role from *Richard III* to *Hamlet*," *Stratford-Upon-Avon Studies* 5 (1963): 9–28. Reprinted in Maxwell, *Elizabethan and Jacobean Drama*, 22–43.

Peter Ure, "The Looking Glass of *Richard II*," *PQ* 34 (April 1955): 219–24.

Van Lann, *The Idiom of Drama*, 218–22.

Watson, *Shakespeare and the Hazards of Ambition*, 34–47.

Winston Weathers, "The Games People Play: A Shakespearean Footnote," *SHR* 1 (March 1967): 87–97.

Joan Webber, "The Renewal of the King's Symbolic Role: From *Richard II* to *Henry V*," *TSLL* 4 (Winter 1963): 530–38.

Samuel Weingarten, "The Name of the King in *Richard II*," *CE* 27 (April 1966): 536–41.

Stanley Wells, "The Lamentable Tale of *Richard II*," *ShStud* 17 (1978–1979): 1–23.

Karl P. Wentersdorf, "Shakespeare's *Richard II*: Gaunt's Part in Woodstock's Blood," *ELN* 18 (March 1980): 99–104.

Tadao Yamamoto, "The Verbal Structure of *Richard the Second*, *ZAA* 12, no. 2 (1964): 163–72.

Young, *Immortal Shadow*s, 196–99.

Richard III

A. A. Ansari, "*Richard III* and 'the irons of wrath,'" *ACM* 1, no. 1 (1988): 14–32.

Aerol Arnold, "The Recapitulation Dream in *Richard III* and *Macbeth*," *SQ* 6 (Winter 1955): 51–56.

M. M. Badawi, "The Paradox of *Richard III*," *Bulletin of the Faculty of Arts* (Alexandria University) 12 (1958): 49–68.

Charles Barberm, "'You' and 'Thou' in Shakespeare's *Richard III*," *LeedsSE* 12 (1981): 273–89.

Bernard Beckerman, "Scene Patterns in *Doctor Faustus* and *Richard III*," in Honigmann, *Shakespeare and His Contemporaries*, 31–41.

Steven Berkowitz, "'Men Were Deceivers Ever' (*Much Ado* 2. 3. 63): Buchanan's *Baptistes*, Shakespeare's *Richard III* and the Uses of Deception, from More to Shakespeare," in *A Collection of Papers Presented in the First National Conference of English and American Literature* (Taichung, Taiwan: National Chung Hsing University, 1986), 39–53.

Ralph Berry, "*Richard III*: Bonding the Audience," in Gray, *Mirror up to Shakespeare*, 114–27.

Berry, *Shakespearean Structures*, 17–19.

David Bevington, "'Why Should Calamity Be Full of Words/' The Efficacy of Cursing in *Richard III*," *ISJR* 56 (March 1981): 9–21.

Travis Bogard, "Shakespeare's Second Richard," *PMLA* 70 (March 1955): 192–209.

A. R. Braunmuller, "Early Shakespearian Tragedy and Its Contemporary Context: Cause and Emption in *Titus Andronicus*, *Richard III*, and 'The Rape of Lucrece,'" in Bradbury and Palmer, *Shakespearian Tragedy*, 96–128.

Dolores M. Burton, "Discourse and Decorum in the First Act of *Richard III*," *ShakS* 14 (1981): 55–84.

David R. Carlson, "The Princes' Embrace in *Richard III*," *SQ* 41 (Autumn 1990): 344–47.

Geoffrey Carnall, "Shakespeare's Richard III and St. Paul," *SQ* 14 (Spring 1963): 1866–88.

Wolfgang Clemen, "Anticipation and Foreboding in Shakespeare's Early Histories," *ShS* 6 (1953): 26–30.

Wolfgang Clemen, "Tradition and Originality in Shakespeare's *Richard III*," *SQ* 5 (Summer 1954): 247–58.

Scott Colley, "Richard III and Herod," *SQ* 37 (Winter 1986): 451–58.

Gillian M. Day, "'Determined to Prove a Villain': Theatricality in *Richard III*," *CrSurv* 3, no. 2 (1991): 149–56.

Louis E. Dollarhide, "Two Unassimilated Movements of *Richard III*: An Interpretation," *MissQ* 12 (Winter 1960–1961): 40–46.

John W. Draper, "Patterns of Tempo in *Richard III*," *NM* 50, no. 1 (1949): 1–12.

Peggy Endel, "Profane Icon: The Throne Scene of Shakespeare's *Richard III*," *CompD* 20 (summer 1986): 115–23.

Inga-Stina Ewbank, "*Richard III* (c. 1591), *Gustav III* (1902), and the Drama of Nationalism," in Newey and Thompson, *Literature and Nationalism*, 98–110.

Ann D. Ferguson, "A Brief Comparison of Supernatural Elements in *Richard III* and *Macbeth*," *GorR* 9 (Summer 1966): 184–92.

Dorothy Norris Foote, "Shakespeare's *Richard III*, IV, iv, 174–177," *Expl* 23 (November 1964): 23.

Alistair Fox, "Richard III's Pauline Oath: Shakespeare's Response to Thomas More," *Moreana* 57 (March 1978): 13–23.

R. Gerber, "Elizabethan Convention and Psychological Realism in the Dream and Last Soliloquy of *Richard III*," *ES* 40 (August 1959): 294–300.

Gomez, *The Alienated Figure in Drama*, 23–26.

Mary J. H. Gross, "Some Puzzling Speech Prefixes in *Richard III*," *PBSA* 71 (March 1977): 73–75.

Hallett and Hallett, *Analyzing Shakespeare's Action*, 12–17, 19–20, 90–91.

James P. Hammersmith, "The Melodrama of *Richard III*," *ES* 70 (February 1989): 28–36.

Mildred E. Hartsock, "Shakespeare's *Richard III*, IV, iv, 164–79," *Expl* 20 (May 1962): 71.

R. Chris Hassel, Jr., "Last Words and Last Things: St. John, Apocalypse, and Eschatology in *Richard III*," *ShS* 18 (1986): 25–40.

R. Chris Hassel, Jr., "Military Oratory in *Richard III*," *SQ* 35 (Spring 1984): 53–61.

R. Chris Hassel, Jr., "Providence and the Text of *Richard III*," *UCrow* 6 (1986): 84–93.

R. Chris Hassel, Jr., "Richard versus Richmond: Aesthetic Warfare in *Richard III*," *DSGW* 121 (1985): 106–16.

Robert B. Heilman, "Saiety and Conscience: Aspects of *Richard III*," *AR* 24 (Spring 1964): 57–73.

Hibbard, *Making of Shakespeare's Dramatic Poetry*, 82–88.

Richard Hosley, "More About 'Tents on Bosworth Field,'" *SQ* 7 (1956): 458–59.

Houston, *Shakespearean Sentences*, 25–30.

Clifford Chalmers Huffman, "'Unvalued Jewels': The Religious Perspective in *Richard III*," *BuR* 26, no. 2 (1982): 58–73.

Daniel E. Hughes, "The 'Worm of Conscience' in *Richard III* and *Macbeth*," *EJ* 55 (1966): 845–52.

Maurice Hunt, "Ordering Disorder in *Richard III*," *SCRev* 6 (Winter 1989): 11–29.

Emrys Jones, "Bosworth Eve," *EIC* 25 (January 1975): 38–54.

Kastan, *Shakespeare and the Shapes of Time*, 93–96.

Terrance Brophy Kearns, "'Brief Abstract and Record of Tedious Days': The Aged in *Richard III*," *PAPA* 13 (Spring 1987): 25–34.

Knight, *The Olive and the Sword*, 16–20.

Knight, *The Sovereign Flower*, 21–25.

Murray Krieger, "The Dark Generations of *Richard III*," *Criticism* 1 (Winter 1959): 32–48.

Bridget Gellert Lyons, "'Kings Games': Stage Imagery and Political Symbolism in *Richard III*," *Criticism* 20 (Winter 1978): 17–30.

Andrew MacDonald, and Gina MacDonald, "The Necessity of Evil: Shakespeare's Rhetorical Strategy in *Richard III*," *ShStud* 19 (1980–1981): 55–69.

Andrew MacDonald, and Gina MacDonald, "The Necessity of the Wooing of Anne in *Richard III*," *UDR* 15 (Spring 1981): 125–28.

McCollum, *Tragedy*, 192–93.

McDonnell, *The Aspiring Mind*, 187–206.

Russ McDonald, "*Richard III* and the Tropes of Treachery," *PQ* 68 (Autumn 1989): 465–83.

John J. McLaughlin, "Richard III as Punch," *SCR* 10, no. 1 (1977): 79–86.

E. H. Meyerstein, "*Richard III*, I.i.32," *RES* 22 (January 1946): 53.

Madonne M. Miner, "'Neither mother, wife, nor England's queen': The Roles of Women in *Richard III*," in Lenz, et al., *The Woman's Part: Feminist Criticism of Shakespeare*, 5–55.

William C. Morris, "Consistency in *Richard III*," *Drama Critique* 7 (Winter 1964): 40–46.

Wolfgang G. Muller, "The Villain as Rhetorican in Shakespeare's *Richard III*," *Anglia* 102, no. 1 (1984): 37–59.

Anthony P. Narkin, "Day-Residue and Christian References in Clarence's Dream," *TSLL* 9 (Summer 1967): 147–50.

Norman Nathan, "The Marriage of Richard and Anne," *N&Q* 200 (February 1955): 55–56.

Michael Neill, "Shakespeare's Halle of Mirrors: Play, Politics, and Psychology in *Richard III*," *ShakS* 8 (1975): 99–129.

Bernard J. Paris, "Richard III: Shakespeare's First Great Mimetic Character," *AJES* 8 (April 1983): 40–67.

Howard Parsons, "*Richard III*," *N&Q* 200 (April 1955): 175–76.

Pye, *Royal Phantasm*, 82–105.

Michael Quinn, "Providence in Shakespeare's Yorkist Plays," *SQ* 10 (winter 1959): 45–46, 50–52.

Ribner, *The English History Play*, 116–24.

James A. Riddell, "Hastings' 'foot-cloth horse' in *Richard III*," *ES* 56 (April 1975): 29–31.

Marvin Rosenberg, "*Richard III*," in *KM 80*, 122–28.

Rossiter, *Angel with Horns*, 1–22.

Pierre Sahel, "The Coup d'etat of Shakespeare's *Richard III*: Politics and Dramatics," *AJES* 10 (April 1985): 1–8.

Betty A, Schellenberg, "Conflicting Paradigms and the Progress of Persuasion in *Richard III*," *CahiersE* 37 (April 1990): 59–68.

Shaw, *Plays and Players*, 142–51.

Donald R. Shupe, "The Wooing of Lady Anne: Psychological Inquiry," *SQ* 29 (Spring 1978): 28–36.

Paul N. Siegel, "Richard III as Businessman," *SJW* 114 (Spring 1978): 101–06.

Jennifer Strauss, "Determined to Prove a Villain: Character, Action and Irony in *Richard III*," *Komos* 1, no. 2 (1967): 115–20.

Henri Suhamy, "The Religious Dimension of *Richard III*," *MCRel* 9 (1991): 115–22.

Gary Taylor, "'Praestat difficilior lectio': *All's Well That Ends Well* and *Richard III*," *RenSt* 2 (March 1988): 27–46.

Gordon K. Thomas, "Is Frailty the Name of Woman? A Reconsideration of *Richard III* 1.2," *Encyclia* 64 (1987): 95–101.

Eustace M. Tillyard, *Some Mystical Elements in English Literature—The Clark Lectures, 1959–1960* (London: Chatto & Windus, 1961), 57–61.

William John Tucker, "Irish Aspects of Shakespeare," *Catholic World* 156 (March 1943): 702.

Peter Ure, "Character and Role from Richard III to Hamlet," *Stratford-Upon-Avon Studies* 5 (1963): 13–19.

John W. Velz, "Episodic Structure in Four Tudor Plays: A Virtue of Necessity," *CompD* (Summer 1972): 87–102.

Marguerite Waller, "Ursurpation, Seduction, and the Problematics of the Proper: A 'Deconstructive,' 'Feminist' Rereading of the Seductions of Richard and Anne in Shakespeare's *Richard III*," in Ferguson, Quilligan, and Vickers, *Rewriting the Renaissance*, 159–74.

Watson, *Shakespeare and the Hazards of Ambition*, 15–34.

Karl Weber, "Shakespeare's *Richard III*, I.iv.24–33," *Expl* 38 (Fall 1980): 24–26.

Wiggins, *Journeymen in Murder*, 39–42, 116–21.

Philip Williams, "*Richard the Third*: The Battle Orations," in *English Studies in Honor of James Southall Wilson*, 125–30.

J. Dover Wilson, "Shakespeare's *Richard III* and the *True Tragedy of Richard the Third*, 1594," *SQ* 3 (October 1952): 299–306.

J. Dover Wilson, "The Composition of the Clarence Scenes in *Richard III*," *MLR* 53 (April 1958): 211–14.

J. Dover Wilson, "A Note on *Richard III*: The Bishop of Ely's Strawberries," *MLR* 52 (October 1957): 563–64.

Gerald H. Zuk, "A Note on Richard's Anxiety Dream," *AI* 14 (Spring 1957): 37–39.

Romeo and Juliet

Barry B. Adams, "The Prudence of Prince Escalus," *ELH* 35 (March 1968): 32–50.

James Andreas, "'To See How a Jest Shall Come About!' Generic Modulation in *Romeo and Juliet*," *PMPA* 12 (1987): 1–8.

Alex Aronson, "A Note on Shakespeare's Dream Imagery," *Visrirbharati Quarterly* 18 (August–October 1952): 171–72.

Jackson G. Barry, "Poem or Speech? The Sonnet as Dialogue in *Love's Labour's Lost* and *Romeo and Juliet*," *PLL* 19 (Winter 1983): 13–36.

Klaus Bartenschlager, "The Love-Sick Tree: A Note on *Romeo and Juliet* 1.1.119 and *Othello* IV.3.39," *ES* 59 (July 1978): 116–18.

Klaus Bartenschlager, "Three Notes on *Romeo and Juliet*," *Anglia* 100, no. 4 (1982): 422–25.

A. Jonathan Bate, "An Herb by Any Other Name: *Romeo and Juliet*, IV.iv.5–6," *SQ* 33 (Autumn 1982): 336.

Roy A. Battenhouse, "Shakespearean Tragedy: A Christian Interpretation," in Scott, *The Tragic Vision and the Christian Faith*, 89–93.

Greg Bentley, "Poetics of Power: Money as Sign and Substance in *Romeo and Juliet*," *EIRC* 17 (1991): 145–66.

David M. Bergeron, "Sickness in *Romeo and Juliet*," *CLAJ* 20 (September 1977): 356–64.

James Black, "The Visual Artistry of *Romeo and Juliet*," *SEL* 15 (Spring 1975): 245–56.

Georges A. Bonnar, "*Romeo and Juliet*: A Possible Significance?" *RES* 2 (October 1951): 319–27.

Ronald B. Bond, "Love and Lust in *Romeo and Juliet*," *WascanaR* 15 (Fall 1980): 22–31.

Lawrence Edward Bowling, "The Thematic Framework of *Romeo and Juliet*," *PMLA* 64 (March 1949): 208–20.

Terry Box, "Shakespeare's *Romeo and Juliet*," *Expl* 47 (Fall 1988): 4–5.

Gerry Brenner, "Shakespeare's Politically Ambitious Friar," *ShakS* 13 (1980): 47–58.

Randolph M. Bulgin, "Drama Imagery in Shakespeare's *Romeo and Juliet*," *Shenandoah* 11 (Winter 1960): 23–38.

H. Edward Cain, "An Emendation in *Romeo and Juliet*," *ShAB* 17 (January 1942): 57–60.

H. Edward Cain, "'Parting' and Justice in *Romeo and Juliet*," *TSL* 7 (Spring 1962): 99–104.

H. Edward Cain, "*Romeo and Juliet*: A Reinterpretation," *ShAB* 22 (October 1944): 163–92.

H. Edward Cain, "A Technique of Motivation in *Romeo and Juliet*," *ShAB* 21 (October 1946): 186–90.

Jill Calaco, "The Window Scenes in *Romeo and Juliet* and Folk Songs of the Night Visit," *SP* 83 (Spring 1986): 138–57.

Bert Cardullo, "The Friar's Flaw, the Play's Tragedy: The Experiment of *Romeo and Juliet*," *CLAJ* 28 (December 1985): 404–14.

William C. Carroll, "'We Were Born to Die': *Romeo and Juliet*," *CompD* 15 (Spring 1981): 54–71.

Joseph S. Chang, "The Language Paradox in *Romeo and Juliet*," *ShakS* 3 (1968): 22–42.

Raymond Chapman, "Double Time in *Romeo and Juliet*," *MLR* 44 (July 1949): 371–74.

James L. Clark, "Style and Convention in *Romeo and Juliet*," in Quinn, *How to Read Shakespearean Tragedy*, 33–88.

Henning Cohen, "Shakespeare's *Romeo and Juliet*, V, iii, 112–115," *Expl* 8 (December 1949): 24.

Michael J. Collins, "Teaching *Romeo and Juliet*" 'The Change of Fourteen Years,'" *CrSurv* 3, no. 2 (1991): 186–93.

H. Coombes, *Literature and Criticism*, 127–29.

Marjorie K. Cox, "Adolescent Process in *Romeo and Juliet*," *PsyR* 63, no. 3 (1976): 379–92.

T. J. Cribb, "The Unity of *Romeo and Juliet*," *ShS* 34 (1981): 93–104.

Taylor Culbert, "A Note on *Romeo and Juliet*, I. iii. 89–90," *SQ* 10 (Winter 1959): 129–32.

Edgar F. Daniels, and Ralph Haven Wolfe, "Shakespeare's *Romeo and Juliet* V.iii.83–86," *Expl* 35 (Winter 1977): 14.

Leonard F. Dean, "Shakespeare's *Romeo and Juliet*, II, i, 34–35," *Expl* 3 (April 1945): 44.

Sara Munson Deats, "The Conspiracy of Silence in Shakespeare's Verona: *Romeo and Juliet*," in Deats and Lenker, *Youth Suicide Prevention*, 71–91.

Alan C. Dessen, "Much Virtue in As: Elizabethan Stage Locales and Modern Interpretation," in Thompson and Thompson, *Shakespeare and the Sense of Performance*, 132–38.

John W. Draper, "Contrast of Tempo in the Balcony Scene," *ShAB* 22 (July 1947): 130–35.

Tom F. Driver, "The Shakespearean Clock: Time and the Vision of Reality in *Romeo and Juliet* and *The Tempest*," *SQ* 15 (Autumn 1964): 363–67.

Charles Edelman, "A Note on the Opening Stage Direction of *Romeo and Juliet*, I.i," *SQ* 39 (Autumn 1988): 361–62.

Edward F. Edinger, "*Romeo and Juliet*: A Coniunctio Drama," in *The Shaman from Elko: Papers in Honor of Joseph L. Henderson on His Seventy-Fifth Birthday*, ed. Gareth Hall, Virginia Detloff, Thomas Kirsch, William McGuire, and Louis Stewart (San Francisco: Jung Institute, 1978), 67–80.

Barbara L. Estrin, "Romeo, Juliet and the Art of Naming Love," *ArielE* 12 (April 1981): 31–49.

Bertraud Evans, "The Brevity of Friar Laurence," *PMLA* 65 (September 1950): 841–65.

Robert O. Evans, "*Romeo and Juliet* II.i.13: Further Commentary," *NM* 64, no. 2 (1963): 390–400.

Frank Fabry, "Shakespeare's Witty Musician: *Romeo and Juliet*, IV.v.114–17," *SQ* 22 (Summer 1982): 182–83.

Kirby Farrell, "Love, Death, and Patriarchy in *Romeo and Juliet*," in Holland, Homan, and Paris, *Shakespeare's Personality*, 86–102.

Ferguson, *Trope and Allegory*, 13–15.

Eleanor Stratton Fliess, and Robert Fleiss, "Shakespeare's Juliet and Her Name," *AI* 33 (Fall 1976): 244–60.

Edward H. Friedman, *Romeo and Juliet* as Tragicomedy: Lope's *Castelvines y Monteses* and Rojas Zorrilla's *Los Bandos de Verona*," *NuR* 33, no. 1 (1989): 82–96.

Berry Gaines, "Another Example of Dialect from the Nurse in *Romeo and Juliet*," *SQ* 32 (Spring 1981): 96–97.

Saad M. Gamal, "*A Midsummer Night's Dream* and *Romeo and Juliet*, Some Parallels," *CairoSE* (1963–64): 109–17.

Allan P. Green, "Shakespeare's *Romeo and Juliet* V.iii.81–86," *Expl* 34 (December 1976): Item 57.

J. C. Grey, "*Romeo and Juliet* and Some Renaissance Notion of Love, Time, and Death," *DR* 48 (Spring 1968): 58–69.

Hallett and Hallett, *Analyzing Shakespeare's Action*, 20–23, 26–29, 139–41, 144–45.

Harriet Hawkins, "Likeness with Difference: Patterns of Action in *Romeo and Juliet, Julius Caesar*, and *Macbeth*," *MEJ* 6, no. 2 (1968): 1–13.

Hawkins, *Likeness of Truth*, 141–44, 151–52.

Hawkins, *Poetic Freedom and Poetic Truth*, 14–15, 18–19.

Robert B. Heilman, "To Know Himself: An Aspect of Tragic Structure," *REL* 5 (April 1964): 36–39.

Elton F. Henley, "Relevance of Mercutio's Queen Mab Speech in *Romeo and Juliet* I.iv.53–94," *LAngQ* 4 (Fall–Winter 1965): 29–32.

William A. Henry, "Theme and Image in *Romeo and Juliet*," *Thoth* 3 (Winter 1962): 13–17.

Hibbard, *Making of Shakespeare's Dramatic Poetry*, 120–32.

Norman Holland, "Romeo's Dream and the Paradox of Literary Realism," *L&P* 13 (Fall 1963): 97–103.

Joan Ozark Holmer, "'Myself Condemned and Myself Excus'd': Tragic Effects in *Romeo and Juliet*," *SP* 88 (Summer 1991): 345–62.

Joan Ozark Holmer, "'O, What Learning Is!': Some Pedagogical Practices for *Romeo and Juliet*," *SQ* 41 (Summer 1990): 187–94.

Richard Hesley, "The 'Good Night, Good Night' Sequence in *Romeo and Juliet*," *SQ* 5 (January 1954): 96–98.

Richard Hosley, "How Many Children Had Lady Capulet?" *SQ* 18 (Spring 1967): 3–6.

Houston, *Shakespearean Sentences*, 44–51.

Maurice Hunt, "'Use and Abuse' in *Romeo and Juliet*," *JRMMRA* 5 (January 1984): 119–32.

Geoffrey Hutchings, "Love and Grace in *Romeo and Juliet*," *ESA* 20, no. 1 (1977): 95–106.

R. W. Ingram, "Magical Pauses and the Vision Scenes in Shakespeare's Last Plays," in McNeir and Greenfield, *Pacific Coast Studies in Shakespeare*, 234–47.

Jackson, *This is Love?*, 15–20.

Jepson, *Ethical Aspects of Tragedy*, 84–87.

Coppélia Kahn, "Coming of Age in Verona," *MLS* 8 (Winter 1977–78): 5–22. Reprinted in Lenz, et al., *The Woman's Part*, 171–93.

Harry Keil, "Scabies and the Queen Mab Passage in *Romeo and Juliet*," *JHI* 18 (June 1957): 394–96, 407–10.

R. M. Keils, "Romeo and Juliet's Rings of Frea," *Missouri English Bulletin* 32, no. 1 (1975): 39–42.

Janusz Kilinski, "Elements of Neo-Platonism in William Shakepeare's *Romeo and Juliet*," *SAP* 17 (1984): 271–77.

Philip C. Kolin, "Shakespeare's *Romeo and Juliet*, I.ii.34–101," *Expl* 40 (Summer 1982): 12–13.

Stanley J. Kozikowski, "Fortune and Men's Eyes in *Romeo and Juliet*," *CP* 10, no. 1 (1977): 45–49.

David Laird, "The Generation of Style in *Romeo and Juliet*," *JEGP* 63 (April 1964): 204–13.

John Lawlor, "*Romeo and Juliet*," *Stratford-Upon-Avon Studies* 3 (1961): 123–44.

Clifford Leech, "The Moral Tragedy of *Romeo and Juliet*," in Henning, et al., *English Renaissance Drama*, 59–75.

Lawrence Lerner, "Shakespeare and Love: *Romeo and Juliet*," in Sharma, *Essays on Shakespeare in Honour of A. A. Ansari*, 11 /–35.

Jill L. Levenson, "The Defintion of Love: Shakespeare's Phrasing in *Romeo and Juliet*," *ShakS* 15 (1982): 21–36.

Jill L. Levenson, "*Romeo and Juliet*: Tragical-Comical-Lyrical History," *PPMRC* 12–13 (1987–1988): 31–46.

Harry Levin, "Form and Formality in *Romeo and Juliet*," *SQ* 11 (Winter 1960): 3–11.

Harry Levin, *Shakespeare and the Revolution of the Times: Perspective and Commentary* (New York: Oxford University Press, 1976), 103–20.

Richard Levin, "'Littera Canina' in *Romeo and Juliet* and 'Michaelmas Term,'" *N&Q* 207 (September 1962): 333–34.

Frederick M. Link, "*Romeo and Juliet*: Character and Tragedy," *BUSE* 1 (Spring–Summer 1955): 9–19.

John B. Lord, "Comic Scenes in Shakespearean Tragedy," *WCSC* 32 (September 1964): 235.

Charles B. Lower, "*Romeo and Juliet*, IV.v: A Stage Direction and Purposeful Comedy," *ShakS* 8 (1975): 177–94.

Herbert McArthur, "Romeo's Loquacious Friend," *SQ* 10 (Winter 1959): 35–44.

Gary M. McCowan, "'Runnawayes Eyes' and Juliet's Epithalamium," *SQ* 27 (Summer 1976): 150–70.

Philip C. McGuire, "On the Dancing in *Romeo and Juliet*," *Ren&R* 5 (May 1981): 87–97.

Waldo F. McNeir, "The Closing of the Capulet Tomb," *SN* 28 (1956): 3–8.

Waldo F. McNeir, "Shakespeare, *Romeo and Juliet*, III, I, 40–44," *Expl* 11 (May 1953): 48.

Milton Mark, *The Enjoyment of Drama*, 103–05.

Edgar Martner, "'Conceit Brags of His Substance, Not of Ornament': Some Notes on Style in *Romeo and Juliet*," in Fabian and von Rosador, *Shakespeare: Text, Language, Criticism*, 180–92.

Thomas Moisan, "'O Any Thing, of Nothing, First Create!': Gender and Patriarchy and the Tragedy of *Romeo and Juliet*," in Kehler and Baker, *In Another Country*, 113–36.

Thomas Moisan, "Rhetoric and the Rehearsal of Death: The 'Lamentations' Scene in *Romeo and Juliet*," *SQ* 34 (Autumn 1983): 389–404.

Thomas Moisan, "Shakespeare's Chaucerian Allegory: The Quest for Death in *Romeo and Juliet* and the *Pardoner's Tale*," in Donaldson and Kollmann, *Chaucerin Shakespeare: Adaptation and Transformation*, 131–49.

Henry A. Myers, "*Romeo and Juliet* and *A Midsummer Night's Dream*: Tragedy and Comedy," in *Tragedy*, 110–28. Reprinted in Barnet, *Aspects of the Drama*, 35–43.

A. K. Nardo, "*Romeo and Juliet* Up against the Wall," *Paunch* 48–49 (1977): 126–32.

Nicholl, *The Chemical Theatre*, 72–73.

J. M. Nosworthy, "The Two Angry Families of Verona," *SQ* 3 (July 1952): 219–26.

W. J. Olive, "Twenty Good Nights," *SP* 47 (April 1950): 180–89.

Avraham Oz, "What's in a Good Name? The Case of *Romeo and Juliet* as a Bad Tragedy," in Charney, *"Bad" Shakespeare*, 133–42.

Philip Parsons, "Shakespeare and the Mask," *ShS* 16 (1963): 124–31.

Douglas L Peterson, "*Romeo and Juliet* and the Art of Moral Navigation," in McNeir and Greenfield, *Pacific Coast Studies in Shakespeare*, 33–46.

E. C. Pettet, "The Imagery of *Romeo and Juliet*," *English* 8 (Autumn 1950): 121–26.

Praz, *The Flaming Heart*, 157–60.

Prior, *The Language of Tragedy*, 61–73.

Irving Ribner, "'Then Denie you Starres': A Reading of *Romeo and Juliet*," in Bennett, Cargill, and Hall, *Studies in the English Renaissance Drama*, 269–86.

Edward W. Rosenheim, Jr., *What Happens in Literature* (Chicago: University of Chicago Press, 1961), 97–108.

Ross, *Philosophy in Literature*, 255–63.

Annette T. Rottenberg, "The Early Love Drama," *CE* 23 (April 1962): 579–82.

Martha Tuck Rozett, "The Comic Structures of Tragic Endings: The Suicide Scenes in *Romeo and Juliet* and *Antony and Cleopatra*," *SQ* 36 (Summer 1985): 152–64.

Kiernan Ryan, "*Romeo and Juliet*: The Language of Tragedy," in *The Taming of the Text: Exploration in Language and Culture*, ed. Willie vam Peer (London: Routledge, 1988), 106–21.

Joseph Satin, "*Romeo and Juliet* as Renaissance *Vita Nuova*," *Discourse* 3 (April 1960): 67–85.

Ernest Schanzer, "Atavism and Anticipation in Shakespeare's Style," *EIC* 7 (July 1957): 244–45.

Stephen Shapiro, "*Romeo and Juliet*: Reversals, Contraries," *CE* 25 (April 1964): 498–501.

Shaw, *Plays and Players*, 41–49.

Paul N. Siegel, "Christianity and the Religion of Love in *Romeo and Juliet*," *SQ* (Autumn 1961): 371–92.

Gunnar Sjogren, " 'Sirrah, Go Hire Me Twenty Cunning Crooks,' " *SQ* 12 (Spring 1961): 161–63.

Ann Pasternak Slater, "Petrarchanism Come True in *Romeo and Juliet*; Proceedings of Third Congress of International Shakespeare Association," in Habicht, Palmer, and Pringle, *Images of Shakespeare*, 129–50.

R. L. Smallwood, "*Romeo and Juliet* V.iii.107–08," *SQ* 26 (Autumn 1975): 298–99.

R. L. Smallwood, " '*Tis Pity She's a Whore* and *Romeo and Juliet*," *CahiersE* 20 (October 1981): 49–70.

Hallett Smith, "The Poetry of the Lyric Group: *Richard II*, *Romeo and Juliet*, *A Midsummer Night's Dream*," in Highfill, *Shakespeare's Craft*, 69–93.

James C. Smith, "Ptolemy and Shakespeare: The Astrological Influences of *Romeo and Juliet*," *SPWVSRA* 7 (1982): 66–70.

Smith, *Dualities in Shakespeare*, 79–109.

Robert Matcalf Smith, "Three Interpretations of *Romeo and Juliet*," *ShAB* 23 (April 1948): 60–77.

Warren Smith. "Romeo's Final Dream," *MLR* 62 (March 1967): 79–83.

Edward Snow, "Language and Sexual Difference in *Romeo and Juliet*," in Erickson and Kahn, *Shakespeare's 'Rough Magic*,' 168–92.

Theodore Spencer, "The Isolation of the Shakespearean Hero," *SR* 52 (July/Sept 1944): 315–16.

R. Stamm, "The First Meeting of the Lovers in Shakespeare's *Romeo and Juliet*," *ES* 67 (February 1986): 2–13.

R. Stamm, "The Orxhard Scene (II.ii) in Shakespeare's *Romeo and Juliet* Revisited: A Study in Dramatic Configuration; Festschrift fur Siegfried Korninger," in Rauchbauer, *A Yearbook of Studies in English Language and Literature 1985/86*, 237–48.

Marilyn Stewart, "Myth and Tragic Action in *La Celestina* and *Romeo and Juliet*," in *The Existential Coordinates of the Human Condition: Poetic—Epic—Tragic: The Literary Genre*, ed. Anna-Teresa Tymieniecka (Dordrecht: Reidel, 1984), 425–33.

J. L. Styan, *The Dark Comedy* (Cambridge: Cambridge University Press, 1962), 18–20.

Styan, *The Elements of Drama*, 25–26, 66–67, 70–72, 129–30, 233–34.

Wylie Sypher, "Romeo and Juliet Are Dead: Melodrama of the Clinical," *NYLF* 7 (1980): 179–86.

G. Thomas Tanselle, "Time in *Romeo and Juliet*," *SQ* 15 (Autumn 1964): 349–62.

Geoffrey Thomas, *The Theatre Alive*, 161–63.

Sidney Thomas, "*Romeo and Juliet*, IV.i.83," *SQ* 28 (Winter 1977): 524–25.

William B. Toole, "The Nurse's 'Vast Irrelevance': Thematic Foreshadowing in *Romeo and Juliet*," *SAB* 45 (January 1980): 21–30.

Alison Wall, "The Feud and Shakespeare's *Romeo and Juliet*: A Reconsideration," *SSEng* 5 (1979–80): 84–95.

Nathaniel Wallace, "Cultural Tropology in *Romeo and Juliet*," *SP* 88 (Summer 1991): 329–44.

Stanley Wells, "Juliet's Nurse: The Uses of Inconsequentiality," in Edwards, Ewbank, and Howard, *Shakespeare's Styles*, 51–66.

Gayle Whittier, "The Sonnet's Body and the Body Sonnetized in *Romeo and Juliet*," *SQ* 40 (Spring 1989): 27–41.

Wiggins, *Journeyman in Murder*, 149–52.

George Walton Williams, "A Note on *Romeo and Juliet*," *N&Q* 207 (September 1962): 181–82.

Philip Williams, Jr., "The Rosemary Theme in *Romeo and Juliet*," *MLN* 195 (April 1953): 400–03.

Bruce W. Young, "Haste, Consent, and Age at Marriage: Some Implications of Social History for *Romeo and Juliet*," *ISJR* 62 (December 1988): 459–74.

Young, *Immortal Shadows*, 25–28.

Calin Zarojanu, "A Mathematical-Linguistic Approach to Shakespeare's *Romeo and Juliet*," *RPL* 26 (January–June 1981): 65–78.

Sir Thomas More
(with Munday)

Louis Marder, "Stylometry 'Proves' Entire 'Sir Thomas More' is All Shakespeare's," *ShN* 30 (September 1980): 29–30.

Thomas Merriam, "The Authorship of *Sir Thomas More*," *ALLCB* 10 (March 1982): 1–7.

G. Harold Metz, "Stylometric Analysis and *Sir Thomas More*," *ShN* 31 (February 1981): 6.

Paul Ramsey, "The Literary Evidence for Shakespeare as Hand D in the Manuscript Play *Sir Thomas More*: A Re-Re-Reconsideration," *UCrow* 11 (1991): 131–55.

George T. Wright, "Can *Sir Thomas More* Be By Shakespeare?" *Moreana* 19 (December 1982): 89–90.

The Taming of the Shrew

Stuart E. Baker, "Masks and Faces in *The Taming of the Shrew*," *NETJ* 1, no. 1 (1990): 45–59.

Bamborough, *The Little World of Man*, 68–69.

Tita French Baumlin, "Petruchio the Sophist and Language as Creation in *The Taming of the Shrew*," *SEL* 29 (Spring 1989): 237–57.

John C. Bean, "Comic Structure and the Humanizing of Kate in *The Taming of the Shrew*," in Lenz, et al., *The Woman's Part*, 65–78.

Peter Berek, "Text, Gender, and Genre in *The Taming of the Shrew*," in Charney, *"Bad" Shakespeare*, 91–104.

Ronald Berman, "Shakespeare Comedy and the Uses of Reason," *SAQ* 63 (Winter 1964): 4–9.

M. C. Bradbrook, "Dramatic Role as Social Image: A Study of *The Taming of the Shrew*," *ShJE* 94 (1958): 132–50.

Charles Brooks, "Shakespeare's Romantic Shrews," *SQ* 11 (Summer 1960): 351–56.

Richard A. Burt, "Charisma, Coercion, and the Comic Form in *The Taming of the Shrew*," *Criticism* 26 (Autumn 1984): 295–311.

Terry Ann Craig, "Petruchio as Exorcist: Shakespeare and Elizabethan Demonology," *SPWVSRA* 3 (1978): 1–7.

George Cheatham, "Imagination, Madness, and Magic: *The Taming of the Shrew* as Romantic Comedy," *ISJR* 59 (November 1985): 221–32.

George Cheatham, "Shakespeare's *The Taming of the Shrew*," *Expl* 42 (Spring 1984): 12.

Marilyn M. Cooper, "Implicature, Convention, and *The Taming of the Shrew*," *Poetics* 10 (February 1981): 1–14.

Marvin Felheim, and Philip Traci, Realism in *The Taming of the Shrew*," *Interpretations* 12 (March 1980): 100–13.

Fineman, *The Subjectivity Effect*, 120–42.

Charles R. Forker, "Immediacy and Remoteness in *The Taming of the Shrew* and *The Tempest*," in Kay and Jacobs, *Shakespeare's Romances Reconsidered*, 134–48.

French, *Shakespeare's Division of Experience*, 76–80.

Bryan A. Garner, "Shakespeare's *The Taming of the Shrew*, V.ii.54," *Expl* 41 (Spring 1983): 16–17.

Shirley Nelson Garner, "*The Taming of the Shrew*: Inside or Outside the Joke?" in Charney, *"Bad" Shakespeare*, 105–19.

Hager, *Shakespeare's Political Animal*, 127–34.

Joan Hatrwig, "Horses and Women in *The Taming of the Shrew*," *HLQ* 45 (February 1982): 285–94.

Carol F. Heffernan, "*The Taming of the Shrew*: The Bourgeoisie in Love," *ELWIU* 12 (Spring 1985): 3–14.

Robert B. Heilman, "The *Taming* Untamed, or, The Return of the Shrew," *MLQ* 27 (June 1966): 147–61.

SHAKESPEARE, WILLIAM, *The Taming of the Shrew*

Hibbard, *Making of Shakespeare's Dramatic Poetry*, 96–99.

Richard Hosley, "Was There a 'Dramatic Epilogue' to *The Taming of the Shrew*?" *SEL* 1 (Spring 1961): 17–34.

Raymond A. Houk, "Shakespeare's Heroic Shrew," *ShAB* 18 (October 1943): 175–86.

Raymond A. Houk, "Strata in *The Taming of the Shrew*," *SP* 39 (April 1942): 291–302.

J. Dennis Huston, "'To Make a Puppet': Play and Play-Making in *The Taming of the Shrew*," *ShakS* 9 (1976): 73–88.

Jackson, *This Is Love?*, 26–31.

Margaret Jones-Davies, "The Disfiguring Power of Figures in *The Taming of the Shrew*," *SGG* 21 (1980–1981): 223–31.

Coppelia Kahn, "*The Taming of the Shrew*: Shakespeare's Mirror of Marriage," *MLS* 5 (Spring 1975): 88–102.

Carolyn Kane, "'Household Government' and *The Taming of the Shrew*," *PAPA* 15 (April 1989): 37–47.

Dorothea Kehler, "Echoes of the Induction in *The Taming of the Shrew*," *RenP 1985* (1986): 31–42.

Randall Martin, "Kates for the Table of the Mind: A Social Metaphor in *The Taming of the Shrew*," *ESC* 17 (Spring 1991): 1–20.

James P. McGlone, "Shakespeare's Intent in *The Taming of the Shrew*," *WasnanaR* 13 (Fall 1978): 79–88.

Margaret Lael Mikesell, "'Love Wrought These Miracles': Marriage and Genre in *The Taming of the Shrew*," *RenD* 20 (1989): 141–67.

Newman, *Fashioning Femininty*, 35–50.

Karen Newman, "Renaissance Family Politics and Shakespeare's *The Taming of the Shrew*," *ELR* 16 (Spring 1986): 86–100.

Marianne L. Novy, "Patriarchy and Play in *The Taming of the Shrew*," *ELR* 9 (Summer 1979): 264–80.

L. E. Orange, "The Punning of *The Shrew*," *SoQ* 3 (October 1965): 295–98.

Velvet D. Pearson, "In Search of a Liberated Kate in *The Taming of the Shrew*," *RMRLL* 44, no. 3 (1990): 229–42.

Marion Perret, "'A Hair of the Shrew . . .,'" *HSL* 11, no. 1 (1979): 36–40.

Marion Perret, "Of Sows' Ears and Silk Purses: Transformation Images in *The Taming of the Shrew*," *ISJR* 54 (May 1980): 431–39.

Robert A. Ravich, "A Psychoanalytic Study of Shakespeare's Early Plays," *Psychoanalytic Quarterly* 33 (July 1964): 399–400.

Robert A. Ravich, "Shakespeare and Psychiatry," *L&P* 14 (Summer/Fall 1964): 102.

Irving Ribner, "Morality of Farce: *The Taming of the Shrew*," in *Essays in American and English Literature Presented to Bruce Robert McElderry, Jr.*, ed. Max F. Schluz, William D. Templeman, and Charles R. Metzger (Athens: Ohio University Press, 1968), 165–76.

Jeanne Addison Roberts, "Horses and Hermaphrodites: Metamorphoses in *The Taming of the Shrew*," *SQ* 34 (Spring 1983): 159–71).

Niall Rudd, "*The Taming of the Shrew*: Notes on Some Classical Allusions," *Hermathena* 129 (Winter 1980): 23–28.

Norman Sanders, "Themes and Imagery in *The Taming of the Shrew*," *RenP 1962* (1963): 63–72.

C. C. Seronsy, "'Supposes' as the Unifying Theme in *The Shrew*," *SQ* 14 (Winter 1963): 15–30.

John W. Shroeder, "*The Taming of a Shrew* and *The Taming of the Shrew*: A Case Reopened," *JEGP* 57 (July 1958): 424–43.

Michael W. Shurgot, "From Fiction to Reality: Character and Stagecraft in *The Taming of the Shrew*," *TJ* 33 (October 1981): 327–40.

Camille Wells Slights, "The Raw and the Cooked in *The Taming of the Shrew*," *JEGP* 88 (April 1989): 168–89.

B. J. Sokol, "A Spenserian Idea in *The Taming of the Shrew*," *ES* 66 (1985): 310–16.

George C. Taylor, "Two Notes on Shakespeare," in Maxwell, *Renaissance Studies in Honor of Hardin Craig*, 181–84.

Sidney Thomas, "Note on *The Taming of the Shrew*," *MLN* 64 (February 1949): 94–96.

W. B. Thorne, "Folk Elements in *The Taming of the Shrew*," *QQ* 75 (Spring 1968): 482–96.

E. M. W. Tillyard, "Some Consequences of a Lacuna in *The Taming of the Shrew*," *ES* 43 (October 1962): 330–35.

E. M. W. Tillyard, "The Fairy-Tale Elements in *The Taming of the Shrew*," in Bloom, *Shakespeare 1564–1964*, 101–14.

Sybil Truchet, "A Sacramental Reading of *The Taming of the Shrew*," in *Aspects du théâtre anglais (1594–1730)*, ed. Nadia Rigaud (Aix-en-Provence: Université de Provence, 1987), 1–10.

Stanley Well, and Gary Taylor, "No Shrew, A Shrew, and The Shrew: Internal Revision in *The Taming of the Shrew*," in Fabian and von Rosador, *Shakespeare: Text, Language, Criticism*, 351–79.

The Tempest

K. M. Abenheimer, "Shakespeare's *Tempest*—A Psychological Analysis," *Psychoanalytic Review* 33 (October 1946): 399–415.

Richard Adams, "*The Tempest* and the Concept of the Machiavellian Playwright," *ELR* 8 (Spring 1978): 43–66.

Don Cameron Allen, *Image and Meaning* (Baltimore: Johns Hopkins University Press, 1960), 42–66.

A. A. Ansari, "The Ambivalence of Caliban," *AJES* 1 (July 1975): 228–43.

Alex Aronson, "A Note on Shakespeare's Dream Imagery," *Visuabharati Quarterly* 18 (August–October 1952): 168–69.

Arthos, *Shakespeare's Use of Drama and Vision*, 173–99.

Wallace A. Bacon, "A Note on *The Tempest*, IV, I," *N&Q* 192 (August 1947): 343–44.

Francis Barker, and Peter Hulme, "Nymphs and Reapers Heavily Vanish: The Discursive Con-Texts of *The Tempest*," in Drakakis, *Alternative Shakespeares*, 191–205.

Walter J. Bate, *From Classic to Romantic* (New York: Harper & Row, 1946), 124–25.

Bernard Baum, "*The Tempest* and *The Hairy Ape*: The Literary Incarnation of Mythos," *MLQ* 14 (September 1953): 258–73.

Ellen R. Belton, "'When No Man Was His Own': Magic and Self-Discovery in *The Tempest*," *UTQ* 55 (Winter 1985–1986): 127–40.

Karol Berger, "Prospero's Art," *ShakS* 10 (1977): 211–39.

David M. Bergeron, "The Tempest/*The Tempest*," *ELWIU* 7 (Spring 1980): 3–9.

Edward I. Berry, "Prospero's 'Brave Spirit,'" *SP* 76 (Winter 1979): 36–48.

Berry, *Poet's Grammar*, 76–78.

Francis Berry, "Shakespeare's Directive to the Player of Caliban," *N&Q* 202 (March 1957): 27.

Ralph P. Boas, "Shakespeare's *The Tempest*, V, I, 181–184," *Expl* 2 (October 1943): 3.

Ronald B. Bond, "Labour, Ease, and *The Tempest* as Pastoral Romance," *JEGP* 77 (October 1978): 330–42.

H. E. Bowen, "'I'll Break My Staff . . . I'll Drown My Book,'" *RenP 1960* (1961): 47–56.

Lawrence E. Bowling, "The Theme of Natural Order in *The Tempest*," *CE* 12 (January 1951): 203–09.

David G. Brailow, "Prospero's 'Old Brain': The Old Man as Metaphor in the *Tempest*," *ShakS* 14 (1981): 285–303.

Curt Breight, "'Treason Doth Never Prosper': *The Tempest* and the Discourse of Treason," *SQ* 41 (Winter 1990): 1–28.

Brockbank, *On Shakespeare*, 303–40.

Philip Brockbank, "*The Tempest*: Conventions of Art and Empire," in Brown and Harris, *Later Shakespeare*, 183–202.

Reuben A. Brower, *The Fields of Light* (New York: Oxford University Press, 1951), 13–14, 95–122, 210–15.

Reuben A. Brower, "The Heresy of Plot," *English Institute Essays* (1951): 62–69.

J. R. Brown, "A Study of *The Tempest*," *ShN* 4 (December 1954): 49.

Paul Brown, "'This Thing of Darkness I Acknowledge Mine': The Tempest and the Discourse of Colonialism," in Dollimore and Sinfield, *Political Shakespeare*, 48–71.

Diana Brydon, "Re-Writing *The Tempest*," *WLWE* 23 (Winter 1984): 75–88.

Bullough, *Mirror of Minds*, 87–89.

Marray W. Bundy, "The Allegory of *The Tempest*," *WCSC* 32 (September 1964): 189–206.

A. S. Cairncross, "*The Tempest*, 3, I, 15 and *Romeo and Juliet*, 1, I, 121–128," *SQ* 7 (December 1956): 448–50.

Paul A. Cantor, "Propero's Republic: The Politics of Shakespeare's *The Tempest*," in Alvis and West, *Shakespeare as Political Thinker*, 239–55.

Paul A. Cantor, "Shakespeare's *The Tempest*: The Wise Man as Hero," *SQ* 31 (Winter 1980): 64–75.

Carroll Camden, "Songs and Choruses in *The Tempest*," *PQ* 41 (January 1962): 114–22.

Diljit K. Chatha, "Major Aspects of Shakespeare's Artistry in *The Tempest*," *CLAJ* 22 (September 1979): 254–63.

B. D. Cheadle, "Prospero and the Dream of Bounty," *ESA* 20, no.1 (1977): 53–61.

David R. Clark, "*Ecclesiasticus* and Prospero's Epilogue," *SQ* 17 (Winter 1966): 79–81.

Clemen, *Shakespeare's Dramatic Art*, 140–45.

Hardin Craig, "Magic in *The Tempest*," *PQ* 47 (Winter 1968): 8–15.

Hardin Craig, "Prospero's Renunciation," *ShN* 3 (April 1953): 13.

David Z. Crookes, "Shakespeare's *The Tempest*, III.iii.95–102," *Expl* 40 (Fall 1981): 14.

John P. Cutts, "The Role of Music in *The Tempest*," *ShN* 9 (February 1959): 4.

D'Amico, *The Moor in English Renaissance Drama*, 197–211.

Clifford Davidson, "Ariel and the Magic of Prospero in *The Tempest*," *SUS* 10 (1978): 229–37.

Clifford Davidson, "The Masque within *The Tempest*," *NDEJ* 10 (Spring 1976): 12–17.

Frank Davidson, "*The Tempest*: An Interpretation," *JEGP* 62 (July 1963): 501–17.

Dawson, *Indirections*, 156–71.

Margreta De Grazia, "*The Tempest*: Gratuitous Movement or Action without Kibes and Pinches," *ShakS* 14 (1981): 249–65.

E. J. Devereux, "Sacramental Imagery in *The Tempest*," *HAB* 19 (Spring 1968): 50–62.

Bonamy Dobree, "*The Tempest*," *E&S* 5 (1952): 13–25.

E. Sue Doss, "Humanity Is Enough," *UCrow* 1 (1978): 64–68.

J. W. Draper, "Humor and Tempo in *The Tempest*,'" *NM* 52, no. 7–8 (1951): 205–17.

J. W. Draper, "'Indian' and 'Indies' in Shakespeare," *NM* 56, no. 3–4 (1955): 107–12.

James P. Driscoll, "The Shakespearean Metastance: The Perspective of *The Tempest*," *BuR* 25, no. 1 (1980): 154–69.

Tom F. Driver, "The Shakespearean Clock: Time and the Vision of Reality in *Romeo and Juliet* and *The Tempest*," *SQ* 15 (Autumn 1964): 363–64, 367–70.

Eagleton, *Shakespeare and Society*, 155–69.

Darlene Mathis Eddy, "The Brave Diligence: The Harmonies of *The Tempest*," *BSUF* 16 (Autumn 1975): 12–25.

Egan, *Drama within Drama*, 90–119.

Harry Epstein, "The Divine Comedy of *The Tempest*," *ShakS* 8 (1975): 279–96.

Barbara L. Estrin, "Telling the Magician from the Magic in *The Tempest*," *BuR* 25, no. 1 (1980): 170–87.

John T. Fain, "Ariel's Song," *ShN* 4 (December 1954): 50.

Ian Ferguson, "Contradictory Natures: The Function of Prospero, His Agent and His Slave in *The Tempest*," *JDECU* 28 (September 1990): 1–9.

L. T. Fitz, "The Vocabulary of the Environment in *The Tempest*," *SQ* 26 (Winter 1975): 42–47.

Karen Flagstad, "'Making This Place Paradise': Prospero and the Problem of Caliban in *The Tempest*," *ShakS* 18 (1986): 205–33.

R. F. Fleissner, "The Endgame in *The Tempest*," *PLL* 21 (Summer 1985): 331–35.

R. F. Fleissner, "On Fetching Caliban's 'Young Scamels,'" *SUS* 10 (1978): 169–72.

M. K. Flint, and E. J. Dobson, "Weak Masters," *RES* 10 (February 1959): 58–60.

Foakes, *Shakespeare*, 144–72.

Charles O. Fox, "A Crux in *The Tempest*," *N&Q* 202 (December 1957): 515–16.

French, *Shakespeare's Division of Experience*, 319–30.

Timothy Fuller, "Temporal Royalties and Virtue's Airy Voice in *The Tempest*," *IJPP* 11 (Winter 1983): 207–24.

Robert C. Fulton, III, "*The Tempest* and the Bermuda Pamphlets: Source and Thematic Intention," *Interpretations* 10 (March 1978): 1–10.

Barry Gaines, and Michael Lofaro, "What Did Caliban Look Like?" *MissFR* 10, no. 2 (1976): 175–86.

Sand M. Gamal, "The Function of Song in Shakespeare's Comedies," *CairoSE* (1961–1962): 120.

Marjorie Garber, "The Eye of the Storm: Structure and Myth in Shakespeare's *Tempest*," *HUSL* 8 (1980): 13–43.

Judith K. Gardiner, "Shakespeare's *The Tempest* IV.i.76–82 (Iris and Hymen)," *Expl* 35 (Fall 1977): 19–20.

Stanton B. Garner, Jr., "*The Tempest*: Language and Society," *ShS* 32 (1979): 177–87.

Carol Gesrier, "*The Tempest* as Pastoral Romance," *SQ* 10 (Autumn 1959): 531–39.

Christopher Gillie, "*The Tempest*," *The Use of English* 7 (Autumn 1955): 37–41.

Ernest B. Gilman, "'All Eyes': Prospero's Inverted Masque," *RenQ* 33 (1980): 214–30.

Harold C. Goddard, "The Meaning of the *Tempest*," in *The Creative Reader*, ed. Robert W. Stallman and R. E. Walters (New York: Ronald, 1954), 633–42.

E. Gohn, "*The Tempest*: Theme and Structure," *ES* 45 (April 1964): 116–25.

R. A. D. Grant, "Providence, Authority, and the Moral Life in *The Tempest*," *ShakS* 16 (1983): 235–63.

Gayle Greene, "'Excellent Dumb Discourse': Silence and Grace in Shakespeare's *Tempest*," *SN* 50, no.2 (1978): 193–205.

Gayle Green, "Margaret Laurence's *Diviners* and Shakespeare's *Tempest*: The Uses of the Past," in Novy, *Women's Re-Visions of Shakespeare*, 165–82.

Robin Grove, "A New Master, a New Man in *The Tempest*," *CR* 18 (1976): 101–13.

Grudin, *Mighty Opposites*, 185–211.

Robert Grudin, "Prospero's Masque and the Structure of *The Tempest*," *SAQ* 71 (Autumn 1972): 401–09.

Hager, *Shakespeare's Political Animal*, 127–34.

Grace R. W. Hall, "The Enigmatical 'Third' in Shakespeare's *The Tempest*," *Selected Proceedings from the Northeast Regional Conference on Christianity and Literature* 2 (1990): 48–51.

John E. Hankins, "Caliban the Beastial Man," *PMLA* 62 (September 1947): 793–801.

Abby Jane Dubman Hansen, "Shakespeare's *The Tempest* (Coral in Full Fadom Five)," *Expl* 35 (Fall 1977): 19–20.

P. G. Harris, "A Temperate in a Torrid Zone," *Makerere Journal* 1 (1958): 55–71.

G. B. Harrison, "*The Tempest*," *Stratford Papers on Shakespeare* 3 (1962): 212–38.

Thomas P. Harrison, Sr., "The 'Broom-Groves' in *The Tempest*," *ShAB* 20 (January 1945): 39–45.

Thomas P. Harrison, Sr., "A Note on *The Tempest*: A Sequel," *MLN* 58 (June 1943): 422–26.

Jeffrey P. Hart, "Prospero and Faustus," *BUSE* 2 (Winter 1956): 197–206.

Geoffrey H. Hartman, *Criticism in the Wilderness* (New Haven and London: Yale University Press, 1980), 96–98.

Hawkes, *Shakespeare's Talking Animals*, 194–212.

Hawkins, *Likeness of Truth in Elizabethan and Restoration Drama*, 1–3, 7–9, 27–29, 38–48, 56–57.

Agnes Heller, "Shakespeare and Human Nature," *New Hungarian Quarterly* 5 (Spring 1964): 20–21.

Richard H. Henze, "*The Tempest*: Rejection of a Vanity," *SQ* 23 (Autumn 1972): 420–34.

C. Hilberry, "*The Tempest*, Act IV," *CE* 23 (April 1962): 586–88.

Richard Hillman, "Chaucer's Frankiln's Magician and *The Tempest*: An Influence beyond Appearances?" *SQ* 34 (Autumn 1983): 426–32.

Richard Hillman, "*The Tempest* as Romance and Anti-Romance," *UTQ* 55 (Winter 1985–1986): 141–60.

F. D. Hoeniger, "Prospero's Storm and Miracle," *SQ* 7 (Winter 1956): 33–38.

Masao Hondo, "The Meaning of Magic and Masque in *The Tempest*," in Milward and Anzai, *Poetry and Drama in the Age of Shakespeare*, 167–83.

Edwin Honig, *Dark Conceit—The Making of Allegory* (Evanston, IL: Northwestern University Press, 1959), 37–38.

Hoy, *The Hyacinth Room*, 273–81.

Maurice Hunt, "'The Backward Voice': Puns and the Comic Subplot of *The Tempest*," *MLS* 12 (Fall 1982): 64–74.

Maurice Hunt, "Contrary Comparisons in *The Tempest*," *BuR* 25, no. 1 (1980): 132–41.

Eleanor N. Hutchens, "The Transfer of Power in *King Lear* and *The Tempest*," *REL* 4 (April 1963): 82–93.

W. Stacy Johnson, "The Genesis of Ariel" *SQ* 2 (July 1951): 205–10.

H. W. Jones, "*The Tempest*, I, I, 13–17," *N&Q* 195 (July 1950): 293–94.

Kastan, *Shakespeare and the Shapes of Time*, 141–44.

Dennis C. Kay, "Ganzalo's 'Lasting Pillars': *The Tempest*," *SQ* 35 (Summer 1984): 322–24.

Alvin Kernan, "Meaning and Emptiness in *King Lear* and *The Tempest*," *RenD* 18 (1987): 225–36.

G. Wilson Knight, "Caliban as Red Man," in Edwards, Ewbank, and Howard, *Shakespeare's Styles*, 205–20.

Knight, *The Crown of Life*, 203–55.

Knight, *The Golden Labyrinth*, 83–85, 126–28, 348–49.

Knight, *The Olive and the Sword*, 65–68.

G. W. Knight, "On the Mystic Symbolism of Shakespeare," *Aryan Path* 35 (October 1964): 458.

Knight, *The Sovereign Flower*, 69–73.

Bernard Knox, "*The Tempest* and the Ancient Comic Tradition," *English Institute Essays* (1954): 52–73. Reprinted in *VQR* 31 (Winter 1955): 73–89.

Peter Knox-Shaw, "'The Man in the Island': Shakespeare's Concern with Projection in *The Tempest*," *Theoria* 61 (October 1983): 23–36.

Helge Kokeritz, "The Pole-Clipt Vineyard, *The Tempest*, IV, I, 68," *MLR* 39 (April 1944): 178–79.

E. P. Kuhl, "Shakespeare and the Founders of America: *The Tempest*," *PQ* 41 (January 1962): 123–46.

Earle Labor, and Lorelle Bender, "Mandala Symbolism in *The Tempest*," *ShN* 37 (Fall 1987): 32.

Fred Langman, "An Approach to *The Tempest*," *SSEng* 2 (1976–77): 24–37.

François Laroque, "*Othello, The Tempest* and the Grotesque," *Cycnos* 5 (1989): 45–62.

Jacqueline E. M. Latham, "The Magic Banquet in *The Tempest*," *ShakS* 12 (1979): 215–27.

Jaqueline E. M. Latham, "*The Tempest* and King James's Daemonologie," *ShS* 28 (1975): 117–23.

Martha Laurent, "Shakespeare's *The Tempest*, V, I, 134–148," *Expl* 22 (April 1964): 65.

Clifford Leech, "Shakespeare's Comic Dukes," *REL* 5 (April 1964): 113–14.

Lorie Jerrell Leininger, "Cracking the Code of *The Tempest*," *BuR* 25, no. 1 (1980): 121–31.

Lorie Jerrell Leininger, "The Miranda Trap: Sexism and Racism in Shakespeare's *Tempest*," in Lenz, et al., *The Woman's Part*, 285–94.

John LeVay, "Shakespeare's *The Tempest*," *Expl* 46 (Summer 1988): 9–11.

Richard Levin, "Anatomical Geography in *The Tempest*, IV. I. 235–238," *N&Q* 209 (April 1964): 142–46.

Mary Loeffelholz, "Miranda in the New World: *The Tempest* and Charlotte Barnes's *The Forest Princess*," in Novy, *Women's Re-Visions of Shakespeare*, 58–75.

Mary Loeffelholz, "Two Masques of Ceres and Proserpine: *Comus* and *The Tempest*," in *Re-Membering Milton: Essays on the Texts and Traditions*, ed. Mary Nyquist and Margaret W. Ferguson (New York: Methuen, 1987), 35–42.

John R. Long, "The Dramatic Functions of the Music in *The Tempest*," *ShN* 2 (March/April 1952): 11.

Joseph A. Longo, "Prospero and Miranda: The Dialectics of Change in *The Tempest*," *UCrow* 2 (1979): 74–83.

Leo Lowenthal, *Literature and the Image of Man—Sociological Studies in the European Drama and Novel* (Boston: Beacon, 1957), 57–97, 221–29.

Maxwell S. Luria, "Standing Water and Sloth in *The Tempest*," *ES* 49 (1968): 328–31.

William G. Madsen, "The Destiny of Man in *The Tempest*," *EUQ* 20 (Fall 1964): 175–82.

A. Lynne Magnusson, "Interruption in *The Tempest*," *SQ* 37 (Winter 1986): 52–65.

John M. Major, "*Comus* and *The Tempest*," *SQ* 10 (Spring 1959): 177–84.

Mann, *The Elizabethan Player*, 41–42.

SHAKESPEARE, WILLIAM, *The Tempest*

Leo Marx, "Shakespeare's American Fable," *MR* 2 (Autumn 1960): 40–71.

Katherine Eisaman Maus, "Arcadia Lost: Politics and Revision in *The Tempest*," *RenD* 13 (1982): 189–209.

Russ McDonald, "Reading *The Tempest*," *ShS* 43 (1991): 15–28.

D. S. McGovern, "'Tempus' in *The Tempest*," *English* 32 (Summer 1983): 201–14.

Jerry L. McGuire, "Shakespeare's *Tempest*: Rhetoric and Poetics," *AI* 39 (Summer 1982): 219–37.

James A. McPeek, "The Genesis of Caliban," *PQ* 25 (October 1946): 378–81.

Barbara Melchiori, "Still Harping on My Daughter," *EM* 11 (1960): 65–72.

Stephen Merton, "*The Tempest* and *Troilus and Cressida*," *CE* 7 (December 1945): 143–50.

Peter Milward, "Gonzalo's 'Merry Fooling,'" *ShStud* 11 (1972–73): 28–36.

Lee Mitchell, "Shakespeare's Legerdemain," *Speech Monographs* 16 (August 1949): 144–50, 152–53, 157–61.

Lee Mitchell, "Two Notes on *The Tempest*," *ETJ* 2 (October 1950): 228–34.

Michael Neill, "Rememberance and Revenge: *Hamlet, Macbeth* and *The Tempest*," in Donaldson, *Jonson and Shakespeare*, 35–56.

Nelson, *Play Within a Play*, 30–34.

Nicholl, *The Chemical Theatre*, 238–39.

John Northam, "Waiting for Prospero," in Axton and Williams, *English Drama*, 188–202.

Frances St. Anne O'Keefe, "Caliban's Dream: *Kainos* and *Kairos* in *The Tempest*," *ABR* 19 (September 1968): 370–85.

Stephen K. Orgel, "New Uses of Adversity: Tragic Experience in *The Tempest*," in Bower, *In Defense of Reading*, 110–32.

Stephen Orgel, "Prospero's Wife," in Greenblatt, *Representing the English Renaissance*, 217–29.

Howard Parsons, "Further Emendations in *The Tempest*," *N&Q* 195 (February 1950): 74–75.

Howard Parsons, "Further Emendations in *The Tempest*," *N&Q* 196 (February 1951): 54–55.

Howard Parsons, "Shakespeare's *Tempest*: A Further Emendation," *N&Q* 194 (October 1949): 424.

Howard Parsons, "Shakespeare's *Tempest*: An Emendation," *N&Q* 194 (March 1949): 121–22.

Howard Parsons, "Shakespeare's *Tempest*: An Emendation," *N&Q* 194 (July 1949): 303.

Howard Parsons, "*The Tempest*: Further Emendations," *N&Q* 195 (July 1950): 294–95.

Michael Payne, "Magic and Politics in *The Tempest*," in Homan, *Shakespeare and the Triple Play*, 43–57.

Alice Hall Petry, "Knowledge in *The Tempest*," *MLS* 11 (Winter 1980–81): 27–32.

James E. Phillips, "*The Tempest* and the Renaissance Idea of Man," *SQ* 15 (Spring 1964): 147–59. Reprinted in McManaway, *Shakespeare 400*, 147–59.

A. M. Potter, "Possession, Surrender, and Freedom in *The Tempest*," *Theoria* 61 (October 1983): 37–49.

Manas Kumar Ray, "Into Something Rich and Strange: Shakespeare, Shakespeare Criticism, and *The Tempest*," *JDECU* 19, nos. 1–2 (1983–1984): 21–44.

M. M. Reese, "Masters and Men: Some Reflections on *The Tempest*," *AJES* 11 (July 1986): 162–66.

Mary Ellen Rickey, "Prospero's Living Drolleries," *RenP 1963* (1964): 35–42.

Jeanne Addison Roberts, "'Wife' or 'Wise': *The Tempest* 1.1786," *SB* 31 (1978): 203–08.

James E. Robinson, "Time and *The Tempest*," *JEGP* 63 (April 1964): 255–67.

B. W. Rose, "*The Tempest*: A Reconsideration of its Meaning," *ESA* 1 (September 1958): 205–17.

H. Sachs, *The Creative Unconscious* (Cambridge, MA: Science-Art Publishers, 1951), 243–323.

Gary Schmidgall, "The Catastrophe of *The Tempest*," *UCrow* 4 (1982): 61–72.

Gary Schmidgall, "The Discovery at Chess in *The Tempest*," *ELN* 23 (June 1986): 11–16.

I. J. Semper, "Shakespeare's Religion Once More," *Catholic World* 156 (February 1943): 595.

SHAKESPEARE, WILLIAM, *The Tempest*

M. A. Shaaber, "A Living Drollery (*Tempest*, III, iii, 21)," *MLN* 60 (June 1945): 387–91.

Shaw, *Plays and Players*, 275–79.

Percy Simpson, "The Supposed Crux in *The Tempest*," *RES* 22 (July 1946): 224–25.

Clifford Siskin, "Freedom and Loss in *The Tempest*," *ShS* 30 (1977): 147–55.

C. J. Sisson, "The Magic of Prospero," *ShS* 11 (1958): 70–77.

Meredith Anne Skura, "Discourse and the Individual: The Case of Colonialism in *The Tempest*," *SQ* 40 (Winter 1989): 42–69.

George Slover, "Magic, Mystery, and Make-Believe: An Analogical Reading of *The Tempest*," *ShakS* 11 (1978): 175–206.

Smith, *Shakespeare's Romances*, 134–38.

Smith, *Dualities in Shakespeare*, 215–28.

Irwin Smith, "Ariel as Ceres," *SQ* 9 (Summer 1958): 430–32.

Soellner, *Shakespeare's Patterns*, 354–83.

Robert Speaight, "Shakespeare and Politics," *Essays by Divers Hands* 24 (1948): 18–20.

Robert Speaight, "Nature and Grace in *The Tempest*," *Dublin Review* 227 (1953): 28–51.

Theodore Spencer, "The Isolation of the Shakespearean Hero," *SR* 59 (Winter 1951): 67–71.

David Sundelson, "'So rare a wonder'd father': Prospero's *Tempest*," in Schwartz and Kahn, *Representing Shakespeare*, 33–53.

James Sutherland, "How the Characters Talk," in Sutherland and Hurtsfield, *Shakespeare's World*, 116–35.

Ann Thompson, "'Miranda, Where's Your Sister?': Reading Shakespeare's *The Tempest*," in *Feminist Criticism: Theory and Practice*, ed. Susan Sellers, Linda Hutcheon, and Paul Perron (Toronto: University of Toronto Press, 1991), 45–55.

Barbara Tovey, "Shakespeare's Apology for Imitative Poetry: *The Tempest* and *The Republic*," *IJPP* 11 (Summer 1983): 275–316.

Traister, *Heavenly Necromancers*, 125–49.

Derek Traversi, "*The Tempest*," *Scrutiny* 16 (June 1949): 127–57.

Raymond A. Urban, "Why Caliban Worships the Man in the Moon," *SQ* 27 (Spring 1976): 203–05.

Kurt Tetzeli von Rosador, "The Power of Magic: From *Endimion* to *The Tempest*," *ShS* 43 (1991): 1–13.

James Walter, "From *Tempest* to *Epilogue*: Augustine's Allegory in Shakespeare's Drama," *PMLA* 98 (January 1983): 60–76.

Burton J. Weber, "The Ordering of *The Tempest*," *WascanaR* 10 (Summer 1975): 3–20.

West, *The Court and the Castle*, 49–58.

Robert H. West, "Ariel and the Outer Mystery," in Bloom, *Shakespeare 1564–1964*, 115–23.

Glynne Wickham, "Masque and Anti-masque in *The Tempest*," *E&S* 28 (1975): 1–14.

Deborah Willis, "Shakespeare's *Tempest* and the Discourse of Colonialism," *SEL* 29 (Spring 1989): 277–89.

Robert F. Wilson, Jr., "The Boatswain's Rule: The Opening Scene of *The Tempest*," *LWU* 12 (June 1980): 258–66.

H. S. Wilson, "Action and Symbol in *Measure for Measure* and *The Tempest*," *SQ* 4 (October 1953): 381–84.

Neil H. Wright, "Reality and Illusion as a Philosophical Pattern in *The Tempest*," *ShakS* 10 (1977): 241–70.

Paul Yachnin, "Shakespeare and the Idea of Obedience: Gonzalo in *The Tempest*," *Mosaic* 24 (Spring 1991): 1–18.

Alan R. Young, "Prospero's Table: The Name of Shakespeare's Duke of Milan," *SQ* 30 (Autumn 1979): 408–10.

Young, *The Heart's Forest*, 146–91.

David Young, "Where the Bee Sucks: A Triangular Study of *Doctor Faustus*, *The Alchemist*, and *The Tempest*," in Kay and Jacobs, *Shakespeare's Romances Reconsidered*, 149–66.

Young, *Immortal Shadows*, 246–48.

Rose A. Zimbardo, "Form and Disorder in *The Tempest*," *SQ* 14 (Winter 1963): 49–58.

David H. Zucker, "Miranda's Nature and Her Education," *Thoth* 5 (Spring 1964): 55–61.

Timon of Athens

A. A. Ansari, "The Protagonist's Dilemma in *Timon of Athens*," *AJES* 11 (July 1986): 142–61.

Babb, *Elizabethan Malady*, 94–95.

Bamborough, *The Little World of Man*, 18–19, 115–16.

David M. Bergeron, "*Timon of Athens* and Morality Drama," *CLAJ* 10 (March 1967): 81–88.

Berry, *Shakespearean Structures*, 101–19.

William H. Bizley, "Language and Currency in *Timon of Athens*," *Theoria* 44 (February 1975): 21–42.

Lesley W. Brill, "Truth and *Timon of Athens*," *MLQ* 40 (March 1979): 17–36.

Brockbank, *On Shakespeare*, 3–29.

Cartelli, *Marlowe, Shakespeare*, 181–98.

Michael Chorost, "Biological Finance in Shakespeare's *Timon of Athens*," *ELR* 21 (Autumn 1991): 349–70.

A. S. Collins, "*Timon of Athens*: A Reconsideration," *RES* 22 (April 1946): 96–108.

David Cook, "*Timon of Athens*," *ShS* 16 (1963): 83–94.

Clifford Davidson, "*Timon of Athens*: The Iconography of False Friendship," *HLQ* 43 (February 1980): 181–200.

Leo Paul S. DeAlvarez, "*Timon of Athens*" in Alvis and West, *Shakespeare as Political Thinker*, 157–59.

John W. Draper, "Patterns of Tempo in *Timon*," *ShAB* 23 (October 1948): 188–94.

John W. Draper, "Subjective Conflict in Shakespearean Tragedy," *NM* 61, no. 2 (1960): 217.

R. P. Draper, "*Timon of Athens*," *SQ* 8 (Spring 1957): 195–200.

Robert C. Elliott, *The Power of Satire: Magic, Ritual, Art* (Princeton: Princeton University Press, 1960), 141–67, 180–81.

Ellis-Fermor, *Frontiers of Drama*, 74–75.

Una Ellis-Fermor, "*Timon of Athens*: An Unfinished Play," *RES* 18 (July 1942): 270–83.

Avi Erlich, "Neither to Give nor to Receive: Narcissism in *Timon of Athens*," in *CUNY English Forum*, vol. 1, ed. Saul N. Brody and Harold Schechter (New York: AMS, 1985), 215–30.

French, *Shakespeare's Division of Experience*, 279–85.

Robert C. Fulton III, "Timon, Cupid, and the Amazons," *ShakS* 9 (1976): 283–99.

Leonard Goldstein, "Alcibiades' Revolt in *Timon of Athens*," *ZAA* 15, no. 3 (1967): 256–78.

Andor Gomme, "*Timon of Athens*," *EIC* 9 (April 1959): 107–25.

Susan Handelman, "*Timon of Athens*: The Rage of Disillusion," *AI* 36 (Spring 1979): 45–68.

Robert B. Heilman, "From Mine Own Knowledge: A Theme in the Late Tragedies," *CentR* 8 (Winter 1964): 36–39.

Holloway, *The Story of the Night*, 121–23, 131–34.

E. A. Honigmann, "*Timon of Athens*," *SQ* 12 (Winter 1961): 3–20.

Hilda H. Hulme, "Two Notes on the Interpretation of Shakespeare's Text," *N&Q* 204 (October 1959): 354–55.

John Dixon Hunt, "Shakespeare and the Paragone: A Reading of *Timon of Athens*," in Habicht, Palmer, and Pringle, *Images of Shakespeare*, 47–63.

Henry D. Janzen, "Shakespeare's *Timon of Athens* III.vi," *Expl* 36 (Fall 1978): 3–4.

Edward D. Johnson, "*Timon of Athens*," *Baconiana* 30 (October 1946): 158.

Coppelia Kahn, "'Magic of Bounty': *Timon of Athens*, Jacobean Patronage, and Material Power," *SQ* 38 (Winter 1987): 34–57.

Knight, *The Golden Labyrinth*, 78–81, 83–84, 242–46.

Kinght, *The Olive and the Sword*, 48–51.

G. Wilson Knight, "*Timon of Athens* and Buddhism," *EIC* 30 (November 1980): 105–23.

G. Wilson Knight, "The Pilgrimage of Hate: An Essay on *Timon of Athens*," in *The Wheel of Fire*, 207–39.

Knight, *The Sovereign Flower*, 53–57.

G. Wilson Knight, "*Timon of Athens*," *REL* 2 (October 1961): 9–18.

Helge Kokeritz, "Five Shakespeare Notes," *RES* 23 (October 1947): 312–13.

Clifford Leech, "Shakespeare's Greeks," *Stratford Papers on Shakespeare* 4 (1963): 4–8, 15–18.

Ruth Levitsky, "*Timon*: Shakespeare's *Magnyfycence* and an Embryonic *Lear*," *ShakS* 11 (1978): 107–21.

Agostino Lombardo, "The Two Utopias if *Timon of Athens*," *ShJE* 120 (1984): 85–89.

J. C. Maxwell, "*Timon of Athens*," *Scrutiny* 15 (Summer 1948): 195–208.

W. M. Merchant, "*Timon* and the Conceit of Art," *SQ* 6 (Summer 1954): 249–58.

W. M. Merchant, "The Harmony of Disenchantment," *Stratford Papers on Shakespeare* 4 (1963): 117–25.

Ninian Mellsmphy, "Wormwood in the Wood outside Athens: *Timon* and the Problem for the Audience," in Charney, *"Bad" Shakespeare*, 166–75.

Robert S. Miola, "Timon in Shakespeare's Athens," *SQ* 31 (Winter 1980): 21–30.

Minerva Neiditz, "Primary Process Mentation and the Structure of *Timon of Athens*," *HSL* 11, no. 1 (1979): 24–35.

Marianna da Vinci Nichols, "*Timon of Athens* and the Rhetoric of NO," *CahiersE* 9 (April 1965): 29–40.

Winifred M. T. Nowottny, "Acts IV and V of *Timon of Athens*," *SQ* 10 (Autumn 1959): 493–97.

E. C. Pettet, "*Timon of Athens*: The Disruption of Feudal Morality," *RES* 23 (October 1947): 321–36.

Pogson, *In the East*, 78–84.

Fitzroy Pyle, "Hostilius: *Timon of Athens*, III, ii. 70," *N&Q* 197 (February 1952): 48–49.

Jarold W. Ramsey, "Timon's Imitation of Christ," *ShakS* 2 (1966): 167–73.

Daniel W, Ross, "'What a Number of Men Eats Timon': Consumption in *Timon of Athens*," *ISJR* 59 (August 1985): 273–84.

Robert Roth, "Another World of Shakespeare," *MP* 49 (August 1951): 51–57.

John Joseph Ruszkiewicz, "Liberality, Friendship, and *Timon of Athens*," *Thoth* 16, no. 1 (1975–76): 3–17.

John Joseph Ruszkiewicz, "'Traffic's Thy God': Wealth and Rhetoric in *Timon of Athens*," *CCTEP* 51 (September 1986): 20–26.

Paul N. Siegel, "Shakespeare and the Neochivarlric Cult of Honror," *CentR* 8 (Winter 1964): 65–70.

William W. E. Slights, "Genera mixta and *Timon of Athens*," *SP* 74 (1977): 39–62.

M. W. A. Smith, "The Authorship of *Timon of Athens*," *Text* 5 (1991): 195–240.

R. Swigg, "*Timon of Athens* and the Growth of Discrimination," *MLR* 62 (October 1967): 387–94.

James N. Tidwell, "Shakespeare's 'Wappen'd Widow,'" *N&Q* 195 (April 1950): 139–40.

J. J. M. Tobin, "Apuleius and *Timon of Athens*," *RRWL* 1, no. 4 (1980): 1–5.

Ralph Tutt, "Dog Imagery in *The Two Gentlemen from Verona*, *King Lear* and *Timon of Athens*," *The Serif* 1 (October 1964): 15–16, 18–21.

Lewis Walker, "Fortune and Friendship in *Timon of Athens*," *TSLL* 18 (Winter 1977): 577–600.

Lewis Walker, "Money in *Timon of Athens*," *PQ* 57 (Spring 1978): 269–71.

Lewis Walker, "*Timon of Athens* and the Morality Tradition," *ShakS* 12 (1979): 159–77.

John M. Wallace, "*Timon of Athens* and the Three Graces: Shakespeare's Senecan Study," *MP* 83 (January 1986): 349–63.

Malcolm Warre, "'Smoke and Luke-Warm Water': A Note on *Timon of Athens*," *Anglia* 82, no. 4 (1964): 342–44.

D. Douglas Waters, "Shakespeare's *Timon of Athens* and Catharsis," *UCrow* 8 (1988): 93–105.

Robert Wilcher, "*Timon of Athens*: A Shakespearian Experiment," *CahiersE* 34 (October 1988): 61–78.

Titus Andronicus

John Crawford Adams, "Shakespeare's Revisions in *Titus Andronicus*," in McManaway, *Shakespeare 400*, 177–90.

Joseph S. G. Bolton, "A Plea for 3½ Rejected Shakespearian Lines," *SQ* 23 (Spring 1972): 261–63.

A. Robin Bowers, "Emblem and Rape in Shakespeare's 'Lucrece' and *Titus Andronicus*," *SIcon* 10 (1984–1986): 79–96.

A. R. Braunmuller, "Early Shakespearian Tragedy and Its Contemporary Context: Caus and Emotion in *Titus Andronicus*, *Richard III*, and 'The Rape of Lucrece,'" in Bradbury and Palmer, *Shakespearian Tragedy*, 96–128.

Ronald Broude, "Four Forms of Vengeance in *Titus Andronicus*," *JEGP* 78 (July 1979): 494–507.

Ronald Broude, "Roman and Goth in *Titus Andronicus*," *ShakS* 6 (1970): 27–34.

Richard T. Brucher, "Tragedy, Laugh on: Comic Violence in *Titus Andronicus*," *RenD* 10 (1979): 71–91.

Jane S. Carducci, "Shakespeare's *Titus Andronicus*: An Experiment in Expression," *CahiersE* 31 (April 1987): 1–9.

Karen Cummingham, "'Scars Can Witness': Trials by Ordeal and Lavinia's Body in *Titus Andronicus*," in *Women and Violence in Literature: An Essay Collection*, ed. Katherine Anne Ackley (New York: Garland, 1990), 139–62.

John P. Cutts, "Shadow and Substance: Structural Unity in *Titus Andronicus*," *CompD* 2 (Summer 1968): 161–72.

D'Amico, *The Moor in English Renaissance Drama*, 135–48.

Arun Kumar Dasgupta, "A Note on *Titus Andronicus* II. I. 1–11," *SQ* 12 (Summer 1961): 340–41.

Clifford Davidson, "A Reading of *Titus Andronicus*," *SUS* 10 (1978): 93–100.

William H. Desmonde, "The Ritual Origin of Shakespeare's *Titus Andronicus*," *International Journal of Psychoanalysis* 36 (March–April 1955): 61–65.

Roslyn Lander Donald, "Formulas and Their Imitations: *The Spanish Tragedy* and *Titus Andronicus*," *PAPA* 4 (Summer 1978): 8–13.

Mary Laughlin Faucett, "Arms/Words/Tears: Language and the Body in *Titus Andronicus*," *ELH* 50 (June 1983): 261–77.

Richard Findlater, "Shakespearean Atrocities," *Twentieth Century* 158 (October 1955): 364–72.

Brian Gibbons, "The Human Body in *Titus Andronicus* and Other Early Shakespeare Plays," *DSGW* 125 (1989): 209–22.

Douglas E. Green, "Interpreting 'Her Martyt'd Signs': Gender and Tragedy in *Titus Andronicus*," *SQ* 40 (Summer 1989): 317–26.

W. W. Greg, "Alteration of Act I of *Titus Andronicus*," *MLR* 48 (October 1953): 439–40.

Ann Haaker, "Non sine causa: The Use of Emblematic Method and Iconology in the Thematic Structure of *Titus Andronicus*," *RORD* 13–14 (1970–1971): 143–68.

A. C. Hamilton, "*Titus Andronicus*: The Form of Shakespearean Tragedy," *SQ* 14 (Summer 1963): 201–13.

Jorgen Wildt Hansen, "*Titus Andronicus* and Logos," *OL* 31, no. 1 (1976): 110–24.

William T. Hastings, "The Hardboiled Shakespeare," *ShAB* 17 (July 1942): 114–25.

Hibbard, *Making of Shakespeare's Dramatic Poetry*, 41–53.

Jane Hiles, "A Margin for Error: Rhetorical Context in *Titus Andronicus*," *Style* 21 (Spring 1987): 62–75.

B. F. Hill, "The Composition of *Titus Andronicus*," *ShS* 10 (1957): 60–70.

Clifford C. Huffman, "*Titus Andronicus*: Metamorphosis and Renewal," *MLR* 67 (October 1967): 730–41.

B. Clark Hulse, "Wresting the Alphabet: Oratory and Action in *Titus Andronicus*," *Criticism* 21 (April 1979): 106–18.

Maurice Hunt, "Compelling Art in *Titus Andronicus*," *SEL* 28 (Spring 1988): 197–218.

G. K. Hunter, "Sources and Meanings in *Titus Andronicus*," in Gray, *Mirror up to Shakespeare*, 171–88.

R. W. Ingram, "'Their noise be our instruction': Listening to *Titus Andronicus* and *Coriolanus*," in Gray, *Mirror up to Shakespeare*, 277–94.

Heather James, "Cultural Disintegration in *Titus Andronicus*: Mutilating Titus, Vergil, and Rome," in Redmond, *Violence in Drama*, 123–40.

Laura Jepsen, "A Footnote on 'Hands' in Shakespeare's *Titus Andronicus*," *Florida State University Studies* 19 (1955): 7–10.

Robert Johnson, "*Titus Andronicus*: The First of the Roman Plays," in Sharma, *Essays on Shakespeare in Honour of A. A. Ansari*, 80–87.

Eldred Jones, "Aaron and Melancholy in *Titus Andronicus*," *SQ* 14 (Spring 1963): 178–79.

Jones, *Othello's Countrymen*, 49–60.

Judith M. Karr, "The Pleas in *Titus Andronicus*," *SQ* 14 (Summer 1963): 278–79.

Gillian Murray Kendall, "'Lend Me Thy Hand': Metaphor and Mayhem in *Titus Andronicus*," *SQ* 40 (Spring 1989): 299–316.

Robert A. Law, "The Roman Background of *Titus Andronicus*," *SP* 40 (April 1943): 145–53.

Pierre Legouis, *Titus Andronicus*, III.i.298–9," *ShS* 28 (1975): 71–74.

James G. McManaway, "Writing in Sand in *Titus Andronicus* IV, i," *RES* 9 (May 1985): 172–73.

G. Harold Metz, "A Stylometric Comparison of Shakespeare's *Titus Andronicus*, *Pericles*, and *Julius Caesar*," *ShN* 29 (October 1979): 42.

Robert S. Miola, "*Titus Andronicus* and the Mythos of Shakespeare's Rome," *ShakS* 14 (1981): 85–98.

Douglas H. Parker, "Shakespeare's Use of Comic Conventions in *Titus Andronicus*," *UTQ* 56 (October 1987): 486–97.

D. E. Parrott, "Further Observations on *Titus Andronicus*," *SQ* 1 (January 1950): 27–29.

Nancy L. Paxton, "Daughters of Lucrece: Shakespeare's Response to Ovid in *Titus Andronicus*; Proceedings of the IXth Congress of the International Comparative Literature Association, 1," in *Classic Models in Literature*, ed. Zoran Konstantinovic, Warren Anderson, and Walter Dietze (Innsbruck: Institut fur Sprachwissenschaft der Universität Innsbruck, 1981), 217–24.

Hereward T. Price, "'Do Good,'" *N&Q* 207 (September 1962): 410.

Hereward T. Price, "The Yew-Tree in *Titus Andronicus*," *N&Q* 208 (March 1963): 98–99.

Robert A. Ravich, "A Psychoanalytic Study of Shakespeare's Early Plays," *Psychoanalytic Quarterly* 33 (July 1964): 396–97.

Shapiro, *Rival Playwrights*, 119–22.

William W. E. Slights, "The Sacrificial Crisis in *Titus Andronicus*," *UTQ* 49 (January 1979): 18–32.

Kristian Smidt, "Levels and Discontinuities in *Titus Andronicus*: Essays in Honour of Irene Simon," in Maes-Jelinek, Michel, and Michel-Michot, *Multiple Worlds, Multiple Words*, 283–93.

Gordon Ross Smith, "The Credibility of Shakespeare's Aaron," *L&P* 10 (Winter 1960): 11–13.

Alan Sommers, "Wilderness of Tigers: Structure and Symbolism in *Titus Andronicus*," *EIC* 10 (July 1960): 275–89.

Stephen J. Teller, "Lucius and the Babe: Structure in *Titus Andronicus*," *MQ* 19 (1978): 343–54.

Ann Thompson, "Philomel in *Titus Andronicus* and *Cymbeline*," *ShS* 31 (1978): 23–32.

Tokson, *The Popular Image of the Blackman in English Drama*, 47–48, 66–67, 97–98, 121–22, 127–28.

Albert H. Tricomi, "The Mutilated Garden in *Titus Andronicus*," *ShakS* 9 (1976): 89–106.

Eugene M. Waith, "The Ceremonies of *Titus Andronicus*," in Gray, *Mirror up to Shakespeare*, 159–70.

Eugene M. Waith, "The Metamorphosis of Violence in *Titus Andronicus*," *ShS* 10 (1957): 39–49.

Gerald Weales, "*Titus Andronicus*, Private Eye," *Southwest Review* 44 (Summer 1959): 225–59.

Grace Starry West, "Going by the Book: Classical Allusions in Shakespeare's *Titus Andronicus*," *SP* 79 (Winter 1982): 62–77.

David Willbern, "Rape and Revenge in *Titus Andronicus*," *ELR* 8 (Summer 1978): 159–82.

Marion Wynne-Davies, "'The Swallowing Womb': Consumed and Consuming Women in *Titus Andronicus*," in Wayne, *The Matter of Difference*, 129–51.

Troilus and Cressida

Jane Adamson, "Drama in the Mind: Shakespeare's *Troilus and Cressida*," *CR* 27 (1985): 3–17.

A. A. Ansari, "The Problem of Identity in *Troilus and Cressida*," *AJES* 3 (October 1978): 199–214.

Carolyn Asp, "In Defense of Cressida," *SP* 74 (Summer 1977): 406–17.

Carolyn Asp, "Transcendence Denied: The Failure of Role Assumption in *Troilus and Cressida*," *SEL* 18 (Spring 1978): 257–74.

Aerol Arnold, "The Hector-Andromache Scene in Shakespeare's *Troilus and Cressida*," *MLQ* 14 (December 1953): 355–40.

William B. Bache, "Affirmation in *Troilus and Cressida*," *Discourse* 10, no. 4 (1967): 446–55.

Bamborough, *The Little World of Man*, 126–27.

C. C. Barfoot, "*Troilus and Cressida*: 'Praise us as we are tested,'" *SQ* 39 (Winter 1988): 45–57.

Roy A. Battenhouse, "Shakespearean Tragedy: A Christian Interpretation," in Nathan A. Scott, Jr., *The Tragic Vision and the Christian Faith*, 78–81, 86–87.

John Bayley, "Time and the Trojans," *EIC* 25 (January 1975): 55–73.

Harry Berger, Jr., "*Troilus and Cressida*: The Observer as Basilisk," *CompD* 2 (Summer 1968): 122–36.

Berry, *Poet's Grammar*, 65–67.

James Binney, "Shakespeare's Heroic Warriors," *Discourse* 11, no. 2 (1968): 257–68.

David-Everett Blythe, "Shakespeare's *Troilus and Cressida*, III.ii.192," *Expl* 41 (Summer 1983): 6.

Guy Boas, "*Troilus and Cressida* and the Time Scheme," *New English Review* 13 (November 1946): 529–35.

Andrew Bongiorno, "*Troilus and Cressida* as One of a Kind," *ShN* 2 (September 1952): 26.

Helmut Bonheim, "Shakespeare's 'Goose of Winchester,'" *PQ* 51 (Autumn 1972): 940–41.

A. Bonjour, "Hector and the 'One in Sumptuous Armour,'" *ES* 45 (April 1964): 104–08.

William R. Bowden, "The Human Shakespeare and *Troilus and Cressida*," *SQ* 8 (Spring 1957): 167–77.

M. C. Bradbrook, "What Shakespeare Did to Chaucer's *Troilus and Cressida*," *SQ* 9 (Summer 1958): 311–19.

Bradshaw, *Shakespeare's Skepticism*, 74–76.

Bredbeck, *Sodomy and Interpretation*, 33–48.

Harold Brooks, "*Troilus and Cressida*: Its Dramatic Unity and Genre," in Mahon and Pendleton, *"Fanned and winnowed opinions,"* 6–25.

M. M. Burns, "*Troilus and Cressida*: The Worst of Both Worlds," *ShakS* 13 (1980): 105–30.

Canfiled, *Word as Bond in English Literature*, 260–72.

Cartelli, *Marlowe, Shakespeare*, 147–51.

Cecil Williamson Cary, "Burlesque as a Method of Irony in Shakespeare's *Troilus* and *All's Well That End's Well*," *SMC* 5 (Summer 1975): 203–14.

Chandhuri, *Infirm Glory*, 146–54.

Linda Charnes, "'So Unsecret to Ourselves': Notorious Identity and the Material Subject in Shakespeare's *Troilus and Cressida*," *SQ* 40 (Autumn 1989): 413–40.

Larry R. Clarke, "'Mars His Heart Inflam'd with Venus': Ideology and Eros in Shakespeare's *Troilus and Cressida*," *MLQ* 50 (September 1989): 209–26.

Douglas Cole, "Myth and Anti-Myth: The Case of *Troilus and Cressida*," *SQ* 31 (Winter 1980): 76–84.

Hardy M. Cook, "*Troilus and Cressida*: Shakespeare's World of Disorder," *SPWVSRA* 8 (1983): 21–28.

John D. Cox, "The Error of Our Eye in *Troilus and Cressida*," *CompD* 10 (Summer 1976): 147–71.

F. Quinland Daniels, "Order and Confusion in *Troilus and Cressida* I, iii," *SQ* 12 (Summer 1961): 285–91.

Kris Davis-Brown, "Shakespeare's Use of Chaucer in *Troilus and Cressida*: 'That the will is infinite, and the execution confined,'" *SCB* 48 (Summer 1988): 15–34.

Dawson, *Indirections*, 77–86.

Barbara Heliodora C. de M. F. de Almieda, "*Troilus and Cressida*: Romantic Love Revisited," *SQ* 15 (Autumn 1964): 327–32.

Wilbur D. Dunkel, "Shakespeare's Troilus," *SQ* 2 (October 1951): 331–34.

Juliet Dusinberre, "*Troilus and Cressida* and the Definition of Beauty," *ShS* 36 (1983): 85–95.

Frederick D. Dyer, "The Destruction of Pandare," *CCP* 1 (September 1964): 123–33.

Eagleton, *Shakespeare and Society*, 13–38.

Elaine Eldridge, "Moral Order in Shakespeare's *Troilus and Cressida*: The Case of the Trojans," *Anglia* 104, no. 1 (1986): 33–44.

Ellis-Fermor, *Frontiers of Drama*, 56–76, 92–93.

W. R. Elton, "Shakespeare's Ulysses and the Problem of Value," *ShakS* 2 (1966): 95–111.

G. Blakemore Evans, "Pandarus' House?: *Troilus and Cressida*, III. Ii; IV. Ii; IV. Iv," *MLN* 62 (January 1947): 33–35.

Barbara Everett, "The Inaction of *Troilus and Cressida*," *EIC* 32 (April 1982): 119–39.

Kristina Faber, "Shakespeare's *Troilus and Cressida*: Of War and Lechery," *CLQ* 26 (June 1990): 133–48.

Kristina Faber, "*Troilus and Cressida*: 'The Expense of Spirit in a Waste of Shame,'" *CCTEP* 52 (September 1987): 61–69.

Willard Farnham, "Troilus in Shapes of Infinite Desire," *SQ* 15 (Spring 1964): 257–64. Reprinted in McManaway, *Shakespeare 400*, 257–64.

Christopher Flannery, "*Troilus and Cressida*: Poetry or Philosophy?" in Alvis and West, *Shakespeare as Political Thinker*, 145–56.

Richard A. Fly, "Cassandra and the Language of Prophecy in *Troilus and Cressida*," *SQ* 26 (Spring 1975): 157–71.

Richard A. Fly, "'Suited in Like Conditions as our Argument': Imitative Form in Shakespeare's *Troilus and Cressida*," *SEL* 15 (Spring 1975): 273–92.

R. A. Foakes, "The Ending of *Troilus and Cressida*," in *KM 80*, 51–52.

Foakes, *Shakespeare*, 43–62.

R. A. Foakes, "Stage Images in *Troilus and Cressida*," in Thompson and Thompson, *Shakespeare and the Sense of Performance*, 150–61.

R. A. Foakes, "*Troilus and Cressida* Reconsidered," *UTQ* 32 (January 1962): 142–54.

J. Karl Franson, "An Antenor-Aeneas Conspiracy in Shakespeare's *Troilus and Cressida*," *StHum* 9 (June 1978): 43–47.

French, *Shakespeare's Division of Experience*, 154–65.

Elizabeth Freund, "'Ariachne's Broken Woof': The Return of Citation in *Troilus and Cressida*," in Parker and Hartman, *Shakespeare and the Question of Theory*, 19–36.

Lester D. Friedman, "Shakespeare's Ambiguous Hero: A Re-Examination of Hector," *Thoth* 12, no. 2 (1972): 50–58.

Jean Gagen, "Hector's Honor," *SQ* 19 (Spring 1968): 129–37.

A. Gerard, "Meaning and Structure in *Troilus and Cressida*," *ES* 40 (June 1959): 144–57.

René Girard, "The Politics of Desire in *Troilus and Cressida*," in Parker and Hartman, *Shakespeare and the Question of Theory*, 188–209.

Girard, *Theatre of Envy*, 121–66.

Marvin Glasser, "Baroque Formal Elements in Shakespeare's *Troilus and Cressida*," *UCrow* 6 (1986): 54–70.

Gomez, *The Alienated Figure in Drama*, 46–47.

Lawrence D. Green, "'We'll Dress Him Up in Voices': The Rhetoric of Disjunction in *Troilus and Cressida*," *QJS* 70 (February 1984): 23–40.

Gayle Greene, "Language and Value in Shakespeare's *Troilus and Cressida*," *SEL* 21 (Spring 1981): 271–85.

Gayle Greene "Shakespeare's Cressida: 'A kind of self,'" in Lenz, et al., *The Woman's Part*, 133–49.

Grudin, *Mighty Opposites*, 77–89.

Robert Grudin, "The Soul of State: Ulyssean Irony in *Troilus and Cressida*," *Anglia* 93, no. 1 (1975): 55–69.

Jay Leon Halio, "Traitor in *All's Well* and *Troilus and Cressida*," *MLN* 72 (June 1957): 408–09.

H. A. Hargreaves, "An Essentially Tragic *Troilus and Cressida*," *HAB* 18 (Summer 1967): 49–60.

Richard C. Harrier, "Troilus Divided," in Bennett, Cargill, and Hall, *Studies in the English Renaissance Drama*, 142–56.

Hawkins, *Poetic Freedom and Poetic Truth*, 78–80.

Tinsley Helton, "Paradox and Hypothesis in *Troilus and Cressida*," *ShakS* 10 (1977): 115–31.

Gilbert Highet, *The Anatomy of Satire* (Princeton: Princeton University Press, 1962), 123–24.

Arlin J. Hiken, "Texture in *Troilus and Cressida*," *ETJ* 19 (September 1967): 367–69.

Ernest A. J. Honigmann, "The Date and Revision of *Troilus and Cressida*," in *Textual Criticism and Literary Interpretation*, ed. Jerome J. McGann (Chicago: University of Chicago Press, 1985), 38–54.

Houston, *Shakespearean Sentences*, 130–42.

David J. Howser, "Armor and Motive in *Troilus and Cressida*," *RenD* 4 (1971): 121–34.

Hilda Hulme, "Three Notes: *Troilus and Cressida* V. Vii. 11; *Midsummer Night's Dream*, II. I. 54; *Measure for Measure* II. I. 39," *JEGP* 57 (October 1958): 921–22.

Zvi Jagendord, "All against One in *Troilus and Cressida*," *English* 31 (Autumn 1982): 199–210.

David M. Jago, "The Uniqueness of *Troilus and Cressida*," *SQ* 29 (Winter 1978): 20–27.

James, *The Dream of Learning*, 55–57.

David E. Jones, "'Mad Idolatry': Love in *Troilus and Cressida*,' *Drama Criticism* 7 (Winter 1964): 8–12.

Paul A. Jorgensen, "Divided Command in Shakespeare," *PMLA* 70 (September 1955): 750–61.

David Kaula, "Will and Reason in *Troilus and Cressida*," *SQ* 12 (Summer 1961): 271–83.

Paul M. Kendall, "Inaction and Ambivalence in *Troilus and Cressida*," in *English Studies in Honor of James Southall Wilson*, 131–46.

Frank Kermode, "'Opinion' in *Troilus and Cressida*," in Kappeler and Bryson, *Teaching the Text*, 164–79.

Frank Kermode, "Opinion, Truth and Value," *EIC* 5 (April 1955): 181–87.

Johannes Kleinstuck, "Ulysses' Speech on Degree as Related to the Play of *Troilus and Cressida*," *Neophil* 43 (January 1959): 58–63.

G. Wilson Knight, "The Philosophy of *Troilus and Cressida*," in *The Wheel of Fire*, 47–72.

L. C. Knights "*Troilus and Cressida* Again," *Scrutiny* 18 (Autumn 1951): 144–57.

A. S. Knowland, "*Troilus and Cressida*," *SQ* 10 (Summer 1959): 353–65.

John M. Kopper, "Troilus at Pluto's Gates: Subjectivity and the Duplicity of Discourse in Shakespeare's *Troilus and Cressida*," in Atkins and Bergeron, *Shakespeare and Deconstruction*, 149–72.

Linda LaBranche, "Visual Patterns and Linking Analogues in *Troilus and Cressida*," *SQ* 37 (Autumn 1986): 440–50.

Margaret Lacy, *The Jacobean Problem Play*, 1–6, 165–98.

F. H. Langman, "*Troilus and Cressida*," in Donaldson, *Jonson and Shakespeare*, 57–73.

William W. Lawrence, "Troilus, Cressida and Thersites," *MLR* 37 (October 1942): 422–37.

Clifford Leech, "Shakespeare's Greeks," *Stratford Papers on Shakespeare* 4 (1963): 4–15.

Rolf P. Lessenich, "Shakespeare's *Troilus and Cressida*: The Vision of Decadence," *SN* 49, no. 2 (1977): 221–32.

Jill L. Levinson, "Shakespeare's *Troilus and Cressida* and the Monumental Tradition in Tapestries and Literature," *RenD* 7 (1976): 43–84.

Vernon P. Loggins, "Rhetoric and Action in *Troilus and Cressida*," *CLAJ* 35 (September 1991): 93–108.

Agostino Lombardo, "Fragments and Scraps: Shakespeare's *Troilus and Cressida*," in *The European Tragedy of Troilus*, ed. Piero Boitani (Oxford: Claredon Press, 1989), 199–217.

Stephen J. Lynch, "Hector and the Theme of Honor in *Troilus and Cressida*," *UCrow* 7 (1987): 68–79.

Charles Lyons, "Cressida, Achilles, and the Finite Deed," *EA* 20 (July 1968): 233–42.

Clifford P. Lyons, "The Hector-Achilles Encounters in Shakespeare's *Troilus & Cressida*," in *Guldalderstudier. Festskrift til Gustav Albeck den 5. juni 1966*, ed. Henning Hoirup, Aage Jorgensen, and Peter Skautrup (Aarhus: Universitetsforlaget), 67–79.

Miller MacLure, "Shakespeare and the Lonely Dragon," *UTQ* 24 (January 1955): 112–14.

William Main, "Character Amalgam in Shakespeare's *Troilus and Cressida*," *SP* 58 (April 1961): 170–78.

Eric S. Mallin, "Emulous Factions and the Collapse of Chivalry: *Troilus and Cressida*," *Representations* 29 (Winter 1990): 145–79.

J. W. McCutchan, " 'Time's Wallet,' " *N&Q* 192 (October 1947): 430–31.

Neil Megaw, "Shakespeare's *Troilus and Cressida*, I, iii, 354–356," *Expl* 15 (May 1957): 52.

Neil Megaw, "The Sneaking Fellow: *Troilus and Cressida*," *N&Q* 201 (November 1956): 469–70.

W. M. Merchant, "The Harmony of Disenchantment," *Stratford Papers on Shakespeare* 4 (1963): 111–25.

Stephen Merton, "*The Tempest* and *Troilus and Cressida*," *CE* 7 (December 1945): 143–50.

George W. Meyer, "Order Out of Chaos in Shakespeare's *Troilus and Cressida*," *TSE* 4 (Spring 1954): 45–56.

J. Hillis Miller, "Ariachne's Broken Woof," *GaR* 31 (Spring 1977): 44–60.

Brian Morris, "The Tragic Structure of *Troilus and Cressida*," *SQ* 10 (Autumn 1959): 481–91.

Kenneth Muir, "*Troilus and Cressida*," *ShS* 8 (1955): 28–39.

Muller, *The Spirit of Tragedy*, 180–85.

Mildred Brand Munday, "Prejorative Patterns in Shakespeare's *Troilus and Cressida*," *Bucknell University Studies* 5, no. 3 (1955): 39–49.

Barry Nass, "'Yet in the Trial Much Opinion Dwells': The Combat between Hector and Ajax in *Troilus and Cressida*," *ES* 65 (April 1984): 1–10.

Winifred M. T. Nowottny, "'Opinion' and 'Value' in *Troilus and Cressida*," *EIC* 4 (July 1954): 282–96.

J. C. Oates, "The Ambiguity of *Troilus and Cressida*," *SQ* 17 (Spring 1966): 141–50.

James Ogden, "Satire and Sympathy in *Troilus and Cressida*," in Sharma, *Essays on Shakespeare in Honour of A. A. Ansari*, 222–30.

Arlene N. Okerlund, "In Defense of Cressida: Character as Metaphor," *WS* 7, no. 3 (1980): 1–17.

Ornstein, *Moral Vision of Jacobean Tragedy*, 240–49.

Roger Owens, "The Seven Deadly Sins in the Prologue to *Troilus and Cressida*," *SJQ* 116 (Spring 1980): 85–92.

T. M. Pearce, "'Another Knot, Five-Finger-Tied': Shakespeare's *Troilus and Cressida*, V. Ii, 157," *N&Q* 205 (January 1960): 18–19.

Anthony G. Petti, "The Fox, the Ape, the Humble Bee and the Goose," *Neophil* 44 (July 1960): 208–11, 213–15.

Helen Puriton Pettigrew, "*Troilus and Cressida*: Shakespeare's Indictment of War," *WVUPP* 5 (January 1947): 34–48.

Jeffrey L. Porter, "Shakespeare and the Motives of Rhetoric: The Failure of Speech in *Troilus and Cressida*," *PostS* 4 (1987): 55–64.

Abbie Findlay Potts, "*Cynthia's Revels*, *Poetaster* and *Troilus and Cressida*," *SQ* 5 (Summer 1954): 297–302.

Neil Powell, "Hero and Human: The Problem of Achilles," *CritQ* 21 (Summer 1979): 17–28.

Robert K. Presson, "The Structural Use of a Traditional Theme in *Troilus and Cressida*," *PQ* 31 (April 1952): 180–88.

Norman Rabkin, "*Troilus and Cressida*: The Use of the Double Plot," *ShakS* 1 (1965): 265–82.

Victor B. Reed, "*Troilus and Cressida* IV. ii, 56," *NM* 57, no. 3–4 (1956): 128–32.

Mary Ellen Rickey, "'Twixt Dangerous Shores': *Troilus and Cressida* Again," *SQ* 15 (Winter 1964): 3–14.

A. P. Riemer, "Some Shakespearean Boxes (*Troilus and Cressida* V.i.15–6)," *SSEng* 12 (1986–1987): 119.

Hugh Robertson, "*Troilus and Cressida* and *Measure for Measure* in Their Age: Shakespeare's Thought in Its Context," in Jowitt and Taylor, *Self and Society*, 3–26.

Leo Rockas, "'Lechery eats itself': *Troilus and Cressida*," *ArielE* 8 (January 1977): 17–32.

Rossiter, *Angel with Horns*, 129–51.

A. P. Rossiter, "*Troilus and Cressida*," *ShN* 5 (February 1955): 3.

Willim Ronald Runyan, "Parallel Hierarchies in *Troilus and Cressida*," *BWVACET* 5 (Spring–Summer 1979): 13–17.

Mark Sacharoff, "The Orations of Agamemnon and Nestor in Shakespeare's *Troilus and Cressida*," *TSLL* 14 (Winter 1972): 223–34.

James Sandoe, "*Troilus and Cressida*," *ShN* 8 (September 1958): 28.

Elias Schwartz, "Tonal Equivocation and the Meaning of *Troilus and Cressida*," *SP* 69 (June 1972): 304–19.

William O. Scott, "Self-Difference in *Troilus and Cressida*," in Atkins and Bergeron, *Shakespeare and Deconstruction*, 129–48.

William P. Shaw, "*Troilus and Cressida*, V.iv.–V.x.: Giving Chaos a Name and a Local Habitation," *SPWVSRA* 2 (1977): 24–48.

Paul N. Siegel, "Shakespeare and the Neo-Chivalric Cult of Honor," *CentR* 8 (Winter 1964): 51–56.

Don Smith, "Truth and Seeming Truth: The Language of *Measure for Measure* and *Troilus and Cressida*," in Jowitt and Taylor, *Self and Society*, 45–60.

J. Oates Smith, "Essence and Existence in Shakespeare's *Troilus and Cressida*," *PQ* 46 (January 1967): 167–85.

R. J. Smith, "Personal Identity in *Troilus and Cressida*," *ESA* 6 (March 1963): 7–26.

Richard C. Snyder, Discovering a 'Dramaturgy of Human Relationships' in Shakespearean Metadrama: *Troilus and Cressida*; Collection of Essays from the Ohio Shakespeare Conference, 1981, Wright State University, Dayton, Ohio," in Cary and Limouze, *Shakespeare and the Arts*, 199–216.

Soellner, *Shakespeare's Patterns*, 195–214.

Rudolf Stamm, "The Glass of Pandar's Praise; The Word Scenery, Mirror Passages, and Reported Scenes in Shakespeare's *Troilus and Cressida*," *E&S* 17 (1964): 55–77.

W. B. Stanford, *The Ulysses Theme* (Oxford: Blackwell, 1963), 164–71.

Frederick W. Sternfeld, "*Troilus and Cressida*: Music for the Play," *English Institute Essays* (1952): 107–37.

David Lloyd Stevenson, "The Love-Game Comedy," *CUSECL* 164 (1946): 215–22.

Mihoko Suzuki, "'Truth Tired with Iteration': Myth and Fiction in Shakespeare's *Troilus and Cressida*," *PQ* 66 (Spring 1987): 153–74.

Hamish F. G. Swanston, "The Baroque Element in *Troilus and Cressida*," *DUJ* 19 (December 1957): 14–23.

Yasunari Takada, "How To Do Things with 'Fall-Out' Systems in *Troilus and Cressida*," *ShStud* 20 (1981–1982): 33–58.

Hawley C. Taylor, "The Stoic Philosophy and Shakespeare's *Troilus and Cressida*." *SJS* 4 (Spring 1978): 82–93.

Thompson and Thompson, *Shakespeare*, 13–46.

Karl F. Thompson, "The Feast of Pride in *Troilus and Cressida*," *N&Q* 203 (May 1958): 193–94.

Karl F. Thompson, "*Troilus and Cressida*: The Incomplete Achilles," *CE* 27 (April 1966): 532–36.

Karl F. Thompson, "The Unknown Ulysses," *SQ* 19 (Spring 1968): 125–28.

Grant L. Voth, and Oliver H. Evans, "Cressida and the World of the Play," *ShakS* 8 (1975): 231–39.

Grant L. Voth, and Oliver H. Evans, "Ulysses and 'Particular Will' in Shakespeare's *Troilus and Cressida*," *SJW* 113 (Summer 1977): 149–57.

Thomas G. West, "The Two Truths of *Troilus and Cressida*," in Alvis and West, *Shakespeare as Political Thinker*, 127–43.

Douglas B. Wilson, "The Commerce of Desire: Freudian Narcissism in Chaucer's *Troilus and Criseyde* and Shakespeare's *Troilus and Cressida*," *ELN* 21 (January 1983): 11–22.

Robert E. Wood, "The Dignity of Morality: Marlowe's Dido and Shakespeare's Troilus," *ShakS* 11 (1978): 95–105.

Robert E. Wood, "*Troilus and Cressida*: The Tragedy of a City," *PQ* 56 (Winter 1977): 65–81.

R. A. Yoder, "'Sons and Daughters of the Game': An Essay on Shakespeare's *Troilus and Cressida*," *ShS* 25 (1972): 11–25.

Twelfth Night

Barry B. Adams, "Orsino and the Spirit of LoveL Text, Syntax, and Sense in *Twelfth Night*, I.i.1–15," *SQ* 29 (Winter 1978): 52–59.

Yoshitaka Arakawa, "Disturbing Elements in *Twelfth Night*," *SES* 5 (1980): 18–28.

Masazumi Araki, "A Fantastical Perspective of A(b/d): The Suppressed 'Incest' Theme in *Twelfth Night*," *ShStud* 19 (1979–1980): 29–56.

Babb, *Elizabethan Malady*, 170–71.

Surabhi Banerjee, "Feste the Fool in Shakespeare's *Twelfth Night*," *JDECU* 18, no. 1 (1982–1983): 80–83.

Barber, *Shakespeare's Festive Comedy*, 240–269.

Alan W. Bellringer, "*Twelfth Night: or What You Will*: Alternatives," *DUJ* 43 (December 1981): 1–13.

Bentley, *The Play*, 285–89, 366–71.

E.M. Blistein, "The Object of Scorn: An Aspect of the Comic Antagonist," *WHR* 14 (Spring 1960): 317–22.

Ralph P. Boas, "Shakespeare's *Twelfth Night*, II, iii, 25–27," *Expl* 3 (February 1945): 29.

M. Keith Booker, "'Nothing That Is So Is So': Dialogic Discourse and the Voice of the Woman in *The Clerk's Tale* and *Twelfth Night*," *Exemplaria* 3 (Fall 1991): 519–37.

Stephen Booth, "*Twelfth Night* 1.1: The Audience as Malvolio," in Erickson and Kahn, *Shakespeare's 'Rough Magic,'* 149–67.

Sandra Braude, "Harmony in Illyria: A Study of Twin Themes of Love and Music in Shakespeare's *Twelfth Night*," *CRUX* 17 (February 1983): 29–35.

Charles Brooks, "Shakespeare's Heroine-Actresses," *ShJE* 96 (1960): 141–43.

Jane K. Brown, "Double Plotting in Shakespeare's Comedies: The Case of *Twelfth Night*," in *Aesthetic Illusion: Theoretical and Historical Approaches*, ed. Frederick Burwick and Walter Pape (Berlin: de Gruyter, 1990), 313–23.

Burke, *The Philosophy of Literary Form*, 291–95.

Edward Burns, "'And call upon my soul within the house': Rhetoric and Response in *Twelfth Night*," in *KM 80*, 28–30.

Carroll Camden, "Three Notes on Shakespeare," *MLN* 72 (March 1957): 251–52.

D. Allen Carroll, "Fabian's Grudge against Malvolio," *SQ* 26 (Winter 1975): 62–66.

William C. Carroll, "The Ending of *Twelfth Night* and the Tradition of Metamorphosis," *NYLF* 5–6 (1980): 49–61.

Maurice Charney, "Comic Premises of *Twelfth Night*," *NYLF* 1 (1978): 151–65.

Maurice Charney, "*Twelfth Night* and the 'Natural Perspective' of Comedy," in Durry, Ellrodt, and Jones-Davies, *De Shakespeare à T. S. Eliot*, 43–51.

Clemen, *Shakespeare's Dramatic Art*, 166–72.

Hennig Cohen, "Shakespeare's *Twelfth Night*, I, v, 128–130," *Expl* 14 (November 1955): 12.

Lee Sheriden Cox, "The Riddle of *Twelfth Night*," *SQ* 13 (Summer 1962): 360.

Milton Crane, "*Twelfth Night* and Shakespearean Comedy," *SQ* 6 (Winter 1955): 1–8.

Dimiter Daphinoff, "'None Can Be Called Deformed but the Unkind': Disruption of Norms in *Twelfth Night*," in Bridges, *On Strangeness*, 99–112.

Dawson, *Indirections*, 73–76.

Alan Downer, "Feste's Night," *CE* 13 (February1952): 258–65.

Terence Eagleton, "Language and Reality in *Twelfth Night*," *CritQ* 9 (Autumn 1967): 217–28.

Lydia Forbes, "What You Will?" *SQ* 13 (Autumn 1962): 475–85.

René E. Fortin, "*Twelfth Night*: Shakespeare's Drama of Initiation," *PLL* 8 (Spring 1972): 135–46.

Barbara Freedman, "Separation and Fusion in *Twelfth Night*," in Charney and Reppen, *Psychoanalytic Approaches to Literature and Film*, 96–119.

French, *Shakespeare's Division of Experience*, 111–18.

Elizabeth Freund, "*Twelfth Night* and the Tyranny of Interpretation," *ELH* 53 (Decemeber 1986): 471–89.

Sand M. Gamal, "The Function of Song in Shakespeare's Comedies," *CairoSE* (1961–1962): 118–19.

Anthony Gash, "Shakespeare's Comedies of Shadow and Substance: Word and Image in *Henry IV* and *Twelfth Night*," *W&I* 4 (January 1988): 626–62.

A. Gerard, "Shipload of Fools: A Note on *Twelfth Night*," *ES* 45 (April 1964): 109–15.

Christopher Gillie, "*Twelfth Night*," *The Use of English* 4 (Spring 1953): 136–40.

Girard, *Theatre of Envy*, 8–20.

Jonathan Goldberg, "Textual Properties," *SQ* 37 (Summer 1986): 213–217.

Henk Gras, "*Twelfth Night, Every Man out of His Humour*, and the Middle Temple Revels of 1597–98," *MLR* 84 (October 1989): 545–64.

Hager, *Shakespeare's Political Animal*, 76–87.

Hallett and Hallett, *Analyzing Shakespeare's Action*, 29–30, 114–16, 128–30, 163–64, 194–95.

Niels Bugge Hansen, "The Comedy of Language and the Language of Comedy: Observations on the Connection between Plot, Theme and Language in *Twelfth Night*," in *Essays Presented to Knud Schibsbye on His 75th Birthday, 29 November 1979*, ed. Michael Chestnutt, Claus Færch, Torben Thrane, and Graham D. Caie (Copenhagen: Akademisk, 1979), 160–63.

Geoffrey H. Hartman, "Shakespeare's Poetical Character in *Twelfth Night*," in Parker and Hartman, *Shakespeare and the Question of Theory*, 37–53.

Terence Hawkes, "Comedy, Orality, and Duplicity: *A Midsummer Night's Dream* and *Twelfth Night*," *NYLF* 5–6 (1980): 155–63.

Nancy K. Hayles, "Sexual Disquise in *As You Like It* and *Twelfth Night*," *ShS* 32 (1979): 63–72.

Theodore C. Hoepfner, "M.A.O.I.—*Twelfth Night*," *N&Q* 203 (May 1958): 193.

Norman N. Holland, "Cuckhold or Counsellor in *Twelfth Night*, I. V. 56," *SQ* 8 (Winter 1957): 127–29.

John Hollander, "*Twelfth Night* and the Morality of Indulgence," *SR* 67 (Spring 1959): 220–38.

J. Dennis Houston, "'When I Came to Man's Estate': *Twelfth Night* and the Problems of Identity," *MLQ* 33 (June 1972): 274–88.

Howarth, *The Tiger's Heart*, 94–100.

Maurice Hunt, "Love, Disguise, and Knowledge in *Twelfth Night*," *CLAJ* 32 (June 1989): 484–93.

Maurice Hunt, "*Twelfth Night* and the Annunciation," *PLL* 25 (Summer 1989): 264–71.

Harold Jenkins, "Shakespeare's *Twelfth Night,*" *Rice Institute Pamphlets* 45 (January 1959): 19–42.

Edward D. Johnson, "Malvolio's Cryptic Word M.O.A.I.," *Baconiana* 30 (January 1946): 26–28.

Evan Jones, "Daring Wind and Rain: *Twelfth Night* and *King Lear,*" *SoRA* 8 (1975): 125–37.

T. J. Kelly, "*Twelfth Night,*" *CR* 19 (1977): 54–70.

Frank Kermode, "The Mature Comedies," *Stratford-Upon-Avon Studies* 3 (1961): 224–27.

J. F. Killeen, "*Twelfth Night*, I.iii.42: '*Castiliano vulgo,*' " *SQ* 28 (Winter 1977): 92–93.

Walter N. King, "Shakespeare and Parmenides: The Metaphysics of *Twelfth Night,*" *SEL* 8 (Spring 1968): 283–306.

Knight, *The Golden Labyrinth*, 67–69.

Thomas Kranidas, "Malvolio on Desire," *SQ* 15 (Autumn 1964): 450–51.

Albert C. Labriola, "*Twelfth Night* and the Comedy of Festive Abuse," *MLS* 5 (Spring 1975): 5–20.

M. E. Lamb, "Ovid's *Metamorphoses* and Shakespeare's *Twelfth Night,*" *NYLF* 5–6 (1980): 63–77.

Jon S. Lawry, "*Twelfth Night* and 'Salt Waves Fresh in Love,'" *ShakS* 6 (1970): 89–108.

Clifford Leech, "Shakespeare's Comic Dukes," *REL* 5 (April 1964): 108–10.

Inge Leimberg, "'M.O.A.I.' Trying to Share the Joke in *Twelfth Night* 2.5 (A Critical Hypothesis)," *Connotations* 1 (March 1991): 78–93.

Harry Levin, "The Underplot of *Twelfth Night,*" in Durry, Ellrodt, and Jone-Daves, *De Shakespeare à T. S. Eliot*, 53–59.

Richard A. Levin, "'It Was Not I': Defense Mechanisms in *Twelfth Night,*" *UCrow* 7 (1987): 50–57.

Richard A. Levin, "*Twelfth Night, The Merchant of Venice*, and Two Alternate Approaches to Shakespearean Comedy," *ES* 59 (January 1978): 336–43.

Cynthia Lewis, "'A Faustian Riddle?' Anagrammatic Names in *Twelfth Night,*" *ELN* 22 (June 1985): 32–37.

Cynthia Lewis, "Viola, Antonia, and Epiphany in *Twelfth Night*," *ELWIU* 13 (Fall 1986): 187–200.

Thad Jenkins Logan, "*Twelfth Night*: The Limits of Festivity," *SEL* 22 (Spring 1982): 223–38.

M. M. Mahood, "Talk of the Devil," *TLS* 16 (June 1966): 541.

Cristina Malcolmson, "'What You Will': Social Mobility and Gender in *Twelfth Night*," in Wayne, *The Matter of Difference*, 29–57.

F. H. Mare, "A Footnote to *Twelfth Night*, Act I, Scene 3," *N&Q* 204 (September 1959): 306–07.

Julian Markels, "Shakespeare's Confluence of Tragedy and Comedy: *Twelfth Night* and *King Lear*," *SQ* 15 (Spring 1964): 75–88.

Robert C. Melzi, "From Lelia to Viola," *RenD* 9 (1966): 67–81.

W. M. Merchant, "Shakespeare's Theology," *REL* 5 (October 1964): 84–85.

S. Nagarajan, "'What You Will': A Suggestion," *SQ* 10 (Winter 1959): 61–67.

Martin Orkin, "Right-Seeing and the Matriculation *Twelfth Night*," *CRUX* 17 (July 1983): 40–49.

Laurie E. Osborne, "The Texts of *Twelfth Night*," *ELH* 57 (March 1990): 37–61.

D. J. Palmer, "Art and Nature in *Twelfth Night*," *CritQ* 9 (Autumn 1967): 201–12.

D. J. Palmer, "*Twelfth Night* and the Myth of Echo and Narcissus," *ShS* 32 (1979): 73–78.

Douglas H. Parker, "Shakespeare's Female Twins in *Twelfth Night*: In Defence of Olivia," *ESC* 13 (1987): 23–34.

T. M. Pearce, "Shakespeare's *Twelfth Night*, II, v, 5–7," *Expl* 7 (December 1948): 19.

Vincent F. Petronella, "Anamorphic Naming in Shakespeare's *Twelfth Night*," *Names* 35 (September–December): 1987): 139–46.

Beryl C. Pogson, "The Esoteric Meaning of *Twelfth Night*," *Baconiana* 32 (Spring 1948): 65–71.

Alex Potter, "Shakespeare's *Twelfth Night*," *CRUX* 12 (February 1978): 46–53.

Arnold W. Preussner, "Waiting in *Hamlet* and *Twelfth Night*," *HSt* 10 (Summer–Winter 1988): 95–103.

John Edwards Price, "'Because I Would Followe the Fashion': Rich's *Farewell to the Military Profession* and Shakespeare's *Twelfth Night*," *ISJR* 62 (December 1988): 397–406.

J. M. Purcell, "*Twelfth Night*, II, ii, 27–28," *N&Q* 203 (September 1958): 375–76.

Fitzroy Pyle, "*Twelfth Night, King Lear* and *Arcadia*," *MLR* 43 (October 1948): 444–52.

E. Royle, "The Pattern of Play in *Twelfth Night*," *Theoria* 23 (April 1964): 1–12.

L. G. Salinger, "The Design of *Twelfth Night*," *SQ* 9 (Spring 1958): 117–39.

Winifred Schleiner, "The Feste-Malvolio Scene in *Twelfth Night* against the Background of Renaissance Ideas about Madness and Possession," *DSGW* 126 (1990): 48–57.

Winifred Schleiner, "Orsino and Viola: Are the Names of Serious Characters in *Twelfth Night* Meaningful?" *ShakS* 16 (1983): 135–41.

Elias Schwartz, "*Twelfth Night* and the Meaning of Shakespearean Comedy," *CE* 28 (May 1967): 508–14, 519.

Melvin Seiden, "Malvolio Reconsidered," *UR* 28 (Winter 1961): 105–13.

Amritjit Singh, "Time in *Twelfth Night*," *RUSEng* 11 (January 1978): 9–16.

Camille Slights, "The Principle of Recompense in *Twelfth Night*," *MLR* 77 (October 1982): 537–46.

Smith, *Dualities in Shakespeare*, 110–22.

Strong, *The Sacred River*, 60–61.

Joseph Summers, "The Masks of *Twelfth Night*" *UR* 22 (Autumn 1955): 25–31.

Homer Swander, "*Twelfth Night*: Critics, Players, and Script," *ETJ* 16 (May 1964): 114–21.

Edmund M. Taft, "Love and Death in *Twelfth Night*," *ISJR* 60 (July 1986): 407–16.

Marion A. Taylor, "'He That Did the Tiger Board,'" *SQ* 15 (Winter 1964): 110–13.

Mark Taylor, "Letters and Readers in *Macbeth, King Lear*, and *Twelfth Night*," *PQ* 69 (1990): 31–53.

Karl F. Thompson, "Shakespeare's Romantic Comedies," *PMLA* 67 (December 1952): 1079–81, 1090–93.

Peter Thomson, "*Twelfth Night*: The Music of Time," in Sharma, *Essays on Shakespeare in Honour of A. A. Ansari*, 211–21.

Stanley Wells, "Reunion Scenes in *The Comedy of Errors* and *Twelfth Night*; Festschrift fur Siegfried Korninger," in Rauchbauer, *A Yearbook of Studies in English Language and Literature 1985/86*, 267–76.

Karl P. Wentersdorf, "The 'Passy Measures Panyn' Crux in *Twelfth Night*: Is Emendation Necessary?" *SQ* 35 (Winter 1984): 82–86.

Karl P. Wentersdorf, "Shakespeare and Carding: Notes on Cruxes in 1 *Henry IV* and in *Twelfth Night*," *SQ* 36 (Spring 1985): 215–19.

David Willbern, "Malvolio's Fall," *SQ* 29 (Winter 1978): 85–90.

Charles Williams, "The Use of the Second Person in *Twelfth Night*," *English* 9 (Spring 1953): 125–28.

Porter Williams, Jr., "Mistakes in *Twelfth Night* and Their Resolution: A Study in Some Relationships of Plot and Theme," *PMLA* 76 (June 1961): 193–99.

Robert F. Willson, Jr., "'And mine is a sad one': Antonio as Stranger in *Twelfth Night*," *ShakB* 2 (September–October 1984): 5–7.

James O. Wood, "'*Maluolios* A Peg-A-Ramsie,'" *ELN* 5 (January 1967): 11–15.

Linda Woodbridge, "'Fire in Your Heart and Brimstone in Your Liver': Towards an Unsaturnalian *Twelfth Night*," *SoRA* 17 (1984): 270–91.

Elizabeth M. Yearling, "Language, Theme, and Character in *Twelfth Night*," *ShS* 35 (1982): 79–86.

Young, *Immortal Shadows*, 218–22.

The Two Gentlemen of Verona

Johannes Adam Bastiaenen, *Moral Tone of Jacobean and Caroline Drama*, 16–18.

Kenneth C. Bennett, "Stage Action and the Interpretation of *The Two Gentlemen of Verona*," *SJW* 116 (Spring 1980): 93–100.

Greg Bentley, "Shakespeare's *Two Gentlemen of Verona*," *Expl* 46 (Summer 1988): 7–9.

Berry, *Shakespearean Structures*, 101–19.

Charles Brooks, "Shakespeare's Heroine-Actresses," *ShJE* 96 (1960): 134–37.

H. F. Brooks, "Two Clowns in a Comedy (to say Nothing of the dog): Speed, Launce (and Crab) in *The Two Gentlemen of Verona*," *E&S* 16 (1963): 91–111.

O. J. Campbell, "*The Two Gentlemen of Verona* and Italian Comedy," *UMSS* (1964): 47–64.

French, *Shakespeare's Division of Experience*, 83–87.

Sand M. Gamal, "The Function of Song in Shakespeare's Comedies," *CairoSE* 1961/62): 114, 117.

René Girard, "Love Delights in Praises: A Reading of *The Two Gentlemen of Verona*," *PL* 13 (1989): 231–47.

Gerard, *Theatre of Envy*, 8–20.

Hibbard, *Making of Shakespeare's Dramatic Poetry*, 99–102.

Arthur Holmberg, "*The Two Gentlemen of Verona* and the Paradox of Salvation," *BRMMLA* 36, no. 1 (1982): 5–22.

Richard J. Jaarsma, "The 'Lear Complex' in *The Two Gentlemen of Verona*," *L&P* 22, no. 2 (1972): 199–202.

Frederick Kiefer, "Love Letters in *The Two Gentlemen of Verona*," *ShakS* 18 (1986): 65–85.

Clifford Leech, "Shakespeare's Comic Dukes," *REL* 5 (April 1964): 105–08.

Peter Lindenbaum, "Education in *The Two Gentlemen of Verona*," *SEL* 15 (Spring 1975): 229–44.

Nemerov, *Poetry and Fiction*, 25–33.

Thomas A. Perry, "Proteus, Wry-Transformed Traveler," *SQ* 5 (January 1954): 33–40.

Thomas A. Perry, "*The Two Gentlemen of Verona* and the Spanish *Diana*," *MP* 87 (August 1989): 73–76.

Jim C. Pogue, "*The Two Gentlemen of Verona* and Henry Wooton's *A Courtlie Controversie of Cupid's Cantels*," *ESRS* 10 (June 1962): 17–28.

Praz, *The Flaming Heart*, 152–56.

Dale G. Priest, "Subjectivity in *Two Gentlemen of Verona*," *EIRC* 6 (1980): 28–46.

Robert A. Ravich, "A Psychoanalytic Study of Shakespeare's Early Plays," *Psychoanalytic Quarterly* 33 (July 1964): 402–04.

William Rossky, "*The Two Gentlemen of Verona* as Burlesque," *ELR* 12 (Autumn 1982): 210–19.

Woong-jae Shin, "*Two Gentlemen of Verona* and Diana enamorada: Shakespeare's Class-Oriented Modifications of His Sources," *JELL* 35 (Novemeber 1989): 717–33.

Edward Sichi, Jr., "Religious Imagery in *The Two Gentlemen of Verona*: Or, Why Does Proteus Get the Girl?" *SPWVSRA* 6 (1981): 42–49.

Camille Wells Slights, "Shakespeare and the Courtesy Book Tradition," *ShakS* 16 (1983): 13–31.

William E. Stephenson, "The Adolescent Dream-World of *The Two Gentlemen of Verona*," *SQ* 17 (Spring 1966): 165–68.

Paul R. Thomas, "The Marriage of True Minds: Ideal Friendship in *Two Gentlemen of Verona*," *ISJR* 57 (1982): 187–92.

Karl F. Thompson, "Shakespeare's Romantic Comedies," *PMLA* 67 (December 1952): 1079–81, 1085–88, 1091–93.

Ralph M. Tutt, "Dog Imagery in *The Two Gentlemen of Verona, King Lear*, and *Timon of Athens*," *The Serif* 1 (October 1964): 15–18.

K. Tetzeli von Rosador, "Plotting the Early Comedies: *The Comedy of Errors, Love's Labour's Lost, The Two Gentlemen of Verona*," *ShS* 37 (1984): 13–22.

Stanley Wells, "The Failure of *The Two Gentlemen of Verona*," *ShJE* 99 (1963): 161–73.

The Two Noble Kinsmen

John P. Cutts, "Shakespeare's Song and Masque in *The Two Noble Kinsmen*," *EM* 18 (Spring 1967): 55–85.

Smith, *Homosexual Desire in Shakespeare's England*, 69–72.

Glynne Wickham, "*The Two Noble Kinsmen* or *A Midsummer Night's Dream, Part II*?" *ETh* 7, no. 2 (1980): 167–96.

The Winter's Tale

Richard H. Abrams, "Leonte's Enemy: Madness in *The Winter's Tale*," in *Aspects of Fantasy: Selected Essays from the Second International Conference on the Fantastic in Literature and Film*, ed. William Coyle (Westport, CT: Greenwood, 1986), 155–62.

Rudolf Almasy, "'Go Together You Precious Winters All': A Reading of Shakespeare's *The Winter's Tale*," *WVUPP* 27 (January 1981): 120–27.

James R. Andreas, "'Music Awake Her: Strike Tis Time': Generic Modulation in *The Winter's Tale*," *TPB* 21 (July 1984): 24–25.

A. A. Ansari, "The Mockery of Art in *The Winter's Tale*," *AJES* 4 (July 1979): 124–41.

Stanford S. Apseloff, "Shakespeare's *Othello*, II.i.253–58 and *The Winter's Tale*, I.ii.115 and 125–25," *Expl* 42 (Spring 1984): 12–13.

Anna Baldwin, "From the *Clerk's Tale* to *The Winter's Tale*," in *Chaucer Traditions: Studies in Honour of Derek Brewer*, ed. Ruth Morse and Barry Windeatt (Cambridge: Cambridge University Press, 1990), 199–212.

Anne Barton, "Leontes and the Spider: Language and Speaker in Shakespeare's Last Plays," in Edwards, Ewbank, and Hunter, *Shakespeare's Styles*, 131–50.

Eben Bass, "*The Winter's Tale*: Great Difference Betwixt Bohemia and Sicilia," *MSE* 6, no. 1–2 (1977): 15–24.

Roy Battenhouse, "Theme and Structure in *The Winter's Tale*," *ShS* 33 (1980): 123–38.

A. F. Bellette, "Truth and Utterance in *The Winter's Tale*," *ShS* 31 (1978): 65–75.

Peter Berek, "'As We Are Mock'd with Art': From Scorn to Transfiguration," *SEL* 8 (Spring 1978): 289–305.

David M. Bergeron, "Hermione's Trial in *The Winter's Tale*," *EiT* 3 (November 1984): 3–12.

David M. Bergeron, "The Restoration of Hermione in *The Winter's Tale*," in Kay and Jacobs, *Shakespeare's Romances Reconsidered*, 125–33.

John D. Bernard, "The Pastoral Vision of *The Winter's Tale*," *ISJR* 53 (May 1979): 219–25.

Berry, *Shakespearean Structures*, 120–35.

Berry, *Poet's Grammar*, 69–74.

Dennis Biggins, "'Exit Pursued by a Beare': A Problem in *The Winter's Tale*," *SQ* 13 (Winter 1962): 3–13.

Adrien Bonjour, "The Final Scene in *The Winter's Tale*," *ES* 33 (October 1952): 193–208.

M. C. Bradbrook, "Dramatic Romance as Open Form in *The Winter's Tale*," in Durry, Ellrodt, and Jones-Davies, *De Shakespeare à T. S. Eliot*, 81–92.

J. A. Bryant, "Shakespeare's Allegory: *The Winter's Tale*," *SR* 63 (Spring 1955): 202–22.

J. A. Bryant, "*The Winter's Tale* and the Pastoral Tradition," *SQ* 14 (Autumn 1963): 387–98.

R. J. A. Bunnett, "*The Winter's Tale*," *Baconiana* 33 (April 1949): 104–07.

Robert Burchfield, "The Bare Infinitives in *The Winter's Tale*," in Fabian and von Rosador, *Shakespeare: Text, Language, Criticism*, 34–56.

Michael D. Bristol, "In Search of the Bear: Spatiotemporal Form and the Heterogeneity of Economies in *The Winter's Tale*," *SQ* 42 (Winter 1991): 145–67.

Joan M. Byles, "*The Winter's Tale, Othello*, and *Troilus and Cressida*: Narcissism and Sexual Betrayal," *AI* 36 (Winter 1979): 80–93.

Ellen M. Caldwell, "Animating Word and Spectacle in the Masque Scenes of *The Winter's Tale*," *ISJR* 58 (May 1984): 281–88.

Canfield, *Word as Bond in English Literature*, 52–66.

Louise G. Clubb, "The Tragicomic Bear," *CLS* 41 (1972): 17–30.

Derek Cohen, "Patriarchy and Jealousy in *Othello* and *The Winter's Tale*," *MLQ* 48 (September 1987): 207–23.

David G. Collins, "The Function of Art in Shakespeare's *The Winter's Tale*," *BSUF* 23 (Summer 1982): 55–59.

Scott Colley, "Leontes' Search for Wisdom in *The Winter's Tale*," *SoAR* 48 (January 1983): 43–53.

Cunningham, *Woe or Wonder*, 34–36, 113–14.

Harry Curtis, Jr., "The Year Growing Ancient: Formal Ambiguity in *The Winter's Tale*," *CLAJ* 23 (June 1980): 431–37.

Elaine Cuvelier, "'Perspective' in *The Winter's Tale*," *CahiersE* 23 (April 1983): 35–46.

Irene G. Dash, "Bohemia's 'Sea Coast' and the Babe Who Was 'Lost Forever,'" *LOS* 3 (1976): 102–09.

Clifford Davidson, "The Iconography of Illusion and Truth in *The Winter's Tale*; Collection of Essays from the Ohio Shakespeare Conference, 1981, Wright State University, Dayton, Ohio," in Cary and Limouze, *Shakespeare and the Arts*, 73–91.

Dawson, *Indirections*, 147–55.

Eagleton, *Shakespeare and Society*, 139–55.

Philip Edwards, "'Seeing Is Believing': Action and Narration in *The Old Wives Tale* and *The Winter's Tale*," in Honigmann, *Shakespeare and His Contemporaries*, 79–83.

Egan, *Drama within Drama*, 56–89.

Walter F. Eggers, Jr., "Genre and Affective Distance: The Example of *The Winter's Tale*," *Genre* 10 (Winter 1977): 29–46.

John Ellis, "Rooted Affection: The Genesis of Jealousy in *The Winter's Tale*," *CE* 25 (April 1964): 545–47.

Peter B. Erickson, "Patriarchal Structures in *The Winter's Tale*," *PMLA* 97 (1982): 819–29.

Barbara L. Estrin, "The Foundling Plot: Stories in *The Winter's Tale*," *MLS* 7 (Winter 1977): 27–38.

Inga-Stina Ewbank, "The Triumph of Time in *The Winter's Tale*," *REL* 5 (April 1964): 83–100.

Howard Felperin, "'Tongue-Tied Our Queen?' The Deconstruction of Presence In *The Winter's Tale*," in Parker and Hartman, *Shakespeare and the Question of Theory*, 3–18.

Foakes, *Shakespeare*, 118–44.

Charles O. Fox, "Clocks and Dials," *ShN* 1 (May 1951): 10.

French, *Shakespeare's Division of Experience*, 313–18.

Charles Frey, "Interpreting *The Winter's Tale*," *SEL* 18 (Spring 1978): 307–29.

Charles Frey, "Tragic Structure in *The Winter's Tale*: Affective Dimension," in Kay and Jacobs, *Shakespeare's Romances Reconsidered*, 113–24.

Northrop Frye, *Fables of Identity—Studies in Poetic Mythology.* (New York: Harcourt, Brace, 1963), 107–18.

Sand M. Gamal, "The Function of Song in Shakespeare's Comedies," *CairoSE* (1961/62): 119–20.

C. O. Gardner, "Three Notes on *The Winter's Tale*," *Theoria* 54 (January 1980): 51–66.

Garner, *The Absent Voice*, 80–99.

C. O. Gardner, "Time and Presence in *The Winter's Tale*," *MLQ* 46 (September 1985): 347–67.

René Girard, "The Crime and Controversy of Leontes in *The Winter's Tale*," *R&L* 22 (1990): 193–219.

René Girard, "Jealousy in *The Winter's Tale*," in Cazelles, *Alphonse Juilland: D'une passion l'autre*, 39–62.

Patricia Southard Gourlay, "'O my most sacred lady': Female Metaphor in *The Winter's Tale*," *ELR* 5 (Autumn 1975): 375–95.

Carryll Grantley, "*The Winter's Tale* and Early Religious Drama," *CompD* 20 (Spring 1986): 17–37.

Andrew Gurr, "The Bear, the Statue, and Hysteria in *The Winter's Tale*," *SQ* 34 (Autumn 1983): 420–25.

Hager, *Shakespeare's Political Animal*, 121–26.

John K. Hale, "The Maturing of Romance in *The Winter's Tale*," *Parergon* 23 (1985): 147–62.

Richard L. Harp, "*The Winter's Tale*: An 'Old Tale' Begetting Wonder," *DR* 58 (1978): 295–308.

Edward L. Hart, "A Mixed Consort: Leontes, Angelo, Helena," *SQ* 15 (Winter 1964): 75–79.

Jonathan Hart, "Alienation, Double Signs with a Difference: Conscious Knots in *Cymbeline* and *The Winter's Tale*," *CIEFLB* 1 (June 1989): 58–78.

Hawkins, *Poetic Freedom and Poetic Truth*, 80–82.

Neil Heims, Shakespeare's *The Winter's Tale*," *Expl* 46 (Summer 1988): 6–7.

Robert R. Hellenga, "The Scandal of *The Winter's Tale*," *ES* 57 (April 1976): 11–18.

R. P. Hewett, *Reading and Response*, 120–27.

Charles W. Hieatt, "The Function of Structure in *The Winter's Tale*," *YES* 8 (1978): 238–48.

Richard W. Hillman, "The 'Gillyvors' Exchange in *The Winter's Tale*," *ESC* 5 (Spring 1979): 16–23.

F. David Hoeniger, "The Meaning of *The Winter's Tale*," *UTQ* 20 (October 1950): 11–26.

Eve Horowitz, "'The Truth of Your Own Seeming': Women and Language in *The Winter's Tale*," *UES* 26 (September 1988): 7–14.

Maurice Hunt, "Leontes' 'Affection' and Renaissance 'Intention': *Winter's Tale* I.ii.135–146," *UMSE* 4, no. 1 (1983): 49–55.

Maurice Hunt, "The Three Seasons of Mankind: Age, Nature, and Art in *The Winter's Tale*," *ISJR* 58 (May 1984): 299–309.

Maurice Hunt, "'Standing in Rich Place': The Importance of Context in *The Winter's Tale*," *RMRLL* 38, no. 1 (1984): 13–33.

Myles Hurd, "Shakespeare's Paulina: Characterization and Craftsmanship in *The Winter's Tale*," *CLAJ* 26 (June 1983): 303–10.

Bertram L. Joseph, "Character and Plot," *DramaS* 4 (Spring–Fall 1964): 546–48.

Mitsuru Kamachi, "'Would Her Name Were Grace': A Reconsideration of the *The Winter's Tale*," *ShStud* 18 (1979–1980): 57–71.

Mythili Kaul, "The Old Shepherd's Speech in *The Winter's Tale*," *UCrow* 7 (1987): 96–100.

David Kaula, "Autolycus' Trumpery," *SEL* 16 (Spring 1986): 287–303.

Nicholas K. Kiessling, "*The Winter's Tale*, II.iii.103–7: An Allusion to the Hag-Incubus," *SQ* 28 (Winter 1977): 93–95.

Han Kim, "A Study of Shakespeare's View of Time and Human Salvation: With Reference to *The Winter's Tale*," *JELL* 35 (August 1989): 537–57.

Knight, *The Crown of Life*, 76–128.

Knight, *The Golden Labyrinth*, 82–84.

L. C. Knights, "'Integration' in *The Winter's Tale*," *SR* 84 (Winter 1976): 595–613. Reprinted in Durry, Ellrodt, and Jones-Davies, *De Shakespeare à T. S. Eliot*, 93–104.

Theresa M. Krier, "The Triumph of Time: Paradox in *The Winter's Tale*," *CentR* 26 (Autumn 1982): 341–53.

Stuart M. Kurland, "'We Need No More of Your Advice': Political Realism in *The Winter's Tale*," *SEL* 31 (Spring 1991): 365–86.

Mary Ellen Lamb, "Ovid and *The Winter's Tale*: Conflicting Views toward Art: Essays in Honor of S. F. Johnson," in Elton and Long, *Shakespeare and Dramatic Tradition*, 69–87.

Maydee G. Lande, "*The Winter's Tale*: A Question of Motive," *AI* 43 (1986):51–65.

F. H. Langman, "*Winter's Tale*," *SoRA* 9 (1976): 195–204.

François Laroque, "Pagan Ritual, Christian Liturgy, and Folk Customs in *The Winter's Tale*," *CahiersE* 22 (October 1982):25–33.

Kathleen Latimer, "The Communal Action of *The Winter's Tale*," in *The Terrain of Comedy*, ed. Louise Cowan (Dallas, TX: Dallas Institute of Humanities and Culture, 1984), 125–42.

John Lawlor, "Pandosto and the Nature of Dramatic Romance," *PQ* 41 (January 1962): 96–113.

Peter Lindenbaum, "Time, Sexual Love, and the Uses of the Pastoral in *The Winter's Tale*," *MLQ* 33 (March 1972): 3–22.

Fredric M. Litto, "The Coherence of the Oracle of Delphi in *The Winter's Tale*," *EAA* 5–6 (1981–1982): 163–71.

A. Lynne Magnusson, "Finding Place for a Faultless Lyric: Verbal Virtuosity in *The Winter's Tale*," *UCrow* 9 (1989): 96–106.

Michael H. Markel, "Why Hermione Lives but Desdemona Dies: An Approach to Shakespearian Genre Definition," *PAPA* 4 (Summer 1978): 50–56.

Cynthia Marshall, "Dualism and the Hope of Reunion in *The Winter's Tale*," *Soundings* 69 (Autumn 1986): 294–309.

Louis L. Martz, "Shakespeare's Humanist Enterprise: *The Winter's Tale*," in Carey, *English Renaissance Studies Presented to Dame Helen Gardner*, 114–31.

P. Marudanayagam, "Shakespeare's *The Winter's Tale*," *Expl* 41 (Spring 1983): 18–19.

S. R. Maveety, "What Shakespeare Did with *Pandosto*: An Interpretation of *The Winter's Tale*," in McNeir and Greenfield, *Pacific Coast Studies in Shakespeare*, 263–79.

David McCandless, "'Verily Bearing Blood': Pornography, Sexual Love, and the Reclaimed Feminine in *The Winter's Tale*," *EiT* 9 (November 1990): 61–81.

John C. McCloskey, "Shakespeare's *The Winter's Tale*," *Expl* 23 (Spring 1965): Item 40.

Russ McDonald, "Poetry and Plot in *The Winter's Tale*," *SQ* 36 (Summer 1985): 315–29.

Bruce McIver, "Shakespeare's Miraculous Deception: Transcendence in *The Winter's Tale*," *MSpr* 73 (1979): 341–51.

Barbara Melchiori, "Still Harping on My Daughter," *EM* 11 (Spring 1960): 63–64.

Ronald M. Meldrum, "Dramatic Intention in *The Winter's Tale*," *HAB* 19 (Summer 1968): 52–60.

Stephen J. Miko, "*The Winter's Tale*," *SEL* 29 (Spring 1989): 259–75.

Bernard Moro, and Michelle Willems, "Death and Rebirth in *Macbeth* and *The Winter's Tale*," *CahiersE* 21 (April 1982): 35–48.

William R. Morse, "Metacriticism and Materiality: The Case of Shakespeare's *The Winter's Tale*," *ELH* 58 (June 1991): 283–304.

Norman Nathan, "Leontes' Provocation," *SQ* 19 (Winter 1968(: 19–24.

Carol Thomas Neely, "*The Winter's Tale*: The Triumph of Speech," *SEL* 15 (Spring 1975): 321–38.

Carol Thomas Neely, "Women and Issue in *The Winter's Tale*," *PQ* 57 (1978): 181–94.

Mary Pollingue Nichols, "*The Winter's Tale*: The Triumph of Comedy over Tragedy," *IJPP* 9 (1981): 169–90.

J. H. P. Pafford, "Music, and the Songs in *The Winter's Tale*," *SQ* 10 (Spring 1959): 161–75.

Daryl W. Palmer, "Entertainment, Hospitality, and Family in *The Winter's Tale*," *ISJR* 59 (February 1985): 253–61.

Natalie Parsons, "Shakespeare's Ladies: Paulina in *Winter's Tale*," *Baconiana* 34 (October 1950): 228–30.

D'Orsay W. Pearson, "Witchcraft in *The Winter's Tale*: Paulina as 'Alcahueta y un Poquito Hechizera,'" *ShakS* 12 (1979): 195–213.

Ace G. Pilkington, "Romance and Fantasy in *The Winter's Tale*," *Encyclia* 58 (1981): 79–84.

Alex Potter, "The Concept of Time in *The Winter's Tale*," *ShSA* 3 (1989): 58–66.

Dennis R. Preston, "Language and the Structure of *The Winter's Tale*," *KN* 25, no. 4 (1978): 421–32.

Richard Proudfoot, "Verbal Reminiscence and the Two-Part Structure of *The Winter's Tale*," *ShS* 29 (1976): 67–78.

R. F. Rashbrook, "*The Winter's Tale*," *N&Q* 192 (November 1947): 520–21.

A. P. Riemer, "Deception in *The Winter's Tale*," *SSEng* 13 (1987–1988): 21–38.

Leo Rockas, "'Browzing of Ivy': *The Winter's Tale*," *ArielE* 6 (January 1975): 3–16.

Henri Roddier, "A Freudian Detective's Shakespeare," *MP* 48 (November 1950): 129–30.

Martha Ronk, "Recasting Jealousy: A Reading of *The Winter's Tale*," *L&P* 36, no. 1 (1990): 50–77.

Murry M. Schwartz, "*The Winter's Tale*: Loss and Transformation," *AI* 32 (Summer 19075): 145–99.

Ernest Schanzer, "The Structural Pattern of *The Winter's Tale*," *REL* 5 (April 1964): 72–82.

William O. Scott, "Seasons and Flowers in *The Winter's Tale*," *SQ* 14 (Autumn 1963): 411–17.

Paul N. Siegel, "Leontes a Jealous Tyrant," *RES* 1 (October 1950): 302–07.

Hallett Smith, "Leontes' Affectio," *SQ* 14 (Spring 1963): 163–66.

Strong, *The Sacred River*, 58.

Richard Studing, "Spectacle and Masque in *The Winter's Tale*," *EM* 21 (Spring 1972): 55–80.

Edward W. Tayler, *Nature and Art in Renaissance Literature* (New York: Columbia University Press, 1964), 121–41.

Michael Taylor, "Innocence in *The Winter's Tale*," *ShakS* 15 (1982): 227–42.

Michael Taylor, "Shakespeare's *The Winter's Tale*: Speaking in the Fereedom of Knowledge," *CritQ* 14 (Spring 1972): 49–56.

David Thatcher, "*The Winter's Tale*, I.ii.186," *SN* 59 (Summer 1987): 207–08.

W. B. Thorne, "'Things Newborn': A Study of the Rebirth Motif in *The Winter's Tale*," *HAB* 19 (Spring 1968): 34–43.

Michio Tokumi, "*The Winter's Tale* in the Social Context," *SELL* 39 (February 1989): 1–11.

Roger J. Trienens, "The Inception of Leontes' Jealousy in *The Winter's Tale*," *SQ* 4 (July 1953): 321–26.

Marion Trousdale, "Style in *The Winter's Tale*," *CritQ* 18 (Winter 1976): 25–30.

S. Viswanathan, "Theatricality and Mimesis in *The Winter's Tale*: The Instance of 'taking one by the hand,'" in Nagarajan and Viswanathan, *Shakespeare in India*, 42–52.

Frederick O. Waage, "Be Stone No More: Italian Cinquecento Art and Shakespeare's Last Plays," *BuR* 25, no. 1 (Spring 1980): 56–87.

David Ward, "Affection, Intention, and Dreams in *The Winter's Tale*," *MLR* 82 (October 1987): 545–54.

Watson, *Shakespeare and the Hazards of Ambition*, 225–74.

Thomas Ramey Watson, "Shakespeare's *Winter's Tale*," *Expl* 40 (Fall 1981): 11–13.

Douglas B. Wilson, "Euripides' *Alcestis* and the Ending of Shakespeare's *The Winter's Tale*," *ISJR* 58 (May 1984): 345–55.

Harold S. Wilson, "Nature and Art in *The Winter's Tale*," *ShAB* 18 (July 1943): 114–20.

Richard Wincor, "Shakespeare's Festival Plays," *SQ* 1 (October 1950): 219–23, 26–33.

SAMPSON, WILLIAM, *The Vow Breaker*

Ellen F. Wright, "'We Are Mock'd with Art': Shakespeare's Wintry Tale," *ELWIU* 6 (Spring 1979): 147–59.

Laurence Wright, "When Does the Tragi-Comic Disruption Start? *The Winter's Tale* and Leontes' 'Affection,'" *ES* 70 (July 1989): 225–32.

T. Wright, "Bohemia's Sea Coast in *The Winter's Tale*," *Baconiana* 38 (December 1954): 117–24.

Young, *The Heart's Forest*, 104–45.

SAMPSON, WILLIAM

The Vow Breaker; or, The Fair Maiden of Clifton

Adams, *English Domestic or Homiletic Tragedies*, 173–77.

SHIRLEY, JAMES

The Bird in a Cage

Kim Walker, "New Prison: Representing the Female Actor in Shirley's *The Bird in a Cage*, (1633)," *ELR* 21 (Autumn 1991): 385–400.

The Cardinal

D. S. Bland, "A Word in Shirley's *The Cardinal*," *RES* 4 (October 1953): 358–59.

A. P. Hogan, "Thematic Analysis of *The Cardinal*: A New Perspective on Shirley," *TES* 5 (1975): 75–85.

Lucow, *James Shirley*, 129–36.

Changes; or, Love in a Maze

Robert R. Reed, Jr., "James Shirley and the Sentimental Comedy," *Anglia* 73, no. 2 (1955): 149–70.

The Constant Maid

Beverly DeBord, "The Stage as Mirror of Society: The Widow in Two Seventeenth Century Comedies," *SPWVSRA* 10 (1985): 71–78.

The Duke's Mistress

Butler, *Theatre and Crisis*, 42–44.

The Example

Nathan Cogan, "James Shirley's *The Example* (1634): Some Reconsiderations," *SEL* 17 (Spring 1977): 317–31.

Robert R. Reed, Jr., "James Shirley and the Sentimental Comedy," *Anglia* 73, no. 2 (1955): 149–70.

The Gamesters

Richard Levin, "Measure beyond Measure and *The Gamesters*," *RN* 18, no. 1 (1965): 1–3.

Robert R. Reed, Jr., "James Shirley and the Sentimental Comedy," *Anglia* 73, no. 2 (1955): 149–70.

The Gentleman of Venice

Lucow, *James Shirley*, 100–03.

Hyde Park

Richard Levin, *The Multiple Plot in English Renaissance Drama*, 96–100.

Richard Levin, "The Triple Plot of *Hyde Park*," *MLR* 62 (January 1967): 17–27.

Robert R. Reed, Jr., "James Shirley and the Sentimental Comedy," *Anglia* 73, no. 2 (1955): 149–70.

Frieder Stadtfeld, "'Fortune', 'providence' and 'manners' in James Shirley's *Hyde Park*," *Anglia* 93, no. 2 (1975): 111–39.

Wells, *Elizabethan and Jacobean Playwrights*, 183–86.

Albert Wertheim, "Games and Courtship in James Shirley's *Hyde Park*," *Anglia* 90, no. 1 (1972): 71–91.

The Lady of Pleasure

Butler, *Theatre and Crisis*, 166–74.

SHIRLEY, JAMES, *The Opportunity*

Richard Levin, *The Multiple Plot in English Renaissance Drama*, 99–102.

Lucow, *James Shirley*, 123–29.

Kenneth Richards, "Satire and Values in James Shirley's *The Lady of Pleasure*," in *A Tribute to George Coffin Taylor*, ed. Arnold Williams (Chapel Hill: University of North Carolina Press, 1952), 168–77.

Tony J. Stafford, "Shirley's *The Lady of Pleasure*: The Dialectic of Earth and Sky," *JRMMRA* 4 (January 1983): 125–34.

The Opportunity

Loftis, *Renaissance Drama in England and Spain*, 251–52.

Saint Patrick of Ireland

J. M. Flood, "An Elizabethan Dramatist on St. Patrick," *Irish Monthly* 76 (September 1948): 421–46.

The Traitor

Joseph W. Donohue, Jr., *Dramatic Character in the English Romantic Age* (Princeton: Princeton University Press, 1970), 29–35.

The Triumph of Peace

Lawrence Venuti, "The Politics of Allusion: The Genry and Shirley's *The Triumph of Peace*," *ELR* 16 (Winter 1986): 182–205.

The Witty Fair One

Leech, *Shakespearian Tragedies*, 190–94.

Robert R. Reed, Jr., "James Shirley and the Sentimental Comedy," *Anglia* 73, no. 2 (1955): 149–70.

The Young Admiral

Loftis, *Renaissance Drama in England and Spain*, 249–51.

SIDNEY, SIR PHILIP

The Four Foster Children of Desire

Glynne Wickham, "*Love's Labor's Lost* and *The Four Foster Children of Desire*, 1581," *SQ* 36 (Spring 1985): 49–55.

Hager, *Dazzling Images*, 184–87.

The Lady of May

Alan Hager, "Phomboid Logic: Anti-Idealism and a Cure for Recusancy in Sidney's *Lady of May*," *ELH* 57 (Fall 1990): 485–502. Reprinted in Hager, *Dazzling Images*, 41–52.

Patrick J. Hogan, "Neoplatonic Elements in Sidney's Masque-like *Lady of May*," *SNew* 1 (1980): 53–57.

Christopher Martin, "Impeding the Progress: Sidney's *The Lady of May*," *ISJR* 60 (February 1986): 395–405.

Louis Adrian Montrose, "Celebration and Insinuation: Sir Philip Sidney and the Motives of Elizabethan Courtship," *RenD* 8 (1977): 3–35.

S. K. Orgel, "Sidney's Experiment in the Pastoral: *The Lady of May*," *JWCI* 26 (July 1963): 198–203.

Penny Pickett, "Sidney's Use of *Phaedrus* in *The Lady of May*," *SEL* 16 (Spring 1976): 33–50.

Robert E. Stillman, "Justice and the 'Good Word' in Sidney's *The Lady of May*," *SEL* 24 (Spring 1984): 23–38.

SKELTON, JOHN

Magnificence

Bevington, *From "Mankind" to Marlowe*, 132–37.

William O. Harris, "The Thematic Importance of Skelton's Allusion to Horace in *Magnyfycence*," *SEL* 3 (Winter 1963): 1–8.

Robert S. Kinsman, "Skelton's *Magyfycence*: The Strategy of the 'Olde Sayde Sawe,'" *SP* 63 (January 1966): 99–125.

Paula Neuss, "Proverbial Skelton," *SN* 54 (Autumn 1982): 237–46.

STEVENSON, WILLIAM, *Gammer Gurton's Needle*

Leigh Winser, "*Magnyfycence* and the Characters of Sottie," *SCJ* 12 (Fall 1981): 85–94.

STEVENSON, WILLIAM

Gammer Gurton's Needle

Bevington, *From "Mankind" to Marlowe*, 33–34.

Douglas Duncan, "*Gammar Gurton's Needle* and the Concept of Human Parody," *SEL* 27 (Spring 1987): 177–96.

Anthony Graham-White, "Elizabethan Punctuation and the Actor: *Gammar Gurton's Needle* as a Case Study," *TJ* 34 (March 1982): 96–106.

Reginald W. Ingram, "*Gammar Gurton's Needle*: Comedy Not Quite of the Lowest Order?" *SEL* 7 (Spring 1967): 257–68.

Stanley J. Kozikowski, "Comedy Ecclesiastical and Otherwise in *Gammar Gurton's Needle*," *Greyfriar* 18 (1975): 5–18.

Stanley J. Kozikowski, "Stevenson's *Gammar Gurton's Needle*," *Expl* 38 (Summer 1980): 37–39.

N. Lindsay McFadyen, "What Was Really Lost in *Gammar Gurton's Needle?*" *RenP 1981* (1982): 9–13.

J. W. Robinson, "The Art and Meaning of *Gammar Gurton's Needle*," *RenD* 14 (1983): 45–77.

Bernard Spivack, *Shakespeare and the Allegory of Evil*, 322–27. Reprinted in Bluestone and Rabkin, *Shakespeare's Contemporaries*, 1–5.

John W, Velz, "Scatology and Moral Meaning in Two English Renaissance Plays," *SCRev* 1 (Spring–Summer 1984): 4–21.

Barrett Jere Whiting, "Diccon's French Cousin," *SP* 42 (Winter 1945): 31–40.

TAILOR, ROBERT

Hog Hath Lost His Pearl

Mann, *The Elizabethan Player*, 178–86.

TAYLOR, JOHN

The Triumphs of Fame and Honor

Sheila Williams, "A Lord Mayor's Show by John Taylor, the Water Poet," *BJRL* 41 (Winter 1959): 501–31.

TOURNEUR, CYRIL

The Atheist's Tragedy

Henry H. Adams, "Cyril Tourneur on Revenge," *JEGP* 48 (January 1949): 72–87.

Jobesh Bhattacharyya, "The Tragedies of Cyril Tourneur and the Medieval Moral Tradition," *Criticism & Research* 8 (1987–1988): 349–62.

Jackson I. Cope, "Tourneur's *Atheist Tragedy* and the Jig of 'Singing Simkin,'" *MLN* 70 (December 1955): 571–73.

Huston Diehl, "'Reduce Thy Understanding to Thine Eye': Seeing and Interpreting in *The Atheist's Tragedy*," *SP* 78 (Winter 1981): 47–60.

Inga-Stina Ekcblad, "An Approach to Tourneur's Imagery," *MLR* 54 (October 1959): 489–98.

Eliot, *Essays on Elizabethan Drama*, 121–29.

Gomez, *The Alienated Figure in Drama*, 34–36.

William E. Gruber, "Building a Scene: The Text and Its Representation in *The Atheist's Tragedy*," *CompD* 19 (Summer 1985): 193–208.

Frank Howson, "Horror and the Macabre in Four Elizabethan Tragedies: *The Revenger's Tragedy*, *The Duchess of Malfi*, *The Second Maiden's Tragedy*, *The Atheist's Tragedy*," *CahiersE* 10 (April 1968): 1–12.

R. J. Kaufmann, "Theodicy, Tragedy, and the Psalmist: Tourneur's *Atheist's Tragedy*," *CompD* 3 (Autumn 1969): 241–62. Reprinted in Davidson, Gianakaris, and Stroupe, *Drama in the Renaissance*, 192–215.

Knight, *Golden Labyrinth*, 102–03.

Clifford Leech, "*The Atheist's Tragedy* as a Dramatic Comment on Chapman's *Bussy* Plays," *JEGP* 52 (October 1953): 525–30.

Levin, *The Multiple Plot in English Renaissance Drama*, 75–85.

TOURNEUR, CYRIL, *The Revenger's Tragedy*

Glen A. Love, "Morality and Style in *The Atheist's Tragedy*," *HAB* 15 (Spring 1964): 38–45.

R. E. R. Madelaine, "Stage Imagery in *The Atheist's Tragedy*," in Brissenden, *Shakespeare and Some Others*, 123–45.

Murray, *A Study of Cyril Tourneur*, 57–143.

Robert Ornstein, "*The Atheist's Tragedy* and Renaissance Naturalism," *SP* 51 (April 1954): 194–207.

Ornstein, *Moral Vision of Jacobean Tragedy*, 118–27.

Parrott, and Ball, *Short View of Elizabethan Drama*, 218–22.

Ribner, *Jacobean Tragedy*, 86–96.

Simpson, *Studies in Elizabethan Drama*, 172–76.

Wells, *Elizabethan and Jacobean Playwrights*, 31–34.

The Revenger's Tragedy

Henry H. Adams, "Cyril Tourneur on Revenge," *JEGP* 48 (January 1949): 72–87.

Jonas A. Barish, "The True and False Families of *The Revenger's Tragedy*," in Henning, Kimbrough, and Knowles, *English Renaissance Drama*, 142–54.

Kellie Harrison Bean, "Tourneur's *The Revenger's Tragedy*," *Expl* 47 (Winter 1989): 8–11.

Berry, *Poet's Grammar*, 80–86.

Jobesh Bhattacharyya, "The Tragedies of Cyril Tourneur and the Medieval Moral Tradition," *Criticism and Research* 8 (1987–1988): 349–62.

Rick Bowers, "Tourneur's *The Revenger's Tragedy*, III.v.69–82," *Expl* 42 (Spring 1984): 10–11.

Laura G. Broomley, "The Lost Lucrece: Middleton's *The Ghost of Lucrece*," *PLL* 21 (Summer 1985): 258–74.

Richard T. Brucher, "Fantasies of Violence: *Hamlet* and *The Revenger's Tragedy*," *SEL* 21 (Spring 1981): 257–70.

Larry S. Champion, "Tourneur's *The Revenger's Tragedy* and the Jacobean Tragic Perspective," *SP* 72 (Summer 1975): 299–321.

Michael Cordner, "Stamping on a Duke: *The Revenger's Tragedy* III.v," *N&Q* 37 (June 1990): 205–06.

T. W. Craik, "*The Revenger's Tragedy*," *EIC* 6 (October 1956): 482–85.

Inga-Stina Ekeblad, "An Approach to Tourneur's Imagery," *MLR* 54 (October 1959): 489–98.

Eliot, *Essays on Elizabethan Drama*, 121–25, 129–33.

Robert C. Evans, "Women and the Meaning of *The Revenger's Tragedy*," *PostS* 4 (1987): 65–73.

Laurie A. Finke, "Painting Women: Images of Femininity in Jacobean Tragedy," *TJ* 36 (October 1984): 357–70.

George L. Geckel, "Justice in *The Revenger's Tragedy*," *RenP 1972* (1973): 75–82.

Gomez, *The Alienated Figure in Drama*, 53–58.

Christine Gomez, "The Malcontent Outsider in British Drama—Jacobean and Modern," *AJES* 12 (April 1987): 53–74.

D. C. Gundy, "Tourneur's *The Revenger's Tragedy*, II.ii.216–18," *Expl* 44 (Spring 1986): 11–12.

R. V. Holdsworth, "Middleton and William Perkins: A Biblical Echo in *The Revenger's Tragedy*," *N&Q* 21 (March 1985): 61–63.

Frank Howson, "Horror and the Macabre in Four Elizabethan Tragedies: *The Revenger's Tragedy*, *The Duchess of Malfi*, *The Second Maiden's Tragedy*, *The Atheist's Tragedy*," *CahiersE* 10 (April 1968): 1–12.

Ronald Huebert, "*The Revenger's Tragedy* and the Fallacy of the Excluded Middle," *UTQ* 48 (January 1978): 10–22.

Peter Hyland, "The Disguised Revenger and *The Revenger's Tragedy*," *SoRA* 15 (1982): 254–62.

Misuro Kamachi, "Vindice *Vindicatus*: The Hidden Trickster in *The Revenger's Tragedy*," *ShStud* 16 (1977–1978): 1–17.

Arthur L. Kistner, and M. K. Kistner, "Morality and Inevitability in *The Revenger's Tragedy*," *JEGP* 71 (April 1972): 36–46.

Knight, *Golden Labyrinth*, 101–02.

Peter Lisca, "*The Revenger's Tragedy*: A Study in Irony," *PQ* 38 (April 1959): 242–51.

J. C. Maxwell, "Two Notes on *The Revenger's Tragedy*," *MLR* 44 (October 1949): 545.

TOURNEUR, CYRIL, *The Revenger's Tragedy*

Scott McMillin, "Acting and Violence: *The Revenger's Tragedy* and Its Departures from *Hamlet*," *SEL* 24 (Spring 1984): 275–91.

Mann, *The Elizabethan Player*, 49–50.

Dieter Mehl, "Corruption, Retribution and Justice in *Measure for Measure* and *The Revenger's Tragedy*," in Honigmann, *Shakespeare and His Contemporaries*, 114–28.

Michael E. Mooney, "'This Luxurious Circle': Figurenposition in *The Revenger's Tragedy*," *ELR* 13 (Spring 1983): 162–81.

D. C. Muecke, "Aspects of Baroque Time and *The Revenger's Tragedy*," in Brissenden, *Shakespeare and Some Others*, 104–22.

Murray, *A Study of Cyril Tourneur*, 173–257.

Allardyce Nicoll, "*The Revenger's Tragedy* and the Virtue of Anonymity," in Hosley, *Essays on Shakespeare and Elizabethan Drama*, 309–16.

J. C. Oates, "The Comedy of Metamorphosis in *The Revenger's Tragedy*," *Bucknell University Studies* 11 (December 1962): 38–52.

Robert Ornstein, "The Ethical Design of *The Revenger's Tragedy*," *ELH* 21 (June 1954): 81–93.

Ornstein, *Moral Vision of Jacobean Tragedy*, 105–18.

Parrott, and Ball, *A Short View of Elizabethan Tragedy*, 215–18.

Howard Pearce, "*Virtù* and *Poesis* in *The Revenger's Tragedy*," *ELH* 43 (March 1976): 19–37.

John Peter, "*The Revenger's Tragedy*," *EIC* 6 (October 1956): 485–86.

John Peter, "*The Revenger's Tragedy* Reconsidered," *EIC* 6 (April 1956): 131–43.

Prior, *The Language of Tragedy*, 136–44.

P. Ramamoorthy, "*King Lear* and *The Revenger's Tragedy* as Theatre of Cruelty," *AJES* 9 (July 1984): 155–62.

Ribner, *Jacobean Tragedy*, 75–86.

Erik Ryding, "Tourneur's *The Revenger's Tragedy*, I.i.12–13," *Expl* 41 (Fall 1982): 20–21.

Leo G. Salingar, "Tourneur and the Tragedy of Revenge," in *The New Pelican Guide to English Literature, Vol. 2: The Age of Shakespeare*, ed. Boris Ford (Harmondsworth: Penguin, 1982), 436–56.

Leslie Sanders, "*The Revenger's Tragedy*: A Play on the Revenge Tragedy," *Ren&R* 10 (February 1973): 25–36.

Samuel Schoenbaum, "*The Revenger's Tragedy*: Jacobean Dance of Death," *MLQ* 15 (September 1954): 201–07.

Scott, *Renaissance Drama*, 31–46.

J. L. Simmons, "The Tongue and Its Office in *The Revenger's Tragedy*," *PMLA* 92 (January 1977): 56–58.

M. W. A. Smith, "*The Revenger's Tragedy*: The Derivation and Interpretation of Statistical Results for Resolving Disputed Authorship," *CHum* 21 (January–March 1987): 21–55.

Peter Stallybrass, "Reading the Body: *The Revenger's Tragedy* and the Jacobean Theatre of Consumption," *RenD* 18 (1987): 121–48.

William L. Stull, "'This Metamorphosde Tragoedie': Thomas Kyd, Cyril Tourneur, and the Jacobean Theatre of Cruelty," *Ariel* 14 (July 1983): 35–49.

Eugene M. Waith, "The Ascription of Speeches in *The Revenger's Tragedy*," *MLN* 57 (February 1952): 119–21.

Wells, *Elizabethan and Jacobean Playwrights*, 34–38.

Stephen Wigler, "If Looks Could Kill: Fathers and Sons in *The Revenger's Tragedy*," *CompD* 9 (Autumn 1975): 206–25.

Stephen Wigler, "'Tis Well He Died; He Was a Witch': A Note on *The Revenger's Tragedy*, V.iii.117," *ELN* 14 (June 1977): 17–20.

Lillian Wilds, "The Revenger as Dramatist: A Study of the Character-as-Dramatist in *The Revenger's Tragedy*," *BRMMLA* 30, no. 3 (1976): 113–22.

Nancy G. Wilds, "'Of Rare Fire Compact': Image and Rhetoric in *The Revenger's Tragedy*," *TSLL* 17 (Spring 1975): 61–74.

TOWNSHEND, AURELIAN

Albion's Triumph

Kogan, *The Hieroglyphic King*, 138–49.

Tempe Restored

Hassell, *Renaissance Drama & the English Church Year*, 136–37.

Kogan, *The Hieroglyphic King*, 149–59.

UDALL, NICHOLAS

Jack Juggler

Takao Kuya, "Determining Authorship Based on the Similarities of Rime Words: With Special Reference to the Dramatic Works Often Attributed to Nicholas Udall," *SELL* 25 (March 1985): 75–114.

Jacob and Esau

Richard Leighton Greene, "Carols in Tudor Drama," in Rowland, *Chaucer and Middle English Studies*, 357–65.

Takao Kuya, "Determining Authorship Based on the Similarities of Rime Words: With Special Reference to the Dramatic Works Often Attributed to Nicholas Udall," *SELL* 25 (March 1985): 75–114.

Ralph Roister Doister

Catherine A. Hebert, "Udall's *Ralph Roister Doister*," *Expl* 37 (Winter 1979): 20.

Edwin S. Miller, "Roister Doister's 'Funeralls,'" *SP* 43 (January 1946): 42–58.

William Perry, "The Prayer for the Queen in *Roister Doister*," *Studies in English* (University of Texas) 27 (June 1948): 222–33.

A. W. Plunestlad, "Satirical Parody in *Roister Doister*: A Reinterpretation," *SP* 60 (April 1963): 141–54.

Frank Towne, "*Roister Doister*'s Assault on *The Castle of Perseverance*, *WSCS* 18 (December 1950): 175–80.

Respublica

Takao Kuya, "Determining Authorship Based on the Similarities of Rime Words: With Special Reference to the Dramatic Works Often Attributed to Nicholas Udall," *SELL* 25 (March 1985): 75–114.

Douglas F. Rutledge, "*Respublica*: Rituals of Status Elevation and the Political Mythology of Mary Tudor," *MRDE* 5 (Spring 1991): 55–68.

WAGER, ?

The Cruel Debtor

Blackburn, *Biblical Drama*, 128–31.

WAGER, LEWIS

The Life and Repentaunce of Mary Magdalene

Bevington, *From "Mankind" to Marlowe*, 94–99, 171–75.

Blackburn, *Biblical Drama*, 131–36.

Mark Eccles, "William Wager and His Plays," *ELN* 18 (June 1981): 258–62.

Peter Happé, "The Protestant Adaptation of the Saint Play," in Davidson, *The Saint Play in Medieval Europe*, 205–40.

Paula Neuss, "The Sixteenth-Century English 'Proverb' Play," *CompD* 18 (Spring 1984): 1–18.

Paul White, "Lewis Wager's *Life and Repentaunce of Mary Magdalene* and John Calvin," *N&Q* 28 (December 1981): 508–12.

WAGER, WILLIAM

Enough Is as Good as a Feast

Adams, *English Domestic or Homiletic Tragedies*, 59–63.

Bevington, *From "Mankind" to Marlowe*, 158–61.

Paula Neuss, "The Sixteenth-Century English 'Proverb' Play," *CompD* 18 (Spring 1984): 1–18.

The Longer Thou Livest the More Fool Thou Art

Bevington, *From "Mankind" to Marlowe*, 91–99, 163–65.

WAGER, WILLIAM, *The Trial of Treasure*

The Trial of Treasure

Leslie M. Olives, "William Wager and *The Trial of Treasure*," *HLQ* 9 (August 1946): 419–30.

WALPUL, GEORGE

Tide Tarrieth No Man

Bernard Beckerman, "Playing the Crowd: Structure and Soliloquy in *Tide Tarrieth No Man*," in Gray, *Mirror up to Shakespeare*, 128–37.

Bevington, *From "Mankind" to Marlowe*, 149–51.

Mann, *The Elizabethan Player*, 23–25.

WARNER, WILLIAM

Albions England

Nancy A. Gutierrez, "An Allusion to 'India' and Pearls," *SQ* 36 (Summer 1985): 220.

WATSON, THOMAS

Absalom

Blackburn, *Biblical Drama*, 81–88.

WEBSTER, JOHN

Appius and Virginia
(with Heywood)

Adams, *English Domestic or Homiletic Tragedy*, 75–78.

Cope, *Dramatury of the Daemonic*, 41–44.

Inga-Stina Ekeblad, "Storm Imagery in *Appius and Virginia*," *N&Q* 3 (March 1956): 5–7.

Forker, *The Skull Beneath the Skin*, 200–24.

Richard Leighton Greene, "Carols in Tudor Drama," in Rowland, *Chaucer and Middle English Studies*, 357–65.

P. Happé, "Tragic Themes in Three Tudor Moralities," *SEL* 5 (Spring 1965): 207–27.

Haworth, *English Hymns and Ballads*, 137–48.

R. G. Howarth, "Webster's *Appius and Virginia*," *PQ* 46 (Winter 1967): 135–37.

Mina Irgat, "Disease Imagery in the Plays of J. Webster," *Litera* 2 (1955): 2–24.

Melvin Seiden, "Two Notes of Webster's *Appius and Virginia*," *PQ* 35 (October 1956): 408–17.

Rosemary Woolf, "The Influence of the Mystery Plays upon the Popular Tragedies of the 1650's," *RenD* 6 (1973): 89–105.

A Cure for a Cuckold

Inga-Stina Ekeblad, "Webster's Constructional Rhythm," *ELH* 24 (September 1957): 165–76.

Forker, *The Skull Beneath the Skin*, 171–89.

Mina Irgat, "Disease Imagery in the Plays of J. Webster," *Litera* 2 (1955): 2–24.

Murray, *A Study of John Webster*, 215–36.

Pearson, *Tragedy and Tragicomedy in the Plays of John Webster*, 115–32.

The Devil's Law Case; or, When Women Go to Law the Devil Is Full of Business

Berry, *The Art of John Webster*, 151–67.

Lee Bliss, "Destructive Will and Social Chaos in *The Devil's Law-Case*," *MLR* 72 (October 1977): 513–25.

Bliss, *The World's Perspective*, 171–88.

D. C. Gunby, "*The Devil's Law-Case:* An Interpretation," *MLR* 63 (October 1968): 545–58.

Forker, *The Skull Beneath the Skin*, 370–450.

Haworth, *English Hymns and Ballads*, 117–36.

Mina Irgat, "Disease Imagery in the Plays of J. Webster," *Litera* 2 (1955): 2–24.

Akiko Kusunoki, "A Study of *The Devil's Law Case* with Special Reference to the Controversy over Women," *ShStud* 21 (1982–83): 1–33.

McLeod, *Dramatic Imagery*, 122–53.

Murray, *A Study of John Webster*, 185–214.

Pearson, *Tragedy and Tragicomedy in the Plays of John Webster*, 96–114.

Schuman, *Theatre of Fine Devices*, 99–112.

The Duchess of Malfi

D. P. V. Akrigg, "A Phase in Webster," *N&Q* 193 (October 1948): 454.

Alexander W. Allison, "Ethical Themes in *Duchess of Malfi*, *SEL* 4 (Spring 1964): 263–73.

Susan C. Baker, "The Static Protagonist in *The Duchess of Malfi*," *TSLL* 22 (Autumn 1980): 343–57.

Catherine Belsey, "Emblem and Antithesis in *The Duchess of Malfi*," *RenD* 11 (1980): 115–34.

Ellen R. Belton, "The Function of Antonio in *The Duchess of Malfi*," *TSLL* 18 (Winter 1976): 474–85.

Kimberly W. Bentson, "*The Duchess of Malfi*: Webster's Tragic Vision," *GyS* 3, no. 1 (1976): 20–36.

David M. Bergeron, "The Wax Figures in *The Duchess of Malfi*," *SEL* 18 (Spring 1978): 331–39.

Berry, *The Art of John Webster*, 107–50.

Michael R. Best, "A Precarious Balance: Structure in *The Duchess of Malfi*," in Brissenden, *Shakespeare and Some Others*, 159–77.

Bliss, *The World's Perspective*, 137–70.

Roy Booth, *John Webster's Heart of Glass,"* English 40 (Spring 1991): 97–113.

Rick Bowers, "The Cruel Mathematics of *The Duchess of Malfi*," *ESC* 16 (Autumn 1990): 369–83.

M. C. Bradbrook, *English Dramatic Form: A History if Its Development* (New York: Barnes & Noble, 1965), 103–06.

M. C. Bradbrook, "Fate and Chance in *The Duchess of Malfi*," in *Aspects of Dramatic Form*, 73–88.

M. C. Bradbrook, "Two Notes Upon Webster," *MLR* 42 (July 1947): 281–91.

Elizabeth Brennan, "The Relationship Between Brother and Sister in the Plays of John Webster," *MLR* 58 (October 1963): 488–94.

Lois E. Bueler, "Webster's Excellent Hyena," *PQ* 59 (Winter 1980): 107–11.

James L. Calderwood, "*The Duchess of Malfi*: Styles of Ceremony," *EIC* 12 (April 1962): 133–47.

Cecil, *Poets and Story Tellers*, 34–43.

Cecil W. Davis, "The Structure of *The Duchess of Malfi*: An Approach," *English* 12 (Autumn 1958): 89–93.

Christy Desmet, " 'Neither Maid, Widow, nor Wife': Rhetoric of the Woman Controversy in *Measure for Measure* and *The Duchess of Malfi*," in Kehler and Baker, *In Another Country*, 71–92.

Bettie Anne Doebler, "Continuity in the Art of Dying: *The Duchess of Malfi*," *CompD* 14 (Summer 1980): 203–15.

James P. Driscoll, "Integrity of Life in *The Duchess of Malfi*," *DramS* 6 (May 1967): 42–53.

Leslie Duer, "The Landscape of Imagination in *The Duchess of Malfi*," *MLS* 10 (Winter 1980): 3–9.

Leslie Duer, "The Painter and the Poet: Visual Design in *The Duchess of Malfi*," *Emblematica* 1 (Fall 1986): 293–316.

Inga-Stina Ekeblad, "The 'Impure Art' of John Webster," *RES* 9 (August 1958): 253–67.

Inga-Stina Ekeblad, "A Webster's Villain: A Study of Character Imagery in *The Duchess of Malfi*," *Orpheus* 3 (September 1956): 126–33.

William Empson, "Mine Eyes Dazzle," *EIC* 14 (January 1964): 80–86.

M. Emslie, "Motives in *Malfi*," *EIC* 9 (October 1959): 391–405.

Anat Feinberg, "Observation and Theatricality in Webster's *The Duchess of Malfi*," *ThR* 6 (Winter 1980–1981): 36–44.

Frank B. Fieler, "The Eight Madmen in *The Duchess of Malfi*," *SEL* 7 (Spring 1967): 343–50.

Laurie A. Finke, "Painting Women: Images of Femininity in Jacobean Tragedy," *TJ* 36 (October 1984): 357–70.

Forker, *The Skull Beneath the Skin*, 296–369.

Forker, "'Three Fair Medals Cast in One Figure': *Discordia Concors* as a Principle of Characterization in *The Duchess of Malfi*," *ISJR* 61 (February 1987): 373–81.

Forker, "Webster and Barnes: The Source of the Ceremony of the Cardinal's Arming in *The Duchess of Malfi* Once More," *Anglia* 106, no. 3–4 (1988): 415–20.

Shirley Nelson Garner, "'Let Her Paint an Inch Thick': Painted Ladies in Renaissance Drama and Society," *RenD* 20 (1989): 123–39.

Louis D. Gianetti, "A Contemporary View of *The Duchess of Malfi*," *CompD* 3 (Autumn 1969): 297–307.

Goodwyn, *Image Pattern and Moral Vision*, 36–69, 98–117.

Gomez, *The Alienated Figure in Drama*, 60–64, 122–25.

John Gouws, "Shakespeare, Webster and the Moriturus Lyric in Renaissance England," *ShSA* 3 (1989): 45–57.

Gayle Greene, "Women on Trial in Shakespeare and Webster: 'The Mettle of (Their) Sex,'" *Topic* 36 (Spring 1982): 5–19.

D. C. Gunby, "*The Duchess of Malfi*: A Theological Approach," in *John Webster*, ed. Brian Morris (London: Benn, 1970), 181–204.

R. W. Hamilton, "Webster and Horace," *N&Q* 35 (March 1988): 63–64.

Anne M. Haselkorn, "Sin and the Politics of Penitence: Three Jacobean Adultresses," in Haselkorn and Travitsky, *The Renaissance Englishwoman in Print*, 119–36.

Hawkins, *Likeness of Truth in Elizabethan and Restoration Drama*, 15–17.

Hawkins, *Poetic Freedom and Poetic Truth*, 27–29, 51–54.

Haworth, *English Hymns and Ballads*, 98–116.

James F. Henke, "John Webster's Motif of 'Consuming': An Approach to the Dramatic Unity and Tragic Vision of *The White Devil* and *The Duchess of Malfi*," *NM* 76 (September 1975): 625–41.

Henry Herring, "The Self and Madness in Marlowe's *Edward II* and Webster's *The Duchess of Malfi*," *JMRS* 9 (Fall 1981): 307–23.

Frank Howson, "Horror and the Macabre in Four Elizabethan Tragedies: *The Revenger's Tragedy*, *The Duchess of Malfi*, *The Second Maiden's Tragedy*, *The Atheist's Tragedy*," *CahiersE* 10 (April 1968): 1–12.

Maurice Hunt, "The Spiritual Echoes of *The Duchess of Malfi*," *ELWIU* 14 (Summer 1987): 171–87.

Maurice Hunt, "Webster and Jacobean Medicine: The Case of *The Duchess of Malfi*," *ELWIU* 16 (Spring 1989): 33–49.

Mina Irgat, "Disease Imagery in the Plays of J. Webster," *Litera* 2 (1955): 2–24.

Theodora A. Jankowski, "Defining/Confining the Duchess: Negotiating the Female Body in John Webster's *The Duchess of Malfi*," *SP* 87 (Spring 1990): 221–45.

Lisa Jardine, "*The Duchess of Malfi*: A Case Study in the Literary Representation of Women," in Kappeler and Bryson, *Teaching the Text*, 203–17.

Victor M. K. Kelleher, "Notes on *The Duchess of Malfi*," *UES* 10 (September 1972): 113–15.

Frederick Kiefer, "The Dance of the Madmen in *The Duchess of Malfi*," *JMRS* 17 (Fall 1987): 211–33.

Kinght, *Golden Labyrinth*, 107–10.

G. Wilson Knight, *Shakespearean Dimensions* (Brighton, Eng.: Harvester Press, 1984), 174–203.

F. H. Langman, "Truth and Effect in *The Duchess of Malfi*," *SSEng* 6 (1980–1981): 30–48.

Clifford Leech, "An Addendum on Webster's *Duchess*," *PQ* 37 (April 1958): 253–56.

Clifford Leech, "John Webster—A Critical Study," *Hogarth Lectures on Literature* 16 (1951): 29–89.

Leech, *Shakespeare's Tragedies*, 23–26.

Cynthia Lewis, "'Wise Men, Folly-Fall'n': Characters Named Antonio in English Renaissance Drama," *RenD* 20 (1989): 197–236.

George L. Lewis, "Elements of Medival Horror Tragedy in *The Duchess of Malfi*," *Central States Speech Journal* 13 (Winter 1961): 106–11.

John Loftis, "Lope de Vega's and Webster's Amalfi Plays," *CompD* 16 (Spring 1982): 64–78.

Joan M. Lord, "*The Duchess of Malfi*: 'The Spirit of Greatness' and 'of Woman,'" *SEL* 16 (Spring 1976): 305–17.

Christina Luckyj, "'Great Women of Pleasure': Main Plot and Subplot in *The Duchess of Malfi*," *SEL* 27 (Spring 1987): 267–83.

Luckyj, *A Winter's Snake*, 18–23, 39–50, 80–84, 86–90, 94–100, 136–45.

Jane Marie Luecke, *"The Duchess of Malfi*: Comic and Satiric Confusion in a Tragedy," *SEL* 4 (Spring 1964): 275–90.

David Luisi, "The Function of Bosola in *The Duchess of Malfi*," *ES* 53 (Decmebr 1972): 509–13.

Susan McCloskey, "The Price of Misinterpretation in *The Duchess of Malfi*," in Markley and Fine, *From Renaissance to Restoration*, 34–55.

McLeod, *Dramatic Imagery*, 75–121.

Kathleen McLuskie, "Drama and Sexual Politics: The Case of Webster's Duchess," in Redmond, *Drama, Sex and Politics*, 77–91.

McPeek, *The Black Book of Knaves*, 91–93.

Margaret Lael Mikesell, "Catholic and Protestant Widows in *The Duchess of Malfi*," *Ren&R* 7 (November 1983): 265–79.

Margaret Lael Mikesell, "Matrimony and Change in Webster's *The Duchess of Malfi*," *JRMMRA* 2 (January 1981): 97–111.

Adair Mill, "John Webster as Moralist," *Litera* 3 (1956): 12–34.

Giles Mitchell, and Eugene Wright, "Duke Ferdinand's Lycanthropy as a Disguise Motive in Webster's *The Duchess of Malfi*," *L&P* 25, no. 2 (1975): 117–23.

J. R. Mulryne, *"The White Devil* and *The Duchess of Malfi*," *Stratford-Upon-Avon Studies* 1 (1960): 201–65.

Murray, *A Study of John Webster*, 118–84.

Michael Neill, "Monuments and Ruins as Symbols in *The Duchess of Malfi*," in Redmond, *Drama and Symbolism*, 71–87.

Marianne Nordfors, "Science and Realism in John Webster's *The Duchess of Malfi*," *SN* 49, no. 2 (1977): 233–42.

Ornstein, *Moral Vision of Jacobean Tragedy*, 140–48.

Parrott, and Ball, *A Short View of Elizabethan Tragedy*, 228–32.

Pearson, *Tragedy and Tragicomedy in the Plays of John Webster*, 84–95.

Dennis R. Preston, "Imagery in *The Duchess of Malfi*," *SAP* 7, no. 2 (1976): 109–20.

Prior, *The Language of Tragedy*, 121–35.

Dale B. J. Randall, "The Rank and Earthy Background of Certain Physical Symbols in *The Duchess of Malfi*," *RenD* 18 (1987): 171–203.

Wayne A. Rebhorn, "Circle, Sword, and the Futile Quest: The Nightmare World of Webster's *Duchess of Malfi*," *CahiersE* 27 (April 1985): 53–66.

Ribner, *Jacobean Tragedy*, 108–22.

Ribner, "Webster's Italian Tragedies," *TDR* 5 (March 1961): 106–18.

Brian Richardson, "Words Made Flesh: Imagery as Causality in Drama," in Hartigan, *Within the Dramatic Spectrum*, 160–67.

J. S. Sastri, "The Latest Motive for Ferdinand's Conduct in *The Duchess of Malfi*," *OJES* 2 (1962): 13–28.

J. S Sastri, "Webster's Masque of Madmen: An Examination," *IJES* 3, no. 1 (1962): 33–43.

Schuman, *Theatre of Fine Devices*, 25–33, 42–47, 82–86.

John L. Selzer, "Merit and Degree in Webster's *The Duchess of Malfi*," *ELR* 11 (Winter 1981): 70–80.

Phoebe S. Spinard, "Coping with Uncertainty in *The Duchess of Malfi*," *EIRC* 6 (1980): 47–63.

Sara Jayne Steen, "The Crime of Marriage: Arabella Stuart and *The Duchess of Malfi*," *SCJ* 22 (Spring 1991): 61–76.

S. W. Sullivan, "The Tendency to Rationalize in *The Duchess of Malfi*," *YES* 4 (1974): 77–84.

Winifred H. Sullivan, "The Madmen's Song and Dance in *The Duchess of Malfi*," *LPer* 8 (November 1988): 14–27.

C. G. Thayer, "The Ambiguity of Bosola," *SP* 54 (April 1957): 162–71.

Cynthia Thomiszer, "Paris' Choice and *The Duchess of Malfi*," *RenP* 1981 (1982): 43–49.

Sybil Truchet, "Action and Inertia in *The Duchess of Malfi*," *BSEAA* 27 (November 1988): 115–21.

S. Velissariou, "Clytaemnestra and *The Duchess of Malfi*: Female Aberration in Aeschylus and Webster," in *Working Papers in Linguistics and Literature*, ed. A. Kakouriotis and R. Parkin-Gounelas (Thessaloniki: Aristotle University Press, 1989), 237–52.

P. F. Vernon, "The Duchess of Malfi's Guilt," *N&Q* 208 (September 1963): 335–38.

Frank W. Wadsworth, "'Rough Music' in *The Duchess of Malfi*: Webster's Dance of Madmen and Charivari Tradition," in *Rite, Drama, Festival, Spectacle:*

WEBSTER, JOHN, *The Fair Maid of the Inn*

Rehearsals towards a Theory of Cultural Performance, ed. John J. MacAloon (Philadelphia: Institute for the Study of Human Issues, 1984), 58–75.

Frank W. Wadsworth, "Webster's *The Duchess of Malfi* in Light of Some Contemporary Ideas on Marriage and Remarriage," *PQ* 35 (October 1956): 394–407.

Wells, *Elizabethan and Jacobean Playwrights*, 45–49.

Frank Whigham, "Sexual and Social Mobility in *The Duchess of Malfi*," *PMLA* 100 (March 1985): 167–86.

George Whiteside, "John Webster: A Fruedian Interpretation of His Two Great Tragedies," in Pope, *The Analysis of Literary Texts*, 201–11.

Wiggins, *Journeymen in Murder*, 173–82.

Charles Wilkinson, "Twin Structures in John Webster's *The Duchess of Malfi*," *L&P* 31, no. 2 (1981): 52–65.

The Fair Maid of the Inn

Forker, *The Skull Beneath the Skin*, 189–200.

Northward Ho
(with Dekker)

Larry S. Champion, "Westward-Northward: Structural Development of Dekker's Ho Plays," *CompD* 16 (Fall 1982): 251–66.

Charles R. Forker, "*Westward Ho* and *Northward Ho:* A Revaluation," *PAPA* 6 (Summer 1980): 1–42.

Sir Thomas More

Gordon C. Cyr, "Shakespeare' vs. Webster as *More*'s Author: A Heretical View," *ShN* 31 (September–November 1981): 27.

Westward Ho
(with Dekker)

Larry S. Champion, "Westward-Northward: Structural Development of Dekker's Ho Plays," *CompD* 16 (Fall 1982): 251–66.

Charles R. Forker, "*Westward Ho* and *Northward Ho:* A Revaluation," *PAPA* 6 (Summer 1980): 1–42.

The White Devil

G. P. V. Akrigg, "Webster's Devil in Crystal," *N&Q* 199 (February 1954): 52.

Sven Backman, "Devil and Jewel: A Note on a Possible Pun in *The White Devil*," *MSpr* 78 (1984): 205–09.

Berry, *The Art of John Webster*, 83–106.

Bliss, *The World's Perspective*, 96–136.

Gail Bradbury, "Webster's 'Lapwing': A Significant Allusion in *The White Devil*," *N&Q* 26 (May 1986): 148.

Laura G. Bromley, "The Rhetoric of Feminine Identity in Webster," in Kehler and Baker, *In Another Country*, 50–70.

John R. Brown, "The Papal Election in John Webster's *The White Devil* (1612)," *N&Q* 202 (November 1957): 490–94.

Harry Bruder, "Alalogic Form and Webster's *White Devil*," *PAPA* 5 (Summer–Fall 1979): 41–47.

Cecil, *Poets and Story Tellers*, 27–37, 41–43.

Larry S. Champoin, "Webster's *The White Devil* and the Jacobean Tragic Perspective," *TSLL* 16 (Winter 1974): 447–62.

R. W. Dent, "The White Devil, or Vittoria Corombona?" *RenD* 9 (1966)" 179–203.

Rupin W. Desai, "'Spectacles fashioned with such perspective art': A Phenomenological Reading of Webster's *The White Devil*," *MRDE* 1 (Summer 1984): 187–98.

Ewa Elandt-Jankowska, "John Webster's *The White Devil*: A Study in Black Humor and Laughter as Audience Response," *SAP* 17 (1984): 208–17.

Forker, *The Skull Beneath the Skin*, 104–09, 254–95.

H. Bruce Franklin, "The Trial Scene in Webster's *The White Devil* Examined in Terms of Renaissance Rhetoric," *SEL* 1 (Spring 1961): 35–52.

Sylvia Freedman, "*The White Devil* and the Fair Woman with a Black Soul," in *Jacobean Poetry and Prose: Rhetoric, Representation and the Popular Imagination* ed. Clive Bloom (New York: St. Martin's, 1988), 151–63.

WEBSTER, JOHN, *The White Devil*

Arthur Freeman, "A Note on *The White Devil*," *N&Q* 205 (November 1960): 421.

Arthur Freeman, "*The White Devil*, I.ii.295: An Emandation," *N&Q* 208 (March 1963): 101–02.

Roma Gill, "'Quaintly Done': A Reading of *The White Devil*," *E&S* 19 (1966): 41–59.

Gomez, *The Alienated Figure in Drama*, 58–60.

Goodwyn, *Image Pattern and Moral Vision*, 16–33, 69–76, 80–96.

Gayle Greene, "Women on Trial in Shakespeare and Webster: 'The Mettle of (Their) Sex,'" *Topic* 36 (Spring 1982): 5–19.

Clive Hart, "Wildfire, St. Anthony's Fire, and *The White Devil*," *N&Q* 15 (December 1968): 375–76.

Anne M. Haselkorn, "Sin and the Politics of Penitence: Three Jacobean Adultresses," in Haselkorn and Travitsky, *The Renaissance Englishwoman in Print*, 119–36.

Haworth, *English Hymns and Ballads*, 80–97.

James F. Henke, "John Webster's Motif of 'Consuming': An Approach to the Dramatic Unity and Tragic Vision of *The White Devil* and *The Duchess of Malfi*," *NM* 76 (September 1975): 625–41.

Jerome W. Hogan, "Webster's *The White Devil* V.iv.118–121," *Expl* 33 (Winter 1974): Item 25.

R. V. Holdsworth, "Another Echo of Hamlet in *The White Devil*," *N&Q* 24 (July 1977): 204–05.

George Holland, "The Function of the Minor Characters in *The White Devil*," *PQ* 52 (Winter 1973): 43–54.

James R. Hurt, "Inverted Rituals in Webster's *The White Devil*," *JEGP* 61 (January 1962): 42–47.

Mina Irgat, "Disease Imagery in the Plays of J. Webster," *Litera* 2 (1955): 2–24.

Ann Rosalind Jones, "Italians and Others: Venice and the Irish in Coryat's *Crudities* and *The White Devil*," *RenD* 18 (1987): 101–19.

Ann Rosalind Jones, "'Italians and Others': *The White Devil* (1612)," in Kastan and Stallybrass, *Staging the Renaissance*, 251–62.

Jones, *Othello's Countrymen*, 24–25, 78–80.

A. L. Kistner, and M. K. Kistner, "Traditional Structures in *The White Devil*," *ELWIU* 12 (Fall 1985): 171–88.

A. L. Kistner. And M. K. Kistner, "*The White Devil* and John Webster," *SN* 61 (Spring 1989): 13–21.

Knight, *Golden Labyrinth*, 104–06.

Norma Kroll, "The Democritean Universe in Webster's *The White Devil*," in Davidson, Gianakaris, and Stroupe, *Drama in the Renaissance*, 236–54.

B. J. Layman, "The Equilibrium of Opposites in *The White Devil*," *PMLA* 74 (September 1959): 336–47.

Clifford Leech, "John Webster—A Critical Study," *Hogarth Lectures on Literature* 16 (1951): 29–89.

Luckyj, *A Winter's Snake*, 5–17, 30–39, 58–68, 114–25.

McLeod, *Dramatic Imagery*, 30–74.

Susan H. McLeod, "Duality in *The White Devil*," *SEL* 20 (Spring 1980): 271–85.

Adair Mill, "John Webster as Moralist," *Litera* 3 (1956): 12–34.

Henry Mooschein, "A Note on *The White Devil*," *N&Q* 13 (July 1966): 296.

John Mulryan, "The Tortoise and the Lady in Vincenzo Cartari's *Imagini* and John Webster's *The White Devil*," *N&Q* (March 1991): 78–79.

John Mulryan, "'What is Truth/ said jesting Pilate': The Truth of Illusion in Shakespeare and Webster," in Jones-Davies, *Vérité et illusion*, 57–73.

J. R. Mulryne, "*The White Devil* and *The Duchess of Malfi*," *Stratford-Upon-Avon Studies* 1 (1960): 201–26.

Murray, *A Study of John Webster*, 31–117.

Ornstein, *Moral Vision of Jacobean Tragedy*, 129–40.

Parrott, and Ball, *A Short View of Elizabethan Tragedy*, 225–28.

Pearson, *Tragedy and Tragicomedy in the Plays of John Webster*, 56–60.

Ribner, *Jacobean Tragedy*, 97–108.

Ribner, "Webster's Italian Tragedies," *TDR* 5 (March 1961): 106–18.

Schuman, *Theatre of Fine Devices*, 18–25, 34–40, 55–58.

Stilling, *Love and Death in Renaissance Tragedy*, 224–35.

Thomas B. Stroup, "Flamineo and the Comfortable Words," *RenP 1963* (1964): 12–16.

WEVER, R., *Lusty Juventus*

S. W. Sullivan. "The Tendency to Rationalize in *The White Devil* and *The Duchess of Malfi*," *YES* 4 (1974): 77–84.

Tokson, *The Popular Image of the Blackman in English Drama*, 85–87.

Frank W. Wadsworth, "Webster's *The White Devil*, III, ii, 75–80," *Expl* 11 (February 1953)" Item 28.

Wells, *Elizabethan and Jacobean Playwrights*, 45–49.

George Whiteside, "John Webster: A Freudian Interpretation of His Two Great Tragedies," in Pope, *The Analysis of Literary Texts*, 201–11.

Wiggins, *Journeymen in Murder*, 166–73.

WEVER, R.

Lusty Juventus

Bevington, *From "Mankind" to Marlowe*, 143–46.

Yukihiro Takemoto, "A Study of Prodigal Son Plays, II: The Revitalization of the Godly Traditions," *Lang&C* 10 (1989): 1–18.

WHETSTONE, GEORGE

Promos and Cassandra

Jan Kott, "Head for Maidenhead, Maidenhead for Head: The Structure of Exchange in *Measure for Measure*," in Conejero, *En torno a Shakespeare*, 93–113.

English Mirror

H. D. Purcell, "Whetstone's *Englysh Myrror* and Marlowe's *Jew of Malta*," *N&Q* 13 (July 1966): 288–90.

WILKINS, GEORGE

The Miseries of Enforced Marriage

Leanore Lieblein, "The Context of Murder in English Domestic Plays, 1590–1610," *SEL* 23 (Spring 1983): 181–96.

G. H. Blayney, "An Aural Error in G. Wilkins's *The Miseries of Enforced Marriage*?" *N&Q* 28 (April 1981): 171–72.

Pericles
(with Shakespeare)

John Arthos, "*Pericles, Prince of Tyre*: A Study in the Dramatic Use of Romantic Narrative," *SQ* 4 (Summer 1953): 257–70.

Babb, *English Malady*, 105–06.

G. A. Barker, "Themes and Variations in Shakespeare's *Pericles*," *ES* 44 (December 1963): 401–14.

Brockbank, *On Shakespeare*, 283–302.

Kwang Soon Cho, "Shakespeare's Control of Audience Response: Dramatic Techniques in *Pericles*," *JELL* 36 (November 1990): 729–48.

Danby, *Poets on Fortune's Hill*, 87–103.

H. Neville Davies, "*Pericles* and the Sherley Brothers," in Honigmann, *Shakespeare and His Contemporaries*, 94–113.

Stephen Dickey, "Language and Role in *Pericles*," *ELR* 16 (1986): 550–56.

Mary Judith Dunbar, "'To the judgement of your eye': Iconography and the Theatrical Art of *Pericles*; Proceedings of the 2nd Congress of the International Shakespeare Association, 1981," in *Shakespeare, Man of the Theatre*, ed. Kenneth Muir, Jay L. Halio, and D. J. Palmer (Newark and London: University of Delaware Press; Associated University Presses, 1983), 86–97.

Philip Edwards, "An Approach to the Problem of *Pericles*," *ShS* 5 (1952): 25–49.

Walter F. Eggers, Jr., "Shakespeare's Gower and the Role of the Authorial Presenter," *PQ* 54 (July 1975): 434–43.

Bertrand Evans, "The Poem of *Pericles*," *University of California Publications English Studies* 11 (1955): 35–56.

Inga-Stina Ewbank, "'My Name is Marina': The Language of Recognition," in Edwards, Ewbank, and Howard, *Shakespeare's Styles*, 111–30.

Nona Fienberg, "Marina in *Pericles*: Exchange Values and the Art of Moral Discourse," *ISJR* 57 (1982): 153–61.

Howard Felperin, "Shakespeare's Miracle Play," *SQ* 18 (Summer 1967): 363–74.

Annette C. Flowers, "Disguise and Identity in *Pericles, Prince of Tyre*," *SQ* 26 (1975): 30–41.

WILKINS, GEORGE, *Pericles*

French, *Shakespeare's Division of Experience*, 297–306.

Elena Glazov-Corrigan, "The New Function of Language in Shakespeare's *Pericles*: Oath Versus 'Holy Word,'" *ShS* 43 (1991): 131–40.

P. Golden, "Antiochus' Riddle in Gower and Shakespeare," *RES* 6 (July 1955): 245, 248–51.

Phyllis Gorfain, "Puzzle and Artifice: The Riddle as Metapoetry in *Pericles*," *ShS* 29 (1976): 11–20.

Sara Hanna, "Christian Vision and Iconography in *Pericles*," *UCrow* 11 (1991): 92–116.

Haselkorn, *Prostitution in Elizabethan and Jacobean Drama*, 51–53.

Richard Hillman, "Shakespeare's Gower and Gower's Shakespeare: The Larger Debt of *Pericles*," *SQ* 36 (Winter 1985): 427–37.

F. David Hoeniger, "Gower and Shakespeare in *Pericles*," *SQ* 33 (Winter 1982): 461–79.

Hilda M. Hulme, "Two Notes on the Interpretation of Shakespeare's Text," *N&Q* 204 (October 1959): 354.

Maurice Hunt, "A Looking Glass for *Pericles*," *ELWIU* 13 (Spring 1986): 3–11.

Maurice Hunt, "'Opening the Book of Monarch's Faults': *Pericles* and Redemptive Speech," *ELWIU* 12 (Fall 1985): 155–70.

Maurice Hunt, "*Pericles* and the Emblematic Imagination," *StHum* 17 (June 1990): 1–20.

Cynthia Marshall, "The Seven Ages of Pericles," *JRMMRA* 8 (January 1987): 147–62.

MacD. P. Jackson, "George Wilkins and the First Two Acts of *Pericles*: New Evidence from Function Words," *L&LC* 6 (1991): 155–63.

MacD. P. Jackson, "*Pericles*, Acts I and II: New Evidence for George Wilkins," *NQ* 37 (June 1990): 192–96.

Robert J. Kane, "A Passage in *Pericles*," *MLN* 68 (June 1953): 483–84.

Akira Kataoka, "*Pericles*: A Quest of Purity," *SELL* 24 (March 1984): 19–41.

Maqbool H. Khan, "The Design of Wonder in *Pericles*," *AJES* 3 (April 1978): 80–106.

Knight, *The Crown of Life*, 32–75.

Knight, *The Golden Labyrinth*, 82–84.

Anthony J. Lewis, "'I feed on mother's flesh': Incest and Eating in *Pericles*," *ELWIU* 15 (Fall 1988): 147–63.

John H. Long, "Laying the Ghosts in *Pericles*," *SQ* 7 (Winter 1956): 39–42.

Louis Marder, "Stylometric Analysis and the *Pericles* Problem," *ShN* 26 (December 1976): 46.

Barbara Melchiori, "Still Harping on My Daughter," *EM* 11 (Spring 1960): 60–63.

Patricia K. Meszaros, "*Pericles*: Shakespeare's Divine Musical Comedy; Collection of Essays from the Ohio Shakespeare Conference, 1981, Wright State University, Dayton, Ohio," in Cary and Limouze, *Shakespeare and the Arts*, 3–20.

G. Harold Metz, "A Stylometric Comparison of Shakespeare's *Titus Andronicus*, *Pericles*, and *Julius Caesar*," *ShN* 29 (Fall 1979): 42.

Kenneth Muir, "*Pericles* II, v," *N&Q* 194 (August 1948): 362.

Kenneth Muir, "The Problem of *Pericles*," *ES* 30 (June 1949): 65–83.

J. R. Mulryne, "'To Glad Your Ear and Please Your Eyes': *Pericles* at the Other Place," *CritQ* 24 (Winter 1979): 31–40.

Norman Nathan, "Pericles and Jonah," *N&Q* 201 (January 1956): 10–11.

Eric Sams, "The Painful Misadventures of *Pericles* Acts I–II," *N&Q* 38 (March 1991): 67–70.

Gerald J. Schiffhorst, "The Imagery of *Pericles* and What It Tells Us," *BSUF* 8 (Autumn 1967): 61–70.

Simpson, *Studies in Elizabethan Drama*, 17–22.

M. W. A. Smith, "The Authorship of Acts I and II of *Pericles*: A New Approach Using the First Words of Speeches," *CHum* 22 (January 1988): 23–41.

M. W. A. Smith, "An Initial Investigation of the Authorship of *Pericles*: Statistics Support Scholars: Shakespeare Did Not Write Acts I & II," *ShN* 33 (Fall 1983): 32.

M. W. A. Smith, "A Procedure to Determine Authorship Using Pairs of Consecutive Words: More Evidence for Wilkens's Participation in *Pericles*," *CHum* 23 (April 1989): 113–29.

Kay Stockholder, "Sex and Authority in *Hamlet*, *King Lear* and *Pericles*," *Mosaic* 18 (Summer 1985): 17–29.

Michael Taylor, "'Here is a thing too young for such a place': Innocence in *Pericles*," *ArielE* 13 (July 1982): 3–19.

WILKINS, GEORGE, *The Travels of the Three English Brothers*

Sidney Thomas, "The Problem of *Pericles*," *SQ* 34 (1983): 448–50.

J. M. Tomkins, "Why Pericles?" *RES* 3 (October 1952): 315–24.

James O. Wood, "The Case of Shakespeare's *Pericles*," *SJS* 6 (Summer 1980): 39–58.

James O. Wood, "Shakespeare, *Pericles*, and the Genevan Bible," *PCP* 12 (1977): 82–89.

Alan R. Young, "A Note on Tournament Impresas in *Pericles*," *SQ* 36 (Autumn 1985): 453–56.

The Travels of the Three English Brothers, Sir Thomas, Sir Anthony, Mr. Robert Shirley
(with Day)

H. Neville Davies, "*Pericles* and the Sherley Brothers," in Honigmann, *Shakespeare and His Contemporaries*, 94–113.

Mann, *The Elizabethan Player*, 68–73.

WILMOT, ROBERT

Gismond of Salerne

Ernest G. Griffin, "*Gismond of Salerne*: A Critical Appreciation," *RES* 4 (April 1963): 94–107.

WILSON, ROBERT

The Cobbler's Prophecy

G. M. Cameron, *Robert Wilson and the Plays of Shakespeare* (Riverton, N.Z.: Privately printed, 1982), 10–15.

J. A. Lavin, "Two Notes on *The Cobbler's Prophecy*," *N&Q* 9 (April 1962): 137–39.

Talbert, *Elizabethan Drama*, 18–24.

Three Ladies of London

J. A. B. Somerset, "*As You Like It*, III.iii.10–13, and *King Lear*, II.iv.125: Analogues from Robert Wilson's *Three Ladies of London*," *N&Q* 29 (April 1982): 116–18.

WOODES, NATHANIEL

The Conflict of Conscience

Bevington, *From "Mankind" to Marlowe*, 245–51.

Oliver Leslie, "John Foxe and *The Conflict of Conscience*," *RES* 25 (January 194): 1–9.

WROTH, LADY MARY

Love's Victorie

Margaret Anne McLaren, "An Unknown Continent: Lady Mary Wroth's Pastoral Drama 'Loves Victorie,'" in Haselkorn and Travitsky, *The Renaissance Englishwoman in Print*, 276–94.

Carolyn Ruth Swift, "Feminine Self-Definition in Lady Mary Wroth's *Love's Victorie* (c. 1621)," *ELR* 19 (Spring 1989): 171–88.

YARRINGTON, ROBERT

Two Lamentable Tragedies

Adams, *English Domestic or Homiletic Tragedies*, 108–14.

Wiggins, *Journeymen in Murder*, 116–21.

Main Sources Consulted

Books listed as main sources are those in which we have found numerous explications—usually five or more. Citations for books with fewer explications are included with full publication information in the Checklist itself. Periodicals listed as main sources are those that frequently publish drama explications. For periodical abbreviations, see the list following the preface.

Accent 8 (Autumn 1947)–16 (Spring 1956).

Acta Neophilologicia 13 (January 1980).

ADAMS, HENRY HITCH. *English Domestic or Homiletic Tragedy 1575–1642*. New York: Columbia University Press.

AERS, LESLEY, and **NIGEL WHEALE**, eds. *Shakespeare and the Changing Curriculum*. London: Routledge, 1991.

ALI, FLORENCE. *Opposing Absolutes: Conviction and Convention in John Ford's Plays*. Salzburg: University of Salzburg, 1974.

Aligarh Critical Miscellany 1 (1988)–3, no. 1 (1990).

Aligarh Journal of English Studies 1 (July 1975)–14 (April 1989).

Allegorica 1 (Summer 1976)–6 (Winter 1981).

MAIN SOURCES CONSULTED

ALLEN, DAVID G., and **ROBERT A. WHITE,** eds. *Traditions and Innovations: Essays on British Literature of the Middle Ages and the Renaissance.* Newark: University of Delaware Press, 1990.

ALTMAN, JOEL B. *The Tudor Play of Mind: Rhetorical Inquiry and the Development of Elizabethan Drama.* Berkeley: University of California Press, 1978.

ALVIS, JOHN, and **THOMAS G. WEST,** eds. *Shakespeare as Political Thinker.* Durham, NC: Carolina Academic Press, 1981.

American Benedictine Review 18 (December 1967)–30 (June 1979).

American Imago 5 (November 1948)–45 (Fall 1988).

American Journal of Psychoanalysis 42 (Spring 82)–49 (September 1989).

American Journal of Semiotics 3, no. 2 (1984),

American Political Science Review 51 (June 1957)–54 (June 1960).

American Scholar 36 (1967).

Analysis Quanderni di Anglistica 4 (1986).

ANDERSON DONALD K., JR., ed. *"Concord in Discord": The Plays of John Ford, 1586–1986.* New York: AMS, 1986.

Anglica 1 (August 1946)–6 (October 1957).

Annual Shakespeare Lectures of the British Academy (1951)–(1955).

Annuale Mediaevale 12 (1971)–166 (1979).

Antioch Review 24 (Spring 1964).

Archiv för das Studium der Neuren Sprachen und Literaturen 203 (1966)–226 (1989).

ArielE: A Review of International English Literature 3 (January 1972)–15 (January 1984).

Arizona Quarterly 12 (Spring 1956)–20 (Winter 1964).

ARTHOS, JOHN. *Shakespeare's Use of Dream and Vision.* Totowa, NJ: Rowman and Littlefield, 1977.

ASIBONG, EMMANUEL B. *Comic Sensibility in the Plays of Christopher Marlowe.* Elms Court, Devon: Arthur Stockwell, 1979.

Aryan Path 35 (1964).

ASP, CAROLYN. *A Study of Thomas Middleton's Tragicomedies.* Salzburg: University of Salzburg, 1974.

510

Assaph: Studies in the Arts 1, no. 1 (1984)–6, no. 3 (1989).

Assays: Critical Approaches to Medieval and Renaissance Texts 2 (1982)–4 (1987).

ATKINS, G. DOUGLAS, and DAVID M. BERGERON, eds. *Shakespeare and Deconstruction*. New York: Peter Lang, 1988.

Atlantis: A Women's Studies Journal/Journal d'Etudes sur la Femme 9 (Spring 1984)–11 (Autumn 1985).

AUS-Papers in English and American Studies 3 (1984).

AXTON, MARIE, and RAYMOND WILLIAMS, eds. *English Drama: Forms and Development: Essays in Honour of Muriel Clara Bradbrook*. Cambridge: Cambridge University Press, 1977.

BABB, LAWRENCE. *The Elizabethan Malady*. East Lansing: Michigan State College Press, 1951.

Baconiana 29 (October 1945)–40 (November 1956).

BAILEY, MARGERY. *Ashland Studies for Shakespeare, 1952*. Ashland: University of Oregon Press, 1955.

BAINES, BARBARA J. *Thomas Heywood*. Boston: Twayne, 1984.

Ball State University Forum 6 (Fall 1965)–26 (Fall 1985).

BAMBOROUGH, J. *The Little World of Man*. New York and London: Longmans, Green, 1952.

BARBER, C. L. *Shakespeare's Festive Comedy: A Study of Dramatic Form and Its Relation to Social Custom*. Princeton: Princeton University Press, 1959.

BARBER, CHARLES. *Theme of Honour's Tongue: a Study of Social Attitudes in the English Drama from Shakespeare to Dryden*. Gothenburg, Sweden: University of Gothenburg, 1985.

BARISH, JONAS A. *Ben Jonson: A Collection of Critical Essays*. Englewood Cliffs, NJ: Prentice-Hall, 1963.

———. *Ben Jonson and the Language of Prose Comedy*. Cambridge, MA: Harvard University Press, 1960.

BARKER, FRANCIS, PETER HULME, and MARGARET IVERSON, eds. *The Uses of History: Marxism, Postmodernism, and the Renaissance*. Manchester: Manchester University Press, 1991.

BARNES, GERALDINE, JOHN GUNN, SONYA JENSEN, and LEE JOBLING, eds. *Words and Wordsmiths: A Volume for H. L. Rogers*. Sydney: University of Sydney, 1989.

BARNET, SYLVAN, ed. *Aspects of Drama.* Boston: Little, Brown, 1962.

BARRY, PATRICIA S. *The King in Tudor Drama.* Salzburg: University of Salzburg, 1977.

BARTON, ANNE. *Ben Jonson, Dramatist.* Cambridge: Cambridge University Press, 1984.

BASTIAENEN, JOHANNES ADAM. *The Moral Tone of Jacobean and Caroline Drama.* New York: Haskell House, 1966.

BATTENHOUSE, HENRY W. *Poets of Christian Thought.* New York: Ronald, 1947.

BEARDSLEY, MONROE C. *Aesthetics: Problems in the Philosophy of Criticism.* New York: Harcourt, Brace, 1958.

BEAURLINE, L. A. *Jonson and Elizabethan Comedy: Essays in Dramatic Rhetoric.* San Marino, CA: Huntington Library, 1978.

BEMENT, PETER. *George Chapman: Action and Contemplation in His Tragedies.* Salzburg: University of Salzburg, 1974.

BENNETT, JOSEPHINE W., OSCAR CARGILL, and **VERNON HALL JR.,** eds. *Studies in English Renaissance Drama in Memory of Karl Julius Holzknecht.* New York: New York University Press, 1959.

BENTLEY, ERIC, ed. *The Importance of Scrutiny.* New York: Stewart, 1948.

———. *The Play.* New York: Prentice-Hall, 1962.

BERGERON, DAVID M. *English Civic Pagentry, 1558–1642.* Columbia: University of South Carolina Press, 1971.

———, ed. *Pagentry in the Shakespearean Theater.* Athens: University of Georgia Press, 1985.

BERRY, FRANCIS. *Poet's Grammar.* London, Routledge, 1958.

BERRY, RALPH. *The Art of John Webster.* The Hague: Mouton, 1969.

———. *Shakespearean Structures.* London: Macmillan, 1981.

BEVINGTON, DAVID M. *From "Mankind" to Marlowe.* Cambridge, MA: Harvard University Press, 1962.

———, and **JAY L. HALIO,** eds. *Shakespeare, Patterns of Excelling Nature: Shakespeare Criticism in Honor of America's Bicentennial from the International Shakespeare Association Congress, Washington, DC, April 1976.* Newark: University of Delaware Press, 1978.

BLACKBURN, RUTH H. *Biblical Drama Under the Tudors.* The Hague and Paris: Mouton, 1971.

BLISS, LEE. *The World's Perspective: John Webster and the Jacobean Drama.* New Brunswick, NJ: Rutgers University Press, 1983.

BLOOM, EDWARD A., ed. *Shakespeare 1564–1964: A Collection of Essays by Various Hands.* Providence, RI: Brown University Press, 1966.

BLOOM, HAROLD, ed. *Christopher Marlowe.* New York: Chelsea House, 1986.

BLOW, SUSAN. *Rhetoric in the Plays of Thomas Dekker.* Salzburg: University of Salzburg Press, 1972.

BLUESTONE, MAX, and **NORMAN RABKIN**, eds. *Shakespeare's Contemporaries.* Englewood Cliffs, NJ: Prentice-Hall, 1961.

BOAS, FREDERICK S. *Introduction to Stuart Drama.* Oxford: Clarendon Press, 1953.

BODKIN, MAUD. *Archetypal Patterns in Poetry.* New York: Oxford University Press, 1961.

Boston Public Library Quarterly 5 (July 1953).

Boston University Studies in English 1 (Spring 1955)–5 (Winter 1961).

Boundary 7, no. 2 (1979).

BOWER, RUEBEN A., and **RICHARD POIRIER**, eds. *In Defense of Reading—A Reader's Approach to Literary Criticism.* New York: Dutton, 1962.

BOYCE, B. *Theophrastan Character in England to 1642.* Cambridge, MA: Harvard University Press, 1947.

BRADBROOK, MURIEL C. *The Growth and Structure of Elizabethan Comedy.* Berkeley: University of California Press, 1960.

BRADBURY, MALCOLM, and **DAVID PALMER.** *Shakespearian Tragedy.* New York: Holmes & Meier, 1984.

BRADLEY, A. C. *Oxford Lectures on Poetry.* New York: St. Martin's, 1963.

BRADSHAW, GRAHAM. *Shakespeare's Skepticism.* Brighton, Sussex: Harvester Press, 1987.

BRAHMER, MIECZYSLAW, STANISLAW HELSTYNKI, and **JULIAN KRYZANOWSKI**, eds. *Studies in Language and Literature in Honour of Margaret Schlauch.* Warsaw: Panstwowe Wydawnictwo Naukowe, 1966.

BRANDT, BRUCE EDWARD. *Christopher Marlowe and the Metaphysical Problem Play.* Salzburg: University of Salzburg, 1985.

BRAUNMULLER, A. R. *George Peele.* Boston: Twayne, 1980.

————, and **J. C. BULMAN**, eds. *Comedy from Shakespeare to Sheridan: Change and Continuity in the English and European Dramatic Tradition.* Newark and London: University of Delaware Press, Associated University Presses, 1986.

BREDBECK, GREGORY W. *Sodomy and Interpretation: Marlowe to Milton.* Ithaca, NY, and London: Cornell University Press, 1991.

BRIDGES, MARGARET. *On Strangeness.* Tubingen: Narr, 1990.

Brigham Young University Studies 166 (1976)–19 (1979).

BRINK, JEAN R., MARYANNE C. HOROWITZ, and **ALLISON P. COUD-ERT**, eds. *Playing with Gender: A Renaissance Pursuit.* Urbana: University of Illinois Press, 1991.

————, **ALLISON P. COUDERT**, and **MARYANNE HOROWITZ**, eds. *The Politics of Gender in Early Modern Europe.* Kirksville, MO: Sixteenth Century Journal Publications, 1989.

BRISSENDEN, ALAN, ed. *Shakespeare and Some Others: Essays on Shakespeare and Some of His Contemporaries.* Adelaide: University of Adelaide, 1976.

British Journal of Medical Psychology 20 (1945).

BROCKBANK, PHILIP. *On Shakespeare: Jesus, Shakespeare and Karl Marx, and Other Essays.* Oxford: Basil Blackwell, 1989.

BROOKS, CLEANTH, ed. *Tragic Themes in Western Literature—Seven Essays.* New Haven: Yale University Press, 1955.

————, and **ROBERT HEILMAN.** *Understanding Drama.* New York: Henry Holt, 1961.

BROOKS-DAVIES, DOUGLAS. *The Mercurian Monarch: Magical Politics from Spenser to Pope.* Manchester: Manchester University Press, 1983.

BROWN, JOHN RUSSEL. *Dramatis Personae—A Retrospective Show.* New York: Viking, 1963.

————, and **BERNARD HARRIS**, eds. *Later Shakespeare.* London and New York: Arnold; St. Martin's, 1966.

BRYAN, ROBERT A., ALTON C. MORRIS, A. A. MURPHEE, and **AUBREY L. WILIAMS**, eds. *All These to Teach: Essays in Honor of C. A. Robertson.* Gainesville: University of Florida Press, 1965.

Bucknell Review 14, no. 2 (1966)–33, no. 1 (1989).

Bucknell University Studies 5, no. 3 (1955)–12 (March 1964).

Bulletin de la Société d'Etudes Anglo-Américaines des XVII et XVIII Siècles 27 (November 1988).

Bulletin of the John Rylands University of Manchester 41 (Winter 1959)–71 (Spring 1989).

Bulletin of the New York Public Library 66 (December 1962).

Bulletin of Research in the Humanities 85 (Winter 1982).

Bulletin of the Rocky Mountain Modern Language Society 30, no. 3 (1976)–36, no. 1 (1982).

Bulletin of the West Virginia Association of College English Teachers 5 (Spring–Summer 1979)–8 (Spring 1983).

Bulletin for the Association for Literary & Linguistic Computing 10 (March 1982).

BULLOUGH, GEOFFREY. *Mirror of Minds—Changing Psychological Beliefs in English Poetry*. London: University of London, 1962.

BURKE, KENNETH. *Perspectives by Incongruity*. Bloomington: Indiana University Press, 1964.

———. *The Philosophy of Literary Form*. New York: Vintage, 1957.

BUTLER, MARTIN. *Theatre and Crisis, 1632–1642*. Cambridge: Cambridge University Press, 1973.

Cahiers de l'Institute de Linguistique de Louvin 14, no. 1–2 (1988).

Cahiers Elisbethains 9 (April 1965)–39 (April 1991).

CAIE, GRAHAM D., and **HOLGER NORGAARD**, eds. *A Literary Miscellany Presented to Eric Jacobsen*. Copenhagen: University of Copenhagen Press, 1988.

Cairo Studies in English (1960)–(1963–1964).

Caliban 17 (1980)–21 (1984).

California English Journal 3, no. 1 (1967).

Cambridge Journal 1 (February 1948)–5 (August 1952).

Cambridge Quarterly 2 (1967)–18 (1989).

Canadian Review of Comparative Literature/Revue Canadienne de Litterature Comparative 17 (September–December 1990).

CANFIELD, J. DOUGLAS. *Word as Bond in English Literature from the Middle Ages to the Restoration*. Philadelphia: University of Pennsylvania Press, 1989.

CAREY, JOHN, ed. *English Renaissance Studies Presented to Dame Helen Gardner in Honor of Her Seventieth Birthday*. Oxford: Clarendon Press, 1980.

Caribbean Quarterly 8 (September 1962).

CARTELLI, THOMAS. *Marlowe, Shakespeare, and the Economy of Theatrical Experience*. Philadelphia: University of Pennsylvania Press, 1991.

CARY, CECIL WILLIAMSON, and **HENRY S. LIMOUZE**, eds. *Shakespeare and the Arts*. Washington, DC: University Press of America, 1982.

Catholic Historical Review 8 (Fall 1973).

Catholic World 156 (1943).

Cauda Pavonis 5 (Spring 1986).

CAZELLES, BRIGITTE. *Alphone Juillard: D'une passion l'autre*. Saratoga, CA: Anma Libri, 1987.

CEA Critic: An Official Journal of the College English Association 31, no. 1 (1968)–38, no. 3 (1975).

CECIL, DAVID. *Poets and Story Tellers*. New York: Macmillan, 1949.

Celestinesca 4 (May 1980).

Centennial Review 4 (Winter 1960)–33 (Winter 1989).

Central Institute of English and Foreign Languages Bulletin 1 (1984).

Central States Speech Journal 12 (Autumn 1960)–13 (Winter 1961).

CHAMPION, LARRY S. *Ben Jonson's "Dotages": A Reconsideration of the Late Plays*. Lexington: University of Kentucky Press, 1967.

———. *Thomas Dekker and the Traditions of English Drama*. New York: Peter Lang, 1985.

———. *Tragic Patterns in Jacobean and Caroline Drama*. Knoxville: University of Tennessee Press, 1977.

CHAN, MARY. *Music in the Theatre of Ben Jonson*. Oxford: Clarendon Press, 1980.

CHANDURI, SUKANTA. *Infirm Glory: Shakespeare and the Renaissance Image of Man*. Oxford: Clarendon Press, 1981.

CHARNEY, MAURICE, ed. *"Bad" Shakespeare: Revaluations of the Shakespeare Canon*. Rutherford, NJ: Farleigh Dickinson University Press, 1988.

————, and **JOSEPH REPPEN**, eds. *Psychoanalytic Approaches to Literature and Film*. Rutherford, NJ: Farleigh Dickinson University Press, 1987.

Chaucer Review 10 (Summer 1975)–21 (Fall 1986).

Chicago Review 15 (1962).

Christian Scholar 47 (Fall 1964).

Christianity and Literature 21 (Spring 1978)–37 (Winter 1988).

Cithera 13 (1974).

The City College Papers 1 (September 1964).

The Claflin College Review 1, no. 2 (1977)–3, no. 2 (1979).

Classic and Modern Literature 2 (1982).

Classica et Mediaevalia 30 (1969).

Classical Bulletin 5 (Spring 1980).

CLAY, CHARLOTTE N. *The Role of Anxiety in English Tragedy, 1580–1642*. Salzburg: University of Salzburg, 1974.

CLEMEN, WOLFGANG. *English Tragedy Before Shakespeare*. London: Methuen, 1961.

————. *Shakespeare's Dramatic Art: Collected Essays*. London: Methuen, 1972.

CLIO 11 (Winter 1982)–16 (Fall 1986).

CLURMAN, HAROLD. *Lies Like Truth*. New York: Macmillan, 1958.

Colby Literary Quarterly 12 (June 1976)–26 (June 1990).

COLEMAN, ANTHONY, and **ANTONY HAMMOND**, eds. *Poetry and Drama, 1570–1700: Essays in Honour of Harold F. Brooks*. London: Methuen, 1981.

College English 4 (November 1942)–33 (April 1972).

College Language Association Journal 1 (March 1958)–35 (September 1991).

College Literature 1 (Spring 1974)–16 (Summer 1989).

COLLEY, JOHN SCOTT. *John Marston's Theatrical Drama*. Salzburg: University of Salzburg, 1974.

Colorado Quarterly 11 (Spring 1956).

Columbia University Forum 5 (Fall 1962)–7 (Winter 1964).

Columbia University Studies in English and Comparitive Literature 164 (1946)–168 (1955).

Comitatus 2 (Spring 1971)–15 (Spring 1984).

Communique 5, no. 2 (1980).

Comparative Drama 1 (Summer 1966)–25 (Summer 1991).

Comparative Literature (Oregon) 8 (Winter 1957)–34 (Summer 1982).

Comparative Literature Studies 14 (January 1944)–41 (January 1972).

Computers and the Humanities 21 (January 1987)–23 (April 1989).

Conference of College Teachers of English Studies 47 (September 1982)–56 (September 1991).

CONEJERO, MANUEL A., ed. *En torno a Shakespeare: Homenaje a T. J. B. Spenser.* Valencia: Universidad de Valencia, Institución Shakespeare, 1980.

CONFREY, BURTON. *The Moral Mission of Literature.* Manchester, NH: Magnificent Press, n. d.

Connotations: A Journal for Critical Debate 1 (1991).

CONOVER, JAMES H. *Thomas Dekker: An Analysis of Dramatic Structure.* The Hague: Mouton, 1969.

COOMBES, H. *Literature and Criticism.* London: Chatto & Windus, 1956.

COPE, JACKSON I. *Dramaturgy of the Daemonic: Studies in Antigeneric Theatre from Ruzante to Grimaldi.* Baltimore and London: Johns Hopkins University Press, 1984.

———. *Theatre and the Dream: From Metaphor to Form in Renaissance Drama.* Baltimore: Johns Hopkins University Press, 1973.

Coranto 5, no. 1 (1967).

CORNELIUS, R. M. *Christopher Marlowe's Use of the Bible.* New York: Peter Lang, 1984.

COX, JOHN D. *Shakespeare and the Dramaturgy of Power.* Princeton: Princeton University Press, 1989.

CRAIG, HARDIN. *The Written Word.* Chapel Hill: University of North Carolina Press, 1953.

CRANE, MILTON, ed. *Shakespeare's Art: Seven Essays.* Chicago and London: University of Chicago Press, 1973.

Criterion 17, no. 1 (1973).

Critical Inquiry 15 (Spring 1989).

Critical Review 15 (1972)–27 (1985).

The Critical Quarterly 1 (Autumn 1959)–28 (Spring–Summer 1986).

Critical Survey 1, no. 1 (1989)–1, no. 3 (1991).

Criticism: A Quarterly Review of Literature 1 (Winter 1959)–33 (Winter 1991).
Criticism and Research 8 (1987–1988).

CRUPI, CHARLES W. *Robert Green.* Boston: Twayne, 1986.

CRUX 10 (April 1973)–22 (April 1988).

CUNNINGHAM, JAMES. *Woe or Wonder: The Emotional Effect of Shakespearean Tragedy.* Denver: University of Denver Press, 1951.

CURRY, JOHN VINCENT. *Deception in Elizabethan Comedy.* Chicago: Loyola University Press, 1955.

CUTTS, JOHN P. *The Left Hand of God: A Critical Interpretation of the Plays of Christopher Marlowe.* Haddonfield, NJ: Haddonfield House, 1973.

Cycnos 5 (1989).

Dacca University Studies 12 (June 1964).

Daedalus 108, no. 3 (1979).

DAICHES, DAVID. *Critical Approaches to Literature.* Englewood Cliffs, NJ: Prentice-Hall, 1956.

Dalhousie Review 41 (Winter 1961–1962)–64 (Winter 1984–1985).

D'AMICO, JACK. *The Moor in English Renaissance Drama.* Tampa: University of South Florida Press, 1991.

DANBY, J. F. *Poets on Fortune's Hill.* London: Faber, 1952.

DAVIDSON, ARTHUR. *The Solace of Literature.* London: Mitre, 1948.

DAVIDSON, CLIFFORD. *The Saint Play in Medieval Europe.* Kalamazoo: Medieval Institute Publications, Western Michigan University, 1986.

———, and **JOHN STROUPE**, eds. *The Drama in the Middle Ages: Comparative and Critical Essays, Second Series.* New York: AMS, 1990.

———, **C. J. GIANKARIS**, and **JOHN H. STROUPE**, eds. *The Drama in the Middle Ages: Comparative and Critical Essays.* New York: AMS, 1982.

————, **C. J. GIANKARIS**, and **JOHN H. STROUPE**, eds. *Drama in the Renaissance: Comparative and Critical Essays.* New York: AMS, 1986.

DAWSON, ANTHONY B. *Indirections: Shakespeare and the Art of Illusion.* Toronto: University of Toronto Press, 1978.

DEATS, SARA MUNSON, and **LAGRETA TALLENT LENKER**, eds. *Youth Suicide Prevention: Lessons from Literature.* New York: Plenum, 1989.

DENNIS, NIGEL F. *Dramatic Essays.* London: Eidenfield & Nicholson, 1962.

DENNY, MELVILLE. *Medieval Drama.* London: Arnold; New York: Crane, Russak, 1973.

DESSEN, ALAN C. *Jonson's Moral Comedy.* Evanston, IL: Northwestern University Press, 1971.

Deutsch Shakespeare-Gesellschaft West: Jahrbuch 111 (1975)–126 (1990).

Diacritics 18 (Winter 1988)–20 (Spring 1990).

Diogenes 11 (Summer 1962).

Discourse 5 (Autumn 1963)–13, no. 3 (1970).

Dock Leaves 4 (Summer 1953).

DOLLIMORE, JONATHAN, and **ALAN SINFIELD**, eds. *Political Shakespeare: New Essays in Cultural Materialism.* Manchester: Manchester University Press, 1985.

DONALDSON, E. TALBOT, and **JUDITH KOLLMANN**, eds. *Chaucerian Shakespeare: Adaption and Transformation.* Detroit: Michigan Consortium for Medieval and Early Modern Studies, 1983.

DONALDSON, IAN. *Jonson and Shakespeare.* London: Macmillan, 1983.

————. *The World Upside-Down: Comedy from Jonson to Fielding.* Oxford: Clarendon Press, 1970.

DORAN, MADELEINE. *Shakespeare's Dramatic Language.* Madison: University of Wisconsin Press, 1976.

DRAKAKIS, JOHN, ed. *Alternative Shakespeares.* London: Methuen, 1985.

Drama Critique 2 (November 1959)–7 (Winter 1964).

The Drama Review (formerly *Tulane Drama Review*) 2 (May 1956)–8 (Summer 1964).

Drama Survey 3 (May 1963)–5 (August 1966).

Dublin Magazine 24 (January–March 1949).

Durham University Journal 7 (March 1945)–46 (December 1982).

DURANT, JACK M., and **M. THOMAS HESTER**, eds. *A Fair Day in the Affections: Literary Essays in Honor of Robert B. White*. Raleigh, NC: Winston, 1980,

DURRY, MARIE-JEANNE, ROBERT ELLORDT, and **MARIE-THERESE JONES-DAVIES**, eds. *De Shakespeare à T. S. Eliot: Melanges offerts à Henri Fluchère*. Paris: Didier, 1976.

Dutch Quarterly Review of Anglo-American Letters 8 (1978)–19 (1989).

EAGLETON, TERENCE. *Shakespeare and Society: Critical Studies in Shakespearean Drama*. New York: Schocken, 1967.

EASTMAN, FRED. *Christ in the Drama*. New York: Macmillan, 1947.

Edda: Nordisk Tidsskrift for Litteraturforskning/Scandinavian Journal of Literary Research 4 (Autumn 1987).

EDENS, WALTER, CHRISTOPHER DURER, **WALTER F. EGGERS, JR., DUNCAN HARRIS**, and **KEITH HULL**, eds. *Teaching Shakespeare*. Princeton: Princeton University Press, 1977.

Educational Theatre Journal 2 (October 1950)–30 (October 1978).

EDWARDS, PHILIP. *Threshold of a Nation: A Study in English and Irish Drama*. Cambridge: Cambridge University Press, 1979.

———, **INGA-STINA EWBANK**, and **G. K. HUNTER**. *Shakespeare's Styles: Essays in Honor of Kenneth Muir*. Cambridge: Cambridge University Press, 1980.

EGAN, ROBERT. *Drama within Drama: Shakespeare's Sense of His Art*. New York and London: Columbia University Press, 1975.

ELAM, KEIR. *Semiotics of Theatre and Drama*. London: Routledge, 1988.

ELIOT, T. S. *Essays on Elizabethan Drama*. New York: Haskel, 1964.

———. *Selected Essays*. New York: Harcourt, Brace, 1950.

Elizabethan Theatre 7, no. 2 (1980).

ELLIS-FERMOR, UNA. *The Frontiers of Drama*. London: Methuen, 1946.

ELTON, W. R., and **WILLIAM B. LONG**, eds. *Shakespeare and the Dramatic Tradition*. Newark: University of Delaware Press, 1989.

Emblematica: An Interdisciplinary Journal of Emblem Studies 1 (1986).

Emory University Press 8 (October 1952)–20 (Fall 1964).

Emporia State Research Studies 10 (January 1962)–32 (Fall 1983).

ENCK, JOHN J. *Jonson and the Comic Truth.* Madison: University of Wisconsin Press, 1957.

enclitic 2, no. 1 (1978).

Encyclia: The Journal of the Utah Academy of Science, Arts, and Letters 58 (1981)–66 (1989).

English Institute Essays (1951)–(1964).

English Journal (Urbana, IL) 39 (1950)–55 (1966).

English: Journal of the English Association 6 (Summer 1947)–40 (Spring 1991).

English Language Notes 2 (March 1965)–27 (December 1989).

English Literary Renaissance 1 (Summer 1971)–21 (Autumn 1991).

English Literature and Language 13 (1976)–23 (1986).

English Miscellany 2 (Spring 1951)–28–29 (1979–80).

English Record 41, no. 1 (1990).

English Studies 28 (July 1947)–72 (April 1991).

English Studies in Africa 1 (September 1958)–26, no. 1 (1983).

English Studies in Canada 1 (Spring 1975)–17 (September 1991).

English Studies in Honor of James Southall Wilson. Charlottesville: University Press of Virginia, 1951.

ERICKSON, PETER, and **COPPÉLIA KAHN**, eds. *Shakespeare's "Rough Magic": Essays in Honor of C. L. Barber.* Newark and London: University of Delaware Press; Associated University Presses, 1985.

ERSKIN-HILL, HOWARD. *The Augustian Idea in English Literature.* London: Arnold, 1983.

Essays and Studies by Members of the English Association 1 (1948)–37 (1984).

Essays by Divers Hands 24 (1948).

Essays in Arts and Sciences 5 (April 1976)– 16 (May 1987).

Essays in Criticism 1 (October 1951)–41 (October 1991).

Essays in Foreign Languages and Literature 26 (1980)–29 (1981).

Essays in Literature 3 (Spring 1976)–18 (Spring 1991).

Essays in Theatre 3 (November 1984)–9 (November 1990).

Estudos Anglo-Americanos 1 (1977)–5–6 (1981–1982).

Etc. 19 (October 1962).

Etudes Anglaises: Grabde Bretagne, Etats Unis 11 (January 1959)–43 (September 1990).

Exemplaria: A Journal of Theory in Medieval and Renaissance Studies 1 (Fall 1989)–3 (Fall 1991).

Explicator 1 (June 1943)–49 (Winter 1991).

Explorations in Renaissance Culture 5 (1979)–17 (1991).

FABIAN, BERNARD, and **KURT TETZELI VON ROSADOR,** eds. *Shakespeare: Text, Language, Criticism: Essays in Honor of Marvin Spevack.* Hildesheim: Olms, 1987.

Faith & Reason 3, no. 2 (1977).

FARLEY-HILLS, DAVID. *The Comic in Renaissance Comedy.* Totowa, NJ: Barnes & Noble, 1981.

FARR, DOROTHY M. *John Ford and the Caroline Theatre.* London: Macmillan, 1979.

————. *Thomas Middleton and the Drama of Realism: A Study of Some Representative Plays.* Edinburgh: Oliver and Boy, 1973.

FERGUSON, FRANCIS. *The Human Image in Dramatic Literature—Essays.* Garden City, NY: Doubleday, 1957.

————. *Trope and Allegory: Themes Common to Dante and Shakespeare.* Athens: University of Georgia Press, 1977.

FERGUSON, MAUREEN QUILLIGAN, and **NANCY J. VICKERS,** eds. *Rewriting the Renaissance: The Discourse of Sexual Difference in Early Modern Europe.* Chicago: University of Chicago Press, 1986.

Fifteenth-Century Studies 6 (1979)–17 (1991).

FINEMAN, JOEL. *The Subjective Effect in Western Literary Tradition: Essays Towards the Release of Shakespeare's Will.* Cambridge, MA, and London: MIT Press, 1991.

FINKELPEARL, PHILIP J. *John Marston of the Middle Temple: An Elizabethan Dramatist in His Social Setting.* Cambridge, MA: Harvard University Press, 1969.

FISCH, HAROLD. *The Dual Image—A Study in the Figure of the Jew in English Literature.* London: Lincolns-Prager, 1959.

FLORBY, GUNILLA. *The Painful Passage to Virtue: A Study of George Chapman's "The Tragedy of Bussy D'Ambois" and "The Revenge of Bussy D'Ambois."* Lund: CWK Gleerup, 1982.

Florida State University Studies 19 (1955).

Florilegium: Carleton University Annual Papers on Late Antiquity and the Middle Ages 5 (March 1983)–7 (June 1985).

FOAKES, R. A. *Shakespeare, The Dark Comedies to the Last Plays: From Satire to Celebration.* Charlottesville: University Press of Virginia, 1971.

Folklore (London, Eng.) 63, no. 1 (1952)–93 (Spring 1982).

FORKER, CHARLES R. *The Skull Beneath the Skin: The Achievement of John Webster.* Carbondale: Southern Illinois University Press, 1986.

Forum (Houston, TX) 4 (October 1967)–12, no. 2 (1974).

Forum for Modern Language Studies 1 (July 1965)–19 (October 1983).

FRENCH, MARILYN. *Shakespeare's Division of Experience.* New York: Summit Books, 1981.

FRICKE, DONNA G., and **DOUGLAS C. FRICKE,** eds. *Aeolian Harps: Essays in Honor of Maurice Browning Cramer.* Bowling Green, OH: Bowling Green University Press, 1976.

FRIEDENREICH, KENNETH, ed. *"Accompaninge the players": Essays Celebrating Thomas Middleton, 1580–1980.* New York: AMS, 1983.

————, **ROMA GILL,** and **CONSTANCE B. KURIYAMA,** eds. *"A poet and a filthy play-maker": New Essays on Christopher Marlowe.* New York: AMS, 1988.

Furman Studies 7 (May 1960)–9 (November 1961).

GAGEN, JEAN E. *The New Woman—Her Emergence in English Drama, 1600–1730.* New York: Twayne, 1954.

GARNER, STANTON B., JR. *The Absent Voice: Narrative Comprehension in the Theatre.* Chicago: University of Chicago Press, 1989.

GARRETT, MARTIN. *"A Diamond, Though Set in Horn": Philip Massinger's Attitude to Spectacle.* Salzburg: University of Salzburg, 1984.

GECKLE, GEORGE L. *John Marston's Drama: Themes, Images, Sources.* Rutherford, NJ: Farleigh Dickinson University Press, 1980.

GEDO, JOHN E., and **GEORGE R. POLLOCK**, eds. *Psychoanalysis: The Vital Issues.* Vol. I: *Psychoanalysis as an Intellectual Discipline.* New York: International Universities Press, 1984.

Genre 5 (Spring 1972)–15 (Spring–Summer 1982).

Georgetown Law Journal 70 (1982).

Georgia Review 31 (Spring 1977)–36 (Summer 1982).

Gettysburg Review 3 (Winter 1990).

GILBERT, ALLAN H. *The Principles and Practice of Criticism.* Detroit: Wayne State University Press, 1991.

GODSHALK, W. L. *The Marlovian World Picture.* The Hague: Mouton, 1974.

GOLDBERG, JONATHAN. *James I and the Politics of Literature.* Baltimore: Johns Hopkins University Press, 1983.

GOMEZ, CHRISTINE. *The Alienated Figure in Drama: From Shakespeare to Pinter.* New Dehli: Reliance, 1991.

GOODMAN, PAUL. *The Structure of Literature.* Chicago: University of Chicago Press, 1954.

GOODWYN, FLOYD LOWELL, JR. *Image Patterns and Moral Vision in John Webster.* Salzburg: University of Salzburg, 1977.

Gordon Review 9 (1966).

GRAHAM, PARRY. *The Golden Age Restor'd: The Culture of the Stuart Court, 1603–1642.* Manchester: Manchester University Press, 1981.

GRANT, THOMAS MARK. *The Comedies of George Chapman: A Study in Development.* Salzburg: University of Salzburg, 1972.

GRAY, J. C., ed. *Mirror up to Shakespeare: Essays in Honour of G. R. Hibbard.* Toronto: University of Toronto Press, 1984.

GREENBLATT, STEPHEN, ed. *The Power of Forms in the English Renaissance.* Norman, OK: Pilgrim, 1982.

———, ed. *Representing the English Renaissance.* Berkeley, London, and Los Angeles: University of California Press, 1988.

Greyfriar: Siena Studies in Literature 6 (1963)–36 (April 1975).

GRUDIN, ROBERT. *Mighty Opposites: Shakespeare and the Renaissance Contrarity.* Berkeley, Los Angeles, and London: University of California Press, 1979.

Gypsy Scholar: A Graduate Forum for Literary Criticism 1, no. 2 (1974)–3, no. 1 (1976).

HABICHT, WERNER, D. J. PALMER, and **ROGER PRINGLE,** eds. *Images of Shakespeare.* Newark: University of Delaware Press, 1988.

HAGER, ALAN. *Dazzling Images: The Masks of Sir Philip Sidney.* Newark: University of Delaware Press, 1991.

————. *Shakespeare's Political Animal: Schema and Schemata in the Canon.* Newark: University of Delaware Press, 1990.

HALLETT, CHARLES A. *Middleton's Cynics: A Study into the Moral Psychology of the Mediocre Mind.* Salzburg: University of Salzburg, 1975.

————, and **ELAINE S. HALLETT.** *Analyzing Shakespeare's Action.* Cambridge and New York: Cambridge University Press, 1991.

————. *The Revenger's Madness: A Study of Revenge Tragedy Motifs.* Lincoln: University of Nebraska Press, 1980.

Hamlet Studies 1 (Spring 1979)–13 (Summer–Winter 1991).

HAPPÉ, PETER, ed. M*edieval English Drama: A Casebook.* London: Macmillan, 1984.

HARRIS, ANTHONY. *Night's Black Agents: Witchcraft and Magic in Seventeenth-Century Drama.* Manchester: Manchester University Press, 1980.

HARRISON, GEORGE. *Elizabethan Plays and Players.* Ann Arbor: University of Michigan Press, 1956.

HARRISON, THOMAS P., ARCHIBALD A. HILL, ERNEST C. MOSSNER, and **JAMES SLEDD,** eds. *Studies in Honor of DeWitt T. Starnes.* Austin: University of Texas Press, 1967.

HASELKORN, ANNE M. *Prostitution in Elizabethan and Jacobean Drama.* Troy, NY: Whitston, 1983.

————, and **BETTY S. TRAVITSKY,** eds. *The Renaissance Englishwoman in Print: Counterbalancing the Canon.* Amherst: University of Massachusetts Press, 1990.

HASSEL, R. CHRIS, J. *Renaissance Drama & the English Church Year.* Lincoln: University of Nebraska Press, 1979.

HAWKES, TERENCE. *Shakespeare's Talking Animals: Language and Drama in Society.* London: Arnold, 1973.

HAWKINS, HARRIET. *Likeness of Truth in Elizabethan and Restoration Drama.* Oxford: Clarendon Press, 1972.

————. *Poetic Freedom and Poetic Truth: Chaucer, Shakespeare, Marlowe, Milton.* Oxford: Clarendon Press, 1976.

HAWORTH, PETER. *English Hymns and Ballads.* Oxford: Blackwell, 1947.

HAWTHORN, RICHMOND Y. *Tragedy, Myth, and Mystery.* Bloomington: University of Indiana Press, 1962.

Hebrew University Studies in Literature and the Arts 3 (1975)–8 (1980).

Helios (Lubbock, TX) 5, no. 1 (1977).

HENN, THOMAS R. *The Harvest of Tragedy.* London: Methuen, 1956.

HENNING, STANDDISH, ROBERT KIMBROUGH, and **RICHARD KNOWLES,** eds. *English Renaissance Drama: Essays in Honor of Madeleine Doran and Mark Eccles.* Carbondale: Southern Illinois University Press, 1976.

Hermathena: A Trinity Dublin Review 129 (Winter 1980).

HEUBERT, RONALD. *John Ford: Baroque English Dramatist.* Montreal and London: McGill-Queen's University Press, 1977.

HEWITT, R. P. *Reading and Response—An Approach to the Criticism of Literature.* London: George G. Harrap, 1960.

HIBBARD, GEORGE RICHARD, ed. *The Elizabethan Theatre V.* Toronto: Macmillan; Hamden, CT: Archon, 1975.

————, ed. *The Elizabethan Theatre VII.* Hamden, CT: Archon, 1980.

————. *The Making of Shakespeare's Dramatic Poetry.* Toronto: University of Toronto Press, 1981.

HIGHET, GILBERT. *The Powers of Poetry.* New York: Oxford University Press, 1960.

HIGHFILL, PHILIP H., JR., ed. *Shakespeare's Craft: Eight Lectures.* Carbondale: Southern Illinois University Press for George Washington University, 1982.

Hispania 43 (December 1960).

Hogarth Lectures on Literature 16 (1951).

HOGG, JAMES, ed. *Elizabethan Miscellany* 3. Salzburg: University of Salzburg, 1981.

————, ed. *Recent Research in Ben Jonson.* Salzburg: University of Salzburg, 1976.

HOLLAND, NORMAN N., SIDNEY HOMAN, and **BERNARD J. PARIS,** eds. *Shakespeare's Personality*. Berkeley: University of Northern California Press, 1989.

HOLLOWAY, JOHN. *The Story of the Night*. Lincoln: University of Nebraska Press, 1961.

HOMAN, SIDNEY. *Shakespeare and the Triple Play: From Study to Stage to Classroom*. Lewisburg, PA: Bucknell University Press, 1988.

HONIGMANN, E. A. J., ed. *Shakespeare and His Contemporaries: Essays in Comparison*. Manchester: Manchester University Press, 1986.

Hopkins Review 1 (Summer 1948).

Horizontes: Revista de la Universidad Catolica de Puerto Rico 27 (October 1963)–36 (April 1975).

HOSLEY, RICHARD, ed. *Essays on Shakespeare and Elizabethan Drama in Honor of Hardin Craig*. Columbia: University of Missouri Press, 1962.

HOUSTON, JOHN PORTER. *Shakespearean Sentences: A Study in Style and Syntax*. Baton Rouge: Louisiana State University Press, 1988.

HOWARD, DOUGLAS, ed. *Philip Massinger: A Critical Reassessment*. Cambridge: Cambridge University Press, 1985.

HOWARD, JEAN E., and **MARION F. O'CONNOR**, eds. *Shakespeare Reproduced: The Text in History and Ideology*. New York: Methuen, 1987.

HOWARTH, HERBERT. *The Tiger's Heart: Eight Essays on Shakespeare*. New York: Oxford University Press, 1970.

HOWE, QUINCEY, JR., ed. *Humanitas: Essays in Honor of Ralph Ross*. Claremont, CA: Scripps College Press, 1977.

HOY, CYRUS H. *The Hyacinth Room*. New York: Knopf, 1964.

Hudson Review 2 (Summer 1949)–22 (Winter 1969–1970).

Humanities Association Bulletin 14 (Fall 1963)–25 (Summer 1974).

Humanities in Society 4 (Spring–Summer 1981).

HUNTER, G. K. *Dramatic Ideas and Cultural Tradition: Studies in Shakespeare and His Contemporaries*. New York: Barnes & Noble, 1978.

Huntington Library Quarterly 9 (January 1946)–54 (Winter 1991).

The Illif Review 41 (Spring 1989).

Illinois Studies in Language and Literature 34 (March 1950).

Indian Journal of English Studies 3, no. 1 (1962)–4, no. 1 (1963).

International Journal of Psychoanalysis 29 (March–April 1948)–36 (March–April 1955).

International Jounal of Women's Studies 4 (January–February 1981).

Interpretation: A Journal of Political Philosophy 7 (Fall 1978)–18 (Fall 1990).

Interpretations (Memphis, TN) 10, no. 1 (1979)–12 (March 1980).

Iowa State Journal of Research 53 (May 1979)–62 (December 1988).

Irish Monthly 73 (May 1949)–79 (February 1951).

ISELIN, PIERRE, and **JEAN-PIERRE MOREAU**, eds. *Le Songe d'une nuit été at "La Duchesse de Malfi": Texte et représentation*. Limoges: Université de Limoges, 1989.

Italian Quarterly 27 (Summer 1986).

JACKSON, GABRIELE BERNHARD. *Vision and Judgement in Ben Jonson's Drama*. New Haven: Yale University Press, 1968.

JACKSON, STONEY. *This Is Love?* New York: Pageant, 1958.

Jahrbuch der Deutschen Schillergesellschaft (1984).

JAMES, D. G. *The Dream of Learning*. New York: Oxford University Press, 1951.

JENSEN, EJNER J. *John Marsten, Dramatist: Themes and Imagery in the Plays*. Salzburg: University of Salzburg, 1979.

JEPSEN, LAURA. *Ethical Aspects of Tragedy*. Gainsville: University of Florida Press, 1953.

Jewish Quarterly 1 (Summer 1953).

JOHANSSON, STIG, and **BJORN TYSDAHL**, eds. *Papers from the First Nordic Conference for English Studies*, Oslo, 17–19 September 1980. Oslo: *University of Oslo*, 1981.

John Donne Journal 5, no. 1–2 (1986).

JOHNSON, MARILYN L. *Images of Women in the Works of Thomas Heywood*. Salzburg: University of Salzburg, 1974.

JOHNSTON, MARK D., and **SAMUEL M. RILEY**, eds. *Proceedings of the Illinois Medieval Association*. Vol. 2. Normal: Graduate School, Illinois State University, 1985.

JONES, ELDRED. *Othello's Countrymen: The African in English Renaissance Drama.* London: Oxford University Press, 1965.

JONES-DAVIES, MARIE THÉRÈSE, ed. *Du Texte a la scene: Languages du théâtre.* Paris: Touzot, 1983.

————, ed. *Vérité et illusion dans le théâtre au temps de la Renaissance.* Paris: Touzot, 1983.

Journal of African Civilizations 7 (November 1985).

Journal of American Folklore 94 (October–December 1981).

Journal of the American Academy of Religion 51 (March 1983).

Journal of the Australian Language and Literature Association 39 (May 1963)–72 (November 1989).

Journal of Commonwealth Literature 12, no. 2 (1977)–25, no. 1 (1990).

Journal of Communication 7 (Winter 1957).

Journal of English (Sana's University) 5 (1978).

Journal of English and German Philology 41 (April 1942)–88 (July 1989).

Journal of English Language and Literture 35 (May 1989)–37 (December 1991).

Journal of English Literary History 9 (March 1942)–58 (June 1991).

Journal of English Studies 2 (March 1979).

Journal of Evolutionary Psychology 1 (June 1979)–9 (August 1988).

Journal of General Education 6 (October 1951)–34 (Spring 1982).

Journal of the Department of English (Calcutta) 17, no. 2 (1981–1982)–28 (September 1990).

Journal of the History of Ideas 7 (April 1946)–33 (April 1972).

Journal of King Saud University Arts 11, no. 1 (1984).

Journal of Medieval and Renaissance Studies 4 (Autumn 1974)–17 (Spring 1987).

Journal of Popular Culture 14 (Summer 1980).

Journal of the Rocky Mountain Medieval and Renaissance Association 2 (January 1981)–11 (January 1990).

Journal of the University of Saugar 6, no. 6 (1951)–7, no. 7 (1952).

Journal of Warburg and Courtland Institutes 9 (March 1943)–34 (September 1971).

JOWETT, J. A., and **R. K. S. TAYLOR,** eds. *Self and Society in Shakespeare's "Troilus and Cressida" and "Measure for Measure."* Bradford, Eng.: University of Leeds Center for Adult Education, 1982.

KAMPS, IVO, ed. *Shakespeare Left and Right.* New York: Routledge, 1991.

KAPPELER, SUSANNE, and **NORMAN BRYSON.** *Teaching the Text.* London: Routledge, 1983.

KASTEN, DAVID SCOTT. *Shakespeare and the Shapes of Time.* Hanover, NH: University Press of New England, 1982.

————, and **PETER STALLYBRASS,** eds. *Staging the Renaissance: Interpretations of Elizabethan and Jacobean Drama.* New York: Routledge, 1991.

KAUFMANN, R. J. *Richard Brome, Caroline Playwright.* New York: Columbia University Press, 1961.

KAY, CAROL MCGINNIS, and **HENRY E. JACOBS,** eds. *Shakespeare's Romances Reconsidered.* Lincoln: University of Nebraska Press, 1977.

Keats-Shelley Journal 32 (Summer 1983).

KEHLER, DOROTHEA, and **SUSAN BAKER,** eds. *In Another Country: Feminist Perspectives on Renaissance Drama.* Metuchen, NJ: Scarecrow, 1991.

Kentucky Philological Association Bulletin 11 (January 1984)–12 (January 1985).

Kentucky Review 8 (Summer 1988).

Kenyon Review 12 (Spring 1950)–48 (Fall 1986).

KIEFER, FREDERICK. *Fortune and Elizabethan Tragedy.* San Marino, CA: Huntington Library, 1983.

KIRK, RUDOLPH, and **C. F. MAIN,** eds. *Essays in Literary History.* New Brunswick, NJ: Rutgers University Press, 1960.

KISTNER, A. L., and **M. K. KISTNER.** *Middleton's Tragic Themes.* New York: Peter Lang, 1984.

KM 80: A Birthday Album for Kenneth Muir, Tuesday, 5 May 1987. Liverpool: Liverpool University Press, n.d.

KNIGHT, G. WILSON. *The Crown of Life.* New York: Oxford University Press, 1947.

————. *Explorations.* New York: New York University Press, 1964.

————. *The Golden Labyrinth:* A Study of British Drama. London: Phoenix House, 1962.

————. *The Imperial Theme*. London: Methuen, 1961.

————. *The Olive and the Sword*. London: Oxford University Press, 1943.

————. *The Sovereign Flower*. London: Butler & Tanner, 1958.

————. *The Wheel of Fire*. New York: World, 1962.

KNIGHTS, L. C. *Drama and Society in the Age of Jonson*. London: Chatto & Windus, 1947.

KOGAN, STEPHEN. *The Hieroglyphic King: Wisdom and Idolatry in the Seventeenth-Century Masque*. Rutherford, NJ: Farleigh Dickinson University Press, 1986.

Komos 1, no. 2 (1968)–3, no. 1 (1973).

KRONENBERGER, LOUIS. *The Thread of Laughter*. New York: Knopf, 1952.

KURIYAMA, CONSTANCE BROWN. *Hammer or Anvil: Psychological Patterns in Christopher Marlowe's Plays*. New Brunswick, NJ: Rutgers University Press, 1980.

Kwaralnik Neeofilologiczny 8, no. 3 (1961)–25, no. 4 (1978).

LACY, M. S. *Jacobean Problem Play*. Ann Arbor: University of Michigan Press, 1956.

LANDA, M. J. *The Jew in Drama*. London: King, n.d.

Landfall 18 (March 1964).

Language and Culture 2 (1982)–12 (1991).

Language and Literature 1, no. 2 (1972).

Language & Style 9 (Winter 1974)–20 (Spring 1987).

Language Quarterly 4 (Fall–Winter 1965)–25 (Fall–Winter 1986).

Lapis 6 (January 1980).

LEASKA, MITCHELL. *The Voice of Tragedy*. New York: Speller, 1963.

LEAVIS, FRANK. *The Common Pursuit*. London: Chatto & Windus, 1944.

LEECH, CLIFFORD, ed. *Marlowe: A Collection of Critical Essays*. Englewood Cliffs, NJ: Prentice-Hall, 1964.

————, ed. *Shakespeare's Tragedies and Other Studies in Seventeenth Century Drama*. London: Chatto & Windus, 1961.

Leeds Studies in English 11 (Spring 1980)–20 (Summer 1989).

Legacy 3, no. 1 (1976).

LEGGATT, ALEXANDER. *Ben Jonson: His Vision and His Art.* London: Methuen, 1981.

LEINWAND, THEODORE B. *The City Staged: Jacobean Comedy, 1603–1613.* Madison: University of Wisconsin Press, 1986.

LENZ, CAROLYN, RUTH SWIFT, GAYLE GREENE, and **CAROL THOMAS NEELY,** eds. *The Woman's Part: Feminist Criticism of Shakespeare.* Urbana: University of Illinois Press, 1980.

LESSER, SIMON O. *Fiction and the Unconscious.* Boston: Beacon Press, 1957.

Letras de Deusto 9 (1979).

LEVIN, CAROL J., ed. *Ambiguous Realities: Women in the Middle Ages and Renaissance.* Detroit: Wayne State University Press, 1987.

LEVIN, HARRY. *The Overreacher: A Study of Christopher Marlowe.* Cambridge, MA: Harvard University Press, 1952.

LEVIN, RICHARD. *The Multiple Plot in English Renaissance Drama.* Chicago: University of Chicago Press, 1971.

LEVICH, MARVIN, ed. *Aesthetics and the Philosophy of Criticism.* New York: Random House, 1963.

LEWALSKI, BARBARA KIEFER, ed. *Renaissance Genres: Essays on Theory, History, and Interpretation.* Cambridge, MA: Harvard University Press, 1986.

Life and Letters Today 36 (January 1943)–52 (February 1947).

LINDLEY, DAVID. *The Court Masque.* Manchester: Manchester University Press, 1984.

———. *Thomas Campion.* Leiden, The Netherlands: Brill, 1986.

Litera 2 (1955)–3 (1956).

Literary Criterion 1 (Summer 1959)–26, no. 1 (1991).

Literary and Linquistic Computing 6 (1991).

The Literary Half-Yearly 5 (July 1964).

Literary Onomastic Studies 3 (1976).

Literatur in Wissenschaft und Unterricht 19 (June 1977)–12 (June 1980).

Literature and Belief 7 (March 1987).

Literature and History 7 (Spring 1981)–12 (Autumn 1986).

MAIN SOURCES CONSULTED

Literature and Medicine 7 (Spring 1988).

Literature and Psychology 5 (May 1956)–36, no. 1 (1990).

Literature and Theology 1 (March 1987).

Literature in Performance 8 (November 1988).

Lock Haven Review 13, no. 1 (1972).

LOFTIS, JOHN. *Renaissance Drama in England and Spain: Topical Allusion and History Plays.* Princeton: Princeton University Press, 1987.

LOGAN, GEORGE M., and **GORDON TESKEY,** eds. *Unfolded Tales: Essays on Renaissance Romance.* Ithaca, NY: Cornell University Press, 1989.

Lore & Language 3 (January 1982).

LUCAS, FRANK L. *Literature and Psychology.* London: Cassell, 1951.

LUCKYJ, CHRISTINA. *A Winter's Snake: Dramatic Form in the Tragedies of John Webster.* Athens: University of Georgia Press, 1989.

LUCOW, BEN. *James Shirley.* Boston: Twayne, 1981.

MACCARTHY, DESMOND. *Humanities.* London: MacGibbon & Kee, 1953.

MACHIN, RICHARD, and **CHRISTOPHER NORRIES,** eds. *Post-Structuralist Readings of English Poetry.* Cambridge: Cambridge University Press, 1987).

MACLURE, MILLAR. *George Chapman: A Critical Study.* Toronto: University of Toronto Press, 1966.

Madison Quarterly 2 (March 1942).

MAES-JELINEK, HENA, PIERRE MICHEL, and **PAULETTE MICHEL-MICHOT.** *Multiple Worlds, Multiple Words.* Liège: Université of Liège, 1987.

MAGNUSSON, A. L., and **C. E. MCGEE,** eds. *The Elizabethan Theatre, XI.* Port Credit, Ont.: Meany, 1990.

MAHON, JOHN W., and **THOMAS A. PENDLETON,** eds. *"Fanned and winnowed opinions": Shakespeare Essays Presented to Harold Jenkins.* London: Methuen, 1987.

MAHOOD, M. M. *Poetry and Symbolism.* London: J. Cape, 1950.

Mainstream 15 (June 1962).

Makerere Journal 1 (1958)–6 (1962).

Maledicta: The International Journal of Verbal Aggression 2 (Summer 1978)–8 (Winter 1984–1985).

Mandrake 1 (February 1947).

Manitoba Arts Review 8 (Winter 1952)–14 (Winter 1958–1959).

MANN, DAVID. *The Elizabethan Player: Contemporary Stage Representation.* London and New York: Routledge, 1991.

MARCUS, LEAH S. *The Politics of Mirth: Jonson, Herrick, Milton, Marvell, and the Defense of the Old Holiday Pastimes.* Chicago: University of Chicago Press, 1986.

MARKLEY, R., and **L. FINE**, eds. *From Renaissance to Restoration: Metamorphosis of the Drama.* Cleveland, OH: Bellflower Press, 1984.

MARX, MILTON. *The Enjoyment of Drama.* New York: Appleton-Century-Crofts, 1947.

Maryland English Journal 6, no. 2 (1968).

MASINGTON, CHARLES G. *Christopher Marlowe's Tragic Vision: A Study in Damnation.* Athens: University of Ohio Press, 1972.

Massachusetts Review 2 (Summer 1961)–23 (Spring 1982).

Massachusetts Studies in English 3, no. 1 (1971)–6, no. 1–2 (1977).

MAXWELL, B., ed. *Renaissance Studies in Honor of Hardin Craig.* Stanford, CA: Stanford University Press, 1942.

MAXWELL, J. C., ed. *Elizabethan and Jacobean Drama: Critical Essays by Peter Ure.* Liverpool: Liverpool University Press, 1974.

MCCOLLOM, WILLIAM G. *Tragedy.* New York: Macmillan, 1963.

MCDONNELL, R. F. *The Aspiring Mind.* Ann Arbor: University of Michigan Press, 1958.

MCELROY, JOHN F. *Parody and Burlesque in the Tragicomedies of Thomas Middleton.* Salzburg: University of Salzburg, 1972.

MCIVER, R. M., ed. *Great Moral Dilemmas in Literature, Past and Present.* New York: Harper & Row, 1956.

MCLEOD, SUSAN H. *Dramatic Imagery in the Plays of John Webster.* Salzburg: University of Salzburg, 1977.

MCMANAWAY, JAMES G., ed. *Joseph Quincy Adams Memorial Studies.* Washington, DC: Folger Shakespeare Library, 1948.

————, ed. *Shakespeare 400: Essays by American Scholars on the Anniversary of the Poet's Birth.* New York: Holt, Rinehart, 1964.

McNeese Review 8 (Spring 1956)–32 (Winter 1988–1989).

MCNEIR, WALDO F., and **THELMA N. GREENFIELD**, eds. *Pacific Coast Studies in Shakespeare*. Eugene: University of Oregon Press, 1966.

MCPEEK, JAMES A. S. *The Black Book of Knaves and Unthrifts in Shakespeare and Other Renaissance Authors*. Hartford: University of Connecticut Press, 1969.

MEAGHER, JOHN C. *Method and Meaning in Jonson's Masques*. Notre Dame, IN: Notre Dame University Press, 1966.

Medievalia 1 (Spring 1975)–7 (October 1981).

Medievalia et Humanistica 8 (March 1977)–10 (1981).

Medieval & Renaissance Drama in England 1 (Summer 1984)–5 (Spring 1991).

Medieval English Theatre 6 (July 1984)–8 (December 1986).

Medieval Studies 28 (1966)–39 (1977).

Medium Aevum 28, no. 1 (1969).

Menninger Quarterly 6, no. 1 (1952).

Michigan Academy of Science, Arts, and Letters 42 (1956)–49 (1964).

Middle English Texts 3 (July 1981)–7 (July 1985).

Mid-Hudson Language Studies 1 (Spring 1978).

Midwest Quarterly 19 (1978)–22 (1980).

MIGNON, ELIZABETH L. *Crabbed Age and Youth*. Durham, NC: Duke University Press, 1947.

Milton Quarterly 6 (March 1972)–25 (December 1991).

Milton Studies 4 (1972)–26 (1991).

MILWARD, PETER, ed. *Poetry and Faith in the English Renaissance*. Tokyo: Renaissance Institute, Sophia University, 1987.

——, and **TETSUO ANZAI**, eds. *Poetry and Drama in the Age of Shakespeare: Essays in Honor of Professor Shonosuke Ishii's Seventieth Birthday*. Tokyo: Sophia University, 1982.

Minnesota Review 2 (October 1961).

Mississippi Folklore Register 10, no. 2 (1976).

Mississippi Quarterly 12 (Winter 1960–1961)–14 (Spring 1963).

Missouri English Bulletin 32, no. 1 (1975).

Modern Drama 24 (September 1981).

Modern Language Notes 57 (January 1942)–91 (December 1976).

Modern Language Quarterly 3 (September 1942)–50 (September 1989).

Modern Language Review 37 (January 1942)–84 (October 1989).

Modern Language Studies 5 (Spring 1975)–21 (Spring 1991).

Modern Philology 45 (May 1948)–87 (August 1989).

Moderna Sprak 58 (1964)–78 (1989).

Moreana 11 (June 1974)–27 (September 1990).

MORRIS, BRIAN, ed. *Christopher Marlowe.* London: Benn, 1968.

————, ed. *John Webster.* London: Benn, 1970.

Mosaic 9 (Spring 1976)–24 (Spring 1991).

Motif 4 (October 1982).

MUIR, EDWIN. *Essays on Literature and Society.* London: Hogarth, 1965.

MUIR, KENNETH. *Shakespeare as Collaborator.* London: Methuen, 1960.

————, **JAY L. HALIO**, and **D. J. PALMER**. *Shakespeare, Man of the Theatre.* London: Associated University Presses, 1983.

MULLANY, PETER F. *Religion and the Artifice of Jacobean and Caroline Drama.* Salzburg: University of Salzburg, 1977.

MULLER, HERBERT J. *The Spirit of Tragedy.* New York: Knopf, 1956.

MURRAY, PETER B. *A Study of Cyril Tourneur.* Philadelphia: University of Pennsylvania Press, 1964.

————. *A Study of John Webster.* The Hague: Mouton, 1969.

Music and Letters 54 (January 1973)–67 (April 1986).

Mythes, Croyances et Religions dans le Monde Anglo-Saxon 9 (1991).

NAGARAJAN, S., and **S. VISWANATHAN**, eds. *Shakespeare in India.* Delhi: Oxford University Press, 1987.

Names 22 (June 1974)–35 (September–December 1987).

NEILL, MICHAEL, ed. *John Ford: Critical Re-Visions.* Cambridge: Cambridge University Press, 1988.

NELSON, ROBERT J. *Play Within a Play.* New Haven: Yale University Press, 1958.

NEMEROV, HOWARD. *Poetry and Fiction: Essays.* New Brunswick, NJ: Rutgers University Press, 1963.

Neophilologus 30 (October 1946)–84 (December 1983).

Neuphilologische Mitteilungen 50, no. 1 (1949)–91, no. 2 (1991).

NEUSS, PAULA, ed. *Aspects of Early English Drama.* Totowa, NJ: Barnes & Noble, 1983.

New Comparison 2 (Autumn 1986)–5 (Summer 1988).

New England Theatre Journal 1, no. 1 (1990).

New Hungarian Quarterly 5 (Spring 1964).

New Literary History 5 (1974)–9 (978).

New Orleans Review 2 (Spring 1979)–11 (Fall–Winter 1984).

New Literary Forum 1 (1978)–2 (1980).

NEWEY, VINCENT, and ANN THOMPSON, eds. *Literature and Nationalism.* Liverpool: Liverpool University Press, 1991.

NEWMAN, KAREN. *Fashioning Femininity and English Renaissance Drama.* Chicago: University of Chicago Press, 1991.

NICHOL, CHARLES. *The Chemical Theatre.* London and Boston: Routledge, 1980.

NICHOLL, ALLARDYCE. *English Drama.* Cambridge: Cambridge University Press, 1952.

Nimbus 3 (Summer 1956).

The Norseman 7 (September–October 1949).

North Carolina Folklore Journal 20 (Spring 1972)–22 (Spring 1974.

North Dakota Quarterly 28 (Winter 1960)–57 (Fall 1989).

Notes and Queries 192 (August 1947)–N.S. 38 (March 1991).

Notre Dame English Journal 10 (Spring 1976)–14 (Summer 1982).

NOVY, MARIANNE, and CAROL THOMAS NEELY, eds. *Women's Revisions of Shakespeare: On the Responses of Woolf, Rich, H. D., George Eliot, and Others.* Urbana: University of Illinois Press, 1990.

NUTALL, A. D. A *New Mimesis: Shakespeare and the Representation of Reality.* London and New York: Methuen, 1983.

OLSON, ELDER. *Tragedy and the Theory of Drama.* Detroit: Wayne State University Press, 1961.

O'NEILL, JUDITH, ed. *Critics on Marlowe: Readings in Literary Criticism.* Coral Gables, FL: University of Miami Press, 1970.

Orbis Litterarum 4, no. 2 (1946)–45, no. 4 (1990).

ORBISON, TUCKER. *The Tragic Vision of John Ford.* Salzburg: University of Salzburg, 1974.

ORGEL, STEPHEN. *The Jonsonian Masque.* Cambridge, MA: Harvard University Press, 1965.

———, ed. *The Renaissance Imagination: Essays and Lectures by D. J. Gordon.* Berkeley: University of California Press, 1975.

Orion 2, no. 1 (1945).

Orpheus 3 (September 1956)–6, no. 1 (1959).

ORNSTEIN, ROBERT. *The Moral Vision of Jacobean Tragedy.* Madison: University of Wisconsin Press, 1960.

Osmania Journal of English Studies 2 (1962)–17 (1981).

Pacific Coast Philology 4 (January 1969)–21 (November 1986).

Pamietnik Literacki 13 (1989).

Papers of the Bibliographic Society of America 71 (March 1977)–84 (December 1990).

Papers on Language and Literature 2 (Summer 1966)–26 (Summer 1990).

Parergon: Bulletin of the Australian Association of Medieval and Renaissance Studies 14 (January 1976)–29 (April 1991).

PARFITT, GEORGE. *Ben Jonson: Public Poet and Private Man.* New York: Barnes & Noble, 1976.

PARKER, PATRICIA, and **GEOFFREY HARTMAN,** eds. *Shakespeare and the Question of Theory.* New York: Methuen, 1985.

PARROTT, THOMAS MARC, and **ROBERT H. BALL.** *A Short View of Elizabethan Drama.* New York: Scribners, 1943.

PARRY, GRAHAM. *The Golden Age Restor'd: The Culture of the Stuart Court, 1603–42.* Manchester: Manchester University Press, 1981.

PARTRIDGE, EDWARD B. *The Broken Compass: A Study of the Major Comedies of Ben Jonson.* New York: Columbia University Press, 1958.

MAIN SOURCES CONSULTED

Paunch 25 (1966)–48–49 (1977).

PEARSON, JACQUELINE. *Tragedy and Tragicomedy in the Plays of John Webster.* Manchester: Manchester University Press, 1980.

Pennsylvania English 11 (Spring 1985).

The Personalist 41 (August 1960)–48, no. 1 (1967).

Perspective 1 (Winter 1948).

Philologica Pragensia 1 (1963)–24, no. 4 (1981).

Philological Quarterly 21 (April 1942)–70 (Spring 1991).

Philology East and West 18 (February 1968)–36 (October 1986).

Philosophy and Literature 5 (Fall 1981)–7 (October 1983).

The Phoenix 2 (Autumn 1948).

Poet Lore 48 (Spring 1942)–52 (Spring 1946).

Poetics: International Review for Theory 6 (Autumn 1977)–10 (February 1981).

Poetics Today 5 (1984).

Poetry Magazine 92 (June 1958).

Post Script: Essays in Film and Humanities 4 (1987).

POPE, RANDOLPH D. *The Analysis of Literary Texts: Current Trends in Methodology.* Ypsilanti, MI: Bilingual Press, 1979.

PRAZ, MARIO. *The Flaming Heart.* Garden City, NY: Anchor, 1950.

PRIOR, MOODY E. *The Language of Tragedy.* New York: Columbia University Press, 1947.

Proceedings of the American Philosophical Association 133 (September 1989).

Proceedings of the British Academy 32 (1946)–70 (1984).

Proceedings of the Leeds Philosophical and Literary Society 7 (July 1952).

Proceedings of the PMR Conference 3 (1978)–12 (1987&1988).

Psychonanalytic Quarterly 11 (October 1942)–33 (July 1964).

Psychoanalytic Review 30 (October 1943)–42 (April 1955).

Psychology Review 55, no. 1 (1968)–65, no. 3 (1978).

Publication of the Modern Language Association 61 (September 1946)–100 (March 1985).

Publications of the Arkansas Philological Association 4 (Summer 1978)–15 (April 1989).

Publications of the Missouri Philological Association 3 (1978)–13 (1988).

PYE, CHRISTOPHER. *The Royal Phantasm: Shakespeare and the Politics of Spectacle*. London and New York: Routledge, 1990.

Quaderni di Filologia Germanica della Facoltà di Lettere e Filosofia dell'Università di Bologna 3 (1984).

Quarterly Journal of Speech 28 (October 1942)–70 (Spring 1984).

Queens Quarterly 58 (Spring 1951)–90 (Spring 1980).

QUINN, EDWARD, ed. *How to Read Shakespearean Tragedy*. New York: Harper, 1978.

Rajasthan University Studies in English 11 (January 1978).

RAO, G. NAGESWARA, ed. *The Laurel Bough: Essays Presented in Honor of Professor M. V. Rama Sarma*. Bombay: Blackie, 1983.

Raritan: A Quarterly Review 2 (Summer 1982)–11 (Summer 1991).

RAUCHBAUER, OTTO, ed. *A Yearbook in English Language and Literature 1985/86*. Vienna: Braunmuller, 1986.

RE: Artes Liberalis 4, no. 2 (1971).

REAL: Yearbook of Research in English and American Literature 7 (1970).

Records of Early English Drama Newsletter 3 (January 1978).

Recovering Literature 4, no. 1 (1975).

REDMOND, JAMES, ed. *Drama and Symbolism*. Cambridge: Cambridge University Press, 1982.

———. *Drama, Sex and Politics*. Cambridge: Cambridge University Press, 1985.

———, ed. *The Theatrical Space*. Cambridge: Cambridge University Press, 1987.

REIK, THEODOR. *The Secret Self*. New York: Farrar, Straus, 1952.

Religion and Literature 22 (1990).

Renaissance and Modern Studies 11 (1968)–19 (1975).

MAIN SOURCES CONSULTED

Renaissance and Reformation 2 (February 1978)–15 (Winter 1991).

Renaissance and Renascences in Western Literature: A Quarterly Newsletter of Classical Influences 1, no. 4 (1980).

Renaissance Bulletin 13 (1986).

Renaissance Drama 1 (1968)–21 (1990).

Renaissance News 18, no. 1 (1965).

Renaissance Papers (1954)–(1989).

Renaissance Quarterly 22 (1969)–42 (Spring 1989).

Renaissance Studies 2 (March 1988).

Renascence: Essays on Value in Literature 30 (Autumn 1978)–39 (Winter 1987).

Representations 18 (Spring 1987)–29 (Winter 1990).

Research Opportunities in Renaissance Drama 13–14 (1970–1971)–27 (1984).

Research Studies (Washington State University) 36 (1968).

Res Publica Litterarum: Essays in the Classical Tradition 2 (1979).

Review of English Literature (Leeds) 2 (October 1961)–8 (July 1967).

Review of English Studies 18 (July 1942)–N.S. 41 (November 1990).

Revista Canaria de Estudios Ingleses 12 (April 1986).

Revista di Litterature Moderne e Comparativ 2 (September–December 1947)–30 (1977).

Revue de Literature Comparee 29 (July–September 1955).

Revue del' Roumaine Linguistique 25 (January–June 1980)–26 (January–June 1981).

Revue de l'Université d'Ottowa 38 (1968).

RHODES, NEILL. *Elizabethan Grotesque*. London: Routledge, 1980.

RIBNER, IRVING. *The English History Play in the Time of Shakespeare*. Princeton: Princeton University Press, 1957.

———. *Jacobean Tragedy: The Quest for Moral Order*. New York: Barnes & Noble, 1962.

Rice Institute Pamphlets 31 (January 1944)–46 (January 1960).

Rocky Mountain Review of Language and Literature 38, no. 1 (1984)–44, no. 3 (1990).

Romanian Review 33 (July 1979).

ROSS, LAWRENCE J. *Philosophy in Literature*, Syracuse, NY: Syracuse University Press, 1949.

ROSSITER, A. P. *Angel with Horns and Other Shakespeare Lectures.* New York: Theatre Arts Books, 1961.

ROSTON, MURRAY. *Biblical Drama in England from the Middle Ages to the Present Day.* London: Faber, 1968.

ROWE, GEORGE E. *Thomas Middleton & the New Comedy Tradition.* Lincoln: University of Nebraska Press, 1979.

ROWSE, A. L. *Christopher Marlowe: A Biography.* London: Macmillan, 1964.

ROWLAND, BERYL, ed. *Chaucer and Middle English Studies in Honour of Rossell Hope Robbins.* London: Allen & Unwin; Kent, OH: Kent State University Press, 1974.

Royal Society of Canada Proceedings and Transactions 43 (June 1949).

SACCIO, PETER. *The Court Comedies of John Lyly: A Study in Allegorical Dramaturgy.* Princeton: Princeton University Press, 1969.

SAID, EDWARD W., ed. *Literature and Society.* Baltimore: Johns Hopkins University Press, 1980.

Salmaguni 88–89 (1990–1991).

SALMONS, JUNE, and **WALTER MORETTI,** eds. *The Renaissance in Ferrara and Its European Horizons/Il Rinascimento a Ferrarara e I suoi orizzonti europei.* Cardiff and Ravenna: University of Wales Press; Lapucci: Edizione del Girasole, 1984.

San Jose Studies 4 (Spring 1978)–10 (Fall 1984).

SCHELL, EDGAR T. *Strangers and Pilgrims: From "The Castle of Perserverance" to "King Lear."* Chicago: University of Chicago Press, 1983.

SCHOENBAUM, S. *Shakespeare and Others.* Washington, DC: Folger Shakespeare Library, 1985.

SCHORER, MARK, ed. *Criticism—The Foundations of Modern Judgement.* New York: Harcourt, Brace, 1962.

SCHUMAN, SAMUEL. *"The Theatre of Fine Devices": The Visual Drama of John Webster.* Salzburg: University of Salzburg, 1982.

SCHWARTZ, MURRAY M. and **COPÉLIA KAHN,** eds. *Representing Shakespeare: New Psychoanalytic Essays.* Baltimore: Johns Hopkins University Press, 1980.

Science & Society 10 (Summer 1946)–27 (Winter 1963).

SCOTT, MICHAEL. *John Marston's Plays: Theme, Structure and Performance*. London: Macmillan, 1978.

————. *Renaissance Drama and the Modern Audience*. London: Macmillan, 1982.

SCOTT, NATHAN A., JR. *The Tragic Vision and the Christian Faith*. New York: Association Press, 1957.

Scrutiny 10 (April 1942)–18 (Winter 1952).

SEIDEL, MICHAEL, and **EDWARD MENDELSON**, eds. *Homer to Brecht: The European Epic and Dramatic Traditions*. New Haven: Yale University Press, 1977.

Selected Papers from the West Virginia Shakespeare and Renaissance Association 2 (1977)–10 (1985).

SELZ, WILLIAM A., ed. *Medieval Drama: A Collection of Festival Papers*. Vermillion: University of South Dakota Press, 1969.

SENSABAUGH, G. F. *The Tragic Muse of John Ford*. New York: Benjamin Bloom, 1944.

Serif 1 (October 1964)–4, no. 3 (1967).

The Seventeenth Century 6 (Autumn 1991).

Seventeenth Century News 23 (Winter 1965)–36 (Spring 1978).

Sewanee Review 52 (Summer 1974)–75 (Winter 1967).

Shakespeare Association Bulletin 17 (January 1942)–24 (January 1949).

Shakespeare Bulletin 2 (July–August 1984)–9 (Winter 1991).

Shakespeare Jahrbuch (Weimar, GDR) 87 (1951)–120 (1984).

Shakespeare Newsletter 1 (October 1951)–38 (Fall–Winter 1988).

Shakespeare Quarterly 1 (January 1950)–42 (Winter 1991).

Shakespeare in Southern Africa 3 (1989)–4 (1990–1991).

Shakespeare Studies (New York) 1 (1972)–19 (1991).

Shakespeare Studies (Tokyo) 1 (1962)–25 (1986–1987).

Shakespeare Survey 2 (1949)–43 (1991).

Shakespeare Yearbook 1 (1990)–2 (1991).

SHALVI, ALICE, and **A. A. MENDILOW**, eds. *Studies in English Language and Literature*. Jerusalem: The Hebrew University, 1966.

SHAPIRO, JAMES. *Rival Playwrights: Marlowe, Jonson, Shakespeare*. New York: Columbia University Press, 1991.

SHARMA, T. R., ed. *Essays on Shakespeare in Honour of A. A. Ansari*. Meerut, India: Shalaba, 1986.

SHAW, GEORGE BERNARD. *Plays and Players*. New York: Oxford University Press, 1958.

Shenandoah 11 (Winter 1966).

SHEPHERD, SIMON. *Amazons and Warrior Women: Varieties of Feminism in Seventeenth-Century Drama*. New York: St. Martin's, 1981.

SHERBO, ARTHUR. *English Sentimental Drama*. East Lansing: Michigan State University Press, 1957.

Sidney Newsletter 1 (1980).

Signs 4 (1978).

Signal 1, no. 1 (1978).

SIMPSON, PERCY. *Studies in Elizabethan Drama*. Oxford: Clarendon Press, 1955.

Sixteenth Century Journal 10 (Spring 1979)–22 (Spring 1991).

SLOTE, BERNICE, ed. *Myth and Symbol—Critical Approaches and Applications*. Lincoln: University of Nebraska Press, 1963.

SMITH, BRUCE R. *Homosexual Desire in Shakespeare's England: A Cultural Poetics*. Chicago and London: University of Chicago Press, 1991.

SMITH, HALLETT. *Shakespeare's Romances: A Study of Some Ways of the Imagination*. San Marino, CA: The Huntington Library, 1972.

SMITH, MARION BODWELL. *Dualities in Shakespeare*. Toronto: University of Toronto Press, 1966.

Social Research 30 (Spring 1963).

SOELLNER, ROLF. *Shakespeare's Patterns of Self-Knowledge*. Columbus: Ohio State University Press, 1972.

Sophia English Studies 1 (1976)–9 (1984).

Soundings 64 (Winter 198x)–70 (Spring–Summer 1987).

South Atlantic Quarterly 47 (October 1948)–85 (Autumn 1986).

MAIN SOURCES CONSULTED

South Atlantic Review 48 (January 1983)–54 (May 1988).

South Atlantic Review (formerly *South Atlantic Bulletin*) 39 (November 1974)–55 (November 1990).

South Central Bulletin 34 (Summer 1974)–48 (Summer 1988).

South Central Review 1 (Spring–Summer 1984)–7 (Spring 1990).

Southern Folklore Quarterly 36 (January 1972)–41 (June 1977).

Southern Humanities Review 2 (December 1968)–13 (September 1979).

Southern Quarterly 3 (October 1965)–16 (October 1977).

Southern Review (Australia) 2 (1967)–19 (1986).

Southern Speech Journal 6 (Spring 1960).

Southwest Review 44 (Summer 1959).

Speculum 26 (October 1951)–58 (July 1983).

Speech Monographs 16 (August 1949).

STALLMAN, R. W. *Critiques and Essays in Criticism.* New York: Ronald, 1949.

Standpunte 36 (October 1983).

Statistical Methods in Linguistics 2 (January 1963).

STAVIG, MARK. *John Ford and the Traditional Moral Order.* Madison: University of Wisconsin Press, 1968.

STEANE, J. B. *Marlowe: A Critical Study.* Cambridge: Cambridge University Press, 1964.

STEINER, GEORGE. *The Death of Tragedy.* New York: Knopf, 1961.

STILLING, ROGER. *Love and Death in Renaissance Tragedy.* Baton Rouge: Louisiana State University Press, 1976.

STOLL, E. E. *From Shakespeare to Joyce.* New York: Doubleday, 1944.

―――. *Shakespeare and Other Masters.* Cambridge, MA: Harvard University Press, 1962.

Stratford Papers on Shakespeare 2 (1961)–5 (1964).

Stratford-Upon-Avon Studies 1 (1960)–5 (1965).

STRONG, L. A. G. *The Sacred River.* London: Methuen, 1945.

STRONG, ROY. *Henry, Prince of Wales and England's Lost Renaissance.* London: Thames and Hudson, 1986.

Structuralist Review 2 (1981).

Studia Anglica Posnanieusia 6, no. 1–2 (1975)–18 (1986).

Studia Germanica Gandensia 21 (1980–1981).

Studia Mystica 7 (Winter 1984).

Studia Neophilologica 14 (Winter 1941–1942)–63 (Summer 1991).

Studies in Bibliography: Papers of the Bibliographical Society of the University of Virginia 31 (1978)–36 (1983).

Studies in English (University of Texas 21) (1942)–35 (1956).

Studies in English Language and Literature 23 (April 1974)–39 (February 1989).

Studies in English Literature, 1500–1900 1 (Spring 1961)–31 (Spring 1991).

Studies in the Humanities 5 (September 1976)–17 (June 1990).

Studies in Iconography 2 (1972)–10 (1984–85).

Studies in the Literary Imagination 5, no. 1 (1972)–6, no. 1 (1973).

Studies in Medieval Culture 5 (Summer 1975)–12 (1982).

Studies in Philology 39 (April 1942)–88 (Summer 1991).

Studies in the Renaissance 5 (1958)–8 (1961).

Studies in Scottish Literature 3 (March 1966)–7 (March 1970).

STYAN, J. L. *The Elements of Drama.* Cambridge: Cambridge University Press, 1960.

Style (DeKalb, IL) 5 (Summer 1971)–21 (Spring 1987).

SubStance: A Review of Theory and Literary Criticism 36 (1982).

Susquehanna University Studies 10 (1978)–21 (1989).

SUTHERLAND, JAMES, and **JOEL HURTSFIELD,** eds. *Shakespeare's World.* London and New York: Arnold; St. Martin's, 1964.

SWEENEY, JOHN GORDON, III. *Jonson and the Psychology of Public Theatre.* Princeton: Princeton University Press, 1984.

Sydney Studies in English 1 (1975–1976)–14 (1988–1989).

TALBERT, ERNEST W. *Elizabethan Drama and Shakespeare's Early Plays.* Chapel Hill: University of North Carolina Press, 1963.

TAYLOR, GARY. *To Analyze Delight: A Hedonist Criticism of Shakespeare.* Newark: University of Delaware Press, 1985.

TAYLOR, JEROME, and **ALAN H. NELSON,** eds. *Medieval English Drama: Essays Critical and Contextual.* Chicago and London: University of Chicago Press, 1972.

Tennessee Folklore Society Bulletin 26 (September 1960).

Tennessee Philological Bulletin: Proceedings of the Annual Meeting of the Tennessee Philological Association 21 (1984).

Tennessee Studies in Literature 5 (Spring 1960)–23 (Spring 1977).

Texas A & I University Studies 2 (January 1969).

Texas Studies in Literature and Language 1 (Winter 1960)–30 (Fall 1988).

Text: Transactions of the Society for Textual Research 3 (1987)–5 (1991).

Text & Presentation 11 (1991).

Textual Practice 5 (Spring 1991).

Thalia: Studies in Literary Humor 1 (Fall–Winter 1978)–9 (Spring–Summer 1986).

THAYER, C. G. *Ben Jonson: Studies in the Plays.* Norman: University of Oklahoma Press, 1963.

Theatre Annual 44 (1989–1990).

Theatre Journal 29 (April 1976)–42 (October 1990).

Theatre Notebook 26 (January 1972).

Theatre Research International 6 (1980–1981)–16 (1991).

Theatre Survey 13, no. 2 (1972)–32 (November 1991).

Theology 50 (1957).

Theoria 17 (1955)–69 (May 1987).

THOMPSON, ANN, and **JOHN O. THOMPSON.** *Shakespeare: Meaning and Metaphor.* Brighton, Sussex: Harvester Press, 1987.

THOMPSON, MARVIN, and **RUTH THOMPSON,** eds. *Shakespeare and the Sense of Performance: Essays in the Tradition of Performance Criticism in Honor of Bernard Beckerman.* Newark: University of Delaware Press, 1989.

Thoth: Syracuse University Graduate Studies in English 1 (Fall 1959)–16, no. 3 (1976).

Thought Currents in English Literature 54 (1981).

TILLYARD, EUSTACE M. *Essays Literary and Educational.* London: Chatto & Windus, 1962.

Times Literary Supplement (London) 4 (November 1965)–20 (June 1980).

TOKSON, ELLIOT H. *The Popular Image of the Blackman in English Drama, 1550–1688.* Boston: G. K. Hall, 1982.

Topic: A Journal of the Literary Arts (Washington, PA) 13 (Spring 1962)–36 (Spring 1982).

TOWNSON, FREDA. *Apologie for "Bartholomew Fayre."* New York: Modern Language Association of America, 1947.

TRAISTER, BARBARA H. *Heavenly Necromancers: The Magician in English Renaissance Drama.* Columbia: University of Missouri Press, 1984.

Transactional Mental Health Research Newsletter 19 (January 1977).

TRAVIS, PETER W. *Dramatic Design in the Chester Cycle.* Chicago and London: University of Chicago Press, 1982.

Tri-Quarterly (Evanston, IL) 8 (1967).

TRICOMI, ALBERT H. *Early Drama to 1600.* Binghamton: Center for Medieval and Early Renaissance Studies, State University of New York, 1987.

Trivium 9 (1974)–21 (1986).

Tulane Studies in English 4 (Spring 1954)–22 (Spring 1974).

Tulsa Studies in Women's Literature 10 (Fall 1991).

Unisa English Studies 2 (May 1968)–29 (September 1991).

Unitas: A Quarterly for the Arts and Sciences (Manilla, Philippines) 64 (June 1991).

Universitas 2, no. 2 (1964).

University of California Publications, English Studies 10 (1954)–11 (1955).

University of Colorado Studies in English 2 (Summer 1945).

University of Dayton Review 10 (autumn 1974)–15 (Spring 1981).

University of Denver Quarterly 10, no. 2 (1975).

University of Hartford Studies in Literature: A Journal of Interdisciplinary Criticism 9, no. 3 (1977)–20, no. 1 (1988).

University of Miami Publications in English and American Literature 1 (March 1953)–7 (March 1964).

University of Mississippi Studies in English 1, no. 1 (1960)–16, no. 1 (1988).

University of Missouri Studies 19, no. 2 (1944)–21, no. 1 (1946).

University of Saga Studies in English 18 (March 1990).

University of Toronto Quarterly 12 (July 1943)–58 (October 1989).

University of West Virginia Bulletin: Philological Studies 4 (1943).

University of Windsor Review 1 (January 1965).

University Review (Kansas City) 20 (Winter 1953)–35 (Winter 1967).

The Upstart Crow 1 (1978)–11 (1991).

The Use of English 4 (Spring 1953)–18 (Summer 1967).

VAN LANN, THOMAS F. *The Idiom of Drama*. Ithaca, NY: Cornell University Press, 1970.

Vanderbilt Studies in the Humanities 2 (1954).

Viator 17 (December 1986).

Virginia English Bulletin 36 (Winter 1986).

Virginia Quarterly Review 28 (Winter 1952)–60 (Winter 1984).

Visuabharati Quarterly 19 (August–October 1952).

WAITH, EUGENE. *The Herculean Hero in Marlowe, Chapman, Shakespeare and Dryden*. New York: Columbia University Press, 1962.

―――. *The Pattern of Tragicomedy in Beaumont and Fletcher.* New Haven: Yale University Press, 1952.

WALLACE, A. DAYLE, ed. *Studies in Honor of John Wilcox*. Detroit: Wayne State University Press, 1958.

Wascana Review 10 (Summer 1975)–15 (Fall 1980).

Washington State College Research Studies 18 (December 1950)–32 (September 1964).

WATSON, ROBERT N. *Ben Jonson's Parodic Strategies: Literary Imperialism in the Comedies*. Cambridge, MA, and London: Harvard University Press, 1987.

―――. *Shakespeare and the Hazards of Ambition*. Cambridge, MA, and London: Harvard University Press, 1984.

WAYNE, VALERIE, ed. *The Matter of Difference: Materialist Feminist Criticism of Shakespeare*. Ithaca, NY: Cornell University Press, 1991.

WEIL, JUDITH. *Christopher Marlowe: Merlin's Prophet.* Cambridge: Cambridge University Press, 1977.

WEISINGER, HERBERT. *The Agony and the Triumph.* East Lansing: University of Michigan Press, 1964.

WELLEK, RENÉ, and **ALVARO RIBEIRO,** eds. *Evidence in Literary Scholarship: Essays in Memory of James Marshall Osborn.* Oxford: Clarendon Press, 1980.

WELLS, HENRY. *Elizabethan and Jacobean Playwrights.* New York: Columbia University Press, 1964.

WEST, REBECCA. *The Court and the Castle—Some Treatments of a Recurring Theme.* New Haven: Yale University Press, 1957.

West Virginia University Philological Papers 5 (January 1945)–27 (1981).

Western Humanities Review 12 (Summer 1958)–18 (Winter 1964).

Western Speech 20 (Winter 1956).

WHITE, HOWARD B. *Antiquity Forgot: Essays on Shakespeare, Bacon, and Rembrandt.* The Hague and Boston: Martinus Nijhoff, 1978.

Wichita State University Bulletin 41, no. 1 (1965).

WIGGINS, MARTIN. *Journeymen in Murder: The Assassin in English Renaissance Drama.* Oxford: Clarendon Press, 1991.

WILLIAMS, CHARLES. *The Image of the City.* New York: Oxford University Press, 1958.

WILLIAMS, PAUL A., ed. *The Fool and the Trickster: Studies in Honour of Enid Welsford.* Cambridge: Brewer, 1978.

WILLIAMS, RAYMOND. *Drama in Performance.* Chester Springs, PA: Dufours, 1954.

Wind & Rain 4 (March 1947).

WOMACK, PETER. *Ben Jonson.* Oxford: Basil Blackwell, 1986.

Women's Studies 7, no. 3 (1980)–9, no. 2 (1982).

Word and Image 3 (January 1987)–4 (January 1988).

World Literature Written in English 23 (1984).

Works and Days: Essays in the Socio-Historical Dimensions of Literature and the Arts 7 (Fall 1989).

Xavier University Studies 7, no. 3 (1968)– 1, no. 1 (1971).

MAIN SOURCES CONSULTED

Yale Review 32 (December 1942)–72 (Summer 1983).

Yale Studies in English 138 (1958).

Yearbook of Cooperative Criticism 10 (1983).

Yearbook in English Studies 1 (1971)–21 (1991).

Yearbook of Italian Studies (1972).

Yiddish 4 (Winter 1982).

YOUNG, DAVID. *The Heart's Forest: A Study of Shakespeare's Pastoral Plays.* New Haven and London: Yale University Press, 1972.

YOUNG, STARK. *Immortal Shadows.* New York: Scribners, 1948.

Zeitschrift für Anglistik und Amerikanstik 10, no. 2 (1962)–36, no. 1 (1988).

ZUCKER, DAVID HARD. *Stage and Image in the Plays of Christopher Marlowe.* Salzburg: University of Salzburg, 1972.